Managing Human Resources

Productivity, Quality of Work Life, Profits

Managing Human Resources

Productivity, Quality of Work Life, Profits

Sixth Edition

Wayne F. Cascio
Graduate School of Business Administration
University of Colorado at Denver

Boston   Burr Ridge, IL   Dubuque, IA   Madison, WI   New York   San Francisco   St. Louis
Bangkok   Bogotá   Caracas   Kuala Lumpur   Lisbon   London   Madrid   Mexico City
Milan   Montreal   New Delhi   Santiago   Seoul   Singapore   Sydney   Taipei   Toronto

McGraw-Hill Higher Education

*A Division of The **McGraw-Hill** Companies*

MANAGING HUMAN RESOURCES:
PRODUCTIVITY, QUALITY OF WORK LIFE, PROFITS

Published by McGraw-Hill/Irwin, a business unit of The McGraw-Hill Companies, Inc. 1221 Avenue of the Americas, New York, NY, 10020. Copyright © 2003, 1998, 1995, 1992, 1989, 1986 by The McGraw-Hill Companies, Inc. All rights reserved. No part of this publication may be reproduced or distributed in any form or by any means, or stored in a database or retrieval system, without the prior written consent of The McGraw-Hill Companies, Inc., including, but not limited to, in any network or other electronic storage or transmission, or broadcast for distance learning.

Some ancillaries, including electronic and print components, may not be available to customers outside the United States.

This book is printed on acid-free paper.

domestic   1 2 3 4 5 6 7 8 9 0 DOW/DOW 9 0 8 7 6 5 4 3 2
international   1 2 3 4 5 6 7 8 9 0 DOW/DOW 9 0 8 7 6 5 4 3 2

ISBN 0-07-231716-7

Publisher: *John E. Biernat*
Senior sponsoring editor: *John Weimeister*
Editorial assistant: *Tammy Higham*
Senior marketing manager: *Ellen Cleary*
Project manager: *Destiny Rynne*
Production supervisor: *Gina Hangos*
Coordinator freelance design: *Mary L. Christianson*
Producer, Media technology: *Mark Molsky*
Supplement producer: *Betty Hadala*
Photo research coordinator: *David A. Tietz*
Photo researcher: *Amy Bethea*
Cover designer: *Artemio Ortiz*
Cover image: *SIS/© Jose Ortega*
Typeface: *10/12 Melior*
Compositor: *GAC/Indianapolis*
Printer: *R. R. Donnelley & Sons Company*

Library of Congress Cataloging-in-Publication Data

Cascio, Wayne F.
   Managing human resources : productivity, quality of work life, profits / Wayne F. Cascio.—6th ed.
    p. cm.
   Includes bibliographical references and index.
   ISBN 0-07-231716-7 (alk. paper)—ISBN 0-07-112311-3 (Internationally ed. : alk. paper)
   1. Personnel management I. Title.
HF5549.C2975 2003
658.3—dc21
                                                         2001056218

INTERNATIONAL EDITION ISBN 0-07-112311-3

Copyright © 2003. Exclusive rights by The McGraw-Hill Companies, Inc. for manufacture and export. This book cannot be re-exported from the country to which it is sold by McGraw-Hill.

The International edition is not available in North America.

www.mhhe.com

To Tanni Lee
Endless joy

ABOUT THE AUTHOR

WAYNE F. CASCIO earned his B.A. degree from Holy Cross College, his M.A. degree from Emory University, and his Ph.D. in industrial/organizational psychology from the University of Rochester. Since then he has taught at Florida International University, the University of California–Berkeley, and the University of Colorado–Denver, where he is at present professor of management.

Professor Cascio is past president both of the Human Resources Division of the Academy of Management, and of the Society for Industrial and Organizational Psychology. He is a fellow of both the Academy of Management and the American Psychological Association, and holds a Diplomate in industrial/organizational psychology from the American Board of Professional Psychology. He is a member of the Board of Directors of the Society for Human Resource Management Foundation.

Professor Cascio's editorial board memberships have included the *Journal of Applied Psychology, Academy of Management Review, Journal of Management, International Journal of Selection and Assessment, Human Performance, Organizational Dynamics,* and *Asia-Pacific Journal of Human Resources.* He has consulted with a wide variety of organizations on six continents, and periodically he testifies as an expert witness in employment discrimination cases. Professor Cascio is an active researcher and is the author or editor of six books on human resource management.

CONTENTS IN BRIEF

CONTENTS

BOXES AND SPECIAL FEATURES

PREFACE

I did not write this book for students who aspire to be specialists in human resource management (HRM). Rather, I wrote it for students of general management whose jobs inevitably will involve responsibility for managing people, along with capital, material, and information assets. A fundamental assumption, then, is that all managers are accountable to their organizations in terms of the impact of their HRM activities, and they are expected to add value by managing their people effectively. They are also accountable to their peers and to their subordinates in terms of the quality of work life that they are providing.

As a unifying theme for the text, I have tried to link the content of each chapter to three key outcome variables—productivity, quality of work life, and profits. This relationship should strengthen the student's perception of HRM as an important function affecting individuals, organizations, and society.

Each chapter incorporates the following distinguishing features:

- In keeping with the orientation of the book toward general managers, each chapter opens with a section called "Questions This Chapter Will Help Managers Answer." This section provides a broad outline of the topics that each chapter addresses.
- Following the chapter opener is the first part of a split-sequence vignette, often from the popular press, that illustrates the topic "human resource management in action." Events in the vignette are designed to sensitize the reader to the subject matter of the chapter. The events in the vignette lead to a climax, but then the vignette stops—like a two-part television drama. The reader is asked to predict what will happen next, and to anticipate alternative courses of action.
- The text for the chapter follows—replete with concepts, research findings, court decisions, company examples, and international comparisons.
- Each chapter includes an "Ethical Dilemma" box. Its purpose is to identify issues relevant to the topic under discussion, on which different courses of action may be desirable and possible. The student must choose a course of action and defend the rationale for doing so.
- As in the fifth edition, in each chapter an "Implications for Management Practice" box provides insights into the ways in which issues presented in the chapter affect the decisions that managers must make. The "Impact" boxes reinforce the link between each chapter's contents and the strategic

objectives—productivity, quality of work life, and the bottom line—that influence all HR functions.
- Near the end of each chapter, the vignette introduced at the outset continues, allowing the reader to compare his or her predictions with what actually happened.

Ultimately the aim of each chapter is to teach prospective managers to *make decisions* based on accurate diagnoses of situations that involve people—in both domestic and global contexts. Familiarity with relevant theory, research, and practice enhances the ability of students to do this. Numerous real-world applications of concepts allow the student to learn from the experiences of others, and the dynamic design of each chapter allows the student to move back and forth from concept to evidence to practice—then back to evaluating concepts—in a continuous learning loop.

WHAT'S NEW IN THE SIXTH EDITION?

HR texts have sometimes been criticized for overemphasizing the HR practices of large organizations. There is often scant advice for the manager of a small business, who wears many hats and whose capital resources are limited. To address this issue, I have made a conscious effort to provide examples of effective HRM practices in small businesses in almost every chapter.

This was no cosmetic revision. I examined every topic and every example in each chapter for its continued relevance and appropriateness. I added dozens of new company examples, updated legal findings from each area, and cited the very latest research findings in every chapter. More than one-third of the references are new. As in previous editions, I have tried to make the text readable, neither too simplistic nor too complex.

The book still includes 16 chapters, although the order has shifted slightly. I moved the financial impact of HR activities up to Chapter 2, since it is important for students of general management to appreciate the magnitude of the impact of effective people management on costs, on revenues, and, ultimately, on share prices. Cases and exercises still appear in each chapter, although most of the chapter-opening cases are new. McGraw-Hill/Irwin's Management Website <http://auth.mhhe.com/business/management/more> contains a wealth of additional materials that students and instructors may find to be helpful. New to this edition is a list of key terms discussed in each chapter. Key terms are printed in boldface in the text and listed at the end of the chapter. A glossary at the end of the book also helps students to locate definitions of important terms quickly.

A final consideration is the treatment of international issues. While there are merits to including a separate chapter on this topic, as well as interspersing international content in each chapter, I do not see this as an either-or matter. I have done both, recognizing the need to frame domestic HR issues in a global context (e.g., recruitment, staffing, compensation, labor-management relations). At the same time, the book covers international issues (e.g., cultural differences, selection, training, and compensation of expatriates) in more depth in a separate chapter.

NEW TOPICS IN THE SIXTH EDITION

- Chapter 1 includes a new chapter-opening case, "The 21st Century Corporation," plus extensive coverage of how the Internet, e-commerce, globalization, and the backlash against globalization are influencing the strategic responses of organizations. It also includes a new ethical dilemma that highlights the conflict between American and foreign cultural values.

- Chapter 2 now focuses exclusively on the financial impact of HRM activities. It includes a new chapter-opening vignette, "Linking Worker Beliefs to Increased Productivity and Profitability," as well as applications to the costing of employee turnover, attitudes, work-life programs, training, high-performance work practices, and organizational culture.

- Chapter 3 explores the legal context of employment decisions. It includes a new chapter-opening vignette, "Sealed without a Kiss—Responding to a Letter Charging Your Company with Unlawful Discrimination." There have been many new regulatory developments, as well as many new developments in the case law that affects employment decisions, and I have rewritten the chapter extensively to reflect these.

- The focus of Chapter 4 is on diversity at work. The chapter-opening vignette, as well as extensive material in the chapter itself, emphasize key factors that make the business case for having a diverse workforce. The chapter addresses specific issues and company-based strategies for finding and keeping members of Generations X and Y, African Americans, Hispanic Americans, Asian Americans, women, workers with disabilities, older workers, and gay and lesbian employees.

- Chapter 5 focuses on analyzing work and planning for people. It includes new material on the Occupational Information Network (O*Net), and on workforce planning in the new millennium, and it addresses the issue of succession planning in small as well as large organizations.

- I have extensively rewritten Chapter 6, "Recruiting," beginning with the chapter-opening vignette, to reflect new strategies that companies and job seekers are using to find each other. New research findings on the effectiveness of recruitment sources and factors that affect recruitment success inform the student, as do new company examples. Finally, a new ethical dilemma addresses the issues associated with online résumés and personal privacy.

- From the new chapter-opening vignette, "Organizational Culture—Key to Staffing 'Fit,'" throughout the panoply of staffing methods, Chapter 7 reflects the very latest research findings, new technology, and practical strategies that companies are using to inform their staffing decisions. To help provide international perspective, an updated application illustrates the Japanese approach to staffing.

- Chapter 8, "Workplace Training," begins with a new chapter-opening vignette, "E-Learning Helps Small Organizations Act Like Big Ones." It also includes new company examples, "Action Learning at Vulcan Materials Company," and "Executive Coaching: Does It Pay Off?"

- Chapter 9, "Performance Management," also begins with a new chapter-opening vignette, "Performance Reviews: Perilous Curves Ahead." It emphasizes the critical need to align performance management with the strategic direction of an organization, and it includes an extensive new section on multirater or 360-degree feedback.

- Managing careers is the focus of Chapter 10, which includes an updated chapter-opening vignette, "Self-Reliance: Key to Career Management for the 21st Century," as well as updated company examples on mergers, acquisitions, and the demise of corporate loyalty, and a new company example, "Up-or-Out Promotions in Professional Service Firms."

- Chapter 11, "Pay and Incentive Systems," includes an updated chapter-opening vignette, "The Trust Gap," updated research findings on alternatives to pay systems based on job evaluation (market-based pay and competency-based pay) and on stock options as incentives, plus a new company example, "What Are You Worth?" The Internet has made pay rates for jobs at all levels more transparent than ever before, and this new company example addresses that issue.

- Chapter 12 includes a new section on how diversity in the workforce means diversity in benefits preferences, the latest strategies companies are using to control health-care costs, updated information about Social Security, and cash-balance pension plans. It also includes a new company example, "How Canadian Imperial Bank of Commerce (CIBC) Controls Disability Costs."

- Chapter 13 focuses exclusively on union representation and collective bargaining. Major emphasis is on understanding the U.S. industrial relations system. A new section, "A Brief History of U.S. Labor Relations," provides historical context, and issues associated with contract administration have been incorporated into this chapter. To provide international perspective, the chapter includes new data on union membership in other countries, and a new section on how laws and foreign-owned firms affect layoffs in the United States.

- Chapter 14 addresses procedural justice and ethics. It includes an updated chapter-opening vignette on alternative dispute resolution, and an entirely new section, "Why Address Procedural Justice?" that illustrates the theory and forms of procedural justice, including international comparisons. There is also a new ethical dilemma, "When a Soon-to-Be-Laid-Off Employee Asks for Advice," plus a completely revised and updated treatment of privacy issues in the workplace.

- Chapter 15, on job safety and health, includes new company examples on best practices in reducing repetitive stress injuries, updated information about Union Carbide and the Bhopal disaster, and the role of multinationals in upholding health and safety standards in less developed countries. The chapter also includes new research findings and information on AIDS and business, violence at work, substance abuse, employee assistance programs, and company-based health-promotion activities.

- Chapter 16, on international dimensions of HRM, remains a capstone for the book. It includes a new chapter-opening vignette, "What's It Like to Be a Global Manager?" as well as new information about global corporations, the backlash against globalization, and what multinational corporations can do to avoid the backlash. The chapter includes a new international example "HRM in the European Union," and a new international application, "How to Stay Safe Abroad." Every topic in the chapter has been thoroughly updated.

HELP FOR INSTRUCTORS

Several important supplements are available to help you use this book more effectively.

- The website for the book includes URLs and links to companies mentioned in the text. It is <www.mhhe.com/cascio6e>.
- An instructor's manual–test bank includes suggested course outlines for both 10- and 16-week terms, chapter outlines (in transparency-master forms), answers to the "Challenge" questions that follow the chapter-opening vignettes, answers to end-of-chapter discussion questions, and comments on end-of-chapter cases and exercises. The test bank contains true-false, multiple-choice, fill-in-the-blank, and short-answer questions for each chapter. Approximately 1,200 questions are included. Each is classified according to level of difficulty and includes a text page reference.
- Computerized testing software includes advanced features that allow the instructor to add and edit questions online; to save and reload tests; to create up to 99 versions of each test; to attach graphics to questions; to import and export ASCII files; and to select questions on the basis of type, level of difficulty, or key words. The program is password protected, and can be networked.
- Slides, using Power Point presentation software, include tables, figures, and content from each chapter of the text, thereby providing an easy-to-follow outline for classroom presentations. Color transparencies are also available.
- Videos to supplement each chapter of the text are available from the McGraw-Hill/Irwin Management Series.
- Access to McGraw-Hill/Irwin's management website, http//auth.mhhe.com/business/management/more/.

ORGANIZATION AND PLAN OF THE BOOK

The chart on the inside of the front cover provides an organizing framework for the book. The organization of the parts is designed to reflect the fact that HRM is an integrated, goal-directed set of managerial functions, not just a collection of techniques.

The text is based on the premise that all organizations operate in multiple environments, competitive, legal, social, and organizational. Three broad HR processes, acquisition, deployment, and adjustment and change, provide the framework within which specific HR functions—employment; development; compensation; labor-management accommodation; and safety, health, and international implications—are carried out. All this is done to achieve three critical strategic objectives: productivity, quality of work life, and profits.

Part 1, "Environment," includes Chapters 1 through 4. It provides the backdrop against which students will explore the nature and content of each HRM function. These first four chapters paint a broad picture of the competitive, legal, social, and organizational environments in which people-management activities take place. They also describe key economic and noneconomic factors that affect productivity, quality of work life, and profits. This is the background against which the remaining five parts (12 chapters) of the book unfold.

Logically, "Employment," Part 2, is the first step in the HRM process, as a firm acquires the talent to operate. Analyzing work, planning for people, recruiting, and staffing are key components of the employment process. The broad process of deployment comprises Part 3, "Development," and Part 4, "Compensation." Finally, Part 5, "Labor-Management Accommodation," and Part 6, "Safety, Health, and International Implications," deal with the broad process of adjustment and change.

In teaching HRM courses at both graduate and undergraduate levels, I use this conceptual framework as a roadmap throughout the course. I believe that it is important for students to grasp the big picture, as well as to understand how the topics in question fit into the broader scheme of HRM functions. I have found that referring to the framework frequently throughout the course, to show students where we have been and where we are going, helps them adopt a more systematic, strategic perspective in addressing any given HRM issue.

ACKNOWLEDGMENTS

Many people played important roles in the development of this edition of the book, and I am deeply grateful to them. Ultimately any errors of omission or commission are mine, and I bear responsibility for them.

Several people at McGraw-Hill/Irwin were especially helpful. Publisher John Biernat, Senior Sponsoring Editor John Weimeister, and Marketing Manager Ellen Cleary provided advice, support, and encouragement. Developmental Editor Tracy Jensen, Editoral Assistant Tammy Higham, and Project Manager Destiny Rynne were ever vigilant to ensure that all phases of the book's production stayed on schedule. It has been a pleasure to work with each of these individuals. Finally, the many reviewers of the current and previous editions of the text provided important insights and helped improve the final product. Their guidance and feedback have helped make the book what it is today, and each deserve special thanks:

- Helen LaVan, DePaul University
- Keith G. Dayton, Kelley School of Business.
- Adrienne Colella, Texas A&M University.
- John Lenti, University of South Carolina.
- Kevin D. Carlson, Virginia Polytechnic University.
- Janis M. Pasquali, Anderson Graduate School of Management.
- Trevor Bain, University of Alabama.
- Dwight D. Frink, University of Mississippi.

Wayne F. Cascio

ENVIRONMENT

To manage people effectively in today's world of work one must understand and appreciate the significant competitive, legal, and social issues. The purpose of Chapters 1 through 4 is to provide insight into these issues. They provide both direction for and perspective on the management of human resources in the new millennium.

1. HUMAN RESOURCES IN A GLOBALLY COMPETITIVE BUSINESS ENVIRONMENT

2. THE FINANCIAL IMPACT OF HUMAN RESOURCE MANAGEMENT ACTIVITIES

3. THE LEGAL CONTEXT OF EMPLOYMENT DECISIONS

4. DIVERSITY AT WORK

HUMAN RESOURCES IN A GLOBALLY COMPETITIVE BUSINESS ENVIRONMENT

1

Questions This Chapter Will Help Managers Answer

1. What will 21st-century corporations look like?
2. What people-related business issues must managers be concerned about?
3. Which features will characterize the competitive business environment in the foreseeable future, and how might we respond to them?
4. What people-related problems are likely to arise as a result of changes in the forms of organizations? How can we avoid these problems?
5. What are the human resource (HR) implications of our firm's business strategy?

THE 21ST-CENTURY CORPORATION*

Sparked by new technologies, particularly the Internet, the corporation is undergoing a radical transformation that is nothing less than a new industrial revolution. This time around, the revolution is reaching every corner of the globe and in the process, rewriting the rules laid down by Alfred P. Sloan, Jr. (the legendary chairman of General Motors), Henry Ford, and other Industrial Age giants. The 21st-century corporation that emerges will in many ways be the polar opposite of the organizations these leaders helped shape.

Many factors are driving change, but none is more important than the rise of Internet technologies. Like the steam engine or the assembly line, the Net has already become an advance with revolutionary consequences, most of which we have only begun to feel. The Net gives everyone in the organization, from the lowliest clerk to the chairman of the board, the ability to access a mind-boggling array of information—instantaneously from anywhere. Instead of seeping out over months or years, ideas can be zapped around the globe in the blink of an eye. That means that the 21st-century corporation must adapt itself to management via the Web. It must be predicated on constant change, not stability; organized around networks, not rigid hierarchies; built on shifting partnerships and alliances, not self-sufficiency; and constructed on technological advantages, not bricks and mortar.

The organization chart of the large-scale enterprise had long been defined as a pyramid of ever-shrinking layers leading to an omnipotent chief executive officer (CEO) at its apex. The 21st-century corporation, in contrast, is far more likely to look like a web: a flat, intricately woven form that links partners, employees, external contractors, suppliers, and customers in various collaborations. The players will grow more and more interdependent, and managing this intricate network will be as important as managing internal operations.

In contrast to factories of the past 100 years that produced cookie-cutter products, the company of the future will tailor its products to each individual by turning customers into partners and giving them the technology to design and demand exactly what they want. Mass customization will result in waves of individualized products and services, as well as huge savings for companies, which no longer will have to guess what and how much customers want.

Intellectual capital will be critical to business success. The advantage of bringing breakthrough products to market first will be shorter than ever because technology will let competitors match or exceed them almost instantly. To keep ahead of the steep new-product curve, it will be crucial for businesses to attract and retain the best thinkers. Companies will need to build a deep reservoir of talent—including both employees and free agents—to succeed in this new era. But attracting and retaining top talent will require more than just huge paychecks. Organizations will need to create the kinds of cultures and reward systems that keep the best minds engaged. The old

---

Sources: J. A. Byrne, Management by web, *BusinessWeek,* Aug. 28, 2000, pp. 84–96; G. Colvin, Managing in the info era, *Fortune,* Mar. 6, 2000, pp. F6–F9; J. Pfeffer and J. F. Veiga, Putting people first for organizational success, *Academy of Management Executive,* 1999, *13*(2) pp. 37–48; J. A. Byrne, Visionary vs. visionary, *BusinessWeek,* Aug. 28, 2000, pp. 210–214.

command-and-control hierarchies are fast crumbling in favor of organizations that empower vast numbers of people and reward the best of them as if they were owners of the enterprise.

It's Global.　In the beginning, the global company was defined as one that simply sold its goods in overseas markets. Later, global companies assumed a manufacturing presence in numerous countries. The company of the future will call on talent and resources—especially intellectual capital—wherever they can be found around the globe, just as it will sell its goods and services around the globe. Indeed, the very notion of a headquarters country may no longer apply, as companies migrate to places of greatest advantage. The new global corporation might be based in the United States but do its software programming in Sri Lanka, its engineering in Germany, and its manufacturing in China. Every outpost will be connected seamlessly by the Net, so that far-flung employees and freelancers can work together in real time.

It's about Speed.　All this work will be done in an instant. "The Internet is a tool, and the biggest impact of that tool is speed," says Andrew S. Grove, chairman of Intel Corporation. That means the old, process-oriented company must revamp radically. With everything from product cycles to employee turnover on fast-forward, there is simply not enough time for deliberation or bureaucracy.

The 21st-century corporation will not have one ideal form. Some corporations will be completely virtual, wholly dependent on a network of suppliers, manufacturers, and distributors for their survival. Others, less so. Some of the most successful companies will be very small and very specialized. Others will be gargantuan in size, scope, and complexity. Table 1–1 presents a summary of these changes.

If people are so critical to business success in the 21st-century organization, what will it take to attract and retain the best? According to John T. Chambers, CEO of Cisco Systems, Inc.: "The reason people stay at a company is that it's a great place to work. It's like playing on a great sports team. Really good players want to be around other really good players. Secondly, people like to work for good leadership. So creating a culture of leaders that people like is key. And the third is, are you working for a higher purpose than an IPO or a paycheck? Our higher purpose is to change the way the world works, lives, and plays."

So if firms are to produce profits through people, what should they do? In the case conclusion at the end of the chapter, we will examine seven practices of successful organizations.

Challenges

1. In Table 1–1, which dimensions of the 21st-century prototype model require effective skills in managing people?
2. How might the Internet change the ways that employees and managers interact?
3. If the 21st-century prototype model of organizations is to be successful, how must companies change their approaches to managing people?

Table 1–1

WHAT A DIFFERENCE A CENTURY CAN MAKE: CONTRASTING VIEWS OF THE CORPORATION

Characteristic	20th Century	21st Century
Organization	The pyramid	The web or network
Focus	Internal	External
Style	Structured	Flexible
Source of strength	Stability	Change
Structure	Self-sufficiency	Interdependencies
Resources	Atoms—physical assets	Bits—information
Operations	Vertical integration	Virtual integration
Products	Mass production	Mass customization
Reach	Domestic	Global
Financials	Quarterly	Real time
Inventories	Months	Hours
Strategy	Top down	Bottom up
Leadership	Dogmatic	Inspirational
Workers	Employees	Employees and free agents
Job expectations	Security	Personal growth
Motivation	To compete	To build
Improvements	Incremental	Revolutionary
Quality	Affordable best	No compromise

THE ENTERPRISE IS THE PEOPLE

Organizations are managed and staffed by people. Without people, organizations cannot exist. Indeed, the challenge, the opportunity, and also the frustration of creating and managing organizations frequently stem from the people-related problems that arise within them. People-related problems, in turn, frequently stem from the mistaken belief that people are all alike, that they can be treated identically. Nothing could be further from the truth. Like snowflakes, no two people are exactly alike, and everyone differs physically and psychologically from everyone else. Sitting in a sports arena, for example, will be tall people, small people, fat people, thin people, people of color, white people, elderly people, young people, and so on. Even within any single physical category there will be enormous variability in psychological characteristics. Some will be outgoing, others reserved; some will be intelligent, others not so intelligent; some will prefer indoor activities, others outdoor activities. The point is that these differences demand attention so that each person can maximize his or her potential, so that organizations can maximize their effectiveness, and so that society as a whole can make the wisest use of its human resources.

This book is about managing people, the most vital of all resources, in work settings. Rather than focus exclusively on issues of concern to the human resource specialist, however, we will examine human resource management (HRM) issues in terms of their impact on management in general. A changing world order has forced us to take a hard look at the ways we manage people. Research has shown time and again that HRM practices can make an important, practical difference in terms of three key organizational outcomes: productivity, quality of work life, and profit. This is healthy. Each chapter in this book considers the impact of a different aspect of human resource management on these three broad themes. To study these impacts, we will look at the latest theory and research in each topical area, plus examples of actual company practices.

This chapter begins by considering what human resources management is all about, how it relates to the work of the line manager, and how it relates to profits. Then we will consider some current competitive challenges in the business environment, emphasizing the importance of business and human resources (HR) strategy. Managing to achieve strategic objectives has direct implications for productivity and quality of work life. Let's begin by considering the nature of HRM.

MANAGING PEOPLE: A CRITICAL ROLE FOR EVERY MANAGER

Managers are responsible for optimizing all of the resources available to them—material, capital, and human.[1] When it comes to managing people, however, all managers must be concerned to some degree with the following five activities: staffing, retention, development, adjustment, and managing change.

Staffing comprises the activities of (1) identifying work requirements within an organization; (2) determining the numbers of people and the skills mix necessary to do the work; and (3) recruiting, selecting, and promoting qualified candidates.

Retention comprises the activities of (1) rewarding employees for performing their jobs effectively; (2) ensuring harmonious working relations between employees and managers; and (3) maintaining a safe, healthy work environment.

Development is a function whose objective is to preserve and enhance employees' competence in their jobs by improving their knowledge, skills, abilities, and other characteristics; HR specialists use the term "competencies" to refer to these items.

Adjustment comprises activities intended to maintain compliance with the organization's HR policies (e.g., through discipline) and business strategies (e.g., cost leadership).

Managing change is an ongoing process whose objective is to enhance the ability of an organization to anticipate and respond to developments in its external and internal environments, and to enable employees at all levels to cope with the changes.

Needless to say, these activities can be carried out at the individual, work-team, or larger organizational unit (e.g., department) level. Sometimes they are initiated by the organization (e.g., recruitment efforts or management development programs), and sometimes they are initiated by the individual or work team (e.g., voluntary retirement, safety improvements). Whatever the case, the responsibilities for carrying out these activities are highly interrelated. Together, these activities constitute the **HRM system**. To understand how each of the major activities within HRM relates to every other one, consider the following scenario.

As a result of a large number of unexpected early retirements, the Hand Corporation finds that it must recruit extensively to fill the vacated jobs. The firm is well aware of the rapid changes that will be occurring in its business over the next 5 to 10 years, so it must change its recruiting strategy in accordance with the expected changes in job requirements. It also must develop selection procedures that will identify the kinds of competencies required of future employees. Compensation policies and procedures may have to change because job requirements will change, and new incentive systems will probably have to be developed. Since the firm cannot identify all the competencies that will be required 5 to 10 years from now, it will have to offer new training and development programs along the way to satisfy those needs. Assessment procedures will necessarily change as well, since different competencies will be required in order to function effectively at work. As a result of carrying out all this activity, the firm may need to discharge, promote, or transfer some employees to accomplish its mission, and it will have to provide mechanisms to enable all remaining employees to cope effectively with the changed environment.

It is surprising how that single event, an unexpectedly large number of early retirees, can change the whole ballgame. So it is with any system or network of interrelated components. Changes in any single part of the system have a reverberating effect on all other parts of the system. Simply knowing that this will occur is healthy, because then we will not make the mistake of confining our problems to only one part. We will recognize and expect that whether we are dealing with problems of staffing, training, compensation, or labor relations, all parts are interrelated. In short, the systems approach provides a conceptual framework for integrating the various components within the system and for linking the HRM system with larger organizational needs.

To some, the activities of staffing, retention, development, and adjustment are the special responsibilities of the HR department. But these responsibilities also lie within the core of every manager's job throughout any organization—and because line managers have **authority** (the organizationally granted right to influence the actions and behavior of the workers they manage), they have considerable impact on the ways workers actually behave. This implies two things: (1) a broad objective of HRM is to optimize the usefulness (i.e., the productivity) of all workers in an organization, and (2) a special objective of the HR department is to help line managers manage those workers more effectively. The HR department accomplishes this special objective through policy initiation and formulation, advice, service, and control in close communication and coordination with line managers. To be sure, each of the responsibilities of HRM is shared by the HR department and the line managers, as shown in Table 1–2.

In the context of Table 1–2, note how line and HR managers share people-related business activities. Generally speaking, HR provides the technical expertise in each area, while line managers (or, in some cases, self-directed work teams) use this expertise in order to manage people effectively. In a small business, however, line managers are responsible for both the technical and the managerial aspects of HRM. For example, in the area of retention, line managers are responsible for treating employees fairly, resolving conflicts, promoting teamwork, and providing pay increases based on merit. To do these things

Table 1–2		
HRM ACTIVITIES AND THE RESPONSIBILITIES OF LINE MANAGERS AND THE HR DEPARTMENT		
Activity	**Line management responsibility**	**HR department responsibility**
Staffing	Providing data for job analyses and minimum qualifications; integrating strategic plans with HR plans at the unit level (e.g., department, division); interviewing candidates, integrating information collected by the HR department, making final decisions on entry-level hires and promotions	Job analysis, human resource planning, recruitment; compliance with civil rights laws and regulations; application blanks, written tests, performance tests, interviews, background investigations, reference checks, physical examinations
Retention	Fair treatment of employees, open communication, face-to-face resolution of conflict, promotion of teamwork, respect for the dignity of each individual, pay increases based on merit	Compensation and benefits, employee relations, health and safety, employee services
Development	On-the-job training, job enrichment, coaching, applied motivational strategies, performance feedback to subordinates	Development of legally sound performance management systems, morale surveys, technical training; management and organizational development; career planning, counseling; HR research
Adjustment	Discipline, discharge, layoffs, transfers	Investigation of employee complaints, outplacement services, retirement counseling
Managing change	Provide a vision of where company or unit is going and the resources to make the vision a reality	Provide expertise to facilitate the overall process of managing change

effectively, the HR department has the responsibility for devising a compensation and benefits system that employees will perceive as attractive and fair. It also must establish merit-increase guidelines that will apply across departments, and provide training and consultation to line managers on all employee relations issues—such as conflict resolution and team building.

Why Does Effective HRM Matter?

There exists a substantial and growing body of research evidence showing a strong connection between how firms manage their people and the economic results they achieve. This evidence is drawn from large samples of companies from multiple industries, studies of the 5-year survival rates of initial public offerings, and research from the automobile, apparel, semiconductor, steel, oil refining, and service industries.[2] For example, a comprehensive study of work practices and financial performance was based on a survey of over 700 publicly held firms in all major industries. The study examined the use of "best practices" in the following areas:

- Personnel selection
- Job design
- Information sharing
- Performance appraisal
- Promotion systems
- Attitude assessment
- Incentive systems
- Grievance procedures
- Labor–management participation

Based on an index of "best-practice" prevalence, firms using more progressive policies in these areas were generally found to have superior financial performance. The 25 percent of firms scoring highest on the index performed substantially higher on key performance measures, as shown below:

Performance measure	Bottom 25%	2d 25%	3d 25%	Top 25%
Annual return to shareholders	6.5	6.8	8.2	9.4
Gross return on capital	3.7	1.5	4.1	11.3

The top 25 percent of firms—those using the largest number of "best practices"—had an annual shareholder return of 9.4 percent, versus 6.5 percent for firms in the bottom 25 percent. Firms in the top 25 percent had an 11.3 percent gross rate of return on capital, more than twice as high as that of the remaining firms. After accounting for other factors likely to influence financial performance (such as industry characteristics), the human resource index remained significantly related to both performance measures.[3]

As this study shows, adoption of high-performance work practices can have an economically significant effect on the market value of a firm. How large an effect? Recent work indicates a range of $15,000 to $45,000 per employee,[4] and shows that such practices can affect the probability of survival of a new firm by as much as 22 percent.[5] The extent to which these practices actually will pay off depends on the skill and care with which the many HR practices available are implemented to solve real business problems and to support a firm's operating and strategic initiatives.

Such high-performance work practices provide a number of important sources of enhanced organizational performance.[6] People work harder because of the increased involvement and commitment that comes from having more control and say in their work. They work smarter because they are encouraged to build skills and competence. They work more responsibly because their employers place more responsibility in the hands of employees farther down in the organization. What's the bottom line in all this? HR systems have important, practical impacts on the survival and financial performance of firms, and on the productivity and quality of work life of the people in them.

Now that we know what HRM is and why it matters, the next step is to understand some significant features of the competitive business environment in which HRM activities take place. Four such features are globalization, technology, electronic commerce (e-commerce), and demographic changes.

FEATURES OF THE COMPETITIVE BUSINESS ENVIRONMENT

Globalization

At its core, the **globalization** of business refers to the free movement of capital, goods, services, ideas, information, and people across national boundaries. Markets in every country have become fierce battlegrounds where both domestic and foreign competitors fight for market share. Foreign competitors can be formidable. For example, Coca-Cola earns more than 80 percent of its revenues from outside the United States. The 500 largest firms in the world employ almost 44 million people; they gross almost $13,000 billion in revenues and $554 billion in profits; and the total value of their assets exceeds $44 billion.[7]

The Backlash Against Globalization.   In no small part, the booming U.S. economy of recent years has been fueled by globalization. Open borders have allowed new ideas and technology to flow freely around the globe, accelerating productivity growth and allowing U.S. companies to be more competitive than they have been in decades. Yet there is a growing fear on the part of many people that globalization benefits big companies instead of average citizens—of America or any other country.[8] In the public eye, multinational corporations are synonymous with globalization. In all their far-flung operations, therefore, they bear responsibility to be good corporate citizens, to preserve the environment, to uphold labor standards, to provide decent working conditions and competitive wages, to treat their employees fairly, and to contribute to the communities in which they operate. Doing so will make a strong case for continued globalization.

Implications of Globalization for HRM.   As every advanced economy becomes global, a nation's most important competitive asset becomes the skills and cumulative learning of its workforce. Globalization, almost by definition, makes this true. Virtually all developed countries can design, produce, and distribute goods and services equally well and equally fast. Every factor of production other than workforce skills can be duplicated anywhere in the world. Capital moves freely across international boundaries, seeking the lowest costs. State-of-the-art factories can be erected anywhere. The latest technologies move from computers in one nation, up to satellites parked in space, and back down to computers in another nation—all at the speed of electronic impulses. It is all fungible—capital, technology, raw materials, information—all except for one thing, the most critical part, the one element that is unique about a nation or a company: its workforce. A workforce that is knowledgeable and skilled at doing complex things keeps a company competitive and attracts foreign investment.[9]

In fact, the relationship forms a virtuous circle: well-trained workers attract global corporations, which invest and give the workers good jobs; the good jobs, in turn, generate additional training and experience. We must face the fact that, regardless of the shifting political winds in Tokyo, Berlin, Washington, Beijing, or Budapest, the shrunken globe is here to stay. Today Tokyo is closer than the town 100 miles away was 30 years ago (after all, long-distance phone use did not become routine until the 1970s).

And tomorrow? Our networks of suppliers, producers, distributors, service companies, and customers will be so tightly linked that we will not be able to tell one locale from another. No political force can stop, or even slow down for long, the borderless economy.[10] The lesson for managers is clear: Be ready or be lost.

Technology

It is no exaggeration to say that modern technology is changing the ways we live and work. The information revolution will transform everything it touches—and it will touch everything. Information and ideas are key to the new creative economy, because every country, every company, and every individual depends increasingly on knowledge. People are cranking out computer programs and inventions, while lightly staffed factories churn out the sofas, the breakfast cereals, the cell phones. The five fastest-growing occupations in the United States are all computer related, according to projections by the Bureau of Labor Statistics. That agency also projects that, by 2005, the percentage of workers employed in industry will fall below 20 percent, the lowest level since 1850. Meanwhile the share of U.S. capital spending devoted to information technology has more than tripled since 1960, from 10 percent to more than 35 percent.[11]

In the creative economy, the most important intellectual property isn't software or music. It's the intellectual capital that resides in people. When assets were physical things like coal mines, shareholders truly owned them. But when the most vital assets are people, there can be no true ownership. The best that corporations can do is to create an environment that makes the best people want to stay.[12] Therein lies the challenge of managing human resources.

Figure 1–1

The online
revolution.
(*Source:* G. Anders,
Buying frenzy, *The
Wall Street Journal,*
July 12, 1999, p. R6.)

THE ONLINE REVOLUTION

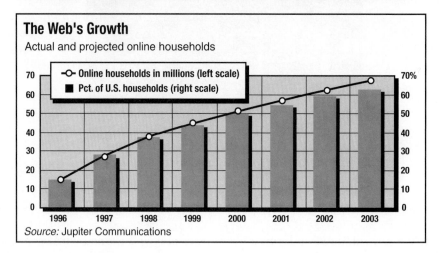

The Web's Growth
Actual and projected online households

Legend:
- Online households in millions (left scale)
- Pct. of U.S. households (right scale)

Source: Jupiter Communications

Impact of New Technology on HRM.   Perhaps the most central use of technology in HRM is an organization's **human resources information system** (HRIS). Indeed, as technology integrates with traditionally labor-intensive HR activities, HR professionals are seeing improvements in response time and efficiency of the report information available. Dozens of vendors offer HRIS applications ranging from benefits enrollment to applicant tracking, time and attendance records, training and development, payroll, pension plans, and employee surveys.[13] Such systems are moving beyond simply storing and retrieving information to include broader applications such as report generation, succession planning, strategic planning, career planning, and evaluating HR policies and practices. In this sense, today's HRIS are tools for management control and decision making.

E-Commerce

Consider this forecast: "The Internet will change the relationship between consumers and producers in ways more profound than you can yet imagine. The Internet is not just another marketing channel; it's not just another advertising medium; it's not just a way to speed up transactions. The Internet is the foundation for a new industrial order. The Internet will empower consumers like nothing else ever has. . . . The Web will fundamentally change customers' expectations about convenience, speed, comparability, price, and service."[14]

Whether it's business-to-business (B2B) or business-to-consumer (B2C), electronic commerce (e-commerce) is taking off. As an example, consider Enron Corporation of Houston, Texas. Once a distributor of natural gas through its extensive pipeline system, the company launched Web-based Enron Online in November 1999. By July 2000 it had revolutionized the energy-trading business, tallying more than $1 billion in average daily trading transactions. More than 800 products were being traded on Enron Online, including natural gas, electricity, coal, plastics, and even excess bandwidth.[15] Even after the company filed for bankruptcy in late 2001, Enron Online remained its most prized asset.

In the automobile industry, consider this scenario from former Ford Motor Co. CEO Jac Nasser. He pictures the day when a buyer hits a button to order a custom-configured Ford Mustang online, transmitting a slew of information directly to the dealer who will deliver it, the finance and insurance units who will underwrite it, the factory that will build it, the suppliers that provide its components, and the Ford designers brainstorming future models. To buyers it will mean getting just what they ordered, delivered right to their doorstep in days.[16] Although there are plenty of risks associated with this scenario,[17] e-commerce is encouraging the reinvention of manufacturing, and it would be foolish to underestimate the ultimate outcome.

Figure 1–1 illustrates the extent of the online revolution. The percentage of households online has rocketed from about 15 percent in 1996 to an estimated 60+ percent in 2003. At present, both B2B and B2C transactions comprise only about 1 percent of commercial and retail transactions.[18] However, the Internet is still in its infancy, and many experts expect that eventually it will be a major factor in pricing. The idea is that prices will be driven downward as B2B online markets allow an endless number of suppliers to bid competitively for contracts with big manufacturers.

Retail e-commerce sites, so the thinking goes, will cut consumer prices by pitting a multitude of sellers against one another, allowing Web-surfing buyers to identify quickly the lowest possible price for any good. Web-based search engines will provide buyers with more information—and bargaining power—about products than ever before. Whether those predictions come to pass will depend on several factors, the most important of which is how much economic activity finally does move online.[19] The value of goods ordered over the Internet and shipped to homes was $20 billion in 1999, about 1 percent of traditional retail sales. That is expected to rise to $180 billion by 2004.[20] As you read this, and as you ponder the future of e-commerce, consider one inescapable fact: All the people who make e-commerce possible are knowledge workers. The organizations they work for still have to address the human resource challenges of attracting, retaining, and motivating them to perform well.

Demographic Changes and Increasing Cultural Diversity

Employers are facing a chronic shortage of skilled help. The mix as well as the numbers of people available to work are changing rapidly, as Figures 1–2 and 1–3 illustrate. As Figure 1–2 shows, there will be a 6.5 percent decrease in the

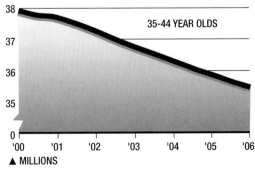

Figure 1–2

The shrinking workforce.
(*Source: Business-Week,* Jan. 10, 2000, p. 8.)

35-44 YEAR OLDS

▲ MILLIONS

DATA: BUREAU OF LABOR STATISTICS/HUN-SCANLON ADVISORS

Figure 1–3

America's chang-
ing complexion.
(*Source: Business-
Week,* Aug. 28, 2000,
p. 79.)

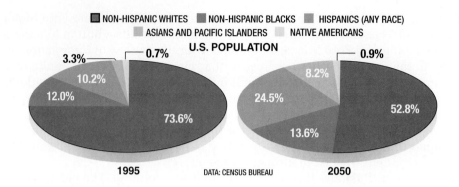

population of 35–44-year-olds between 2000 and 2006. Over the next 50 years, non-Hispanic whites will be a slim majority of the U.S. population. Hispanics will make up nearly a quarter of the population, with Asians, African Americans, and, to a much lesser extent, Native Americans comprising the rest (see Figure 1–3). Currently, female participation has jumped to 60 percent from 50 percent two decades ago, and the long-term trend toward earlier retirement has recently been reversed. Only 10 percent want to stop working altogether when they retire from their jobs.[21]

Implications for HRM.   These trends have two key implications for managers: (1) the reduced supply of workers will make finding and keeping employees a top priority. (2) The task of managing a culturally diverse workforce, of harnessing the motivation and efforts of a wide variety of workers, will present a continuing challenge to management.

   The organizations that thrive will be the ones that embrace the new demographic trends instead of fighting them. That will mean even more women and minorities in the workforce—and in the boardrooms as well. Currently there are 350,000 unfilled jobs in the U.S. information-technology industry. IBM's head of global diversity characterizes this as a "war for talent" as he ticks off various IBM projects to develop talent among women, African Americans, Asians, homosexuals, and other groups. "None of this is charitable."

RESPONSES OF FIRMS TO THE NEW COMPETITIVE REALITIES

In today's world of fast-moving global markets and fierce competition, the windows of opportunity are often frustratingly brief.[22] "Three-C" (i.e., command, control, compartmentalization) logic dominated industrial society's approach to organizational design throughout the 19th and 20th centuries, but trends such as the following are accelerating the shift toward new forms of organization for the 21st century:[23]

- Smaller companies that employ fewer people.
- The shift from vertically integrated hierarchies to networks of specialists.
- Technicians, ranging from computer repair specialists to radiation therapists, replacing manufacturing operatives as the worker elite.

Work in the 21st century requires constant learning and higher-order thinking, as more jobs shift from manufacturing to services.

- Pay tied less to a person's position or tenure in an organization and more to the market value of his or her skills.
- A change in the paradigm of doing business from making a product to providing a service, often by part-time or temporary employees.
- Outsourcing of activities that are not core competencies of a firm (e.g., payroll).
- The redefinition of work itself: constant learning, more higher-order thinking, less nine-to-five mentality.

In response to these changes, many firms are doing one or more of the following: developing new forms of organization, restructuring (including downsizing), adopting principles of total quality management, reengineering their work processes, and building flexibility into work schedules and rules. Let's briefly consider each of these.

New Forms of Organization

One example of a new organizational form that is evolving from these changes is the **virtual organization,** where teams of specialists come together to work on a project—as in the movie industry—and disband when the project is finished. Virtual organizations are already quite popular in consulting, in legal defense, and in sponsored research. They are multisite, multiorganizational, and dynamic.[24] More common in the information age, however, is the **virtual workplace** in which employees operate remotely from each other and from managers.[25] They work anytime, anywhere—in real space or in cyberspace. The widespread availability of electronic mail (e-mail), teleconferencing, faxes, and intranets (within-company information networks) facilitates such arrangements. Compelling business reasons, such as reduced real estate expenses, increased productivity, higher profits, improved customer service, access to global markets, and environmental benefits, drive their implementation. Jobs in sales, marketing, project engineering, and consulting seem to be best suited for virtual workplaces because individuals in these jobs already work with their clients by phone, or at the clients' premises. Such jobs are service- and knowledge-oriented, they are dynamic, and they evolve according to customer requirements.

A third example of a new organizational form is the *modular corporation*—that's right, modular. The basic idea is to focus on a few core competencies—those a company does best, such as designing and marketing computers or copiers—and to outsource everything else to a network of suppliers.[26] If design and marketing are core competencies, then manufacturing or service units are modular components. They can be added or taken away with the flexibility of switching parts in a child's Lego set. Does the modular corporation work? As an example, consider Dell Computer.

COMPANY EXAMPLE

DELL COMPUTER

The Modular Corporation in Action

Dell prospers by remaining perfectly clear about what it is and what it does. "We are a really superb product integrator. We're a tremendously good sales-and-logistics company. We're not the developer of innovative technology."[27] Says CEO Michael Dell, "We can grow at a rapid rate by focusing on our core business." Grow it has, from $3.4 billion in sales in fiscal 1995 to $25.3 billion in 2000.[28]

Dell sells IBM-compatible personal computers (PCs) in competition with Compaq, Apple, and IBM. While others rely primarily on computer stores or dealers, Dell sells directly to consumers, who read about the products on the company's web page, in newspaper ads, or in catalogs. Buyers either order online or call a toll-free number and place their orders with a staff of well-trained salespeople.

Dell doesn't build a zillion identical computers, flood them out to retailers, and hope you like what you see. Instead, it waits until it has your custom order (and your money), then orders components from suppliers and assembles the parts. At its OptiPlex factory in Austin, Texas, 84 percent of orders are built, customized, and shipped within 8 hours. Some components, such as the monitor or speakers, may be sent directly from the supplier to your home (never passing through Dell) and arrive on your doorstep at the same time as everything else.[29] In 1999, for example, Dell custom-assembled more than 25,000 different computer configurations for buyers.[30] By eliminating intermediaries—and the retailer's typical 13 percent markup—Dell can charge lower prices than its rivals.[31]

Modular companies are flourishing in two industries that sell trendy products in a fast-changing marketplace: apparel (Nike and Reebok are modular pioneers) and electronics. Such companies work best when they accomplish two objectives: (1) collaborating smoothly with suppliers and (2) choosing the right specialty. Companies need to find loyal, reliable vendors they can trust with trade secrets, and they need the vision to identify what customers will want, not just what the company is technically good at. For example, Dell deals with hundreds of suppliers, but about 90 percent of its parts and components come from two dozen companies. It works closely with them to make sure the parts are designed for snap-in assembly and for just-in-time delivery.[32]

Restructuring, Including Downsizing

Restructuring can assume a variety of forms, of which downsizing is probably the most common. Companies can restructure by selling or buying plants or lines of business, or by laying off employees. **Downsizing,** the planned elimination of positions or jobs, has had, and will continue to have, profound effects on organizations, managers at all levels, employees, labor markets, customers, and shareholders. Based on the type of restructuring in question, one study examined its effects on profitability and stock returns of the 500 largest companies listed on the New York Stock Exchange (Standard & Poor's S&P 500) over a 12-year period. It began by classifying the companies each year into one of five categories: stable employers, employment or asset downsizers or upsizers. Researchers then observed the subsequent effects over the following 3 years.[33] In terms of profitability (return on assets), employment downsizers were performing about as well as their industries prior to the downsizing, but their employment cuts did not enable them to outperform their industries in years 0, 1, or 2. In contrast, stable employers consistently outperformed their industries in years 0, 1, and 2.

In terms of stock performance, upsizers generated stock returns that were 50 percent higher than the stable employers in the year they increased employment, and their cumulative stock returns were 20 percentage points higher than those of stable employers over the 3-year period of the study. In contrast, downsizing companies as a group performed no better than the stable employers over the same 3-year period.

Employment downsizers reduced their work forces by an average of 11 percent. Relative to their industries, they were able to attain a return on assets that was only 0.3 percent above their industry average by year 2. The benefits of employment downsizing seem small when compared to the human cost. The message to employers is clear: Don't try to shrink your way to prosperity. Instead, the best way to prosper is by growing your business.

Total Quality Management

Total quality management (TQM) is a set of principles and practices whose core ideas include understanding customer needs, doing things right the first time, and striving for continuous improvement. The TQM revolution began in the 1980s, based on the principles of statistical quality control for manufacturing processes developed by W. Edwards Deming.[34] Motorola, Xerox, and Ford pioneered its application in the United States.

The group problem-solving focus of TQM encourages employee empowerment by using the job-related expertise and ingenuity of the workforce. Cross-functional teams develop solutions to complex problems, often shortening the time taken to design, develop, or produce products and services. Since a team may not include a representative of management, the dividing line between labor and management often becomes blurred in practice, as workers themselves begin to solve organizational problems. Thus adoption of TQM generally requires cultural change within the organization as management reexamines its past methods and practices in light of the demands of the new philosophy.[35]

Unfortunately, TQM programs have not been the final answer to customer satisfaction and productivity improvement. In many cases managers view quality as a quick fix and are disillusioned when results prove difficult to achieve. It generally takes 3 to 5 years before TQM principles become institutionalized,[36] and some managers are unwilling to make that kind of commitment. When TQM initiatives do work, it is often because managers have made major changes to their philosophies and HR programs. In fact, organizations known for the quality of their products and services strongly believe that employees are key to those results.

Reengineering

More recently, organizations have moved beyond TQM programs to a more comprehensive approach to redesigning business processes called reengineering. **Reengineering** is the fundamental rethinking and radical redesign of business processes to achieve dramatic improvements in cost, quality, and speed.[37] A process is a collection of activities (such as procurement, order fulfillment, product development, or credit issuance), that takes one or more kinds of input and creates an output that is of value to a customer. Customers may be internal or external. Consider credit issuance as an example. Instead of the separate jobs of credit checker and pricer, the two may be combined into one "deal structurer." Such integrated processes may cut response time and increase efficiency and productivity. Employees involved in the process are responsible for ensuring that customers' requirements are met on time and with no defects, and they are empowered to experiment in ways that will cut cycle time and reduce costs. Result: Less supervision is needed, while workers take on broader responsibilities and a wider purview of activities.

HR issues are central to the reengineering of business processes.[38] Reengineering requires that managers create an environment and an organizational culture that embraces, rather than resists, change. The effectiveness of such efforts depends on effective leadership and communication, both of which are people-related business processes. In fact, changes in job analyses, selection, training, performance management, career planning, compensation, and labor relations are all necessary in order to complement and support reengineering efforts.

Flexibility

For all the emphasis on the "New Economy," most jobs are still modeled on the clock-punching culture of the industrial past. Middle-income parents are now logging 260 more hours a year on the job than they did a decade ago. In the aggregate, Americans are now working more hours than the Japanese.[39] For many of them, however, 9 A.M. to 5 P.M. isn't working anymore. Time is employees' most precious commodity. They want the flexibility to control their own time—where, when, and how they work. They want balance in their lives between work and leisure. Flexibility in schedules is the key, as organizations strive to retain talented workers in a hot job market.

Small business owners in particular are finding that flexibility on hours is a cheap benefit that allows them to compete with large companies whose schedules may be more rigid. As a result, many are hiring members of a group once shunned by employers—mothers of young children. "We're learning that the trade-off if they have to leave work for something child-related is loyalty in

Ethical Dilemma
Conflict between American and Foreign Cultural Values

Each chapter of this book contains a brief scenario that illustrates a decision-making situation that could result in a breach of acceptable behavior. Such situations pose ethical dilemmas. To be ethical is to conform to moral standards or to conform to the standards of conduct of a given profession or group (e.g., medicine, auditing). Ethical decisions about behavior take account not only of one's own interests but also, equally, the interests of those affected by a decision. What would you recommend in response to the following situation?[43]

You are the director of HR for a large, southwestern teaching hospital. This hospital has a cooperative program with a major teaching hospital in Saudi Arabia. Each year several doctors from your hospital spend the year in Saudi Arabia teaching and doing research. The stay in Saudi Arabia is generally considered both lucrative and professionally rewarding.

This morning you had a visit from two of the doctors in the hospital who had been rejected for assignment to Saudi Arabia. They were very upset, as they are both very qualified and ambitious. You had carefully explained to them that while the selection committee was impressed with their abilities, the members had decided that, since they were Jewish, it would be best if they were disqualified from consideration. In spite of vigorous protests from the two doctors, you had held your ground and supported the committee's decision. However, as you sit at home reading that evening, the situation replays itself in your mind, and you think about the decision and feel a little uncertain.

Is the director of HR correct in supporting the committee's decision? What criteria should the committee, and the director of HR, use to make a decision such as this? What would you recommend?

---

return for that flexibility," says Susan Lyon, president of Lyon & Associates, a small advertising and marketing firm in San Diego.[40]

Despite the fact that only 53 percent of U.S. employers offer flextime to their employees,[41] a recent poll found 56 percent of managers reporting that employees with flexible schedules are more productive per hour. That kind of positive buzz is what is driving work redesign processes to enhance flexibility at companies such as Ernst & Young, Hewlett-Packard, Bank of America, and Lucent Technologies.[42]

People make organizations go. How the people are selected, trained, and managed determines to a large extent how successful an organization will be. As you can certainly appreciate by now, the task of managing people in today's world of work is particularly challenging in light of the competitive realities we have discussed. To survive, let alone compete, firms need a strategy to compete, and HR strategy must be consistent with it. We will examine these ideas in more detail in the sections below.

COMPETITIVE STRATEGIES

The means that firms use to compete for business in the marketplace and to gain competitive advantage are known as **competitive strategies.**[44] Competitive strategies may differ in a number of ways, including the extent to which firms emphasize innovation, quality enhancement, cost reduction, and speed.[45]

While it might appear logical that the different types of strategies require different types of HR practices,[46] the research evidence on this issue is mixed.[47] This has led some authors to recommend that firms adopt a set of "best practices" regardless of their competitive strategy.[48] Others emphasize the need to focus on activities that are most crucial to the implementation of the competitive strategy chosen.[49] However, these two perspectives are not necessarily mutually exclusive, for a firm's performance may be enhanced even more when best practices are matched to the requirements inherent in a firm's competitive strategy.[50] The important lesson for managers is that *human resources represent a competitive advantage that can increase profits when managed wisely.* Let us now consider alternative competitive strategies in more detail, along with their HR management implications.

Innovation strategy is used to develop products or services that differ from those of competitors. Its primary objective is to offer something new and different. Enhancing product or service quality is the primary objective of the **quality-enhancement strategy,** while the objective of a **cost-reduction strategy** is to gain competitive advantage by being the lowest cost producer of goods or provider of services. Finally, the objective of a **speed strategy,** or time-based strategy, is to be the fastest innovator, producer, distributor, and responder to customer feedback. Innovation strategy emphasizes managing people so that they work *differently;* quality-enhancement strategy emphasizes managing people so that they work *smarter;* cost-reduction strategy emphasizes managing people so that they work *harder;* and speed strategy emphasizes managing people so that they work *more efficiently* by changing the way work is done.

While it is convenient to think of these four competitive strategies as pure types applied to entire organizations, business units, or even functional specialties, the reality is more complex. As the following example illustrates, various combinations of the four strategies are often observed in practice.

As is well known, Ford Motor Co. has emphasized employee involvement since the early 1980s. In October 1978, Philip Caldwell, then president of Ford, made the following statement at a meeting of top executives: "Our strategy for the years ahead will come to nothing unless we ask for greater participation of our work force. Without motivated and concerned workers, we're not going to lower our costs as much as we need to—and we aren't going to get the product quality we need."[51] Elements of both cost-reduction and quality-enhancement strategies are evident in Caldwell's statement.

EMPLOYEE BEHAVIORS AND HUMAN RESOURCE STRATEGIES APPROPRIATE TO EACH COMPETITIVE BUSINESS STRATEGY

Chief executive officers need HR executives who have a clear sense of strategic direction, know the services required by the business, and understand the initiatives it should be taking toward organizational change.[52]

In practical terms, strategic HRM means getting everybody from the top of the organization to the bottom doing things to implement the strategy of the business effectively. The idea is to use people most wisely with respect to the strategic needs of the organization. This does not just happen, as the following sections demonstrate.

Innovation Strategy

Under a competitive strategy of innovation, the implications for managing people may include selecting highly skilled individuals, giving employees more discretion, using minimal controls, making greater investments in human resources, providing more resources for experimentation, allowing and even rewarding occasional failure, and appraising performance for its long-run implications. Innovative firms such as Sun Microsystems, Hewlett-Packard, 3M, Raytheon, and PepsiCo illustrate this strategy.[53]

Because the innovation process depends heavily on individual expertise and creativity, employee turnover can have disastrous consequences.[54] Moreover, firms pursuing this strategy are likely to emphasize long-term needs in their training programs for managers and to offer training to more employees throughout the organization.[55] If they do not, turnover is likely to increase, as a recent survey revealed. Among employees who say their company offers poor training, 41 percent plan to leave within a year, versus only 12 percent who rate training opportunities as excellent. Likewise, 35 percent of employees who do not receive regular mentoring plan to look for another job within 12 months, versus just 16 percent of those with regular mentoring.[56] The same survey found the cost of losing a typical worker to be $50,000. So a 1,000-worker company with poor training could lose as much as $14.5 million, while nonexistent mentoring could cost $9.5 million (not all dissatisfied employees will actually leave).

Desired role behaviors of employees suggest that any assessment of contributions of the HR function should focus attention primarily on the economic payoff of selection and training programs and also on reducing controllable turnover, especially among high performers who are not easy to replace. Because innovation strategy requires a long-term orientation that focuses on the personal and professional development of employees, HR activities that involve work-life programs, employee assistance programs, or wellness programs could help achieve success. Supportive organizational cultures, which underlie each of these approaches, are critical components of retention efforts.[57]

Quality-Enhancement Strategy

The profile of behaviors appropriate for a quality-enhancement strategy includes: relatively repetitive and predictable behaviors; a longer-term focus; a modest amount of cooperative, interdependent behavior; a high concern for quality with a modest concern for quantity of output; a high concern for how goods or services are made or delivered; low risk-taking activity; and commitment to the goals of the organization.[58]

Because quality enhancement typically involves greater employee commitment and fuller use of employees' abilities, fewer employees are needed to produce the same level of output. This phenomenon has been observed at such firms as L. L. Bean, Corning Glass, Honda, and Toyota.[59]

It is well known that the productivity gains resulting from improved selection or training can be expressed in various ways: in dollars, in increases in output, in decreases in hiring needs, or in savings in payroll costs.[60] Since fewer workers *may* be needed after the implementation of valid selection programs, managers may wish to focus on the change in staffing requirements (along with the associated cost savings) as one outcome of a quality-enhancement strategy.

Since reliable and predictable behavior is important to the implementation of this strategy, another objective is to minimize absenteeism, tardiness, and turnover. Cost savings associated with any HR programs designed to control these undesirable behaviors should therefore be documented carefully. Moreover, opportunities to participate in formal and informal training programs tend to promote a long-term commitment to the goals of the organization and flexibility to change on the part of employees.

In summary, to be consistent with a quality-enhancement strategy, HR strategy should focus on using highly valid selection and training programs, on promoting positive changes in employees' attitudes and in their lifestyles, and on decreasing absenteeism and controllable turnover.

Cost-Reduction Strategy

Given the highly competitive markets that firms confront every day, cost control has become a mantra for organizations everywhere. Firms pursuing a cost-reduction strategy are characterized by tight fiscal and management controls, minimization of overhead, and pursuit of economies of scale. The primary objective is to increase productivity by decreasing the unit cost of output per employee. Strategies for reducing costs include reducing the number of employees; reducing wage levels; using part-time workers, subcontractors, or automation; changing work rules, and permitting flexibility in job assignments.[61]

The profile of role behaviors in the context of a cost-reduction strategy includes relatively repetitive and predictable behaviors, a relatively short-term focus, primarily autonomous or individual activity, a modest concern for quality coupled with a high concern for quantity of output (goods or services), emphasis on results, low risk-taking, and stability. In addition, there is minimal use of training and development.

Sometimes managers adopt cost-reduction strategies in rather desperate situations, as their firms struggle to survive.[62] More commonly, though, cost reduction is used in combination with other strategies to keep companies prosperous. As an example, Ford Motor Company assigns managers to "100-day" projects to attack costs or other problems. At Ford's Escort factory in Wayne, Michigan, for example, one group studied how to reduce the $585,000 the plant spent each year on Kevlar gloves to protect workers who handle sheet metal and glass. By figuring out how to have the $4.72-a-pair gloves washed so they could be worn more than once, the group saved 50 cents a car, or $115,000 a year.[63]

Speed Strategy

"The computer, the fax, and the microwave are not going to go away; they are going to get faster or be replaced by new technologies that do even more than they do and are faster yet. Demands by consumers for more choices, and faster, more comprehensive services . . . would seem to underline the need for speed in development, production, and delivery of products and services."[64]

The first imperative under such a strategy is to select highly skilled individuals who are committed to speed management and whose beliefs, attitudes, and values related to time are consistent with those the organization is seeking. Both workers and managers must embrace change, rather than resist it; company culture must support their efforts; and both work groups and cross-functional teams must share the same norms about time. A fluid, networked organizational structure, rather than the old "command, control, and compartmentalization" system, is most appropriate. Finally, all HR systems, including staffing, training, reward, and performance management, must support the speed-management philosophy.

As an example of speed strategy in action, consider Dell Computer's approach to business-to-business e-commerce. Dell applies its customer-obsessed direct-sales practices and enhances them using the Web to take care of annoying details. The company's main weapon is its Premier Page Program, which serves over 5,000 U.S. companies. When Dell wins a corporate customer with more than 400 employees, it will build that customer's Premier Page. The page is little more than a set of smaller Web pages, often linked to the customer's intranet, which let approved employees go online to configure personal computers (PCs), pay for them, and track their delivery status. About $5 million of Dell PCs are ordered this way every day. Premier Pages provide access to instant technical support and Dell sales representatives. There is no more waiting on hold. The pages reduce ordering errors, and they free Dell employees to do things only they can do—such as talking face-to-face with customers and selling merchandise. One corporate customer, Bayer Corporation, had the following to say about Dell's sales representative: "He solicits input. He knows the heartbeat of Bayer. He's there to solve our problems, not just get commissions."[65] That's speed strategy in action, but it's also innovation, quality enhancement, and cost control. People are essential ingredients of Dell's hybrid strategy, for they are the sources of innovation and renewal.

Throughout this section we have been emphasizing the need to align a firm's general business strategy with its HRM strategy. Federal Express and United Parcel Service illustrate this interplay nicely.

EMPLOYMENT SYSTEMS AND BUSINESS STRATEGIES AT FEDEX AND UPS[66]   COMPANY EXAMPLE

Explanations for what makes firms competitive are turning more frequently to the notion of "core competencies" that are unique to firms.[67] In this example, let us consider some unique competencies that differentiate services and, in turn, drive the competitiveness of the two firms in question.

Although both Federal Express (FedEx) and United Parcel Service (UPS) are in the shipping business, it is difficult to find two companies with people-management practices that are more different. FedEx has no union, and its workforce is managed using the latest HRM tools. For example, both individual and group performance are assessed, and both influence pay. The company has

pay-for-suggestion systems, quality-of-work-life (QWL) programs, and a variety of other arrangements that empower employees and increase their involvement. Employees at FedEx have played an important role in helping design the organization of work and the way technology has been used.

UPS, on the other hand, uses none of these HRM practices. Employees have no direct say over issues regarding how work is organized. Their jobs are designed by industrial engineers according to time-and-motion studies. The performance of each employee is measured and evaluated against company standards for each task, and employees receive daily feedback on their performance. The only effort at employee involvement is collective bargaining over contract terms through the Teamsters' Union, which represents drivers. Management, rather than the union, appears to be the force maintaining this system of work organization. It has shown little interest in moving toward work systems such as the kind used at FedEx.

The histories of the two companies help explain the difference in management practices. FedEx was founded by Fred Smith, a Yale graduate with a background in economics. At UPS, on the other hand, virtually every executive, including CEO James Kelly, began by driving a truck. Says one logistics consultant, "The UPS guys get ahead by scrambling all the time. They get promoted and hustle like mad and yell at the drivers to make their section profitable and get their bonus. They don't care about image. They're tough. Their attitude is, 'Whaddaya mean I can't drive through that brick wall?' "[68]

The material rewards for working at UPS are substantial, and may more than offset the low levels of job enrichment and the tight supervision. The company pays the highest wages and benefits in the industry. It also offers employees gain-sharing and stock ownership plans. Once-private UPS raised $5.4 billion in November 1999 in the largest IPO ever, although UPS employees still have a large equity stake in the company. In contrast to FedEx, UPS fills virtually all positions (98 percent) from within the company, offering entry-level drivers excellent long-term prospects for advancement.

As a result of these material rewards, UPS employees are highly motivated and loyal to the company, despite a 16-day strike in 1997. With 326,000 employees, versus 141,000 at FedEx, UPS drivers, the most important work group in the delivery business, make 12.4 million daily deliveries, versus 4.5 million at FedEx. Although FedEx hauls far fewer packages than UPS, 71 percent of them go by plane, not truck. This means that FedEx's yield, or revenue per package, is much higher.[69]

Why does it make sense for UPS to rely on highly engineered systems that are generally thought to contribute to poor morale and motivation, but then to offset the negative effects with strong material rewards? FedEx, in contrast, offers an alternative model with high levels of morale and motivation and lower material rewards. Differences in technology do not explain it. FedEx is known for its pioneering investments in information systems (it was the first to install elaborate scanning and tracking equipment, which enabled it to tell customers exactly where their package was), but UPS has responded recently with its own wave of computerized operations. Yet the basic organization of work at UPS has not changed.

In fact, the employment systems in these two companies are driven by their business strategies. FedEx is the smaller of the two, operating until recently with only one hub in Memphis and focusing on the overnight package delivery service as its platform product. UPS, in contrast, has a much larger scale of business. With 150,000 trucks and 610 planes, versus 43,500 trucks and 637 planes for FedEx, UPS has a much larger overall share of the on-time delivery business (55 percent of the market, versus 25 percent for FedEx).[70]

The scale and scope of business at UPS demand an extremely high level of coordination across its network of delivery hubs, coordination that is achievable only through a highly regimented and standardized approach to job design. Changes in practices and procedures essentially have to be systemwide to be effective. Such coordination is compatible with the systemwide process of collective bargaining but not with significant levels of autonomy of the kind associated with shop-floor decision making by employees.

FedEx, on the other hand, historically had only one hub, which meant that there were fewer coordination problems. This allowed considerable scope for autonomy and participation in shaping work decisions at the group level.

What is the lesson in this example? When it comes to managing people, there may be no single set of "best practices" for all employers. Firms that are in competition with one another work hard to differentiate their products and services and to find niches in markets where they are protected from competition. Differentiating products and services is one of the essential functions of strategic management. Distinctive human resource practices encourage differentiation by shaping the core competencies that determine how firms compete.

Each chapter of this book focuses on a different aspect of HRM and considers its impact on three important outcomes: productivity, quality of work life, and profits. In the next two sections we will examine the concepts of productivity and quality of work life. In the next chapter we will focus on the contribution of effective HRM to profits.

PRODUCTIVITY: WHAT IS IT AND WHY IS IT IMPORTANT?

In general, **productivity** is a measure of the output of goods and services relative to the input of labor, capital, and equipment. The more productive an industry, the better its competitive position because its unit costs are lower. When productivity increases, businesses can pay higher wages without boosting inflation. Productivity increases in 2000 were higher than in any period in the past 25 years, largely due to the effect of information technology.[71] This is the way standards of living improve. Improving productivity simply means getting more out of what is put in. It does not mean increasing production through the addition of resources, such as time, money, materials, or people. It is doing better with what you have. Improving productivity is not working harder; it is working smarter. Today's world demands that we do more with less—fewer people, less money, less time, less space, and fewer resources in general. These ideas are shown graphically in Figure 1–4 and illustrated in the company example below.

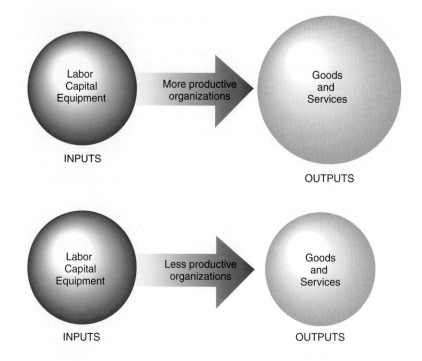

COMPANY EXAMPLE   **IMPROVING PRODUCTIVITY AT GTE CORPORATION72**

Evidence from a wide range of industries shows that productivity gains are real
and ongoing. Whether they are manufacturing semiconductors, offering banking
services, or keeping track of medical records, U.S. companies are doing more
with less. GTE Corporation's operations in Florida's Tampa-Sarasota region are
more the rule than the exception. Over the past 5 years, the area's population
and telephone system have grown by about 7 percent annually, yet GTE still employs the same number of service people, about 250. Laptops let repair crews
plan their daily schedules efficiently and allow customers to get a more accurate
time of arrival from the repair folks. The staff backing up these technicians has
dropped from 45 to 11 as software-driven "expert" systems take customer requests and arrange them in the most efficient order. Indeed, one survey of nearly
400 companies found that the return on investment in information systems
could exceed 50 percent.

Productivity Improvement: Steps Managers Can Take
While information technology clearly drives improvements in productivity, so
also does effective management. Some steps managers can take include:

- Efforts to rebuild employee loyalty that has been eroded by downsizing, restructuring, and mergers. Firms like Xerox, Monsanto, and United Technologies are doing it by boosting training budgets for survivors and overhauling
  pay plans to give survivors a bigger stake in the company's success.[73]
- Helping to make both unionized and nonunionized workers aware that their
  rewards depend ultimately on production.

QUALITY OF WORK LIFE THROUGH QUALITY RELATIONSHIPS

Figure 1–5

Quality of work life through quality relationships, as practiced by the Adolph Coors Company of Golden, Colorado.

"Quality In All We Are And All We Do"

- Recognizing that there is no "quick fix" approach. Worker training, work redesign, product reengineering—all must be linked to the priorities of the business plan and integrated into a comprehensive productivity-improvement strategy.
- Recognizing the crucial importance of continuous improvements in quality (an important aspect of productivity improvement) through prevention of errors. Doing this requires a reshaping of attitudes from the boardroom to the loading dock, so that quality becomes more important than simply getting a product out the door.

Greater productivity benefits organizations directly (i.e., it improves their competitive position relative to that of rivals), and it benefits workers indirectly (e.g., in higher pay and improved purchasing power). But many workers want to see a tighter connection between working smarter and the tangible and psychological rewards they receive from doing their jobs well. They want to see significant improvements in their quality of work life.

QUALITY OF WORK LIFE: WHAT IS IT?

There are two ways of looking at what **quality of work life** means.[74] One way equates QWL with a set of objective organizational conditions and practices (e.g., promotion-from-within policies, democratic supervision, employee involvement, safe working conditions). An example of this approach is shown in Figure 1–5. The other way equates QWL with employees' perceptions that they are safe, relatively well satisfied, and able to grow and develop as human beings. This way relates QWL to the degree to which the full range of human needs is met.

IMPACT OF EFFECTIVE HRM ON PRODUCTIVITY, QUALITY OF WORK LIFE, AND THE BOTTOM LINE

Labor markets were tight in the 1990s. For most of that decade, downsizing set the tone for the modern employment contract. As companies frantically restructured to cope with slipping market share or heightened competition, they tore up old notions of paternalism. They told employees, "Don't expect to spend your life at one company anymore. You are responsible for your own career, so get all the skills you can and prepare to change jobs, employers, even industries. As for the implicit bond of loyalty that might have existed before, well, forget it," said employers. "In these days of fierce global competition, loyalty is an unaffordable luxury."[76]

Today, after several years of tight labor markets, employers have changed their tune. Now it's, "Don't leave. We need you. Work for us—you can build a career here." Employers are going to great lengths to persuade employees that they want them to stay for years. According to a recent survey, employees are less loyal to their companies, and they tend to put their own needs and interests above those of their employers. More often they are willing to trade off higher wages and benefits for flexibility and autonomy, job characteristics that allow them to balance their lives on and off the job. Almost 9 out of every 10 workers live with family members, and nearly half care for dependents, including children, elderly parents, or ailing spouses.[77] Among employees who switched jobs in the last 5 years, pay and benefits rated in the bottom half of 20 possible reasons why they did so. Factors rated highest were "nature of work," "open communication," and "effect on personal/family life." What are the implications of these results? When companies fail to factor in quality-of-work-life issues and quality-of-life issues when introducing any of the popular schemes for improving productivity, the only thing they may gain is a view of the backs of their best people leaving for friendlier employers.[78]

In many cases these two views merge: Workers who like their organizations and the ways their jobs are structured will feel that their work fulfills them. In such cases, either way of looking at one's quality of work life will lead to a common determination of whether a good QWL exists. However, because people differ and because the second view is quite subjective—it concedes, for example, that not everyone finds such things as democratic decision making and self-managed work teams to be important components of a good QWL—we will define QWL in terms of employees' perceptions of their physical and mental well-being at work.

Current Status of QWL Efforts

In theory, QWL is simple—it involves giving workers the opportunity to make decisions about their jobs, the design of their workplaces, and what they need to make products or to deliver services most effectively. It requires managers to treat workers with dignity. Its focus is on employees and management operating the business together.

In practice, its best illustrations can be found in the auto, steel, food, electronics, and consumer products industries, in plants characterized by self-managing work teams, flat organizational structures, and challenging roles for

IMPLICATIONS FOR MANAGEMENT PRACTICE

The trends we have reviewed in this chapter suggest that the old approaches to managing people may no longer be appropriate responses to economic or social reality. A willingness to experiment with new approaches to managing people is healthy. To the extent that the newer approaches do enhance productivity, QWL, and profits, everybody wins. Competitive issues cannot simply be willed away, and because of this we may see even more radical experiments in organizations. The traditional role of the manager may be blurred further as workers take a greater and greater part in planning and controlling work, not simply doing what managers tell them to do. For ex-

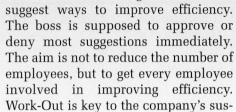

ample, under its Work-Out program, General Electric holds corporate "town meetings" at which lower-level blue- and white-collar employees and even customers grill bosses and suggest ways to improve efficiency. The boss is supposed to approve or deny most suggestions immediately. The aim is not to reduce the number of employees, but to get every employee involved in improving efficiency.

Work-Out is key to the company's sustained productivity growth in the 21st century. Programs such as GE's suggest that human resource management, an essential part of the jobs of all managers, will play an even more crucial role in the future world of work.

all. It requires a willingness to share power, extensive training for workers and managers, and considerable patience by all involved. Workers must get to know the basics of cost, quality, profits, losses, and customer satisfaction by being exposed to more than a narrowly defined job—they must learn to think and act like businesspeople.[75] Managers must come to understand their new role: leaders, helpers, and information gatherers. None of this is simple or easily done, and it may take several years to become fully integrated into a business. Now that we understand the concepts of productivity and QWL, let's examine the impact of effective HRM on them as well as on the bottom line.

BUSINESS TRENDS AND HR COMPETENCIES

Over the past decade, organizations have become more complex, dynamic, and fast-paced. As a result, senior managers recognize that attracting, retaining, and managing people effectively is more important than ever. In leading-edge companies, HR professionals play four key roles[79]:

1. **Strategic partners** show concern for multiple stakeholders, including employees, customers, shareholders, and society at large. They understand how money gets made, spent, and lost in a global context. They educate managers about the value of people as an organizational resource, and about the consequences of both effective and ineffective HRM.
2. **Innovators** help their organizations create an environment that supports continuous learning and improvement. Rather than relying on what others are doing, they create new approaches to managing people.

3. **Collaborators** know how to create win-win situations. They share rather than compete, and work effectively inside as well as outside the organization.
4. **Change facilitators** anticipate the need for change, and prepare their organizations to deal with it. They think conceptually and articulate their ideas clearly. They execute changes in strategy, and energize others to accept and embrace change.

Human Resource Management in Action: Conclusion

THE 21ST CENTURY CORPORATION

Management systems that produce profits through people seem to share seven dimensions in common. Let's briefly examine each one.

1. **Employment security.** Such security is fundamental to most other high-performance management practices. The reason is that innovations in work practices or other forms of worker–management cooperation or productivity improvement are not likely to be sustained over time when workers fear that by increasing productivity they will work themselves out of a job. Additionally, if the goal is to avoid layoffs, organizations will be motivated to hire sparingly in order to keep their labor forces smaller and more productive.
2. **Selective hiring.** This requires several things, the first of which is having a large applicant pool from which to select. Second, the organization needs to be clear about the most critical skills and attributes in the applicant pool. At Southwest Airlines, for example, applicants for flight attendant positions are evaluated in interviews on the basis of initiative, judgment, adaptability, and their ability to learn. Third, the skills and abilities sought should be consistent with particular job requirements and the organization's approach to the market (e.g., high customer service). Fourth, they screen on attributes that are difficult to change through training. For example, technical skills are easier to acquire than teamwork and a service attitude.
3. **Self-managed teams and decentralization are basic elements of organization design.** Teams substitute peer-based control for hierarchical control of work. They also make all the people in a firm feel accountable and responsible for the operation and success of the enterprise, not just a few people in senior management. This increased sense of responsibility stimulates more initiative and effort on the part of everyone involved. By substituting peer for hierarchical control, teams permit removal of layers of hierarchy and the absorption of tasks previously performed by administrative specialists. The tremendously successful natural foods grocery store chain, Whole Foods Markets, is organized on the basis of teams. It attributes much of its success to that arrangement.
4. **Comparatively high compensation contingent on organizational performance.** It is simply not true that only certain industries can or should pay high wages. The Home Depot has been extremely successful and profitable. It operates in a highly competitive environment, and even though it emphasizes everyday low pricing as an important part of its business strategy, it pays its staff comparatively well for the retail industry. It hires

more experienced people with building-industry experience, and it expects its sales associates to provide a higher level of customer service. Broad-based stock ownership also figures prominently in high-performance work systems. Firms such as Wal-Mart, AES Systems, and Microsoft encourage share ownership, but that is only one part of a broader philosophy and culture that incorporates other practices such as training, information sharing, and delegation of responsibility.

5. **Extensive training.** Training is an essential component of high-performance work systems because these systems rely on front-line employee skill and initiative to identify and resolve problems, to initiate changes in work methods, and to take responsibility for quality. Firms such as the Men's Wearhouse (an off-price specialty retailer of men's tailored business attire and accessories) and Motorola use training as a source of competitive advantage. Motorola mandates 40 hours of training per employee per year. It is simply part and parcel of the overall management process of these firms.

6. **Reduced differences in status.** The fundamental premise of high-performance management systems is that organizations perform at a higher level when they are able to tap the ideas, skill, and effort of all their people. Reducing the status distinctions that separate individuals and groups, causing some to feel less valued, helps make all members of an organization feel important and committed. Sam Walton, founder of Wal-Mart, was one of the most underpaid CEOs in the United States. He wasn't poor, for he owned stock in his company. He also encouraged stock ownership for his employees. Having his fortune rise and fall along with those of other employees produced a sense of common fate and reduced status differences.

7. **Sharing of information.** The sharing of information on such things as financial performance, strategy, and operational measures conveys to an organization's people that they are trusted. Even motivated and trained people cannot contribute to enhancing organizational performance if they don't have information on important dimensions of performance and training on how to use and interpret that information. John Mackey, CEO of Whole Foods Markets, states: "If you're trying to create a high-trust organization . . . an organization where people are all-for-one and one-for-all, you can't have secrets."

It may appear easy to create a high-performance organization, but if that were so, then all firms would be as successful as the ones mentioned here. Don't be fooled. Implementation of these ideas in a systematic, consistent fashion is tough, and it remains rare enough to be an important source of competitive advantage for firms in a number of industries. The message at this century's dawn is that management is a human art and getting more so as information technology takes over routine tasks. Progressive managers understand that they will provide competitive advantage by tapping employees' most essential humanity, their ability to create, judge, imagine, and build relationships. As you can see from this case, management of 21st-century organizations will be fast-paced, exciting, and full of people-related business challenges.

SUMMARY

People are a major component of any business, and the management of people (human resource management, or HRM) is a major part of every manager's job. It is also the specialized responsibility of the HR department. In fact, we use the term "strategic HRM" to refer to the wisest possible use of people with respect to the strategic focus of the organization. HRM involves five major areas: staffing, retention, development, adjustment, and managing change. Together they compose the HRM system, for they describe a network of interrelated components. The HRM function is responsible for maximizing productivity, quality of work life, and profits through better management of people.

The competitive business environment of the 21st century will be characterized by factors such as an aging and changing workforce in a high-tech workplace that demands and rewards ever-increasing skill, and increasing global competition in almost every sector of the economy. In response, new organization forms, such as the virtual corporation, the virtual workplace, and the modular corporation, are appearing. The new forms imply a redistribution of power, greater participation by workers, and more teamwork. Firms are also restructuring, reengineering, implementing total quality management, and building flexibility into work schedules in order to support their competitive strategies. Such strategies may involve innovation, quality enhancement, cost reduction, or speed. The challenge of attracting, retaining, and motivating people has never been greater.

One of the most pressing demands we face today is for productivity improvement—getting more out of what is put in; doing better with what we have; and working smarter, not harder. Nevertheless, increased productivity does not preclude a high quality of work life (QWL). QWL refers to employees' perceptions of their physical and psychological well-being at work. It involves giving workers the opportunity to make decisions about their jobs, the design of their workplaces, and what they need to make products or to deliver services most effectively. Its focus is on employees and management operating a business together. HR professionals can help by serving as strategic partners, innovators, collaborators, and change facilitators.

DISCUSSION QUESTIONS

1–1. What are the HRM implications of globalization, technology, and e-commerce?

1–2. How will demographic changes and increasing cultural diversity affect the ways that organizations manage their people?

1–3. Considering everything we have discussed in this chapter, describe management styles and practices that will be effective for businesses in the next decade.

1–4. What difficulties do you see in shifting from a hierarchical, departmentalized organization to a leaner, flatter one in which power is shared between workers and managers?

1–5. How can effective HRM contribute to improvements in productivity and quality of work life?

KEY TERMS

staffing	development
retention	adjustment

managing change	competitive strategies
HRM system	innovation strategy
authority	quality-enhancement strategy
globalization	cost-reduction strategy
human resource information system	speed strategy
virtual organization	productivity
virtual workplace	quality of work life
restructuring	strategic partners
downsizing	collaborators
total quality management	innovators
reengineering	change facilitators

APPLYING YOUR KNOWLEDGE

*Employee Participation and Customer Satisfaction**   *Case 1–1*

"Joe and I virtually share everything. We sit together. We're in meetings together. We're together even when we're apart." So says R. Timothy Epps, vice president of people systems at Saturn Corporation. The partner to which he refers is Joseph D. Rypkowski, a vice president of the United Auto Workers (UAW). This partnering between management and labor is the crux of Saturn Corporation's revolutionary idea. Not only are Epps and Rypkowski "paired," but so are Saturn's president and the UAW's top boss. From the top management level down through the ranks, both represented and nonrepresented workers have partners, and, unlike many other organizations with adversarial labor–management relations, the UAW and Saturn's management work together as teams in virtually every facet of the operation. According to Epps, "We're committed to an entirely different set of beliefs. One is to have UAW involvement in all aspects of the business. The other crucial principle is that we believe those people affected by a decision should be involved in that decision."

Saturn Corporation is a wholly owned subsidiary of General Motors (GM). GM's market share in the United States is down to 29.4 percent, and GM, the largest industrial corporation in the world, has been struggling of late. GM is Detroit's high-cost producer. Saturn is part of GM's strategy to get its North American automobile business back in gear.

The genesis of the Saturn experiment in teamwork occurred in February of 1984 with the establishment of Group 99. This group consisted of 99 employees representing a broad cross-section of UAW members, GM managers, and staff from over 50 plants around the country.

The goal of Group 99 was to study other top-performing, globally successful corporations, and to create a new approach to building a small car in the United States. The

---

Adapted from: D. A. Aaker, Building a brand: The Saturn story, *California Management Review, 36*(2), 1994, 114–133; R. Blumenstein, GM's first-quarter profit soared 76%, aided by strength in North America, *The Wall Street Journal*, Apr. 15, 1997, pp. A3, A5; S. Rubinstein, M. Bennett, & T. Kochan, The Saturn partnership: Co-management and the reinvention of the local union, in B. E. Kaufman & M. M. Kleiner (eds.), *Employment representation,* ILR Press, Ithaca, NY, 1992; Saturn Company web page, *www.saturn.com;* GM: Why strong profits aren't good enough, *BusinessWeek,* Dec. 27, 1999, p. 56; G. L. White, Late to the fair, Saturn is set to unveil small SUV, *The Wall Street Journal*, Oct. 6, 2000, pp. B1, B4.

hope was that this step would enable GM to compete effectively in the small-car market, something it had been unable to do in the past.

After visiting and studying about 60 benchmark companies, Group 99 concluded that employees did their best work and were most committed when they felt they were part of the decision-making process. Their recommendation was that Saturn, with its headquarters in Troy, Michigan, and its manufacturing operations in Spring Hill, Tennessee, would have to operate with a totally new and different philosophy. According to Epps, "The primary goal is to create a culture in which employees accept ownership for the direct labor functions they perform, but to also create a culture that reaches out and helps them understand the systems that support them."

To enable Saturn to operate with a completely new philosophy, GM created Saturn as a separate subsidiary on January 7, 1985. This autonomy allowed a new structure to be put into place and is a crucial step in Saturn's success. The company operates according to five shared values: commitment to customer enthusiasm, commitment to excel, teamwork, trust and respect for the individual, and continuous improvement.

General Motors sees Saturn as a possible model for future GM plants. Former chairman Roger Smith indicated that the techniques that GM would learn from the Saturn experiment would eventually be replicated throughout the company, "improving the efficiency and competitiveness of every plant we operate. . . . Saturn is the key to GM's long-term competitiveness, survival, and success as a domestic producer."

Along with a different approach to its employees, Saturn has taken a much different approach toward its customers. It begins with the now-famous "no-dicker-sticker"—a fixed price for each automobile sold. This eliminates the price haggling many customers resent. Saturn salespeople are called "sales consultants" and they do not work on commission. The consultants receive considerable training, including team-building skills, orientation toward partnering with the factory, and treating customers as intelligent human beings. This approach has enabled Saturn to build up some of the strongest brand-loyalty and customer-satisfaction ratings in the auto industry.

Saturn's customer orientation is illustrated in the way it handled a recall in June 1993. At that time, the company discovered that a wire may not have been properly grounded on all models produced prior to April 1993. The publicity surrounding the recall was generally positive. For one thing, the recall was not mandated by the government. Instead, it was voluntary, and it was handled expeditiously. After two weeks, about half the cars were repaired. By comparison, a major recall by a competitor about the same time was only about one-third complete after a year. Finally, Saturn dealers handled the recall with grace and good humor. One chartered a bus to a local baseball game. When the bus returned, the cars had been repaired and washed. Another had a barbecue for customers while their cars were being fixed. A third offered theater tickets. The result of all this? Marketing studies undertaken by the J. D. Power Company showed that customer satisfaction did not decline at all as a result of the recall. In fact, several dimensions of customer satisfaction (e.g., "takes care of customers," "good dealer") ratings actually improved.

One key is that the UAW has also committed to the Saturn experiment, and has signed a historic labor agreement in an attempt to minimize confrontation. "Traditionally, in my experience," explains Rypkowski, "production employees felt that the corporation had very deep pockets and that their input wasn't welcome. It didn't matter whether they provided input. Therefore, who cared if the systems that supported them or the operations around them were inefficient, because it didn't matter."

The UAW has accepted some fundamental philosophical approaches to running the Saturn plant that are quite different. "We are trying to get more involvement in decision making and ownership for activities that have traditionally been performed by management or resource people," explains Rypkowski.

In the new approach to management at Saturn, these tasks are performed by people who produce the product. For example, assembly-line workers are responsible for quality control; budgeting; materials handling; and, to some degree, ordering their own materials. Team members even hire their own new team members.

"We've broadened the scope of their responsibilities so they have a bigger and better picture of what it takes to run the business," says Rypkowski. "Even though their piece of running the business may be relatively small, they gain a better appreciation for what the organization has to do and what it costs in dollars."

The ultimate goal at Saturn is to have self-directed work teams in which consensus is used to make decisions. Currently, there are about 150 work teams, consisting of approximately 15 people each.

Saturn's mission statement makes it clear that the intent is to allow employees to be involved in decision making in areas that affect them. Presently, decisions are reached by the "70 percent comfortable" rule of consensus: each team member must feel at least 70 percent comfortable with a decision.

"All you have to do is tell somebody that once," says Rypkowski. "They hear that, and they're going to hold you to it. Once you make that statement, you had better be prepared to follow through because people take it very seriously."

At Saturn, there is no shortage of interest and involvement. In fact, it is not uncommon now for employees to ask how their input was taken into consideration any time a decision is made that affects them. But people's willingness to take responsibility and their ability to do so can be two different things. Employees may *want* to be involved, but are they *able* to perform in these tasks?

Questions

1. What aspects of quality-of-work-life (QWL) programs does the experiment at the Saturn plant illustrate?
2. How can Saturn ensure that employees have not only the willingness to take responsibility but also the ability to do so?
3. In this case, a completely new company was started with considerable autonomy from General Motors. Why do you think so many large organizations turn to "green field" operations such as this when undertaking major changes in corporate culture and operations? Do you foresee any problems down the road for GM in this regard?

REFERENCES

1. Campbell, J. P., Dunnette, M. D., Lawler, E. E., III, & Weick, K. E., Jr. (1970). *Managerial behavior, performance, and effectiveness.* NY: McGraw-Hill.
2. Pfeffer, J. (1998). *The human equation: Building profits by putting people first.* Boston, MA: Harvard Business School Press, chap. 2. See also Cascio, W. F. (2000). *Costing human resources: The financial impact of behavior in organizations* (4th ed.). Cincinnati, OH: South-Western College Publishing.
3. Huselid, M. A. (1995). The impact of human resource management practices on turnover, productivity, and corporate financial performance. *Academy of Management Journal, 38,* pp. 635–672.
4. Davidson, W. N., III, Worrell, D. L., & Fox, J. B. (1996). Early retirement programs and firm performance. *Academy of Management Journal, 39,* pp. 970–984.
5. Welbourne, T. M., & Andrews, A. O. (1996). Predicting the performance of initial public offerings: Should human resource management be in the equation? *Academy of Management Journal, 39,* pp. 891–919.

6. Pfeffer, J., & Veiga, J. F. (1999). Putting people first for organizational success. *Academy of Management Executive, 13*(2), pp. 37–49.

7. The world's largest corporations: The global 500 by the numbers. (2000, July 24). *Fortune*, pp. 232–234, F1–F24.

8. Backlash: Behind the anxiety over globalization. (2000, April 24). *BusinessWeek*, pp. 38–43, 202.

9. Reich, R. B. (1990, Jan.–Feb.). Who is us? *Harvard Business Review,* pp. 53–64.

10. Borderless management: Companies strive to become truly stateless. (1994, May 23). *BusinessWeek*, pp. 24–26.

11. Coy, P. (2000, Aug. 28). The creative economy. *BusinessWeek*, pp. 76–82.

12. Ibid.

13. For Web addresses and contact information for vendors, see the HRIS Buying Guide. (2000, April). *HR Magazine*, pp. 181–200.

14. Hamel, G., & Sampler, J. (1998, Dec. 7). The E-corporation. *Fortune*, pp. 80–92.

15. Smith, R., & Lucchinetti, A. (2000, Aug. 28). Sink or swim. *The Wall Street Journal*, pp. A1, A10. See also *Fortune's* fastest growing companies. (2000, Sept. 4). *Fortune*, pp. 180–186.

16. At Ford, E-commerce is job 1. (2000, Feb. 28). *BusinessWeek*, pp. 74–78.

17. Ibid.

18. Blackmon, D. A. (2000, July 17). Price buster: E-commerce hasn't had an impact on the economy's overall price structure. Yet. *The Wall Street Journal*, pp. R12, R26.

19. Ibid.

20. O'Reilly, B. (2000, Feb. 7). They've got mail! *Fortune*, pp. 101–112.

21. Most in survey want to keep working after retiring. (2000, Sept. 29). *The Denver Post*, p. 8A. See also Coy, op. cit.

22. Byrne, J. A. (1993, Feb. 8). The virtual corporation. *BusinessWeek,* pp. 98–103.

23. Colvin, G. (2000, March 6). Managing in the info era. *Fortune*, pp. F6–F9. See also Kiechel, W., III (1993, May 17). How we will work in the year 2000. *Fortune,* pp. 38–52.

24. Snow, C. C., Lipnack, J., & Stamps, J. (1999). The virtual organization: Promises and payoffs, large and small. In C. L. Cooper and D. M. Rousseau (eds.), *The virtual organization*, pp. 15–30. NY: Wiley.

25. Cascio, W. F. (2000). Managing a virtual workplace. *Academy of Management Executive, 13*(3), pp. 81–90.

26. Spee, J. C. (1995, Mar.). Addition by subtraction: Outsourcing strengthens business focus. *HRMagazine,* pp. 38–43. See also Tully, S. (1993, Feb. 8). The modular corporation. *Fortune,* pp. 106–108, 112–114.

27. Mort Topfer, former vice chairman of Dell, as quoted in Morris, B. (2000, Oct. 16). Can Michael Dell escape the box? *Fortune*, pp. 92–110.

28. Morris, op. cit. See also McWilliams, G. (2000, Aug. 31). System upgrade. *The Wall Street Journal*, pp. A1, A8.

29. O'Reilly, op. cit.

30. At Ford, E-commerce is job 1, op. cit.

31. Dial Dell for servers (1996, Sept. 16). *BusinessWeek*, p. 102. See also Tully, op. cit.

32. Ibid.

33. Morris, J. R., Cascio, W. F., & Young, C. E. (1999, Winter). Downsizing after all these years: Questions and answers about who did it, how many did it, and who benefited from it. *Organizational Dynamics*, pp. 78–87.

34. Walton, M. (1986). *The Deming management method.* NY: Perigee.

35. Brophy, B. (1986, Sept. 29). New technology, high anxiety. *U.S. News & World Report*, pp. 54, 55.

36. Walton, op. cit.

37. Hammer, M., & Champy, J. (1993). *Reengineering the corporation.* NY: Harper Business.

38. White, J. B. (1996, Nov. 26). Next big thing: Re-engineering gurus take steps to remodel their stalling vehicles. *The Wall Street Journal*, pp. A1, A10.
39. Flexibility: The answer to burnout (2000, Sept. 20). *BusinessWeek*, p. 162.
40. Johnson, R. (2000, Sept. 19). Employers now vie to hire moms with young children. *The Wall Street Journal*, p. B2.
41. What employers are offering their employees (2000). *Workplace Visions*, no. 4, p. 3.
42. Conlin, M. (2000, Sept. 20). Nine to 5 isn't working anymore. *BusinessWeek*, pp. 94–98.
43. Taylor, S., & Eder, R. W. (2000). U.S. expatriates and the Civil Rights Act of 1991: Dissolving boundaries. In M. Mendenhall & G. Oddou (eds.), *Readings and cases in international human resource management* (3d ed.). Cincinnati, OH: South-Western College Publishing, pp. 251–279.
44. Porter, M. E. (1985). *Competitive advantage*. New York: Free Press. See also Hitt, M. A., Ireland, R. D., & Hoskisson, R. E. (2001). *Strategic management: Competitiveness and globalization* (4th ed.). Cincinnati, OH: South-Western College Publishing.
45. Vinton, D. E. (1992). A new look at time, speed, and the manager. *Academy of Management Executive*, *6*(4), pp. 7–16. See also Schuler, R. S., & Jackson, S. E. (1987). Linking competitive strategies with human resource management practices. *Academy of Management Executive*, *1*(3), pp. 207–219.
46. Jackson, S. E., & Schuler, R. S. (1990). Human resource planning. *American Psychologist*, *45*, 223–239.
47. Becker, B., & Gerhart, B. (1996). The impact of human resource management on organizational performance: Progress and prospects. *Academy of Management Journal*, *39*, pp. 779–801. See also Gerhart, B., Trevor, C., & Graham, M. (1996). New directions in employee compensation research. In G. R. Ferris (ed.), *Research in personnel and human resources management*, *14*. Greenwich, CT: JAI Press, pp. 143–203.
48. See, for example, Pfeffer, J. (1994). *Competitive advantage through people*. Boston: Harvard Business School Press.
49. Cappelli, P., & Crocker-Hefter, A. (1996). Distinctive human resources are firms' core competencies. *Organizational Dynamics*, *24*(3), pp. 7–22.
50. Youndt, M. A., Snell, S. A., Dean, J. W., Jr., & Lepak, D. P. (1996). Human resource management, manufacturing strategy, and firm performance. *Academy of Management Journal*, *39*, pp. 836–866.
51. Banas, P. A. (1988). Employee involvement: A sustained labor/management initiative at the Ford Motor Company. In J. P. Campbell and R. J. Campbell (eds.), *Productivity in organizations*. San Francisco: Jossey-Bass, pp. 388–416 (quotation source: p. 391).
52. Ulrich, D. (1998, Jan.–Feb.). A new mandate for human resources. *Harvard Business Review*, pp. 124–134.
53. Brown, E. (1999, May 24). Nine ways to win on the Web. *Fortune*, pp. 112–125. See also Schuler & Jackson, op. cit.
54. Kanter, R. M. (1985, Winter). Supporting innovation and venture development in established companies. *Journal of Business Venturing*, *1*, pp. 47–60.
55. Jackson, S. E., Schuler, R. S., & Rivero, J. C. (1989). Organizational characteristics as predictors of personnel practices. *Personnel Psychology*, 42, pp. 727–736.
56. Reingold, J. (1999, Mar. 1). Why your workers might jump ship. *BusinessWeek*, p. 8.
57. Shellenbarger, S. (1997, Dec. 21). For keeping employees, money isn't everything. *San Francisco Chronicle,* p. J1.
58. Schuler & Jackson, op. cit.
59. Taylor, A. III. (1990, Nov. 19). Why Toyota keeps getting better and better and better. *Fortune*, pp. 66–79.
60. Cascio, W. F. (1989). Using utility analysis to assess training outcomes. In I. L. Goldstein (ed.), *Training and development in organizations* (pp. 63–88). San Francisco: Jossey-Bass.

61. Schuler & Jackson, op. cit.
62. Richman, L. S. (1993, Sept. 20). When will the layoffs end? *Fortune*, pp. 54–56.
63. Simison, R. L. (1999, Jan. 13). Ford rolls out new model of corporate culture. *The Wall Street Journal*, pp. B1, B4.
64. Vinton, D. E. (1992). A new look at time, speed, and the manager. *Academy of Management Executive*, *6*(4), pp. 7–16.
65. Brown, op. cit., p. 114.
66. Cappelli, P., & Crocker-Hefter, A. (1996, Winter). Distinctive human resources are firms' core competencies. *Organizational Dynamics*, pp. 7–22.
67. Prahalad, C. K., & Hamel, G. (1990, May–June). The core competencies of the corporation. *Harvard Business Review*, pp. 79–91.
68. O'Reilly, op. cit.
69. Ibid.
70. Ibid.
71. Productivity: It just keeps going. (2000, Feb. 21). *BusinessWeek*, p. 176. See also Coy, op. cit.
72. Riding high: Corporate America now has an edge over its global rivals (1995, Oct. 9). *BusinessWeek*, p. 142.
73. *Survivors* White, J. B., & Lublin, J. S. (1996, Sept. 27). Some companies try to rebuild loyalty. *The Wall Street Journal*, pp. B1, B2.
74. Lawler, E. E., & Mohrman, S. A. (1985, Jan.–Feb.). Quality circles: After the fad. *Harvard Business Review*, pp. 65–71.
75. Case, J. (1995, June). The open-book revolution. *Inc.*, pp. 26–43.
76. We want you to stay. Really. *BusinessWeek*, June 22, 1998, pp. 67–72.
77. Johnson, A. A. (1999, Feb.). *Strategic meal planning: Work-life initiatives for building strong organizations*. Paper presented at the conference on integrated health, disability, and work/life initiatives. New York.
78. Noble, B. P. (1993, Sept. 11). Quality-of-life is getting to be key work issue. *The New York Times*, p. A6.
79. Schuler, R. S., Jackson, S. E., & Storey, J. (2000). HRM and its link with strategic management. In J. Storey (ed.), *Human resource management: A critical text*. London: International Thomson, chap. 7.

2 THE FINANCIAL IMPACT OF HUMAN RESOURCE MANAGEMENT ACTIVITIES

Questions This Chapter Will Help Managers Answer

1. Can behavior costing help improve our business?
2. If I want to know how much money employee turnover is costing us each year, what factors should I consider?
3. How do employees' attitudes relate to customer satisfaction and revenue growth?
4. What's the business case for work-life programs?
5. Is there evidence that high-performance work policies are associated with improved financial performance?

LINKING WORKER BELIEFS TO INCREASED PRODUCTIVITY AND PROFITABILITY[1]

An in-depth study by the Gallup Organization, the Princeton, N.J.–based polling and research firm, identified 12 worker beliefs that play the biggest role in triggering a profitable, productive workplace. Its multiyear study was based on an analysis of data from more than 100,000 employees in 12 industries.

Analysis showed a consistent, reliable relationship between the 12 beliefs and outcomes such as profits, productivity, employee retention, and customer loyalty. For example, work groups that have these positive attitudes are 50 percent more likely to achieve customer loyalty and 44 percent more likely to produce above-average profitability.

Gallup analyzed employee data to determine how well the respondents' organizations support the 12 employee statements. Organizations whose support of the statements ranked in the top 25 percent averaged 24 percent higher profitability, 29 percent higher revenue, and 10 percent lower employee turnover than those that scored lowest on the statements. Here are the 12 basic belief statements that underlie the most important worker attitudes:

1. I know what is expected of me at work.
2. I have the materials and equipment I need to do my work right.
3. At work I have the opportunity to do what I do best every day.
4. In the last 7 days I have received recognition or praise for doing good work.
5. My supervisor, or someone at work, seems to care about me as a person.
6. There is someone at work who encourages my development.
7. In the last 6 months someone at work has talked to me about my progress.
8. At work, my opinions seem to count.
9. The mission or purpose of my company makes me feel my job is important.
10. My fellow employees are committed to doing quality work.
11. I have a best friend at work.
12. This last year I have had opportunities at work to learn and grow.

According to Curt Coffman, a Gallup senior vice president and workplace consultant, the best news is that the 12 beliefs can be coaxed forth with good management techniques. "These are all something that we can really do something about. Unlike pay issues, which most managers and workers have no control over, every individual team member can do something to help create these beliefs."

For instance, consider belief number 4. Although it requires long-term commitment, managers can deliver on this, at very little cost. Belief number 7 is even less time-consuming. Interestingly, researchers found significant variances between work groups or operating units within the same company. "What becomes clear from this investigation is that while we tend to celebrate great companies, in reality there are only great managers," Coffman said. In fact, it is on the front line that the hard work of building a stronger workplace gets done. Gallup has studied thousands of great managers and has identified the key behaviors that the best managers seem to share in helping to trigger these beliefs. In the conclusion to this chapter-opening vignette, we will consider what these key behaviors might be.

Challenges

1. What kinds of organizational policies might help to support these beliefs?
2. What can a manager do in his or her everyday behavior to encourage these beliefs?
3. Why is it that work groups that hold these beliefs are 50 percent more likely to achieve customer loyalty? What might be the link?

In business settings, it is hard to be convincing without data. If the data are developed systematically and comprehensively and are analyzed in terms of their strategic implications for the business or business unit, they are more convincing. The chapter-opening vignette demonstrates how the beliefs of workers on 12 issues affect company profitability and turnover. In this chapter we will examine methods used to assess the costs and benefits of HR activities in six key areas: absenteeism, turnover, employee attitudes, work-life programs, training, and high-performance work practices.

Orientation

As emphasized earlier, the focus of this book is *not* on training HR specialists. Rather, it is on training line managers, who must, by the very nature of their jobs, manage people and work with them to accomplish organizational objectives. Consequently, the purpose of this chapter is not to show how to measure the effectiveness of the HR department; the purpose is to show how to assess the costs and benefits of relevant HR activities. The methods can and should be used in cooperation with the HR department, but they are not the exclusive domain of that department. They are general enough to be used by any manager in any department to measure the costs and benefits of employee behavior.

This is not to imply that dollars are the only barometer of the effectiveness of HR activities. The payoffs from some activities, such as managing diversity and providing child care, must be viewed in a broader social context. Furthermore, the firm's strategy and goals must guide the work of each business unit and of that unit's HR management activities. For example, to emphasize its outreach efforts to the disadvantaged, a firm might adopt a conscious strategy of *training* workers for entry-level jobs, while *selecting* workers who already have the skills to perform higher-level jobs. To make the most effective use of the information that follows, keep these points in mind. We begin this chapter by describing a general approach to attaching economic estimates to the consequences of employee behaviors. This method is known as **behavior costing.**

THE BEHAVIOR COSTING APPROACH

This approach assigns dollar estimates to behaviors, such as the absenteeism, turnover, and job performance, of employees and managers. Behavior costing does not measure the value of an employee or manager as an asset, but rather it considers the economic consequences of his or her behavior. This is an expense model of HR accounting,[2] and, contrary to popular belief, there are methods for determining the costs of employee behavior in all HR management activities—behaviors associated with the attraction, selection, retention, development, and utilization of people in organizations. It is the approach taken in this chapter to assessing the costs and benefits of the activities of all employees, managerial as well as nonmanagerial. We will apply standard cost-accounting procedures to employee behavior. To do this, we must first identify each of the elements of behavior to which we can assign a cost; and each behavioral cost element must be separate and mutually exclusive from the others. To begin, let's consider the definitions of some key terms.

Some Definitions

The costing methods described below are based on several definitions and a few necessary assumptions. To begin with, there are, as in any costing situation, both controllable and uncontrollable costs, and there are direct and indirect measures of these costs.

Direct measures refer to actual costs, such as the accumulated, direct cost of recruiting.

Indirect measures do not deal directly with cost; they are usually expressed in terms of time, quantity, or quality.[3] In many cases indirect measures can be converted to direct measures. For example, if we know the length of time per preemployment interview plus the interviewer's hourly pay, it is a simple matter to convert time per interview into cost per interview.

Indirect measures have value in and of themselves, and they also supply part of the data needed to develop a direct measure. As a further example, consider the direct and indirect costs associated with mismanaged organizational stress, as shown in Table 2–1.[4] The direct costs listed in the left-hand column of Table 2–1 can all be expressed in terms of dollars. To understand this concept, consider just two items: the costs associated with work accidents and with grievances. Figure 2–1 presents just some of the direct costs associated with accidents; it is not meant to be exhaustive, and it does not include such items as lost time, replacement costs, institution of "work to rule" by co-workers if they feel the firm is responsible, the cost of the safety committee's investigation, and the costs associated with changing technology or job design to prevent future accidents. The items shown in the right-hand column of Table 2–1 cannot be expressed as easily in dollar terms, but they are no less important, and the cost of these indirect items may in fact be far larger than the direct costs. Both direct and indirect costs, as well as benefits, must be considered to apply behavior-costing methodology properly.

Controllable versus Uncontrollable Costs

In any area of behavior costing, some types of costs are controllable through prudent HR decisions, while other costs are simply beyond the control of the organization. Consider employee turnover as an example. To the extent that people leave for reasons of "better salary," "more opportunity for promotion and career development," or "greater job challenge," the firm incurs **controllable costs** associated with turnover. That is, the firm can alter its HR management practices to reduce the voluntary turnover. However, if the turnover is due to such factors as death, poor health, or spouse transfer, the firm incurs **uncontrollable costs.**

Table 2–1

DIRECT AND INDIRECT COSTS ASSOCIATED WITH MISMANAGED STRESS

Direct costs	Indirect costs

Participation and membership:
  Absenteeism
  Tardiness
  Strikes and work stoppages
	Loss of vitality:
	  Low motivation
	  Dissatisfaction

Performance on the job:
  Quality of productivity
  Quantity of productivity
  Grievances
  Accidents
  Unscheduled machine downtime
    and repair
  Material and supply
    overutilization
  Inventory shrinkages
	Communication breakdowns:
	  Decline in frequency of contact
	  Distortions of messages
	
	Faulty decision making
	
	Quality of work relations:
	  Distrust
	  Disrespect
	  Animosity

Compensation awards	Opportunity costs

Source: B. A. Macy & P. H. Mirvis, *Evaluation Review, 6*(3), Figure 4–5. Copyright © 1982 by Sage Publications, Inc. Reprinted by permission.

The point is that in human resource costing, the objective is not simply to *measure* costs but also to *reduce* the costs of human resources by devoting resources to the more "controllable" factors. To do this, we must do two things well:

1. Identify, for each HR decision, which costs are controllable and which are not.
2. Measure these costs at Time 1 (prior to some intervention designed to reduce controllable costs) and then again at Time 2 (after the intervention).

Hence the real payoff from determining the cost of employee behaviors lies in being able to demonstrate a financial gain from the wise application of human resource management methods.

The following sections present both hypothetical and actual company examples of behavior costing in the areas of absenteeism, turnover, employee attitudes, work-life programs, training, and high-performance work practices. Then we present two macro-level assessments of the financial impact of high-performance work practices, one focusing on organizational culture and the other on how HR factors affect the probability of survival of initial public offerings (IPOs). The focus will be on methods and outcomes rather than on alternative HR management approaches that might be used to reduce costs or increase profits in each area. (We discuss such approaches in subsequent chapters throughout the book.)

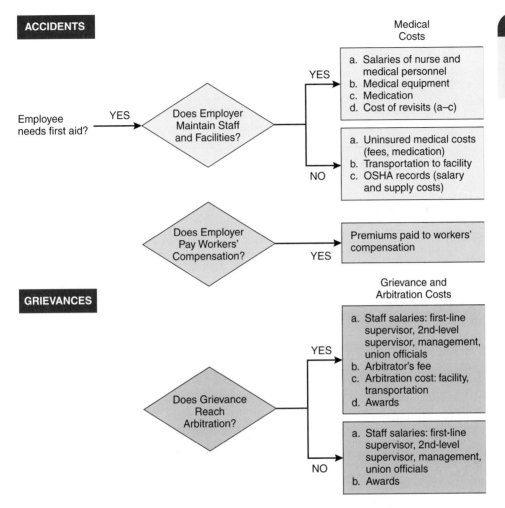

Figure 2–1

The costs of accidents and grievances.

COSTING EMPLOYEE ABSENTEEISM

In any human resource costing application, it is important first to define exactly what is being measured. From a business standpoint, **absenteeism** *is any failure of an employee to report for or to remain at work as scheduled, regardless of reason.* The term "as scheduled" is very significant, for it automatically excludes vacations, holidays, jury duty, and the like. It also eliminates the problem of determining whether an absence is "excusable" or not. Medically verified illness is a good example. From a business perspective, the employee is absent and is simply not available to perform his or her job; that absence will cost money. How much money? In year 2000 dollars, the cost of unscheduled absences in U.S. workplaces was about $800 *per employee per year.*[5] For every 100 employees, that's $80,000. Figures like that get management's attention.

   Would it surprise you to learn that the leading causes of absenteeism are family-related issues? Personal illness, the reason you might expect to be the main justification for calling in sick, is actually true only in about 1 in 5 cases. Other causes are personal needs (about 1 in 5 cases), stress (about 1 in 6 cases), and entitlement mentality (about 1 in 6 cases).[6]

Figure 2–2

Total estimated cost of employee absenteeism.
(*Source:* W. F. Cascio, *Costing human resources: The financial impact of behavior in organizations* [4th ed.], South-Western College Publishing, Cincinnati, OH, 2000, p. 63. Used with permission.)

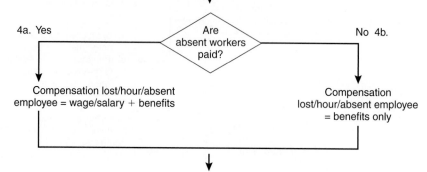

1. Compute total employee hours lost to absenteeism for the period.

2. Compute weighted average wage or salary/hour/absent employee.

3. Compute cost of employee benefits/hour/employee.

4a. Yes   Are absent workers paid?   No 4b.

Compensation lost/hour/absent employee = wage/salary + benefits

Compensation lost/hour/absent employee = benefits only

5. Compute total compensation lost to absent employees (1. × 4a. or 4b., as applicable).

6. Estimate total supervisory hours lost to employee absenteeism.

7. Compare average hourly supervisory salary + benefits.

8. Estimate total supervisory salaries lost to managing absenteeism problems (6. × 7.).

9. Estimate all other costs incidental to absenteeism.

10. Estimate total costs of absenteeism (Σ5., 8., 9.).

11. Estimate total cost of absenteeism/employee (10. ÷ total no. employees).

Figure 2–2 is a flowchart that shows how to estimate the total cost of employee absenteeism over any period. To illustrate the computation of each cost element in Figure 2–2, let us use as an example a hypothetical 1,800-employee firm called Mini-Mini-Micro Electronics; hour and dollar amounts for each element are shown in Table 2–2. An item-by-item explanation follows.

Item 1: Total Hours Lost to Employee Absenteeism for the Period. Assume that employee absenteeism accounts for 1.75 percent of scheduled work hours (about average for manufacturing firms in the United States),[7] which will be applied to total scheduled work hours. Also assume an 8-hour day and a 5-day week. Hours of scheduled work time per employee per year may be determined by subtracting 2 weeks' vacation hours and 5 paid holidays from total work hours:

$$\text{Total hours of work per year} = 40 \text{ hours} \times 52 \text{ weeks} = 2{,}080 \text{ hours}$$
$$2 \text{ weeks of vacation} = 40 \text{ hours} \times 2 \text{ weeks} = 80 \text{ hours}$$
$$5 \text{ paid holidays} = 40 \text{ hours} \times 5 \text{ days} = 40 \text{ hours}$$
$$\text{Scheduled work hours per year per employee} =$$
$$2{,}080 \text{ hr} - 80 \text{ hr} - 40 \text{ hr} = 1{,}960 \text{ hr}$$

Table 2–2

COST OF EMPLOYEE ABSENTEEISM AT MINI-MINI-MICRO ELECTRONICS.

Item	Mini-Mini-Micro Electronics
1. Total hours lost to employee absenteeism for the period	61,740 hr
2. Weighted-average wage or salary per hour per absent employee	$19.30/hr
3. Cost of employee benefits per hour per absent employee	$6.755/hr
4. Total compensation lost per hour per absent employee:	
a. if absent workers are paid (wage or salary plus benefits)	$26.055/hr
b. if absent workers are not paid (benefits only)	—
5. Total compensation lost to absent employees (total hours lost × 4a or 4b, whichever applies)	$1,608,635.75
6. Total supervisory hours lost on employee absenteeism	8820 hr
7. Average hourly supervisory wage, including benefits	$32.063/hr
8. Total supervisory salaries lost to managing problems of absenteeism (hours lost × average hourly supervisory wage—item 6 × item 7)	$282,791.25
9. All costs incidental to absenteeism and not included in items 1 through 8	$200,000
10. Total estimated cost of absenteeism— summation of items 5, 8, and 9	$2,091,427
11. Total estimated cost of absenteeism per employee (total estimated costs ÷ total number of employees)	$1,161.90 per employee absence

To calculate total scheduled work hours per year, multiply the hours of scheduled work time per employee by the number of employees:

1,960 hr × 1,800 employees = 3,528,000 total scheduled work hours per year

To determine total work hours lost to absenteeism, multiply total scheduled hours by 1.75 percent:

3,528,000 hr × 0.0175 = 61,740 work hours lost per year

Item 2: Weighted-Average Wage or Salary per Hour per Absent Employee. Employers that have systems in place for employees to report their absences can determine the exact wage or salary per hour per absent employee. Others might use the following procedure to estimate a weighted-average wage or salary per hour per absentee:

Occupational group	Approximate percentage of total absenteeism	Average hourly wage	Weighted average wage
Blue-collar workers	.55	$19.05	$10.48
Clerical workers	.35	16.20	$ 5.67
Management and professional	.10	31.50	$ 3.15
Total weighted-average pay per employee per hour			$19.30

Item 3: Cost of Employee Benefits per Hour per Absent Employee. The cost of benefits is included in the calculations because benefits consume, on average, more than a third of total compensation (see Chapter 12). Ultimately, we want to be able to calculate the total compensation lost as a result of absenteeism. Since our primary interest is in the cost of benefits per absentee, we multiply the weighted-average hourly wage by the benefits as a percentage of base pay. (If benefits differ as a function of union-nonunion or exempt-nonexempt status, a weighted-average benefit should be computed in the same manner as was done to compute a weighted-average wage.) For Mini-Mini-Micro, the cost of benefits per hour per absentee is

$$\$19.30 \times 0.35 = \$6.755$$

Item 4: Total Compensation Lost per Hour per Absent Employee. This amount is determined by adding the weighted-average hourly wage and the hourly cost of benefits (assuming that absent workers are paid). Some firms (e.g., Honda USA) do not pay absentees: "No work, no pay." In such instances, only the cost of benefits should be included in the estimate of total compensation lost per hour per absent employee. For Mini-Mini-Micro, where absent workers *are* paid, the compensation lost per hour for each absent employee is

$$\$19.30 + \$6.755 = \$26.055$$

Item 5: Total Compensation Lost to Absent Employees. This amount is simply total hours lost multiplied by total compensation lost per hour:

$$61,740 \text{ hr} \times \$26.055/\text{hr} = \$1,608,635.75$$

Note that the first five items shown in Figure 2–2 refer to the costs associated with absentees themselves. The next three items refer to the firm's costs of managing employee absenteeism.

Item 6: Total Supervisory Hours Lost on Employee Absenteeism. Three factors determine this category of lost time:

A = Estimated average number of hours lost per supervisor per day managing absenteeism problems

B = Total number of supervisors who deal with absenteeism problems

C = *Total number of working days in the period for which absentee costs are being analyzed (including all shifts and weekend work)*

The supervisor's time is "lost" because, instead of planning, scheduling, and troubleshooting productivity problems, he or she must devote time to non-productive activities associated with managing absenteeism problems. The actual amount of time lost can be determined by having supervisors keep diaries indicating how they spend their time or by conducting structured interviews with experienced supervisors.

To calculate supervisory hours lost, multiply $A \times B \times C$. For Mini-Mini-Micro Electronics, the data needed for this calculation are as follows:

Estimate of A = 30 minutes, or 0.50 hour, per day

Estimate of B = 72 supervisors

(Of the firm's 1,800 employees, 10 percent, or 180, are supervisors, and 40 percent of the 180, or 72, of the supervisors deal regularly with absenteeism problems.)

Estimate of C = 245 days per year

Supervisory hours lost in dealing with absenteeism = 0.50 hour per day × 72 supervisors × 245 days per year

= 8820 supervisory hours lost per year

Item 7: Average Hourly Supervisory Wage, Including Benefits. For those supervisors who deal regularly with absenteeism problems, assume that their average hourly wage is $23.75 plus 35 percent benefits ($8.313), or $32.063 per hour.

Item 8: Total Cost of Supervisory Salaries Lost to Managing Problems of Absenteeism. To determine this cost, multiply the total supervisory hours lost by the total hourly supervisory wage:

8,820 hours × $32.063 per hour = $282,791.25

Item 9: All Costs Incidental to Absenteeism and Not Included in Items 1 through 8. Assume that Mini-Mini-Micro spends $200,000 per year in absenteeism-related costs that are not associated with either absentees or supervisors. These costs are associated with elements such as overtime premiums; wages for temporary help; machine downtime; production losses; inefficient materials usage by temporary substitute employees; and, for very large organizations, permanent labor pools to fill in for absent workers.

Item 10: Total Estimated Cost of Employee Absenteeism—Summation of Items 5, 8, and 9. This cost is the sum of the three costs determined thus far: costs associated with absent employees (item 5) plus costs associated with the management of absenteeism problems (item 8) plus other absenteeism-related costs (item 9). For Mini-Mini-Micro Electronics, the total yearly cost is

$$\$1,608,635.75 + \$282,791.25 + \$200,000 = \$2,091,427$$

Item 11: Total Estimated Cost of Absenteeism per Employee. This amount is the total yearly cost divided by the number of employees:

$$\$2,091,427 \div 1800 \text{ employees} = \$1,161.90$$

Interpreting the Costs of Absenteeism

Perhaps the first questions management will ask upon seeing absenteeism cost figures are: What do they mean? Are we average, above average, below average? Unfortunately, there are no industry-specific figures on the costs of employee absenteeism. Certainly, these costs will vary depending on the type of firm, the industry, and the level of employee that is absent (unskilled versus skilled or professional workers). As a benchmark, however, consider that the average employee in the United States has about seven unscheduled absences per year, while the average British employee has about eight per year.[8]

Remember that the dollar figure determined above (we will call it the "Time 1" figure) becomes meaningful as a baseline from which to measure the financial gains realized as a result of a strategy to reduce absenteeism. At some later time (we will call this "Time 2"), the total cost of absenteeism should be measured again. The difference between the Time 2 figure and the Time 1 figure, minus the cost of implementing the strategy to reduce absenteeism, represents net gain.

Other questions that often arise at this point are: Are these dollars real? Since supervisors are drawing their salaries anyway, what difference does it make if they have to manage absenteeism problems? True, but what is the best possible gain from them for that pay? Let's compare two firms, A and B, identical in regard to all resources and costs—supervisors get paid the same, work the same hours, manage the same size staff, and produce the same kind of product. But absenteeism in A is very low, and in B it is very high. The paymasters' records show the same pay to supervisors, but the accountants show higher profits in A than in B. Why? Because the supervisors in firm A spend less time managing absenteeism problems. They are more productive because they devote their energies to planning, scheduling, and troubleshooting. Instead of putting in a 10- or 12-hour day (which the supervisors in firm B consider "normal"), they wrap things up after only 8 hours. In short, reducing the number of hours that supervisors must spend managing absenteeism problems has two advantages. One, it allows supervisors to maximize their productivity, and two, it reduces the stress and the wear and tear associated with repeated 10- to 12-hour days, which, in turn, enhances the quality of work life of supervisors.

COSTING EMPLOYEE TURNOVER

Organizations need a practical procedure for measuring and analyzing the costs of employee turnover, especially because top managers view the costs of hiring, training, and developing employees as investments that must be evaluated just like other corporate resources. The objective in costing human resources is not just to measure the relevant costs, but also to develop methods and programs to reduce the costs of human resources by managing the more controllable aspects of those costs.

Turnover may be defined as *any permanent departure beyond organizational boundaries*[9]—a broad and ponderous definition. Not included as turnover within this definition, therefore, are transfers within an organization and temporary layoffs. The rate of turnover in percentage over any period can be calculated by the following formula:

$$\frac{\text{Number of turnover incidents per period}}{\text{Average work force size}} \times 100\%$$

Nationwide in 1999, for example, monthly turnover rates averaged about 1 percent, or 12 percent annually.[10] However, this figure most likely represents both controllable turnover (controllable by the organization) and uncontrollable turnover. Controllable turnover is "voluntary" on the part of the employee, while uncontrollable turnover is "involuntary" (due, e.g., to retirement, death, or spouse transfer). Furthermore, turnover may be *functional,* where the employee's departure produces a benefit for the organization, or *dysfunctional,* where the departing employee is someone the organization would like to retain.

High performers who are difficult to replace represent dysfunctional turnovers; low performers who are easy to replace represent functional turnovers. The crucial issue in analyzing turnover, therefore, is not how many employees leave but rather the performance and replaceability of those who leave versus those who stay.[11]

In costing employee turnover, first determine the total cost of all turnover and then estimate the percentage of that amount that represents controllable, dysfunctional turnover—resignations that represent a net loss to the firm and that the firm could have prevented. Thus, if total turnover costs $1 million and 50 percent is controllable and dysfunctional, $500,000 is our Time 1 baseline measure. To determine the net financial gain associated with the strategy adopted prior to Time 2, compare the total gain at Time 2, say $700,000, minus the cost of implementing the strategy to reduce turnover, say $50,000, with the cost of turnover at Time 1 ($500,000). In this example, the net gain to the firm is $150,000. Now let's see how the total cost figure is derived.

Components of Turnover Costs

There are three broad categories of costs in the basic turnover costing model: separation costs, replacement costs, and training costs. This section presents only the cost elements that make up each of these three broad categories. Those who wish to investigate the subject more deeply may seek information on the more detailed formulas that are available.[12]

Separation Costs

Following are four cost elements in separation costs:

1. **Exit interview,** including the cost of the interviewer's time and the cost of the terminating employee's time.

2. **Administrative functions related to termination,** for example, removal of the employee from the payroll, termination of benefits, and turn-in of company equipment.
3. **Separation pay,** if applicable.
4. **Increased unemployment tax,** which may come from either or both of two sources. First, in states that base unemployment tax rates on each company's turnover rate, high turnover will lead to a higher unemployment tax rate. Suppose a company with a 10 percent annual turnover rate was paying unemployment tax at a rate of 5 percent on the first $7,000 of each employee's wages in 2000. But in 2001, because its turnover rate jumped to 15 percent, the company's unemployment tax rate may increase to 5.5 percent. Second, replacements for those who leave will result in extra unemployment tax being paid. Thus a 500-employee firm with no turnover during the year will pay the tax on the first $7,000 (or whatever the state maximum is) of each employee's wages. The same firm with a 20 percent annual turnover rate will pay the tax on the first $7,000 of the wages of 600 employees.

The sum of these four cost elements represents the total separation costs for the firm.

Replacement Costs

There are eight cost elements associated with replacing employees who leave:

1. **Communicating job availability.**
2. **Preemployment administrative functions,** for example, accepting applications and checking references.
3. **Entrance interview,** or perhaps multiple interviews.
4. **Testing** and/or other types of assessment procedures.
5. **Staff meetings,** if applicable, to determine whether replacements are needed, to recheck job analyses and job specifications, to pool information on candidates, and to reach final hiring decisions.
6. **Travel and moving expenses,** for example, travel for all applicants and travel plus moving expenses for all new hires.
7. **Postemployment acquisition and dissemination of information,** for example, all the activities associated with in-processing new employees.
8. **Medical examinations,** if applicable, either performed in-house or contracted out.

The sum of these eight cost elements represents the total cost of replacing those who leave.

Training Costs

This third component of turnover costs includes three elements:

1. **Informational literature** (e.g., an employee handbook).
2. **Instruction in a formal training program.**
3. **Instruction by employee assignment** (e.g., on-the-job training).

Table 2–3

PRODUCTIVITY LOSS OVER EACH THIRD OF THE LEARNING PERIOD FOR FOUR JOB CLASSIFICATIONS

Classification	Weeks in learning period	Productivity loss during each third of the learning period		
		1	2	3
Managers and partners	24	75%	40%	15%
Professionals and technicians	16	70	40	15
Office and clerical workers	10	60	40	15
Broker trainees	104	85	75	50

Note: The learning period for the average broker trainee is 2 years, although the cost to the firm is generally incurred only in the first year. It is not until the end of the second year that the average broker trainee is fully productive.

The sum of these three cost elements represents the total cost of training replacements for those who leave.

Note two important points. One, if there is a formal orientation program, the per-person costs associated with replacements for those who left should be included in the first cost element, *informational literature.* This cost should reflect the per-person, amortized cost of developing the literature, not just its delivery. Do not include the total cost of the orientation program unless 100 percent of the costs can be attributed to employee turnover.

Two, probably the major cost associated with employee turnover, *reduced productivity during the learning period,* is generally not included along with the cost elements *instruction in a formal training program* and *instruction by employee assignment.* The reason for this is that formal work-measurement programs are not often found in employment situations. Thus it is not possible to calculate accurately the dollar value of the loss in productivity during the learning period. If such a program does exist, then by all means include this cost. For example, a major brokerage firm did a formal work-measurement study of this problem and reported the results shown in Table 2–3. The bottom line is that we want to be conservative in our training cost figures so that we can defend every number we generate.

The Total Cost of Turnover

The sum of the three component costs—separation, replacement, and training—represents the total cost of employee turnover for the period in question. Other factors could also be included in the tally, such as the uncompensated performance differential between leavers and their replacements, but that is beyond the scope of this book.[13]

Remember, *the purpose of measuring turnover costs is to improve management decision making.* Once turnover figures are known, managers have a sound basis for choosing between current turnover costs and instituting some type of turnover-reduction strategy. These might include actions such as the following: appoint a retention czar whose job is to help build a supportive culture and employee commitment,[14] provide realistic job previews, and institute merit-based rewards to retain high performers).[15]

As an example of the impact of turnover costs on management, consider the results Corning, Inc., found when it tallied only its out-of-pocket expenses for turnover, such as interview costs and hiring bonuses. That number, $16 to $18 million annually, led to an investigation into the causes of turnover and, in turn, to new policies on flexible scheduling and career development.[16]

Think about the fully loaded cost of turnover. It includes not just separation and replacement costs, but also an exiting employee's lost leads and contacts, the new employee's depressed productivity while he or she is learning, and the time coworkers spend guiding him or her. The combined effect of those factors can easily cost 150 percent or more of the departing person's salary.[17] In fact, Merck & Company, the pharmaceutical giant, found that, depending on the job, turnover costs were 1.5 to 2.5 times the annual salary paid.[18]

Obviously, there are opportunities in this area for enterprising managers to make significant bottom-line contributions to their organizations. For example, one way to reduce turnover, especially among employees who seek opportunities for personal growth and professional development, is to provide training. Indeed, among employees who say their company offers poor training, 41 percent plan to leave within a year, versus only 12 percent of those who rate their firm's training opportunities as excellent.[19] At firms such as Hewlett-Packard, IBM, and Skyway Express, training is an important component of each firm's competitive strategy. We will describe methods of assessing the costs and benefits of training in the next section.

FINANCIAL EFFECTS OF EMPLOYEE ATTITUDES

Attitudes are internal states that focus on particular aspects of or objects in the environment. They include three elements: *cognition*, the knowledge an individual has about the focal object of the attitude; the *emotion* an individual feels toward the focal object; and an *action* tendency, a readiness to respond in a predetermined manner to the focal object.

For example, **job satisfaction** is a multidimensional attitude; it is made up of attitudes toward pay, promotions, coworkers, supervision, the work itself, and so on. Another attitude is **organizational commitment**—a bond or linking of an individual to the organization that makes it difficult to leave.[20]

Managers are interested in employees' job satisfaction and commitment principally because of the relationship between attitudes and behavior. They assume that employees who are dissatisfied with their jobs and who are not committed strongly to their organizations will tend to be absent or late for work, to quit more often, and to place less emphasis on customer satisfaction than those whose attitudes are positive. Poor job attitudes therefore lead to lowered productivity and organizational performance. Evidence indicates that this is, in fact, the case, and that management's concern is well placed.[21]

Behavior Costing and Employee Attitudes

Sears, Roebuck & Co. applied behavior-costing methodology to study the relationship between employee attitudes, customer behavior, and profits. In retailing, there is a chain of cause and effect running from employee behavior to customer behavior to profits. Employee behavior, in turn, depends to a large extent on attitude. What is different about the Sears model is that instead of trying to relate employee attitudes directly to financial outcomes, the model treats customer behavior as a critical intervening variable.

Measures, Data, and a Causal Model. Over two quarters Sears managers collected survey data from employees and customers and financial data from 800 of its stores. A team of consulting statisticians then factor-analyzed the data into meaningful clusters, and used causal pathway modeling to assess cause-effect relationships. Based on initial results, Sears adjusted the model and continued to collect data for a new iteration at the end of the next quarter.

How did Sears benefit from the model? It could see how employee attitudes drove not just customer service, but also employee turnover and the likelihood that employees would recommend Sears and its merchandise to friends, family, and customers. It discovered that an employee's ability to see the connection between his or her work and the company's strategic objectives was a driver of positive behavior. It also found that asking customers whether Sears is a "fun place to shop" revealed more than a long list of more specific questions would. It began to see exactly how a change in training or business literacy affected revenues.

Although Sears used a 70-item questionnaire to assess employees' attitudes, it found that a mere 10 of those questions captured the predictive relationship between employee attitudes, behavior toward the customer, and customer satisfaction. Items such as the following predicted an employee's attitude about his or her job:

- I like the kind of work I do.
- I am proud to say I work at Sears.
- How does the way you are treated by those who supervise you influence your *overall attitude* about your job?

Items such as the following predicted an employee's attitude about the company:

- I feel good about the future of the company.
- I understand our business strategy.
- Do you see a connection between the work you do and the company's strategic objectives?

In summary, Sears produced a model, revised it three times, and created a kind of balanced scorecard for the company—the Sears Total Performance Indicators (TPIs)—that showed pathways of causation all the way from employee attitudes to profits. The company conducts interviews and collects data continually, assembles its information quarterly, and recalculates the impacts on its model annually to stay abreast of the changing economy, changing

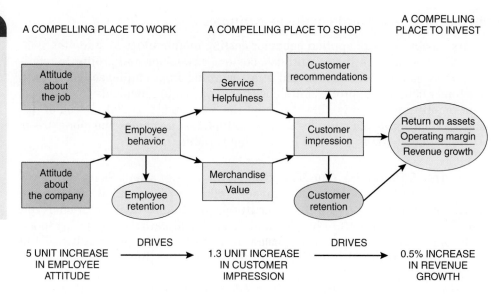

Figure 2–3

Revised model: The employee-customer-profit chain.
(*Source:* A. J. Rucci, S. P. Kirn, & R. T. Quinn, The employee-customer-profit chain at Sears, *Harvard Business Review,* Jan.–Feb., 1998, p. 91. Used with permission.)

demographics, and changing competitive circumstances. The revised model (see Figure 2–3) helps Sears managers run the company.

For example, consider the quality of management as a driver of employee attitudes. The model shows that a 5-unit improvement in employee attitudes will drive a 1.3-unit improvement in customer satisfaction in the next quarter, which in turn will drive a 0.5 percent improvement in revenue growth. If Sears knew nothing about a local store except that employee attitudes had improved by 5 units on its survey instrument, it could predict with confidence that if revenue growth in the district as a whole were 5 percent, revenue growth at this particular store would be 5.5 percent. Every year an outside accounting firm audits these numbers as closely as it audits financial measures.

Impact on Managers' Behavior and on the Firm. In a revolutionary step, Sears now bases all long-term executive incentives on the TPI. Such incentives are now based on nonfinancial as well as on financial performance—one-third on employee measures, one-third on customer measures, and one-third on traditional investor measures. At the level of the firm, employee satisfaction on Sears's TPI rose 4 percent, and customer satisfaction by almost 4 percent in one year. The 4 percent improvement translated into more than $200 million in additional revenues for that year. That increased Sears' market capitalization (price per share times the number of shares outstanding) by nearly one-quarter of a billion dollars.

Realizing the Full Benefits of the Model. The challenge of realizing the full benefit of the model includes three important components: (1) creating and refining the employee-customer-profit model and the measurement system that supports it; (2) creating management alignment around the use of the model to run the company; and (3) deploying the model so as to build business literacy and trust among employees. This implies that any retailer could copy the Sears measures, even the modeling techniques, and still fail to realize much benefit from the model, because the mechanics of the system are not in themselves enough to make it work. At Sears, the new business model altered the logic and culture of the business. Indeed, the process of altering the logic is what changed the culture.[22]

FINANCIAL EFFECTS OF WORK-LIFE PROGRAMS

Although these programs were originally termed "work-family" programs, this book uses the term "work-life" programs, to reflect a broader perspective of this issue. The term "work life" recognizes the fact that employees at every level in an organization, whether parents or nonparents, face personal or family issues that can affect their performance on the job.[23] A **work-life program** includes any employer-sponsored benefit or working condition that helps an employee to balance work and nonwork demands. At a general level, such programs span five broad areas[24]:

1. **Child- and dependent-care benefits** (e.g., on-site or near-site child- or elder-care programs, summer and weekend programs for dependents).
2. **Flexible working conditions** (e.g., flextime, job sharing, teleworking, part-time work, compressed work weeks).
3. **Leave options** (e.g., maternity, paternity, adoption leaves, sabbaticals, phased re-entry or retirement schemes).
4. **Information services and HR policies** (e.g., cafeteria benefits; life-skill educational programs such as parenting skills, health issues, financial management, and retirement; exercise facilities; professional and personal counseling).
5. **Organizational cultural issues** (e.g., an organizational culture that is supportive with respect to the nonwork issues of employees, coworkers, and supervisors who are sensitive to family issues).

Who Adopts Work-Life Programs?   A recent study sought to identify characteristics of organizations that are associated with the adoption of work-life programs.[25] Five such characteristics were investigated: organizational size (measured on a 10-point scale from 1, fewer than 25 employees, to 10, more than 8,000 employees), the percentage of women in the organization, the percentage of employees under age 35 in the organization, public- versus private-sector ownership, and the organization's track record in HR management (good versus poor).

Only two of the five characteristics were associated with the adoption of work-life programs. Larger organizations were better able to provide a broad base of work-life benefits than smaller organizations. Larger organizations tended to adopt more policies related to individual support (e.g., personal counseling, relocation assistance), leave, life-career strategies, and child and dependent care benefits than were smaller organizations. Similarly, organizations rated as having good track records in HR management tended to implement more flexible work options, individual growth, and life-career policies. However, the percentage of women in the organization, the percentage of employees under age 35, and public- versus private-sector ownership were unrelated to the adoption of work-life programs.

Company-sponsored child care is a valuable work-life program for many parents.

Work-Life Programs and Employee Behaviors

For purposes of illustration, we will consider the financial effects of only three of the many possible work-life interventions: child care, elder care, and stress.

Child Care. Allied Signal compared the number days missed by parents 12 months prior to the introduction of a child care center versus 12 months after its introduction. The number of days missed dropped from 259 to 30).[26] In a cost-benefit analysis of its sick-child care programs, Honeywell determined that it saved $45,000 over and above the cost of the programs in the first 9 months of operation. Small employers can save money too. Thus a 38-person CPA firm in California found that by providing seasonal on-site child care, it netted an additional $25,000 annual income through increased availability of staff.[27]

A study at a major aerospace firm reported the following savings in the first year of operation of a child care center[28]:

- Reduced absences arising from child care breakdowns: 5.28 days saved per employee, or $243,302.
- Reduced tardiness due to child care problems: 8.37 times late or left early per employee (multiplied by 2 hours), or $96,422.
- Reduced work time spent looking for child care: 7 hours per employee, or $12,900.

The total estimated net savings for this very large employer were $352,624.

Finally, a study of the return on investment (ROI) of back-up child care (i.e., child care used in emergencies or when regular child care is unavailable) at Chase Manhattan Bank revealed the following. Child care breakdowns were the cause of 6,900 days of potentially missed work by parents. Because back-up child care was available, these lost days were not incurred. When multiplied by the average daily salary of the employee in question, gross savings were $1,523,175. The annual cost of the back-up child care center was $720,000, for a net savings of $803,175, and a **return on investment (ROI),** or economic gains divided by program costs, of better than 110 percent.[29]

Elder Care.   At the national level, a study by Metropolitan Life Insurance Company of employer costs for elder care provided by full-time employees found that the aggregate cost to U.S. employers was almost $400 million per year. This was based on the number of full-time caregivers by gender, the median weekly wage in the United States by gender, and a finding that 10.5 percent of employed caregivers were absent a minimum of 6 days per year performing caregiving responsibilities, such as taking their older relatives to the doctor or other health care visits, visiting them, or arranging for services.[30]

The same study also examined the aggregate cost to U.S. employers of partial absenteeism—arriving late for work, leaving early, or extending lunch breaks—in order to meet elder care responsibilities. Among caregivers employed full time, 59 percent reported that they had to adjust their schedules in these ways. Fully 22 percent of caregivers are unable to make up this time by working late, coming in on weekends, or taking work home.[31] Experts on caregiving estimate that, on average, caregivers lose a minimum of 1 hour per week or 50 hours per year that cannot be made up. Based on the number of full-time caregivers by gender, the median weekly wage in the United States by gender, the number experiencing partial absenteeism (59 percent), and the number unable to make up 50 hours per year (22 percent), the total cost to employers was estimated to exceed $488 million.

Some caregivers find that their elder care responsibilities are so great that they have to quit their jobs. In the MetLife study, over 17 percent of caregivers fell into that category. At a broader level, Johnson & Johnson found that policies on time and leave were very significant in employees' decisions to stay with the firm, *even if they personally had not used them.* This is not atypical, and it is consistent with other published research.[32] The fact is that people are more committed to organizations that offer work-life programs, regardless of the extent to which they personally might benefit from them. In one group of employers with work-life programs, 78 percent reported that the programs helped their companies retain valuable employees. At Nations Bank, two-thirds of employees on flexible schedules said they would have left without these policies.[33]

Stress. In a study of organizations with and without work-life programs, Northwestern Mutual life found employees in companies that did not have supportive policies were twice as likely to report burnout and stress.[34] Employer-sponsored work-life programs do not erase the difficulties of balancing responsibilities, but they do provide resources that help employees to manage and solve their own problems.

Open communication policies and supportive work environments combine to reduce work-life stress. Thus a recent survey found that the top six retention practices as rated by employees were: salary increases (number 1), health care (number 2), open communications policy and base salary (tied for number 3), 401(k) plan (number 5), and flexible work schedules (number 6).[35]

It is not just the policies but also the environment in which they are implemented that makes the biggest difference for employees. Thus an evaluation of Johnson & Johnson's work-life programs found that, while employees appreciated and made use of the company's array of progressive policies, the factors most often associated with people's ability to balance work and nonwork roles were a supportive supervisor and workplace culture.[36]

Cautions in Making the Business Case for Work-Life Programs. While the results of the studies just presented may seem compelling, keep in mind three important considerations. One, recognize that no one set of facts and figures will make the case for all firms. It depends on the highest priority of the organization in question: Is it primarily attraction and public image, retention of talent, or the costs versus benefits of alternative programs?

Two, don't rely on isolated facts to make the business case. Considered by itself, any single study or fact is only one piece of the total picture. It is important to develop a dynamic understanding of the importance of the relationship between work and personal life. Doing so requires a focus on an organization's overall culture and values, not just on programs or statistics. Often a combination of quantitative information along with employees' experiences, in their own words (qualitative information that brings statistics to life), is most effective.

Three, don't place work-life initiatives under an unreasonable burden of proof. Decision makers may well be skeptical even after all the facts and costs have been presented to them. This suggests that more deeply rooted attitudes and beliefs may underlie the skepticism—such as a belief that addressing personal concerns may erode service to clients or customers, or that people will take unfair advantage of the benefits, or that work-life issues are just women's issues. Constructing a credible business case means addressing attitudes and values as well as assembling research.[37]

COSTING THE EFFECTS OF TRAINING ACTIVITIES

At the most basic level, the task of evaluation is counting—counting clients, counting errors, counting dollars, counting hours, and so forth. The most difficult tasks of evaluation are deciding which things should be counted and developing routine methods for counting them. Managers should count the things that will provide the most useful feedback. Managers assess the results of training to determine whether it is worth the cost. Training valuation (in financial terms) is not easy, but the technology to do it is available and well developed.[38]

A manager may have to value training in two types of situations: one in which only indirect measures of dollar outcomes are available and one in which direct measures of dollar outcomes are available.

Indirect Measures of Training Outcomes

Indirect measures of training outcomes are more common than direct measures. That is, many studies of training outcomes report improvements in job performance or decreases in errors, scrap, and waste. Relatively few studies report training outcomes directly in terms of dollars gained or saved. Indirect measures can often be converted into estimates of the dollar impact of training, however, by using a method known as utility analysis. Although the technical details of the method are beyond the scope of this chapter,[39] following is a summary of one such study.

A large, U.S.-based multinational firm conducted a 4-year investigation of the effect and utility of its corporate managerial, sales, and technical training functions. The study is noteworthy, for it adopted a strategic focus by comparing the payoffs from different types of training in order to assist decision makers in allocating training budgets and specifying the types of employees to be trained.[40]

Project History.   The CEO, a former research scientist, requested a report on the dollar value of training. He indicated that training should be evaluated experimentally, strategically aligned with the business goals of the organization, and thus demonstrated to be a worthwhile investment for the company. Thus the impetus for this large-scale study came from the top of the organization.

Methodological Issues.   In a project of this scope and complexity, it is necessary to address several important methodological issues. The first concerns the outcomes or **criteria** to use in judging each program's effectiveness. Training courses that attempt to influence the supervisory style of managers may affect a large percentage of the tasks that compose the job. Conversely, a course designed to affect sales of a specific product may only influence a few of the tasks in the sales representative's job. The researchers corrected for this issue to ensure that the estimate of economic payoff for each training program only represented the value of performance on specific job elements.

A second issue that must be considered when assessing the effectiveness of alternative training programs is the **transfer of trained skills** from the training to the job. For the training to have value, skills must be generalized to the job (i.e., exhibited on the job) and such transfer must be maintained for some period of time. To address the issue of transfer, the measure of performance on all training programs was behavioral performance on the job. Performance was assessed by means of a survey completed by each trainee's supervisor (for most courses), peers (i.e., Hazardous Energy Control), or subordinates (i.e., Team Building) before and after training.

Because it was not possible to assess the length of training's effects in this study, decision makers assumed that training's effect (and economic utility) was maintained without decay or growth for precisely one year. In addition, the researchers calculated **break-even values,** which indicate the length of time the observed effect would need to be maintained in order to recover the cost of the training program.[41]

Training Programs Evaluated.   A sample of 18 high-use or high-cost courses was selected based on the recommendation of the training departments throughout the organization. Managerial training courses were defined as courses developed for individuals with managerial or supervisory duties. Sales training courses were defined as programs designed to enhance the performance of sales representatives by affecting sales performance or support of their own sales. Technical training courses (e.g., Hazardous Energy Control, In-House Time Management) were defined as courses not specifically designed for sales or supervisory personnel.

Of the 18 programs, 8 evaluation studies used a **control group design** in which training was provided to one group and not provided to a second group that was similar to the trained group in terms of relevant characteristics. The remaining 10 training program evaluations relied on a **pretest–posttest only design,** in which a control group was not used and the performance of the trained group alone was evaluated before and after the training program.

Results.   Over all 18 programs, assuming a normal distribution of performance on the job, the average improvement was about 17 percent (.54 of a standard deviation, or SD). However, for technical and sales training it was higher (.64 SD), and for managerial training it was lower (.31 SD). Thus training in general was effective.

The mean ROI was 45 percent for the managerial training programs, and 418 percent for the sales and technical training programs. However, one inexpensive time-management program developed in-house had an ROI of nearly 2,000 percent. When the economic utility of that program is removed, the overall average ROI of the remaining training programs was 84 percent and the ROI of sales and technical training was 156 percent.

Time to Break-Even Values.   There was considerable variability in these values. Break-even periods ranged from a few weeks (e.g., time management, written communications) to several years (supervisory skills, leadership skills). Several programs were found to have few positive or even slightly negative effects, and thus would never yield a financial gain.

Conclusions.   This study compared the effectiveness and economic utility of different types of training across sales, technical, and managerial jobs. The estimated cost of the 4-year project, including the fully loaded cost of rater time, as well as the cost of consulting, travel, and materials, was approximately $500,000. This number may seem large. However, over the same time period, the organization spent over $240 million on training. Thus the cost of the training program evaluation was approximately 0.2 percent of the training budget during the same period. Given budgets of this magnitude, some sort of accountability is prudent.

Despite the overall positive effects and utility of the training, there were some exceptions. The important lesson to be learned is that it is necessary to evaluate the effect and utility of each training program before drawing overall conclusions about the impact of training. It would be simplistic to claim that "training is a good investment" or that "training is a waste of time and money."[42]

Direct Measures of Training Outcomes

When **direct measures of training outcomes** are available, standard valuation methods are appropriate. The following study valued the results of a behavior-modeling training program (described more fully below) for sales representatives in relation to the program's effects on sales performance.[43]

Study Design.   A large retailer conducted a behavior-modeling program in two departments, Large Appliances and Radio/TV, within 14 of its stores in one large metropolitan area. The 14 stores were matched into seven pairs in terms of size, location, and market characteristics. Stores with unusual characteristics that could affect their overall performance, such as declining sales or recent changes in management, were not included in the study.

The training program was then introduced in seven stores, one in each of the matched pairs, and not in the other seven stores. Other kinds of ongoing sales training programs were provided in the control-group stores, but the behavior-modeling approach was used only in the seven experimental-group stores. In the experimental-group stores, 58 sales associates received the training, and their job performance was compared with that of 64 sales associates in the same departments in the control-group stores.

As in most sales organizations, detailed sales records for each individual were kept on a continuous basis. These records included total sales as well as hours worked on the sales floor. Since all individuals received commissions on their sales and since the value of the various products sold varied greatly, it was possible to compute a job performance measure for each individual in terms of average commissions per hour worked.

There was considerable variation in the month-to-month sales performance of each individual, but sales performance over 6-month periods was more stable. In fact, the average correlation between consecutive sales periods of 6 months each was about .80 (where 1.00 equals perfect agreement). Hence the researchers decided to compare the sales records of participants for 6 months before the training program was introduced with the results achieved during the same 6 months the following year, after the training was concluded. All sales promotions and other programs in the stores were identical, since these were administered on an areawide basis.

The Training Program Itself.   The program focused on specific aspects of sales situations, such as "approaching the customer," "explaining features, advantages, and benefits," and "closing the sale." The training itself proceeded according to the following procedure. First the trainers presented guidelines (or "learning points") for handling each aspect of a sales interaction. Then the trainees viewed a videotaped situation in which a "model" sales associate followed the guidelines in carrying out that aspect of the sales interaction with a customer. The trainees then practiced the same situation in role-playing rehearsals. Their performance was reinforced and shaped by their supervisors, who had been trained as their instructors.

Study Results.   Of the original 58 trainees in the experimental group, 50 were still working as sales associates 1 year later. Of the remaining 8 associates, 4

Figure 2–4

Changes in per-hour commissions before and after the behavior-modeling training program.

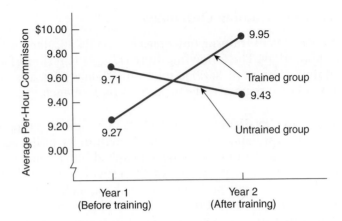

had been promoted during the interim, and 4 others had left the company. In the control-group stores, only 49 of the original 64 were still working as sales associates 1 year later. Only 1 had been promoted, and 14 others had left the company. Thus the behavior-modeling program may have had a substantial positive effect on turnover, since only about 7 percent of the trained group left during the ensuing year, as compared to 22 percent of those in the control group. (This result had not been predicted.)

Figure 2–4 presents the changes in average per-hour commissions for participants in both the trained and the untrained groups from the 6-month period before the training was conducted to the 6-month period following the training. Note in Figure 2–4 that the trained and untrained groups did not have equal per-hour commissions at the start of the study. While the stores that members of the two groups worked in were matched at the start of the study, sales commissions were not. Sales associates in the trained group started at a lower point than did sales associates in the untrained group. Average per-hour commissions for the trained group increased over the year from $9.27 to $9.95 (from $17.20 to $18.47 in year 2000 dollars); average per-hour commissions for the untrained group declined over the year from $9.71 to $9.43 (from $18.02 to $17.49 in year 2000 dollars). In other words, the trained sales associates increased their average earnings by about 7 percent, whereas those who did not receive the behavior-modeling training experienced a 3 percent decline in average earnings. This difference was statistically significant. Other training outcomes (e.g., trainee attitudes, supervisory behaviors) were also assessed, but, for our purposes, the most important lesson was that the study provided objective evidence to indicate the dollar impact of the training on increased sales.

The program also had an important secondary effect on turnover. Since all sales associates are given considerable training (which represents an extensive investment of time and money), it appears that the behavior modeling contributed to *cost savings* in addition to *increased sales*. As noted in the previous discussion of turnover costs, an accurate estimate of these cost savings requires that the turnovers be separated into controllable and uncontrollable, because training can affect only controllable turnover.

Finally, the use of objective data as criterion measures in a study of this kind does entail some problems. As pointed out earlier, the researchers found that a 6-month period was required to balance out the month-to-month variations in sales performance resulting from changing work schedules, sales promotions, and similar influences that affected individual results. It also took some vigilance to ensure that the records needed for the study were kept in a consistent and conscientious manner in each store. According to the researchers, however, these problems were not great in relation to the usefulness of the study results. "The evidence that the training program had a measurable effect on sales was certainly more convincing in demonstrating the value of the program than would be merely the opinions of participants that the training was worthwhile."[44]

THE FINANCIAL IMPACT OF HIGH-PERFORMANCE WORK PRACTICES

In an effort to enhance their competitiveness, some firms have instituted **high-performance work practices**. Such practices provide workers with the information, skills, incentives, and responsibility to make decisions that are essential for innovation, quality improvement, and rapid response to change. They seem particularly appropriate given the attributes that characterize today's economic environment. These include an unusual reliance on front-line workers; the treatment of workers as assets to be developed, not costs to be cut; new forms of worker–management collaboration that break down adversarial barriers; and the integration of technology and work in ways that will cause machines to serve human beings and not vice versa.[45] In a nationally representative sample of 700 private-sector establishments in the United States, 37 percent had a majority of front-line workers engaged in two or more high-performance work practices.[46] Thus, while the absolute number of firms that have adopted such practices still constitutes a minority, if managers are to be able to argue forcefully for greater investments in people, they must be able to demonstrate that the benefits of implementing such practices outweigh the costs. Do such programs pay off?

High-Performance Work Practices and Organizational Performance

A substantial amount of research has been conducted on the relationship between productivity and high-performance work practices, such as the use of valid staffing procedures, organizational cultures that emphasize team orientation and respect for people, employee involvement in decision making, compensation linked to firm or worker performance, and training. The evidence indicates that such practices are usually associated with increases in productivity (defined as output per worker), as well as with a firm's long-term financial performance.[47] However, these effects are most pronounced when such work practices are implemented together as a system.[48] As an example, let us consider the impact of organizational culture on employee retention and HR costs.

Organizational Culture, Employee Retention, and HR Costs

Does organizational culture matter to new employees? That was the research question in a study that investigated the retention rates of 904 college graduates hired by six public accounting firms over a 6-year period.[49] Organizational culture values varied considerably across the six firms, from high task orientation (i.e., high orientation toward detail and stability) to high interpersonal orientation (i.e., high concern for a team orientation and respect for individuals).

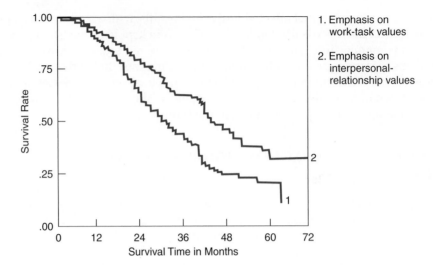

Figure 2–5

Voluntary survival rates in two organizational cultures.
(*Source:* J. E. Sheridan, Organizational culture and employee retention, *Academy of Management Journal, 35,* 1992, p. 1049.)

New employees stayed an average of 45 months in the cultures emphasizing interpersonal relationships, but only 31 months in the cultures emphasizing work-task values (see Figure 2–5). This is a 14-month difference in median survival time. The next task was to translate the difference in time into a measure of profits forgone (i.e., opportunity losses).

Using the firms' average billing fees, along with hiring, training, and compensation costs, mean profits per professional employee ranged from $58,000 during the first year of employment to $67,000 during the second year and $105,000 during the third. A firm therefore incurs an opportunity loss of only $9,000 ($67,000 − $58,000) when a new employee replaces a 2-year employee, but a $47,000 loss ($105,000 − $58,000) when a new employee replaces a 3-year employee.

If it is assumed that both strong and weak performers generated the same average level of profits in each year of employment and that annual profits were distributed uniformly between those with 31 and those with 45 months' seniority, it is possible to estimate the opportunity loss associated with the 14-month difference in median survival time. This difference translated into an opportunity loss of approximately $44,000 per new employee [($47,000 − $9,000/12) × 14] between the firms having the two different types of cultural values. This is roughly $55,000 per new employee in year 2000 dollars. Considering the total number of new employees hired by each office over the 6-year period of the study, the study indicates that a firm emphasizing work-task values incurred opportunity losses of approximately $6 to $9 million ($7.6 to $11.4 million in year 2000 dollars) more than a firm emphasizing interpersonal-relationship values.

The Causal Effect of Management Practices on Performance

Evidence that management practices affect performance comes from a study of the 5-year survival rate of 136 nonfinancial companies that initiated their public offerings in the U.S. stock market in 1988.[50] By 1993, some 5 years later, only 60 percent of these companies were still in existence. Empirical analysis controlled statistically for factors such as size, industry, and even profits. Results showed that both the value the firm placed on human resources—such as whether the company cited employees as a source of competitive advantage—and how the or-

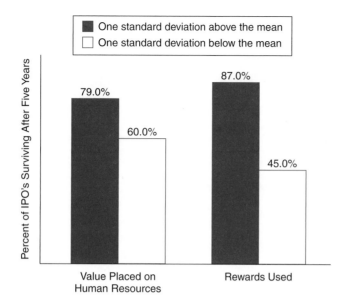

Figure 2–6

Probability of an initial public offering firm's survival after 5 years. (*Source:* Based on information from T. Welbourne & A. Andrews, Predicting performance of initial public offering firms: Should HRM be in the equation? *Academy of Management Journal, 39,* 1996, 910–911.)

ganization rewarded people—such as stock options for all employees and profit sharing—were significantly related to the probability of survival.

As Figure 2–6 demonstrates, the results were important in a practical sense as well. The difference in survival probability for firms one standard deviation above and one standard deviation below the mean (those in the upper and lower 16 percent of all firms in the sample, respectively) on valuing human resources was almost 20 percent. The difference in survival depending on where the firm scored on rewards was even more dramatic, with a difference in 5-year survival probability of 42 percent between firms in the upper and lower tails of the distribution.

As these examples show, adoption of high-performance work practices can have an economically significant effect on the market value of the firm. How large an effect? Recent work indicates a range of $15,000 to $45,000 per employee.[51] For example, an analysis of the financial impact of HR systems across 702 firms revealed that a 1-SD improvement in the HR system was associated with an increase in shareholder wealth of $41,000 per employee—about a 14 percent market value premium.[52]

The extent to which these practices actually will pay off depends on the skill and care with which the many HR practices available are implemented to solve real business problems and to support a firm's operating and strategic initiatives.

LINKING WORKER BELIEFS TO INCREASED PRODUCTIVITY AND PROFITABILITY

Human Resource Management in Action: Conclusion

The very best managers seem to share four key behaviors that help to trigger the 12 worker beliefs that underlie a profitable, productive workplace.

1. **Select for talent.** Gallup defines talents as patterns of thoughts, feelings, and behaviors that come naturally to an individual. The best managers identify talents that are needed for a particular position, and then find people who fit the role. This means looking beyond a person's knowledge

IMPACT OF HUMAN RESOURCE MANAGEMENT ACTIVITIES ON PRODUCTIVITY, QUALITY OF WORK LIFE, AND THE BOTTOM LINE

There is a growing consensus among managers in many industries that the future success of their firms may depend more on the skill with which human problems are handled than on the degree to which their firms maintain leadership in technical areas. For example, consider the average return to shareholders by *Fortune* magazine's list of the 100 Best Companies to Work for in America. Of the 61 firms in the group that are publicly traded, they outperformed the Russell 3000, an index of large and small companies that mirrors the 100 Best over both 5- and 10-year periods. Over 5 years, the 100 Best returned an average of 27.5 percent versus 17.3 percent for the Russell 3000. Over 10 years, the 100 Best returned an average of 23.4 percent versus 14.8 percent for the Russell 3000.

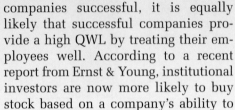

While it could be that well-treated employees who enjoy a high quality of work life make companies successful, it is equally likely that successful companies provide a high QWL by treating their employees well. According to a recent report from Ernst & Young, institutional investors are now more likely to buy stock based on a company's ability to attract talented people. Talented people want challenging work, opportunities for professional growth and development, and high QWL. Institutional investors are betting cash that companies providing that kind of an environment will be successful in the marketplace.[53]

and skills to size up whether a job really "fits" the person. For example, positions involving sales or customer service require "woo," or the talent for establishing trust with someone quickly upon meeting them. In filling these jobs great managers look for people who possess "woo."

2. **Define the right outcomes.** Managers who do this best establish very clear objectives, so employees know exactly what they need to attain, they make sure that employees have the resources to do their jobs well (e.g., equipment, information, budget, staff), and then they allow employees to pave their own paths. The best managers don't define the steps for their employees and don't legislate style.

3. **Focus on strengths.** Gallup senior vice president Coffman calls this approach "trying to bring out what God left in, rather than trying to put back what God forgot." Rather than identifying workers' weaknesses and attempting to fix them, where the gains will be short lived, focus on strengths. Identify and reinforce strengths, and then figure out where your workers' strengths will serve the company best.[54]

4. **Find the right fit.** According to Coffman, "Talent never becomes 'talented' without being given a role for it to shine." The best managers continually encourage their employees to look in the mirror and assess themselves in order to find the kind of work that will bring out their best talents.

SUMMARY

The purpose of this chapter was to illustrate the financial impact of human resource management activities. To do so, we adopted the methodology of behav-

Ethical Dilemma
Survey Feedback: Nice or Necessary?

Is it unethical to ask employees for their opinions, attitudes, values, or beliefs on an attitude survey and then subsequently not to give them any feedback about the results? We know that survey results that are not fed back to employees are unlikely to be translated into action strategies, and that it is poor management practice to fail to provide feedback.[55] Is it unethical as well? (*Hint:* See the definition of ethical decision making in Chapter 1.)

IMPLICATIONS FOR MANAGEMENT PRACTICE

How can such substantial gains in productivity, quality, and profits as we have described in this chapter occur? They happen because high-performance management practices provide a number of sources for enhanced organizational performance.[56]

1. People work harder because of the increased involvement and commitment that come from having more control and say in their work. Managers who adopt democratic leadership styles influence employees' perceptions of personal control over their work.

2. People work smarter because they are encouraged to build skills and competence. Managers have considerable influence over the opportunities for professional growth and development of their employees.

3. Finally, people work more responsibly because more responsibility is placed in the hands of employees further down in the organization. Again, managers who delegate responsibility appropriately can foster such feelings of responsibility on the part of their subordinates. These practices work not because of some mystical process, but because they are grounded in sound social science principles that are supported by a great deal of evidence. Managers should use them to create win-win scenarios for themselves and for their people.

ior costing. Behavior costing does not measure the value of employees and managers as assets, but rather the economic consequences of their behavior, for example, to be absent or to quit. Applying behavior costing methodology properly requires that both direct and indirect costs be considered. However, the objective is not simply to measure these costs; it is also to reduce them by devoting resources to show costs that are controllable. The chapter presented behavior-costing methods in five key areas of employee behavior—absenteeism, turnover, employee attitudes, work-life programs, and employee training—and then examined the financial impact of high-performance work practices on organization-level outcomes. Firms that implement more such practices tend to be more profitable and to provide higher returns to shareholders than those that implement fewer or none of them. However, these effects are most pronounced when such work practices are implemented together as a system.

To illustrate this, we examined two longitudinal studies, one on organization culture, and one on the survival of a sample of firms after their initial public offerings (IPOs). With respect to organizational culture, results indicated that over a 6-year period, a public accounting firm emphasizing work-task values incurred opportunity losses of approximately $6 to $9 million ($7.6 to $11.4 million in year 2000 dollars) more than a firm emphasizing interpersonal-relationship values. With respect to IPOs, 5 years after going public, 60 percent of the firms survived. Results showed that both the value the firm placed on human resources—such as whether the company cited employees as a source of competitive advantage—and how the organization rewarded people—such as stock options for all employees and profit sharing—were significantly related to the probability of survival. Management practices had a causal effect on the performance of firms.

DISCUSSION QUESTIONS

2–1. What is behavior costing methodology? How can it be useful to an operating manager?

2–2. Discuss three controllable and three uncontrollable costs associated with absenteeism.

2–3. Why should efforts to reduce turnover focus only on controllable costs?

2–4. In making the business case for work-family programs, what points would you emphasize?

2–5. Given the positive financial returns from high-performance work practices, why don't more firms implement them?

KEY TERMS

behavior costing	work-life program
direct measures	return on investment (ROI)
indirect measures	indirect measures of training outcomes
controllable costs	criteria
uncontrollable costs	transfer of trained skills
absenteeism	break-even values
turnover	control group design
attitudes	pretest–posttest only design
job satisfaction	direct measures of training outcomes
organizational commitment	high performance work practices

APPLYING YOUR KNOWLEDGE

Case 2–1   **Absenteeism at ONO, Inc.**

ONO, Inc., is an auto supply company with 11 employees. In addition, there are two supervisors and Fred Donofrio, the owner and general manager. Last year, ONO did $3 million in business and earned $150,000 in profits ($225,000 before taxes). The auto supply business is extremely competitive, and owners must constantly be on the lookout for ways to reduce costs in order to remain profitable.

Employee salaries at ONO average $17 an hour, and benefits add another 33 percent to these labor costs. The two supervisors earn an average of $26 an hour, with a similar level (percentage) of benefits. Employees receive 2 weeks of vacation each year and 12 days of paid sick leave.

Over the last 2 years, Fred Donofrio has noted an increasing rate of absenteeism among his 11 employees (there seems to be no similar problem with the two supervisors). Last week, he asked Cal Jenson, his most senior supervisor, to go through the records from last year and determine how much absenteeism had cost ONO. Further, he asked Cal to make any recommendations to him that seemed appropriate depending on the magnitude of the problem.

Cal determined that ONO lost a total of 539 employee labor-hours (67.375 days) to absenteeism last year (this figure did not, of course, include vacation time). Further, he estimated that he and the other supervisor together averaged 1.5 hours in lost time whenever an employee was absent for a day. This time was spent dealing with the extra problems (rescheduling work, filling in for missing workers, etc.) that an absence created. On several occasions last year, ONO was so short of help that temporary workers had to be hired or present employees had to work overtime. Cal determined that the additional costs of overtime and outside help last year totaled $1,100. Cal is now in the process of preparing his report to Fred Donofrio.

Questions

1. What figure will Cal Jenson report to Fred Donofrio for the amount that absenteeism cost ONO last year?
2. Is absenteeism a serious problem at ONO? Why or why not?
3. What recommendations for action could Cal Jenson make to Fred Donofrio?

REFERENCES

1. Micco, L. (1998, Sept.). Gallup study links worker beliefs, increased productivity. *HR News,* p. 16.
2. Mirvis, P. H., & Macy, B. A. (1976). Measuring the quality of work and organizational effectiveness in behavioral-economic terms. *Administrative Science Quarterly, 21,* pp. 212–226.
3. Fitz-enz, J. (1984). *How to measure human resources management.* New York: McGraw-Hill.
4. For more on this issue see DeFrank, R. S., & Ivancevich, J. M. (1998). Stress on the job: An executive update. *Academy of Management Executive, 12, pp.* 55–66. See also DeFrank, R. S., Konopaske, R., & Ivancevich, J. M. (2000). Executive travel stress: Perils of the road warrior. *Academy of Management Executive, 14*(2), pp. 58–71. See also Sauter, S. L., & Murphy, L. R. (eds.) (1995). *Organizational risk factors for job stress.* Washington, DC: American Psychological Association.
5. VanDerWall, S. (1998, Nov.). Survey finds unscheduled absenteeism hitting 7-year high. *HR News,* p. 14.
6. Ibid.
7. Bulletin to management (1999, 4th quarter). Washington, DC: Bureau of National Affairs.

8. Workplace epidemic: Absenteeism rises for third year in a row (1996, Feb. 27). *The Wall Street Journal,* p. A1. See also Cost of absenteeism for British employers (1995, Dec.). *Manpower Argus,* no. 327, p. 6.

9. Macy, B. A., & Mirvis, P. H. (1983). Assessing rates and costs of individual work behaviors. In S. E. Seashore, E. E. Lawler, P. H. Mirvis, & C. Camann (eds.), *Assessing organizational change.* New York: Wiley, pp. 139–177.

10. Bulletin to management, op. cit.

11. Martin, D. C., & Bartol, K M. (1985). Managing turnover strategically. *Personnel Administrator, 30*(11), pp. 63–73.

12. Cascio, W. F. (2000). *Costing human resources: The financial impact of behavior in organizations* (4th ed.). Cincinnati, OH: South-Western College Publishing.

13. For more on this subject, see ibid.

14. Tired of employee turnover? Just appoint a retention czar. (1998, Nov. 10). *The Wall Street Journal*, p. A1.

15. For additional strategies, see Griffeth, R. W., Hom, P. W., & Gaertner, S. (2000). A meta-analysis of antecedents and correlates of employee turnover: Update, moderator tests, and research implications for the next millennium. *Journal of Management, 26,* pp. 463–488.

16. Solomon, J. (1988, Dec. 29). Companies try measuring cost savings from new types of corporate benefits. *The Wall Street Journal,* p. B1.

17. Branch, S. (1998, Nov. 9). You hired 'em. But can you keep 'em? *Fortune,* pp. 247–250.

18. Solomon, op. cit.

19. Why your workers might jump ship (1999, Mar. 1). *BusinessWeek*, p. 8.

20. Mathieu, J. E., & Zajac, D. M. (1990). A review and meta-analysis of the antecedents, correlates, and consequences or organizational commitment. *Psychological Bulletin, 108* (2), pp. 171–194.

21. Ryan, A. M., Schmit, M. J., & Johnson, R. (1996). Attitudes and effectiveness: Examining relations at an organizational level. *Personnel Psychology, 49,* pp. 853–883. See also Cohen, A. (1993). Organizational commitment and turnover: A meta-analysis. *Academy of Management Journal, 36,* 1140–1157. See also Ostroff, C. (1992). The relationship between satisfaction, attitudes, and performance: An organizational-level analysis. *Journal of Applied Psychology, 77,* pp. 963–974.

22. Rucci, A. J., Kirn, S. P., & Quinn, R. T. (1998, Jan.–Feb.). The employee-customer-profit chain at Sears. *Harvard Business Review*, pp. 82–97.

23. Edwards, J. R., & Rothbard, N. P. (2000). Mechanisms linking work and family: Clarifying the relationship between work and family constructs. *Academy of Management Review, 25,* pp. 178–199.

24. Bardoel, E. A., Tharenou, P., & Moss, S. A. (1998). Organizational predictors of work-family practices. *Asia Pacific Journal of Human Resources, 36*(3), pp. 31–49.

25. Ibid.

26. Bright Horizons Family Solutions (1997). The financial impact of on-site child care. Port Washington, NY: Author.

27. Johnson, A. A. (1995, August). The business case for work-family programs. *Journal of Accountancy*, pp. 53–57.

28. Bright Horizons Family Solutions, op. cit.

29. Ibid.

30. The MetLife study of employer costs for working caregivers (1997, June). Westport, CT: Metropolitan Life Insurance Co.

31. Scharlach, A. E. (1994). Caregiving and employment: Competing or complementary roles? *The Gerontologist, 34,* pp. 378–385.

32. Grover, S. L., & Crooker, K. J. (1995). Who appreciates family-responsive human resource policies: The impact of family-friendly policies on the organizational attachment of parents and non-parents. *Personnel Psychology, 48,* pp. 271–288.

33. Johnson, op. cit.
34. Ibid.
35. Society for Human Resource Management. (1997). What keeps employees from quitting? Alexandria, VA: Author.
36. Families and Work Institute (1993). *An evaluation of Johnson & Johnson's work-life programs.* NY: Author.
37. Johnson, op. cit.
38. Cascio, op. cit. See also Cascio, W. F. (1989). Using utility analysis to assess training outcomes. In I. L. Goldstein (ed.), *Training and development in organizations.* San Francisco: Jossey-Bass, pp. 63–88.
39. Cascio, op. cit. See also Boudreau, J. W. (1991). Utility analysis for decisions in human resource management. In M. D. Dunnette & L. M. Hough (eds.), *Handbook of industrial and organizational psychology* (vol. 2). San Francisco: Jossey-Bass, pp. 621–745. For a contrarian view, see Skarlicki, D. P., Latham, G. P., & Whyte, G. (1996). Utility analysis: Its evolution and tenuous role in human resource management decision making. *Canadian Journal of Administrative Sciences, 13*(1), pp. 13–21. *See also Latham, G. P., & Whyte, G. (1994). The futility of utility analysis. Personnel Psychology, 47,* pp. 31–46.
40. Morrow, C. C., Jarrett, M. Q., & Rupinski, M. T. (1997). An investigation of the effect and economic utility of corporate-wide training. *Personnel Psychology, 50,* pp. 91–119.
41. For more on break-even analysis, see Boudreau, J. W. (1984). Decision theory contributions to HRM research and practice. *Industrial Relations, 23,* pp. 198–217.
42. Morrow et al., op. cit.
43. Meyer, H. H., & Raich, J. S. (1983). An objective evaluation of a behavior modeling training program. *Personnel Psychology, 36,* pp. 755–761.
44. Ibid., p. 761.
45. Forecasting the future of the American workplace (1993, Sept.). *American Workplace, 1*(1), pp. 1, 4.
46. Osterman, P. (1994). How common is workplace transformation, and can we explain who adopts it? *Industrial and Labor Relations Review, 47*(2), pp. 173–188.
47. Pfeffer, J. (1998). *The human equation: Building profits by putting people first.* Boston: Harvard Business School Press. Terpstra, D. E., & Rozell, E. J. (1993). The relationship of staffing practices to organizational-level measures of performance. *Personnel Psychology, 46,* pp. 27–48. See also Gerhart, B., & Milkovich, G. T. (1990). Organizational differences in managerial compensation and firm performance. *Academy of Management Journal, 33, pp.* 663–691.
48. Pfeffer, op. cit. Bae, J., & Lawler, J. J. (2000). Organizational and HRM strategies in Korea: Impact on firm performance in an emerging economy. Ferris, G. R., Hochwarter, W. A., Buckley, M. R., Harrell-Cook, G., & Frink, D. (1999). Human resources management: Some new directions. *Journal of Management, 25,* pp. 385–415. Delery, J. E., & Doty, D. H. (1996). Modes of theorizing in strategic human resource management: Tests of universalistic, contingency, and configurational performance predictions. *Academy of Management Journal, 39,* pp. 802–835.
49. Sheridan, J. E. (1992). Organizational culture and employee retention. *Academy of Management Journal, 35,* pp. 1036–1056.
50. Welbourne, T. M., & Andrews, A. O. (1996). Predicting the performance of initial public offerings: Should human resource management be in the equation? *Academy of Management Journal, 39, pp.* 891–919.
51. Davidson, W. N., III, Worrell, D. L., & Fox, J. B. (1996). Early retirement programs and firm performance. *Academy of Management Journal, 39, pp.* 970–984
52. Huselid, M. A., & Becker, B. E. (1997). The impact of high performance work systems, implementation effectiveness, and alignment with strategy on shareholder wealth. Unpublished paper, Rutgers University, pp. 18–19.

53. Grant, L. (1998, Jan. 12). Happy workers, high returns. *Fortune*, p. 81.

54. The founder and chairman of SRI Gallup, Donald Clifton, has written a book on this very theme. Clifton, D. O., & Nelson, P. (1992). *Soar with your strengths*. NY: Delacorte Press.

55. Kraut, A. I. (1996). *Organizational surveys*. San Francisco: Jossey-Bass. See also Does survey feedback make a difference? (1993, Fall). *Decisions . . . Decisions,* pp. 1, 2.

56. Pfeffer, J., & Veiga, J. F. (1999). Putting people first for organizational success. *Academy of Management Executive, 13*(2), pp. 37–48.

3 THE LEGAL CONTEXT OF EMPLOYMENT DECISIONS

Questions This Chapter Will Help Managers Answer

1. How are employment practices affected by the civil rights laws and Supreme Court interpretations of those laws?

2. What should be the components of an effective policy to prevent sexual harassment?

3. What obligations does the Family and Medical Leave Act impose on employers? What rights does it grant to employees?

4. When a company is in the process of downsizing, what strategies can it use to avoid complaints of age discrimination?

5. What should senior management do to ensure that job applicants or employees with disabilities receive "reasonable accommodation"?

You flip through your mail at the office and run across an envelope with the dreaded return address of the federal Equal Employment Opportunity Commission (EEOC). As you slowly tear open the envelope, perspiration beads on your forehead. When you remove the contents you learn that it is exactly what you feared: a charge of discrimination. What should you do now?

The Charge

EEOC proceedings usually begin with a written charge of discrimination that employers receive in the mail. After you, as the employer, receive the charge, immediately assess its merits. To look for any procedural defects, ask the following four questions.

1. Was the charge filed within the time allowed? If your state has a fair employment agency, charges must be filed within 300 days of the last date on which the alleged discrimination occurred. If your state does not have a fair employment agency, charges must be filed within 180 days.
2. Does the charge name the proper employer (the company for which the charging party either worked or applied to work) as the respondent? If not, the charge may have been sent to the wrong company by accident. Also, if the employee making the charge is a temp, the charge might incorrectly name your company, rather than the agency for which the temporary employee works.
3. Is your company subject to federal antidiscrimination statutes? The EEOC enforces four federal laws: Title VII of the Civil Rights Act of 1964, the Americans with Disabilities Act (ADA), the Age Discrimination in Employment Act (ADEA), and the Equal Pay Act (EPA). Only companies with 15 or more employee are subject to Title VII and the ADA. Only companies with 20 or more employees are subject to the ADEA. However, the EPA applies to virtually every private-sector employer and most public-sector employers.

After checking for procedural errors, investigate the factual allegations of the charge. Start by reviewing company records—such as the employment file of the person who filed the charge. If a job applicant filed the charge, review that person's application, résumé, the job advertisements, and any other relevant documents. Employment documents most often relevant to EEOC charges include records of production, discipline, attendance, and performance evaluations.

Also review the employment files of other persons whose situations might be comparable to those of the charging party. Thus, if the charging party was discharged for poor attendance, review the files of other employees with comparable attendance records to ensure that none were treated more favorably

---

**Source:* Adapted from T. S. Bland, Sealed without a kiss, *HRMagazine, 45*(10), 2000, pp. 85–92.

than the charging party. If so, be sure there is a legitimate business reason for the discrepancy. If there is none, the EEOC may use this disparate treatment to find that the company behaved in a discriminatory manner.

Next, review any company policies or guidelines relevant to the EEOC charge to ensure that the company followed them. Failure to do so, in the eyes of the EEOC, may be evidence that the company acted discriminatorily.

Finally, interview any persons who might have firsthand knowledge of the charge. Make it clear that you are merely engaging in a fact-finding investigation and that there will be no retaliation against those interviewed for providing unfavorable information about the company.

Preparing a Response

Once you have all the facts relevant to the charge, you are ready to prepare a response. In most cases, you make one of three possible responses:

1. Agree to mediate the charge, if invited to do so by the EEOC.
2. Make a settlement offer to the charging party through the EEOC without participating in the formal mediation process.
3. Prepare a "position statement," which sets forth the company's version of events, and file it with the EEOC.

Unless you choose one of the first two alternatives, the EEOC will require you to submit a written position statement explaining why your organization took the alleged adverse action against the person bringing the charge.

Your goal in preparing the position statement is to convince the EEOC that no discrimination occurred and that there is no cause to conduct an "on-site" investigation at the company's premises. Such a statement generally includes the following sections:

- A brief description of the company's business.
- A description of the position the charging party held with the company. If the charging party was an applicant, describe the position to which the individual applied.
- A description of any rules, policies, or procedures you believe are applicable to the charge. For example, if the charge involves sexual harassment, briefly describe your organization's anti-harassment policy and attach a copy of it to the position statement.
- Next describe in chronological order the events that led to any adverse action taken against the charging party. Make it clear that the adverse action was based on legitimate, non-discriminatory reasons. One way to do this is to show that the company took similar actions with comparable employees who are not members of a protected class.

As emphasized in a recent Supreme Court case, *Reeves v. Sanderson Plumbing* (197 F.3d 688), companies should always tell employees and the EEOC the truthful reason for any adverse action taken. Under the *Reeves* ruling, employers that fail to provide honest reasons for the adverse actions they take against employees will have a very difficult time getting their cases dismissed without a jury trial. In the conclusion to this case at the end of the chapter we will learn what happens after the company files its position statement with the EEOC.

Challenges

1. What factors might a company consider in deciding whether to accept mediation or to make a settlement offer to the charging party?
2. Why might the company try to avoid an "on-site" investigation?
3. Why might the company try to avoid a jury trial?

SOCIETAL OBJECTIVES

As a society, we espouse equality of opportunity, rather than equality of outcomes. That is, the broad goal is to provide for all Americans, regardless of race, age, gender, religion, national origin, or disability, an equal opportunity to compete for jobs for which they are qualified. The objective, therefore, is equal employment opportunity (EEO), not equal employment (EE), or equal numbers of employees from various subgroups. For Americans with disabilities, the nation's goals are to ensure equality of opportunity, full participation, independent living, and economic self-sufficiency.

The U.S. population, as well as its workforce, is a diverse lot. Even among native-born English speakers, at least 22 different dialects of English are spoken in the United States! Whenever the members of such heterogeneous groups must work together, the possibility of unfair discrimination exists. Civil rights laws have been passed at the federal and state levels to provide remedies for job applicants or employees who feel they have been victims of unfair discrimination. From a managerial perspective, it is important to understand the rights as well as the obligations of employers, job candidates, and employees. Indeed, understanding these laws and their management implications is critical for all managers, not just for HR professionals. As we will see, ignorance in this area can turn out to be very expensive. Let's begin by considering the meaning of EEO and the forms of unfair discrimination.

EEO AND UNFAIR DISCRIMINATION: WHAT ARE THEY?

Civil rights laws, judicial interpretations of the laws, and the many sets of guidelines issued by state and federal regulatory agencies have outlawed discrimination based on race, religion, national origin, age, sex, and physical disability. In short, they have attempted to frame national policy on *equal employment opportunity*. Although no law has ever attempted to define precisely the term *discrimination*, in the employment context it can be viewed broadly as the giving of an unfair advantage (or disadvantage) to the members of a particular group in comparison with the members of other groups.[1] The disadvantage usually results in a denial or restriction of employment opportunities, or in an inequality in the terms or benefits of employment.

It is important to note that whenever there are more candidates than available positions, it is necessary to select some candidates in preference to others. Selection implies exclusion; and as long as the exclusion is based on what can be demonstrated to be job-related criteria, that kind of discrimination is entirely proper. It is only when candidates are excluded on a prohibited basis, one that is not related to the job (e.g., age, race, gender), that unlawful and unfair discrimination exists. In short, EEO implies at least two things:

1. **Evaluation of candidates for jobs in terms of characteristics that really do make a difference between success and failure** (e.g., in selection, promotion, performance appraisal, or layoff).
2. **Fair and equal treatment of employees on the job** (e.g., equal pay for equal work, equal benefits, freedom from sexual harassment).

Despite federal and state laws on these issues, they represent the basis of an enormous volume of court cases, indicating that stereotypes and prejudices do not die quickly or easily. Discrimination is a subtle and complex phenomenon that may assume two broad forms:

1. **Unequal (disparate) treatment** is based on an intention to discriminate, including the intention to retaliate against a person who opposes discrimination, has brought charges, or has participated in an investigation or a hearing. There are three major subtheories of discrimination within the disparate treatment theory:
   a. Cases that rely on **direct evidence** of the intention to discriminate. Such cases are proved with direct evidence of:
      Pure bias based on an open expression of hatred, disrespect, or inequality, knowingly directed against members of a particular group. Blanket exclusionary policies—for example, deliberate exclusion of an individual whose disability (e.g., an inability to walk) has nothing to do with the requirements of the job she is applying for (financial analyst).
   b. Cases that are proved through **circumstantial evidence** of the intention to discriminate (see *McDonnell Douglas v. Green* test, p. 85), including those that rely on statistical evidence as a method of circumstantially proving the intention to discriminate systematically against classes of individuals.
   c. **Mixed-motive cases** (a hybrid theory) that often rely on both direct evidence of the intention to discriminate on some impermissible basis (e.g., gender, race, disability) and proof that the employer's stated legitimate basis for its employment decision is actually just a pretext for illegal discrimination.
2. **Adverse impact (unintentional) discrimination** occurs when identical standards or procedures are applied to everyone, despite the fact that they lead to a substantial difference in employment outcomes (e.g., selection, promotion, layoffs) for the members of a particular group, and they are unrelated to success on a job. For example, use of a minimum height requirement of 5 feet, 8 inches for police cadets. That requirement would have an adverse impact on Asians, Hispanics, and women. The policy is neutral on its face but has an adverse impact. To use it, an employer would need to show that the height requirement is necessary to perform the job.

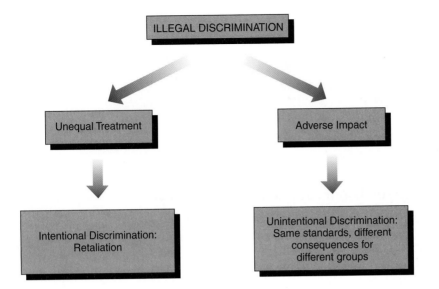

Figure 3–1

Major forms
of illegal
discrimination.

These two forms of illegal discrimination are illustrated graphically in Figure 3–1.

THE LEGAL CONTEXT OF HUMAN RESOURCE DECISIONS

Now that we understand the forms that illegal discrimination can take, let's consider the major federal laws governing employment. Then we will consider the agencies that enforce the laws, as well as some important court cases that have interpreted them. The federal laws that we will discuss fall into two broad classes:

1. Laws of broad scope that prohibit unfair discrimination.
2. Laws of limited application, for example, those that require nondiscrimination as a condition for receiving federal funds (contracts, grants, revenue-sharing entitlements).

The particular laws that we shall discuss within each category are the following:

Laws of broad scope	Laws of limited application
Thirteenth and Fourteenth Amendments to the U.S. Constitution	Executive Orders 11246, 11375, and 11478
Civil Rights Acts of 1866 and 1871	Rehabilitation Act of 1973
Equal Pay Act of 1963	Vietnam Era Veterans Readjustment Act of 1974
Title VII of the Civil Rights Act of 1964	Uniformed Services Employment and Reemployment Rights Act of 1994
Civil Rights Act of 1991	

Cont. on page 82

Laws of broad scope (cont.)	Laws of limited application (cont.)
Age Discrimination in Employment Act of 1967, as amended in 1986 Immigration Reform and Control Act of 1986 Americans with Disabilities Act of 1990 Family and Medical Leave Act of 1993	

The Thirteenth and Fourteenth Amendments

The Thirteenth Amendment prohibits slavery and involuntary servitude. Any form of discrimination may be considered an incident of slavery or involuntary servitude and thus be liable to legal action under this amendment.[2] The Fourteenth Amendment guarantees equal protection of the law for all citizens. Both the Thirteenth Amendment and the Fourteenth Amendment granted to Congress the constitutional power to enact legislation to enforce their provisions. It is from this source of constitutional power that all subsequent civil rights legislation originates.

The Civil Rights Acts of 1866 and 1871

These laws were enacted on the basis of the provisions of the Thirteenth and Fourteenth Amendments. The Civil Rights Act of 1866 grants all citizens the right to make and enforce contracts for employment, and the Civil Rights Act of 1871 grants all citizens the right to sue in federal court if they feel they have been deprived of any rights or privileges guaranteed by the Constitution and other laws.

Until recently, both of these civil rights acts were viewed narrowly as tools for solving Reconstruction-era racial problems. This is no longer so. In *Johnson v. Railway Express Agency, Inc.*, the Supreme Court held that, while the Civil Rights Act of 1866 on its face relates primarily to racial discrimination in the making and enforcement of contracts, it also provides a federal remedy against racial discrimination in private employment.[3] It is a powerful remedy. The Civil Rights Act of 1991 amended the Civil Rights Act of 1866 so that workers are protected from intentional discrimination in all aspects of employment, not just hiring and promotion. Thus racial harassment is covered by this civil rights law. The Civil Rights Act of 1866 allows for jury trials and for compensatory and punitive damages* for victims of intentional racial and ethnic discrimination, and it covers both large and small employers, even those with fewer than 15 employees.

The 1866 law also has been used recently to broaden the definition of racial discrimination originally applied to African Americans. In a unanimous decision, the Supreme Court ruled that race was equated with ethnicity during the legislative debate after the Civil War, and therefore Arabs, Jews, and other ethnic

---

*Punitive damages are awarded in civil cases to punish or deter a defendant's conduct and are separate from compensatory damages, which are intended to reimburse a plaintiff for injuries or harm.

groups thought of as "white" are not barred from suing under the 1866 act. The Court held that Congress intended to protect identifiable classes of persons who are subjected to intentional discrimination solely because of their ancestry or ethnic characteristics. Under the law, therefore, race involves more than just skin pigment.[4]

The Equal Pay Act of 1963

This act was passed as an amendment to an earlier compensation-related law, the Fair Labor Standards Act of 1938. For those employees covered by the Fair Labor Standards Act, the Equal Pay Act requires that men and women working for the same establishment be paid the same rate of pay for work that is substantially equal in skill, effort, responsibility, and working conditions. Pay differentials are legal and appropriate if they are based on seniority, merit, systems that measure the quality or quantity of work, or any factor other than sex (for example, shift differentials, completion of a job-related training program). Moreover, in correcting any inequity under the Equal Pay Act, employers must raise the rate of lower-paid employees, not lower the rate of higher-paid employees.[5]

Thousands of equal-pay suits have been filed (predominantly by women) since the law was passed. For individual companies the price can be quite high. For example, in 1999 Texaco agreed to pay a record $3.1 million to female employees who consistently had been paid less than their male counterparts. That amount included $2.2 million in back pay and interest and $900,000 in salary increases.[6]

Title VII of the Civil Rights Act of 1964

The Civil Rights Act of 1964 is divided into several sections, or titles, each dealing with a particular facet of discrimination (e.g., voting rights, public accommodations, public education). Title VII is most relevant to the employment context, for it prohibits discrimination on the basis of race, color, religion, sex, or national origin in all aspects of employment (including apprenticeship programs). Title VII is the most important federal EEO law because it contains the broadest coverage, prohibitions, and remedies. Through it, the **Equal Employment Opportunity Commission (EEOC)** was created to ensure that employers, employment agencies, and labor organizations comply with Title VII.

Some may ask why we need such a law. As an expression of social policy, the law was passed to guarantee that people would be considered for jobs not on the basis of the color of their skin, their religion, their gender, or their national origin, but rather, on the basis of the abilities and talents that are necessary to perform a job.

In 1972, the coverage of Title VII was expanded. It now includes almost all public and private employers with 15 or more employees, except (1) private clubs, (2) religious organizations (which are allowed to discriminate on the basis of religion in certain circumstances), and (3) places of employment connected with an Indian reservation. The 1972 amendments also prohibit the denial, termination, or suspension of government contracts (without a special hearing) if an employer has followed and is now following an affirmative action plan accepted by the federal government for the same facility within the past 12 months. **Affirmative action** refers to those actions appropriate to overcome the effects of past or present policies, practices, or other barriers to equal employment opportunity.[7]

Finally, back-pay awards in Title VII cases are limited to 2 years prior to the filing of a charge. For example, if a woman filed a Title VII claim in 1995, and the matter continued through investigation, conciliation, trial, and appeal until 2000, she might be entitled to as much as 7 years' back pay, from 1993 (2 years prior to the filing of the charge) until the matter was resolved in her favor. The 2-year statute of limitations begins with the *filing* of a charge of discrimination.

Elected officials and their appointees are excluded from Title VII coverage, but they are still subject to the Fourteenth Amendment, to the Civil Rights Acts of 1866 and 1871, and to the Civil Rights Act of 1991. The following are also specifically exempted from Title VII coverage:

1. **Bona fide occupational qualifications (BFOQs)**. Discrimination is permissible when a prohibited factor (e.g., gender) is a bona fide occupational qualification for employment, that is, when it is considered "reasonably necessary to the operation of that particular business or enterprise." The burden of proof rests with the employer to demonstrate this. (According to one HR director, the only legitimate BFOQs that she could think of are sperm donor and wet nurse!) Both the EEOC and the courts interpret BFOQs quite narrowly.[8] Preferences of the employer, coworkers, or clients are irrelevant and do not constitute BFOQs. Moreover, BFOQ is not a viable defense to a Title VII race claim.

2. **Seniority systems**. Although there are a number of legal questions associated with their use, Title VII explicitly permits bona fide seniority, merit, or incentive systems "provided that such differences are not the result of an intention to discriminate."

3. **Preemployment inquiries**. Inquiries regarding such matters as race, sex, or ethnic group are permissible as long as they can be shown to be job related. Even if not job related, some inquiries (e.g., regarding race or sex) are necessary to meet the reporting requirements of federal regulatory agencies. Applicants provide this information on a voluntary basis.

4. **Testing**. An employer may give or act upon any professionally developed ability test. If the results demonstrate adverse impact against a protected group, then the test itself must be shown to be job related (i.e., valid) for the position in question.

5. **Preferential treatment**. The Supreme Court has ruled that Title VII does not require the granting of preferential treatment to individuals or groups because of their race, sex, religion, or national origin on account of existing imbalances:

    The burden which shifts to the employer is merely that of proving that he based his employment decision on a legitimate consideration, and not an illegitimate one such as race . . . . Title VII forbids him from having as a goal a work force selected by any proscribed discriminatory practice, but it does not impose a duty to adopt a hiring procedure that maximizes hiring of minority employees.[9]

6. **National security**. Discrimination is permitted under Title VII when it is deemed necessary to protect the national security (e.g., against members of groups whose avowed aim is to overthrow the U.S. government).

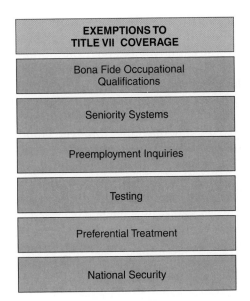

EXEMPTIONS TO TITLE VII COVERAGE
Bona Fide Occupational Qualifications
Seniority Systems
Preemployment Inquiries
Testing
Preferential Treatment
National Security

Figure 3–2

The six exemptions to Title VII coverage.

Initially it appeared that these exemptions (summarized in Figure 3–2) would blunt the overall impact of the law significantly. However, it soon became clear that they would be interpreted very narrowly both by the EEOC and by the courts.

Litigating Claims of Unfair Discrimination

If someone decides to bring suit under Title VII, the first step is to establish a prima facie case of discrimination (i.e., a body of facts presumed to be true until proved otherwise). However, the nature of prima facie evidence differs depending on the type of case brought before the court. If an individual alleges that a particular employment practice had an **adverse impact** on all members of a class that he or she represents, prima facie evidence is presented when adverse impact is shown to exist. Usually this is demonstrated by showing that the selection rate for the group in question is less than 80 percent of the rate of the dominant group (e.g., white males), and that the difference is statistically significant. If the individual alleges that he or she was treated differently from others in the context of some employment practice (i.e., **unequal treatment discrimination**), a prima facie case is usually presented either through direct evidence of the intention to discriminate or by circumstantial evidence. The legal standard for circumstantial evidence is a four-part test first specified in the *McDonnell Douglas v. Green* case,[10] wherein a plaintiff must be able to demonstrate that:

1. She or he has asserted a basis protected by Title VII, the Age Discrimination in Employment Act, or the Americans with Disabilities Act.
2. She or he was somehow harmed or disadvantaged (e.g., by not receiving a job offer or a promotion).
3. She or he was qualified to do the job or to perform the job in a satisfactory manner.
4. Either a similarly situated individual (or a group other than that of the plaintiff) was treated more favorably than the plaintiff, or the matter complained of involved an actual (rather than a nonexistent) employment opportunity.

Once the court accepts prima facie evidence, the burden of producing evidence shifts back and forth from plaintiff (the complaining party) to defendant (the employer). First, the employer is given the opportunity to articulate a legitimate, nondiscriminatory reason for the practice in question. Following that, in an unequal treatment case, the burden then shifts back to the plaintiff to show that the employer's reason is a pretext for illegal discrimination. In an adverse impact case, the plaintiff's burden is to show that a less discriminatory alternative practice exists and that the employer failed to use it. A similar process is followed in age discrimination cases.

The Civil Rights Act of 1991[11]

This act overturned six Supreme Court decisions issued in 1989. Following are key provisions that are likely to have the greatest impact in the context of employment.

Monetary Damages and Jury Trials

A major effect of this act is to expand the remedies in discrimination cases. Individuals who feel they are the victims of intentional discrimination based on race, gender (including sexual harassment), religion, or disability can ask for compensatory damages for pain and suffering, as well as for punitive damages, and they may demand a jury trial. In the past, only plaintiffs in age discrimination cases had the right to demand a jury.

Compensatory and punitive damages are available only from nonpublic employers (public employers are still subject to compensatory damages up to $300,000), and not for adverse impact (unintentional discrimination) cases. Moreover, they may not be awarded in an Americans with Disabilities Act (ADA) case when an employer has engaged in good-faith efforts to provide a reasonable accommodation. Thus, the 1991 Civil Rights Act provides the sanctions for violations of the ADA. The total amount of damages that can be awarded depends on the size of the employer's workforce:

Number of employees	Maximum combined damages per complaint
15–100	$ 50,000
101–200	100,000
201–500	200,000
More than 500	300,000

In a 1999 decision, *Kolstad v. American Dental Association*, the U.S. Supreme Court held that the availability of punitive damages depends on the motive of the discriminator, rather than the nature of the conduct (the extent to which it is "egregious" or "outrageous"). Further, employers should not be assessed punitive damages if they implement in good faith sound antidiscrimination policies and practices. It is not enough simply to distribute a well-crafted policy. Supervisors must be trained to use it, and there should be consequences for failing to do so.[12]

Adverse Impact (Unintentional Discrimination) Cases

The act clarifies each party's obligation in such cases. As we noted earlier, when an adverse impact charge is made, the plaintiff must identify a specific employment practice as the cause of discrimination. If the plaintiff is successful in demonstrating adverse impact, the burden of producing evidence shifts to the employer, who must prove that the challenged practice is "job-related for the position in question and consistent with business necessity."

Protection in Foreign Countries

Protection from discrimination in employment, under Title VII of the 1964 Civil Rights Act and the Americans with Disabilities Act, is extended to U.S. citizens employed in a foreign facility owned or controlled by a U.S. company. However, the employer does not have to comply with U.S. discrimination law if to do so would violate the law of the foreign country. To be covered under this provision, the U.S. citizen must be employed overseas in a firm controlled by an American employer.[13]

Racial Harassment

As we noted earlier, the act amended the Civil Rights Act of 1866 so that workers are protected from intentional discrimination in all aspects of employment, not just hiring and promotion.

Challenges to Consent Decrees

Once a court order or consent decree is entered to resolve a lawsuit, nonparties to the original suit cannot challenge such enforcement actions.

Mixed-Motive Cases

In a mixed-motive case, an employment decision was based on a combination of job-related factors as well as unlawful factors, such as race, gender, religion, or disability. Under the Civil Rights Act of 1991, an employer is guilty of discrimination if it can be shown that a prohibited consideration was a motivating factor in a decision, even though other factors, which are lawful, also were used. However, if the employer can show that the same decision would have been reached even without the unlawful considerations, the court may not assess damages or require hiring, reinstatement, or promotion.

Seniority Systems

The act provides that a seniority system that intentionally discriminates against the members of a protected group can be challenged (within 180 days) at any of three points: (1) when the system is adopted, (2) when an individual becomes subject to the system, or (3) when a person is injured by the system.

"Race Norming" and Affirmative Action

The act makes it unlawful "to adjust the scores of, use different cutoff scores for, or otherwise alter the results of employment-related tests on the basis of race, color, religion, sex, or national origin." Prior to the passage of this act, within-group percentile scoring (so-called race norming) had been used extensively to adjust the test scores of minority candidates to make them more comparable to those of nonminority candidates. Under **race norming**, each individual's percentile score on a selection test was computed relative only to others in his or her race or ethnic group, and not relative to the scores of all persons who took the test. The percentile scores (high to low) were then merged into a single list, and the single list of percentiles was presented to those responsible for hiring decisions.

Extension to U.S. Senate and Appointed Officials

The act extends protection from discrimination on the basis of race, color, religion, gender, national origin, age, and disability to employees of the U.S. Senate, political appointees of the president, and staff members employed by elected officials at the state level. Employees of the U.S. House of Representatives are covered by a House resolution adopted in 1988.

The Age Discrimination in Employment Act of 1967 (ADEA)

As amended in 1986, this act prohibits discrimination in pay, benefits, or continued employment for employees age 40 and over, unless an employer can demonstrate that age is a bona fide occupational qualification (BFOQ) for the job in question. Like Title VII, this law is administered by the EEOC. A key objective of the law is to prevent financially troubled companies from singling out older employees when there are cutbacks. In fact the Supreme Court has ruled that an employee over 40 is not required to show that a person under 40 replaced him or her in order to bring a claim of age discrimination.[14] However, according to the EEOC, when there are cutbacks, older workers can waive their rights to sue under this law (e.g., in return for sweetened benefits for early retirement). Under the **Older Workers Benefit Protection Act** (OWBPA), an individual employee who does not have a pending claim has 21 days to consider such a waiver (45 days if terminated during a group reduction in force or if leaving voluntarily through a group incentive program), and 7 days after signing to revoke it.[15] Even after signing a waiver, an employee can still sue for age discrimination if the employer did not comply with OWBPA requirements for obtaining a knowing and voluntary release.[16]

Increasingly, older workers are being asked to sign such waivers in exchange for enhanced retirement benefits. For example, at AT&T Communications, Inc., employees who signed waivers received severance pay equal to 5 percent of current pay times the number of years of service. For those without waivers, the company offered a multiplier of 3 percent.

The Immigration Reform and Control Act of 1986 (IRCA)

This law applies to every employer in the United States, even to those with only one employee. It also applies to every employee—whether full-time, part-time, temporary, or seasonal—and it makes the enforcement of national immigration policy the job of every employer. While its provisions are complex, the basic features of the law fall into four broad categories[17]:

1. Employers may not hire or continue to employ "unauthorized aliens" (that is, those not legally authorized to work in this country).
2. Employers must verify the identity and work authorization of every new employee. Employers may not require any particular form of documentation but must examine documents provided by job applicants (e.g., U.S.

passports for U.S. citizens; "green cards" for resident aliens) showing identity and work authorization. Both employer and employee then sign a form (I-9), attesting under penalty of perjury that the employee is lawfully eligible to work in the United States.

3.   Employers with 4 to 14 employees may not discriminate on the basis of citizenship or national origin. Those with 15 or more employees are already prohibited from national origin discrimination by Title VII. However, this prohibition is tempered by an exception that allows employers to select an applicant who is a U.S. citizen over an alien when the two applicants are equally qualified.

4.   Certain illegal aliens have "amnesty" rights. Those who can prove that they resided in the United States continuously from January 1982 to November 6, 1986 (the date of the law's enactment), are eligible for temporary, and ultimately permanent, resident status.

Penalties for noncompliance are severe. For example, for failure to comply with the verification rules, fines range from $100 to $1000 for each employee whose identity and work authorization have not been verified. The act also provides for criminal sanctions for employers who engage in a pattern or practice of violations, and a 1996 Executive Order prohibits companies that knowingly hire illegal aliens from receiving federal contracts.[18]

The Americans with Disabilities Act of 1990 (ADA)

Passed to protect the estimated 54 million Americans with disabilities,[19] this law applies to all employers with 15 or more employees. People with disabilities are protected from discrimination in employment, transportation, and public accommodation. Title I of the ADA, the employment section, protects approximately 86 percent of the American workforce.[20]

As a general rule, the ADA prohibits an employer from discriminating against a "qualified individual with a disability." A qualified individual is one who is able to perform the **essential** (i.e., primary) **functions** of a job with or without accommodation. **Disability** is a physical or mental impairment that substantially limits one or more major life activities, such as walking, talking, seeing, hearing, or learning. People are protected if they currently have an impairment, have a record of such impairment, or if the employer thinks they have an impairment (e.g., a person with diabetes under control).[21] Rehabilitated drug and alcohol abusers are protected, but current drug abusers may be fired. The alcoholic, in contrast, is covered and must be reasonably accommodated by being given a firm choice to rehabilitate himself or herself or face career-threatening consequences.[22] The law also protects people who have tested positive for the AIDS virus.[23]

In three rulings in 1999 and one in 2002,[24] the U.S. Supreme Court held that, in general, individuals who can function normally with mitigating measures (e.g., eyeglasses to correct near-sightedness, medication to control mental illness) are not protected by the ADA. To be protected, an individual must have an impairment that prevents or severely restricts him or her from doing activities that are of central importance to most people's daily lives.[25] However, if someone is disabled under the law, an employer must try to find a way to help, for example, by granting a short leave of absence or by changing the work schedule. But companies don't have to lower work standards, tolerate misconduct, or give someone a make-work job.[26] Here are five major implications for employers:

1. Any factory, office, retail store, bank, hotel, or other building open to the public will have to be made accessible to those with physical disabilities (e.g., by installing ramps, elevators, telephones with amplifiers). "Expensive" will be no excuse, unless such modifications will lead an employer to suffer an "undue hardship."

2. Employers must make "reasonable accommodations" for job applicants or employees with disabilities (e.g., by restructuring job and training programs, modifying work schedules, or purchasing new equipment that is "user friendly" to sight- or hearing-impaired people).[27] **Qualified job applicants** (i.e., individuals with disabilities who can perform the essential functions of a job with or without reasonable accommodation) must be considered for employment. Practices such as the following may facilitate the process[28]:

   ■ Expressions of commitment by top management to accommodate workers with disabilities.

   ■ Assignment of a specialist within the "EEO–affirmative action" section to focus on "equal access" for people with disabilities.

   ■ Centralizing recruiting, intake, and monitoring of hiring decisions.

   ■ Identifying jobs or task assignments where a specific disability is not a bar to employment.

   ■ Developing an orientation process for workers with disabilities, supervisors, and coworkers.

   ■ Publicizing successful accommodation experiences within the organization and among outside organizations.

   ■ Providing in-service training to all employees and managers about the firm's "equal access" policy, and about how to distinguish "essential" from "marginal" job functions.

   ■ Outreach recruitment to organizations that can refer job applicants with disabilities.

   ■ Reevaluating accommodations on a regular basis.

3. Preemployment physicals will now be permissible only if all employees are subject to them, and they cannot be given until after a conditional offer of employment is made. That is, the employment offer is made conditional upon passing of the physical examination. Further, employers are not permitted to ask about past workers' compensation claims or disabilities in general. However, after describing essential job functions, an employer can ask whether the applicant can perform the job in question.[29]

   Here is an example of the difference between these two types of inquiries: "Do you have any back problems?" clearly violates the ADA because it is not job specific. However, the employer could state the following: "This job involves lifting equipment weighing up to 50 pounds at least once every hour of an 8-hour shift. Can you do that?"

4. Medical information on employees must be kept separate from other personal or work-related information about them.

5. Drug-testing rules remain intact. An employer can still prohibit the use of alcohol and illegal drugs at the workplace and continue to give alcohol and drug tests.

Enforcement

This law is enforced according to the same procedures currently applicable to race, gender, national origin, and religious discrimination under Title VII of the Civil Rights Act of 1964. The enforcement agency is the Equal Employment Opportunity Commission. In cases of intentional discrimination, individuals with disabilities may be awarded both compensatory and punitive damages up to $300,000 (depending on the size of the employer's workforce). Each year, roughly 18,000 complaints are filed with the agency. Of these, the top five areas that workers complain about most often are wrongful discharge (54 percent), lack of reasonable accommodation (32 percent), terms of employment (15 percent), harassment (14 percent), and hiring (8 percent).[30] As the chapter-opening vignette illustrates, this area will be a "hot" one for allegations of illegal discrimination for some time to come.

What will the cost to employers be? According to a 1998 survey by the Job Accommodation Network, the average cost to employers of helping workers with disabilities to overcome their impairments was a mere $935 per person.[31]

The Family and Medical Leave Act of 1993 (FMLA)

The FMLA covers all private-sector employers with 50 or more employees, including part-timers, who work 1,250 hours over a 12-month period (an average of 25 hours per week). The law gives workers up to 12 weeks' unpaid leave each year for birth, adoption, or foster care of a child within a year of the child's arrival; care for a spouse, parent, or child with a serious health condition; or the employee's own serious health condition if it prevents him or her from working. The employer is responsible for designating an absence or leave as FMLA leave, on the basis of information provided by the employee.[32] Employers can require workers to provide medical certification of such serious illnesses and can require a second medical opinion. Employers also can exempt from the FMLA key salaried employees who are among their highest-paid 10 percent. For leave takers, however, employers must maintain health insurance benefits and give the workers their previous jobs (or comparable positions) when their leaves are over. Enforcement provisions of the FMLA are administered by the U.S. Department of Labor.[33] The overall impact of this law was softened considerably by the exemption of some of its fiercest opponents—companies with fewer than 50 employees, or 95 percent of all businesses.[34] Nevertheless, the law still covers about 300,000 employers and 45 million employees in the private sector, and about 15 million more in state and local governments.[35] For employers, FMLA complaints can be costly. How costly? Monetary damages awarded under the FMLA came to $19 million in 1999.[36]

This completes the discussion of "absolute prohibitions" against discrimination. The following sections discuss nondiscrimination as a basis for eligibility for federal funds.

Executive Orders 11246, 11375, and 11478

Presidential executive orders in the realm of employment and discrimination are aimed specifically at federal agencies, contractors, and subcontractors. They have the force of law, even though they are issued unilaterally by the president without congressional approval, and they can be altered unilaterally as well. The requirements of these orders are parallel to those of Title VII.

In 1965, President Lyndon Johnson issued Executive Order 11246, prohibiting discrimination on the basis of race, color, religion, or national origin as a condition of employment by federal agencies, contractors, and subcontractors with contracts of $10,000 or more. Those covered are required to establish and maintain a program of equal employment opportunity in every facility of 50 or more people. Such programs include employment, upgrading, demotion, transfer, recruitment or recruitment advertising, layoff or termination, pay rates, and selection for training.

In 1967, Executive Order 11375, also issued by President Johnson, prohibited discrimination in employment based on sex. Executive Order 11478, issued by President Richard Nixon in 1969, went even further, for it prohibited discrimination in employment based on all the previous factors, plus political affiliation, marital status, or physical disability.

Enforcement of Executive Orders

Executive Order 11246 provides considerable enforcement power, administered by the Department of Labor through its Office of Federal Contract Compliance Programs (OFCCP). Upon a finding by the OFCCP of noncompliance with the order, the Department of Justice may be advised to institute criminal proceedings, and the secretary of labor may cancel or suspend current contracts as well as the right to bid on future contracts. Needless to say, noncompliance can be very expensive.

The Rehabilitation Act of 1973

This act requires federal contractors (those receiving more than $2,500 in federal contracts annually) and subcontractors to actively recruit qualified people with disabilities and to use their talents to the fullest extent possible. The legal requirements are similar to those of the Americans with Disabilities Act.

The purpose of this act is to eliminate *systemic discrimination*, that is, any business practice that results in the denial of equal employment opportunity.[37] Hence the act emphasizes "screening in" applicants, not screening them out. It is enforced by the OFCCP.

The Vietnam Era Veterans Readjustment Act of 1974

Federal contractors and subcontractors are required under this act to take affirmative action to ensure equal employment opportunity for Vietnam-era veterans (August 5, 1964, to May 7, 1975). The OFCCP enforces it.

The Uniformed Services Employment and Reemployment Rights Act of 1994

Regardless of the size of its organization, an employer may not deny a person initial employment, reemployment, promotion, or benefits on the basis of that person's membership or potential membership in the armed service. To be protected, the employee must provide advance notice. Employers need not always rehire a returning service member (e.g., if the employee received a dishonorable discharge, or if changed circumstances at the workplace make reemployment impossible or unreasonable), but the burden of proof will almost always be on the employer. The U.S. Department of Labor administers this law.[38]

Federal Enforcement Agencies: EEOC and OFCCP

The Equal Employment Opportunity Commission is an independent regulatory agency whose five commissioners (one of whom is chairperson) are appointed by the President and confirmed by the Senate for terms of 5 years. No more than three of the commissioners may be from the same political party. Like the OFCCP, the EEOC sets policy and in individual cases determines whether there is "reasonable cause" to believe that unlawful discrimination has occurred. If the EEOC finds reasonable cause, it can sue either on its own behalf or on behalf of a claimant. As far as the employer is concerned, the simplest and least costly procedure is to establish a system to resolve complaints internally. However, if this system fails or if the employer does not make available an avenue for such complaints, an aggrieved individual (or group) can file a formal complaint with the EEOC. The process is shown graphically in Figure 3–3.

Once it receives a complaint of discrimination, the EEOC follows a three-step process: investigation, conciliation, and litigation.[39] As Figure 3–3 indicates, complaints must be filed within 180 days of an alleged violation (300 days if the same basis of discrimination is prohibited by either state or local laws). If that requirement is satisfied, the EEOC immediately refers the complaint to a state agency charged with enforcement of fair employment laws (if one exists) for resolution within 60 days. If the complaint cannot be resolved within that time, the state agency can file suit in a state district court and appeal any decision to a state appellate court, the state supreme court, or the U.S. Supreme Court. As an alternative to filing suit, the state agency may redefer to the EEOC. Again, the EEOC seeks voluntary reconciliation, where the EEOC may serve as mediator. In 1999 for example, the EEOC successfully resolved 4,833 discrimination complaints through voluntary mediation.[40] If mediation fails, EEOC may refer the case to the Justice Department (if the defendant is a public employer) or file suit in federal district court (if the defendant is a private employer). Like state court decisions, federal court decisions may be appealed to one of the 12 U.S. Courts of Appeal (corresponding to the geographical region, or "circuit," in which the case arose, see Figure 3–4). In turn, these decisions may be appealed to the U.S. Supreme Court, although very few cases are actually heard by the Supreme Court. Generally the Court will grant **certiorari** (discretionary review) when two or more circuit courts have reached different conclusions on the same point of law or when a major question of constitutional interpretation is involved. If the Supreme Court denies certiorari, the lower court's decision is binding.

EEOC Guidelines

The EEOC has issued a number of guidelines for Title VII compliance.[41] Among these are guidelines on discrimination because of religion, national origin, gender, and pregnancy; guidelines on affirmative action programs; guidelines on employee selection procedures; and a policy statement on preemployment inquiries. These guidelines are not laws, although the Supreme Court has indicated that they are entitled to "great deference."[42]

Information Gathering

This is another major EEOC function, for each organization in the United States with 100 or more employees must file an annual report (EEO-1) detailing the

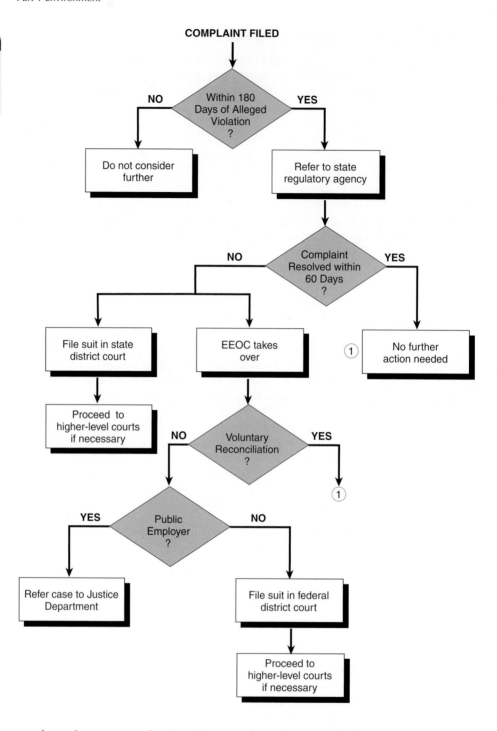

Figure 3–3

Discrimination complaints: the formal process.

number of women and minorities employed in nine different job categories ranging from laborers to managers and professionals. Through computerized analysis of the forms, the EEOC is able to identify broad patterns of discrimination (**systemic discrimination**) and to attack them through class actions. In any given year the EEOC typically receives about 80,000 complaints. Its backlog of cases totaled 40,234 at the end of 1999.[43]

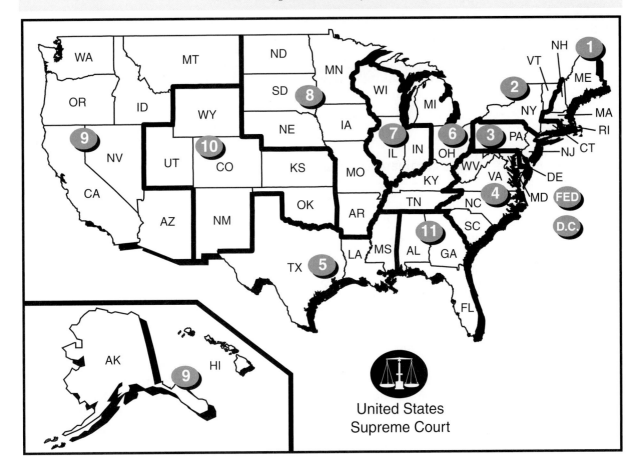

Figure 3–4

The system of Federal Appellate Courts in the United States.
(*Source:* Georgetown University Law Library.)

Office of Federal Contract Compliance Programs (OFCCP)

Contract compliance means that in addition to quality, timeliness, and other requirements of federal contract work, contractors and subcontractors must meet EEO and affirmative action requirements. As we have seen, these requirements cover all aspects of employment.

Companies are willing to go to considerable lengths to avoid the loss of government contracts. More than a quarter of a million companies, employing 27 million workers and providing the government with more than $100 billion in construction, supplies, equipment, and services, are subject to contract compliance enforcement by the OFCCP.[44] Contractors and subcontractors with more than $50,000 in government business and with 50 or more employees must prepare and implement written affirmative action plans.

In jobs where women and minorities are underrepresented in the workforce relative to their availability in the labor force, employers must establish goals and timetables for hiring and promotion. Theoretically, goals and timetables are

Figure 3–5

The distinction between rigid quotas and goals and timetables.

Start

Done by Specific Date

QUOTAS: Inflexible; *MUST* be met in a specified amount of time

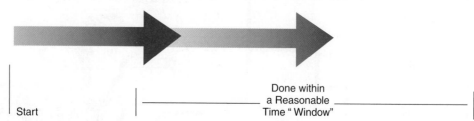

Start

Done within a Reasonable Time " Window"

GOALS AND TIMETABLES: Flexible; *MAY* be met in a realistic amount of time

distinguishable from rigid quotas in that they are flexible objectives that can be met in a realistic amount of time (Figure 3–5). Goals and timetables are not required under the Rehabilitation Act and the Vietnam veterans law.

When a compliance review by the OFCCP does indicate problems that cannot be resolved easily, it tries to reach a conciliation agreement with the employer. Such an agreement might include back pay, seniority credit, special recruitment efforts, promotion, or other forms of relief for the victims of unlawful discrimination.

The conciliation agreement is the OFCCP's preferred route, but if such efforts are unsuccessful, formal enforcement action is necessary. Contractors and subcontractors are entitled to a hearing before a judge. If conciliation is not reached before or after the hearing, employers may lose their government contracts, their payments may be withheld by the government, or they may be debarred from any government contract work. Debarment is the OFCCP's ultimate weapon, for it indicates in the most direct way possible that the U.S. government is serious about equal employment opportunity programs.

Affirmative Action Remedies

In three different cases, the Supreme Court found that Congress specifically endorsed the concept of non-victim-specific racial hiring goals to achieve compliance.[45] Further, the Court noted the benefits of flexible affirmative action rather than rigid application of a color-blind policy that would deprive employers of flexibility in administering human resources. How do employers do in practice? One 7-year study of companies that set annual goals for increasing African-American male employment found that only one-tenth of the goals were achieved. Some may see this as a sign of failure, but it also reflects the fact that the goals were not rigid quotas. "Companies promise more than they can deliver, . . . but the ones that promise more do deliver more."[46]

Employment Case Law: Some General Principles

Although Congress enacts laws, the courts interpret the laws and determine how they will be enforced. Such interpretations define what is called **case law**, which serves as a precedent to guide future legal decisions. And, of course, precedents are regularly subject to reinterpretation.

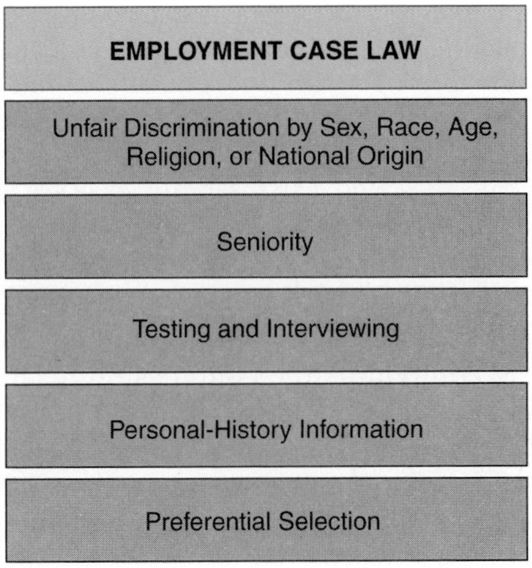

```
┌─────────────────────────────────────────┐
│           EMPLOYMENT CASE LAW            │
├─────────────────────────────────────────┤
│  Unfair Discrimination by Sex, Race, Age,│
│       Religion, or National Origin       │
├─────────────────────────────────────────┤
│               Seniority                  │
├─────────────────────────────────────────┤
│        Testing and Interviewing          │
├─────────────────────────────────────────┤
│      Personal-History Information         │
├─────────────────────────────────────────┤
│          Preferential Selection          │
└─────────────────────────────────────────┘
```

Figure 3–6

Areas making up the main body of employment case law.

In the area of employment, a considerable body of case law has accumulated since 1964. Figure 3–6 illustrates areas in which case law is developed most extensively. Lawsuits affecting virtually every aspect of employment have been filed, and in the following sections we will consider some of the most significant decisions to date.

Sex Discrimination

Suppose you run an organization that has 238 managerial positions—all filled by men. Only one promotional opportunity to a managerial position is available. Suppose that only a 2-point difference in test scores separates the best-qualified man from the best-qualified woman. What do you do? Until a landmark Supreme Court decision (*Johnson v. Santa Clara Transportation Agency*[47]), if you promoted the woman you invited a lawsuit by the man. If you promoted the woman to correct past discrimination (thereby acknowledging past bias), you would invite discrimination suits by women. No longer. The Supreme Court ruled unambiguously that in traditionally sex-segregated jobs, a qualified woman can be promoted over a marginally better-qualified man to promote more balanced representation. The Court stressed the need for affirmative action plans to be flexible, gradual, and limited in their effect on whites and men. The Court also expressed disapproval of strict numerical quotas except where necessary (on a temporary basis) to remedy severe past discrimination.

Many employers are in similar positions. That is, they have not been proved guilty of past discrimination, but they have a significant underrepresentation of women or other protected groups in various job categories. This decision clearly put pressure on employers to institute voluntary affirmative action programs, but at the same time it also provided some welcome guidance on what they were permitted to do.

Pregnancy

The Equal Employment Opportunity Commission's guidelines on the Pregnancy Discrimination Act of 1978 state:

> The basic principle of the Act is that women affected by pregnancy and related con-
> ditions must be treated the same as other applicants and employees on the basis of
> their ability or inability to work. A woman is therefore protected against such prac-
> tices as being fired, or refused a job or promotion, merely because she is pregnant or
> has had an abortion. She usually cannot be forced to go on leave as long as she can
> still work. If other employees who take disability leave are entitled to get their jobs
> back when they are able to work again, so are women who have been unable to
> work because of pregnancy.[48]

Each year, the EEOC receives about 3,600 complaints related to pregnancy
(about 1 out of every 50 complaints the commission receives).[49] However, this
may be only the tip of the iceberg. For example, the National Association of
Working Women in Cleveland handles 15,000 calls a year from women claiming gender-based discrimination, including pregnancy.[50]

Under the law, an employer is never *required* to give pregnant employees
special treatment. If an organization provides no disability benefits or sick
leave to other employees, it is not required to provide them for pregnant employees.[51] While the actual length of maternity leave is now an issue to be determined by the woman's and/or the company's physician, a Supreme Court
decision in *California Federal Savings & Loan Association v. Guerra* upheld a
California law that provides for up to 4 months of unpaid leave for pregnancy
disability.[52]

Economic pressures on employers may make legal action unnecessary in
the future. Evidence now indicates that many employers are doing their best to
accommodate pregnant women through flexible work scheduling and generous
maternity leave policies.[53] Given the number of women of childbearing age in
the workforce and the fact that 85 percent of all women have children,[54] combined with the tight labor markets that employers face, there really is no other
choice.

One large survey of company practices found that new mothers typically
spend 1 to 3 months at home following childbirth, that job guarantees for returning mothers were provided by 35 percent of the companies, and that employers of 501 to 1000 employees are most likely to provide full pay.[55]

What percentage of women use disability benefits fully and then decide not
to return to work? At Corning Glass, Inc., US Bank, and Levi Straus & Co., more
than 80 percent do return to work. Moreover, the provision of maternity leave
benefits has helped establish good rapport with employees.

How much do these extra benefits cost? The Health Insurance Association
of America estimated that the extension of health insurance coverage to
pregnancy-related conditions of women employees and employees' spouses
would increase premiums by an average of 13 percent.[56]

Reproductive Hazards

Another way sex discrimination may be perpetuated is by barring women from
competing for jobs that pose occupational health hazards to their reproductive
systems. In a landmark 1991 decision (*UAW v. Johnson Controls, Inc.*) the
Supreme Court ruled on this issue. It held that such "fetal protection" policies,
which had been used by more than a dozen major companies, including General Motors, DuPont, Monsanto, Olin, Firestone, and B. F. Goodrich, are a form

of illegal sex discrimination that is prohibited by Title VII. At issue was the policy of Johnson Controls, Inc., a car battery manufacturer, that excluded women of childbearing age from jobs involving exposure to lead.[57] The company argued that its policy was based on the BFOQ exception to Title VII, because it was essential to a safe workplace.

The Supreme Court disagreed, ruling that the BFOQ exception is a narrow one, limited to policies that are directly related to a worker's ability to do the job. "Women as capable of doing their jobs as their male counterparts may not be forced to choose between having a child and having a job. . . . Decisions about the welfare of future children must be left to the parents who conceive, bear, support, and raise them rather than to the employers who hire those parents," said the Court.[58]

What are businesses to do? Clearly, they will have to provide more complete information to inform and warn female (and male) workers about fetal health risks on the job. They may also urge women to consult their physicians before starting such assignments. However, the Supreme Court noted that it would be difficult to sue a company for negligence after it abandoned its fetal protection policy if (1) the employer fully informs women of the risk, and (2) it has not acted negligently.[59] Mere exclusion of workers, both unions and managers agree, does not address chemicals remaining in the workplace to which other workers may be exposed. Nor are women more sensitive to reproductive hazards than men. Changing the workplace, rather than the workforce, is a more enlightened policy.

Sexual Harassment

Sexual harassment is not really about sex. It's about power—more to the point, the abuse of power.[61] In the vast majority of cases on this issue, females rather than males have suffered from sexual abuse at work. Such abuse may constitute illegal sex discrimination, a form of unequal treatment on the job. How prevalent is it? More than 15,000 complaints are filed annually with the EEOC, 90 percent of Fortune 500 companies have dealt with sexual harassment complaints, and more than a third have been sued at least once. The cost? An average of $200,000 on each complaint that is investigated in-house and found to be valid. In fact, one consulting firm estimates that the problem costs the average large corporation $6.7 million a year.[62] It is perilous self-deception for a manager to believe that sexual harassment does not exist in his or her own organization.

What is sexual harassment? Although opinions differ,[63] perhaps the clearest definition is that provided by the EEOC: "unwelcome sexual advances, requests for sexual favors, and other verbal or physical conduct of a sexual nature when submission to or rejection of this conduct explicitly or implicitly affects an individual's employment, unreasonably interferes with an individual's work performance, or creates an intimidating, hostile, or offensive work environment."[64]

Actually, a "no-frills" definition can be put into one word: "unwelcome." According to the courts, for behavior to be treated as sexual harassment, the offender has to know that the behavior is unwelcome. If a person wants to file a grievance, therefore, it is important to be able to prove either that he or she told the perpetrator to back off or that the action was so offensive the harasser should have known it was unwelcome.

Ethical Dilemma
Secret Taping of Supervisors: It May Be Legal, but Is It Ethical?

Employees who think a supervisor is out to get them have something new up their sleeves: hidden tape recorders. Secret tapings are on the rise, often by employees trying to protect their jobs, and aided by the availability of cheap miniature recorders. Such taping, often done to support legal claims, outrages and exasperates employers. Defenders counter that secret recording sometimes is the only way to bring out the truth.

Federal law allows secret taping, as long as one of the people being recorded knows about it. At least a dozen states, including New York, have similar state laws. However, in about 14 other states, including California, the law requires that everyone being taped must know that he or she is being recorded.

Most companies confronted with a tape quickly settle out of court. In one case, for example, a pregnant saleswoman's coworkers told her outright that they would force her off the job by making life hard on her at work. The workers were afraid the pregnancy would stop the woman from racking up sales, and they all would lose a bonus as a result. Once the woman sued for pregnancy discrimination, the coworkers lied about threatening her. They said, "We were all happy for her—we gave her a big hug when we found out she was pregnant." But the woman produced a secret tape she had made of the threats and won a $180,000 settlement.

What is a business to do? Issue a policy against covert recording. That way, employees who tape can be fired for breaking company rules. In states where secret taping is illegal, companies can turn the tables on employees by using the recordings against them. Employment lawyers also advise companies to hire experts to make sure the tapes are authentic and have not been edited. How about coworkers and managers? The cheapest and best protection of all is to avoid saying things you would be embarrassed to go into on a witness stand . . . or to see on the evening news.[60]

While many behaviors can constitute sexual harassment, there are two main types:

1. Quid pro quo (you give me this; I'll give you that).
2. Hostile work environment (an intimidating, hostile, or offensive atmosphere).

Quid pro quo harassment exists when the harassment is a condition of employment. For example, consider the case of *Barnes v. Costle:* The plaintiff rebuffed her director's repeated sexual overtures. She ignored his advice that sexual intimacy was the path she should take to improve her career opportunities. Subsequently the director abolished her job. The court of appeals found that sexual cooperation was a condition of her employment, a condition the director did not impose upon males. Therefore, sex discrimination occurred and the employer was liable.[65]

The U.S. Supreme Court has gone even further. In two key rulings in 1998, *Burlington Industries, Inc. v. Ellerth*[66] and *Faragher v. City of Boca Raton,*[67] the Court held that employers always are potentially liable for a supervisor's sexual misconduct toward an employee, even if they knew nothing about that supervisor's conduct. However, in some cases an employer can defend itself by showing that it took reasonable steps to prevent harassment on the job.

Hostile environment harassment was defined by the Supreme Court in the case of *Meritor Savings Bank v. Vinson.*[68] Vinson's boss had abused her verbally as well as sexually. However, since Vinson was making good career progress, the district court ruled that the relationship was a voluntary one having nothing to do with her continued employment or advancement. The Supreme Court disagreed, ruling that whether the relationship was "voluntary" is irrelevant. The key question was whether the sexual advances from the supervisor were "unwelcome." If so, and if they are "sufficiently severe or pervasive to be abusive,"[69] then they are illegal. This case was groundbreaking because it expanded the definition of harassment to include verbal or physical conduct that creates an intimidating, hostile, or offensive work environment or interferes with an employee's job performance. Employers may also be liable for the harassing actions of nonemployees, such as customers, if they fail to take reasonable steps to stop the harassing behavior.[70]

In a 1993 case, *Harris v. Forklift Systems, Inc.*, the Supreme Court ruled that plaintiffs in such suits need not show psychological injury to prevail. While a victim's emotional state may be relevant, she or he need not prove extreme distress. In considering whether illegal harassment has occurred, juries must consider factors such as the frequency and severity of the harassment, whether it is physically threatening or humiliating, and whether it interferes with an employee's work performance.[71]

As we noted earlier, the Civil Rights Act of 1991 permits victims of sexual harassment—who previously could be awarded only missed wages—to collect a wide range of punitive damages and attorney's fees from employers who mishandled a complaint.

Preventive Actions by Employers

What can an employer do to escape, or to at least limit, its liability for the sexually harassing acts of its managers or workers? As we noted earlier, the Supreme Court ruled that employers may escape liability for sexual and other harassment. This is so if they can prove two things. One, they exercised reasonable care to prevent and promptly correct harassing behavior. Two, the employee who suffered the harassment unreasonably failed to take advantage of preventive and corrective opportunities. This suggests that an effective policy should include the following features[72]:

- A firm and clear statement from the chief executive officer to the effect that sexual harassment will not be tolerated.
- A workable definition of sexual harassment that is publicized via staff meetings, bulletin boards, handbooks, and new-employee orientation programs. It should also include concrete examples of inappropriate behaviors (e.g., derogatory comments, demeaning jokes, visual messages, nicknames that refer to a person's membership in any protected group).
- An established complaint procedure to provide a vehicle for employees to report claims of harassment to their supervisors or to a neutral third party, such as the HR department. Include multiple ways to file complaints because the more choices employees have, the less reasonable will be their failure to complain.

- A clear statement of sanctions for violators and protection for those who make charges.
- Prompt, confidential investigation of every claim of harassment, no matter how trivial.
- Preservation of all investigative information, with records of all such complaints kept in a central location.
- Training of all managers and supervisors, including top management, to recognize and respond to complaints, giving them written materials outlining their responsibilities and obligations when a complaint is made.
- Follow-up to determine whether harassment has stopped.[73]

Age Discrimination

The Equal Employment Opportunity Commission's guidelines on age discrimination emphasize that in order to defend an adverse employment action against employees age 40 and over, an employer must be able to demonstrate a "business necessity" for doing so. That is, it must be able to show that age is a factor directly related to the safe, efficient operation of a business. To establish a prima facie case of age discrimination with respect to termination, for example, an individual must show that[74]:

1. She or he is within the protected age group (40 years of age and over).
2. She or he is doing satisfactory work.
3. She or he was discharged despite satisfactory work performance.
4. The position was filled by a person younger than the person replaced.

For example, an employee named Schwager had worked for Sun Oil Ltd. for 18 years, and his retirement benefits were to be vested (i.e., not contingent on future service) at 20 years. When the company reorganized and had to reduce the size of its workforce, the average age of those retained was 35 years, while the average age of those terminated was 45.7 years. The company was able to demonstrate, however, that economic considerations prompted the reorganization and that factors other than age were considered in Schwager's termination. The local manager had to let one person go, and chose Schwager because he ranked lowest in overall job performance among salespeople in his district and did not measure up to their standards. Job performance, not age, was the reason for Schwager's termination. Employers can still fire unproductive workers, but the key is to base employment decisions on ability, not on age.[75]

"Overqualified" Job Applicants

Employers sometimes hesitate to hire an individual who has a great deal of experience for a job that requires few qualifications and may be only an entry-level job. They assume that an overqualified individual will be bored in such a job or is using the job only to get a foot in the door so he or she can apply for another job at a later time. Beware of violating the Age Discrimination in Employment Act! An appeals court has ruled that rejection of an older worker because he or she is overqualified may be a pretext to mask the real reason for rejection—the employee's age. In the words of the court: "How can a person

"ENGLISH-ONLY" RULES—NATIONAL ORIGIN DISCRIMINATION?

Rules that require employees to speak only English in the workplace have come under fire in recent years. Employees who speak a language other than English claim that such rules are not related to the ability to do a job and have a harsh impact on them because of their national origin. At present, the courts have not developed a uniform standard to apply in assessing the validity of English-only rules.[76]

Employers should be careful when instituting such a rule. While it is not necessarily illegal to make fluency in English a job requirement, or to discipline an employee for violating an English-only rule, employers must be able to show there is a legitimate business need for it. Avoid requiring the use of English at all times and in all areas of the workplace.

Inform employees in advance of the circumstances where speaking only in English is required, and of the consequences of violating the rule. (Conversely, many employers would be delighted to have a worker who can speak the language of a non-English-speaking customer.) Otherwise, the employer may be subject to discrimination complaints on the basis of national origin.[77]

overqualified by experience and training be turned down for a position given to a younger person deemed better qualified?"[78]

Seniority

"Seniority" is a term that connotes length of employment. A **seniority system** is a scheme that, alone or in tandem with "nonseniority" criteria, allots to employees ever-improving employment rights and benefits as their relative lengths of pertinent employment increase.[79]

Various features of seniority systems have been challenged in the courts for many years.[80] However, one of the most nettlesome issues is the impact of established seniority systems on programs designed to ensure equal employment opportunity. Employers often work hard to hire and promote members of protected groups. If layoffs become necessary, however, those individuals may be lost because of their low seniority. As a result, the employer takes a step backward in terms of workforce diversity. What is the employer to do when seniority conflicts with EEO?

The U.S. Supreme Court has been quite clear in its rulings on this issue in two landmark decisions, *Firefighters Local Union No. 1784 v. Stotts*[81] (decided under Title VII) and *Wygant v. Jackson Board of Education*[82] (decided under the equal protection clause of the Fourteenth Amendment). The Court ruled that an employer may not protect the jobs of recently hired African-American employees at the expense of whites who have more seniority.[83]

Voluntary modifications of seniority policies for affirmative action purposes remain proper, but where a collective bargaining agreement exists, the consent of the union is required. Moreover, in the unionized setting, courts have made it clear that the union must be a party to any decree that modifies a bona fide seniority system.[84]

Testing and Interviewing

Title VII clearly sanctions the use of "professionally developed" ability tests. Nevertheless, it took several landmark Supreme Court cases to clarify the proper role and use of tests. The first was *Griggs v. Duke Power Co.*, the most significant EEO case ever, which was decided in favor of Griggs.[85] Duke Power was prohibited from requiring a high school education or the passing of an intelligence test as a condition of employment or job transfer because it could not show that either standard was significantly related to job performance:

> What Congress has forbidden is giving these devices and mechanisms controlling force unless they are demonstrably a reasonable measure of job performance. . . . What Congress has commanded is that any tests used must measure the person for the job and not the person in the abstract.[86]

The ruling also included four other general principles:

1. The law prohibits not only open and deliberate discrimination but also practices that are fair in form but discriminatory in operation. That is, Title VII prohibits practices having an adverse impact on protected groups, unless they are job related. This is a landmark pronouncement because it officially established adverse impact as a category of illegal discrimination.

   For example, suppose an organization wants to use prior arrests as a basis for selection. In theory, arrests are a "neutral" practice since all persons are equally subject to arrest if they violate the law. However, if arrests cannot be shown to be job related, and, in addition, if a significantly higher proportion of African Americans than whites is arrested, the use of arrests as a basis for selection is discriminatory in operation.

2. The employer bears the burden of proof that any requirement for employment is related to job performance. As affirmed by the Civil Rights Act of 1991, when a charge of adverse impact is made, the plaintiff must identify a specific employment practice as the cause of the discrimination. If the plaintiff is successful, the burden shifts to the employer.

3. It is not necessary for the plaintiff to prove that the discrimination was intentional; intent is irrelevant. If the standards result in discrimination, they are unlawful.

4. Job-related tests and other employment selection procedures are legal and useful.

The confidentiality of individual test scores has also been addressed both by the profession[87] and by the courts. Thus the Supreme Court affirmed the right of the Detroit Edison Company to refuse to hand over to a labor union copies of aptitude tests taken by job applicants and to refuse to disclose individual test scores without the written consent of employees.[88]

As is well known, interviews are commonly used as bases for employment decisions to hire or to promote certain candidates in preference to others. Must such "subjective" assessment procedures satisfy the same standards of job-relatedness as more "objective" procedures, such as written tests? If they produce an adverse impact against a protected group, the answer is yes, according to the Supreme Court in *Watson v. Fort Worth Bank & Trust*.[89]

As in its *Griggs* ruling, the Court held that it is not necessary for the plaintiff to prove that the discrimination was intentional. If the interview ratings result in adverse impact, they are presumed to be unlawful, unless the employer can show some relationship between the content of the ratings and the requirements of a given job. This need not involve a formal validation study, although the Court agreed unanimously that it is possible to conduct such studies when subjective assessment devices are used.[90] The lesson for employers? Be sure that there is a legitimate, job-related reason for every question raised in an employment or promotional interview. Limit questioning to "need to know," rather than "nice to know," information and monitor interview outcomes for adverse impact. Validate this selection method. It is unwise to wait until the selection system is challenged.

Personal History

Frequently, job qualification requirements involve personal background information. If the requirements have the effect of denying or restricting equal employment opportunity, they may violate Title VII. For example, in the *Griggs v. Duke Power Co.* case, a purportedly neutral practice (the high school education requirement that excluded a higher proportion of African Americans than whites from employment) was ruled unlawful because it had not been shown to be related to job performance. Other allegedly neutral practices that have been struck down by the courts on the basis of non–job relevance include:

- Recruitment practices based on present employee referrals, where the workforce is nearly all white to begin with.[91]
- Height and weight requirements.[92]
- Arrest records, because they show only that a person has been accused of a crime, not that she or he was guilty of it; thus arrests may not be used as a basis for selection decisions,[93] except in certain sensitive and responsible positions (e.g., police officer, school principal).[94]
- Conviction records, unless the conviction is directly related to the work to be performed—for example, a person convicted of embezzlement applying for a job as a bank teller.[95]

Despite such decisions, personal-history items are not unlawfully discriminatory per se, but to use them you must show that they are relevant to the job in question. Just as with employment interviews, collect this information on a need to know, not on a nice to know, basis.

Preferential Selection

In an ideal world, selection and promotion decisions would be color-blind. Thus, social policy as embodied in Title VII emphasizes that so-called **reverse discrimination** (discrimination against whites and in favor of members of protected groups) is just as unacceptable as is discrimination by whites against members of protected groups.[96] In an effort to improve the prospects for advancement of members of protected groups, such as African Americans, can an employer grant them preference in admission to a training program? The case of *United Steelworkers of America v. Weber* addressed this issue.

These people are protesting the passage of an anti-affirmative action law in California.

    Brian Weber, a white lab analyst at Kaiser Aluminum & Chemical Company's Gramercy, Louisiana, plant, sued his company and his union under Title VII after he was bypassed for a crafts-retraining program. Previously the company and the union had jointly agreed to reserve 50 percent of the available places for African Americans.[97] Although there had been years of exclusion of African Americans from such training programs, there was no proven record of bias at the plant on which to justify such a quota. Thus the company and the union were caught in a dilemma. To eliminate the affirmative action plan was to run the risk of suits by minority employees and the loss of government contracts. To retain the plan when there was no previous history of proven discrimination was to run the risk of reverse discrimination suits by white employees. Finally, to admit previous discrimination at the plant in order to justify the affirmative action plan was to invite suits by minority applicants and employees.

    The Supreme Court ruled that employers can give preference to minorities and women in hiring for "traditionally segregated job categories" (i.e., where there has been a societal history of purposeful exclusion of these individuals from the job category). Employers need not admit past discrimination in order to establish voluntary affirmative action programs. The Court also noted that the Kaiser plan was a "temporary measure" designed simply to eliminate a manifest racial imbalance.[98]

Subsequent cases, together with the Civil Rights Act of 1991, have clarified a number of issues left unresolved by Weber:

1. Courts may order, and employers voluntarily may establish, affirmative action plans, including goals and timetables, to address problems of underutilization of women and minorities. Individuals who were not parties to the original suit may not reopen Court-approved affirmative action settlements.
2. The plans need not be directed solely to identified victims of discrimination but may include general, classwide relief.
3. While the courts will almost never approve a plan that would result in whites' losing their jobs through layoffs, they may sanction plans that impose limited burdens on whites in hiring and promotions (i.e., plans that postpone hiring and promotion).
4. Numerically based, preferential programs should not be used in every instance, and they need not be based on an actual finding of discrimination.[99]

Social policy, as articulated in pronouncements by Congress and the courts, clearly reflects an effort to provide a more level playing field that allows women, minorities, and nonminorities to compete for jobs on the basis of merit alone. As Eleanor Holmes Norton, former chair of the EEOC, noted: "Affirmative action alone cannot cure age-old disparities based on race or sex. But if Title VII is allowed to do its work, it will speed the time when it has outlived its usefulness and our country has lived up to its promises."[100]

SEALED WITHOUT A KISS—RESPONDING TO A LETTER CHARGING YOUR COMPANY WITH UNLAWFUL DISCRIMINATION

Human Resource Management in Action: Conclusion

Events Following the Position Statement

Generally the EEOC may choose any of the following courses of action:

- Make a determination without requesting additional information from the company.
- Request additional documentation or other written information from the company.
- Hold a fact-finding conference, usually during an investigation on the company's premises.

If the EEOC requests additional documentation or other written information, it is generally in the company's best interest to provide it. If not, the EEOC may issue a subpoena and force the company to do so. Also, providing the additional information may reduce the likelihood of an on-site investigation.

IMPACT OF LEGAL FACTORS ON PRODUCTIVITY, QUALITY OF WORK LIFE, AND THE BOTTOM LINE

There are both direct and indirect costs associated with unlawful discrimination. For example, sexual harassment can create high levels of stress and anxiety for both the victim and the perpetrator. These psychological reactions can lead to outcomes that increase labor costs for employers. Job performance may suffer, and absenteeism, sick leave, and turnover may increase. Both internal discrimination against present employees and external discrimination against job applicants can lead to costly lawsuits. Litigation is a time-consuming, expensive exercise that no organization wants.[101] Yet organizations have been hit with lawsuits affecting virtually every aspect of the employment relationship, and many well-publicized awards to victims have reached millions of dollars.

Let's not view the legal and social aspects of the HR management process exclusively in negative terms. Most of the present civil rights laws and regulations were enacted as a result of gross violations of individual rights. In most instances, the flip side of unlawful discrimination is good HR practice. For example, it is good practice to use properly developed and validated employment selection procedures and performance appraisal systems. It is good HR practice to treat people as individuals and not to rely on stereotyped group membership characteristics (e.g., stereotypes about women, ethnic groups, older workers, workers with disabilities). Finally, it just makes good sense to pay people equally, regardless of gender, if they are equally qualified and are doing the same work. These kinds of HR practices can enhance productivity, provide a richer quality of work life, and contribute directly to the overall profitability of any enterprise.

Of course if the EEOC request is burdensome, or if it involves trade secrets that you believe are irrelevant to the charge, you can try to convince the EEOC investigator to narrow the scope of the request. Occasionally, despite your best efforts, the EEOC may decide that it is necessary to perform an on-site investigation. If this happens, keep several things in mind.

One, negotiate a mutually agreeable date and time for the inspection. The EEOC is a government agency. It does not have an unfettered right to enter your property, and can do so only with your permission or with a warrant. Use this fact as leverage to negotiate a favorable time for the investigation.

Two, ask the investigator to describe the goals of the investigation, who is to be interviewed, and the job or work areas he or she wishes to observe. Then limit the scope of the investigation to what the investigator has indicated.

Three, before the on-site investigation begins, look over the list of employees the EEOC wishes to contact. If there is anyone on the list whom you have not interviewed, do so now. Emphasize that you are not trying to influence their testimony, that they should tell the truth, and that there will be no retaliation for anything they tell to the EEOC.

Four, designate a company representative who will attend all EEOC interviews of managerial employees. Note, however, that the company representative does not have the right to attend interviews between the EEOC and nonmanagerial employees.

The EEOC's Findings

If the charging party does not interrupt the investigation process by asking the EEOC to issue a right-to-sue notice that allows the charging party to file suit in court, then the EEOC will continue until it reaches a decision on the charge. If the decision is in favor of the employer, the agency will issue a "no-cause" finding, and the matter stops at the EEOC. However, the charging party retains the right to file a discrimination claim in court within 90 days.

If the decision is in favor of the employee, the agency will issue a "cause" finding, and the EEOC will invite the company to engage in a conciliation process. Essentially the EEOC will try to help the parties reach a mutually agreeable settlement. If both parties agree to all terms, the matter is settled, and no lawsuit may be filed except to enforce the settlement agreement, if necessary.

If the conciliation fails, the EEOC will issue the charging party a right-to-sue notice that permits the individual to file a suit in court, or the EEOC itself will file suit against the employer.

SUMMARY

Congress enacted the following laws to promote fair employment. They provide the basis for discrimination suits and subsequent judicial rulings:

- Thirteenth and Fourteenth Amendments to the U.S. Constitution.
- Civil Rights Acts of 1866 and 1871.
- Equal Pay Act of 1963.
- Title VII of the Civil Rights Act of 1964.
- Age Discrimination in Employment Act of 1967 (as amended in 1986).
- Immigration Reform and Control Act of 1986.
- Americans with Disabilities Act of 1990.
- Civil Rights Act of 1991.
- Family and Medical Leave Act of 1993.
- Executive Orders 11246, 11375, and 11478.
- Rehabilitation Act of 1973.
- Uniformed Services Employment and Reemployment Rights Act of 1994.

The Equal Employment Opportunity Commission and the Office of Federal Contract Compliance Programs are the two major federal regulatory agencies charged with enforcing these nondiscrimination laws. The EEOC is responsible both for private and public nonfederal employers, unions, and employment agencies. The OFCCP is responsible for ensuring compliance from government contractors and subcontractors.

A considerable body of case law has developed, affecting almost all aspects of the employment relationship. We discussed case law in the following areas:

- Sex discrimination, sexual harassment, reproductive hazards, and pregnancy.
- Age discrimination.
- National origin discrimination.
- Seniority.

Implications For Management Practice

A manager can easily feel swamped by the maze of laws, court rulings, and regulatory agency pronouncements that organizations must navigate through. While it is true that in the foreseeable future there will continue to be legal pressure to avoid unlawful discrimination, there will be great economic pressure to find and retain top talent.[102] Workforce diversity is a competitive necessity, and employers know it. Progressive managers recognize that now is the time to begin developing the kinds of corporate policies and interpersonal skills that will enable them to operate effectively in multicultural work environments.

- Testing and interviewing.
- Personal history (specifically, pre-employment inquiries).
- Preferential selection.

The bottom line in all these cases is that, as managers, we need to be very clear about job requirements and performance standards, we need to treat people as individuals, and we must evaluate each individual fairly relative to job requirements and performance standards.

DISCUSSION QUESTIONS

3–1. If you were asked to advise a private employer (with no government contracts) of its equal employment opportunity responsibilities, what would you say?

3–2. As a manager, what steps can you take to deal with the organizational impact of the Family and Medical Leave Act?

3–3. Prepare a brief outline of an organizational policy on sexual harassment. Be sure to include grievance, counseling, and enforcement procedures.

3–4. What steps would you take as a manager to ensure fair treatment for older employees?

3–5. Collect two policies on EEO, sexual harassment, or family and medical leave from two different employers in your area. How are they similar (or different)? Which aspects of the policies support the appropriate law?

KEY TERMS

discrimination

equal employment opportunity

unequal treatment

direct evidence

circumstantial evidence

mixed-motive cases

adverse impact

affirmative action

bona fide occupational qualifications

race-norming

essential functions

disability

qualified job applicant

systemic discrimination

case law

quid pro quo harassment

hostile environment harassment

seniority system

reverse discrimination

APPLYING YOUR KNOWLEDGE

A Case of Harassment?   *Case 3–1*

Erin Dempsey was working late trying to finish the analysis of the ticket report for her boss, Ron Hanson. The deadline was tomorrow, and she still had several hours of work to do before the analysis would be finished. Erin did not particularly enjoy working late, but she knew Ron would be expecting the report first thing in the morning. She had been working very hard recently, hoping that she would earn a promotion to senior travel agent at the large urban travel agency where she was employed. Getting the ticket report done on time would be absolutely essential for any promotion opportunities.

Matt Owens, a coworker at the travel agency, was also working late that evening. Suddenly, he appeared in Erin's office uninvited and sat down in the side chair. "Got a big date tonight, eh, Erin?" Matt said with a touch of sarcasm in his voice.

"I'm working very hard on the ticket report tonight, Matt, and I really could use a bit of privacy." Erin had sensed before that Matt was a pest and she hoped that by being rather direct with him he would leave her alone.

"A cute chick like you shouldn't waste a perfectly good Wednesday evening working late."

"Please Matt, I've got work to do."

"Oh come on Erin. I've noticed the way you act when you walk by my office or when we pass in the halls. It's clear that you're dying to go out with me. Some things a guy can just sense. This is your big chance. I'll tell you what. Let's go to dinner at that new intimate French restaurant up on the hill. Afterward we can stop by my place for some music, a fire in the fireplace, and a nightcap. I make a great Black Russian. What do you say?"

Erin was furious. "I say you're an egotistical, self-centered, obnoxious, dirty old man. If you don't get out of here right now, I'm going to call Ron Hanson at home and tell him that you're keeping me from finishing the ticket report."

"Oh my, you're even sexier when you're angry. I like that in a woman."

Erin could see that she was getting nowhere fast with this approach, so she decided to leave the room in hopes that Matt would get the hint and go home. As she stormed through the door, Matt mockingly held the door ajar and said, "After you, sweet thing." He patted Erin on the backside as she passed. Erin stopped in her tracks, turned to Matt, and said, "If you *ever* do that again, I'll . . . ." She was so mad that she couldn't think of an appropriate threat. So instead she just stormed off down the hall and left the building.

The next morning, Erin was waiting in the office of Daryl Kolendich, the owner of the travel agency, when he arrived at work. Erin knew that Ron Hanson would probably be angry that she had gone over his head to the agency owner, but she was so furious with Matt Owens that she wanted immediate action. She described the incident to Daryl and demanded that some sort of disciplinary action be taken with Matt.

"Now calm down, Erin. Let's think through this problem a bit first. Isn't it possible that you can handle this sort of problem yourself? Is it possible that you may in fact have been encouraging Matt to act this way? Look, I understand that you're upset. I would be too, if I were in your shoes. But look at it this way. We've been hiring male travel agents for only the last few years now. Prior to that time there were only female agents, so problems like these never arose. Matt is from an older generation than yours. It takes time for men like him to get used to working on an equal basis with women. Can't you just try to make sure over the next few weeks that you give him no encouragement at all? If you do, I'm sure this problem will take care of itself."

Erin was not at all convinced. "But I *did* make it very clear I was not interested in him. It seemed to make him even more persistent. You're the owner and the boss here, and I'll do what you ask, but it seems to me that it's your responsibility to make sure this kind of sexual harassment doesn't take place in this agency."

"Erin, has your supervisor Ron Hanson ever suggested that your job opportunities here would be improved if you went out with him? Have I ever in any way intimated that a date with me could lead to a promotion for you?"

Erin was silent. It was true that none of the management staff at the agency had been guilty of sexual harassment. In fact, both Ron and Daryl had been highly supportive of her work ever since she arrived. Her annual pay raises had been higher than those of most other coworkers, both male and female.

Daryl broke the silence. "I guess my point is that we don't have a sexual harassment situation here. Please try what I've suggested and let me know in a couple of weeks if you feel it hasn't worked."

Questions

1. What is sexual harassment in the workplace? Was Matt Owens guilty of sexual harassment?
2. If you were Erin Dempsey, what would you do?
3. What is an organization's responsibility in regard to sexual harassment among coworkers or supervisor–subordinate pairs? Do you think that Daryl Kolendich responded appropriately to the problem?
4. Outline a brief personnel policy that an organization could adopt to protect itself from sexual harassment lawsuits.

REFERENCES

1. Jones, J. E., Jr., Murphy, W. P., & Belton, R. (1987). *Discrimination in employment* (5th ed.). St. Paul, MN: West.
2. Friedman, A. (1972). Attacking discrimination through the Thirteenth Amendment. *Cleveland State Law Review, 21,* 165–178.
3. *Johnson v. Railway Express Agency, Inc.* (1975). 95 S. Ct. 1716.
4. Civil rights statutes extended to Arabs, Jews (1987, May 19). *Daily Labor Report,* pp. 1, 2, 6.
5. Bland, T. S. (1999, July). Equal pay enforcement heats up. *HRMagazine,* pp. 138–145.
6. Ibid.
7. Jones et al., op. cit. See also *Bakke v. Regents of the University of California* (1978). 17 FEPC 1000.
8. Privacy and sex discrimination (1992, Apr.). *Bulletin.* Denver: Mountain States Employers Council, Inc., p. 3.
9. *Furnco Construction Corp. v. Waters* (1978). 438 U.S. 567.
10. *McDonnell Douglas v. Green* (1973). 411 U.S. 972.
11. Civil Rights Act of 1991, Public Law No. 102–166, 105 Stat. 1071 (1991). Codified as amended at 42 U.S.C., Section 1981, 2000e *et seq.*
12. Valenza, G. (1999, Nov.–Dec.). The Supreme Court creates a safe harbor from liability for punitive damages. *Legal Report,* pp. 5–8. Washington, DC: Society for Human Resource Management.
13. Taylor, S., & Eder, R. W. (2000). U.S. expatriates and the Civil Rights Act of 1991: Dissolving boundaries. In M. Mendenhall & G. Oddou (eds.), *Readings and cases in international human resource management* (3rd ed., pp. 251–270). Cincinnati, OH: South-Western College Publishing.

14. Age discrimination (1996, May). *Bulletin*. Denver: Mountain States Employers Council, Inc., pp. 3, 4.

15. Pierson, G. C., & Fulkerson, S. R. (1999, March–April). The Older Workers Benefit Protection Act: Are waivers worth the paper they're written on? *Legal Report*, pp. 5–8. Washington, DC: Society for Human Resource Management.

16. EEOC proposes regulations on ADEA waivers (1999, July–Aug.). *Legal Report,* pp. 1–3. Washington, DC: Society for Human Resource Management.

17. Pitfalls of verifying a worker's employment authorization: Are your I-9 forms up to snuff? (1996, Apr.). *Bulletin*. Denver: Mountain States Employers Council, Inc., p. 2. See also Bradshaw, D. S. (1987). Immigration reform: This one's for you. *Personnel Administrator, 32*(4), 37–40.

18. Pitfalls, op. cit.

19. America's largest untapped market: Who they are, the potential they represent (1998, March 2). *Fortune*, pp. S1–S12.

20. Four years after the ADA. (1996, Nov.–Dec.). *Working Age*, p. 2.

21. EEOC definition of term "disability" (1995, May). *Bulletin*. Denver: Mountain States Employers Council, Inc., pp. 1, 3.

22. Drug and alcohol testing: 1996 overview for employers. *Bulletin*. Denver: Mountain States Employers Council, Inc., pp. 1, 3.

23. Americans with Disabilities Act of 1990, Public Law No. 101–336, 104 Stat. 328 (1990). Codified at 42 U.S.C., Section 12101 *et seq.*

24. *Sutton v. United Airlines*, 119 S. Ct. 2139 (1999); *Murphy v. United Parcel Service*, 119 S. Ct. 2133 (1999); *Albertsons v. Kirkingsburg*, 11 S. Ct. 2162 (1999).

25. Greenberger, R. S. (2002, Jan. 9). Supreme Court sets tighter standards for employees with disability claims. *The Wall Street Journal*, p. B4.

26. When workers just can't cope (2000, Oct. 30). *BusinessWeek*, pp. 100, 102.

27. Campbell, W. J., & Reilly, M. E. (2000). Accommodations for persons with disabilities. In J. F. Kehoe (ed.), *Managing selection in changing organizations* (pp. 319–367). San Francisco: Jossey-Bass.

28. Cascio, W. F. (1994). The 1991 Civil Rights Act and the Americans with Disabilities Act of 1990: Requirements for psychological practice in the workplace. In B. D. Sales & G. R. VandenBos (eds.), *Psychology in litigation and legislation.* Washington, DC: American Psychological Association, pp. 175–211.

29. Petesch, P. J. (2000, Nov.). Popping the disability-related question. *HRMagazine,* pp. 161–172.

30. Sharf, J. C., & Jones, D. P. (2000). Employment risk management. In J. F. Kehoe (ed.), *Managing selection in changing organizations* (pp. 271–318). San Francisco: Jossey-Bass.

31. Garland, S. B. (1999, April 26). Protecting the disabled won't cripple business. *BusinessWeek*, pp. 71, 73.

32. Paltell, E. (1999, Sept.). FMLA: After six years, a bit more clarity. *HRMagazine*, pp. 144–150.

33. Shea, R. E. (2000, Jan.). The dirty dozen. *HRMagazine*, pp. 52–56.

34. Most small businesses appear prepared to cope with new family-leave rules (1993, Feb. 8). *The Wall Street Journal*, pp. B1, B2.

35. Brotherton, P. (1996, Apr.). HR exec, FMLA officials disagree on law's impact. *HR News*, p. 10.

36. Billings, D. (2000, Sept.). DOL issues FMLA survey, releases enforcement stats. *HR News*, p. 20.

37. Jackson, D. J. (1978). Update on handicapped discrimination. *Personnel Journal, 57*, 488–491.

38. The Uniformed Services Employment and Reemployment Rights Act of 1994, Public Law 102-353; H.R. 995.

39. Ledvinka, J., & Scarpello, V. G. (1991). *Federal regulation of personnel and human resource management* (2d ed.). Boston: PWS-Kent.

40. Leonard, B. (2000, Jan.). EEOC hails its smallest backlog since 1984. *HR News*, pp. 1, 11.

41. For more information, see *www.eeoc.gov.*

42. *Albemarle Paper Company v. Moody* (1975). 442 U.S. 407.

43. Sharf & Jones, op. cit. See also Leonard, op. cit.

44. Lublin, J. S., & Pasztor, A. (1985, Dec. 11). Tentative affirmative action accord is reached by top Reagan officials. *The Wall Street Journal*, p. 4.

45. *Wygant v. Jackson Board of Education* (1986). 106 S. Ct. 1842; *Local 28 Sheet Metal Workers v. E.E.O.C.* (1986). 106 S. Ct. 3019; *Local 93 Firefighters v. Cleveland* (1986). 106 S. Ct. 3063.

46. Pear, R. (1985, Oct. 27). The cabinet searches for consensus on affirmative action. *The New York Times*, p. E5.

47. *Johnson v. Santa Clara Transportation Agency* (1987, Mar. 26). 107 S. Ct. 1442, 43 FEP Cases 411; *Daily Labor Report*, pp. A1, D1–D19.

48. *Guidelines on discrimination because of sex*, 29CFR1604.11. Appendix to Part 1604—questions and answers on the Pregnancy Discrimination Act (rev. July 1, 1999).

49. Cowan, A. L. (1989, Aug. 21). Women's gains on the job: Not without a heavy toll. *The New York Times*, pp. A1, A14.

50. Fernandez, J. P. (1993). *The diversity advantage.* New York: Lexington.

51. Trotter, R., Zacur, S. R., & Greenwood, W. (1982). The pregnancy disability amendment: What the law provides. Part II. *Personnel Administrator, 27,* 55–58.

52. *California Federal Savings & Loan Association v. Guerra* (1987). 42 FEP Cases 1073.

53. Balancing work and family (1996, Sept. 16). *BusinessWeek*, pp. 74–80.

54. Schwartz, F. N. (1992, Mar.–Apr.). Women as a business imperative. *Harvard Business Review*, pp. 105–113.

55. *Pregnancy and employment: The complete handbook on discrimination, maternity leave, and health and safety.* (1987). Washington, DC: Bureau of National Affairs.

56. Trotter et al., op. cit.

57. Kilborn, P. (1990, Sept. 2). Manufacturer's policy, women's job rights clash. *Denver Post*, p. 2A.

58. Wermiel, S. (1991, Mar. 21). Justices bar "fetal protection" policies. *The Wall Street Journal*, pp. B1, B8. See also Epstein, A. (1991, Mar. 21). Ruling called women's rights victory. *Denver Post*, pp. 1A, 16A.

59. Fetal protection policy voided (1991, May). *Bulletin.* Denver: Mountain States Employers Council, p. 2.

60. Woo, J. (1992, Nov. 3). Secret taping of supervisors is on the rise, lawyers say. *The Wall Street Journal*, pp. B1, B5.

61. Fisher, A. B. (1993, Aug. 23). Sexual harassment: What to do. *Fortune*, pp. 84–88.

62. Ibid. See also Yang, C. (1996, May 13). Getting justice is no easy task. *BusinessWeek*, p. 98.

63. York, K. M. (1989). Defining sexual harassment in workplaces: A policy-capturing approach. *Academy of Management Journal, 32,* 830–850.

64. EEOC (1999). *Guidelines on discrimination because of sex.* 29 C.F.R., Part 1604 (11)(a) (rev. July 1, 1999).

65. *Barnes v. Costle* (1977). 561 F. 2d 983 (D.C. Cir.).

66. 118 S. Ct. 2257 (1998).

67. 118 S. Ct. 2275 (1998).

68. *Meritor Savings Bank v. Vinson* (1986). 477 U.S. 57.

69. Ibid.

70. Morrell, A. J. (2000, Jan.–Feb.). Nonemployee harassment. *Legal Report*, pp. 1–4. Washington, DC: Society for Human Resource Management.

71. Barrett, P. M. (1993, Nov. 10). Justices make it easier to prove sex harassment. *The Wall Street Journal*, pp. A3, A4.

72. Segal, J. A. (1999, Nov.). Strategic planning for Troglodyte-free workplaces. *HRMagazine,* pp. 138–148. See also LaGow, R. (1998, Aug.). High court expands, clarifies employer liability for sex harassment. *HR News,* p. 6. See also Mars v. Venus: A new survey suggests that good training programs can cut sexual harassment (1998, May 4). *BusinessWeek,* p. 8.

73. Lessons learned: The hard way (1996, Apr.). *Bulletin.* Denver: Mountain States Employers Council, pp. 2, 3. See also Sexual Harassment: Preventive measures (1992, Jan.). *Bulletin.* Denver: Mountain States Employers Council, p. 2.

74. *Schwager v. Sun Oil Company of PA* (1979). 591 F. 2d 58 (10th Cir.).

75. Miller, C. S., Kaspin, J. A., & Schuster, M. H. (1990). The impact of performance appraisal methods on age discrimination in employment act cases. *Personnel Psychology, 43,* 555–578.

76. Roffer, M. H., & Sanservino, N. J., Jr. (2000, Sept.). Holding employees' native tongues. *HRMagazine,* pp. 177–184.

77. Ibid. See also Leonard, B. (1995, Sept.). English-only rules. *HR News,* pp. 1, 6. See also English only (1993, July). *Bulletin.* Denver: Mountain States Employers Council, Inc., p. 3.

78. Age discrimination—overqualified (1993, July). *Bulletin.* Denver: Mountain States Employers Council, Inc., p. 2.

79. *California Brewers Association v. Bryant* (1982). 444 U.S. 598, p. 605.

80. See, for example, *Franks v. Bowman Transportation Co.* (1976). 424 U.S. 747; *International Brotherhood of Teamsters v. United States* (1977). 432 U.S. 324; *American Tobacco Company v. Patterson* (1982). 535 F. 2d 257 (CA-4). See also Gordon, M. E., & Johnson, W. A. (1982). Seniority: A review of its legal and scientific standing. *Personnel Psychology, 35,* 255–280.

81. *Firefighters Local Union No. 1784 v. Stotts* (1984). 104 S. Ct. 2576.

82. *Wygant v. Jackson Board of Education* (1986). 106 S. Ct. 1842.

83. Greenhouse, L. (1984, June 13). Seniority is held to outweigh race as a layoff guide. *The New York Times,* pp. A1, B12.

84. Britt, L. P., III (1984). Affirmative action: Is there life after Stotts? *Personnel Administrator, 29*(9), 96–100.

85. *Griggs v. Duke Power Company* (1971). 402 U.S. 424.

86. Ibid., p. 428.

87. Committee on Psychological Tests and Assessment, American Psychological Association (1996, June). Statement on the disclosure of test data. *American Psychologist, 51,* 644–648.

88. Justices uphold utility's stand on job testing (1979, Mar. 6). *The Wall Street Journal,* p. 4.

89. *Watson v. Fort Worth Bank & Trust* (1988). 108 S. Ct. 299.

90. Bersoff, D. N. (1988). Should subjective employment devices be scrutinized? *American Psychologist, 43,* 1016–1018.

91. *EEOC v. Radiator Specialty Company* (1979). 610 F. 2d 178 (4th Cir.).

92. *Dothard v. Rawlinson* (1977). 433 U.S. 321.

93. *Gregory v. Litton Systems, Inc.* (1973). 472 F.2d 631 (9th Cir.).

94. *Webster v. Redmond* (1979). 599 F. 2d 793 (7th Cir.).

95. *Hyland v. Fukada* (1978). 580 F. 2d 977 (9th Cir.). See also Sharf & Jones (2000), op. cit.

96. *McDonald v. Santa Fe Transportation Co.* (1976). 427 U.S. 273.

97. *United Steelworkers of America v. Weber* (1979). 99 S. Ct. 2721.

98. Beyond Bakke: High Court approves affirmative action in hiring, promotion (1979, June 28). *The Wall Street Journal,* pp. 1, 30.

99. Replying in the affirmative (1987, Mar. 9). *Time,* p. 66.

100. Norton, E. H. (1987, May 13). Step by step, the Court helps affirmative action. *The New York Times,* p. A27.

101. Cascio, W. F. (2000). *Costing human resources: The financial impact of behavior in organizations* (4th ed.). See chap. 4, "The high cost of mismanaging human resources (pp. 83–106). Cincinnati, OH: South-Western College Publishing.

102. Humphrey, B., & Stokes, J. (2000, May). The 21st century supervisor. *HRMagazine*, pp. 185–192.

DIVERSITY AT WORK

4

MAKING THE BUSINESS CASE FOR DIVERSITY*

Diversity is more than just a passing blip on America's corporate conscience. It has become something that many companies compete on, and that they are proud of. Yet others remain to be convinced. They want the business justification for diversity to be sound and demonstrable. To do that, it's necessary to address five major issues. Here's how some companies responded.

1. **How does diversity help an organization expand into global markets?** "Our major growth opportunities will occur outside of our North American business. Our objectives for business growth for the next decade indicate that our international business will be as large as our domestic business. Diversity is a business imperative. There is no way to achieve our business strategy unless we develop and utilize diversity in the marketplace to achieve competitive advantage around the world. Just 5 years ago all of our operations were located at U.S. headquarters. Now 4 of our 7 businesses are located outside of the U.S. in different regions of the globe. For us, global diversity has to address the following: (a) race, gender, and ethnic differences as they are manifested in different parts of the world; (b) cultural diversity issues and opportunities as they relate to trade, consumers, and the global economy; and (c), integration at multiple levels of our operating, manufacturing, R&D, sales, IT, and human resource systems" (Procter & Gamble).

2. **How can diversity help build brand equity, increase consumer purchasing, and grow the business?** "Diversity will capitalize on business growth opportunities for our brands. Twenty-three percent of our total sales dollar growth in the year 2001 will come from people of color (e.g., African-Americans, Hispanic-Americans/Latinos, Asian-Pacific Islanders). This equates to $237 million in incremental sales growth from existing brands. This figure does not include new brand introductions" (Fortune 100 consumer products company, Midwest United States).

3. **How does diversity support the organization's human resource strategies?** "We are facing a tremendous threat to our ability to retain top talent. Our attrition rate for our technical managers exceeds 28 percent. The percentages are greater for our technical managers who are under the age of 30, those with 3–8 years tenure, and across all race and gender categories. The dollar impact of losing this talent exceeds $15 million annually. The loss in intellectual capital is incalculable. The notion that our attrition is consistent with industry trends is totally unacceptable. We cannot hire talent fast enough to replace this brain drain. Diversity is a strategic imperative to retaining top talent and reducing our attrition rate by 50% in the next two years. We must identify the compelling factors that ensure we retain that talent for which we have invested so heavily" (Fortune 50 IT company, United States headquartered).

Sources: C. Y. Chen & J. Hickman, America's 50 best companies for minorities, *Fortune*, July 10, 2000, pp. 190–200; Society for Human Resource Management, *Workplace diversity*, Author, Alexandria, VA, 1999; V. J. Weaver, & Dixon-Kheir C., Making the Business Case for Diversity: A Win-Win Proposition, *Mosaics*, Nov.–Dec., 1999, pp. 1, 4, 5, 7; Competitive practices for a diverse workforce, *Fortune*, July 6, 1998, pp. S1–S18.

4. **How does diversity build our corporate image among our consumers?**
   "Diversity in our products, advertising, and promotions and the use of women and minority-owned businesses will demonstrate our commitment to good corporate citizenship, thus demonstrating trust, fairness, and goodwill to our consumers and to the trade. The benefits will be manifested in positive consumer campaigns and publicity for the company. We will be identified as a good corporate citizen that should be supported through increased purchases of our products" (Fortune 100 consumer products company, United States based).

5. **How does diversity enhance operational efficiency?** "Our plant has been given a mandate by corporate to improve significantly our manufacturing process and decrease our operating costs or face being closed or sold. We have three years to become a fully integrated, cost-effective, high-performing manufacturing operation. Our diversity strategy has to help us leverage those differences that have traditionally created barriers. Specifically, we have to explore alternative partnerships with union and management. We have to resolve hostilities between our historically older employees and younger engineers and managers. We have to address the fear and resistance to innovation, and redesign our human resource systems" (Manufacturing plant, Midwest United States).

Of necessity, the building of the business case for diversity in any given company will vary, but companies that have done so tend to adopt a systematic process that includes seven key elements. In the concluding section of this case, we will examine more closely those seven key elements.

Challenges

1. What is the objective of building and managing a diverse workforce?
2. Is there additional information beyond these five issues that you feel is necessary to make the business case for diversity?
3. What steps can you take as a manager to become more effective in a work environment that is more diverse than ever?

The U.S. workforce is diverse—and is becoming more so every year.[1]

- More than half the U.S. workforce now consists of racial (i.e., nonwhite) and ethnic (i.e., people classified according to common traits and customs) minorities, immigrants, and women.
- Women's share of the labor force was 46 percent in 1998; it will be 48 percent by 2008.
- White non-Hispanics accounted for 74 percent of the labor force in 1998. Their share of the labor force in 2008 will decrease modestly to 71 percent.
- The Asian, American Indian, Alaska Native, and Pacific Islanders' share of the labor force will increase from 5 to 6 percent, the Hispanic share will increase from 10 to 13 percent, and the African-American share will hold steady at about 12 percent between 1998 and 2008.
- The labor force age 45–64 will grow faster than the labor force of any other age group as the baby-boom generation (born 1946–1964) continues to age.

At the same time, the labor force age 25–34 is projected to decline by 2.7 million, reflecting the decrease in births in the late 1960s and early 1970s.

These demographic facts do not indicate that a diverse workforce is something a company ought to have. Rather, they tell us that all companies already do have or soon will have diverse workforces.

Unfortunately, attitudes and beliefs about the groups contributing to the diversity change only slowly. To some, workers and managers alike, workforce diversity is simply a problem that won't go away. Nothing can be gained with this perspective. To others, diversity represents an opportunity, an advantage that can be used to compete and win in the global marketplace, as we shall now see.

WORKFORCE DIVERSITY: AN ESSENTIAL COMPONENT OF HR STRATEGY

Managing diversity means establishing a heterogeneous workforce (including white men) to perform to its potential in an equitable work environment where no member or group of members has an advantage or a disadvantage.[2] Managing diversity is not the same thing as managing affirmative action. **Affirmative action (AA)** refers to actions taken to overcome the effects of past or present practices, policies, or other barriers to equal employment opportunity.[3] It is a first step that gives managers the opportunity to correct imbalances, injustices, and past mistakes. Over the long term, however, the challenge is to create a work setting in which each person can perform to his or her full potential and therefore compete for promotions and other rewards on merit alone. Table 4–1 highlights some key differences between equal employment opportunity or affirmative action and diversity.

Table 4–1

MAJOR DIFFERENCES BETWEEN EQUAL EMPLOYMENT OPPORTUNITY OR AFFIRMATIVE ACTION AND DIVERSITY

EEO or AA	Diversity
Government initiated	Voluntary (company-driven)
Legally driven	Productivity driven
Quantitative	Qualitative
Problem focused	Opportunity focused
Assumes assimilation	Assumes integration
Internally focused	Internally and externally focused
Reactive	Proactive

Source: Frequently asked questions, the Diversity Training Group, Herndon, VA. Available at *http://www.diversitydtg.com.*

Figure 4–1

Increased diversity in the workforce meshes well with the evolving changes in organizations and markets.

There are five reasons diversity has become a dominant activity in managing an organization's human resources (see Figure 4–1):

1. The shift from a manufacturing to a service economy.
2. Globalization of markets.
3. New business strategies that require more teamwork.
4. Mergers and alliances that require different corporate cultures to work together.
5. The changing labor market.[4]

The Service Economy

Roughly 87 percent of U.S. employees work in service-based industries (see Table 4–2).[5] Manufacturing will maintain its share of total output, while productivity in this sector increases and the need for additional labor decreases. Virtually all the growth in new jobs will come from service-producing industries. Service-industry jobs, such as in banking, financial services, health services, tourism, and retailing, imply lots of interaction with customers. Service employees need to be able to "read" their customers—to understand them, to anticipate and monitor their needs and expectations, and to respond sensitively and appropriately to those needs and expectations. In the service game, "customer literacy" is an essential skill. Racial- and ethnic-minority customers, in particular, represent a large market segment. For example, a recent study commissioned by the cable television industry found that people of color have $650 billion in spending power and represent 20 percent of all cable subscribers,

Table 4–2

THE SHIFT FROM MANUFACTURING TO SERVICE JOBS, 1973–2008 (EST.)

Year	Manufacturing jobs (%)	Service jobs (%)
1973	26	74
1983	20	80
1993	16	84
1998	13	87
2008 (est.)	12	88

(*Source:* U.S. Bureau of Labor Statistics, Employment projections, 1998–2008.)

generating $6.7 billion in cable-subscriber revenue. The study concluded that racial bias, by any measure, is simply a bad business practice for the cable TV industry or any other enterprise.[6]

A growing number of companies now realize that their workforces should mirror their customers. Similarities in culture, dress, and language between service workers and customers creates more efficient interactions between them and better business for the firm. Maryland National Bank in Baltimore discovered this when it studied the customer retention records for its branches. The branches showing highest customer loyalty recruited locally to hire tellers, who could swap neighborhood gossip. The best of 20 branch managers was located in a distant suburb and was described as dressing "very blue collar. She doesn't look like a typical manager of people. But this woman is totally committed to her customers."[7]

When companies discover they can communicate better with their customers through employees who are similar to their customers, those companies then realize they have increased their internal diversity. And that means they have to manage and retain their new, diverse workforce. There is no going back; diversity breeds diversity. Managing it well is an essential part of HR strategy.

The Globalization of Markets

As organizations around the world compete for customers, they offer customers choices unavailable to them domestically. With more options to choose from, customers have more power to insist that their needs and preferences be satisfied. To satisfy them, firms have to get closer and closer to their customers. Some firms have established a strong local presence (e.g., advertisements for Japanese-made cars that showcase local dealerships and satisfied American owners); others have forged strategic international alliances (e.g., Apple Computer and Sony). Either way, diversity must be managed: by working through domestic diversity (local presence) or by merging national as well as corporate cultures (international alliances). Successful global leaders measure success in this area of cultural learning as they measure other business factors.

Diversity characterizes
many work teams.

For example, the CEO of Switzerland-based Novo Nordisk requires his managers to "buy" and "sell" three best practices to managers in other parts of the world each year on their corporate Intranet. Doing so underscores three valuable lessons. One, we must use technology to move information around the company. Two, we must learn from our colleagues around the globe and share information with them. Three, we must measure these "soft" skills as we measure "hard" business returns, and hold people accountable for them. In short, culture matters.[8]

New Business Strategies That Require More Teamwork

To survive, to serve, and to succeed, organizations need to accomplish goals that are defined more broadly than ever before (e.g., world-class quality, reliability, and customer service). That means carrying out strategies that no one part of the organization can execute. For example, if a firm's business strategy emphasizes speed in every function (in developing new products, producing them, distributing them, and responding to feedback from customers), the firm needs to rely on teams of workers. Teams mean diverse workforces, whether as a result of drawing from the most talented or experienced staff or through deliberately structuring diversity to stimulate creativity.

Firms have found that only through work teams can they execute newly adopted strategies stressing better quality, innovation, cost control, or speed. Indeed, virtual teams, domestic or global, promise new kinds of management challenges. In a virtual team, members are dispersed geographically or organizationally. Their primary interaction is through some combination of electronic communication systems. They may never "meet" in the traditional sense. Further, team membership is often fluid, evolving according to changing task requirements. This has created a rich training agenda, as members from diverse backgrounds must learn to work productively together.[9]

A majority of U.S. companies now use some form of team structure in their organizations, for they have found that work teams promote greater flexibility, reduced operating costs, faster response to technological change, fewer job classifications, better response to new worker values (e.g., empowerment of lower-level workers, increased autonomy and responsibility), and the ability to attract and retain top talent.[10] Teams also facilitate innovation by bringing together experts with different knowledge bases and perspectives,[11] such as in concurrent engineering—a design process that relies on teams of experts from design, manufacturing, and marketing.

Diversity is an inevitable by-product of teamwork, especially when teams are drawn from a diverse base of employees. Young and old, male and female, American-born and non-American-born, better and less well educated—these are just some of the dimensions along which team members may differ. Coordinating team talents to develop new products, better customer service, or ways of working more efficiently is a difficult, yet essential, aspect of business strategy. As the national director of HR for Deloitte & Touche LLP, a management consulting firm, says, "Diversity is good business. If you don't use the best of all talent, you don't make money."[12]

Mergers and Strategic International Alliances

The managers who have worked out the results of all the mergers, acquisitions, and strategic international alliances occurring over the past 20 years know how important it is to knit together the new partners' financial, technological, production, and marketing resources.[13] However, the resources of the new enterprise also include people, and this means creating a partnership that spans different corporate cultures.

A key source of problems in mergers, acquisitions, and strategic international alliances is differences in corporate cultures.[14] According to a Hewitt Associates survey of 218 major U.S. corporations, integrating culture was the top challenge for 69 percent of them.[15] Corporate cultures may differ in many ways, such as the customs of conducting business, how people are expected to behave, and the kinds of behaviors that get rewarded. One observer has called culture "the DNA of an organization—invisible to the naked eye, but critical in shaping the character of the workplace."[16]

When two foreign businesses attempt a long-distance marriage, the obstacles are national cultures as well as corporate cultures. Fifty percent of U.S. managers either resign or are fired within 18 months of a foreign takeover.[17] Many of the managers report a kind of "culture shock." As one manager put it, "You don't quite know their values, where they're coming from, or what they really have in mind for you."[18] Both workers and managers need to understand and capitalize on diversity as companies combine their efforts to offer products and services to customers in far-flung markets.

The Changing Labor Market

You can be sure of this: Over the next 25 years the U.S. workforce will comprise more women, more immigrants, more people of color, and more older

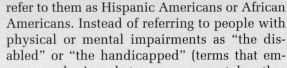

A WORD ABOUT TERMINOLOGY

In recent years, few topics have sparked as much debate as "politically correct" language. Choosing the right words may take a bit more thought and effort, but it is imperative to do so in business communication. After all, it makes no sense to alienate employees and customers by using words that show a lack of respect or sensitivity. Consider just two examples. Instead of referring to dark-skinned people as blacks (whose ethnic origins may be Hispanic or African), it is more appropriate to refer to them as Hispanic Americans or African Americans. Instead of referring to people with physical or mental impairments as "the disabled" or "the handicapped" (terms that emphasize what a person cannot do rather than what he or she can do), it is more appropriate to refer to them as "people with disabilities." Showing respect and sensitivity to differences by means of the language we use in business is the first step toward building upon the capabilities of a diverse work force.

workers.[19] Our workplaces will be characterized by more diversity in every respect. The first step to attaining the advantages of diversity is to teach all employees to understand and value different races, ethnic groups, cultures, languages, religions, sexual orientations, levels of physical ability, and family structures. Skeptical managers, supervisors, and policymakers need to understand that different does not mean deficient.[20] For example, in attempting to resolve a conflict between two employees, workers or managers from different cultures might: (1) dictate a solution; (2) serve as referees, issuing rulings only after hearing from both sides; or (3) stay out of the conflict altogether. Each of these strategies can work under certain circumstances. Different styles do not mean that one is necessarily better than another. Only when employees understand these things will the corporation they work for be able to build the trust that is essential among the members of high-performance work teams. Such teams incorporate practices that provide their members with the information, skills, incentives, and responsibility to make decisions that are essential to innovate, to improve quality, and to respond rapidly to change.[21]

Diversity at Work—A Problem for Many Organizations

Recent studies of the U.S. workforce indicate widespread perceptions of racial and sexual discrimination in the workplace—perceptions that take a heavy toll on job performance. Thus in a recent study, nearly 60 percent of minority executives reported that they have observed a double standard in the delegation of job assignments. Forty-five percent said they personally had been targets of racial or cultural jokes, and 44 percent reported holding back anger for fear of being seen as have a chip on their shoulders.[22] Reports of discrimination correlate with a tendency to feel "burned out," a reduced willingness to take initiative on the job, and a greater likelihood of planning to change jobs. Not surprisingly, therefore, minorities and women quit companies up to 2.5 times as often as white males, costing employers millions of dollars in lost training and productivity.[23] This is hardly the way to build a productive workforce.

So what do minority employees really want? It's simple: inclusion, encouragement, and opportunity.[24] If employers want to promote healthy, cooperative interaction, they must assume the leadership to do so. As we shall see, many have. First, however, it is necessary to understand the concept of culture and its impact on thought and action. Culture is the foundation of group differences. In the following sections we will examine the concept of culture and then focus briefly on some key issues that characterize three racial or ethnic groups (African Americans, Hispanic Americans, and Asian Americans), women, and the six generations that make up the U.S. workforce. As in other chapters, we will present examples of companies that have provided progressive leadership in this area.

Culture—The Foundation of Group Differences

Culture refers to the characteristic behavior of people in a country or region. Culture helps people make sense of their part of the world. It provides them with an identity—one they retain even when they emigrate and that is retained by their children and grandchildren as well.[25]

When we talk about culture, we include, for example, family patterns, customs, social classes, religions, political systems, clothing, music, food, literature, and laws.[26] Understanding the things that make up a person's culture helps diverse peoples to deal more constructively with one another. Conversely, misunderstandings among people of goodwill often cause unnecessary interpersonal problems and have undone countless business deals. We will examine the concept of culture more fully in our final chapter.

"Accepting diversity" means more than feeling comfortable with employees whose race, ethnicity, or gender differ from your own.[27] It means more than accepting their accents or language, their dress or food. What it does mean is learning to value and respect styles and ways of behaving that differ from yours. To manage diversity, there is no room for inflexibility and intolerance—displace them with adaptability and acceptance.

African Americans in the Workforce

African Americans will make up about 12.4 percent of the U.S. civilian workforce in the year 2008.[28] Consider these facts:

- In a 2001 report, according to the U.S. Bureau of the Census, African Americans owned 823,500 businesses in the United States (4 percent of all non-farm businesses), employed more than 718,000 people, and generated $71.2 billion in revenue.[29]
- Spending power of African-American consumers is up 86 percent in the past 10 years, to an estimated $572.1 billion in 2001[30] (see Figure 4–2).
- Fannie Mae, Applied Materials, Merrill Lynch, and American Express all have African-American chief executive officers or heirs apparent.[31]
- The top five companies for African Americans to work for are the New York Times, Avis Rent-A-Car, Advantica (parent company of Denny's), the U.S. Postal Service, and Fannie Mae.[32]

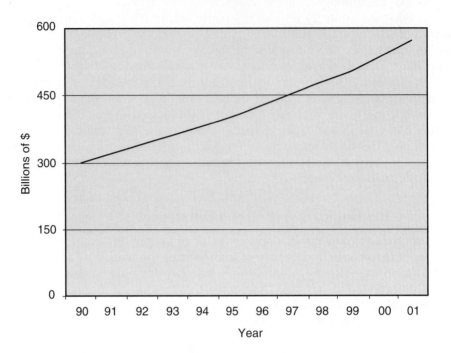

Figure 4–2

African-American buying power in billions of dollars.

African-American Buying Power

Despite these encouraging trends, sometimes progress only comes through the legal system. For example, in November 2000, Coca-Cola Company agreed to a record $192.5 million settlement to a race-discrimination lawsuit that alleged wide disparities in pay, promotions, and performance evaluations. The cost to Coke included $113 million in cash, $43.5 million to adjust salaries of African-American employees over the next 10 years, and $36 million to implement various diversity initiatives and oversight by a seven-member panel of the company's employment practices.[33] Such settlements do lead to improvement. Consider Texaco, Inc., as an example. In November 1996 it agreed to a $175 million settlement of a racial discrimination case filed by African-American employees. By the end of 1999 minorities accounted for 44 percent of new hires, 22 percent of promotions, and *all* employees are now required to attend diversity training. However, the clearest sign that Texaco is moving toward fundamental change may be that nobody at the company seems to think the battle is won. Says Deval Patrick, the company's African-American general counsel: "This is not paradise. With diversity, there is no endgame."[34]

In *Fortune* magazine's list of the top 50 companies for minorities to work for, members of ethnic minorities hold an average of 16 percent of board seats, make up 22 percent of the officials and managers, and pull down 13 percent of the 50 largest paychecks. Those are all key signs that a company has gone beyond political correctness. After all, no company would fill its top slots with unqualified people just to look multicultural! At a broader level, fully 65 percent of the Fortune 1000 largest companies in America have at least one member of an ethnic minority on their board of directors, up from 55 percent in 1998. Among *Fortune*'s list of 100 Best Companies to Work For, the typical company comprises 48 percent female and 25 percent minority employees.[35] As an executive from Cisco Systems noted, "When talented minorities thrive in an organization, it sends a powerful message to up-and-comers in the company."[36]

Among companies that are committed to making diversity a competitive advantage, here are some other practices to consider[37]:

- Hire only those search firms with a solid track record for providing diverse slates of candidates for positions at all levels
- Forge links with colleges and universities with significant numbers of minority students, and bring real jobs to the recruiting table.
- Start formal mentoring and succession programs to ensure that minorities are in the leadership pipeline.
- Include progress on diversity issues in management performance reviews and compensation.
- Set specific goals in critical areas, such as the percentages of minorities and women hired, promoted, and in the overall workforce. Also set goals for the amount of business conducted with outside vendors owned by minorities and women.
- Provide all employees with confidential outlets for airing and settling grievances, for example, telephone and e-mail hot lines.

COMMITMENT TO DIVERSITY AT XEROX[38]

COMPANY EXAMPLE

The philosophy at Xerox is simple: "If you don't value diversity, you can't manage it." This attitude can be traced to Joseph C. Wilson, who founded Xerox and who regularly stressed its social responsibilities and community involvement. David Kearns, the firm's former CEO, expressed its stance: "At Xerox, affirmative action is not a platitude, nor is it a special program. It is a clear-cut, plainly stated corporate business objective." One of the ways in which the company supports diversity is in its recognition and encouragement of a network of local and regional caucus groups (for African Americans, women, and Hispanic Americans). The groups meet on their own time and set their own rules and agendas, serving their members in these ways: (1) as a communication link between the members and upper management; (2) as a vehicle for personal and professional development (e.g., through workshops on topics such as presentation skills or how to run a meeting); (3) as a forum for networking and support within the caucus group (e.g., women relating to women on issues of common concern), (4) by giving members a chance to serve as role models to majority employees for managing diversity, and (5) by representing the corporation in community activities, such as outreach recruitment or presentations to schools or civic associations.

Another diversity strategy at Xerox focuses on how to get minority employees and women into jobs that are pivotal to further advancement. The idea here is to examine the backgrounds of all top executives and identify the key positions they held at lower levels—that is, positions that get people noticed—and to set goals for getting minorities and women into these jobs.

A third goal at Xerox is to transform its total employment from male-dominated to a fully diverse workforce. This means that Xerox is actively striving to achieve and then maintain equitable representation of all employee groups—majority males and females as well as minority males and females—at all grade bands, in all functions, in all functions, and in all organizations. To accomplish this, Xerox has incorporated these objectives into its corporate HR planning, and especially into all decisions regarding hiring, developing, and moving employees at all levels.

Has this approach worked? Yes; Xerox won the 1995 Commerce Department glass ceiling award for removing barriers to minorities and women. In 2000 it ranked number 11 on *Fortune*'s list of America's 50 best companies for minorities. Fully 20 percent of its 50 highest paid executives were minorities, as were 23.4 percent of its managers and officials.[39]

Hispanics in the Workforce

Hispanics, who will compose almost 13 percent of the civilian labor force in the year 2008,[40] experience many of the same disadvantages as African Americans. However, the term Hispanic encompasses a large, diverse group of people who come from distinctively different ethnic and racial backgrounds and who have achieved various economic and educational levels. For example, a third-generation, educated, white Cuban American has little in common with an uneducated Central American immigrant of mainly Native American ancestry who has fled civil upheaval and political persecution. Despite the fact that their differences far outweigh their similarities, both are classified as Hispanic. Why? Largely because of the language they speak (Spanish) or because of their surnames or because of their geographical origins.

Mexicans, Puerto Ricans, and Cubans constitute the three largest groups classified as Hispanic.[41] They are concentrated in four geographic areas: Mexican Americans reside mostly in California and Texas, Puerto Ricans mostly in New York, and a majority of Cuban Americans in Florida. These four states account for 73 percent of the firms owned by Hispanics. Hispanics own a total of 1.2 million businesses in the United States (6 percent of all nonfarm businesses), employing more than 1.3 million people, and generating $186.3 billion in revenue. Labor force participation rates for Hispanics (as a group) are growing rapidly, as Figure 4–3 shows.

Hispanics are also getting wealthier, as mean household income grew 13.4 percent in real terms from 1990 to 2000, to nearly $40,500. Spending power among Hispanics is difficult to measure accurately, partly because of language and education differences, but is estimated at between $273 and $445 billion per year.[42]

To encourage greater representation of Hispanics throughout the corporate structure, companies like Pacific Bell have initiated aggressive recruitment and retention programs.

COMPANY EXAMPLE   MANAGEMENT DIVERSITY AT PACIFIC BELL[43]

Pacific Bell, a telecommunications company operating in California, realized for two basic reasons that it had to change the way it traditionally recruited employees and managers. For one, the population of Hispanics, African Americans, and Asian Americans was increasing rapidly in California, but only a small percentage of these minorities attended college. If Pacific Bell continued

Figure 4–3

Growth of the civilian Hispanic labor force (in millions), 1980–2008 (est.).
(*Source:* Employment projection, 1998–2008, *Statistical abstract of the United States,* U.S. Bureau of Labor Statistics, Washington, DC, 1995.)

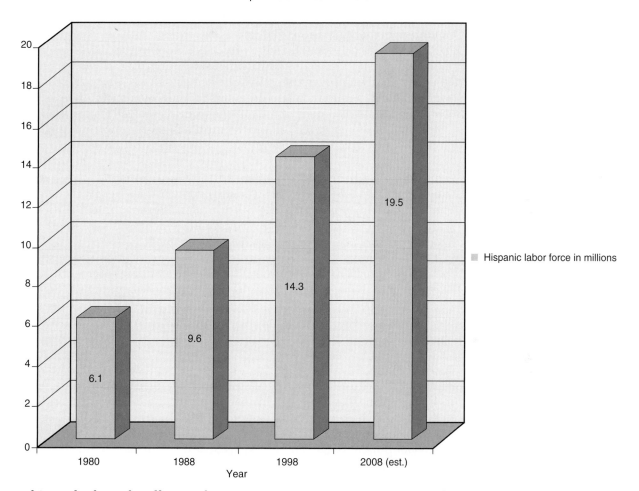

Hispanic labor force in millions

to hire only through college and university campuses, its minority employees as a percentage of its total employees would most likely shrink. This would be especially true for Hispanics, because their population was growing at the fastest rate. Hence, while the percentage of Hispanics in California was growing, the percentage of Hispanics on the payroll of Pacific Bell was decreasing.

The other reason Pacific Bell decided to change its recruitment was based on forecasts by the company's planners that its largest growth in management jobs would be in the high-technology areas of engineering, marketing, and data systems. The work in these management jobs requires advanced technical skills and formal education, and they had traditionally been filled via promotion from lower levels. But the company recognized that promotions could not produce the number of skilled managers needed in the near future. So Pacific Bell developed a new recruitment strategy comprising four components:

1. Internal networking by a group called the Management Recruitment District designed to generate employee referrals, to establish networks of employees who had contacts in the minority communities, to identify employees who could serve as guest speakers for external presentations, and to make presentations at regularly scheduled departmental staff meetings.

2. Advertising directed toward specific ethnic groups. The advertisements showed a diverse group of people employed in marketing, engineering, and management positions. These ads were placed in local and national publications serving the targeted minority communities on a regular basis to demonstrate the company's interest in minority hiring and the fact that it valued employee diversity. The same ads were placed in campus publications to announce appointments for employment interviews.

3. Establishment of contact with small institutions in the California State University system, which tended to enroll a higher proportion of minority students, as well as with Arizona State University and the University of New Mexico, both of which have large Hispanic enrollments. The company established relationships with minority student organizations and faculty (particularly those identified with business or technical fields) to identify issues and to offer support. For example, Pacific Bell developed a video, "Engineering Your Management Future," to tell engineering majors about career paths in management.

4. At the local or national level of professional minority organizations, such as the National Hispanic Council for High Technology Careers, Pacific Bell sought advisors to help develop management candidates. The company even hosted a 3-day conference to address the alarming underrepresentation of Hispanics in the teaching and practice of sciences and engineering.

Pacific Bell also established an internship program (the Summer Management Program) for third-year college students, making them student ambassadors representing Pacific Bell's career opportunities. For managers from minority groups who were already employed, Pacific Bell offered 6-day, off-site training programs conducted by external consultants and designed to help further develop their skills. The programs also provided a safe place for participants to talk about sensitive issues such as covert racism and prejudice, topics not likely to be discussed in the work setting.

Results

Over the program's first 10 years, 1980–1990, minority managers increased from 17.5 percent to 28.2 percent. By 1996, 70 percent of the company's workforce was minority or female.[44] Pacific Bell has a long-term commitment to improving education in California, to recruitment among minorities, and to equal employment opportunity. Thus its Knowledge Network Explorer *www.kn.pacbell.com*) helps schools, libraries, and colleges use Internet and video-conferencing technology. By 2001, the company had installed for free almost 10,000 high-speed Internet access lines in various educational and community facilities throughout California.[45]

Asian Americans in the Workforce

The share of the workforce composed of Asian Americans has increased from 3 percent in 1988 to 4.6 percent in 1998 to an estimated 5.7 percent in 2008.[46] James Cheng, a director in the mergers and acquisitions department of phone company GTE, described a paradox in the positive characterization of Asians as hard working and deferential. The paradox is that such views can be as damaging as negative ones because Asian employees can find themselves relegated to roles as corporate workhorses—not leaders. "You do see at the entry level a lot of Asians in GTE on the technical side," Cheng says. "Why aren't we being pushed toward higher-level positions?"[47] In some companies, they are. In *Fortune*'s 2000 list, the top five companies for Asians to work for are Applied Materials, Union Bank of California, Dole Food, Levi Strauss, and Sun Microsystems. For example, at Applied Materials, a Santa Clara, California, maker of semiconductor equipment, Asians compose 23.5 percent of the workforce. Minorities as a group compose 38.7 percent of the workforce, and 26.1 percent of officials and managers. At Union Bank of California, Asians compose almost 26 percent of the workforce. Minorities as a group compose 54 percent of the workforce, 35.7 percent of officials and managers, and 61 percent of new hires.

At UPS, for example, diversity has paid off handsomely. Jennifer Kannar, a Hong Kong–raised product manager, proposed a bilingual support center to win the business of Korean-American entrepreneurs in Southern California. The company took several months to evaluate the proposal—to Kannar's frustration—but ultimately it approved the center. Kannar is now expanding to include Vietnamese, Chinese, and Japanese businesses. Had UPS not consciously striven for a diverse workforce, it may well have missed the opportunity Kannar saw.[48]

Women in the Workforce

Over the past 30 years, women have raised their expectations and levels of aspiration sharply higher, largely because of the women's movement, coupled with landmark civil rights legislation and well-publicized judgments against large companies for gender discrimination in hiring, promotion, and pay. In 1972, women questioned the possibility of having a family and holding a job at the same time. By the mid-1980s, they took it for granted that they could manage both, and by the mid-1990s, 89 percent of young women said they expect to have both a family and a job.[49] Among *Fortune*'s 2001 list of the 100 Best Companies to Work For, 63 of the companies report that at least 30 percent of supervisory managers are women.[50] Five forces account for the changes:

1. **Changes in the family**. Legalized abortion, contraception, divorce, and a declining birthrate have all contributed to a decrease in the number of years of their lives most women devote to rearing children. Of all women, 85 percent have babies,[51] but 55 percent of mothers with children under 3 years of age now work, as do 75 percent of those whose youngest child is under 18.[52] Fully 70 percent of mothers return to the same jobs after childbirth.[53] Women are also significant providers of

family income, with more than 55 percent of employed women bringing in half or more of it.[54]

The proportion of single-parent family groups with children under age 18 has increased dramatically, and today, single mothers are more likely than married mothers to be employed.[55] This is not surprising, since women head most single-parent families, and most working women have little choice except to work.

2. **Changes in education**. Since World War II, increasing numbers of women have been attending college. Women now earn almost 57 percent of all undergraduate degrees, 58 percent of all masters degrees, and 41 percent of all doctorates. Women also earn about 50 percent of all undergraduate business degrees, and 55 percent of all MBAs.[56]

3. **Changes in self-perception**. Many women juggle work and family roles. This often causes personal conflict, and the higher they rise in an organization, the more that work demands of them in terms of time and commitment.[57] Many women executives pay a high personal price for their organizational status in the form of broken marriages or never marrying at all.[58] For example, a year 2000 study of successful women with MBAs who have risen to within the top three levels of the CEO position in their companies found that only 67 percent were married, compared to 84 percent of men with the same level of success. The gap is even greater when it comes to children. Nearly three-quarters of the men have children, while only 49 percent of the women do.[59] Thus *a major goal of EEO for women is to raise the awareness of these issues among both women and men so that women can be given a fair chance to think about their interests and potential, to investigate other possibilities, to make an intelligent choice, and then to be considered for openings or promotions on an equal basis with men.*[60]

4. **Changes in technology**. Advances in technology, both in the home (e.g., frozen foods, microwave ovens) and in the workplace (e.g., robotics), have reduced the physical effort and time required to accomplish tasks. Through technology more women can now qualify for formerly all-male jobs, and, for some women and for some types of jobs, technology makes virtual work arrangements possible, thus helping the women to balance their work and personal lives.[61]

5. **Changes in the economy**. Although there has been an increasing shift away from goods production and toward service-related industries, there are increasing numbers of female employees in all types of industries. Here are some statistics characterizing these changes[62]:

   - Today, women make up 38 percent of U.S. business owners, double the number 12 years ago.[63]
   - Women-owned businesses include the same types of industries as are in the Fortune 500.
   - The number of jobs in businesses owned by women now surpasses the number of jobs in the businesses represented on the Fortune 500 list.
   - Women held 43 percent of executive, managerial, and administrative jobs in 2000.
   - Between 1995 and 2000, the number of women ages 25–34 in managerial and professional jobs has increased 14.6 percent, to 5 million.

- Only 7 percent of working women now drop out of the workforce in any given year, down from 12 percent in the mid-1970s.
- Among families having annual incomes that reach $45,000 to $55,000, 70 percent have working wives.

The statistics presented thus far imply that women have made considerable economic gains over the past three decades. However, there are also some disturbing facts that moderate any broad conclusions about women's social and economic progress:

- Today, U.S. women make 76 cents for every dollar earned by men. At the current rate of increase, women will not reach wage parity with men until 2017. Although the gap is decreasing, at every educational level women make less than men at the same level, and female-dominated fields do not pay as well as male-dominated fields.[64]
- As a group, women who interrupt their careers for family reasons never again make as much money as women who stay on the job. A study of over 2,400 women aged 30 to 64 (each with one or more gaps in work of at least 6 months) found that those who took a break of 1 year or so lost the same ground in salary as women who dropped out for longer periods. Compared with women who stayed on the job, women who took breaks earned 33 percent less, on average, during the year they returned to work. And the stigma persists: despite working continuously for 11 to 20 years after the dropout interval, these women still earned 10 percent less.[65] (However, women who stay on the job, and do not have children, suffer almost no gender gap in pay, relative to men of the same age.[66])
- Women in paid jobs still bear most of the responsibility for family care and housework.

Conclusions Regarding Women in the Workforce

The clearest picture we need to see from the data reflecting all these changes is this: If all the United States' working women were to quit their jobs tomorrow and stay at home to cook and clean, businesses would disintegrate. There is no going back to the way things were before women entered the workforce. What many people tend to think of as "women's issues" really are business issues, competitiveness issues. Examples: Companies that routinely don't offer child care and flexibility in work scheduling will suffer along with their deprived workers.[67] Women are not less committed employees; working mothers especially are not less committed to their work. Three-quarters of professional women who quit large companies did so because of lack of career progress; only 7 percent left to stay at home with their children.[68] Businesses should react to the kinds of issues reflected in these examples based not on what is the right or wrong thing to do, but on what makes economic sense to do—which usually also is the right thing to do.

It is important that executives see that creative responses to work–family dilemmas are in the best interests of both employers and employees. Adjustments to work schedules (flextime), extended maternity and paternity leaves, and quality day care based near the job come a little closer to workable solutions. Chapter 10 will deal with this issue in greater detail, but for now let's consider some practical steps that IBM is taking.

COMPANY EXAMPLE

IBM—CHAMPION OF GLOBAL DIVERSITY AND FAMILY-FRIENDLY POLICIES[69]

IBM has made the Ten-Best list for working mothers for 12 consecutive years. It continues to set lofty standards by researching new programs and policies, expanding and improving old ones, and extending such efforts worldwide. In keeping with its mission of becoming "the premier global employer for working mothers," IBM recently conducted its first work–life issues survey of employees outside the United States. As a result, IBM is assessing depending care in 11 countries, initiating diversity training in Asia, and launching the Global Partnership for Workforce Flexibility to kick off pilot projects on alternative work arrangements and to examine cultural barriers.

IBM's efforts to advance women through networking groups and leadership training initiatives continue to make steady progress. To develop female technical talent, IBM hosted its first-ever internal conference for Women in Technology; 500 women from 29 countries attended.

In the United States, no company can top IBM's leave for childbirth, which gives mothers and fathers *three years* of job-guaranteed time off with benefits. (However, if business needs require it, parents may be asked to come back part time after one year.) With a dependent care fund of $8.3 million, IBM also ranks high on child care, supporting 47 near-site centers—where employees' children have priority access—and 2,610 family child care homes. Last year it even launched pilot programs in New York and North Carolina that screen nannies for employees who prefer in-home care.

Age-Based Diversity

At present, the U.S. workforce is populated by five different generations of workers, with different, often conflicting values and attitudes.[70] Below is a brief sketch of each.

- The **swing generation** (born roughly between 1910 and 1929) struggled through the Great Depression; fought the good war (World War II); and, following that war, rebuilt the American economy, which would dominate the world for more than 30 years. Most, but not all, members of the swing generation have retired.
- The **silent generation** (born between 1930 and 1945) is demographically smaller. Born in the middle of the Great Depression, too young to have fought in World War II, they were influenced by the swing generation. Because its members were in relatively short supply, they were more heavily in demand. Many went to the best colleges, were courted by corporations, rose rapidly, and were paid more than any other group in history. In return they embraced their elders' values and became good "organization men" (i.e., they gave their hearts and souls to their employers and made whatever sacrifices were necessary to get ahead; in return, employers gave them increasing job responsibility, pay, and benefits). Many members of the silent generation currently hold positions of power (e.g., corporate leaders, members of Congress).

- The **baby-boom generation** (born between 1946 and 1964) currently accounts for 78 million people and 55 percent of the workforce. The boomers believe in rights to privacy, due process, and freedom of speech in the workplace; they also believe that employees should not be fired without just cause and that the best should be rewarded without regard to age, gender, race, position, or seniority. Downsizing (the planned elimination of positions or jobs) has shocked and frustrated many boomers over shrinking advancement opportunities for themselves and created a sense of betrayal as many of their parents were fired or rushed into early retirement. Boomers represent a huge base of knowledge and talent in organizations. They bring years of management and leadership expertise that cannot be replaced easily. Fortunately, few leave voluntarily. Only 3 percent of employees 50 or over change jobs in any given year, compared with 10 percent of the entire labor force and 12 percent of workers ages 25–34.[71]
- **Generation X,** also known as "baby busters" (born between 1965 and 1977), represent approximately 50 million Americans, or about one-third of the workforce. They have grown up in times of rapid change, both social and economic. Hurt more by parental divorce, and having witnessed corporate downsizing firsthand, they tend to be independent, cynical, and do not expect the security of long-term employment. On the other hand, they also tend to be practical, focused, and future oriented. They demand interesting work assignments, and thrive on open-ended projects that require sophisticated problem solving. This is a computer-literate generation. Five characteristics define the kinds of work environments that Gen Xers find most rewarding: (1) control over their own schedules, (2) opportunity to improve their marketable skills, (3) exposure to decision makers, (4) the chance to put their names on tangible results, and (5) clear areas of responsibility.[72]
- **Generation Y** (born between 1977 and 1997) includes offspring of the baby boomers as well as an influx of immigrants throughout the 1990s (one-quarter of whom were under the age of 19). With more than 80 million members, it will have a huge impact on future products, marketing, and management practices. Generation Y has grown up amid more sophisticated technologies, and has been exposed to them earlier than members of Generation X ever were. This is a group that grew up with e-mail, not U.S. mail. Multitasking is easy for them. As an example, consider the typical teenager doing homework on his or her computer: simultaneously using a word processor, surfing the Internet, chatting with friends via instant messaging programs, downloading music, listening to a CD, and talking on the telephone, all while the television is turned on in the background! This implies both good news and bad news for employers. The good news is that Generation Y will be good at engaging in multiple tasks, filtering out distractions, and juggling numerous projects. The bad news? Short attention spans, the constant need for stimulation or entertainment, and a blurring of the lines between work and leisure time while on the job.

MANAGING DIVERSITY

As we have seen, racial and ethnic minorities, women, and immigrants will account for increasingly large segments of the U.S. labor force over time. And there are other large and growing groups—older workers, workers with disabilities, gay and lesbian workers, members of Generation X and Generation Y—that will soon affect the overall makeup of the workforce. Businesses that want to grow will have to rely on this diversity. Let us consider some practical steps that managers can take to prepare for these forthcoming changes.

Racial and Ethnic Minorities

To derive maximum value from a diverse workforce, not merely to tolerate it, corporations now realize that it's not enough just to start a mentoring program or put a woman on the board of directors. Rather, they have to undertake a host of programs—and not just inside the company. Texaco and Dow Chemical are building ties with minorities as early as high school. Polaroid and Ameritech are investing in employee organizations that monitor corporate policies and work with community groups. More specifically, to attract and retain racial and ethnic minorities, consider taking the following steps[73]:

- **Focus** on bringing in the best talent, not on meeting numerical goals.
- **Establish** mentoring programs among employees of same and different races.
- **Hold** managers accountable for meeting diversity goals.
- **Develop** career plans for employees as part of performance reviews.
- **Promote** minorities to decision-making positions, not just to staff jobs.
- **Diversify** the company's board of directors.

Diversity should be linked to every business strategy—for instance, recruiting, selection, placement (after identifying high-visibility jobs that lead to other opportunities within the firm), succession planning, performance appraisal, and reward systems. Companies like Advantica, Levi Strauss & Co., Fannie Mae, Sempra Energy, and Dole Food do that extremely well.[74] Here's an example.

COMPANY EXAMPLE   ## LEVI STRAUSS & COMPANY—DIVERSE BY DESIGN[75]

Levi Strauss & Company (LS&CO.) is proud to be a $6 billion company. But it is just as proud to be recognized as one of the most ethnically and culturally diverse companies in the United States, if not the world. Fully 58 percent of its 23,000 U.S. employees belong to minority groups. Its top management level is 14 percent nonwhite and 30 percent female.

Education is the cornerstone of LS&Co.'s efforts. The company invests in its employees through its Valuing Diversity educational programs, one of which includes a 3.5-day experience. The program is designed to get employees thinking about how to become more tolerant of personal differences and to see the importance of those differences.

The company's ads for job openings encourage minorities and women to apply. When job seekers interview at the company, they often find a person who looks like them on the other side of the desk. Says the African-American manager of internal audits: "You get a feeling that there's opportunity here because of the diversity at senior levels."

LS&CO. also supports in-house networking groups of African Americans, Hispanics, Asian–Pacific Islanders, women, lesbians, and gay men. The Diversity Council, made up of two members of every group, meets regularly with members of the executive committee to raise awareness of diversity issues. Finally, part of every manager's bonus is tied to specific activities and accomplishments that meet the goals of the company's Aspiration Statement, which encourages all employees to aspire to appreciate diversity.

Promoting diversity in the workforce makes good marketing sense for LS&CO. too. As an Asian-American manager of corporate marketing noted: "It's tough to design and develop merchandise for markets you don't understand." On the flip side: When you make a point of valuing other people's contributions, some good ideas for products make their way back to headquarters. The company credits an Argentinian employee for thinking up its Dockers brand of casual pants, which now makes more than $1 billion a year in revenues.

Alas, diversity also has its downside: costly and time-consuming disagreements abound in a company where everyone's ideas are encouraged. Some managers who feel they need command and control become uncomfortable in a less structured, more open and egalitarian organization—which LS&CO. thinks harnesses diversity—and these managers leave the company.

Female Workers

Here are six ways that firms today provide women with opportunities not previously available to them.[76]

1. **Alternative career paths**.   This is especially popular in law and accounting firms that have sanctioned part-time work for professionals. PricewaterhouseCoopers is a champion of this approach.

2. **Extended leave**.   IBM, as we have seen, grants up to 3 years off with benefits and the guarantee of a comparable job on return. However, leave takers must be on call for part-time work during 2 of the 3 years.

3. **Flexible scheduling**.   At NCNB, a bank based in North Carolina, employees create their own schedules and work at home. After 6 months' maternity leave, new mothers can increase their hours at work gradually. Most who choose to cut their hours work two-thirds time and receive two-thirds pay.

4. **Flextime**.   Through its Women's Interests Network, an 825-member task force with chapters in five states, American Express now has a universal framework for employees and their managers to implement flexible work arrangements at all of the company's 1,675 locations. Among U.S. employers, fully 57 percent offer flexible scheduling, but unlike the system at American Express, most are informal arrangements.[77]

5. **Job sharing**.   This is not for everyone, but it may work especially well with clerical positions where the need for coordination of the overall workload is minimal. That is, activities such as filing, faxing, word processing, and photocopying are relatively independent tasks that workers can share. In contrast, development of a new product or a new marketing campaign often requires a continuity of thought and coordinated

action that cannot easily be assigned to different workers or managers. At Steelcase, the office equipment manufacturer, for example, two employees can share title, workload, salary, health benefits, and vacation.

6. **Teleworking** is work carried out in a location that is remote from central offices or production facilities, where the worker has no personal contact with coworkers, but is able to communicate with them using electronic means. It is a popular and rapidly growing alternative to the traditional, office-bound work style. Two of every three Fortune 500 companies now employ teleworkers. Currently 40 million employees telework on a global basis, and by 2003 more than 137 million workers worldwide are expected to telework at least on a part-time basis. Survey results indicate that employees want more opportunities for telework, and that their top priority is to gain the flexibility to control their own time.[78]

Generations X and Y

Here are 10 suggestions for integrating Generations X and Y into the workforce.[79] Explain to them how their work contributes to the bottom line, always provide full disclosure, create customized career paths, allow them to have input into decisions, provide public praise, treat them as sophisticated consumers, encourage the use of mentors, provide access to innovative technology, consider new benefits and compensation strategies, and offer opportunities for community involvement.

In terms of compensation, these generations are used to having and spending money. Cash compensation is a powerful tool, so consider signing bonuses, lucrative merit-increase plans, variable pay, at-risk compensation, stock options, retention bonuses or contracts, and frequent recognition. With respect to community involvement, these generations have high rates of volunteerism. They will look for opportunities to continue this in the context of the workplace.

Older Workers

By 2003, more than half of all workers in the United States will be 40 or older.[80] By 2015, more than a third of all workers will be 50 and over. To be sure, their experience, wisdom, and institutional memories (memories of traditions, of how and why things are done as they are in an organization) represent important assets to firms. As important elements of the diversity "mix," progressive organizations will continue to develop and use these assets effectively. Here are six priorities to consider in order to maximize the use of older workers[81]:

1. **Age and experience profile.**   Executives should look at the age distribution across jobs, as compared with performance measures, to see what career paths for older workers might open in the future and what past performance measures have indicated about the kinds of knowledge, skills, abilities, and other characteristics necessary to hold these positions. Why do this? Because it's important to identify types of jobs where older workers can use their experience and talents most effectively.

2. **Job performance requirements.**   Companies should then define more precisely the types of abilities and skills needed for various posts. While

physical abilities decline with age, especially for heavy lifting, running, or sustained physical exertion (needed in jobs such as firefighting and law enforcement), mental abilities generally remain stable well into the eighties. Clear job specifications must serve as the basis for improved personnel selection, job design, and performance management systems. For example, jobs may be designed for self-pacing, may require periodic updating, or may require staffing by people with certain physical abilities.

3. **Performance management**.   Not only must a firm analyze the requirements of jobs better, there must also be improved ways of managing the performance of workers in those jobs. For example, age biases may be reflected in managers' attitudes. This is known as age grading: subconscious expectations about what people can and cannot do at particular times of their lives. Both Banker's Life and Casualty Co. and Polaroid have teams that audit the appraisals of older workers to check for unfair evaluations. These teams also attempt to redress general age prejudice in the workplace by working with employees and managers at all levels to replace myths about older workers with facts based on evidence.

4. **Workforce interest surveys**.   Once management understands the abilities its older workers have, it must determine what they want. The idea is to survey workers to determine their career goals so that the ones who are capable of achieving their goals won't stall. Not only must management decide that it wants to encourage selectively some older workers to continue with the organization, it must also consider encouraging turnover of workers it doesn't want to continue. And, of course, management must evaluate what effects different incentives will have on the workers it wants to continue and on the ones it doesn't.

5. **Training and counseling**.   To meet the needs of the workforce remaining on the job, firms need to develop training programs to avoid **mid-career plateaus** (i.e., performance at an acceptable but not outstanding level, coupled with little or no effort to improve one's current performance), as well as training programs to reduce **obsolescence** (the tendency for knowledge or skills to become out of date). These programs must reflect the special needs of older workers, who can learn but need to be taught differently (for example, by using self-paced programs instead of lectures).

6. **The structure of jobs**.   To whatever degree management may consider changing older workers' work conditions, such as work pace, or the length or timing of the workday, it should explore the proposed changes jointly with the workforce. After all, multiple generations are likely to be affected by the changes, and boomers, Gen Xers, and Generation Ys are all likely to support what they helped to create.

Workers with Disabilities

A 30-year-old war veteran with a disability called a radio talk show recently to complain that prospective employers wouldn't consider him for jobs despite his outstanding credentials. "How many interviews have you had?" asked the talk show host, who heads a nonprofit organization dedicated to placing people with disabilities in jobs. "Not one" he admitted. "As soon as I tell them I can't walk, type, and other things I can't do, they get off the telephone as quickly as possible."

"I'm not surprised," said the host, "Prospective employers want to know what job applicants can do for them, not what their limitations are. If you can show a prospective employer that you will bring in customers, design a new product, or do something else that makes a contribution, employers will hire you. Your disability won't matter if you can prove that you will contribute to the employer's bottom line."[82]

The fact is that poll after poll of employers demonstrates that they regard most people with disabilities as good workers, punctual, conscientious, and competent, if given reasonable accommodation. Despite this evidence, persons with disabilities are less likely to be working than any other demographic group under age 65. One survey found that two-thirds of persons with disabilities between the ages of 16 and 64 are unemployed. They also work approximately one-third fewer hours than those without disabilities.[83] What can be done?

Perhaps the biggest barrier is employers' lack of knowledge. For example, many are concerned about financial hardship because they assume it will be costly to make architectural changes to accommodate wheelchairs and add equipment to aid workers who are blind or deaf. In fact, statistics show that most accommodations cost less than $1,000 per employee, and 15 percent cost nothing.[84] Consider several possible modifications:

- Placing a desk on blocks, lowering shelves, and using a carousel for files are inexpensive accommodations that enable people in wheelchairs to be employed.
- Telephone amplifiers can be installed for hearing-impaired individuals, and magnifying glasses for the sight-impaired. Much to their delight, employers have found that these systems helped them gain new customers with hearing or sight impairments.[85]
- Flextime, job-sharing, and other modifications to the work schedule that enable mothers with young children to continue to work are also being used to help employees with acquired immunodeficiency syndrome (AIDS), cancer, and other life-threatening diseases to continue to work.[86]

Accommodations like these enable persons with disabilities to work, to gain self-esteem, and to reach their full potential. That is a key objective of diversity at work.

Gay and Lesbian Employees

Throughout this chapter we have emphasized that workforce diversity is a business issue. Either you attract, retain, and motivate the best talent or else you lose business. This is one reason more than 75 percent of Fortune 1,000 firms have elected to add the words "sexual orientation" to their nondiscrimination policies, and why 1 in 8 of all firms—1 in 4 with more than 5,000 workers—offer domestic partner benefits.[87] Well-known companies such as Apple Computer, Fox Broadcasting, Glaxo-Wellcome, Microsoft, Time Warner, and Walt Disney are just a few examples of companies that offer such benefits.

American Express Financial Advisors goes one step further. It has established 17 Diversity Learning Labs in its field locations. The labs receive concentrated funding, resource, and training support from the region and corporate offices. They focus on diverse segments in the African-American, gay and lesbian, Hispanic, and women's markets. Not only are the labs help-

To Prepare for Coming Changes in
Internal Organizational Environments

Develop an age, gender, and race/ethnic
profile of the present workforce

Carefully assess job performance
requirements

Check for possible unfairness in
performance management

Use interest surveys to determine
what current workers want

Provide opportunities for employee
training and career counseling

Explore with workers alternatives
to traditional work patterns

Figure 4–4

Priority listing of
suggested actions
to manage effec-
tively the internal
organizational
environments of
the future.

ing to acquire a more diverse base of clients for the company, but they also are
surfacing some key lessons:

- Targeting diverse clients drives the need for a similarly diverse workforce.
- To drive the diversity initiative throughout the company, it must be integrated into business plans, with a requirement to measure specific results.
- Leaders of the efforts to acquire diverse clients must not only have client-
acquisition expertise in that specific market segment, but also have strong
project-management experience.

   To be sure, the internal expertise and competence fostered by the learning
labs is helping American Express to prosper in its business on a global scale.[88]
As we have seen, the workforce is now and will continue to be more and more
diverse. A list of actions that managers can take to deal with these changes is
presented in Figure 4–4.

MAKING THE BUSINESS CASE FOR DIVERSITY

*Human Resource
Management
in Action:
Conclusion*

You will need to be able to address these seven key components in establishing
the business case for diversity in any given company: situation assessment,
benchmarking, business positioning, leadership and organizational involvement, communication, measurement, and a diversity strategic plan.

1. **Situation assessment** provides a snapshot of the current business environment. It is fundamental to establishing a business case for diversity because it integrates both quantitative and qualitative information about a
   specific diversity issue, group, or the entire organization. It typically includes an assessment of the organization's culture, a review of business
   performance indicators, demographics of the customer or client base, the
   number of languages spoken by customers or clients, product or service

ETHICAL DILEMMA
Does Diversity Management Conflict with Maximizing Shareholder Value?

The main objective of profit-making businesses is to maximize overall returns to shareholders (increases in stock prices plus dividends). Since earnings affect this objective, management needs to determine the extent to which any new program—including any new workforce program—will affect the bottom line. For sound business reasons, having a diverse workforce and managing it properly can increase shareholder value. However, companies generally tend to measure success in these programs by looking at indicators other than the bottom line. Affirmative action programs have been criticized strongly for adding costs to firms but little or no financial benefits.[89] Given the costs involved, can diversity programs be justified over time purely on philosophical and moral grounds (i.e., it's the right thing to do)?

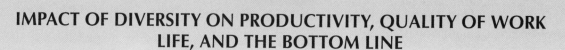

IMPACT OF DIVERSITY ON PRODUCTIVITY, QUALITY OF WORK LIFE, AND THE BOTTOM LINE

All employees, no matter who, no matter at what level, want to be treated with respect. They want to know that their employer values the work they do. That's the most basic thing you must do in managing diversity. When diversity is managed well, as at DuPont, Procter & Gamble, Monsanto, and Allied Signal, productivity and the quality of work life improve. So do stock prices. Researchers examined the effect on stock prices of announcements of U.S. Department of Labor awards for exemplary diversity programs, and also announcements of damage awards from the settlement of discrimination lawsuits. Announcements of awards were associated with significant, positive excess returns that represent the capitalization of positive information concerning improved business prospects. Conversely, damage awards were associated with significant negative stock price changes, which represent the capitalization of negative economic implications associated with discriminatory corporate practices.[90] In addition to the negative impact on stock prices, the direct costs of investigation and litigation of a 75-person class-action lawsuit alleging unfair discrimination exceed $460,000—assuming you win.[91] In terms of specific payoffs, a multicultural team at DuPont gained about $45 million in new business worldwide by changing the way DuPont develops and markets decorating materials like its Corian countertops. Among other things, the team recommended an array of new colors that appealed to overseas customers.[92] Said the chief executive officer of Nutrasweet: "You can't send someone from the north side of Chicago to sell Nutrasweet in Singapore. You need a team to reflect the markets you're going to serve."[93]

IMPLICATIONS FOR MANAGEMENT PRACTICE

1. Workforce diversity is here to stay. There is no going back to the demographic makeup of organizations 20 years ago. To be successful in this new environment, learn to value and respect cultural styles and ways of behaving that differ from your own.

2. Recognize that there are tangible business reasons for making the effective management of workforce diversity a high priority: (a) it is an opportunity to serve the needs of customers better and to penetrate new markets, and (b) diverse teams make it possible to enhance creativity, flexibility, and rapid response to change.

3. To maximize the potential of all members of the workforce, link concerns for diversity to every business strategy: recruitment, selection, placement, succession planning, performance management, and rewards.

4. To retain talented women and minorities, follow the lead of Procter & Gamble in developing long-term career plans that include multiple assignments—and don't be afraid to share the plan with the employees in question. As former CEO John Pepper noted, "So often, people don't know how you feel about them until it's too late."[94]

---

development strategy, statistics on turnover within various groups, recruitment, and trends in current and potential litigation.

2. **Benchmarking** helps answer questions such as: "What is our competition doing?" and "What are the 'best-in-class' diversity practices?" This process examines the diversity practices of other organizations and provides key learning information about their problems as well as their successes.

3. **Business positioning** is often overlooked in building a business case for diversity. Its purpose is to determine how diversity can support business strategies. To do so it is necessary to examine how the business will compete in the marketplace (its strategies), marketing and sales projections, customer and consumer trends, the number of countries in which the organization operates, and financial information. How can a diverse workforce leverage these trends to the company's advantage?

4. **Leadership and organizational involvement** at all levels are necessary to sustain a diversity initiative. This is key to determining how to position diversity with the appropriate sponsorship by top leaders of the organization.

5. **Communication initiatives** address the question of how diversity should be integrated into the communication systems for internal and external customers of the organization, managers, employees, and other relevant stakeholders.

6. **Measurement** is often overlooked. Surveys show that while more than three out of every four organizations support diversity as a corporate undertaking, only half take the time to measure the outcomes of their efforts. Doing so requires a specification in advance of key deliverables and criteria to use in measuring outcomes. Use a comparative process that includes

both baseline data that detail the starting conditions *and* clear objectives against which change can be measured. For example, one objective might be to reduce controllable turnover among females by 25 percent within 2 years. This component answers two important questions, "What will success look like?" and "How will the organization know?"[95]

7. **A diversity strategic plan** focuses on integrating the strategic and tactical elements of the business case for diversity. It answers questions about who, what, and how. It maps out the priorities, the largest areas of impact, and the requirements to move the business case for diversity forward. It becomes the blueprint for selling and communicating the business case for diversity throughout the organization.

SUMMARY

More than half the U.S. workforce now consists of racial and ethnic minorities, immigrants, and women. White, native-born males, as a group, are still dominant in numbers over any other group, but women will compose nearly half the entire workforce by 2008. The Asian, American-Indian, Alaska Native, and Pacific Islanders' share of the labor force will increase from 5 to 6 percent, the Hispanic share will increase from 10 to 13 percent, and the African-American share will hold steady at about 12 percent between 1998 and 2008.

Managing diversity means encouraging a heterogeneous workforce, which includes white men, to perform to its potential in an equitable work environment in which no one group enjoys an advantage or suffers a disadvantage. At least five factors account for the increasing attention companies are paying to diversity: (1) the shift from a manufacturing to a service economy, (2) the globalization of markets, (3) new business strategies that require more teamwork, (4) mergers and alliances that require different corporate cultures to work together, and (5) the changing labor market. Each of these factors can represent opportunities for firms whose managers and employees understand what culture is, and appreciate cultural differences among other employees and managers, and especially the firm's market.

To attract and retain women, as well as persons with disabilities, companies are making available to them alternative career paths, extended leaves, flexible scheduling, flextime, job sharing, and opportunities to telework. In addition, many companies now offer the same benefits to same-sex couples as to heterosexual couples. A different aspect of diversity is generational diversity—important differences in values, aspirations, and beliefs that characterize the swing generation, the silent generation, the baby boomers, Generation X, and Generation Y. To manage older workers effectively, managers should develop an age profile of the workforce, monitor job performance requirements for the kinds of characteristics people need to do their jobs well, develop safeguards against age bias in performance management, conduct workforce interest surveys, provide education and counseling, and consider modifying the structure of jobs.

Finally, to manage diversity effectively, do the following things well: focus on bringing in the best talent, not on meeting numerical goals; establish mentoring programs among employees of same and different races; hold managers accountable for meeting diversity goals; develop career plans for employees as part of performance reviews; promote women and minorities to decision-making positions, not just to staff jobs; and diversify the company's board of directors.

DISCUSSION QUESTIONS

4–1. In your opinion, what are some key business reasons for emphasizing the effective management of a diverse workforce?

4–2. Discuss some possible reasons why deep divisions in the workforce still remain between and among racial and ethnic minorities, between women and men, and across generations.

4–3. What would the broad elements of a company policy include if the objective was to emphasize the management of diversity?

4–4. How should the outcomes of diversity programs be measured?

4–5. Suppose you were asked to enter a debate in which your task was to argue against any special effort to manage workforce diversity. What would you say?

KEY TERMS

ethnic minorities	baby-boom generation
managing diversity	generation X
affirmative action	generation Y
culture	teleworking
EEO for women	age grading
swing generation	mid-career plateaus
silent generation	obsolescence

APPLYING YOUR KNOWLEDGE

The Challenge of Diversity*

Case 4–1

Talk, talk, talk. As Ken Hartman, an African-American midlevel manager at Blahna, Inc., recalls, that's all he got from the white men above him in top management—despite the fact that Blahna had long enjoyed a reputation as a socially responsible company. But that reputation didn't mean much to Hartman as he watched other African-American managers he thought were highly qualified get passed over for plum jobs, and his own career seemed stalled on a lonely plateau. Top management always mouthed diversity, Hartman said, "but in the end, they chose people they were comfortable with for key positions."

The Diversity Track Record

Is this situation uncommon? Not at all. Human resource experts estimate that only 3 percent to 5 percent of U.S. corporations are diversifying their workforces effectively.

*Source: Diversity management: Beyond awareness, *Employee Relations Bulletin,* Aug. 7, 1994, pp. 1–7; R. Mitchell & M. Oneal, Managing by values, *BusinessWeek,* Aug. 1, 1994, pp. 46–52; F. Rice, How to make diversity pay, *Fortune,* Aug. 8, 1994, pp. 78–86.

Employers agree with this assessment. A 1992 survey by the Hay Group showed that only 5 percent of 1405 participating companies thought they were doing a "very good job" of managing the diversity of their workforces.

Such results might surprise those who remember how loudly the diversity drum was beaten several years ago when the Labor Department released its study entitled *Workforce 2000*. This study reported that only 15 percent of the new entrants into the workforce by the year 2000 would be white males. At the time, many companies vowed to master the management of diversity. They spent large sums of money on consultants to whip it into the corporate culture mix. Yet in most cases, the changes never took hold. At many companies, downsizing became the more urgent imperative. At others, the commitment was never really there.

Examples are provided by Maybelline, Microsoft, and advertising agencies. At the former, a new line of cosmetics for women of darker hues was launched in 1990. It was called "Shades of You." The product was a clear winner, garnering about 35 percent of the ethnic cosmetics market despite the fact that few people of color are employed by Maybelline. Maybelline CEO Robert Hiatt asserts, "It is not the makeup of our management that is important; it is paying attention to the market and our customers. We don't even keep track of the number of minorities in our company."

Microsoft fails to push diversity as well. Says Randy Massengale, who heads Microsoft's 2-year-old diversity effort, "The company has been so focused on growth that we have not built all of the human resources infrastructure we need." The result? A much more homogeneous staff than the hip culture at Microsoft might suggest.

Ad agencies, in particular, don't seem to have caught on. A recent survey reveals that fewer than 1 percent of media managers are African American, 2 percent are Hispanic, 3 percent are Asian, and Native Americans are too few to count. This lack of diversity is particularly ironic for an industry that is supposed to know consumer markets.

The way a company deals with a crisis is often what marks it as a leader. AT&T, lavishly praised for its management of diversity during the past decade, was hit hard by a headline-making incident last fall. The company's employee magazine featured a cartoon of customers on various continents making phone calls. The caller in Africa was depicted as an animal. Immediately upon dissemination of the newsletter, the company's switchboard lit up with calls from irate employees, customers, civil rights groups, and legislators.

Tackling the problem head on, AT&T Chairman Robert Allen apologized to all for the "racist" illustration and noted that it was drawn by a freelancer. He vowed to turn the ugly incident into an opportunity to accelerate the pace of workforce diversity at AT&T and immediately went to work developing an action plan to make it happen. The plan appeared in less than 2 months, with a mission "to create a work environment that sets the world-class standard for valuing diversity." Among the steps listed in the six-page plan, all 13 top officers at AT&T will increase their direct interactions with minority employee caucus groups.

The Strategy at Blahna, Inc.

Ken Hartman's firm, Blahna, Inc., has finally gotten the message. The company is now using diversity management strategies to head off conflict and reduce turnover among employees it can ill afford to lose.

Several years ago, Blahna formed a 20-member Committee for Workplace Diversity, chaired by a vice president. The committee was chartered to consider why women and minorities weren't better represented at all levels of the organization. Although the company had a good record of hiring women and minorities, the committee discovered that turnover was 2 to 3 times higher for these groups than it was for white males.

Sample exit interviews revealed that women and minorities left for culture-related reasons—for instance, because they didn't feel valued in their day-to-day work, didn't have effective working relationships, or didn't sense that the work they were being given to do would lead to the fulfillment of their career goals. White males, on the other hand, left for business-related reasons, such as limited opportunities for future advancement.

As a result of this initial investigation, Blahna formed a 25-person Diversity Advisory Committee. The committee determined to take a two-step approach to dealing with diversity issues. The first step was to increase awareness; the second was to build skills for dealing with diversity-related challenges. Both steps involved training conducted by diversity consultants, Hope & Associates.

To date, 60 percent of Blahna's 11,000 employees have gone through a 2-day diversity seminar. Forty percent have gone through a more extensive 6-day training program as well. "The premise of the training is that the more different you are, the more barriers there can be to working well together," explains Blahna's diversity development director. Training sessions do not offer advice on how to get along with Asian Americans, women, or other specific groups. Rather, the emphasis is on learning skills that will make it easier to relate to and communicate with others.

A key part of the training offered by Hope & Associates is the implementation of a "consulting pairs" process. The consulting pairs approach is designed to help trainees take what they've learned in training and apply it on the job. When a conflict—which may or may not be related to diversity—first arises between two peers or a manager and employee, a consulting pair is called in to facilitate discussion and problem solving. The unique feature of this approach is that the consulting pair is selected to match as closely as possible the backgrounds of the individuals who are involved in the conflict. Of course, all proceedings are strictly confidential.

The result? Ken Hartman is a happier guy these days. As president of one of Blahna's divisions, the 48-year-old executive is a step away from joining the ranks of senior management. Life has changed for him since Blahna "stopped talking about values like diversity and began behaving that way."

Questions
1. Why do many companies find increasing and managing diversity to be difficult challenges?
2. What were the key elements in Blahna's successful diversity strategy?
3. Under what circumstances might the consulting pairs approach be most useful?
4. What steps should management take to ensure that the consulting pairs approach is working?

REFERENCES

1. U.S. Bureau of Labor Statistics. *Employment projections, 1998–2008.* See *www.stats.bls.gov,* accessed Apr. 15, 2001.
2. Torres, C., & Bruxelles, M. (1992, Dec.). Capitalizing on global diversity. *HRMagazine,* pp. 30–33.
3. Equal Employment Opportunity Commission (1979, Jan. 19). *Affirmative action guidelines.* Pub. no. 44 FR 4421. Washington, DC: U.S. Government Printing Office.
4. Jackson, S. E., & Alvarez, E. B. (1992). Working through diversity as a strategic imperative. In S. E. Jackson (ed.), *Diversity in the workplace.* New York: Guilford, pp. 13–35.
5. The data for Table 4–2 come from the U.S. Bureau of Labor Statistics. *Employment projections, 1998–2008.* See *www.stats.bls.gov,* accessed Apr. 15, 2001. See also The perplexing case of the plummeting payrolls (1993, Sept. 20). *BusinessWeek,* p. 27.

6. Update column (1999, June 21). *Broadcasting and Cable Magazine*, p. 40.

7. Sellers, P. (1990, June 4). What customers really want. *Fortune*, pp. 58–68.

8. Digh, P. (2000, Jan.–Feb.) Diversity goes global. *Mosaics*, pp. 1, 4, 5.

9. Cascio, W. F. (2000). Managing a virtual workplace. *Academy of Management Review*, *14*(3), 81–90. See also Townsend, A. M., DeMarie, S. M., & Hendrickson, A. R. 1998. Virtual teams: Technology and the workplace of the future. *Academy of Management Executive, 12*(3):17–29.

10. Huszczo, G. E. (1996). *Tools for team excellence: Getting your team into high gear and keeping it there.* Palo Alto, CA: Davies-Black. See also Wellins, R. S., Byham, W. C., & Wilson, J. M. (1991). *Empowered teams.* San Francisco: Jossey-Bass.

11. Watson, W. E., Kumar, K., & Michaelson, L. K. (1993). Cultural diversity's impact on interaction process and performance: Comparing homogeneous and diverse task groups. *Academy of Management Journal*, *36*(3), 590–602.

12. Wall, J., in Affirmative action on the edge (1995, Feb. 13). *U.S. News & World Report*, p. 37.

13. Tetenbaum, T. (1999, Autumn). Beating the odds of merger & acquisition failure. *Organizational Dynamics*, pp. 22–36. See also Cascio, W. F., & Serapio, M. G., Jr. (1991, Winter). Human resources systems in an international alliance: The undoing of a done deal? *Organizational Dynamics*, pp. 63–74.

14. Serapio, M. G., Jr., & Cascio, W. F. (1996). End-games in international alliances. *Academy of Management Executive*, *10*(1), 63–73.

15. Tetenbaum, op. cit.

16. Davenport, T., cited in ibid., p. 26.

17. Marks, M., & Mirvis, P. (1998). *Joining forces: One plus one equals three in mergers, acquisitions, and alliances.* San Francisco: Jossey-Bass. See also McWhirter, W. (1989, Oct. 9). I came, I saw, I blundered. *Time*, pp. 72, 77.

18. Ibid.

19. *Workplace visions: The labor shortage* (2000, Sept.–Oct.). Alexandria, VA: Society for Human Resource Management. See also Sivy, M. (1997, October). What America will look like in 25 years. *Money*, pp. 98–106.

20. Jackson, S. E. (1992). Preview of the road to be traveled. In S. E. Jackson (ed.), *Diversity in the workplace.* New York: Guilford, pp. 4–12.

21. Becker, B. E., Huselid, M. A., & Ulrich, D. (2001). *The HR Scorecard: Linking people, strategy, and performance.* Boston: Harvard Business School Press.

22. Mehta, S. N. (2000, July 10). What minority employees really want. *Fortune*, pp. 181–186.

23. Ibid.

24. Boyacigiller, N. A., Kleinberg, M. J., Phillips, M. E., & Sackman, S. A. (1996). Conceptualizing culture. In B. J. Punnett & O. Shenkar (eds.), *Handbook for international management research.* Cambridge, MA: Blackwell, pp. 157–208.

25. Harris, P. R., & Moran, R. T. (1990). *Managing cultural differences* (3d ed.). Houston: Gulf Publishing.

26. Fernandez, J. P., with Barr, M. (1993). *The diversity advantage.* New York: Lexington Books.

27. U.S. Bureau of Labor Statistics, op. cit.

28. More than 800,000 businesses owned by African-Americans (2001, Mar. 22). *U.S. Department of Commerce News.* pp. 1, 8.

29. Spending power of African-Americans: Up, up, up (2001, Jan. 22). *BusinessWeek*, p. 16.

30. Mehta, op. cit.

31. America's 50 best companies for minorities (2000, July 10). *Fortune*, pp. 190–200.

32. McKay, B. (2000, Nov. 17). Coca-Cola agrees to settle bias suit for $192.5 million. *The Wall Street Journal*, pp. A3, A8.

33. Patrick, D., quoted in Labich, K. (1999, Sept. 6). No more crude at Texaco. *Fortune*, p. 212.

34. Boyle, M. (2001, Jan. 8). How the workplace was won. *Fortune*, pp. 150–153.
35. Garr, D., quoted in Mehta, op. cit., p. 184.
36. Labich (1999), op. cit.
37. Sessa, V. J. (1992). Managing diversity at the Xerox Corporation: Balanced workforce goals and caucus groups. In S. E. Jackson (ed.), *Diversity in the workplace*. New York: Guilford, pp. 37–64.
38. America's 50 best companies for minorities (2000, July 10). *Fortune*, pp. 190–200.
39. U.S. Bureau of Labor Statistics, op. cit.
40. Fernandez with Barr, op. cit.
41. Porter, E., & Nelson, E. (2000, Oct. 13). P&G reaches out to Hispanics. *The Wall Street Journal*, pp. B1, B4. See also Porter, E. (2000, Oct. 13). Why the Latino market is so hard to count. *The Wall Street Journal*, pp. B1, B4.
42. Roberson, L., & Gutierrez, N. (1992). Beyond good faith: Commitment to recruiting management diversity at Pacific Bell. Jackson, op. cit. pp. 65–68.
43. Work week (1996, Sept. 24). *The Wall Street Journal*, p. A1.
44. Knowledge Network Explorer. *www.kn.pacbell.com/*, accessed Apr. 18, 2001.
45. U.S. Bureau of Labor Statistics, op. cit.
46. Cheng, J., quoted in Mehta, S. (2000, July 10). What minority employees really want. *Fortune*, p. 183.
47. Mehta, op. cit.
48. Shellenbarger, S. (1995, May 11). Women indicate satisfaction with role of big breadwinner. *The Wall Street Journal*, pp. B1, B2.
49. The 100 best companies to work for (2001, Jan. 8). *Fortune*, pp. 148–168.
50. Schwartz, F. N. (1992, Mar.–Apr.). Women as a business imperative. *Harvard Business Review*, pp. 105–113.
51. *Workplace visions: Demographics* (1996, Sept.–Oct.). Alexandria, VA: Society for Human Resource Management. See also Richardson, L. (1992, Sept. 2). No cookie cutter answers in "mommy wars." *The New York Times*, pp. B1, B5.
52. Shellenbarger, S. (2000, July 26). Work & family. *The Wall Street Journal*, p. B1.
53. Shellenbarger (1995), op. cit.
54. Pear, R. (2000, Nov. 5). Single moms working more. *The Denver Post*, p. J2.
55. *Digest of educational statistics 2000,* tables 248 and 254. Washington, DC: National Center for Educational Statistics.
56. "Mommy, do you love your company more than me?" (1999, Dec. 20). *BusinessWeek,* p. 175.
57. Sellers, P. (1996, Aug. 5). Women, sex, & power. *Fortune*, pp. 43–57.
58. The new debate over working moms (2000, Sept. 18). *BusinessWeek,* pp. 102–104.
59. Boyle, M. B. (1975). Equal opportunity for women is smart business. *Harvard Business Review, 51,* 85–95.
60. Cascio, op. cit.
61. Women rise in work place, but wage gap continues (2000, April 25). *The Wall Street Journal*, p. A16. See also Pollock, E. J. (2000, Feb. 7). Deportment gap. *The Wall Street Journal*, pp. A1, A20. Roberts, S. (1995, Apr. 27). Women's work: What's new, what isn't. *The New York Times*, p. B6. Dobrzynski, J. H. (1995, April 20). Some action, little talk: Companies embrace diversity but are reluctant to discuss it. *The New York Times*, pp. D1, D4. Sharpe, R. (1994, Mar. 29). The waiting game: Women make strides, but men stay firmly in top company jobs. *The Wall Street Journal*, pp. A1, A8.
62. "Mommy, do you love your company more than me?" op cit.
63. Leinwand, D. (1999, Oct. 11). Debate rages on remedies for women's pay gap. *The Denver Post*, pp. 15A, 18A. See also Crittenden, D. (1995, Aug. 22). Yes, motherhood lowers pay. *The New York Times*, p. A15. Fernandez with Barr, op. cit.
64. Rowland, M. (1992, Aug. 23). Strategies for stay-at-home moms. *The New York Times*, p. 16F.
65. Crittenden, op. cit.

66. Cartwright, C. (1999, Oct.). The 100 best companies for working mothers. *Working Mother*, pp. 26–114. Balancing work and family (1996, Sept. 16). *BusinessWeek*, pp. 74–80.

67. Women entrepreneurs (1994, Apr. 18), *BusinessWeek,* pp. 104–110 op. cit. See also "Mommy, do you love your company more than me?" op. cit.

68. Cartwright, C. (1999, Oct.). The 100 best companies for working mothers. *Working Mother*, pp. 74, 75.

69. The framework for this section was drawn from the following sources: The new workforce: Generation Y (2001). *Workplace Visions*, no. 2, pp. 1–7. Zemke, R., Raines, C., & Filipczak, B. (2000). *Generations at work: Managing the clash of veterans, boomers, Xers, and nexters in your workplace.* NY: AMACOM. Glube, N. (1999, March). Boomers, Gen Xers offer both challenges, potential. *HR News*, pp. 15, 16.

70. Fisher, A. (1996, Sept. 30). Wanted: Aging baby-boomers. *Fortune*, p. 204.

71. Hays, S. (1999, Nov.). Generation X and the art of reward. *Workforce, 78*, 11–13.

72. Labich, op. cit. See also Diversity: Beyond the numbers game (1995, Aug. 14), *BusinessWeek,* pp. 60, 61.

73. America's 50 best companies for minorities (2000, July 10). *Fortune*, p. 190.

74. Ibid. See also Cuneo, A. (1992, Nov. 15). Diverse by design: How good intentions make good business. *BusinessWeek*, p. 72.

75. Cartwright, op. cit. See also Balancing work and family (1996, September 16). *Business Week*, pp. 74–80. See also Wentling, R. M. (1995, May). Breaking down barriers to women's success. *HRMagazine*, pp. 79–85.

76. Kleiman, C. (2000, Nov. 6). Many flex schedules are informal arrangements. *The Denver Post*, p. 2N.

77. Cascio, op. cit. See also The new world of work: Flexibility is the watchword. (2000, Jan. 10). *BusinessWeek,* p. 36. See also Conlin, M. (1999, Sept. 20). 9 to 5 isn't working anymore. *BusinessWeek*, pp. 94–98.

78. The new workforce, op. cit. Zemke et al. (2000). Op. cit. Glube, op. cit.

79. Munk, N. (1999, Feb. 1). Finished at forty. *Fortune*, pp. 50–66.

80. Brotherton, P. (2000, Mar.–Apr.). Tapping into an older workforce. *Mosaics*, pp. 1, 4, 5. See also Few companies pursue strategies that would better utilize older workers (2000, May–June). *Working Age*, pp. 2–3. Thornburg, L. (1995, Feb.). The age wave hits: What older workers want and need. *HRMagazine*, pp. 40–45. Andrews, E. S. (1992, Winter). Expanding opportunities for older workers. *Journal of Labor Research, 13*(1), 55–65.

81. Just one break changes lives of disabled (1994, Oct. 23). *The New York Times*, Special Supplement, The diversity challenge, p. 11.

82. Bruyere, S. M. (2000, Nov.–Dec.). Dealing effectively with disability accommodations. *Mosaics*, pp. 1, 4, 5.

83. Disabled succeed in the workplace (1994, Oct. 23). *The New York Times*, Special Supplement, The diversity challenge, pp. 10–11.

84. Ibid. See also Cascio, W. F. (1994). The Americans with Disabilities Act of 1990 and the 1991 Civil Rights Act: Requirements for psychological practice in the workplace. In B. D. Sales & G. R. VandenBos (eds.), *Psychology in litigation and legislation.* Washington, DC: American Psychological Association, pp. 175–211.

85. See, for example, When workers just can't cope (2000, Oct. 30). *BusinessWeek*, pp. 100, 102.

86. Digh, P. (2001, Apr.). In and out of the corporate closet. Diversity Forum, Society for Human Resource Management, Alexandria, VA. Available at *my.shrm.org/diversity/members/articles.*

87. Employee networks (2001, April). Diversity Forum, Society for Human Resource Management, Alexandria, VA. Available at *my.shrm.org/diversity/orientation.* See also Diversity: Making the business case (1996, Dec. 9). *BusinessWeek*, Special Advertising Section, p. 7.

88. Sharf, J. C., & Jones, D. P. (2000). Employment risk management. In J. F. Kehoe (ed.), *Managing selection in changing organizations.* San Francisco: Jossey-Bass, pp. 271–318. See also Brimelow, P., & Spencer, L. (1993, Feb. 15). When quotas replace merit, everybody suffers. *Forbes*, pp. 80–102.

89. Wright, P., Ferris, S. P., Hiller, J. S., & Kroll. M. (1995). Competitiveness through management of diversity: Effects on stock price valuation. *Academy of Management Journal, 38*, 273–287.

90. Cascio, W. F. (2000). *Costing human resources: The financial impact of behavior in organizations* (4th ed., chap. 4). Cincinnati: South-Western college Publishing.

91. Labich, K. (1996, September 9). Making diversity pay. *Fortune,* pp. 177–180.

92. Dobrzynski, J. H. (1995, April 20), op. cit.

93. Labich, op. cit.

94. For more information on metrics, see Digh, P. (1999, Sept.–Oct.). Creating a new balance sheet: The need for better diversity metrics. *Mosaics*, pp. 1, 4, 5.

EMPLOYMENT

Now that you understand the competitive, legal, and social environments within which HR management activities take place, it is time to address three major aspects of the employment process: analyzing the work to be done, the kinds of skills needed to do the work, and hiring employees. Logically, before an organization can select employees, it needs to be able to specify the kind of work that needs to be done, how it should be done, the number of people needed, and the personal characteristics required to do the work. Chapter 5 addresses these issues. Chapter 6 considers the planning, implementation, and evaluation of recruitment operations. Finally, Chapter 7 examines initial screening and personnel selection—why they are done, how they are done, and how they can be evaluated.

5. ANALYZING WORK AND PLANNING FOR PEOPLE

6. RECRUITING

7. STAFFING

5

ANALYZING WORK AND PLANNING FOR PEOPLE

Questions This Chapter Will Help Managers Answer

1. How is job analysis information useful to the operating manager?
2. How can workforce planning be integrated most effectively with general business planning?
3. What should be the components of a fair information practice policy with regard to information about employees?
4. How can human resource forecasts be most useful?
5. What control mechanisms might be most appropriate to ensure that action plans match targeted needs?

THE ANALYSIS OF WORK—FOUNDATION FOR EMPLOYMENT PRACTICES

Situation:

You are Pat Evans, chief engineer at Western Water Company. Western Water is a small, investor-owned utility company that provides water treatment, water distribution, and water use planning for a small, but growing, area. Each year, Western hires about six junior civil engineers to work in any of the following areas: water service planning, wastewater treatment, facilities planning, design engineering, or construction engineering. However, the number of new hires among civil engineers is expected to grow larger in the coming years, as the population density (and thus the demand for water service) increases in the area served by Western Water.

As chief engineer, you are responsible for all hiring of new engineers. You are concerned that past hiring procedures have been pretty slack—basically a cursory review of courses taken in the engineering curriculum plus an unstructured interview. As a result, Western really doesn't know what its new junior civil engineers can do, what they are looking for in a company, and what particular assignments they are best suited for. To make matters worse, an average of 50 percent of the newly hired junior civil engineers leave the company within 3 years. You are determined to change current practices. As a start, you have asked your HR Department to analyze each of the possible job assignments for junior civil engineers and to report back to you with a list of "common denominators" that seem to cut across all the assignments. That study was begun in July, it is now November 1, and you have just received the results. Western will begin recruiting in earnest next February, and most hiring decisions will be made in March–April, primarily among engineering students who will graduate in May–June. Thus you have several months to develop new hiring procedures to be put into place before the screening and selection of the next group of candidates actually begin.

In response to your request, here is a summary of the broad job dimensions of junior civil engineers that you just received from HR, along with a statement of the personal characteristics necessary to do each of them.

1. **Modeling and calculations.** Applications of professional engineering knowledge in order to develop and test mathematical models of civil engineering activities (e.g., water distribution, quality, and treatment; hydraulic; structural). Knowledge required: civil engineering principles, including mathematics through advanced calculus, statics, dynamics, basic water and wastewater chemistry, engineering economics, structural systems, surveying principles, and construction methods.

2. **Computer software applications.** Use and application of computer software tools ranging from word processing to spreadsheet-based economic analyses to modeling proposed projects. Abilities required: use of computer-based spreadsheets, graphics, word processing, and database management programs. Ability to use civil engineering modeling software, applications-development software, project scheduling, and computer-aided drafting is desirable.

3. **Project planning and management**. Identification of project objectives, scope, feasibility, milestones, and completion schedules, together with preparation of supporting documentation. Monitor and coordinate project activities in order to meet time and cost parameters. Knowledge and abilities required: engineering standard practices, formats of technical reports, water distribution systems, methods of effective presentations, whether oral or written. Must be able to develop cost analyses for projects, set priorities, and schedule activities in a logical, organized manner. Must be able to coordinate activities and work among other engineering sections, vendors, consultants, and contractors.

4. **Written communications.** Preparation of memos, letters, and engineering reports designed to address a variety of audiences, including other engineers, staff members working in maintenance, operations, or clerical positions, public agencies, government bodies, and members of the general public. Knowledge and abilities required: proper English grammar, spelling, punctuation, and sentence structure; ability to organize and compile relevant information to be used in reports; ability to communicate effectively in English in a clear, concise, organized manner, taking into account the abilities and needs of the audience.

5. **Individual and group interactions.** Provision of technical expertise, either by telephone or face to face, to contractors, other engineers, members of the board of directors, government agencies, and applicants for water service. Knowledge and abilities required: engineering terminology, ability to establish and maintain effective working relationships in a variety of contexts (one-on-one or group) and with people from a variety of backgrounds (technical as well as nontechnical); ability to communicate orally in English in a clear, understandable, concise manner, taking into account the needs and abilities of the audience.

6. **Data summary and synthesis.** Integration of information from a variety of sources (e.g., maps, calculations, environmental reports, feasibility studies) in order to provide a basis for technical recommendations or project planning. Abilities required: ability to organize data in order to assemble a written memo; ability to modify existing maps to help visualize a site and surrounding conditions; ability to summarize assumptions used in project design in order to recommend a course of action to superiors.

7. **Problem resolution.** Technical and interpersonal skills needed to achieve workable solutions to civil engineering, economic, or people-related problems. Abilities required: ability to negotiate effectively with a variety of constituencies; ability to listen actively in order to clarify issues and to ask for appropriate information; ability to express one's own position—verbally as well as in writing—including supporting logic and arguments, in order to communicate one's position to other parties.

Just as you finish reading the report, Tracy Garcia, a senior civil engineer at Western, knocks on your door. "Have you read that job analysis report on junior civils yet, Pat?" You reply, "I sure have, and boy, has it given me ideas about new ways of selecting, training, and assessing the performance of our new hires."

Challenges

1. How might the information presented in the job analysis help Western do a better job of recruiting new junior civil engineers?
2. As Pat Evans, what specific selection procedures would you like to see put into place?
3. How might the information in the job analysis report be useful in assessing the performance of new hires?

In order to make intelligent decisions about the people-related needs of a business, two types of information are essential: (1) a description of the work to be done, the skills needed, and the training and experience required for various jobs, and (2) a description of the future direction of a business. Once these are known, it makes sense to forecast the numbers and skills mix of people required at some future time period. We consider the first of these needs, job analysis, in the sections to follow, and the second, human resource planning, in the latter part of the chapter.

ALTERNATIVE PERSPECTIVES ON JOBS

Jobs are frequently the subject of conversation: "I'm trying to get a job"; "I'm being promoted to a new job"; "I'd sure like to have my boss's job." Or, as Samuel Gompers, first president of the American Federation of Labor, once said, "A job's a job; if it doesn't pay enough, it's a lousy job."

Jobs are important to individuals: They help determine standards of living, places of residence, status (values ascribed to individuals because of their positions), and even sense of self-worth. Jobs are important to organizations because they are the vehicles through which work (and thus organizational objectives) is accomplished. The way to manage people to work efficiently is through answers to such questions as:

- Who specifies the content of each job?
- Who decides how many jobs are necessary?
- How are the interrelationships among jobs determined and communicated?
- Has anyone looked at the number, design, and content of jobs from the perspective of the entire organization, the "big picture"?
- What are the minimum qualifications for each job?
- What should training programs stress?
- How should performance on each job be measured?
- How much is each job worth?

Unfortunately, there is often a tendency, even an urgency, to get on with work itself ("Get the job done!") rather than to take the time to think through these basic questions; but this tendency is changing as firms struggle to raise productivity and to cope with such problems as deregulation and global economic competition.

In the spirit of continuous improvement, firms in every developed country around the world are rethinking the fundamental principles that underlie the design of work and the required numbers and skills of people to do the work. For example, in an effort to get a better return on its enormous capital investment, General Motors has instituted around-the-clock production and flexible, lean manufacturing at its Lordstown, Ohio, plant. To do so, it retrained workers to handle a variety of jobs, instead of endlessly repeating a few rote tasks.[1] Job analysis was essential to understand the relationships among the newly enlarged jobs.

The term **job analysis** describes the process of obtaining information about jobs. As the chapter-opening vignette illustrates, this information is useful for a number of business purposes. Regardless of how it is collected, it usually includes information about the tasks to be done on the job, as well as the personal characteristics (education, experience, specialized training) necessary to do the tasks.

An overall written summary of task requirements is called a **job description,** and an overall written summary of worker requirements is called a **job specification.** The result of the process of job analysis is a job description and a job specification. In the past, such job definitions often tended to be quite narrow in scope. Today's organizations, however, emphasize flexibility and more critical thinking in jobs. As an example, consider a job description developed by Mazda executives of assembly line work at their Flat Rock, Michigan, plant:

> They want their new employees to be able to work in teams, to rotate through various jobs, to understand how their tasks fit into the entire process, to spot problems in production, to troubleshoot, articulate the problems to others, suggest improvements, and write detailed charts and memos that serve as a road map in the assembly of the car.[2]

Does that sound like a traditional description of assembly-line work? Hardly. Yet it is typical of the increased mental demands being placed on workers at all levels. Instead of being responsible for simple procedures and predictable tasks, workers are now expected to draw inferences and render diagnoses, judgments, and decisions, often under severe time pressure.[3]

Why Study Job Requirements?

Sound HR management practice dictates that thorough job analyses always be done, for they provide a deeper understanding of the behavioral requirements of jobs. This in turn creates a solid basis on which to make job-related employment decisions.[4] Legally, job analyses play a major role in the defense of employment practices (e.g., interviews, tests, performance appraisal systems) that are challenged, for they demonstrate that the practices in question are "job related." Unfortunately, job analyses are often done for a specific purpose (e.g., training design) without consideration of the many other uses of this information. Some of these other uses, along with a brief description of each, are listed below and shown graphically in Figure 5–1.

Organizational Structure and Design.   By clarifying job requirements and the interrelationships among jobs, responsibilities at all levels can be specified, promoting efficiency and minimizing overlap or duplication.

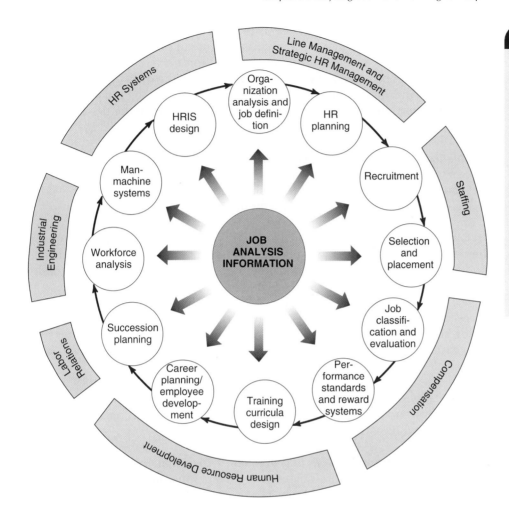

Figure 5–1

Job analysis is the foundation of many human resource management programs. [*Source*: R. C. Page and D. M. Van De Voort, Human resource planning and job analysis. In W. F. Cascio (ed.), *Planning, employment, and placement*, vol. 2 of the ASPA/BNA *Human resource management series.* Washington, DC: Bureau of National Affairs, 1989.]

Human Resource Planning.   Job analysis is the foundation for forecasting the need for human resources as well as for plans for such activities as training, transfer, or promotion. Frequently, job analysis information is incorporated into a human resource information system (HRIS).

Job Evaluation and Compensation.   Before jobs can be ranked in terms of their overall worth to an organization or compared to jobs in other firms for purposes of pay surveys, it is important to understand what they require. Job descriptions and specifications provide such understanding to those who must make job evaluation and compensation decisions.

Recruitment.   The most important information an executive recruiter ("headhunter") or company recruiter needs is full knowledge of the job or jobs in question, and the personal characteristics necessary to perform them.

Selection.   Any method used to select or promote applicants must be based on a keen, meaningful forecast of job performance. An understanding of just what a worker is expected to do on the job, as reflected in job-related interviews or test questions, is necessary for such a meaningful forecast.

Placement.   In many cases, applicants are first selected and then placed in one of many possible jobs. When there is a clear picture of the needs of a job and the abilities of workers to fulfill those needs, selection decisions will be accurate and workers will be placed in jobs where they will be the most productive. That is, selection and placement tend to go hand in hand. On the other side of the selection-placement coin, when there is a blurred picture of the needs of a job, selection decisions will not be accurate, and placement will probably be worse.

Orientation, Training, and Development.   Training a worker can be very costly, as we shall see later. Up-to-date job descriptions and specifications help ensure that training programs reflect actual job requirements. In other words, "What you learn in training today you'll use on the job tomorrow."

Performance Appraisal.   If employees are to be judged in terms of how well they do those parts of their jobs that really matter, the parts that distinguish effective from ineffective performers, it is important to specify critical and noncritical job requirements. Job analysis does this.

Career Path Planning.   If the organization (as well as the individual) does not have a thorough understanding of the requirements of available jobs and how jobs at succeeding levels relate to one another, effective career path planning is impossible.

Labor Relations.   The information provided by job analysis is helpful to both management and unions for contract negotiations, as well as for resolving grievances and jurisdictional disputes.

Engineering Design and Methods Improvement.   To design equipment to perform a specific task reliably and efficiently, engineers must understand exactly the capabilities of the operator and what he or she is expected to do. Job analysis provides this understanding. Similarly, any improvements or proposed new working methods must be evaluated relative to their impact on overall job objectives.

Job Design.   As with methods improvement, changes in the way work is accomplished must be evaluated through a job analysis, focusing on the tasks to be done and on the behaviors required of the people doing the tasks.

Safety.   Frequently, in the course of doing a job analysis, unsafe conditions (environmental conditions or personal habits) are discovered and thus may lead to safety improvements.

Vocational Guidance and Rehabilitation Counseling.   Comprehensive job descriptions and specifications enable men and women to make informed decisions regarding career choices.

Job Classification Systems.   Selection, training, and pay systems are often keyed to job classification systems, also referred to as "job families." Without job analysis information, it is impossible to determine reliably the structure of the relationships among jobs in an organization.

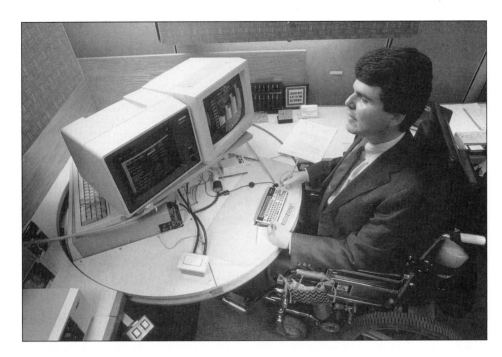

Job analysis identifies essential functions of jobs, as well as the personal characteristics necessary to do them.

Dynamic Characteristics of Jobs

There are two basic things to keep in mind in thinking about what job analysis is and what it should accomplish:

One is the **dynamic characteristics of jobs.** As time goes on, everything changes, and so do jobs. This has been recognized only recently; the popular view of a job was that what it required did not change; a job was a static thing, designed to be consistent although the workers who passed through it were different. Now we know that for a job to produce efficient output, it must change according to the workers who do it. In fact, the nature of jobs might change for three reasons:

- **Time**. For example, lifeguards, ski instructors, and accountants do different things at different times of the year.
- **People**. Particularly in management jobs but also in teaching or coaching, the job is what the incumbent makes of it.
- **Environment and context**. Technology changes jobs—for example, consider how the Internet has changed the jobs of purchasing agents, or how personal computers have changed the jobs of clerk-typists. Thus, a recent job analysis of clerk-typists by the city of Los Angeles revealed that the ability to manipulate electronic files in a Windows-based environment has become more important than typing speed![5] Research also has shown that for the same job performed in different locations, ratings of what people do and the time they spend on various tasks may differ depending on the context in which the work is performed.[6] Context includes, among other things, the extent of use of technology, the extent to which rules and procedures govern work activities, and the overall organizational culture. Job analyses should reflect the context in which work is done, and they should be updated any time that there are significant changes in jobs.

Two, job analysis comprises job specifications and people requirements that should reflect *minimally* acceptable qualifications for job holders. Frequently they do not, reflecting instead a profile of the *ideal* job holder.

How are job specifications set? Typically by consensus among experts—immediate supervisors, job incumbents, and job analysts. Such a procedure is professionally acceptable, but care must be taken to distinguish between required and desirable qualifications. The term required denotes inflexibility; that is, it is assumed that without this qualification, an individual absolutely would be unable to do the job. Desirable implies flexibility; it is "nice to have" this ability, but it is not a "need to have" (see job dimension 2 in the chapter-opening vignette). To be sure, required qualifications will exist in almost all jobs, but care must be exercised in establishing them, for such requirements must meet a higher standard.

LEGALITIES

JOB ANALYSIS AND THE AMERICANS WITH DISABILITIES ACT OF 1990

Job analyses are not legally required under the ADA, but sound professional practice suggests that they be done for three reasons. One, the law makes it clear that job applicants must be able to understand what the essential functions of a job are before they can respond to the question "Can you perform the essential functions of the job for which you are applying?" Essential functions are those that require relatively more time and have serious consequences of error or nonperformance associated with them. A function may be essential because the reason the position exists at all is to perform that function (e.g., a baggage handler at an airport must be able to lift bags weighing up to 70 pounds repeatedly throughout an 8-hour shift). Alternatively, the function may be so highly specialized that it cannot be shifted to others (e.g., in a nuclear power plant, a nuclear engineer must perform inspections, often by crawling through tight spaces). Job analysis is a systematic procedure that can help to identify essential job functions.

Two, existing job analyses may need to be updated to reflect additional dimensions of jobs, namely, the physical demands, environmental demands, and mental abilities required to perform essential functions. Figure 5–2 shows a portion of a checklist of physical demands.

Three, once job analyses are updated as described, a summary of the results is normally prepared in writing in the form of a job description. What may work even better under the ADA, however, is a video job description, to provide concrete evidence to applicants of the physical demands, environmental demands (e.g., temperatures, noise level, working space), or mental demands (e.g., irate customers calling with complaints) of jobs. Candidates who are unable to perform a job because of a physical or mental disability may self-select out, thereby minimizing the likelihood of a legal challenge.

To ensure job-relatedness, be able to link required knowledge, skills, abilities, and other characteristics (measures of which candidates actually are assessed on) to essential job functions. Finally, recognize that under the ADA it is imperative to distinguish "essential" from "nonessential" functions *prior* to announcing a job or interviewing applicants.[7] If a candidate with a disability can

Figure 5–2

Portion of a physical abilities checklist.

Use the symbols below to rate the following activities:

NP   Not present   Activity does not exist

O   Occasionally   Activity exists up to 1/3 of the time

F   Frequently   Activity exists from 1/3 to 2/3 of the time

C   Constantly   Activity exists 2/3 or more of the time

1a. Strength (also enter the percentage of time spent in each activity)

_____ Standing _____ percent

_____ Walking _____ percent

_____ Sitting _____ percent

1b. Also indicate the number of pounds that must be lifted, carried, pushed, or pulled.

_____ Lifting _____ (weight)

_____ Carrying _____ (weight)

_____ Pushing _____ (weight)

_____ Pulling _____ (weight)

2. Climbing _____

3. Balancing _____

4. Stooping _____

5. Kneeling _____

6. Crouching _____

7. Crawling _____

8. Reaching _____

9. Talking (Ordinary) _____ (Other) _____

10. Hearing (Ordinary conversation) _____ (Other) _____

perform the essential functions of a job and is hired, the employer must be willing to make **reasonable accommodations** to enable the person to work.[8] Here are some examples that the ADA defines as "reasonable" accommodation efforts:

- Restructuring a job so that someone else does the nonessential tasks a person with a disability cannot do.
- Modifying work hours or work schedules so that a person with a disability can commute during off-peak periods.
- Reassigning a worker who becomes disabled to a vacant position.
- Acquiring or modifying equipment or devices (e.g., a telecommunications device for the deaf).
- Adjusting or modifying examinations, training materials, or HR policies.
- Providing qualified readers or interpreters.

From a Task-Based to a Process-Based Organization of Work

Traditional task-based "jobs" were packaged into clusters of similar tasks and assigned to specialist workers. Today many firms have no reason to package work that way. Instead, they are unbundling tasks into broader chunks of work that change over time. Such shifting clusters of tasks make it difficult to define a "job," at least in the traditional sense. Practices such as flextime, job sharing, and telecommuting, not to mention use of temporary workers, part-timers, and consultants, have compounded the definitional problem.

At the same time, there is pressure from the online recruiting community to standardize descriptions of work and applicant credentials. Applicants are demanding standardization so that descriptions and titles of their work will be understood by employers they are contacting.[9] At least some firms, however, are moving from a task-based toward a process-based organization of work. A **process** is a collection of activities (such as procurement, order fulfillment, product development, or credit issuance), that takes one or more kinds of input and creates an output that is of value to a customer.[10] Customers may be internal or external. Individual tasks are important parts of the process, but the process itself cuts across organizational boundaries and traditional functions, such as engineering, production, marketing, and finance.

Consider credit issuance as an example. Instead of the separate jobs of credit checker and pricer, the two may be combined into one "deal structurer." Such integrated processes may cut response time and increase efficiency and productivity. Bell Atlantic created a "case team"—a group of people who have among them all of the skills necessary to handle an installation order. Members of the team—who previously were located in different departments and in different geographical areas—were brought together into a single unit and given total responsibility for installing the equipment. Such a process operates, on average, ten times faster than the assembly-line version it replaces. Bell Atlantic, for example, reduced the time it takes to install a high-speed digital service link from 30 days to three.[11]

Employees involved in the process are responsible for ensuring that customers' requirements are met on time and with no defects, and they are empowered to experiment in ways that will cut cycle time and reduce costs. Result: less supervision is needed, while workers take on broader responsibilities and a wider purview of activities. Moreover, the kinds of activities that each worker does are likely to shift over time.

In a process-based organization of work, three things are important:

- Identification of job specifications (i.e., the personal characteristics—knowledge, skills, abilities, and other characteristics—necessary to do the work).
- Identification of the environment, context, and social aspects of work.
- A change in emphasis, from describing jobs to describing roles.

Keep these ideas in mind as you continue reading about the analysis of jobs and work.

How Do We Study Job Requirements?

A number of methods are available to study jobs. At the outset it is important to note that no one of them is sufficient. Rather, it is important to use a combination of them to obtain a total picture of the task and the physical, mental, social, and environmental demands of a job. Here are five common methods of job analysis:

1. **Job performance.** With this approach, an analyst actually does the job under study to get firsthand exposure to what it demands.

2. **Observation.** The analyst simply observes a worker or group of workers doing a job. Without interfering, the analyst records the what, why, and how of the various parts of the job. Usually this information is recorded in a standard format.

3. **Interview.** In many jobs in which it is not possible for the analyst actually to perform the job (e.g., airline pilot) or where observation is impractical (e.g., architect), it is necessary to rely on workers' own descriptions of what they do, why, and how. As with recordings of observations, use a standard format to collect input from all workers sampled to interview. In this way all questions and responses can be restricted to job-related topics. More importantly, standardization makes it possible to compare what different people are saying about the job in question.

4. **Critical incidents**. These are vignettes comprising brief actual reports that illustrate particularly effective or ineffective worker behaviors. For example:

   > On January 14, Mr. Vin, the restaurant's wine steward, was asked about an obscure bottle of wine. Without hesitation, he described the place of vintage and bottling, the meaning of the symbols on the label, and the characteristics of the grapes in the year of vintage.

   After collecting many of these little incidents from knowledgeable individuals, it is possible to abstract and categorize them according to the general job area they describe. The end result is a fairly clear picture of actual job requirements.

5. **Structured questionnaires.** These questionnaires list tasks, behaviors (e.g., negotiating, coordinating, using both hands), or both. Tasks focus on *what* gets done. This is a job-oriented approach. Behaviors, on the other hand, focus on *how* a job is done. This is a worker-oriented, or ability-requirements, approach. Workers rate each task or behavior in terms of whether or not it is performed, and, if it is, they rate characteristics such as frequency, importance, level of difficulty, and relationship to overall performance. The ratings provide a basis for scoring the questionnaires and for developing a profile of actual job requirements.[12] The ability to represent job content in terms of numbers allows relatively precise comparisons across different jobs.[13] One of the most popular structured questionnaires is the Position Analysis Questionnaire (PAQ).

   The PAQ is a behavior-oriented job analysis questionnaire.[14] It consists of 194 items that fall into the following categories:

   - **Information input.** Where and how the worker gets the information to do her or his job.
   - **Mental processes.** The reasoning, planning, and decision making involved in a job.
   - **Work output.** Physical activities as well as the tools or devices used.
   - **Relationships with other persons.**
   - **Job context.** Physical and social.

Figure 5–3

Sample PAQ
items.

	Code	*Importance to This Job*
	DNA	Does not apply
	1	Very minor
	2	Low
	3	Average
	4	High
	5	Extreme

5.3 Personal and Social Aspects

This section includes various personal and social aspects of jobs. Indicate by code the *importance* of these aspects as part of the job.

148 | I Civic obligations (because of the job, the worker assumes, or is expected to assume, certain civil obligations or responsibilities)

149 | I Frustrating situations (job situations in which attempts to deal with problems or achieve job objectives are obstructed or hindered, and may thus contribute to frustration on the part of the worker)

150 | I Strained personal contacts (dealing with individuals or groups in "unpleasant" or "strained" situations, for example, certain aspects of police work, certain types of negotiations, handling certain mental patients)

- **Other job characteristics.** For example, apparel, work continuity, licensing, hours, and responsibility.

The items provide either for checking a job element if it applies or rating it on a scale, such as in terms of importance, time, or difficulty. An example of some PAQ items is shown in Figure 5–3. While structured job analysis questionnaires are growing in popularity, the newest applications are web-based, and use company intranets and computer-generated graphics to help illustrate similarities and differences across jobs and organizational units. An additional benefit is that the products of the job analysis are available anytime, anywhere, to anyone who has access to the company's intranet.[15]

The preceding five methods of job analysis represent the popular ones in use today. Table 5–1 considers the pros and cons of each method. Regardless of the method used, the workers providing job information to the analyst must be experienced and knowledgeable about the jobs in question.[16] However, there seem to be no differences in the quality of information provided by members of different gender or race/ethnic subgroups,[17] or by high as opposed to low performers.[18] Nevertheless, it may well be that in relatively autonomous jobs, such as those of stockbrokers, high and low performers allocate their time quite differently.[19] In terms of the types of data actually collected, the most popular methods today are observation, interviews, and structured questionnaires.

Analyzing Managerial Jobs

Analysis of managerial jobs requires some special considerations. One is that managers tend to adjust the content of their jobs to fit their own style rather than to fit the needs of the work to be done. The result of this is that when it comes to querying them about their work, they will describe what they actually do, having lost sight of what they should be doing. Another consideration is that it is difficult to identify what a manager does over time because her or his activity differs from time to time, perhaps one activity one month or week or day, and then some other activity the following day or week or month. Indeed, managers' activities change throughout the day. As immediate situations or general

Table 5–1

ADVANTAGES AND DISADVANTAGES OF FIVE POPULAR JOB ANALYSIS METHODS

Method	Advantages	Disadvantages
Job performance	With this method there is exposure to actual job tasks, as well as to the physical, environmental, and social demands of the job. It is appropriate for jobs that can be learned in a relatively short period of time.	This method is inappropriate for jobs that require extensive training or are hazardous to perform.
Observation	Direct exposure to jobs can provide a richer, deeper understanding of job requirements than workers' descriptions of what they do.	If the work in question is primarily mental, observations alone may reveal little useful information. Critical, yet rare, job requirements (e.g., "copes with emergencies") simply may not be observed.
Interviews	This method can provide information about standard as well as nonstandard and mental work. Since the worker is also his or her own observer, he or she can report on activities that would not be observed often. In short, the worker can provide the analyst with information that might not be available from any other source.	Workers may be suspicious of interviewers and their motives; interviewers may ask ambiguous questions. Thus distortion of information (either as a result of honest misunderstanding or as a result of purposeful misrepresentation) is a real possibility. For this reason, the interview should never be used as the sole job analysis method.
Critical incidents	This method focuses directly on what people do in their jobs, and thus it provides insight into job dynamics. Since the behaviors in question are observable and measurable, information derived from this method can be used for most possible applications of job analysis.	It takes considerable time to gather, abstract, and categorize the incidents. Also, since by definition the incidents describe particularly effective or ineffective behavior, it may be difficult to develop a profile of average job behavior—our main objective in job analysis.
Structured questionnaires	This method is generally cheaper and quicker to administer than other methods. Questionnaires can be completed off the job, thus avoiding lost productive time. Also, where there are large numbers of job incumbents, this method allows an analyst to survey all of them, thus providing a breadth of coverage that is impossible to obtain otherwise. Furthermore, such survey data often can be quantified and processed by computer, which opens up vast analytical possibilities.	Questionnaires are often time consuming and expensive to develop. Rapport between analyst and respondent is not possible unless the analyst is present to explain items and clarify to misunderstandings. Such an impersonal approach may have adverse effects on respondent cooperation and motivation.

Table 5–2

JOB ANALYSIS METHODS AND THE PURPOSE OR PURPOSES *BEST* SUITED TO EACH

Method	Job descriptions	Development of tests	Development of interviews	Job evaluation	Training design	Performance appraisal design	Career path planning
Job performance		X	X		X	X	
Observation	X	X	X				
Interviews	X	X	X	X	X	X	
Critical incidents	X	X	X		X	X	
Questionnaires:							
Task checklists	X	X	X	X	X	X	
Behavior checklists			X	X	X	X	X

environments change, so will the content of a manager's job, and each such change will affect managers differently in different functional areas, different geographical areas, and different organizational levels (e.g., first-line supervisors versus divisional vice presidents). To analyze them, we must identify and measure the fundamental dimensions along which they differ and change. That is, we must identify what managers actually do on their jobs, and then we must specify behavioral differences due to time, person, and environmental changes.

The Management Position Description Questionnaire (MPDQ) is a 197-item, behavior-based instrument for describing, comparing, classifying, and evaluating executive positions in terms of their content.[20] An example of one portion of the MPDQ is shown in Figure 5–4.

Job Analysis: Relating Method to Purpose

Given such a wide choice among available job analysis methods, the combination of methods to use is the one that best fits the *purpose* of the job analysis research (e.g., staffing, training design, performance appraisal). Table 5–2 is a matrix that suggests some possible match-ups between job analysis methods and various purposes. The table simply illustrates the relative strengths of each method when used for each purpose. For example, the job performance method of job analysis is most appropriate for the development of tests and interviews, training design, and performance appraisal system design.

OCCUPATIONAL INFORMATION

The U.S. Department of Labor published the *Dictionary of Occupational Titles (DOT)* in the 1930s to help deal with the economic crisis of the Great Depression by helping the new public employment system to link skill supply and skill demand. The last version of the DOT, published in 1991, contained descriptive information on more than 12,000 jobs.[21] However, information was job

Part 8
Contacts

To achieve organizational goals, managers and consultants may be required to communicate with employees at many levels within the company and with influential people outside of the company. This part of the questionnaire addresses the nature and level of these contacts.

Directions:

Step 1—Significance

For each contact and purpose of contact noted, indicate how significant a part of your position each represents by assigning a number between 0 to 4 to each block. Remember to consider both the importance and frequency of the contact.

0–Definitely not a part of the position.

1–Minor significance to the position.

2–Moderate significance to the position.

3–Substantial significance to the position.

4–Crucial significance to the position.

Step 2—Other Contacts

If you have any other contacts, please elaborate on their nature and purpose below.

_____
_____
_____
_____
_____
_____
_____
_____
_____
_____
_____
_____

Purpose of Contact

	Share Information regarding past, present, or anticipated activities or decisions.	Influence others to act or decide in a manner consistent with your objectives	Direct the plans, activities, or decisions of others
1. Executives.	10	11	12
2. Group managers (managers report to position).	13	14	15
3. Managers (supervisors report to position).	16	14	18
4. Supervisors (no supervisors report to position).	19	20	21
5. Professional/administrative exempt.	22	23	24
6. Clerical or support staff (nonexempt).	25	26	27
7. Other nonexempt employees.	28	29	30

	Provide/gather Information or promote the organization or its products/services.	Resolve problems.	Sell products/ services.	Negotiate contracts/ settlements, etc.
8. Customers of the company's products or services.	31	32	33	34
9. Representatives of vendors/subcontractors.	35	36	37	38
10. Representatives of other companies or professional organizations and institutions.	39	40	41	42
11. Representatives of labor unions.	43	44	45	46
12. Representatives of influential community organizations.	47	48	49	50
13. Individuals such as applicants or shareholders.	51	52	53	54
14. Representatives of the media, including the press, radio, television, etc.	55	56	57	58
15. National, state, or regional elected government representatives and/or lobbyists.	59	60	61	62
16. Local government officials and/or representatives of departments such as customs, tax, revenue, traffic, procurement, law enforcement, and environment.	63	64	65	66

Figure 5–5

The O*Net
Content Model.
(*Source:* N. G. Peterson, M. D. Mumford, W. C. Borman, P. R. Jeanneret, E. A. Fleishman, K. Y. Levin, M. A. Campion, M. S. Mayfield, F. P. Morgeson, K. Pearlman, M. K. Gowing, A. R. Lancaster, M. B. Silver, & D. M. Dye. Understanding work using the Occupational Information Network (O*Net): Implications for practice and research. *Personnel Psychology, 54,* 2001, p. 458.)

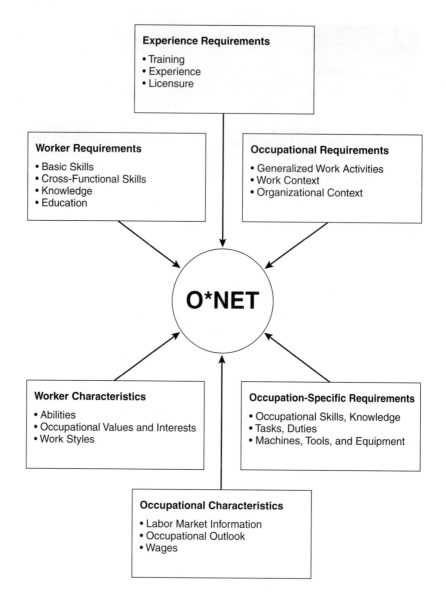

Experience Requirements
• Training
• Experience
• Licensure

Worker Requirements
• Basic Skills
• Cross-Functional Skills
• Knowledge
• Education

Occupational Requirements
• Generalized Work Activities
• Work Context
• Organizational Context

O*NET

Worker Characteristics
• Abilities
• Occupational Values and Interests
• Work Styles

Occupation-Specific Requirements
• Occupational Skills, Knowledge
• Tasks, Duties
• Machines, Tools, and Equipment

Occupational Characteristics
• Labor Market Information
• Occupational Outlook
• Wages

specific, and did not provide a cross-job organizing structure that would allow comparisons of similarities and differences across jobs. Also, by focusing on tasks, or what gets done, the DOT did not indicate directly what personal characteristics workers must have to perform the job, or the context in which the job was performed. To deal with these problems, the U.S. Department of Labor sponsored a large-scale research project called the Occupational Informational Network (O*Net), which incorporates the 60 years of information about jobs and work since the DOT was developed. **O*Net** is a national occupational information system that provides comprehensive descriptions of the attributes of workers and jobs. It is based on four broad design principles: (1) multiple descriptor domains that provide "multiple windows" into the world of work, (2) a common language of work and worker descriptors that covers the entire spectrum of occupations, (3) description of occupations based on a taxonomy from broad to specific, and (4) a comprehensive content model that integrates the previous three principles.

Multiple Windows. These are necessary to allow people to work with the kinds of descriptors that are most useful for the questions they are asking. These descriptors include tasks, abilities, skills, areas of knowledge, and work context. Such organization allows one to ask how specific skills are related to different types of work activities.

Common Language. Since job-specific information can change rapidly, the O*Net uses general descriptors that are more stable. O*Net permits job-specific information, but does so within the organizing structure of broader descriptors, such as generalized work activities (as in the PAQ) like "selling or influencing others" and "assisting or caring for others."

Taxonomies and Hierarchies of Occupational Descriptors. This approach to occupational classification allows information to be summarized and assigned to fewer categories. Because O*Net is concerned with both positions and occupations, a broad range of descriptors was developed. For example, some descriptors focus on key skills needed to perform specific jobs, while others are concerned with broader organizational and contextual factors, such as organizational climate. Descriptors within each content domain were then arranged in a hierarchy.

The O*Net Content Model. This model incorporated the three design principles—multiple windows, common language, and hierarchical taxonomies—to include the major types of cross-job descriptors and to provide a general descriptive framework of occupational information. Figure 5–5 shows the six major domains of the O*Net Content Model and the major categories within each one. Additional references provide more in-depth information about the O*Net system.[22]

THE RELATIONSHIP OF JOB ANALYSIS TO WORKFORCE PLANNING

Having identified the behavioral requirements of jobs, the organization is in a position to identify the numbers of employees and the skills required to do those jobs, at least in the short term. Further, an understanding of available competencies is necessary to allow the organization to plan for the changes to new jobs required by corporate goals. This process is known as workforce planning (WP). It refers to planning for people who will do the organization's work, but who may not be its employees.[23] These are "make-versus-buy" decisions that have become more important in firms as a result of globalization, outsourcing, employee leasing, new technologies, organizational restructuring, and diversity in the workforce. All these factors produce uncertainty—and since it's difficult to be efficient in an uncertain environment, firms develop business and workforce plans to reduce the impact of uncertainty. The plans may be short-term or long-term in nature, but to have a meaningful impact on future operations, it is important to link the business and workforce plans tightly to each other. To understand why, let's consider how WP in the new millennium differs from WP in earlier time periods.

Workforce Planning in the New Millennium

In the past, WP tended to be a reactive process because business needs usually defined human resource needs. For example, in the past a bank might decide to acquire a rival because it made good economic sense. Only after that decision was made would the bank worry about deploying talent in the two firms and integrating the two workforces. Today, major changes in business, economic, and social environments are forcing organizations to integrate business planning with WP and to adopt a longer-term, proactive perspective.[24] For example, according to the vice president of human resources at Liz Claiborne, Inc.:

> Human resources is part of the strategic [business] planning process. It's part of policy development, line extension planning, and merger and acquisition processes. Little is done in the company that doesn't involve us in the planning, policy, or finalization stages of any deal.[25]

Change, as well as the pace of change, is accelerating. Thus at Cisco Systems, executives think not in terms of calendar years, but rather in terms of Internet years, where each calendar year is equivalent to 7 Internet years. Based on this reality, Chief Executive John Chambers says, "Instead of looking at a one-year plan, we began looking at every quarter and adjusting our plan up or down.[26] To address human resource concerns systematically, firms now recognize that they need short-term as well as long-term solutions. As usually practiced, job analysis identifies qualities that employees need to perform existing jobs. Yet rapid changes in technology mean that the jobs of the future will differ radically from those of the present.[27] Methods are available now for identifying skill and ability requirements for jobs that do not yet exist. These are known as future-oriented, or "strategic" job analyses.[28] They can provide additional, relevant information to general business plans. General business plans, in turn, may be strategic or tactical in nature. Let's consider them further in the following section.

Types of Plans: Strategic, Tactical, and Workforce

Strategic planning is not about how to position products and businesses within an industry. Rather, it's about changing industry rules or creating tomorrow's industries, much as Wal-Mart Stores, Inc., did in retailing or Charles Schwab did in the brokerage and mutual fund businesses.[29] Strategic planning for an organization includes:

Defining philosophy. Why does the organization exist? What unique contribution does it make?

Formulating statements of identity, purpose, and objectives. What is the overall mission of the organization? What are its goals? Are the missions and goals of strategic business units consistent with the mission of the organization?

Evaluating strengths, weaknesses, and competitive dynamics. What factors, internal or external, may enhance or inhibit the ability of the organization to achieve its objectives?

Determining design. What are the components of the organization, what should they do, and how should they relate to one another, toward achieving objectives and fulfilling the organization's mission?

Developing strategies. How will the objectives, at every level, be achieved? How will they be measured, not only in quantitative terms of what is to be achieved, but also in terms of time?

Devising programs. What will be the components of each program, and how will the effectiveness of each program be measured?

The biggest benefit of strategic planning is its emphasis on growth, for it encourages managers to look for new opportunities, rather than simply cutting more workers. But the danger of strategic planning is that it may lock companies into a particular vision of the future—one that may not come to pass. This poses a dilemma: how to plan for the future when the future changes so quickly. The answer is to make the planning process more democratic. Instead of relegating strategic planning to a separate staff—as in the past—it needs to include a wide range of people, from line managers to customers to suppliers. Top managers must listen, and must be prepared to shift plans in midstream, if conditions demand it. This is exactly the approach that Cisco Systems takes. Cisco is not wedded to any particular technology, for it recognizes that customers are the arbiters of choice. It listens carefully to its customers, and then offers solutions that customers want. Sometimes this means acquiring other companies to provide the technology that will satisfy customer demands. Indeed, Cisco has acquired more than 40 companies in the last decade. This mindset enables Cisco to move in whatever directions that markets and customers dictate.[30]

Strategic planning differs considerably from short-range tactical (or operational) planning. It involves fundamental decisions about the very nature of the business. Strategic planning may result in new business acquisitions, divestitures of current (profitable or unprofitable) product lines, new capital investments, or new management approaches.[31] It provides direction and scope to tactical planning.

Tactical planning, also known as operational planning, addresses issues associated with the growth of current or new operations, as well as with any specific problems that might disrupt the pace of planned, growth. Purchasing new or additional office equipment to enhance efficiency (e.g., computer hardware or software), coping with the recall of a defective product (e.g., defective brakes in cars), and dealing with the need to design tamper-proof bottle caps (e.g., in the pharmaceutical industry) are examples of tactical planning problems. Beyond the obvious difference in the time frames distinguishing strategic planning and tactical planning, the other difference between the two is the degree of change resulting from the planning—and hence the degree of impact on workforce planning.

Workforce planning parallels the plans for the business as a whole. WP focuses on questions such as: What do the proposed business strategies imply with respect to human resources? What kinds of internal and external constraints will (or do) we face? For example, restrictive work rules in a collective bargaining contract are an internal constraint, while a projected shortfall in the supply of college graduate electrical engineers (relative to the demand for them by employers) is an external constraint. What are the implications for staffing, compensation practices, training and development, and management succession? What can be done in the short run (tactically) to prepare for long-term (strategic) needs?

More on Workforce Planning

Although WP means different things to different people, general agreement exists on its ultimate objective—namely, the most effective use of scarce talent in the interests of the worker and the organization. Thus we may define WP broadly as an effort to anticipate future business and environmental demands on an organization, and to provide qualified people to fulfill that business and satisfy those demands.[32] This general view suggests several specific, interrelated activities that together comprise a WP system. They include:

- **A talent inventory** to assess current human resources (skills, abilities, and potential) and to analyze how they are currently being used.
- **A workforce forecast** to predict future people requirements (the number of workers needed, the number expected to be available based on labor market characteristics, the skills mix required, and internal versus external labor supply).
- **Action plans** to enlarge the pool of people qualified to fill the projected vacancies through such actions as recruitment, selection, training, placement, transfer, promotion, development, and compensation.
- **Control and evaluation** to provide feedback on the overall effectiveness of the human resource planning system by monitoring the degree of attainment of HR objectives.

THE RELATIONSHIP OF WORKFORCE PLANNING TO STRATEGIC AND TACTICAL PLANNING

A variety of WP applications exists.[33] For example, WP itself can be strategic (long-term and general) or tactical (short-term and specific). It may be done organizationwide, or it may be restricted to divisions, departments, or any common employee groups. It may be carried out on a recurring basis (e.g., annually) or only sporadically (e.g., when launching a new product line or at the outset of a capital expansion project). Regardless of its specific application, almost all experts agree that if WP is to be genuinely effective, it must be linked with the different levels of general business planning, not as an end or goal in and of itself, but rather as a means to the end of building more competitive organizations. Line managers direct the overall process. When line managers perceive that HR practices help them achieve their goals, they are more likely to initiate and support WP efforts. Furthermore, the process raises important human resource questions.[34] The relationship between business planning and WP is depicted in Figure 5–6.

The long-range perspective (2 to 5 years or longer, depending on the firm and the industry) of strategic planning flows naturally into the middle-range

Figure 5–6

Impact of three levels of business planning on workforce planning.

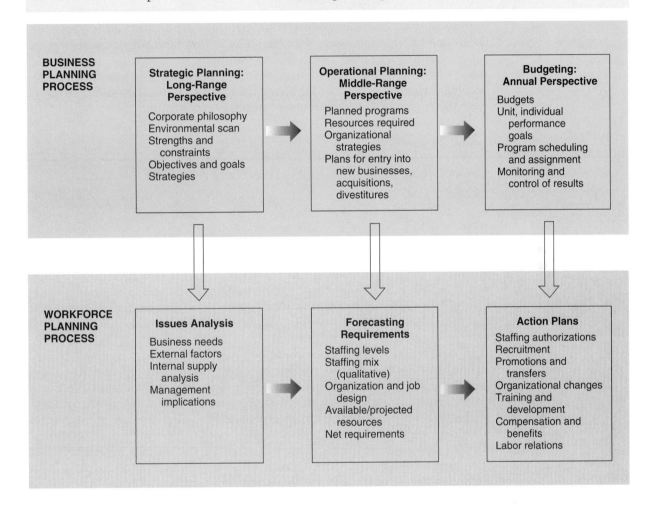

perspective (1 to 2 years) of operational planning. Annual budgeting decisions provide specific timetables, allocations of resources, and standards for implementing strategic and operational plans. As the time frame shortens, planning details become increasingly specific.

At the level of strategic planning, WP is concerned with such issues as assessing the management implications of future business needs, assessing factors external to the firm (e.g., demographic and social trends), and gauging the internal supply of employees over the long run. The focus here is to analyze issues, not to make detailed projections.

At the level of operational, or tactical, planning, WP is concerned with detailed forecasts of employee supply (internal and external to the organization) and employee demand (numbers needed at some future time period). Based on the forecasts, specific action plans can be undertaken. These may involve recruitment, changes in incentives, promotions, training, or transfers. Procedures must be established to control and evaluate progress toward targeted objectives.

Of necessity, Figure 5–6 is an oversimplification. In practice, business objectives (needs) may be long or short term in nature, and workforce forecasts and programs (action plans) must address both types. As a simple example, consider that the personal characteristics of managers that lead to success during the start-up and early growth phases of an organization's life cycle (i.e., short- and intermediate-term horizons) may inhibit performance as the organization matures and stabilizes (i.e., the long-term horizon), but the same personal characteristics may be needed to reinvigorate the organization if it becomes sluggish in responding to the demands of the marketplace. To appreciate this, consider the experience of Apple Computer, Inc.

COMPANY EXAMPLE

CHANGING BUSINESS AND HR NEEDS AT APPLE COMPUTER, INC.

Apple experienced dramatic changes as a company as it moved from an entrepreneurial start-up in the 1970s, through a high-growth phase in the 1980s tied to its Macintosh computers, to its status as a mature, stable competitor in the globally competitive personal computer market in the new millennium. In the 1970s, Apple was launched by technical whizzes and young dreamers, led by Steven Jobs. The major objective was to produce a commercially viable product. In the 1980s, Apple hired John Sculley as CEO to provide marketing savvy and technological vision as the company showed the masses that computing with a graphical user interface could be fun. The Macintosh line had arrived, as had the need for professional marketing expertise. Unfortunately, Sculley's decision not to license the Macintosh operating system in the mid-1980s cost Apple an estimated $20–$40 billion in value. In the 1990s, therefore, Apple realized that it needed a CEO with a proven ability to cut costs, to shorten product development cycles, and to penetrate new markets. When CEO Gilbert Amelio stumbled in Apple's comeback attempt, Steven Jobs returned, to lead the company—again. He paid himself $1 a year from 1997 through 2000, and then was rewarded handsomely for saving the company. Jobs recognized that Apple's challenge in the new millennium, as it had been in the 1970s and 1980s, was to make and market commercially viable products—in a business environment that was totally different from the 1970s environment in which he began.[35]

As Figure 5–6 shows, workforce planning focuses on firm-level responses to people-related business issues over multiple time horizons. What are some examples of such issues, and how can managers identify them? People-related business concerns, or issues, might include, for example, "What types of managers will we need to run the business in the early 21st century, and how do we make sure we'll have them?" At a broader level, issues include the impact of rapid technological change, more complex organizations (in terms of products, locations, customers, and markets), more frequent responses to external forces such as legislation and litigation, demographic changes, and increasing multinational competition. In this scenario, environmental changes drive issues, issues drive actions, and actions encompass programs and processes used to

Human Resource Issue	Analysis: Evidence Options
What is the HR problem, gap, or opportunity identified as a result of changes in the following? • Business environment • Business strategy • Organizational circumstances	What are the dimensions of the issue? • Evidence of the issue • Scope • Coverage/applicability • Potential business impact • Alternative solutions and their pros and cons

Management Actions/Resources	Measures/Targets
What course of action will be implemented? • Strategy of 1–2 years • Specific action programs • Responsibility assigned • Timing for completion • Financial and staff resources required	How will the results be measured? • Outcomes • Measures/evidence • Target levels

Figure 5–7

Data to include on an HR strategy worksheet. (*Source:* R. S. Schuler & J. W. Walker, Human resources strategy: Focusing on issues and actions, *Organizational Dynamics*, Summer 1990, p. 14.)

design and implement them.[36] Issues themselves may be identified with the aid of an HR strategy worksheet, such as that shown in Figure 5–7.

Realistically, HR concerns become business concerns and are dealt with only when they affect the line manager's ability to function effectively. Such concerns may result from an immediate issue, such as downsizing or a labor shortage, or from a longer-term issue that can be felt as if it were an immediate issue, such as management development and succession planning.[37] On the other hand, people-related business issues such as workforce diversity, changing requirements for managerial skills, no-growth assumptions, mergers, retraining needs, and health and safety are issues that relate directly to the competitiveness of an organization and threaten its ability to survive. In short, progressive firms recognize that people-related business issues will have powerful impacts on their strategic business and workforce planning for the foreseeable future.

HR Objectives—Foundation for Workforce Planning

Objectives can be expressed either in behavioral terms ("By the third week of training, you should be able to do these things . . . ") or in end-result terms ("By the end of the next fiscal year, five new retail stores should be open, and each should be staffed by a manager, an assistant manager, and three clerks"). In the context of cost control in compensation, for example, the following questions should prove useful in setting human resource objectives:

- What level will the wage rate for an occupation be?
- How many people will we employ?
- How much more will our firm have to pay to attract more employees?
- How would the number of people our company employs change if the wage were lower? If it were higher?

HR objectives vary according to such things as the type of environment a company operates in, its strategic and tactical plans, and the current design of jobs and employee work behaviors. As examples, consider some of McDonald's human resource objectives: Define jobs narrowly so that they are easy to learn in a short period of time; pay minimum wages to most nonmanagement employees so that the cost of turnover is low; design jobs to minimize decision making by the human operator (e.g., use computer-controlled cooking operations, and item labeling on cash registers).[38]

To be sure, objectives will differ depending on the time frame they represent. Examples of short-term HR objectives include increasing the breadth and depth of the applicant pool, increasing the length of time new hires stay with the organization, and decreasing the amount of time undesirable hires stay with the organization. In the longer term, HR objectives are more likely to include readjusting employees' skills, attitudes, and behaviors to fit major changes in the needs of the business. This happened, for example, as heavily regulated industries, such as cable television, were given the freedom to compete for business in open markets. Different kinds of competencies were needed. Of course, management practices also must change to fit changes in the needs of employees.

In sum, differences in the types of objectives established for the short and long term reflect differences in the types of changes that are feasible with 2 or 3 additional years of time. Setting human resource objectives is art as much as it is science. It requires conscious forethought based on the kind of future the firm wants to create for itself. It requires teamwork, and it cannot be left to serendipity.

TALENT INVENTORIES

Once HR objectives are set, it then becomes useful to compare the numbers, skills, and experience of the current workforce with those desired at some future time period. A talent inventory facilitates assessment of the current workforce; forecasts of workforce supply and demand help to determine future needs. In combination these tools provide powerful planning information for the development of action programs. In both large and small organizations, such information is often computerized. When combined with other databases, it can be used to form a complete human resource information system (HRIS) that is useful in a variety of situations.[39]

Information such as the following is typically included in a profile developed for each manager or non-manager:

- Current position information.
- Previous positions in the company.
- Other significant work experience (e.g., at other companies or in the military).
- Education (including degrees, licenses, and certifications).
- Language skills and relevant international experience.
- Training and development programs attended.
- Community or industry leadership responsibilities.
- Current and past performance appraisal data.
- Disciplinary actions.
- Awards received.

Information provided by individuals may also be included. A major retailer, for example, includes factors that may limit an employee's mobility (e.g., health and family circumstances), as well as willingness to relocate. IBM in-

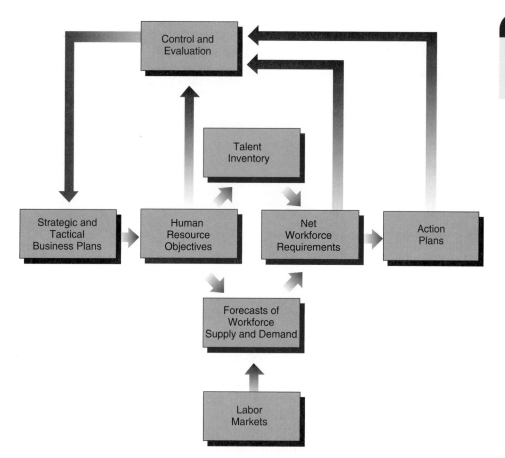

Figure 5–8

An integrated workforce planning system.

cludes the individual's expressed preference for future assignments and locations, including interest in staff or line positions in other IBM locations and divisions.[40]

Talent inventories and workforce forecasts must complement each other; an inventory of present talent is not particularly useful for planning purposes unless it can be analyzed in terms of future workforce requirements. On the other hand, a forecast of workforce requirements is useless unless it can be evaluated relative to the current and projected future supply of workers available internally. Only at that time, when we have a clear understanding of the projected surpluses or deficits of employees in terms of their numbers, their skills, and their experience, does it make sense to initiate action plans to rectify projected problems. Figure 5–8 illustrates such an integrated WP system.

Although secondary uses of the talent inventory data may emerge, it is important to specify the primary uses at the concept-development stage. Doing so provides direction and scope regarding who and what kinds of data should be included.

Some common uses of a talent inventory are: identification of candidates for promotion, management succession planning, assignment to special projects, transfer, training, workforce diversity planning and reporting, compensation planning, career planning, and organizational analysis.

Figure 5–9		
The hottest job prospects: fastest-growing occupations by level of education and training, 1998–2008. *(Source: Occupational Outlook Handbook,* U.S. Department of Labor, Washington, DC, 2000–2001.)	**First professional degree**	Veterinarians, chiropractors, physicians, lawyers, and clergy
	Doctoral degree	Biological scientists, medical scientists, college and university faculty, physicists, and astronomers
	Master's degree	Speech-language pathologists and audiologists, physical therapists, counselors, urban and regional planners, archivists, curators, and conservators
	Work experience plus bachelor's or higher degree	Engineering, science, and computer systems managers; medical and health services managers; management analysts; artists and commercial artists; advertising, marketing, and public relations managers
	Bachelor's	Computer engineers, computer systems analysts, database administrators, physicians assistants, and residential counselors
	Associate degree	Computer support specialists, paralegals and legal assistants, health information technicians, physical therapy assistants and aides, and respiratory therapists
	Post-secondary vocational training	Data processing equipment repairers, surgical technologists, central office and PBX installers and repairers, emergency medical technicians, and manicurists

WORKFORCE FORECASTS

The purpose of workforce forecasting is to estimate labor requirements at some future time period. Such forecasts are of two types: (1) the external and internal supply of labor and (2) the aggregate external and internal demand for labor. We consider each type separately because each rests on a different set of assumptions and depends on a different set of variables.[41]

Internal supply forecasts relate to conditions *inside* the organization, such as the age distribution of the workforce, terminations, retirements, and new hires within job classes. Both internal and external demand forecasts, on the other hand, depend primarily on the behavior of some business factor (e.g., student enrollments, projected sales, product volume) to which human resource needs can be related. Unlike internal and external supply forecasts, demand forecasts are subject to many uncertainties—in domestic or worldwide economic conditions, in technology, and in consumer behavior, to name just a few. The *Occupational Outlook Handbook*, published by the U.S. Department of Labor, focuses on macro-forecasts of aggregate demand for various occupations. Figure 5–9 shows an excerpt of one such forecast for the fastest-growing occupations from 1998 to 2008. In the following sections we will consider several micro- or firm-level workforce forecasting techniques that have proved to be practical and useful.

Forecasting External Workforce Supply

The recruiting and hiring of new employees are essential activities for virtually all firms, at least over the long run. Whether they are due to projected expansion of operations or to normal workforce attrition, forays into the labor market are necessary.

Several agencies regularly make projections of external labor market conditions and estimates of the supply of labor to be available in general categories. These include the Bureau of Labor Statistics of the U.S. Department of Labor, the Engineering Manpower Commission, and the Public Health Service of the

Department of Health and Human Services. For new college and university graduates, the Northwestern Endicott-Lindquist Report is one spected barometers of future hiring decisions. Organizations in both and private sectors are finding such projections of the external labor market be helpful in preventing surpluses or deficits of employees.

As an example, consider these facts. Several years ago, some 47,000 jobs opened up worldwide in the field of computer animation, according to the Roncarelli Report, an industry survey. At the same time, only 14,000 animators graduated from art school. That imbalance between the demand for new workers and the supply of them bids up starting salaries to the point where new hires may earn more than senior people at their companies! Not surprisingly, therefore, these new hires are known as "gold-collar" workers. They are educated, smart, creative, computer literate, equipped with portable skills—and in demand.[42]

Forecasting Internal Workforce Supply

A reasonable starting point for projecting a firm's future supply of labor is its current supply of labor. Perhaps the simplest type of internal supply forecast is the **succession plan,** a concept that has been discussed in the planning literature for decades. Succession plans may be developed for management employees, nonmanagement employees, or both. The process of developing such a plan includes setting a planning horizon, identifying replacement candidates for each key position, assessing current performance and readiness for promotion, identifying career development needs, and integrating the career goals of individuals with company goals. The overall objective, of course, is to ensure the availability of competent executive talent in the future or, in some cases, immediately, as when a key executive dies suddenly.[43] Here is how one firm does it.

SUCCESSION PLANNING IN THE MINISTRY OF TRANSPORTATION AND COMMUNICATIONS (MTC), PROVINCE OF ONTARIO

COMPANY EXAMPLE

MTC, one of the leading transportation authorities in North America, is responsible for the management of a highway network comprising approximately 13,000 miles of provincial roads. It also manages the subsidy allocation for an additional 62,500 miles of municipal roads and is involved in the planning for provincial commuter rail and air services. Major operational activities include planning, design, construction, maintenance, and research related to transportation systems and facilities.

The full-time workforce consists of approximately 2,600 management and 7,700 bargaining-unit employees, although for practical reasons, succession planning has been limited to middle and senior management (about 1,300 positions). Succession planning is one of the responsibilities of every manager.

Current and future business plans and the assessed skills and potential of the management workforce provide the main inputs to the planning system. Meaningful forecasts can be done only for large job families. Hence, MTC's operations have been divided into five primary and eight secondary functions, and

Figure 5–10

Corporate workforce demand forecasting model used at the Ontario Ministry of Transportation and Communications. See text for explanations of the data that go into each column.

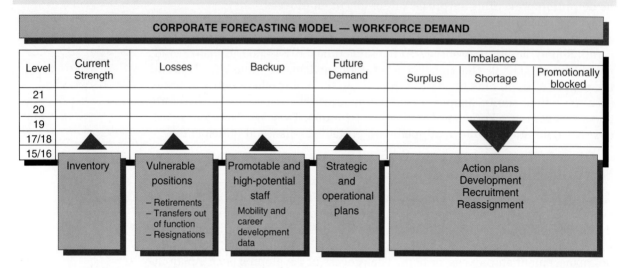

CORPORATE FORECASTING MODEL — WORKFORCE DEMAND

Level	Current Strength	Losses	Backup	Future Demand	Imbalance		
					Surplus	Shortage	Promotionally blocked
21							
20							
19							
17/18							
15/16							

Inventory	Vulnerable positions – Retirements – Transfers out of function – Resignations	Promotable and high-potential staff Mobility and career development data	Strategic and operational plans	Action plans Development Recruitment Reassignment

separate analyses are done for each of these functions. Figure 5–10 illustrates the various data that are used in the forecast to determine potential shortages, surpluses, numbers of promotable staff blocked from promotion (e.g., because there is no higher-level job to progress to in a particular job family), and annual training and development effort required to maintain backup strength.

- Current strength is determined from a talent inventory maintained by the corporate planning group.
- Losses are made up of resignations, dismissals, transfers, and retirements. Resignations, dismissals, and transfers are assessed from historical data, modified by current and future trends. Retirement figures are based on a review of individual retirement ranges.
- Backup is determined from two sources: (1) As part of the annual appraisal process, managers identify those employees who are considered promotable within the next 1-year planning cycle; and (2) in a separate annual process, managers identify high-potential individuals who have the ability to progress to two responsibility levels higher—in more than one function—during a 5-year forecast period.
- Future demand is forecast on the basis of current as well as future business plans. These are determined by MTC's strategic policy committee (composed of the CEO and senior executives) with input from six planning groups.
- Finally, the data for succession planning for each function are manipulated by means of a computerized forecasting model (Figure 5–11). The model was chosen because it is simple to use and flexible enough to be able to analyze situations that vary according to staffing levels, turnover rates, and replacement strategies.[44]

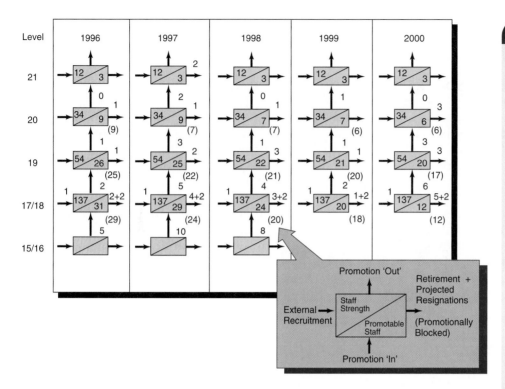

Figure 5–11

Management succession forecasting model used at the Ontario Ministry of Transportation and Communications. An explanation of the numbers in each box is contained in the lower right corner of the figure. For example, at job level 17/18 in 1998, staff strength is 137 persons, of whom 24 are promotable. Four persons were promoted "out," 8 were promoted "in," 1 was recruited externally, 3 retired, 2 were projected to resign, and 20 were promotionally blocked.

What is different about succession planning in today's turbulent business environment? In a nutshell, in specifying position requirements companies are defining more generic competencies (e.g., ability to cut costs and to work with diverse constituencies), rather than specific knowledge and skills. They also are making it clear to individuals that they are responsible for their own career development, with no explicit or implicit promises made to them about future opportunities by the firm.[45]

CEO Succession at General Electric. One of the most closely watched CEO successions took place at GE in 2001, as Jack Welch retired. The process took six and a half years, and during that time Welch and the board of directors broke most of what passes for the rules of corporate succession planning. They never named a chief operating officer or other heir apparent. They never looked at an outsider. They formed no strategic vision of the next 10 years, and they used no common template for measuring the candidates.

What they did was spend an extraordinary amount of time getting to know the contenders, and more time talking with one another about them. Various best-practice guidelines for boards outline succession processes that may require fewer than 100 director-hours. GE's board spent thousands. This is the most striking feature of the process—a staggering amount of human interaction. Outsiders are often curious about the mechanics, but Welch says mechanics aren't the key. "The process is all chemistry, blood, sweat, family, feelings." While it is too soon to know whether the new CEO of GE, Jeffrey Immelt, was the right choice, the two other finalists also became instant CEOs: Robert Nardelli at 3M, and W. James McNerney at Home Depot.[46]

Ethical Dilemma: Should Succession Plans Be Secret?

The issue of secrecy versus openness with regard to succession plans is a thorny one. If firms keep workforce planning information about specific candidates secret, planning may have limited value. Thus at a software company, a senior executive on her way out the door for a president's job at a competitor was told that the firm had expected her to be its next president. Her response? "If I'd known, I would have stayed."

A somewhat different course of events transpired at another firm whose policy was to talk openly about prospective candidates. There, employees learned what the company had in mind for them over the next 3 to 5 years. Subsequently, when they did not get the jobs they thought they were entitled to, employees felt betrayed. Some sued, others left. In your view, is it unethical to share planning information with employees and then not follow the plan? Conversely, do employees have a right to see such information?

SMALL BUSINESSES CONFRONT SUCCESSION PLANNING[47]

General Electric is an example of succession planning in a large firm. But what about small firms, such as family-owned businesses? Only about 30 percent of family businesses outlive their founders, usually for lack of planning. Since many founders of small companies started in the post–World War II boom are now retiring, the question of succession is becoming more pressing. Here are some of the ways families are trying to solve the problem: groom one child from an early age to take over.

- 25 percent plan to let the children compete and choose one or more successors, with help from the board of directors.

- 35 percent plan to groom one child from an early age to take over.
- 15 percent plan to let the children compete and choose one or more successors, without input from a third party.
  - 15 percent plan to form an "executive committee" of two or more children.
  - 10 percent plan to let the children choose their own leader, or leaders.

Suppose the CEO dies suddenly? Plan ahead to establish a committee that would assume immediate control of the company while it searches for a permanent successor. Experts say that naming a successor too quickly can anger employees still coping with the loss of their boss.

Forecasting Workforce Demand

In contrast to supply forecasting, demand forecasting is beset with multiple uncertainties—changes in technology; consumer attitudes and patterns of buying behavior; local, national, and international economies; number, size, and types of contracts won or lost; and government regulations that might open new markets or close off old ones, just to name a few. Consequently, forecasts of workforce demand are often more subjective than quantitative, although in practice a combination of the two is often used. One popular approach to demand forecasting is the Delphi technique.

The Delphi Technique.   The **Delphi technique** is a structured approach for reaching a consensus judgment among experts about future developments in any area that might affect a business (e.g., the level of a firm's future demand for labor). Originally developed as a method to facilitate group decision making, it has also been used in workforce forecasting. Experts are chosen on the basis of their knowledge of internal factors that might affect a business (e.g., projected retirements), their knowledge of the general business plans of the organization, or their knowledge of external factors that might affect demand for the firm's product or service and hence its internal demand for labor. Experts may range from first-line supervisors to top-level managers. Sometimes experts internal to the firm are used, but if the required expertise is not available internally, then one or more outside experts may be brought in to contribute their opinions. To estimate the level of future demand for labor, an organization might select as experts, for example, managers from corporate planning, human resources, marketing, production, and sales.

The Delphi technique was developed during the late 1940s at the Rand Corporation's "think tank" in Santa Monica, California. Its objective is to predict future developments in a particular area by integrating the independent opinions of experts.[48] Face-to-face group discussion among the experts is avoided since differences in job status among group members may lead some individuals to avoid criticizing others and to compromise on their good ideas. To avoid these problems, an intermediary is used. The intermediary's job is to pool, summarize, and then feed back to the experts the information generated independently by all the other experts during the first round of forecasting. The cycle is then repeated, so that the experts are given the opportunity to revise their forecasts and the reasons behind their revised forecasts. Successive rounds usually lead to a convergence of expert opinion within three to five rounds.

In one application, Delphi did provide an accurate 1-year demand forecast for the number of buyers needed for a retailing firm.[49] Here's a set of guidelines to make the Delphi process useful:

- Give the expert enough information to make an informed judgment. That is, give him or her the historical data that have been collected, as well as the results of any relevant statistical analysis that has been conducted, such as staffing patterns and productivity trends.
- Ask the kinds of questions a unit manager can answer. For example, instead of asking for total staffing requirements, ask by what percentage staffing is likely to increase or ask only about anticipated increases in key employee groups, such as marketing managers or engineers.
- Do not require precision. Allow the experts to round off figures, and give them the opportunity to indicate how sure they are of the forecasted figures.
- Keep the exercise as simple as possible, and especially avoid questions that are not absolutely necessary.
- Be sure that all experts have a common understanding of classifications of employees and other definitions.

- Enlist top management's and experts' support for the Delphi process by showing how good forecasts will benefit the organization and small-unit operations, and how they will affect profitability and workforce productivity.[50]

How Accurate Is Accurate?

Accuracy in forecasting the demand for labor varies considerably by firm and by industry type (e.g., utilities versus women's fashions): roughly from 2 to 20 percent error. Certainly factors such as the duration of the planning period, the quality of the data on which forecasts are based (e.g., expected changes in the business factor and labor productivity), and the degree of integration of WP with strategic business planning all affect accuracy. How accurate a labor demand forecast should be depends on the degree of flexibility in staffing the workforce. That is, to the extent that people are geographically mobile, multiskilled, and easily hired, there is no need for precise forecasts.[51]

Matching Forecast Results to Action Plans

Labor demand forecasts affect a firm's programs in many different areas, including recruitment, selection, performance appraisal, training, transfer, and many other types of career enhancement activities. These activities are all "action programs." Action programs help organizations adapt to changes in their environments. In the past decade or so, one of the most obvious changes in the business environment has been the large influx of women, minorities, and immigrants into the workforce. To adapt to these changes, organizations have provided extensive training programs designed to develop these individuals' management skills. Also, they have provided training programs for supervisors and coworkers in human relations skills to deal effectively with members of these underrepresented groups.[52]

Assuming a firm has a choice, however, is it better to *select* workers who already have developed the skills necessary to perform competently or to select workers who do not have the skills immediately but who can be *trained* to perform competently? This is the same type of "make-or-buy" decision that managers often face in so many other areas of business. Managers have found that it is often more cost-effective to buy, rather than to make. This is also true in the context of selection versus training.[53] Put your money and resources into selection. Always strive *first* to develop the most accurate, the most valid selection process that you can, for it will yield higher-ability workers. *Then* apply those action programs that are most appropriate in further increasing the performance of your employees. With high-ability employees, the productivity gain from a training program in, say, spreadsheets, might be greater than the gain from the same program with lower-ability employees. Further, even if the training is about equally effective with well-selected, higher-ability employees and poorly selected, lower-ability employees, the *time* required for training may be less for higher-ability employees. Thus training costs will be reduced, and the net effectiveness of training will be greater when applied along with a highly valid personnel selection process. This point becomes even more relevant if one views training as a strategy for building sustained competitive advantage. Firms that select high-caliber employees, and then commit resources to de-

IMPACT OF JOB ANALYSIS AND WORKFORCE PLANNING ON PRODUCTIVITY, QUALITY OF WORK LIFE, AND THE BOTTOM LINE

As noted earlier, jobs are dynamic, not static, in their requirements. This is especially true of jobs at the bottom and at the top of today's organizations. Entry-level jobs now demand workers with new and different kinds of skills. Even simple clerical work now requires computer knowledge, bank tellers need more knowledge of financial transactions and sales techniques, and foreign competition means that assembly-line workers need more sophisticated understanding of mathematics and better reading and reasoning skills in order to cut costs and improve quality.

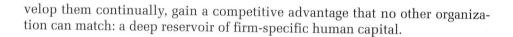

Current information on the behavioral requirements of jobs is critically important if firms are to develop meaningful specifications for selecting, training, and appraising the performance of employees in them and if employees are to perform their jobs successfully. Workforce planning information is no less important, so that firms can institute action plans now to cope with projected HR needs in the future.

What are firms actually doing? A recent survey of 2,100 firms by the Hay Group found that workforce planning was formal and well developed at only 21 percent of the firms. It was undeveloped or rudimentary at another 30 percent. Most firms said that finding and keeping key people is a top priority.[54] However, without solid planning they may miss seeing the need for new talent and the need to develop new ways of selecting and training that talent.

velop them continually, gain a competitive advantage that no other organization can match: a deep reservoir of firm-specific human capital.

CONTROL AND EVALUATION OF WP SYSTEMS

The purpose of control and evaluation is to guide WP activities, identifying deviations from the plan and their causes. For this reason, we need yardsticks to measure performance. Qualitative and quantitative objectives can both play useful roles in WP. Quantitative objectives make the control and evaluation process more objective and measure deviations from desired performance more precisely. Nevertheless, the nature of evaluation and control should always match the degree of development of the rest of the WP process. In newly instituted WP systems, for example, evaluation is likely to be more qualitative than quantitative, with little emphasis placed on control. This is because supply-and-demand forecasts are likely to be based more on "hunches" and subjective opinions than on hard data. Under these circumstances, workforce planners should attempt to assess the following[55]:

- The extent to which they are tuned in to workforce problems and opportunities and the extent to which their priorities are sound.
- The quality of their working relationships with staff specialists and line managers who supply data and use WP results. (How closely do the

workforce planners work with these specialists and line managers on a day-to-day basis?)
- The extent to which decision makers, from line managers who hire employees to top managers who develop long-term business strategy, are making use of WP forecasts, action plans, and recommendations.
- The perceived value of WP among decision makers. (Do they view the information provided by workforce planners as useful to them in their own jobs?)

In more established WP systems, in which objectives and action plans are both underpinned by measured performance standards, key comparisons might include the following[56]:

- Actual staffing levels against forecast staffing requirements.
- Actual levels of labor productivity against anticipated levels of labor productivity.
- Actual personnel flow rates against desired rates.
- Action programs implemented against action programs planned. (Were there more or fewer? Why?)
- The actual results of the action programs implemented against the expected results (e.g., improved applicant flows, lower quit rates, improved replacement ratios).
- Labor and action program costs against budgets.
- Ratios of action program benefits to action program costs.

IMPLICATIONS FOR MANAGEMENT PRACTICE

More and more, workforce issues are seen as people-related business issues. This suggests that as a manager you should do the following:
- Keep a management view, not an HR staff department view, of critical issues and opportunities. Consider a comment by the director of HR at Merck & Co.:
  > Line managers are starting to address the needs of individual and organizational performance—e.g., they know why every job exists in the organization, who the people in these jobs are, and how competent they are; and they know it is important to keep their skills updated. There is a saying at Merck: "Human resources are too important to be left to the HR department." Fully one-third of the performance evaluation of line managers is related to people management.[57]
- Plan within the context of managing the business strategically.

- Execute the strategy—doing so requires effective management consensus, communications designed to educate, and involvement of all parties. This is not a "pie in the sky" recommendation. In a recent survey, almost 60 percent of managers felt that the linkage between HR strategy and business results was either not effective or just "somewhat effective." Only 3 percent rated it "world class."[58]

On the other hand, tight linkage, as at Northwestern Mutual Life Insurance, Mary Kay Cosmetics, and Tandy Corporation—can lead to consistent levels of high performance. As one CEO noted: "We don't make financial, marketing, technical, or human resources decisions—we make business decisions [and] we routinely involve all the functions."[59]

The advantage of quantitative information is that it highlights potential problem areas and can provide the basis for constructive discussion of the issues.

THE ANALYSIS OF WORK—FOUNDATION FOR EMPLOYMENT PRACTICES

One of the new ideas that you, as Pat Evans, had for recruiting junior civil engineers was to develop a video that illustrated each of the seven essential functions of the job: modeling and calculations, computer software applications, project planning and management, written communications, individual and group interactions, summary and synthesis of data, and problem resolution. Using a narrator, a script, and actual engineers at Western, the video would, in your opinion, ensure that job applicants developed a realistic picture of what it's like to work at Western. Since the company always seemed to have many more applicants than positions, you thought that perhaps the video might help to reduce turnover among new hires, if they could get a good idea ahead of time of what they'd be getting into. Just as the company was selective about whom it chose to hire, the video would provide job applicants with information that would help them make informed decisions about their future employer.

Another application of the job dimensions and the video was in selection. You could visualize a "technical oral interview" in which candidates would be asked to describe their experiences in dealing with each of the seven major areas revealed by the job analysis. Interviewers would then ask follow-up questions in a systematic manner in order to elicit relevant information, and, based on the recruiting video job applicants had seen, they too could ask meaningful questions of the interviewers. Finally, it occurred to you that the very same job dimensions identified by the job analysis could, with a little elaboration, also be used as bases for judging the performance of junior civil engineers. You thought: "I love to mine information from a report, and that job analysis report has really been a gold mine for me and for engineering at Western."

SUMMARY

We are witnessing vast changes in the very nature of work itself, as well as in the types and numbers of jobs available. To reduce uncertainty and increase efficiency, careful attention needs to be paid to a thorough understanding of the behavioral requirements of jobs and to workforce planning.

A written summary of the task requirements for a particular job is called a job description, and a written summary of people requirements is called a job specification. Together they compose a job analysis. This information is useful for a variety of organizational purposes ranging from HR planning to career counseling.

Some combination of available job analysis methods (job performance, observation, interviews, critical incidents, structured questionnaires) should be used, for all have both advantages and disadvantages. Key considerations in the choice of methods are the method-purpose fit, cost, practicality, and an overall judgment of the appropriateness of the methods for the situation in question.

Job analysis provides one input to the workforce planning process. Strategic and operational planning provide others. Strategic business planning is the long-range process of setting organizational objectives and deciding on action programs to achieve those objectives. Operational, or tactical, planning deals with the normal, ongoing growth of current operations or with specific problems that temporarily disrupt the pace of normal growth. Annual budgeting decisions provide specific timetables, allocations of resources, and implementation standards. The shorter the planning time frame, the more specific the planning details must be.

Strategic and operational business objectives dictate what HR objectives must be. So also do internal and external labor markets. Workforce planning (WP) parallels general business planning. Broadly speaking, WP is an effort to anticipate future business and environmental demands on an organization and to meet the people requirements dictated by those conditions. This general view suggests several interrelated activities that together compose an integrated WP system. These include (1) an inventory of talent currently on hand, (2) forecasts of labor supply and demand over short- and long-term periods, (3) action plans such as training or job transfer to meet forecasted HR needs, and (4) control and evaluation procedures.

DISCUSSION QUESTIONS

5–1. In your opinion, what are some of the key reasons for the deep changes we are seeing in the way jobs are done?

5–2. Choose a business process (e.g., order fulfillment) and identify the flow of work. How do task-based and process-based work flows differ?

5–3. For purposes of succession planning, what information would you want in order to evaluate "potential"?

5–4. In your opinion, is it more cost-effective to "buy" or to "make" competent employees?

5–5. Why should the output from forecasting models be tempered with the judgment of experienced line managers?

KEY TERMS

job analysis	O*Net
job description	strategic planning
job specification	tactical planning
dynamic characteristics of jobs	workforce planning
reasonable accommodations	succession plan
process	Delphi technique

APPLYING YOUR KNOWLEDGE

Workforce Planning at First Bank   *Case 5–1*

First Bank is a large, federally chartered bank located in a rapidly growing area in the southwestern United States. Over the past several years, First Bank experienced a significant expansion in size and operations, and a rapid influx of new employees at all organizational levels. As it expanded and matured, the bank began to recognize its pressing need for talented, knowledgeable managers. Much talent had been hired from outside the bank over the past several years, but top management had become convinced that the long-run health of the bank depended on its ability to develop managerial talent internally.

Linda Bishop had recently been hired to develop and install a new workforce planning system at First Bank. She had previous experience both in banking and in workforce planning, so she seemed like a logical choice for the job. On the basis of her prior experience, Linda knew that many banking functions cross divisional lines and require managers with broad exposure to important areas within the bank. Further, she knew that division heads operate with a high degree of autonomy, and that divisional and corporate objectives are not always directly aligned. Therefore, Linda knew that the new WP process would have to be corporatewide in scope. Only from that perspective could a planner assess bankwide, long-run workforce needs.

When Linda arrived at her new job, her boss had informed her that the focus of the WP system was to be on management development and succession planning. To emphasize that focus, she was given the title of Director of Management Development and Workforce Planning. The position had corporatewide staff authority over all presently existing activities that related to management development and workforce planning. Today, Linda is thinking about a briefing that she is to give the executive officers of the bank next week. They have asked her to provide them with a statement of the objectives of the new HRP system as she sees it, an outline of the potential benefits that might accrue to the bank, and a list of suggested steps in the implementation of the WP system.

Questions

If you were Linda Bishop, what would you be prepared to say to the executive officers in terms of:
1. The objectives of WP?
2. The potential benefits of WP?
3. Important steps in the implementation of the WP system?

REFERENCES

1. General Motors: Open all night (1992, June 1). *BusinessWeek*, pp. 82, 83.
2. Vobejda, B. (1987, Apr. 4). The new cutting edge in factories. *The Washington Post*, p. A14.
3. Pearlman, K., & Barney, M. F. (2000). Selection for a changing workplace. In J. F. Kehoe (ed.), *Managing selection in changing organizations*. San Francisco: Jossey-Bass, pp. 3–72. See also Goldstein, I. L., & Gilliam, P. (1990). Training system issues in the year 2000. *American Psychologist, 45*, 134–143.

4. Landy, F. J., Shankster-Cawley, L., & Moran, S. K. (1995). Advancing personnel selection and placement methods. In A. Howard (ed.), *The changing nature of work.* San Francisco: Jossey-Bass, pp. 252–289.

5. Wheeler, M. (2000, May). Clerk/typist job analysis. Presentation to the Personnel Testing Council of Southern California, Los Angeles.

6. Lindell, M. K., Clause, C. S., Brandt, C. J., & Landis, R. S. (1998). Relationship between organizational context and job analysis task ratings. *Journal of applied Psychology, 83,* 769–776.

7. Cascio, W. F. (1994). The Americans with Disabilities Act of 1990 and the 1991 Civil Rights Act: Requirements for psychological practice in the workplace. In B. D. Sales & G. R. VandenBos (eds.), *Psychology in litigation and legislation.* Washington, DC: American Psychological Association, pp. 175–211.

8. Campbell, W. J., & Reilly, M. E. (2000). Accommodations for persons with disabilities. In J. F. Kehoe (ed.), *Managing selection in changing organizations.* San Francisco: Jossey-Bass, pp. 319–367.

9. Cappelli, P. (2001, March). Making the most of on-line recruiting. *Harvard Business Review,* pp. 139–146.

10. Hammer, M., & Champy, J. (1993). *Reengineering the corporation.* New York: Harper Business.

11. Ibid.

12. Fleishman, E. A., & Mumford, M. D. (1991). Evaluating classifications of job behavior: A construct validation of the ability requirements scales. *Personnel Psychology, 44,* 523–575.

13. Harvey, R. J. (1991). Job analysis. In M. D. Dunnette & L. M. Hough (eds.), *Handbook of industrial and organizational psychology* (vol. 2.) Palo Alto, CA: Consulting Psychologists Press, pp. 71–163.

14. McCormick, E. J., Jeanneret, P. R., & Mecham, R. C. (1972). A study of job characteristics and job dimensions as based on the Position Analysis Questionnaire (PAQ). *Journal of Applied Psychology, 56,* 347–368.

15. Pearlman & Barney, op. cit.

16. Landy, F. J., & Vasey, J. (1991). Job analysis: The composition of SME samples. *Personnel Psychology, 44,* 27–50. See also DiNisi, A. S., Cornelius, E. T., III, & Blencoe, A. G. (1987). Further investigation of common knowledge effects on job analysis ratings. *Journal of Applied Psychology, 72,* 262–268. See also Friedman, L., & Harvey, R. J. (1986). Can raters with reduced job descriptive information provide accurate Position Analysis Questionnaire (PAQ) ratings? *Personnel Psychology, 39,* 779–789.

17. Schmitt, N., & Cohen, S. A. (1989). Internal analyses of task ratings by job incumbents. *Journal of Applied Psychology, 73,* 96–104.

18. Conley, P. R., & Sackett, P. R. (1987). Effects of using high- versus low-performing job incumbents as sources of job-analysis information. *Journal of Applied Psychology, 72,* 434–437.

19. Borman, W. C., Dorsey, D., & Ackerman, L. (1992). Time-spent responses as time-allocation strategies: Relations with sales performance in a stockbroker sample. *Personnel Psychology, 45,* 763–777.

20. Tornow, W. W., & Pinto, P. R. (1976). The development of a managerial taxonomy: A system for describing, classifying, and evaluating executive positions. *Journal of Applied Psychology, 61,* 410–418.

21. U.S. Department of Labor. (1991). *Dictionary of occupational titles* (4th ed.). Washington, DC: Author.

22. Peterson, N. G., Mumford, M. D., Borman, W. C., Jeanneret, P. R., Fleishman, E. A., Levin, K. Y., Campion, M. A., Mayfield, M. S., Morgeson, F. P., Pearlman, K., Gowing, M. K., Lancaster, A. R., Silver, M. B., & Dye, D. M. (2001). Understanding work using the Occupational Information Network (O*Net): Implications for practice

and research. *Personnel Psychology, 54*, 451–492. See also Peterson, N. G., Mumford, M. D., Borman, W. C., Jeanneret, P. R., & Fleishman, E. A. (eds.) (1999). *An occupational information system for the 21st century: The development of O*Net.* Washington, DC: American Psychological Association.

23. Higgs, A. C., Papper, E. M., & Carr, L. S. (2000). Integrating selection with other organizational processes and systems. In Kehoe (ed.), op. cit., pp. 73–122.

24. Ibid. See also Morgan, R. B., & Smith, J. E. (1996). *Staffing the new workplace.* Chicago: CCH.

25. Connors, K., cited in Lawrence, S. (1989, Apr.). Voice of HR experience. *Personnel Journal*, p. 70.

26. Chambers, quoted in O'Reilly, C. A., III, & Pfeffer, J. (2000). *Hidden value: How great companies achieve extraordinary results with ordinary people.* Boston: Harvard Business School Press, p. 56.

27. Sanchez, J. I. (2000). Adapting work analysis to a fast-paced and electronic business world. *International Journal of Selection and Assessment, 8*(4), 207–215. See also U.S. Bureau of Labor Statistics (2001). *stats.bls.gov.*

28. Pearlman & Barney, op. cit. See also Arvey, R. D., Salas, E., & Gialluca, K. A. (1992). Using task inventories to forecast skills and abilities. *Human Performance, 5*, 171–190. See also Schneider, B., & Konz, A. M. (1989). Strategic job analysis. *Human Resource Management, 38*, 51–64.

29. Hamel, G. (2000). *Leading the revolution.* Boston: Harvard Business School Press. See also Prahalad, C. K., & Hamel, G. (1994). *Competing for the future.* Boston: Harvard Business School Press.

30. O'Reilly & Pfeffer, op. cit.

31. Greer, C. R. (2001). *Strategic human resource management,* (2nd ed.). Upper Saddle River, NJ: Prentice-Hall. See also Walker, J. W. (1992). *Human resource strategy.* New York: McGraw-Hill.

32. Cascio, W. F. (1998). Applied psychology in personnel management (5th ed.). Englewood Cliffs, NJ: Prentice-Hall.

33. Jackson, S. E., & Schuler, R. S. (1990). Human resource planning: Challenges for industrial/organizational psychologists. *American Psychologist, 45*, 223–239.

34. Ulrich, D. (1998, Jan.–Feb.). A new mandate for human resources. *Harvard Business Review*, 124–134. See also Ulrich, D. (1986). Human resource planning as a competitive edge. *Human Resource Planning, 9*(2), 41–50.

35. Colvin, G. (2001, June 25). The great CEO pay heist. *Fortune*, pp. 64–70. See also Apple articulates its internet plans (1996, Aug.). *Macworld*, pp. 27, 28. See also Apple's CEO gets tough (1996, July). *Macworld*, pp. 35–37. See also Strategic planning (1996, Aug. 26), *BusinessWeek,* p. 50.

36. Schuler, R. S., & Walker, J. W. (1990, Summer). Human resources strategy: Focusing on issues and actions. *Organizational Dynamics*, pp. 5–19.

37. Ibid.

38. The man who McDonaldized Burger King (1979, Oct. 8). *BusinessWeek*, pp. 132, 136.

39. See, for example, Kavanagh, M. J., Geutal, H. G., & Tannenbaum, S. I. (1990). *Human resource information systems: Development and application.* Boston: PWS-Kent.

40. Walker, op. cit.

41. Ibid.

42. Vinzant, C. (2000, Sept. 18). How do you say "labor shortage"? *Fortune*, pp. 342–344. See also Munk, N. (1998, Mar. 16). The new organization man. *Fortune*, pp. 63–82.

43. Wing, J. (1996, May). Succession planning smooths return to business-as-usual. *HR News*, p. 11. See also Bennett, A. (1988, Apr. 29). Many companies aren't prepared to deal with sudden death of chief executive. *The Wall Street Journal*, p. 25.

44. Reypert, L. J. (1981). Succession planning in the Ministry of Transportation and Communications, Province of Ontario. *Human Resource Planning, 4,* 151–156.

45. For more on this issue, see Borwick, C. (1993, May). Eight ways to assess succession plans. *HRMagazine,* pp. 109–114.

46. Colvin, G. (2001, Jan. 8). Changing of the guard. *Fortune,* pp. 84–99. See also Running the house that Jack built (2000, Oct. 2). *BusinessWeek,* pp. 130–138.

47. Nothing succeeds like a succession plan (1991, Sept. 30). *BusinessWeek,* pp. 126, 127. See also Wing, op. cit. See also Bennett, A., & Lublin, J. S. (1992, March 17). Predecessor's presence clouds succession plan. *The Wall Street Journal,* pp. B1, B8. See also Brown, B. (1988, Aug. 4). Succession strategies for family firms. *The Wall Street Journal,* p. 23.

48. Dalkey, N. (1969). *The Delphi method: An experimental study of group opinion.* Santa Monica, CA: Rand.

49. Milkovich, G. T., Annoni, A. J., & Mahoney, T. A. (1972). The use of the Delphi procedure in manpower forecasting. *Management Science, 19,* 381–388.

50. Frantzreb, R. B. (1981). Human resource planning: Forecasting manpower needs. *Personnel Journal, 60,* 850–857.

51. Ibid.

52. Wells, S. J. (2001, June). Smoothing the way. *HRMagazine,* pp. 52–58. See also Labich, K. (1996, Sept. 9). Making diversity pay. *Fortune,* pp. 177–180.

53. Schmidt, F. L., Hunter, J. E., & Pearlman, K. (1982). Assessing the economic impact of personnel programs on workforce productivity. *Personnel Psychology, 35,* 333–347.

54. Dreazen, Y. J., & Schlesinger, J. M. (2000, Feb. 7). Job stretching. *The Wall Street Journal,* pp. A1, A6. See also Daniels, C. (2000, Apr. 3). To hire a lumber expert, click here. *Fortune,* pp. 267–270. See also Munk, op. cit.

55. Walker, J. W. (1980). *Human resource planning.* New York: McGraw-Hill.

56. Dyer, L., & Holder, G. W. (1988). A strategic perspective of human resource management. In L. Dyer & G. W. Holder (eds.), *Human resource management: Evolving roles and responsibilities.* Washington, DC: Bureau of National Affairs, pp. 1-1 to 1-46.

57. Schuler & Walker, op. cit., p. 13.

58. American Management Association (1995). *Human resource management survey.* New York: Author.

59. Buller, P. F. (1993). Successful partnerships: HR and strategic planning at eight top firms. In R. S. Schuler (ed.), *Strategic human resources management.* New York: American Management Association, p. 23.

RECRUITING

6

Questions This Chapter Will Help Managers Answer

1. What factors are most important to consider in developing a recruitment policy?
2. Under what circumstances does it make sense to retain an executive search firm?
3. Do alternative recruitment sources yield differences in the quality of employees and in their "survival" rates on the job?
4. How can we communicate as realistic a picture as possible of a job and organization to prospective new employees? What kinds of issues are most crucial to them?
5. If I lose my current job in management, what's the most efficient strategy for finding a new one?

THE ART OF FINDING TALENT*

In a recent survey, executives rated "finding the talent to meet our hiring needs" as their greatest business challenge. Likewise, the International Franchise Association found that 95 percent of its members ranked labor as their number 1 headache. In some cases it is curbing growth and expansion possibilities, and in others it is forcing operators to shut down early for lack of staff. Among high-technology firms in the United States, it is estimated that 800,000 jobs are going unfilled. This has forced employers to use creative recruitment tactics in order to attract competent staff. Here is what two leading-edge companies are doing to find and attract top talent.

Cisco Systems. Cisco's recruiters target "passive job seekers," people who are happy and successful where they are. Since this group is not very accessible, Cisco had to learn how to lure them. It began by holding focus groups with ideal recruitment targets, such as senior engineers and marketing professionals from competitors to find out how they spend their free time (lots of movies), what websites they visit, and how they feel about job hunting (they hate it). Then the real work started.

Cisco learned how to reach potential applicants through a variety of routes not usually used in recruiting, such as infiltrating art fairs, microbrewery festivals, and even home-and-garden shows. In Silicon Valley, the first-time home buyers that such shows attract tend to be young achievers at successful technology companies. Cisco recruiters work the crowds, collecting business cards from prospects and speaking to them informally about their careers.

The way the company uses newspaper help-wanted ads has also changed dramatically. Rather than listing specific job openings, the company runs ads featuring its Internet address and an invitation to apply at Cisco. Directing all job seekers to its website is a major benefit. There it can post hundreds of job openings and lots of information about each one. Since most prospects visit Cisco's website from their jobs, Cisco can even tell where they work.

Relying again on focus groups, Cisco sought to learn how happily employed people could be enticed to interview for a job. The response: "I'd do it if I had a friend who told me he had a better opportunity at Cisco than I have at my present employer." So the company launched its "Make Friends @ Cisco" program to help prospects make a pal at Cisco who could describe what it's like to work there. Although the program is only advertised in local movie theaters, Cisco receives about 150 requests each week from applicants wishing to be introduced to a friend at Cisco. About a third of new hires now come through the friends program.

To accelerate and standardize online résumé submission, Cisco uses a tool called "Profiler" on its employment web page. Profiler asks applicants to

Sources: High hurdles for business, *USA Today,* June 25, 2001 p. 1; D. Morse, Labor shortage has franchisees hustling for workers, *The Wall Street Journal,* Aug. 22, 2000, p. B2; R. E. Thaler-Carter, Diversify your recruitment advertising, *HRMagazine,* June 2001, pp. 93–96; P. Nakache, Cisco's recruiting edge, *Fortune,* Sept. 29, 1997, pp. 275, 276; J. Useem, For sale online: You, *Fortune,* July 5, 1999, pp. 67–78; C. Daniels, To hire a lumber expert, click here, *Fortune,* Apr. 3, 2000, pp. 267–270.

provide educational and employment information by choosing appropriate selections from a series of pull-down menus. Because most people log on to Profiler from work (peak usage of Cisco's employment page occurs between 10 A.M. and 3 P.M.), they risk being caught in the act by a boss who is just dropping by. To deal with this, there is an "Oh No! My Boss Is Coming" button, which quickly fills the screen with "Seven Habits of a Successful Employee." The employment page also includes a virtual tour of the company's campus in Silicon Valley. The entire kit gets prominent play on the company's home page, thus ensnaring curious passers-by.

Home Depot.   The Home Depot, which sells everything from hardware, to lumber, to plumbing supplies for home-improvement projects, automated its hiring and promotion system as one part of the settlement of a sex discrimination lawsuit. For a company with more than 1,000 stores and almost $40 billion in annual revenues, recruiting and hiring are everyday activities.

At a cost of $10 million, the company installed computer kiosks in every store. Computerized staffing would help to ensure that a broader pool of applicants, including women, would be considered for jobs. Job seekers' applications go into a companywide network. In the first 2 years after the system was introduced into all Home Depot stores, the number of female managers increased by 30 percent and the number of minority managers by 28 percent.

Rather than feeling displaced by the system, hiring managers are happy to get help from the computerized system, which handles initial screening. Applicants, who apply at kiosks in stores or by calling a tollfree number, are given a 40-90–minute basic skills test that helps weed out unqualified applicants before live interviews. Managers say that has meant better candidates, which, in turn, has helped reduce turnover by 11 percent.

Other retailers, such as Target, Publix supermarkets, and Hollywood Video, have also automated their application processes, but where the Home Depot breaks new ground is in using its system for promotion decisions as well as for initial hiring decisions. Here's how the promotion system works.

Employees are required to register for jobs they might want in the future, and they are encouraged to update their profiles regularly at the kiosks sitting in employee break rooms. Let's say a cashier wants to become an assistant manager. What he doesn't know is that he needs to work first as a sales associate. The computer will point that out, along with some helpful hints about what to do each step of the way. Managers can interview and promote only people who have registered an interest in the position, and they must interview at least three people. This new way of doing things is not negotiable, and five managers have been dismissed for not using the system, according to a Home Depot lawyer.

The system is networked, so that if someone applies to a Home Depot in Atlanta the application could potentially go to any store within commuting distance. This means store managers have a bigger pool of applicants to choose from, and many say it provides them with great candidates they might never have considered before. In the concluding section to this case, we will examine what a third leading company, GE Medical Systems, is doing to make employee referrals effective, and how it measures the success of its recruiting efforts.

Challenges

1. Why do you think creative approaches to recruitment, like those used at Cisco and Home Depot, are necessary?
2. Finding talent is one thing. Keeping it is another. Do you see any links between employee recruitment and employee retention?
3. What should a company measure to determine whether its recruiting efforts are effective?

Recruitment as a Strategic Imperative

Recruitment is a form of business competition, and it is fiercely competitive. Just as corporations compete to develop, manufacture, and market the best product or service, so they must also compete to identify, attract, and hire the most qualified people. Recruitment is a business, and it is big business.[1] It demands serious attention from management, for any business strategy will falter without the talent to execute it. Certainly the range of recruitment needs is broad. A small manufacturer in a well-populated rural area faces recruitment challenges that are far different from those of a high-technology firm operating in global markets. Both need talent, although different types of talent, to be successful in their respective markets. Regardless of the size of a firm, or what industry it is in, recruitment and selection of people with strategically relevant abilities is more important than ever. Let's begin our treatment by examining the "big picture" of the employee recruitment and selection process, along with some important legal issues. Then we'll focus specifically on the processes of planning, managing, and evaluating recruitment efforts. We will address the special issues associated with recruiting people for international assignments in Chapter 16.

THE EMPLOYEE RECRUITMENT/SELECTION PROCESS

Recruitment begins, as Figure 6–1 indicates, by specifying human resource requirements (numbers, skills mix, levels, time frame), which are the typical result of job analysis and workforce planning (WP) activities. Conceptually (and logically) job analysis precedes WP in Figure 6–1, because, as we noted in Chapter 5, it is necessary to specify the work to be done and the personal characteristics necessary to do the work (knowledge, skills, abilities, and other characteristics) before one can specify the numbers and types of people needed to do the work. Not shown in Figure 6–1, although critically important to the overall recruitment-selection process, are strategic business objectives. For example, recruitment and selection strategies for new employees are likely to differ considerably depending on whether a company's objective in hiring, say, new salespeople, is to identify candidates who are able to execute "cold calls" for new customers as opposed to servicing existing, long-term customers.

The step following recruitment is **initial screening,** which is basically a rapid, rough "selection" process. Sixty years ago, when line supervisors hired factory workers outside the gates of a plant, they simply looked over the candidates and

The employee recruitment and selection process.
*For purposes of clarity and simplicity, relevant activities are shown only for recruitment, screening, and selection—the topics of this and the following chapter.

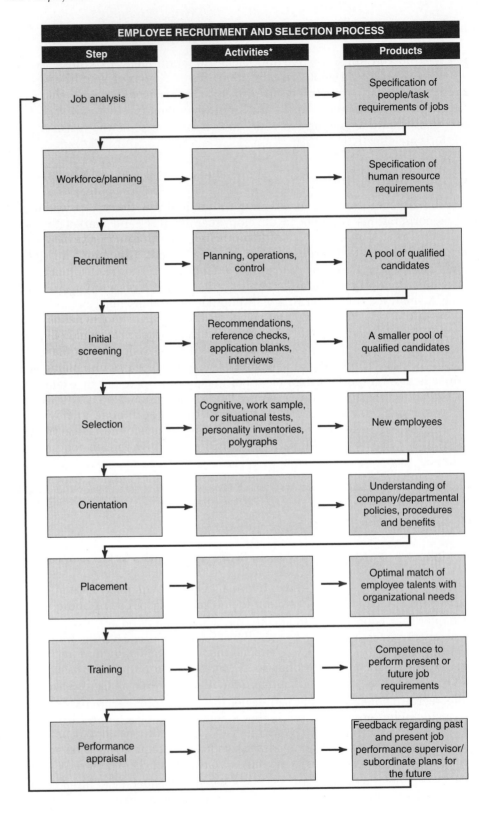

EMPLOYEE RECRUITMENT AND SELECTION PROCESS

Step	Activities*	Products
Job analysis		Specification of people/task requirements of jobs
Workforce/planning		Specification of human resource requirements
Recruitment	Planning, operations, control	A pool of qualified candidates
Initial screening	Recommendations, reference checks, application blanks, interviews	A smaller pool of qualified candidates
Selection	Cognitive, work sample, or situational tests, personality inventories, polygraphs	New employees
Orientation		Understanding of company/departmental policies, procedures and benefits
Placement		Optimal match of employee talents with organizational needs
Training		Competence to perform present or future job requirements
Performance appraisal		Feedback regarding past and present job performance supervisor/ subordinate plans for the future

RECRUITMENT POLICIES

As a framework for setting recruitment policies, let us consider four different possible company postures[2]:

1. **Passive nondiscrimination** is a commitment to treat all races and both sexes equally in all decisions about hiring, promotion, and pay. No attempt is made to recruit actively among prospective minority applicants. This posture fails to recognize that discriminatory practices in the past may block prospective applicants from seeking present job opportunities.

2. **Pure diversity-based recruitment** is a concerted effort by the organization actively to expand the pool of applicants so that no one is excluded because of past or present discrimination. However, the decision to hire or to promote is based on the best-qualified individual, regardless of race or sex.

3. **Diversity-based recruitment with preferential hiring** goes further than pure diversity-based recruitment; it systematically favors women and minorities in hiring and promotion decisions. This is a "soft-quota" system.

4. **Hard quotas** represent a mandate to hire or promote specific numbers or proportions of women or minority-group members.

Both private and government employers find hard quotas an unsavory strategy for rectifying the effects of past or present unfair discrimination. Nevertheless, the courts have ordered "temporary" quotas in instances where unfair discrimination has obviously taken place and where no other remedy is feasible.[3] Temporary quotas have bounds placed on them. For example, a judge might order an employer to hire two African-American employees for every white employee until the number of African-American employees reaches a certain percent of the employer's workforce.

Passive nondiscrimination misses the mark. This became obvious as far back as 1968, when the secretary of labor publicly cited the Allen-Bradley Company of Milwaukee for failure to comply with Executive Order 11246 by not actively recruiting African Americans. The company was so well known in Milwaukee as a good place to work that it usually had a long waiting list of friends and relatives of current employees. As a matter of established business practice, the company preferred to hire referrals from current employees; almost no public recruiting was done for entry-level job openings. As a result, because almost all the present employees were white, so were almost all the referrals.

As noted in the discussion of legal issues in employment in Chapter 3, preferential selection is a sticky issue. However, in several landmark cases the Supreme Court established the following principle[4]: Staffing decisions must be made on a case-by-case basis; race or sex may be taken into account as one factor in an applicant's favor, but the overall decision to select or reject must be made on the basis of a combination of factors, such as entrance test scores and previous performance. That leaves us with pure diversity-based recruitment as a recruitment and selection strategy. Indeed, in a free and open competitive labor market, that's the way it ought to be.

then pointed to various people. "You, you, and you—the rest of you come back another day." That's an example of initial screening, and it was probably done only on the basis of physical characteristics. The **selection process** following initial screening is more rigorous. For example, physical characteristics alone do not provide many clues about a person's potential for management, or for any other kind of work for that matter. What is needed, of course, are samples of behavior, either through tests and personal interviews or through the testimony of others about a candidate, as with reference checks.

Past the selection stage, we are no longer dealing with job candidates, we are dealing with new employees. Typically, the first step in their introduction to company policies, practices, and benefits (technically, this is called "socialization") is an **orientation** program. Orientation may take up several hours or several weeks; it may be formal, informal, or some combination of the two. As we shall see in Chapter 8, orientation has more significant and lasting effects than most people might expect.

Placement occurs after orientation; placement is the assignment of individuals to jobs. In large firms, for example, individuals may be selected initially on the basis of their potential to succeed in general management. After they have been observed and assessed during an intensive management training program, however, the organization is in a much better position to assign them to specific jobs within broader job families, such as marketing, production, or sales. (There are instances in which employees are selected specifically to fill certain positions; these are so-called one-shot selection-placement programs.) The technical expertise and the resources necessary to implement optimal placement programs (select, orient, then place) are found mostly in very large organizations, such as the military.

Once new employees are selected, oriented, and placed, they can be *trained* to achieve a competent level of job performance. As we shall see in the next chapter, training is very big business.

Finally, **performance appraisal,** one component of a performance-management system, provides feedback to employees regarding their past and present job performance proficiency, as well as a basis for improving performance in the future. The first time a new employee's performance is appraised, it is like pushing a button that starts a continuous loop, more precisely a continuous feedback loop, comprising the employee's performance, the manager's appraisal of it, and the communication between the two about performance and appraisal.

Of course, all the phases of recruiting and selecting employees are interrelated. But the final test of all phases comes with the appraisal of job performance. There is no point in reporting that, say, 150 possible candidates were recruited and screened, 90 offers were extended, and 65 candidates were hired and trained, if the first appraisal of their performance indicates that most were inept. Remember that, when you evaluate the performance of new hires, you are doing so within the context of a system, or a network of human resource activities, and you are really appraising recruitment, selection, and training, among other HRM activities.

Recruitment policies ultimately depend on the structure and functioning of internal and external labor markets. Let us therefore discuss labor market issues in some detail.

Developing Recruitment Policies: Labor Market Issues

A **labor market** is a geographical area within which the forces of supply (people looking for work) interact with the forces of demand (employers looking for people) and thereby determine the price of labor.[5] In a tight labor market, demand by employers exceeds the available supply of workers, which tends to exert upward pressure on wages. In a loose labor market, the reverse is true: The supply of workers exceeds employer demand, exerting downward pressure on wages. In recent years the labor market for software developers, computer and electrical engineers, information-technology workers, and aircraft mechanics has been fairly tight; wages for these jobs have been increasing steadily.[6] On the other hand, the labor market for lawyers, steelworkers, and unskilled labor has been fairly loose in recent years, reducing pressure for wage increases for these workers.

Unfortunately, it is not possible to define the geographical boundaries of a labor market in any clear-cut manner.[7] Employers needing key employees will recruit far and wide if necessary. Indeed, for certain types of jobs and certain firms, the Internet has made recruitment from global labor markets a reality. In short, employers do not face a single, homogeneous market for labor, but rather a series of discontinuous, segmented labor markets over which supply-and-demand conditions vary substantially.[8] Economists focus on this fact as the major explanation for wage differences among occupations and among geographical areas.

Of practical concern to managers, however, is a reasonably accurate definition of labor markets for planning purposes. Here are some factors that are important for defining the limits of a labor market[9]:

- Geography.
- Education and/or technical background required to perform a job.
- Industry.
- Licensing or certification requirements.
- Union membership.

Companies may use one or more of these factors to help define their labor markets. Thus an agricultural research firm that needs to hire four veterinarians cannot restrict its search to a local area since the market is national or international in scope. Union membership is not a concern in this market, but licensing and/or certification is. Typically a doctor of veterinary medicine degree is required along with state licensure to practice. Applicants are likely to be less concerned with where the job is located and more concerned with job design and career opportunities. On the other hand, suppose a brewery is trying to hire a journey-level plumber. The brewery will be looking at a labor market defined primarily by geographic proximity, and secondarily by people whose experience, technical background, and (possibly) willingness to join a union after employment qualify them for the job.

Internal versus External Labor Markets

The discussion thus far has concerned the structure and function of external labor markets. Internal labor markets also affect recruitment policies, in many cases more directly, because firms often give preference to present employees in promotions, transfers, and other career-enhancing opportunities. Each employing unit is a separate market. At Delta Air Lines, for example, virtually all jobs above the entry level are filled by internal promotion rather than by outside recruitment. Delta looks to its present employees as its source of labor supply, and workers look to this "internal labor market" to advance their careers. In the internal labor markets of most organizations, employees peddle their talents to available "buyers."[10] Three elements compose the internal labor market:

- Formal and informal practices that determine how jobs are organized and described.
- Methods for choosing among candidates.
- Procedures and authorities through which potential candidates are generated by those responsible for filling open jobs.

In an open internal labor market, every available job is advertised throughout the organization, and anyone can apply. Preference is given to internal candidates by withholding outside advertising until the job has been on the internal market for several days. Finally, each candidate for a job receives an interview.

Recruitment Policies and Labor Market Characteristics

A great deal of research suggests that employers change their policies in response to changes in market conditions.[11] For example, as labor becomes increasingly scarce, employers may change their policies in the following ways:

- Improving the characteristics of vacant positions, for example, by raising salaries or increasing training and educational benefits.
- Reducing hiring standards.
- Using more (and more expensive) recruiting methods.
- Extending searches over a wider geographical area.

As we have seen, legal considerations are an important component of recruitment policies. Workforce utilization is a central issue in this area.

LEGALITIES

WORKFORCE UTILIZATION

Workforce utilization is simply a way of identifying whether or not the composition of the workforce—measured by race and sex—employed in a particular job category in a particular firm is representative of the composition of the entire labor market available to perform that job. To see what considerations this implies, let's consider this situation: There is a town where 10 percent of the females and 15 percent of the African Americans are qualified arc welders. Now let's say that a firm in this town needs and has on staff 20 arc welders, of whom none are female and 3 are African American. If the representation of the workforce reflects the representation of qualified arc welders in the town, we should expect to find $20 \times 0.15 = 3$ African-American arc welders, and $20 \times 0.10 = 2$ female arc welders. Yet no female arc welders are employed at the firm. Now can you begin to see what workforce utilization is all about?

One of the main things that must be considered in workforce utilization is the available labor market, which the courts refer to as the "relevant labor market." In practice, some courts have defined the relevant labor market for jobs that require skills not possessed by the general population as those living within a reasonable commuting or recruiting area for the facility who are in the same occupational classification as the job in question.[12]

In computing workforce utilization statistics, begin by preparing a table, such as Table 6–1, which examines the job group "managers." (Similar analyses must also be done for eight other categories of employees specified by the EEOC.) This table shows that of 90 managers, 20 are African American and 15 are female. However, labor market data indicate that 30 percent and 10 percent of the available labor market for managers are African American and female, respectively. Hence, for workforce representation to reach parity with labor market representation, 0.30×90, or 27, of the managers should be African American and 0.10×90, or 9, should be female. The recruitment goal, therefore, is to hire 7 more African Americans to reach parity with the available labor force. What about the 6 excess female managers? The utilization analysis serves simply as a "red flag," calling attention to recruitment needs. The extra female managers will not be furloughed or fired. However, they may be given additional training, or they may be transferred to other jobs that might provide them with greater breadth of experience, particularly if utilization analyses for those other jobs indicate a need to recruit additional females.

Table 6–1

AFRICAN-AMERICAN AND FEMALE UTILIZATION ANALYSIS FOR MANAGERIAL JOBS

Managers employed by the firm			Percent available in relevant labor market		Utilization*		Goal	
Total	African Americans	Females	African Americans	Females	African Americans	Females	African Americans	Females
90	20	15	30	10	−7 (22%)	+6 (17%)	27	9

*Under the "utilization" column, the −7 for African Americans means that according to the relevant labor market, the African Americans are underrepresented by 7 managers, and the +6 for females means that not only are the females adequately represented, but there are 6 more female managers than needed to meet parity according to the relevant labor market.

At this point, a logical question is, how large a disparity between the composition of the workforce employed and the composition of the available labor market constitutes a prima facie case of unfair discrimination by the employer? Fortunately the Supreme Court has provided some guidance on this question in its ruling in *Hazelwood School District v. United States*.[13] To appreciate the Court's ruling, it is necessary to describe the reasoning behind it. In examining disparities between workforce representation and labor force representation, the first step is to compute the difference between the actual number of employees in a particular job category (e.g., the 20 African-American managers in Table 6–1) and the number expected if the workforce were truly representative of the labor force (27 African-American managers). The Court ruled that if the difference between the actual number and the expected number is so large that the difference would have only 1 chance in 20 of occurring by chance alone, it is reasonable to conclude that race was a factor in the hiring decisions made. If the odds of the difference occurring by chance alone are greater than 1 in 20 (e.g., 1 in 10), it is reasonable to conclude that race was not a factor in the hiring decisions. Statistical tests can be used to compute the probability that the differences occurred by chance.

RECRUITMENT—A TWO-WAY PROCESS

Recruitment frequently is treated as if it were a one-way process—something organizations do to search for prospective employees. This approach may be termed a "prospecting" theory of recruitment. In practice, however, prospective employees and managers seek out organizations just as organizations seek them out. This view, termed a "mating" theory of recruitment, appears more realistic. Recruitment success (from the organization's perspective) and job search success (from the candidate's perspective) both depend on timing. If there is a match between organizational recruitment efforts and a candidate's job search efforts, conditions are ripe for the two to meet.

In order for organizations and candidates actually to meet, however, three other conditions must be satisfied. There must be a common communication medium (e.g., the organization advertises in a trade journal read by the candidate), the candidate perceives a match between his or her personal characteristics and the organization's stated job requirements, and the candidate is motivated to apply for the job. Comprehensive recruitment-planning efforts must address these issues.

RECRUITMENT PLANNING

Recruitment begins with a clear specification of (1) the number of people needed (e.g., through workforce forecasts and utilization analyses), and (2) when they are needed. Implicit in the latter is a time frame—the duration between the receipt of

Table 6–2

AVERAGE TIME SPAN FOR EVENTS IN A RECRUITMENT PIPELINE

Sequence of events		
From	**To**	**Average number of days**
Résumé	Invitation	5
Invitation	Interview	6
Interview	Offer	4
Offer	Acceptance	7
Acceptance	Report to work	<u>21</u>
Total length of the pipeline		43

a résumé and the time a new hire starts work. This time frame is sometimes referred to as the "recruitment pipeline." The "flow" of events through the pipeline is represented as in Table 6–2. The table shows that if an operating manager sends a requisition for a new hire to the HR Department today, it will take almost a month and a half, 43 days on average, before an employee fulfilling that requisition actually starts work. Among organizations with between 1 and 500 employees, one survey found that, in practice, the average length of the pipeline is 41 days.[14] A recent study of Fortune 500 firms found that the average firm cut about 6 days off its hiring cycle by posting jobs online instead of in newspapers, another four days by taking online applications instead of paper ones, and more than a week by screening and processing applications electronically.[15] The HR department must make sure that operating and staff managers realize and understand information such as is represented by this pipeline.

One of the ways that operating and staff managers can be sure that their recruitment needs will fit the length of the recruitment pipeline is by examining the segments of the overall workforce by job group (e.g., clerical, sales, production, engineering, managers). For each of these job groups, the HR department, with the cooperation of operating managers who represent each job group, should examine what has occurred over the past several years in terms of new hires, promotions, transfers, and turnover. This will help provide an index of what to expect in the coming year, other things remaining equal.

INTERNAL RECRUITMENT

In deciding where, when, and how to implement recruitment activities, initial consideration should be given to a company's current employees, especially for filling jobs above the entry level. If external recruitment efforts are undertaken without considering the desires, capabilities, and potential of present employees (e.g., the 6 excess female managers shown in Table 6–1), a firm may incur both short- and long-run costs. In the short run, morale may degenerate; in the long run, firms with a reputation for consistent neglect of in-house talent may find it difficult to attract new employees and to retain experienced ones. This is why soundly conceived action plans (that incorporate developmental and training needs) and management succession plans are so important.

One of the thorniest issues confronting internal recruitment is the reluctance of managers to grant permission for their subordinates to be interviewed for potential transfer or promotion. As one reviewer put it, "Most supervisors are about as reluctant to release a current employee as they are to take a cut in pay."[16] To overcome this aversion, promotion-from-within policies must receive strong top-management support, coupled with a company philosophy that permits employees to consider available opportunities within the organization.

Among the channels available for internal recruitment, the most popular ones are succession plans (discussed in Chapter 5), job posting, employee referrals, and temporary worker pools.

Job Posting

Advertising available jobs internally began in the early days of affirmative action, as a means of providing equal opportunity for women and minorities to compete. It served as a method of getting around the "old boy" network, where jobs sometimes were filled more by "who you knew" than by "what you knew." Today **job posting** is an established practice in many organizations, especially for filling jobs up to the lower executive level.

Openings are published on bulletin boards (electronic or hard-copy) or in lists available to all employees. Interested employees must reply within a specified number of days, and they may or may not have to obtain the consent of their immediate supervisors.[17] Some job-posting systems apply only to the plant or office in which a job is located, while other companies will relocate employees.

Job Posting at Nortel Networks.   Nortel has contracted with Monster.com to create its own job board, called Job Shop. Says the firm's director of internal mobility: "I want to make it drop-dead easy to find your next opportunity internally." The goal is to provide an internal version of what is available in the outside market, thereby redistributing talent within Nortel's growing businesses and preventing employees from leaving for competitors. Any employee can post a résumé on Job Shop without alerting his or her superior, and any manager can post a job opening. The system automatically alerts managers' superiors after openings are posted.[18]

While there are clear advantages to job posting, potential disadvantages arise if employees "game" the system by transferring to new jobs in other company departments or locations that do not require different or additional skills, simply as a way of obtaining grade or salary increases. To avoid this problem, it is critical to establish consistent pay policies across jobs and locations. Further, if no limits are placed on the bidding process, job posting systems can impose substantial administrative costs. Thus, at some firms, employees cannot bid on a new job until at least 1 year after hire, and they must have accrued at least 6 months' tenure in their current jobs before becoming eligible to bid for new ones.[19]

Another problem might arise from poor communication. For example, if employees who unsuccessfully apply for open jobs do not receive feedback that might help them to be more competitive in the future, and if they have to find out through the grapevine that someone else got the job they applied for, a job posting program cannot be successful. The lesson for managers is obvious: Regular communication and follow-up feedback are essential if job posting is to work properly.

Employee Referrals

Referral of job candidates by present employees has been and continues to be a major source of new hires at many levels, including professionals. It is an internal recruitment method, since internal rather than external sources are used to attract candidates. Typically such programs offer a cash or merchandise bonus when a current employee refers a successful candidate to fill a job opening. The logic behind employee referral is that "it takes one to know one." Interestingly, the rate of employee participation seems to remain unaffected by such efforts as higher cash bonuses, cars, or expense-paid trips.[20] This suggests that good employees will not refer potentially undesirable candidates even if the rewards are outstanding.

Employee Referrals at MasterCard.   In 1995, employee referrals accounted for less than 10 percent of all new hires, but by 1999 that number had zoomed to almost 40 percent. MasterCard pays current employees $1,000 for referrals of hourly workers, and $2,000 to $3,000 for referrals of professionals.

What makes this program different, however, is that MasterCard pays its employees *immediately* for anyone hired from their referrals. Initially there was concern that some employees might make bad referrals just to get the money. That concern ended when one employee pointed out that it was employees' responsibility to make the referral, and then it was the responsibility of HR and the hiring manager to make the decision to hire. It's their fault if a bad hiring decision was made, so why punish the employee?

By changing the program to pay the employee immediately upon the hire of a candidate he or she referred, MasterCard generated goodwill among its employees, and within 1 year it quadrupled the number of referrals from present employees. Subsequent research revealed that the referral program pays for itself nearly tenfold in terms of the savings in recruitment and retention costs, and that has helped convince some very skeptical upper managers of the value of the program.[21]

Some firms have created online alumni networks to find and rehire former employees. For example, some 8,000 former employees signed onto New York Life Insurance's alumni network in the first month of its existence. Other sites, such as Referrals.com, pay participants for confidential leads such as tips on colleagues who might be interested in moving to new jobs.[22]

Three factors seem to be instrumental in the prescreening process of referrals: the morale of present employees, the accuracy and detail of job information, and the closeness of the intermediary friend.[23] While employee referrals clearly have advantages, it is important to note that from an EEO perspective, employee referrals are fine as long as the workforce is diverse in gender, race, and ethnicity to begin with. A potential disadvantage, at least for some firms, is that employee referrals tend to perpetuate the perspective and belief systems of the current work force. This may not be the best way to go for organizations that are trying to promote changes in strategy, outlook, or orientation.

Temporary Worker Pools

Unlike workers supplied from temporary agencies, in-house "temporaries" work directly for the hiring organization and may receive benefits, depending on the number of scheduled hours worked per week. Temporary workers (e.g., in clerical jobs, accounting, word processing) help meet fluctuating labor demands due to such factors as illness, vacations, terminations, and resignations. Companies save on commissions to outside agencies, which may be as high as 50 percent or more of a temporary employee's hourly wages.[24]

In the health care field, Hospital Corp. of America operates an internal pool of 2,000 itinerant registered nurses who circulate among the company's 83 hospitals in 19 cities on 13-week assignments. The nurses get a monthly housing allowance, even if they stay with their families or friends, and they keep accruing benefits and seniority rather than starting anew each time they take an assignment.[25]

The Travelers Corporation established a pool of temporaries made up of its own retirees. A recent survey showed the growing popularity of this practice. Almost half the firms surveyed used retirees under some contractual arrangement, about 10 percent allowed retirees to share jobs with other employees, and most retirees continued to receive pension and insurance benefits when they came back to work. About 40 percent of the respondents paid market rates for jobs performed by retirees, while 26 percent paid retirees what they had received at the time they retired.[26]

EXTERNAL RECRUITMENT

To meet demands for talent brought about by business growth, a desire for fresh ideas, or to replace employees who leave, organizations periodically turn to the outside labor market. Keep in mind, however, that the recruitment practices of large and small firms differ considerably. Those of larger firms tend to be more formal and bureaucratic than those of smaller firms. In addition, many job seekers have distinct preferences regarding firm size, and they actively seek those types of employers to the exclusion of those that do not meet their preferences. One might argue, therefore, that large and small firms are separate labor markets.[27] In this section we will describe four of the most popular recruitment sources: university relations, executive search firms, employment agencies, and recruitment advertising. Because they are both time consuming and expensive, large employers are more likely to use university relations and executive search firms.

University Relations

What used to be known as "college recruiting" is now considerably broader in many companies. The companies have targeted certain schools that best meet their needs and have broadened the scope of their interactions with them.[28] Such activities may now include, in addition to recruitment, gifts and grants to the institutions, summer employment and consulting projects for faculty, and invitations to placement officers to visit company plants and offices.

Mobil is a good example of this trend. The company now deals with only about 50 colleges and universities, instead of the 200 or so on its list a few years ago. It also uses separate teams (made up of six to eight people from various Mobil units) for each school. Many of the team members are alumni or alumnae of the school they are assigned to. They help plan the dozen or so campus activities each year, such as providing talent for student organizations, conducting career-information days, holding receptions, and sponsoring ceremonies at which recruiters present Mobil Foundation checks to support some campus activity. The recruitment-team strategy has already helped to increase the number of graduates hired from targeted schools.[29]

COMPANY EXAMPLE

HOW BOOZ, ALLEN & HAMILTON SHOWS WHAT MANAGEMENT CONSULTANTS REALLY DO[30]

Would-be recruits at Booz, Allen & Hamilton go online to view realistic job previews. The firm launched a website featuring consultants as they work on projects for a pro bono client. Viewers can follow consultants' progress, and see how they deal with clients, team members, and their friends and families outside of work. The weekly episodes are edited video clips rather than live streaming video, and each one features interactive questions and answers plus detailed information about each of the project's consultants. While some might criticize this approach for making consultants even more visible to executive recruiters, Booz, Allen is not concerned. Said one partner: "The reality of the workplace right now is that if a headhunter wants to find our staff, they can." How true. Booz, Allen is not alone in promoting online employee videos to applicants. Some firms have 24-hour "recruit cams" tracking the workplace, while others, such as Lehman Brothers Holdings, Inc., feature detailed "day-in-the-life" employee profiles. All are attempting to provide realistic previews to prospective new hires.

To enhance the yield from campus recruitment efforts, employers should consider the following research-based guidelines[31]:

1. Establish a "presence" on college campuses beyond just the on-campus interviewing period (as Mobil has done).
2. Upgrade the content and specificity of recruiting materials. Many are far too general in nature. Instead, provide more detailed information about the characteristics of entry-level jobs, especially those that have had a significant positive effect on the decisions of prior applicants to join the organization. See the company example of Booz, Allen & Hamilton.
3. Devote more time and resources to training on-campus interviewers to answer specific job-related questions of applicants.
4. For those candidates who are invited for on-site company visits, provide itineraries and agendas prior to their arrival. Written materials should answer candidates' questions dealing with travel arrangements, expense reimbursements, and whom to contact at the company and how.
5. Ensure that the attributes of vacant positions are comparable to those of competitors. This is as true for large as for small organizations. Some of the key job attributes that influence the decisions of applicants are the opportunities for creativity or to exercise initiative, promotional opportunities, and long-term income potential. They tend to rank starting salary as less important than these factors.[32]

Executive Search Firms

Such firms are retained typically to recruit for senior-level positions that command salaries over $115,000 (in 2001 dollars) and total compensation packages worth in excess of $160,000. The reasons for doing so may include a need to maintain confidentiality from an incumbent or a competitor, a lack of local resources to recruit executive-level individuals, or insufficient time. To use an executive search consultant most effectively requires time and commitment from the hiring organization. It must allow the consultant to become a company "insider," to develop knowledge and familiarity with the business, its strategic plans, and key players.[33]

Although using an executive search firm has advantages, employers evaluating a search firm should carefully consider the following indications that the firms can do competent work[34]:

- The firm has defined its market position by industries rather than by disciplines or as a jack-of-all-trades.

- The firm understands how your organization functions within the industries served.
- The firm is performance-oriented and compensates the search salesperson substantially on the basis of assignment completion.
- The firm combines the research and recruiting responsibilities into one function. Doing so allows the researcher-recruiter to make a more comprehensive and knowledgeable presentation to targeted candidates on behalf of the client.
- The firm uses primary research techniques for locating sources. Secondary research techniques in the form of computerized databases, files of unsolicited résumés, and directories can identify qualified candidates, but finding top performers requires a more personalized approach. In fact, only one in 300 unsolicited résumés is likely to be shown to a client, and only one in 3,000 of these job seekers may get a job.[35]
- The firm is organized to function as a task force in the search for candidates, particularly where they are being recruited for multiple assignments or when placement speed is essential.
- The firm is a member of the Association of Executive Search Consultants (AESC), and subscribes to AESC's Practice Standards and Code of Ethics.

Compared to other recruitment sources, executive search firms are quite expensive. Total fees may reach 30 to 35 percent of the compensation package of the new hire. Fees are often paid as follows: a retainer amounting to one-third the total fee as soon as the search is commissioned; one-third 60 days into the assignment; and a final third upon completion. If an organization hires a candidate on its own prior to the completion of the search, it still must pay all or some portion of the search firm's fee, unless it makes other arrangements.[36]

Employment Agencies

These are some of the most widely available and mostly widely used outside sources. However, there is great variability in size and quality across agencies. To achieve best results from this channel, cultivate a small number of firms and thoroughly describe the characteristics (e.g., education, training, experience) of candidates needed, the fee structure, and the method of resolving disputes.[37]

Agency fees generally vary from 10 percent of the starting salary for clerical and support staff to 20 to 30 percent of the starting salary for professional, exempt-level hires. Unlike executive search firms, however, employment agencies receive payment only if one of their referrals results in a hire. In addition, most agencies offer prorated refunds if a candidate proves unacceptable. For example, an agency might return 90 percent of its fee if a candidate leaves within 30 days, 60 percent if the new hire lasts between 30 and 60 days, and 30 percent if the new hire leaves after 60 to 90 days on the job.[38] Table 6–3 summarizes the differences between executive search firms and employment agencies.

Recruitment Advertising

When this medium is mentioned, most people think of want ads in the local newspaper. But think again. This medium has become just as colorful, lively, and imaginative as consumer advertising. Today companies approach job

Table 6–3

DIFFERENCES BETWEEN EXECUTIVE SEARCH FIRMS AND EMPLOYMENT AGENCIES

Services	Executive search firms	Employment agencies
Financial arrangements	Fees based on 30 to 35 percent of candidate's salary and time needed to recruit, or a flat rate plus expenses.	Fees based on 20 to 35 percent of candidate's starting salary.
	Retainer fee required; payment due even if opening filled through other sources.	No retainer fee; fee due only if position filled by agency.
	Staff compensation may include salary, bonus, profit sharing, and incentives for business generation.	Staff compensation usually depends on commissions for placements made.
Caseload	Personal consultant handles only three to five cases at once.	Agent works with many open job orders at one time.
	Firms usually handle openings at higher levels of organization.	Agencies typically assigned lower-level vacancies.
Relationship with clients	Firms represent employers only.	Agencies represent employers and job seekers.
	General management involved in decision to retain search firm.	HR department makes decision to use agency.
	Consultant thoroughly researches client organization and position requirements before search.	Agents spend less time on initial research and job specifications. Some assignments handled by phone with no personal contact.
	Firms conduct assignments on an exclusive basis.	Agencies compete with similar companies for placements.
Time commitment	Consultant invests 40 to 50 hours per month on each search.	Limited investment of time on any client, due to lack of guaranteed payment.
Referral rates and guarantees	Two to four highly qualified candidates recommended to each client.	Large numbers of applicants referred to increase odds of a placement.
	Recruitment and evaluation efforts target broad range of candidates, most of whom are not in job market.	Recruitment focuses mainly on candidates actively seeking new employment.
	Process and results oriented.	Placement oriented.
	Reputable firms offer a professional guarantee and commitment to thorough, ethical practices.	Contingency fee arrangement eliminates any obligation to produce results.
Level of client involvement	Minimal HR and management time involvement required.	Considerable HR time required to screen, interview, and evaluate candidates.

Source: J. S. Lord, External and internal recruitment, in W. F. Cascio (ed.), *Human resource planning, employment, and placement.* Bureau of National Affairs, Washington, DC, 1989, pp. 2–87, 2–88.

The Internet is a popular medium among job seekers and employees alike.

candidates in much the same way as prospective customers: carefully identified and targeted, attracted to the company and its brand, and then sold on the job. Corporate home pages on the Internet are often designed with potential recruits in mind, as they're frequently the first place job seekers look when they begin to evaluate companies. GE Power Systems highlights links to information about diversity, employee benefits, and balancing work and family. Accenture (formerly Andersen Consulting) and Enterprise Rent-a-Car are just two of the many companies that provide compelling materials on their websites about why people should work there.[39]

COMPANY EXAMPLE   ## HELP WANTED: ONLINE JOB SEARCH[40]

Consider these facts. Currently more than 90 percent of large corporations in the United States use the Internet to recruit employees, and every day more than 55 million Americans surf the Internet, either for entertainment, business, or commerce purposes. While recruiters are expected to spend $1.7 billion on Internet recruitment by 2003, at the same time spending on more traditional sources, such as classified ads, has declined 26 percent in the past year alone. Job board Monster.com contains more than 11 million résumés of job seekers, and sites such as Hotjobs.com, Headhunter.net, and Telecomcareers.net contain millions more. While the big sites want job seekers to post résumé data in a standardized format to make it easier for prospective employers to search through them, there is a downside to this process. It tends to overlook persons with unique skills or experience. To overcome this problem, niche sites, such as Craigslist.com (rated by Forrester Research as the Net's most efficient job-placement site), Itcareers.com, and Journalismjobs.com, allow job seekers to cut and paste their own résumés. On the flip side, a recent survey by Wetfeet.com, a San Francisco Internet recruiting-services firm, found that many companies posting openings on the web get carried away with slick presentations and tend to neglect things such as easy site navigation and job-interview information. Almost 30 percent of survey respondents eliminated employers from consideration because of bad websites. There are two lessons in all this. One, companies that get the basics right and make it easy for job candidates to use their sites can beat their competitors to the best talent. Two, niche sites that specialize, for example in health care, journalism, or information technology, may be more efficient than broad sites in helping online job seekers to focus their searches.

This is just a brief glimpse into external recruitment sources. Others include career fairs, outplacement firms, former employees, trade shows, co-op and work-study programs, government employment agencies, alumni associations, racial and ethnic organizations, and freestanding, online talent sites. For example, on a typical Monday, the peak day for job hunts, about 4 million people search for work on the job board at Monster.com, the leading online talent site.[41] Conversely, more than 1 million people put their résumés on-line every year.[42]

SPECIAL INDUCEMENTS—RELOCATION AID, HELP FOR THE TRAILING SPOUSE, AND SIGN-ON BONUSES

Especially with higher-level jobs, newly recruited managers expect some form of relocation assistance. Such assistance may include disposal of the residence left behind, lease-breaking expenses, temporary living expenses, and moving costs, to name just a few. Such costs add up quickly. The average cost of relocating a home-owning current employee in 2001 was $57,279. For a home-owning new hire it was $45,948.[43]

Prodded by the emergence of the dual-career family (60 percent of all families[44]), firms are finding that many managers and professionals, men and women alike, are reluctant to relocate unless the spouse will be able to find suitable employment in a new location. "If I can't work, I won't move." That is what more and more companies are hearing from the spouses of prospective transferees, and it is not music to their ears.[45] On average, employers paid about $1,350 in spouse-employment assistance in 2001,[46] primarily for job counseling, fees to placement agencies, contacts outside the company, and to cover the costs of printing résumés.[47]

An increasingly common recruiting inducement, independent of any relocation assistance, is the sign-on bonus. Originally used in the sports world, signing bonuses are now common among executives, professionals (particularly in high-technology firms), and to middle-level executives, as companies seek to buttress the eroding bonds between them and their employees.

What's a company to do if things don't work out and the new person simply walks away with the cash? Firms such as General Electric and Owens-Corning require that the entire amount be repaid if the person leaves within one year, and 50 percent if he or she leaves within 2 years. After that, the repayment gradually drops to zero.[48]

With the explosion of new technologies being developed for internal computer networks and the Internet, high-technology companies are going after all the talent they can find. In fact, competition for experienced workers is so intense that "you have to treat your current employees as though you were recruiting them" [to stave off raids by rivals] says the chief technology officer at Sun Microsystems, Inc.[49] He's right. A project leader at Sun with 6 years experience recently left to join a rival. Why? It offered a $6,000 signing bonus plus 1,500 shares of the company's stock.[50]

Summary Findings Regarding Recruitment Sources

Now that we have examined some of the most popular sources for internal and external recruiting, it seems reasonable to ask "Which sources are most popular with employers and job applicants?" Among employers, evidence indicates that:

- Informal contacts are used widely and effectively at all occupational levels.
- Use of public employment services declines as required skills levels increase.
- The internal market is a major recruitment source except for entry-level, unskilled, and semiskilled workers.
- Larger firms are the most frequent users of walk-ins, write-ins, and the internal market.[51]

However, for recruiting workers from underrepresented groups, a study of 20,000 applicants in a major insurance company revealed that female and African-American applicants consistently used formal recruitment sources (corporate websites, general job-listing sites, advertising) rather than informal ones (walk-ins, write-ins, employee referrals). Nevertheless, informal sources produced the best-quality applicants for all groups (males, females, African Americans, Hispanics, and under and over 40 years of age), and led to proportionately more hires.[52]

Factors Affecting Recruitment Success

A survey of 500 companies revealed how factors such as the source of résumés, type of position, geographic location, and time constraints all can influence recruitment success.[53] With regard to résumés, managers surveyed judged only about 7 percent of incoming résumés to be worth routing to hiring managers. However, the growing use of artificial intelligence software to identify and match applicant characteristics with job requirements may help to improve the overall accuracy of the process.[54]

The rate of invitations to visit varied markedly (from 8 to 60 percent), depending on the type of position in question. Generally, candidates for technical and lower-level positions had the highest invitation rates. However, the invitation rate fell as the level of position rose. About 40 percent of those interviewed received job offers, with candidates for lower-level positions earning the highest offer rates. Nontechnical positions generated twice as many acceptances (82 percent) as technical positions (41 percent).

With respect to geographical location, positions requiring relocation generated fewer acceptances to interview requests and (not surprisingly) fewer employment offers. A final factor that affects recruitment needs is time. Adequate assessment of recruitment needs begins with accurate staffing analysis and forecasting. However, a large number of unexpected retirements, resignations, or terminations may place unrealistic time demands on recruiters. Although time frames differ from job to job and industry to industry, three months from the receipt of a requisition to the new employee's start date is considered an acceptable time period for recruiting a journey-level professional.[55]

Diversity-Oriented Recruiting

Special measures are called for in diversity-oriented recruiting. While it might appear obvious that employers should use women and members of underrepresented groups (1) in their HR offices as interviewers, (2) on recruiting trips to high schools, colleges, and job fairs, and (3) in employment advertisements, these are necessary, but not sufficient, steps. Diverse candidates consider broader factors in their decisions to apply or to remain with organizations. In fact, a recent WetFeet.com study found that, although as many as 44 percent of African-American candidates said they eliminated a company from consideration because of a lack of gender or ethnic diversity, three other diversity-related attributes affected their decisions to apply or remain. These were the ready availability of training and career-development programs, the presence of a diverse upper management, and the presence of a diverse workforce.[56]

Employers need to establish contacts in the groups targeted for recruitment based on credibility between the employer and the contact and credibility between the contact and the targeted groups. Allow plenty of lead time for the contacts in the targeted groups to notify prospective applicants and for the applicants to apply for available positions.

Various community or professional organizations might be contacted (e.g., Society of Mexican-American Engineers and Scientists, National Society of Black Engineers), and leaders of those organizations should be encouraged to visit the employer and to talk with employees. As we saw in Chapter 4, this strategy was used successfully by Pacific Bell in its effort to recruit high-potential Hispanic candidates.[57] Another source is *Outreach and Recruitment Directory: A Resource for Diversity-Related Recruitment Needs.*[58] The directory is available as a hardcover book or as software, and the database can be sorted by a variety of factors, such as job type, location, target population, or specific types of organizations.

For companies that use search firms to recruit executives, some offer an additional 5 percent of the first year's salary—in addition to the usual 30 percent fee—if the search consultant can find qualified minorities to fill a position.[59] Frequent use of the phrase "an equal opportunity–equal access employer" is a "must" in diversity-oriented recruiting. Finally, recognize two things: (1) it will take time to establish a credible, workable diversity-oriented recruitment program, and (2) there is no payoff from passive nondiscrimination.

What are firms actually doing in this area to increase workforce diversity? Kraft General Foods, Phillip Morris, and Dun & Bradstreet are typical. They are revamping their decentralized recruitment systems in order to develop a coordinated recruitment effort. They have begun by gathering data on who, when, and where they recruit, and how they fare with different groups. The goal is to create a consistent corporate image that will support recruiting efforts across the board.[60]

Figure 6–2

Traditional approach to résumé processing.

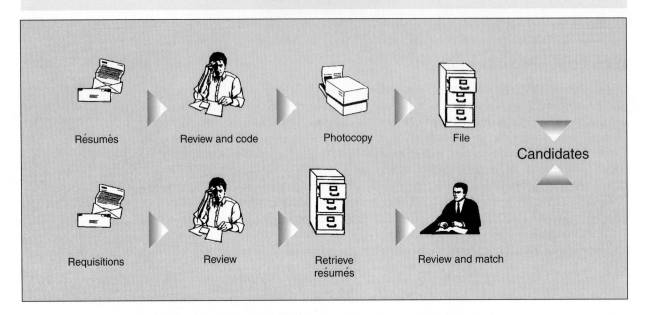

MANAGING RECRUITMENT OPERATIONS

Administratively, recruitment is one of the easiest activities to foul up—with potentially long-term negative publicity for the firm. Traditionally, recruitment was intensively paper based. It proceeded as shown in Figure 6–2. A traditional employment department receives paper résumés, date-stamps them, and distributes them to individual recruiters. The recruiters then manually code, categorize, and file each individual résumé, frequently repeating this manual process hundreds of times a day.

Finding and matching candidates to open requisitions entails more manual paper processing. Papers must then be copied and forwarded to hiring managers for review, tracked manually with notes and comments, and refiled manually. Individuals are identified as future candidates or as employees, if they have been hired. The process is cumbersome and time consuming.

Reengineered Recruitment in the Information Age

With the Resumix6 System from HotJobs.com, Ltd., automation replaces the entire manual process (see Figure 6–3). Resumix6:

- Employs advanced scanning, optical character recognition (OCR), and imaging technologies to capture an exact on-line image of the original résumé (for résumés that are faxed or mailed in hard-copy form).
- Uses KnowledgeBase software that contains 25,000 skills that combine into 10 million practical combinations of search terms to extract key résumé information. It then inputs that information into an applicant résumé database.

Figure 6–3

Reengineered résumé processing with Resumix.

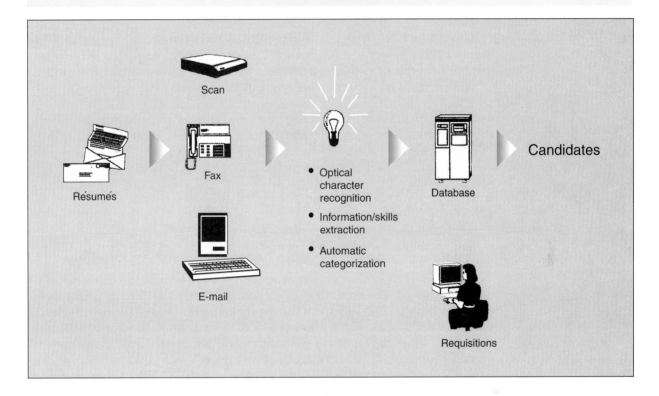

- Provides instant on-line access to résumé and skills information in the database.

After a résumé is processed, Resumix6 creates a résumé summary, containing the key information extracted from the résumé, including name, addresses, telephone numbers; degrees, schools, grade-point averages; work history, including dates, companies, job titles; and up to 80 skills. The KnowledgeBase software recognizes the contextual meanings of words within the résumé. For example, it can distinguish between John Harvard, a candidate; 140 Harvard Street, an address; Harvard University, a school, and Harvard, ID, a town. Simple keyword-based systems are much less efficient, for they will return all résumés containing the word "Harvard," Those résumés will then require subsequent analysis and classification.

Information in the résumé summary is stored in the applicant résumé database. The user searches against the database by building requisitions containing specific skill and experience criteria, and clicking on the search button. Resumix6 then provides a prioritized list of qualified applicants for review. It also can integrate to applicant kiosks, Interactive Voice Response (IVR) systems, and corporate Intranets.

How does the system work in practice? Firms such as Texas Instruments, Disney, Vanguard Group, and United Parcel Service Airlines have found that

Resumix6 has cut their cost per hire by up to 50 percent, and shortened their hiring cycles by an average of 48 percent.[61] That's a competitive advantage!

Evaluation and Control of Recruitment Operations

The reason for evaluating past and current recruitment operations is simple: to improve the efficiency of future recruitment efforts. To do this, it is necessary to analyze systematically the performance of the various recruitment sources. Consider collecting the following kinds of information[62]:

- Cost of operations, that is, labor costs of company recruitment staff, operational costs (e.g., recruiting staff's travel and living expenses, agency fees, advertising expenses, brochures, supplies, and postage), and overhead expenses (e.g., rental of temporary facilities and equipment).
- Cost per hire, by source.
- Number and quality of résumés by source.
- Acceptance/offer ratio.
- Analysis of post-visit and rejection questionnaires.
- Salary offered—acceptances versus rejections.

Cisco Systems is one company that diligently measures the outcomes of its recruiting efforts. For example, Cisco's cost per hire is just $6,556 versus an industry average of $10,800. Even during its high-growth period, from the early 1990s through 2000, Cisco's in-house staff of recruiters remained steady at about 100, while the company's annual rate of hiring rose from 2,000 to 8,000 people. The most important statistic, however, is 45 days. This is the average time it takes Cisco to fill an open job—down from 113 days three years ago. How avidly does Cisco pursue candidates online? It has software that tracks where visitors to its website go after leaving. It then places employment banner ads on those sites.[63]

Which recruitment sources are most *effective*? Over the past 30 years, this is one of the most intensely researched areas in recruitment. However, a recent review of that literature found that alternative sources did not consistently explain differences in subsequent performance, job attitudes, or turnover.[64] However, research with a national sample did reveal that the types of recruitment sources used vary by income and education (higher for applicants identified by recruiters, lower for walk-ins). It also revealed differences by gender (relatively more men were hired via recruiters and more women were hired via newspaper advertisements), and race (relatively more nonwhites were hired via recruiters and relatively more whites were hired via walk-ins and employment agencies).[65]

Indeed, a study of 10 different recruitment sources used by more than 20,000 applicants for the job of insurance agent showed that recruiting source explained only 5 percent of the variation in applicant quality, 1 percent of the variation in the survival of new hires, and none of the variation in commissions.[66] If sources do not differ appreciably on these important characteristics, organizations probably should rely on those that are less costly (e.g., Internet and newspaper ads) and produce higher-quality applicants (informal sources) than more expensive sources (employment agencies). However, regardless of the recruitment sources used to generate applicants, once a final applicant pool has been assembled, organizations can maximize the economic returns of selection by ignoring recruitment sources and using a top-down (i.e., rank order from best to least qualified) selection strategy.[67]

Several studies have examined the recruitment process from the perspective of applicants—how applicants regarded the various sources of information (on-campus interviewer-recruiter, friend, job incumbent, professor) about a job opportunity.[68] The studies investigated whether applicants regarded the information source as credible or not, which sources provided favorable or unfavorable job information, and which sources led to greater acceptances of job offers.

Findings indicated that the on-campus interviewer-recruiter, the first and often the only representative of a company seen by applicants, often was not liked, not trusted, and not perceived as knowing much about the job. Furthermore, applicants were more inclined to believe unfavorable information than favorable information, and they were more likely to accept jobs when the source of information about the job was not the interviewer. Other research has shown that job attributes (supervision, job challenge, location, salary, title) *as well as* recruitment activities (e.g., gender and educational characteristics of recruiter, behavior during the interview) are important to applicants' reactions. In short, recruitment may be viewed as a market exchange process in which employers attempt to differentiate their "products" (job opportunities) among "consumers" (job applicants) who vary in their levels of job-relevant knowledge, abilities, and skills.[69]

Timing issues in recruitment, particularly delays, are important factors in the job choice decisions of applicants.[70] Research indicates that (1) long delays between recruitment phases are not uncommon; (2) applicants react to such delays very negatively, often perceiving that "something is wrong" with the organization; and (3) regardless of their inferences, the most marketable candidates accept other offers if delays become extended. What are the implications of these findings? In a competitive marketplace, top talent disappears quickly. If you want to compete for it, streamline the decision-making process so that you can move fast.

Realistic Job Previews

A conceptual framework that might help explain some of these research findings is that of the **realistic job preview** (RJP).[71] An RJP requires that, in addition to telling applicants about the nice things a job has to offer (e.g., pay, benefits, opportunities for advancement), recruiters must also tell applicants about the unpleasant aspects of the job. For example, "It's hot, dirty, and sometimes you'll have to work on weekends." Research in actual company settings has indicated consistent results.[72] That is, when the unrealistically positive expectations of job applicants are lowered to match the reality of the actual work setting prior to hire, job acceptance rates may be lower and job performance is unaffected, but job satisfaction and survival are higher for those who receive an RJP. These conclusions have held up in different organizational settings (e.g., manufacturing versus service jobs) and when different RJP techniques are used (e.g., plant tours versus video presentations versus written descriptions of the work). In fact, RJPs improve retention rates, on average, by 9 percent.[73]

RJPs administered after hire also have positive effects. They help to reduce turnover, to cope with work demands, and they signal that the employer is concerned about the well-being of its new hires.[74]

Longitudinal research shows that RJPs should be balanced in their orientation. That is, they should enhance overly pessimistic expectations and reduce overly optimistic expectations. Doing so helps to bolster the applicant's perceptions of the organization as caring, trustworthy, and honest.[75]

A final recommendation is to develop RJPs even when there is no turnover problem (proactively rather than reactively). They should employ an audiovisual medium and, where possible, show actual job incumbents.[76]

Nevertheless, RJPs are not appropriate for all types of jobs. They seem to work best (1) when few applicants are actually hired (that is, the selection ratio is low), (2) when used with entry-level positions (since those coming from outside to inside the organization tend to have more inflated expectations than those who make changes internally), and (3) when unemployment is low (since job candidates are more likely to have alternative jobs to choose from).[77]

THE OTHER SIDE OF RECRUITMENT—JOB SEARCH

At some time or another, whether voluntarily or otherwise, almost everyone faces the difficult task of finding a job. Much of this chapter has emphasized recruitment from the organization's perspective. But as we noted at the outset, a

Ethical Dilemma
Online Resumes and Personal Privacy

Millions of people will transmit their résumés over the Internet this year. Is this a recruiting bonanza for employers? In one sense, yes, for they can scan online job boards using keywords to identify candidates with the educational background, training accomplishments, and workplace experience that they need. On the other hand, there are some very serious privacy concerns for job seekers, and employee relations concerns for employers, and they should be recognized.[78]

Résumés posted at one site can be can be traded or sold to other sites, they can be stolen by unscrupulous headhunters or duplicated and reposted by roving "spiders," and current employers can locate them as well. The Internet is so vast that many people think their résumés

are safe there. Think again, for a number of factors can wrest control from a job seeker. Here is one.

In the name of protecting company secrets, some corporations have begun to assign HR staff members to patrol cyberspace in search of wayward workers. Their objective is to reassign employees who are circulating their résumés online, and who therefore have one foot out the electronic door, off sensitive projects. Fair enough. But such a practice can also be viewed as an invasion of an employee's privacy and right to search for a job that might make better use of his or her skills. What do you think? Is it ethical for one's current employer to search the Internet in an effort to identify employees who have posted their résumés online?

mating theory of recruitment—in which organizations search for qualified candidates just as candidates search for organizations—is more realistic. How do people find jobs? Research shows that most people land jobs through personal contacts or networking, rather than through employment agencies or direct mailings of their résumés.[79] This is especially true for executives.[80] At the same time, networking is not necessarily superior to alternative job-search techniques. Keep this in mind as you read the following scenario.

Scenario 1—Unemployed

This scenario has happened all too frequently over the last decade (as a result of mergers, restructurings, and downsizings), and it is expected to occur often this decade as economic conditions change.[81] You are a mid-level executive, well regarded, well paid, and seemingly well established in your chosen field. Then—whammo!—a change in business strategy or a change in economic conditions results in your layoff from the firm you hoped to retire from. What do you do? How do you go about finding another job? According to management consultants and executive recruiters, the following are some of the key things not to do, followed by some suggestions for posting an Internet résumé.[82]

- **Don't panic.** A search takes time, even for well-qualified middle- and upper-level managers. Seven months to a year is not unusual. Be prepared to wait it out.
- **Don't be bitter.** Bitterness makes it harder to begin to search; it also turns off potential employers.
- **Don't kid yourself.** Do a thorough self-appraisal of your strengths and weaknesses, your likes and dislikes about jobs and organizations. Face up to what has happened, decide if you want to switch fields, figure out where you and your family want to live, and don't delay the search itself for long.
- **Don't drift.** Develop a plan, target companies, and go after them relentlessly. Realize that your job is to find a new job. Cast a wide net; consider industries other than your own.
- **Don't be lazy.** The heart of a good job hunt is research. Use reference books, public filings, and annual reports when drawing up a list of target companies. If negotiations get serious, talk to a range of insiders and knowledgeable outsiders to learn about politics and practices. You don't want to wind up in a worse fix than the one you left. Unfortunately, research indicates that only about 5 percent of job applicants do any research on a company before an interview.[83]
- **Don't be shy or overeager.** Since personal contacts are the most effective means to land a job, pull out all the stops to get the word out that you are available. At the same time, resist the temptation to accept the first job that comes along. Unless it's absolutely right for you, the chances of making a mistake are quite high.
- **Don't ignore your family.** Some executives are embarrassed and don't tell their families what's going on. A better approach, experts say, is to bring the family into the process and deal with issues honestly.

- **Don't lie**. Experts are unanimous on this point. Don't lie, and don't stretch a point—either on résumés or in interviews. Be willing to address failures as well as strengths. Discuss openly and fully what went wrong at your old job.
- **Don't jump the gun on salary**. Always let the potential employer bring this subject up first. But once it surfaces, thoroughly explore all aspects of your future compensation and benefits package.
- **If you post a résumé on the Internet,** post a digital version on your own home page and place the word "résumé" in the website address to increase your chance of being noticed by Internet recruiters. Also, place plenty of links to websites of present and former employers, colleges, professional associations, and publications on your digital résumé. Create a simpler version of your résumé to send to a recruiter or potential employer, and let them know a longer version is available. Use smaller, targeted job boards in your field. They can be more effective than the big, brand-name sites.

Those who have been through the trauma of job loss and the challenge of finding a job often describe the entire process as a wrenching, stressful one. Avoiding the mistakes shown above can ensure that finding a new job need not take any longer than necessary.

Scenario 2—Employed, but Searching for a New Job

People who are currently employed may decide to engage in job search for any one or more of the following reasons: to establish a network, to demonstrate their marketability to their current employers, or to develop other job choices to compare with their current positions. A recent study using currently employed managers found that they engaged in more job search behavior to the extent they were more agreeable (trusting, compliant, caring), neurotic (anxious, insecure, poorly emotionally adjusted), and open to experience (imaginative, nonconforming, autonomous). In addition, managers higher in cognitive ability searched more actively, perhaps in an effort to ensure that their "hidden" abilities are recognized.[84] What are the implications of these results for organizations? Assuming that the manager is someone you want to retain, communicate clearly that he or she is valued, and that there are rich opportunities within the organization. This is exactly what Home Depot does.

Home Depot allows all employees, no matter how junior, decision-making authority. In a service industry, that provides an edge over competitors. With 216,000 employees, Home Depot's culture is built from the inside out. More than 90 percent of non-entry-level jobs are filled internally, and only about 12 of the company's 400 department heads came from outside the company. The company calls its sales staff "Associates." As company founders Bernie Marcus and Arthur Blank wrote in *Built to Last,* their history of the company, "'Associate' implies an equal as opposed to a wage slave. We value what the salesperson on the store floor says just as much—sometimes more—than what the district manager says. . . . The salesperson touches the customer more."

Home Depot's stock purchase plan allows all employees to buy stock at any time for a 15 percent discount off the company's stock price, set once a year.

IMPACT OF RECRUITMENT ON PRODUCTIVITY, QUALITY OF WORK LIFE, AND THE BOTTOM LINE

A close fit between individual strengths and interests and organizational and job characteristics almost guarantees a happy "marriage." On the other hand, since the bottom line of recruitment success lies in the number of successful placements made, the effects of ineffective recruitment may not appear for years. For this reason alone, a regular system for measuring and evaluating recruitment efforts is essential. Moreover, it's difficult to manage what you can't measure.[86] Consider that the cost of new college hires varies between $2,000 and $8,500 (in 2001 dollars), and that the first-year turnover rate for new college graduates can be as high as 50 percent at some companies.[87] It seems more important than ever to assess whether such costs are outweighed by easier and improved selection procedures, better employee retention, lower training needs and costs, or higher levels of productivity. Finding, attracting, and retaining top talent is now and will continue to be an important management challenge with direct impacts on productivity, quality of work life, and the bottom line.

The payoff: Home Depot's employee turnover is as much as 20 percent lower than the average in the retail industry.[85]

THE ART OF FINDING TALENT

Human Resource Management in Action: Conclusion

GE Medical Systems invents and makes CT scanners, magnetic resonance imagers, and other biomedical equipment that requires some of the most demanding software coding and electrical engineering anywhere. It's an innovation powerhouse, with more than 80 percent of its equipment sales coming from products no more than 3 years old. The company competes for talent with the likes of Intel, Cisco Systems, Microsoft, and Hewlett-Packard, and hires about 500 technical workers a year.

What is remarkable about GE Medical is that last year it cut its cost of hiring by 17 percent, reduced the time needed to fill a position by between 20 percent and 30 percent, and cut in half the percentage of new hires that don't work out. How did it do this? It did so by developing detailed staffing plans and rigorously measuring the performance of its outside recruiters (e.g., first-pass yield, the percentage of résumés that result in interviews; second-pass yield, the percentage of interviews that result in offers). It also had summer interns grade their programs and their bosses (former summer interns are twice as likely to accept a job offer as other candidates), and it focused major attention on employee referrals.

In terms of employee referrals, fully 10 percent of them result not just in an interview, but in a hire. In comparison, just 1 percent of people whose résumés come into GE Medical are even called for an interview. Nothing else—not headhunters and not internships—even comes close to that kind of yield. The company doubled the number of employee referrals by taking three easy steps:

IMPLICATIONS FOR MANAGEMENT PRACTICE

Talent is what makes firms go. Recruitment is therefore a strategic imperative, and an important form of business competition. Given the substantial costs of recruitment and training, employers must consider the needs of employees if they wish to attract and retain top talent. American Express Travel-Related Services adopted this view in introducing its KidsCheque and FamilyCheque programs to subsidize child care and elder care for employees, over 70 percent of whom are female.[88] Its experience suggests that the following elements should be part of any successful recruitment program:

- Always view recruitment as a long-term strategy.
- Be responsive to employees' needs.
- Develop benefits that genuinely appeal to the employees being hired.
- Promote recruitment benefits to the target audience.
- Audit the recruitment programs in place.

How did the senior HR officer at American Express Travel-Related Services sell the program to hard-nosed senior managers? By emphasizing its business advantages; that is, he presented it less like a typical human resources plan and more like a marketing plan—focusing on the goal of differentiating the company in the labor market and placing it ahead of the competition. He emphasized again and again the importance of acting immediately to obtain a first-mover advantage.

Brands and reputations have always been important in product markets. Today they are just as important in labor markets.[89] American Express has a well-known brand and an excellent reputation. It wanted to leverage both of these in its recruitment efforts.

What were the results of the program? Within weeks of the introduction of the program in Jacksonville, Florida, for example, almost 80 percent of eligible employees had signed up. In addition, the company began to receive résumés from people who had heard about KidsCheque from the local media and who were interested in joining American Express as a result. It also received telephone calls from HR managers at other companies that were interested in instituting similar programs.[90]

1. The program is simple and rewarding—no complex forms and no bureaucracy. The referring employee receives a small goodie like a gift certificate at a local retail store simply for referring a qualified candidate.
2. The company pays the referring employee $2,000 if the person he or she refers is hired, and $3,000 if the new hire is a software engineer. That may seem like a lot of money, but the more often GE pays it, the more money it saves, because it's in lieu of a $15,000 to $20,000 headhunter's fee.
3. The company begins asking new employees for referrals almost from their first day on the job. That's because if the new employee comes from, say, Motorola, for the first 3 months he or she is still a part of Motorola, in a sense, and remembers everybody. Nine months later, he or she is a part of GE. That, of course, is the goal.

SUMMARY

Recruitment begins with a clear statement of objectives, based on the types of knowledge, skills, abilities, and other characteristics that an organization needs. Objectives are also based on a consideration of the gender and ethnic-group representation of the workforce, relative to that of the surrounding labor force. Finally, a recruitment policy must spell out clearly an organization's intention to evaluate and screen candidates without regard to factors such as race, gender, age, or disability, where these characteristics are unrelated to a person's ability to do a job successfully. The actual process of recruitment begins with a specification of workforce requirements—numbers, skills mix, levels, and the time frame within which such needs must be met.

Recruitment may involve internal, external, or both kinds of labor markets. Internal recruitment often relies on succession plans, job posting, employee referrals, or temporary worker pools. Many external recruitment sources are also available. In this chapter we discussed four such sources: university relations, executive search firms, employment agencies, and recruitment advertising. In managing and controlling recruitment operations, consider calculating the cost of operations and analyzing the performance of each recruitment source, since recruitment success is determined by the number of hires who actually perform their jobs successfully.

DISCUSSION QUESTIONS

6–1. What special measures might be necessary for a successful diversity-oriented recruitment effort?

6–2. Discuss the conditions under which realistic job previews are and are not appropriate.

6–3. How would you advise a firm that wants to improve its college recruitment efforts?

6–4. Draft a recruitment ad for a trade journal to advertise a job opening at your company. Have a friend critique it, as well as, if possible, a knowledgeable HR professional from a local company. Summarize their suggestions for improvement and incorporate them into a final draft.

6–5. You have just lost your middle-management job. Outline a procedure to follow in trying to land a new one.

KEY TERMS

recruitment
selection
orientation
placement
performance appraisal
initial screening
passive nondiscrimination
pure diversity-based recruitment

diversity-based recruitment with
    preferential hiring
hard quotas
labor market
workforce utilization
job posting
realistic job preview

APPLYING YOUR KNOWLEDGE

Case 6–1	### *Recruiting at Sandmeyer Steel Company*

Kenneth T. Sandmeyer, a man who patrols the shop floor in a three-piece suit and provides holiday turkeys to all hands, exudes old-school attitudes about how to run a business. But that does not extend to having unusually high employee recruitment standards.

"Don't give us your best and brightest," the 57-year-old head of Sandmeyer Steel Company tells people who may know someone looking for a job. "Give us the people who are average or mediocre and don't know what they want to do with their lives."

Yet Mr. Sandmeyer has trouble finding workers to meet even his modest standards. His predicament is a measure of how hard it is for many American manufacturers to find workers these days, for reasons that embrace culture, education, and demographics.

Indeed, what Mr. Sandmeyer calls the people problem is getting worse in many parts of the country, hastening America's decline as a manufacturer and undermining the ability to compete against countries like Japan and Germany, where factory work has higher status and the numbers of skilled workers are larger.

The problem is particularly bad in urban areas like Philadelphia, where the middle class has higher aspirations, the poor have no skills, and the television-weaned youth of both groups are shocked to discover that the modern factory is still often noisy, smelly, dirty, and uncomfortably hot or cold.

Mr. Sandmeyer calls the people problem his biggest worry in managing his family's stainless steel company in the northeast corner of the city: "It's held down our growth. We have not been able to gain as much market share as we would have, had we had more productive and capable employees."

With imaginative searching that enlisted the aid of a local priest—and has resulted in 30 to 40 percent of its workforce being foreign born—Sandmeyer Steel has largely managed to fill its ranks. It has succeeded despite stiff competition from large employers that typically offer similar pay but more training, more prestige, better fringe benefits, and less physical discomfort.

A newly hired employee with no previous work experience is paid $9.50 an hour. Someone with a year or two of experience and a record of dependability might get $10.50 to $13.50. Mr. Sandmeyer said the tight labor situation has bid up the company's wage costs.

"It's hot and dirty work; it's heavy manufacturing," Sandmeyer acknowledged of his plant. "Instead of air conditioning," he said, "we open every window and door when it gets over 90, and everybody gets free soda."

Questions

1. Serious labor shortages do exist in many places, but these are not the only reasons for the recruiting problems experienced by many small businesses. What are some others?
2. As a manager in such a small business, what sources might you use to find new workers?
3. What special advantages does a small business have over a large one? How can you incorporate these into the recruitment process?

REFERENCES

1. Wellner, A. S. (2001, Jan.). Employers join forces to recruit. *HRMagazine*, pp. 86–96. See also Leonard, B. (2001, Feb.). Recruiting from the competition.

HRMagazine, pp. 78–85. See also Lord, J. S. (1989). External and internal recruitment. In W. F. Cascio (ed.), *Human resource planning, employment, and placement.* Washington, DC: Bureau of National Affairs, pp. 2-73 to 2-102.

2. Seligman, D. (1973, March). How "equal opportunity" turned into employment quotas. *Fortune,* pp. 160–168.

3. Replying in the affirmative (1987, Mar. 9). *Time,* p. 66.

4. *Officers for Justice v. Civil Service Commission* (1992). 979 F. 2d 721 (9th Cir.), cert. denied, 61 U.S.L.W. 3667, 113 S. Ct. 1645 (Mar. 29, 1993). See also Affirmative action upheld by high court as a remedy for past job discrimination (1986, July 3). *The New York Times,* pp. A1, B9.

5. Reynolds, L. G., Masters, S. H., & Moser, C. H. (1986). *Labor economics and labor relations* (9th ed.). Englewood Cliffs, NJ: Prentice-Hall.

6. Kuczynski, S. (2000, June). While supplies last: Scarce, expensive, and in demand, information technology employees are flying off the shelves. *HRMagazine,* pp. 37–44. See also Booming Boeing (1996, Sept. 30). *BusinessWeek,* pp. 118–125.

7. Reynolds et al., op. cit.

8. Sebastian, P. (1988, Sept. 16). Labor pains. *The Wall Street Journal,* pp. 1, 12.

9. Barber, A. E. (1998). *Recruiting employees.* Thousand Oaks, CA: Sage. See also Milkovich, G. T., & Newman, J. G. (1996). *Compensation* (5th ed.). Homewood, IL: Irwin. See also Wallace, M. J., & Fay, C. H. (1988). Compensation theory and practice (2d ed.). Boston: PWS-Kent.

10. Barber, op. cit. See also Baron, J. N., Davis-Blake, A., & Bielby, W. T. (1986). The structure of opportunity: How promotion ladders vary within and among organizations. *Administrative Science Quarterly, 31,* 248–273. See also Stewman, S. (1986). Demographic models of internal labor markets. *Administrative Science Quarterly, 31,* 212–247.

11. For an excellent summary of this research, see Rynes, S. L. (1991). Recruitment, job choice, and post-hire consequences: A call for new research directions. In M. D. Dunnette & L. M. Hough (eds.), *Handbook of industrial and organizational psychology* (2d ed., vol. 2). Palo Alto, CA: Consulting Psychologists Press, pp. 399–444.

12. *Wards Cove Packing Co. v. Antonio,* 109 S. Ct. 2115 (1989). See also Ledvinka, J., & Scarpello, V. G. (1991). *Federal regulation of personnel and human resource management* (2d ed.). Boston: PWS-Kent.

13. *Hazelwood School District v. United States* (1977). 433 U.S. 299.

14. Staffing efficiency quantified (1995, October). *Bulletin.* Denver, CO: Mt. States Employers Council, p. 5.

15. Cappelli, P. (2001, March). Making the most of on-line recruiting. *Harvard Business Review,* pp. 139–146.

16. Lord, op. cit.

17. Farish, P. (1989). Recruitment sources. In Cascio (ed.), op. cit. pp. 2-103–2-134.

18. Cappelli, op. cit., p. 146.

19. Breaugh, J. A. (1992). *Recruitment: Science and practice.* Boston: PWS-Kent.

20. Society for Human Resource Management (2001). *SHRM 2001 employee referral program survey.* Alexandria, VA: Author. See also Lord, op. cit.

21. Leonard, B. (1999, August). Employee referrals should be cornerstone of staffing efforts. *HR News,* p. 54.

22. Cappelli, op. cit.

23. Griffeth, R. W., Hom, P. W., Fink, L. S., & Cohen, D. J. (1997). Comparative tests of multivariate models of recruiting sources effects. *Journal of Management, 23,* 19–36. See also Kirnan, J. P., Farley, J. A., & Geisinger, K. F. (1989). The relationship between recruiting source, applicant quality, and hire performance: An analysis by sex, ethnicity, and age. *Personnel Psychology, 42,* 293–308.

24. Lord, op. cit.

25. Kilborn, P. T. (1990, May 6). Nurses get V.I.P. treatment, easing shortage. *The New York Times*, pp. 1, 28.

26. Farish, op. cit.

27. Barber, A. E., Wesson, M. J., Roberson, Q. M., & Taylor, M. S. (1999). A tale of two job markets: Organizational size and its effect on hiring practices and job search behavior. *Personnel Psychology, 52*, 841–867.

28. Poe, A. C. (2000, May). Face value: Snag students by establishing a long-term, personal presence on campus. *HRMagazine*, pp. 60–68.

29. Farish, op. cit.

30. Silverman, R. E. (2000, Oct. 31). The jungle: What's news in recruitment and pay. *The Wall Street Journal*, p. B18.

31. Poe, op. cit. See also Kolenko, T. A. (1990). College recruiting: Models, myths, and management. In G. R. Ferris, K. M. Rowland, & M. R. Buckley (eds.), *Human resource management: Perspectives and issues* (2d ed.). Boston: Allyn & Bacon, pp. 109–121.

32. Barber, op. cit.

33. Columbia Consulting Group (2000). *Executive search guidelines*. NY: Author.

34. Ibid. See also Lord, op. cit. See also LoPresto, R. (1986). Ethical recruiting. *Personnel Administrator, 31*(11), 90–91.

35. Labor letter (1988, May 10). *The Wall Street Journal*, p. 1.

36. Lord, op. cit.

37. Farish, op. cit.

38. Lord, op. cit.

39. Cappelli, op. cit.

40. Cappelli, 2001, op. cit. See also Salkever, A. (2000, Oct. 9). A better way to float your résumé. *BusinessWeek*, pp. 202–206. See also Silverman, R. E. (2000, Oct. 3). Raiding talent via the web. *The Wall Street Journal*, pp. B1, B16. See also Work week (2000, Apr. 4). *The Wall Street Journal*, p. A1. See also Wildstrom, S. H. (1999, Sept. 20). Wanted: Better job listings. *BusinessWeek*, p. 19. See also Hays, S. (1999). Hiring on the web. *Workforce, 78*(8), 76–84.

41. Cappelli, op. cit.

42. Useem, J. (1999, May 24). Read this before you put a résumé online. *Fortune*, pp. 290, 292.

43. Albus, S. M. (2001, July). 2001 transfer volume and cost survey. *erc.org/MOBILITY_Online/current/0701tvc.shtml.*

44. Two-income couples in the U.S. now the majority (2000, Dec. 14). *The Denver Post*, p. 1A.

45. Peraud, P. (2001, June). Promoting a spouse's right to work. *www.erc.org/Mobility_online/current/0601perraud.shtml.*

46. Albus, op. cit.

47. Collie, H. C. (1998, Mar.). The changing face of corporate relocation. *HRMagazine*, pp. 97–102.

48. Markels, A. (1996, Aug. 21). Signing bonuses rise to counter rich pay plans. *The Wall Street Journal*, pp. B1, B4.

49. Chan, S. (1996, Aug. 9), op. cit. In frenzy to recruit, hi-tech concerns try gimmicks, songs. *The Wall Street Journal,* pp. B1, B3.

50. Ibid.

51. Barber, op. cit. See also Bureau of National Affairs (1988, May). *Recruiting and selection procedures* (PPF Survey 146). Washington, DC: Bureau of National Affairs.

52. Kirnan et al., op. cit. See also Thaler-Carter, R. E. (2001, June). Diversify your recruitment advertising. *HRMagazine,* pp. 92–100.

53. Lord, op. cit.

54. *www.HotJobssoftware.com* (2001, June). Resumix6.

55. Lord, op. cit.

56. Thaler-Carter, op. cit.

57. Roberson, L., & Gutierrez, N. C. (1992). Beyond good faith: Commitment to recruiting management diversity at Pacific Bell. In S. E. Jackson (ed.), *Diversity in the workplace.* New York: Guilford, pp. 65–88.

58. *Outreach and recruitment directory: A resource for diversity-related recruitment needs* (2001). Columbia, MD: Berkshire Associates, Inc.

59. Labor letter (1989, Mar. 21). *The Wall Street Journal,* p. A1.

60. Employers go to school on minority recruiting (1992, Dec. 15). *The Wall Street Journal,* p. B1.

61. *www.HotJobssoftware.com,* op. cit.

62. Wilson, J. B. (2001). Measuring recruitment. In M. J. Fleming & J. B. Wilson (eds.), *Effective HR measurement techniques.* Alexandria, VA: Society for Human Resource Management, pp. 65–76.

63. Useem, J. (1999, July 5). For sale online: You. *Fortune,* pp. 67–78.

64. Barber, op. cit.

65. Vecchio, R. P. (1995). The impact of referral sources on employee attitudes: Evidence from a national sample. *Journal of Management, 21,* 953–965.

66. Kirnan et al., op. cit.

67. Williams, C. R., Labig, C. E., Jr., & Stone, T. H. (1993). Recruitment sources and posthire outcomes for job applicants and new hires: A test of two hypotheses. *Journal of Applied Psychology, 78,* 163–172.

68. Rynes, S. L., Bretz, R. D., Jr., & Gerhart, B. (1991). The importance of recruitment in job choice: A different way of looking. *Personnel Psychology, 44,* 487–521. See also Barber, op. cit., See also Fisher, C. D., Ilgen, D. R., & Hoyer, W. D. (1979). Source credibility, information favorability, and job offer acceptance. *Academy of Management Journal, 22,* 94–103.

69. Maurer, S. D., Howe, V., & Lee, T. W. (1992). Organizational recruiting as marketing management: An interdisciplinary study of engineering graduates. *Personnel Psychology, 45,* 807–833.

70. Rynes et al., op. cit.

71. Popovich, P., & Wanous, J. P. (1982). The realistic job preview as a persuasive communication. *Academy of Management Review, 7,* 570–578.

72. Barber, op. cit. See also Breaugh, op. cit. See also Premack, S. L., & Wanous, J. P. (1985). A meta-analysis of realistic job preview experiments. *Journal of Applied Psychology, 70,* 706–719.

73. Hom, P. W., Griffeth, R. W., Palich, L. E., & Bracker, J. S. (1998). An exploratory investigation into theoretical mechanisms underlying realistic job previews. *Personnel Psychology, 51,* 421–451. See also McEvoy, G. M., & Cascio, W. F. (1985). Strategies for reducing employee turnover. A meta-analysis. *Journal of Applied Psychology, 70,* 342–353.

74. Hom, P. W., Griffeth, R. W., Palich, L. E., & Bracker, J. S. (1999). Revisiting met expectations as a reason why realistic job previews work. *Personnel Psychology, 52,* 97–112.

75. Meglino, B. M., De Nisi, A. S., Youngblood, S. A., & Williams, K. J. (1988). Effects of realistic job previews: A comparison using an enhancement and a reduction preview. *Journal of Applied Psychology, 73,* 259–266.

76. Wanous, J. P. (1989). Installing a realistic job preview: Ten tough choices. *Personnel Psychology, 42,* 117–134.

77. Wanous, J. P. (1980). *Organizational entry: Recruitment, selection and socialization of newcomers.* Reading, MA: Addison-Wesley.

78. Useem, op. cit.

79. Wanberg, C. R., Kanfer, R., & Banas, J. T. (2000). Predictors and outcomes of networking intensity among unemployed job seekers. *Journal of Applied Psychology, 85,* 491–503. See also Granovetter, M. S. (1995). *Getting a job* (2d ed.). Chicago: University of Chicago Press.

80. Work week (2000, Apr. 4). *The Wall Street Journal,* p. A1.

81. Morris, J. R., Cascio, W. F., & Young, C. E. (1999, Winter). Downsizing after all these years. *Organizational Dynamics*, pp. 78–87. See also Uchitelle, L., & Kleinfeld, N. R. (1996, Mar. 3). On the battlefields of business, millions of casualties. *The New York Times*, pp. 1, 14–17.

82. Silverman (2000, Oct. 3). op. cit. When a recruiter comes knocking, be ready to respond (1996, Aug. 6). *The Wall Street Journal*, p. B1. See also Rigdon, J. E. (1992, June 17). Deceptive résumés can be door openers but can become an employee's undoing. *The Wall Street Journal*, pp. B1, B7. See also Cohn, G. (1985, Nov. 19). Advice on what not to do as the search continues. *The Wall Street Journal*, p. 37.

83. Work week. (1995, Oct. 31). *The Wall Street Journal*, p. A1.

84. Boudreau, J. W., Boswell, W. R., Judge, T. A., & Bretz, R. D., Jr. (2001). Personality and cognitive ability as predictors of job search among employed managers. *Personnel Psychology, 54*, 25–50.

85. Stein, N. (2000, May 29). Winning the war to keep talent. *Fortune*, pp. 132–138.

86. Kolenko, op. cit.

87. Breaugh, op. cit.

88. Morrison, E. W., & Herlihy, J. M. (1992). Becoming the best place to work: Managing diversity at American Express Travel-Related Services. In S. E. Jackson (ed.), *Diversity in the workplace*. New York: Guilford, pp. 203–226.

89. Cappelli, op. cit.

90. Ibid.

7 STAFFING

Questions This Chapter Will Help Managers Answer

1. In what ways do business strategy and organizational culture affect staffing decisions?
2. What screening and selection methods are available, and which ones are most accurate?
3. What should be done to improve preemployment interviews?
4. Can work-sample tests improve staffing decisions?
5. What are some advantages and potential problems to consider in using assessment centers to select managers?

ORGANIZATIONAL CULTURE—KEY TO STAFFING "FIT"*

Is there a common denominator among the most admired companies? According to one study, the answer is yes. It's organizational culture—shared values, expectations, and behavior—that set the context of everything a company does. In the most admired companies, such as Asea Brown Boveri, Bristol-Myers Squibb, Intel, J. P. Morgan Chase, 3M, Toyota, and Southwest Airlines, the key priorities were teamwork, customer focus, fair treatment of employees, initiative, and innovation. In average companies the top priorities were minimizing risk, respecting the chain of command, supporting the boss, and making budget. In addition, the most admired companies all have consensus at the top regarding cultural priorities. Rather than giving culture a few lines in the company handbook, the most admired companies live their cultures every day, and they go out of their ways to communicate it both to current employees as well as to prospective new hires. Thus Intel works hard to retain the egalitarianism and cooperative spirit among employees that it started with. In practice that means that there are no reserved parking places, no executive dining rooms, no corner offices—and everyone gets stock options.

By contrast it is all too common for average companies to say they value teamwork, but then to award bonuses only on the basis of individual achievement. According to the Hay Group, the Philadelphia-based management consulting firm that conducted the study, the single best predictor of overall excellence was a company's ability to attract, retain, and motivate talented people. Organizational culture can either facilitate those activities or else inhibit them. It is a key to "fit" between employees and their organizations. New hires consider it in their decisions to accept or not to accept jobs. Not surprisingly, therefore, more and more companies are taking stock of what they stand for, what they are trying to achieve, and how they operate every day to achieve their goals. In the conclusion to this case, we will see what some of these companies are doing in this area.

Challenges

1. What can a company do to communicate its culture to prospective new hires?
2. What might be the role of organizational culture in staffing decisions?
3. How might organizational culture affect the ways that employees deal with coworkers and customers?

The chapter-opening vignette describes the crucial role of organizational culture in attracting, retaining, and motivating employees to perform their best every day. The most progressive companies strive to convey their cultures to

Sources: H. Kelleher, I did it my way, *Fortune*, June 1, 2001; C. A. O'Reilly III and J. Pfeffer, Southwest Airlines: If success is so simple, why is it so hard to imitate? *Hidden Value,* Boston, Harvard Business School Press, 2000, pp. 21–48; What makes a company great? *Fortune,* Oct. 26, 1998, p. 218; J. Muller, Ford: Why it's worse than you think, *BusinessWeek,* June 25, 2001, pp. 80–89; E. Shapiro, Time Warner defines, defends, system of values, *The Wall Street Journal,* Apr. 9, 1999, pp. B1, B4.

new hires as well as to current employees, and the degree of fit of a prospective new hire with the organizational culture plays a major role in staffing decisions. In addition to culture fit, there is a constant need to align staffing decisions with business strategy. As we shall see in this chapter, a wide variety of tools for initial screening and selection decisions is available, and much is known about each one. We will examine the evidence of the relative effectiveness of the tools, so that decision makers can choose those that best fit their long- and short-range objectives. Let us begin by considering the role of business strategy in staffing decisions.

ORGANIZATIONAL CONSIDERATIONS IN STAFFING DECISIONS

Business Strategy

Clearly, there should be a fit between the intended strategy of an enterprise and the characteristics of the people who are expected to implement it. Unfortunately, very few firms actually link strategy and staffing decisions in a structured, logical way. Nevertheless, we can learn how to effect such a fit by considering a two-dimensional model that relates an organization's strategy during the stages of its development to the style of its managers during each stage.[1]

For strategic reasons, it is important to consider the stage of development of a business because many characteristics of a business—such as its growth rate, product lines, market share, entry opportunity, and technology—change as the organization changes. One possible set of relationships between the development stage and the management selection strategies is shown in Figure 7–1. While a model such as this is useful conceptually, in practice the stages might not be so clearly defined, and there are many exceptions.

Organizations that are just starting out are in the *embryonic* stage. They are characterized by high growth rates, basic product lines, heavy emphasis on product engineering, and little or no customer loyalty.

Organizations in the *high-growth* stage are concerned with two things: fighting for market share and building excellence in their management teams. They focus on refining and extending product lines, and on building customer loyalty.

Mature organizations emphasize the maintenance of market share, cost reductions through economies of scale, more rigid management controls over workers' actions, and the generation of cash to develop new product lines. In contrast to the "freewheeling" style of an embryonic organization, there is much less flexibility and variability in a mature organization.

Finally, an *aging* organization struggles to hold market share in a declining market, and it demands extreme cost control obtained through consistency and centralized procedures. Economic survival becomes the primary motivation.

Different management styles seem to fit each of these development stages best. In the embryonic stage there is a need for enterprising managers who can thrive in high-risk environments. These are known as entrepreneurs (Figure 7–1). They are decisive individuals who can respond rapidly to changing conditions.

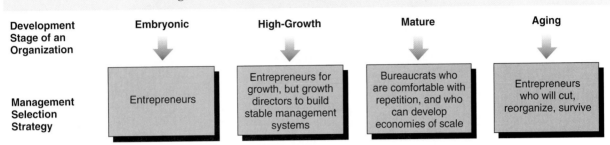

Figure 7–1

The relationship between the development stage of an organization and the management selection strategy that best fits each stage.

Development Stage of an Organization	Embryonic	High-Growth	Mature	Aging
Management Selection Strategy	Entrepreneurs	Entrepreneurs for growth, but growth directors to build stable management systems	Bureaucrats who are comfortable with repetition, and who can develop economies of scale	Entrepreneurs who will cut, reorganize, survive

During the high-growth stage there is still a need for entrepreneurs, but it is also important to select the kinds of managers who can develop stable management systems to preserve the gains achieved during the embryonic stage. We might call these managers "growth directors."

As an organization matures, there is a need to select the kind of manager who does not need lots of variety in her or his work, who can oversee repetitive daily operations, and who can search continually for economies of scale. Individuals who fit best into mature organizations have a "bureaucratic" style of management.

Finally, an aging organization needs "movers and shakers" to reinvigorate it. Strategically, it becomes important to select (again) entrepreneurs capable of doing whatever is necessary to ensure the economic survival of the firm. This may involve divesting unprofitable operations, firing unproductive workers, or eliminating practices that are considered extravagant.

Admittedly, these characterizations are coarse, but they provide a starting point in the construction of an important link between the development stage of an organization and its staffing strategy. Such strategic concerns may be used to supplement job analyses as bases for staffing. This also suggests that *job* descriptions, which standardize and formalize behavior, should be broadened into *role* descriptions that reflect the broader and more changeable strategic requirements of an organization.

Organizational Culture

A logical extension of the mating theory of recruitment (i.e., concurrent search efforts for a match by organizations and individuals) is the mating theory of selection. That is, just as organizations choose people, people choose jobs and organizations that fit their personalities and career objectives and in which they can satisfy needs that are important to them.[2]

In the context of selection, it is important for an organization to describe the dimensions of its "culture"—the environment within which employment decisions are made, and the environment within which employees work on a day-to-day basis. It has been described as the DNA of an organization—invisible to the naked eye, but critical in shaping the character of the workplace.[3] *Culture is the pattern of basic assumptions a given group has invented, discovered, or developed in learning to adapt both to its external and internal environments.* The pattern of assumptions has worked well enough to be considered valid and, therefore, to be taught to new members as the correct way to perceive, think, and feel in relation to those problems. **Organizational culture** is embedded and transmitted through mechanisms such as the following[4]:

1. Formal statements of organizational philosophy and materials used for recruitment, selection, and socialization of new employees.
2. Promotion criteria.
3. Stories, legends, and myths about key people and events.
4. What leaders pay attention to, measure, and control.
5. Implicit and possibly unconscious criteria that leaders use to determine who fits key slots in the organization.

Organizational culture has two implications for staffing decisions. One, cultures vary across organizations; individuals will consider this information if it is available to them in their job-search process.[5] Companies such as IBM and Procter & Gamble have a strong marketing orientation, and their staffing decisions tend to reflect this value. Other companies, such as Sun Microsystems and Hewlett-Packard, are oriented toward R&D and engineering, while still others, such as McDonald's, concentrate on consistency and efficiency. Recruiters assess person-job fit by focusing on specific knowledge, skills, and abilities. They assess person-organization fit by focusing more on values and personality characteristics.[6] By linking staffing decisions to cultural factors, companies try to ensure that their employees have internalized the strategic intent and core values of the enterprise. In this way they will be more likely to act in the interest of the company and as dedicated team members, regardless of their formal job duties.[7]

Two, other things being equal, individuals who choose jobs and organizations that are consistent with their own values, beliefs, and attitudes are more likely to be productive, satisfied employees. This was demonstrated in a study of 904 college graduates hired by six public accounting firms over a 7-year period. Those hired by firms that emphasized interpersonal-relationship values (team orientation, respect for people) stayed an average of 45 months. Those hired by firms that emphasized work-task values (detail, stability, innovation) stayed with their firms an average of 31 months. This 14-month difference in survival rates translated into an opportunity loss of at least $6 million for each firm that emphasized work-task values.

While the firms that emphasized interpersonal relationship values were uniformly more attractive to both strong and weak performers, strong performers stayed an average of 13 months longer in firms that emphasized work-task values (39 months versus 26 months for weak performers). The lesson for managers? Promote cultural values that are attractive to most new employees; don't just select individuals who fit a specific profile of cultural values.[8]

The Logic of Personnel Selection

If variability in physical and psychological characteristics were not so prevalent, there would be little need for selection of people to fill various jobs. Without variability among individuals in abilities, aptitudes, interests, and personality traits, we would expect all job candidates to perform comparably. Research shows clearly that as jobs become more complex, individual differences in output variability also increase.[9] Likewise, if there were 10 job openings available and only 10 qualified candidates, selection again would not be a significant issue since all 10 candidates would have to be hired. Selection becomes a relevant concern only when there are more qualified candidates than there are positions to be filled, for selection implies choice and choice means exclusion.

Since practical considerations (safety, time, and cost) make job tryouts for all candidates infeasible in most selection situations, it is necessary to *predict* the relative level of job performance of each candidate on the basis of available information. As we shall see, some methods for doing this are more accurate than others. However, before considering them, we need to focus on the fundamental technical requirements of all such methods—**reliability** and **validity.**

Reliability of Measurement

The goal of any selection program is to identify applicants who score high on measures that purport to assess knowledge, skills, abilities, or other characteristics that are critical for job performance. Yet we always run the risk of making errors in employee selection decisions. Selection errors are of two types: selecting someone who should be rejected (erroneous acceptance) and rejecting someone who should be accepted (erroneous rejection). These kinds of errors can be avoided by using measurement procedures that are reliable and valid.

A measurement is considered to be reliable if it is consistent or stable, for example:

- **Over time**—such as on a hearing test administered first on Monday morning and then again on Friday night
- **Across different samples of items**—say, on form A and form B of a test of mathematical aptitude; or on a measure of vocational interests administered at the beginning of a student's sophomore year in college and then again at the end of her or his senior year
- **Across different raters or judges working independently**—as in a gymnastics competition

As you might suspect, inconsistency is present to some degree in all measurement situations. In employment settings, people generally are assessed only once. That is, organizations give them, for example, one test of their knowledge of a job or one application form or one interview. The procedures through which these assessments are made must be standardized in terms of content, administration, and scoring. Only then can the results of the assessments be compared meaningfully with one another. Those who desire more specific information about how reliability is actually estimated in quantitative terms should consult the technical appendix at the end of this chapter.

Validity of Measurement

Reliability is certainly an important characteristic of any measurement procedure, but it is simply a means to an end, a step along the way to a goal. Unless a measure is reliable, it cannot be valid. This is so because unless a measure produces consistent, dependable, stable scores, we cannot begin to understand what implications high versus low scores have for later job performance and economic returns to the organization. Such understanding is the goal of the validation process. From a practical point of view, *validity refers to the job-relatedness of a measure*—that is, the strength of the relationship between scores from the measure and some indicator or rating of actual job performance.[10]

Although evidence of validity may be accumulated in many ways, validity always refers to the degree to which the evidence supports inferences that are drawn from scores or ratings on a selection procedure. It is the inferences regarding the specific use of a selection procedure that are validated, not the procedure itself.[11] Hence a user must first specify exactly why he or she intends to use a particular selection procedure (that is, what inferences he or she intends to draw from it). Then the user can make an informed judgment about the adequacy of the available evidence of validity in support of that particular selection procedure when used for a particular purpose.

Scientific standards for validation are described in greater detail in *Principles for the Validation and Use of Personnel Selection Procedures*[12] and *Standards for Educational and Psychological Testing*.[13] Legal standards for validation are contained in the *Uniform Guidelines on Employee Selection Procedures*.[14] For an overview of the various strategies used to validate employee selection procedures, see the Technical Appendix at the end of this chapter.

Quantitative evidence of validity is often expressed in terms of a correlation coefficient (that may assume values between -1 and $+1$) between scores on a predictor of later job performance (e.g., a test or an interview) and a criterion that reflects actual job performance (e.g., supervisory ratings, dollar volume of sales). In employment contexts, predictor validities typically vary between about .20 and .50. In the following sections we will consider some of the most commonly used methods for screening and selection decisions, together with validity evidence for each one.

SCREENING AND SELECTION METHODS

Employment Application Forms

Particularly when unemployment is high, organizations find themselves deluged with applications for employment for only a small number of available jobs. As an example, consider that in 2000, Southwest Airlines received 216,000 résumés, conducted 45,000 interviews, and hired 7,000 new employees! This is not unusual among companies with solid reputations and strong company cultures. Of course when applications are submitted electronically, it is possible to screen them for obvious mismatches by considering answers to questions such as "Are you willing to move?" and "When are you prepared to start work?" In other cases, however, much of the screening is still done by hand.

An important requirement of all employment application forms is that they ask only for information that is valid and fair with respect to the nature of the job. Studies of application forms used by more than 200 organizations indicated that, for the most part, the questions required information that was job related

Ethical Dilemma
Are Work History Omissions Unethical?

Consider the following situation. A job applicant knowingly omits some previous work history on a company's application form, even though the form asks applicants to provide a complete list of previous jobs. However, the applicant is

truthful about the dates of previous jobs he does report. He leaves it to the interviewer to discover and to ask about the gaps in his work history. The interviewer fails to ask about the gaps. Is the job applicant's behavior unethical?

and necessary for the employment decision.[15] On the other hand, more than 95 percent of the forms included one or more legally indefensible questions.

Review employment application forms regularly to be sure that the information they require complies with equal employment opportunity guidelines and case law. For example, under the Americans with Disabilities Act of 1990, an employer may not ask a general question about disabilities on an application form, or whether an applicant has ever filed a workers' compensation claim. However, at a preemployment interview, after describing the essential functions of a job, an employer may ask whether there is any physical or mental reason the candidate cannot perform the essential functions. Here are some guidelines that will suggest which questions to delete[16]:

- Any question that might lead to an adverse impact on the employment of members of groups protected under civil rights law.
- Any question that cannot be demonstrated to be job related or that does not concern a bona fide occupational qualification.
- Any question that could possibly constitute an invasion of privacy.

Some organizations have sought to identify statistically significant relationships between responses to questions on application forms and later measures of job performance (e.g., tenure, absenteeism, theft). Such **weighted application blanks** (WABs) are often highly predictive, yielding validities in the range of .25 to .50.[17] In one study, for example, researchers examined 28 objective questions for a random sample of the employment applications representing 243 current and former circulation-route managers at a metropolitan daily newspaper.[18] A statistical procedure (multiple regression analysis) was used to identify which people were most likely to stay on the job for more than 1 year (the break-even point for employee orientation and training costs). Several interesting findings resulted from the study:

1. Questions on the WAB that best predicted time on the job at the beginning of the study did not predict time on the job several years later. Hence, it is necessary to recheck WAB questions periodically.
2. The statistical analysis showed that items that "conventional wisdom" might suggest or those used by interviewers did not predict employee turnover accurately.

VIDEO RÉSUMÉS?

Yes, video résumés are here—but maybe not to stay. With the popularity of VCRs and PC-based digital video at home and at work, the video résumé may seem like an inevitable development. Candidates can look their best; rehearse answers to questions; and, in general, present themselves in the best possible light. Thus Kforce.com, an electronic job board, allows applicants to submit audio or video clips of themselves for recruiters to use as screening tools.

These efforts, however, get mixed reviews from employers and recruiters, many of whom consider video résumés to be costly gimmicks that fail to provide as much useful information as an ordinary résumé. Here are some of their objections: The answers are shallow rather than in depth, the videos take considerable time to review, and the videos could cause legal problems for employers who reject candidates from protected groups. For these reasons, they have yet to catch on in a big way.

3. An independent check of a new sample of job candidates showed that the WAB was able to identify employees who would stay on the job longer than 1 year in 83 percent of the cases.
4. The length of the time employees stayed on previous jobs was unrelated to their length of stay on their current job.
5. The best predictors were "experience as a sales representative," "business school education," and "never previously worked for this company."

Allstate Insurance uses a similar approach. A person who wants to be an independent agent for Allstate first completes an online application, and the company scores the application against the profile of the model successful agent. The candidate finds out immediately whether the score meets a certain threshold. If it does, there is a second, more detailed questionnaire to fill out. Once again, the applicant learns right away whether the score is high enough. If it is, a face-to-face interview is scheduled.[19]

Executives balk at spending time and money on HR research. Nevertheless, poor hires are expensive. SmithKline Beecham Corporation spends, on average, more than $17,000 (in 2001 dollars) to recruit and train each worker.[20] That's more than $1 million for every 60 workers hired. These kinds of numbers often tend to cast new light on this neglected area.

Recommendations and Reference Checks

Recommendations and reference checks are commonly used to screen outside job applicants. They can provide four kinds of information about a job applicant: (1) education and employment history, (2) character and interpersonal competence, (3) ability to perform the job, and (4) the willingness of the past or current employer to rehire the applicant.

A recommendation or reference check will be meaningful, however, only if the person providing it (1) has had an adequate opportunity to observe the applicant in job-relevant situations, (2) is competent to evaluate the applicant's job performance, (3) can express such an evaluation in a way that is meaningful to the prospective employer, and (4) is completely candid.[21]

Unfortunately, evidence is beginning to show that there is little candor, and thus little value, in written recommendations and referrals, especially those that must, by law, be revealed to applicants if they petition to see them. Specifically, the Family Educational Rights and Privacy Act of 1974 (the Buckley amendment) gives students the legal right to see all letters of recommendation written about them. It also permits release of information about a student only to people approved by the student at the time of the request.

Research suggests that if letters of recommendation are to be meaningful, they should contain the following information[22]:

1. **Degree of writer familiarity with the candidate.**   Time known, and time observed per week.
2. **Degree of writer familiarity with the job in question.**   To help the writer make this judgment, the reader should supply to the writer a description of the job in question.
3. **Specific examples of performance.**   Goals, task difficulty, work environment, and extent of cooperation from coworkers.
4. **Individuals or groups to whom the candidate is compared.**

When seeking information about a candidate from references, consider the following guidelines[23]:

- Request job-related information only; put it in written form to prove that your hire or no-hire decision was based on relevant information.
- Obtain job candidates' written permission to check references prior to doing so.
- Stay away from subjective areas, such as the candidate's personality.
- Evaluate the credibility of the source of the reference material. Under most circumstances, an evaluation by a past immediate supervisor will be more credible than an evaluation by an HR representative.
- Wherever possible, use public records to evaluate on-the-job behavior or personal conduct—e.g., records regarding criminal and civil litigation, driving, or bankruptcy.
- Remember that the courts have ruled that a reference check of an applicant's prior employment record does not violate his or her civil rights as long as the information provided relates solely to work behavior and to reasons for leaving a previous job.

What should you do if you are asked to provide reference information? Here are some useful guidelines:

- Obtain written consent from the employee prior to providing reference data. Fully 89 percent of respondents in a recent survey said they do this now.[24]
- Do not blacklist former employees.
- Keep a written record of all released information.
- Make no subjective statements, such as "He's got a bad attitude." Be specific, such as "He was formally disciplined three times last year for fighting at work."

- So long as you know the facts and have records to back you up, you can feel free to challenge an ex-employee's ability or integrity. But official records are not always candid. A file might show that an executive "resigned," but not that the company avoided a scandal by letting him quit instead of firing him for dishonesty. When there is no supporting data, never even whisper about the employee's sticky fingers.[25]

- If you are contacted by phone, use a telephone "call-back" procedure to verify information provided on a job application by a former employee. Ask the caller to give her or his name and title, the company name, and the nature and purpose of the request. Next, obtain the written consent of the employee to release the information. Finally, call the company back by phone. Do not volunteer any information; say only whether or not the information the caller already has is correct.

- Release only the following general types of information (subject to written consent of the employee): dates of employment, job titles during employment and time in each position, promotions, demotions, attendance record, salary, and reason for termination (no details, just the reason).

Sweetening of résumés and previous work history is common. How common? It has been reported that 20 to 25 percent of all résumés and job applications include at least one major fabrication.[26] The lesson: Always verify key aspects of previous history.

What is the current status of reference checking in practice? Fully two-thirds of companies now say that it has become harder to check applicants' references. Some 44 percent say that a former employer's reluctance to comment hurts applicants' chances of being hired.[27] In large measure this is due to a series of well-publicized suits for slander, such as the $25 million in punitive damages received by a former employee of John Hancock Company, and the $250,000 award upheld by a federal appeals court in Washington, D.C. against a construction company for giving a poor job reference based on hearsay.[28]

On the other hand, employers can be held liable for **negligent hiring** if they fail to check closely enough on a prospective employee who then commits a crime in the course of performing his or her job duties. The employer becomes liable if it knew, or should have known, about the applicant's unfitness to perform the job in question.[29] When courts receive negligent hiring claims they consider: (1) would the risk have been discovered through a thorough background check? (2) Did the nature of the job cause greater risk? (3) Did the employer have a greater responsibility to conduct a thorough background investigation because of the nature of the job? (4) Was the action intentional?[30]

Currently, an employer has no legal duty or obligation to provide information to prospective employers. However, if an employer's policy is to disclose reference information, providing false or speculative information could be grounds for a lawsuit.[31] Reference checking is not an infringement on privacy when fair reference-checking practices are used. It is a sound evaluative tool that can provide objectivity for employers and fairness for job applicants. Figure 7–2 shows the kinds of employment information checked most often.

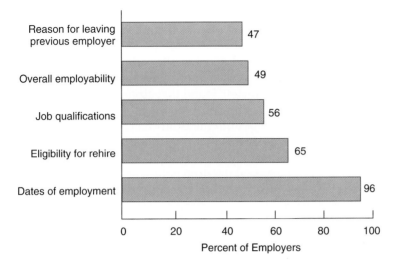

Figure 7–2

Information most
commonly sought
in a reference
check. For exam-
ple, 65 percent of
the employers
sampled reported
that they ask
specifically
whether a candi-
date is eligible to
be rehired by a
former employer.
(*Source:* J. Click,
SHRM survey high-
lights dilemmas of
reference checks,
HR News, July 1995,
p. 13.)

THE USE OF TESTS AND INVENTORIES IN SELECTION

Organizations evaluate and select job candidates on the basis of the results of psychological measurements. The term "measurements" is used here in the broad sense, implying tests and inventories. **Tests** are standardized measures of behavior (e.g., math, vocabulary) that have right and wrong answers, while **inventories** are standardized measures of behavior (e.g., interests, attitudes, opinions) that do not have right and wrong answers. Inventories can be falsified to present an image that a candidate thinks a prospective employer is looking for. Tests cannot be falsified. In the context of personnel selection, tests are preferable, for obvious reasons. Inventories are probably best used for purposes of placement or development because in those contexts there is less motivation for a job candidate to present an image other than what he or she really is. Nevertheless, as we shall see, inventories have been used successfully in selection. What follows is a brief description of available methods and techniques, together with an assessment of their track records to date.

Drug Testing

Drug screening tests, which began in the military and spread to the sports world, are now becoming more common in employment. Ninety-five percent of Fortune 500 companies now make preemployment drug testing a regular part of their prehire procedures.[32]

Critics charge that such screening may not be cost effective, that it violates an individual's right to privacy, and that frequently the tests are inaccurate.[33] Employers counter that the widespread abuse of drugs is reason enough for wider testing.

Do the results of such drug tests forecast certain aspects of later job performance? In the largest reported study of its kind, the U.S. Postal Service took urine samples from 5,465 job applicants. It never used the results to make hiring decisions and did not tell local managers of the findings. When the data were examined 6 months to a year later, workers who had tested positive prior to employment were absent 41 percent more often and were fired 38 percent more often. There were no differences in turnover between those who tested positive and those who did not. These results held up even after adjustment for factors such as age, sex, and race. As a result, the Postal Service implemented preemployment drug testing nationwide.[34] A later review found that absenteeism and involuntary turnover are the outcomes that drug testing forecasts most accurately.[35]

Is such drug testing legal? The Supreme Court has upheld (1) the constitutionality of the government regulations that require railroad crews involved in accidents to submit to prompt urinalysis and blood tests and (2) urine tests for U.S. Customs Service employees seeking drug enforcement posts. The extent to which such rulings will be limited to safety-sensitive positions has yet to be clarified by the Court. Nevertheless, an employer has a legal right to ensure that employees perform their jobs competently and that no employee endangers the safety of other workers. So if illegal drug use either on or off the job may reduce job performance and endanger coworkers, the employer has adequate legal grounds for conducting drug tests.

To avoid legal challenge, consider instituting the following commonsense procedures[36].

1. Inform all employees and job applicants, in writing, of the company's policy regarding drug use.
2. Include the policy, and the possibility of testing, in all employment contracts.
3. Present the program in a medical and safety context. That is, state that drug screening will help improve the health of employees and will also help ensure a safer workplace.
4. Check the testing laboratory's experience, its analytical methods, and the way it protects the security and identity of each sample. Use only federally certified laboratories.
5. If drug testing will be used with employees as well as job applicants, tell employees in advance that it will be a routine part of their employment.
6. If drug testing is done, it should be uniform—that is, it should apply to managers as well as nonmanagers.

COMPANY EXAMPLE   ## PERFORMANCE FACTORS INC. (PFI)

PFI has designed an innovative, computer-based assessment program to determine an employee's fitness for work. PFI's Factor 1000 software, which tests a worker's hand-eye coordination, could provide an effective alternative to blood tests and urinalysis, which many regard as an invasion of personal privacy. The test, which demands considerable concentration and skill, requires the employee to center a moving object between two posts on the computer screen; employees are able to manipulate the object by turning a small knob while the computer monitors and records their performance. Results of each employee's performance are compared with a companywide baseline average.

One company that uses Factor 1000 is Silicon Valley's Ion Implant Services, Inc. Each day before work, delivery drivers line up to stand in front of a computer to play the short video game. But it's not a game. Unless the machine prints a receipt confirming that the drivers have passed the video test, they can't climb behind the wheel.

Does Factor 1000 work? According to *BusinessWeek*, R. F. White, a California petroleum distributor, used Factor 1000 for a year and found that accidents dropped 67 percent, errors fell 92 percent, and workers' compensation claims declined 64 percent. Not surprisingly, PFI's business has been good. It now tests workers who perform a range of tasks, from machine tooling to driving tour buses to handling poisonous gases and high-voltage equipment (*Business-Week,* June 3, 1996, p. 36).

Two Controversial Selection Techniques

Handwriting Analysis

Handwriting analysis (graphology) is reportedly used as a hiring tool by 85 percent of French companies.[37] In Israel, graphology is more widespread than any other personality measurement. Its use is clearly not as widespread in the United States, although sources estimate that more than 3,000 U.S. firms retain handwriting analysts as employment consultants. Such firms generally require job applicants to provide a one-page writing sample. Experts then examine it (at a cost of $60 to $500) for 3 to 10 hours. They assess more than 300 personality traits, including enthusiasm, imagination, and ambition.[38] Are the analysts' predictions valid? In one study involving the prediction of sales success, 103 writers supplied two samples of their handwriting—one "neutral" in content, the second autobiographical. The data were then analyzed by 20 professional graphologists to predict supervisors' ratings of each salesperson's job performance, each salesperson's own ratings of his or her job performance, and sales productivity. The results indicated that the type of script sample did not make any difference. There was some evidence of interrater agreement, but there was no evidence for the validity of the graphologists' predictions.[39] Similar findings have been reported in other well-controlled studies and in meta-analyses (statistical cumulations) of such studies.[40] In short, there is little to recommend the use of handwriting analysis as a predictor of job performance.

Polygraph Examinations

Advocates claim that polygraph (literally, "many pens") examinations are accurate in more than 90 percent of criminal and employment cases *if* interpreted by a competent examiner. Critics claim that the tests are accurate only two-thirds of the time and are far more likely to be unreliable for a subject who is telling the truth.[41]

Prior to 1988, some 4 million polygraph tests were administered each year, 70–80 percent of them for preemployment selection purposes.[42] However, a federal law passed in 1988, the Employee Polygraph Protection Act, severely restricts the use of polygraphs in the employment context (except in the case of firms providing security services and those manufacturing controlled substances). It permits polygraph examinations of current employees only under very restricted circumstances. The prohibition is a huge setback for the polygraph industry, causing it to lose about 85 percent of its $100 million in annual revenues.[43] Indeed, arbitrators had long held that the refusal of an employee to submit to a polygraph exam does not constitute "just cause" for discharge, even when the employee has agreed in advance (e.g., on a job application) to do so on request.[44]

Integrity Tests

Shrinkage—an industry term for losses due to bookkeeping errors and employee, customer, and vendor theft—is estimated to make up almost 2 percent of annual sales.[45] Employee theft alone is estimated to cause up to 30 percent of all business failures.[46] In 2000 the average value of goods taken per shoplifting incident was $128, and it was $1,023 per incident of employee theft. In the aggregate, the cost of theft to the nation's retailers was $29 billion.[47] With statistics like these, it should come as no surprise that written **integrity tests** are being used by an estimated 25 percent of employers.[48] They are of two types.[49] Overt integrity tests (clear purpose tests) are designed to assess directly attitudes toward dishonest behaviors. The second type, personality-based measures (disguised-purpose tests) aim to predict a broad range of counterproductive behaviors at work (disciplinary problems, violence on the job, excessive absenteeism, and drug abuse, in addition to theft).

Do they work? Yes—as demonstrated by a meta-analysis (a statistical cumulation of research results across studies) of 665 validity coefficients that used 576,460 test takers. The average validity of the tests, when used to predict supervisory ratings of performance, was .41. The results for overt integrity and personality-based tests were similar. However, the average validity of overt tests for predicting theft per se was much lower—.13. For personality-based tests, there were no validity estimates available for the prediction of theft alone. Thus theft appears to be less predictable than broadly counterproductive behaviors, at least by overt integrity tests.[50] The validity of integrity tests for predicting drug and alcohol abuse per se is about .30.[51] Finally, since there is no correlation between race and integrity test scores, such tests might well be used in combination with general mental ability test scores to comprise a broader selection procedure.[52]

Despite these encouraging findings, a least three key issues have yet to be resolved[53]: (1) there are almost no data regarding the types of classification errors made by these measures; (2) while "fake-ability" or impression management has been observed on honesty tests,[54] many such tests do not contain lie scales to detect response distortion; and (3) many writers in the field apply the same language and logic to integrity testing as to ability testing. Yet there is an important difference: While it is possible for an individual with poor moral behavior to "go straight," it is certainly less likely that an individual who has demonstrated a lack of intelligence will "go smart." If they are honest about their past, therefore, reformed individuals with a criminal past may be "locked into" low scores on integrity tests (and therefore be subject to classification error). Thus the broad validation evidence that is often acceptable for cognitive ability tests may not hold up in the public policy domain for integrity tests.

Mental Ability Tests

The major types of mental ability tests used in business today include measures of general intelligence; verbal, nonverbal, and numerical skills; spatial relations

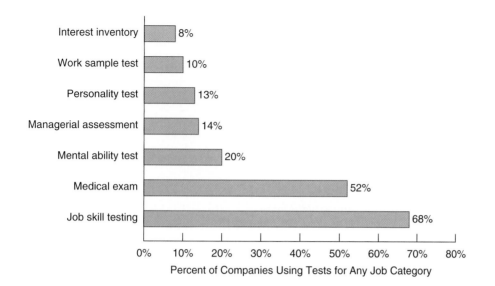

Figure 7–3

Most common tests and examinations used for selection.
(*Source:* 2001 AMA Survey on workplace testing, American Management Association, New York, 2001, p. 2.)

ability (the ability to visualize the effects of manipulating or changing the position of objects); motor functions (speed, coordination); mechanical information, reasoning, and comprehension; clerical aptitudes (perceptual speed tests); and inductive reasoning (the ability to draw general conclusions on the basis of specific facts). When job analysis shows that the abilities or aptitudes measured by such tests are important for successful job performance, the tests are among the most valid predictors currently available (see Figure 7–3 and Table 7–1). For administrative convenience and for reasons of efficiency, many tests today are administered on personal computers, either at a dedicated physical location (such as a company office) or using web-based assessments.[55] While job applicants tend to prefer multimedia, computer-based tests,[56] it is important to ensure that they measure the same characteristics as the paper-and-pencil versions of the same tests.[57]

With respect to the selection of managers, 70 years of research indicate that successful managers are forecast most accurately by tests of their intellectual ability, by their ability to draw conclusions from verbal or numerical information, and by their interests.[58] Further research has found two other types of mental abilities that are related to successful performance as a manager: fluency with words and spatial relations ability.[59]

Validity Generalization

A traditional belief of testing experts is that validity is situation specific. That is, a test with a demonstrated validity in one setting (e.g., selecting bus drivers in St. Louis) might not be valid in another, similar setting (e.g., selecting bus drivers in Atlanta), possibly as a result of differences in specific job tasks, duties, and behaviors. Thus it would seem that the same test used to predict bus driver success in St. Louis and in Atlanta would have to be validated separately in each city.

Two decades of research have cast serious doubt on this assumption.[60] In fact, it has been shown that the major reason for the variation in validity coefficients across settings is the size of the samples—they were too small. When the

Table 7–1

AVERAGE VALIDITIES OF ALTERNATIVE PREDICTORS OF JOB PERFORMANCE

Measure	Validity*
General mental ability tests	.51
Work sample tests	.54
Integrity tests	.41
Conscientiousness tests	.31
Employment interviews (structured)	.51
Employment interviews (unstructured)	.38
Job knowledge tests	.48
Job tryout procedure	.44
Peer ratings	.49
Ratings of training and experience	.45
Reference checks	.26
Job experience (years)	.18
Biographical data	.35
Assessment centers	.37
Points assigned to training and experience	.11
Years of education	.10
Interests	.10
Graphology	.02
Age	−.01

*Validity is based on cumulative findings that have been summarized using meta-analysis. Validity is expressed as a correlation coefficient that varies from −1 to +1.
Source: Adapted from F. L. Schmidt & J. E. Hunter, The validity and utility of selection methods in personnel psychology: Practical and theoretical implications of 85 years of research findings, *Psychological Bulletin, 124,* 1998, p. 265.

effect of sampling error is removed, the validities observed for similar test-job combinations across settings do not differ significantly. In short, the results of a validity study conducted in one situation can be generalized to other situations as long as it can be shown that jobs in the two situations are similar.

Since thousands of studies have been done on the prediction of job performance, **validity generalization** allows us to use this database to establish definite values for the average validity of most predictors. The average validities for predictors commonly in use are shown in Table 7–1.

Personality Measures

"**Personality**" is the set of characteristics of a person that account for the consistent ways that he or she responds to situations. Five personality characteristics particularly relevant to performance at work are known as the "Big Five." They are: neuroticism, extraversion, openness to experience, agreeableness, and conscientiousness.[61] **Neuroticism** concerns the degree to which an individual is insecure, anxious, depressed, and emotional, versus calm, self-confident, and cool. **Extraversion** concerns the degree to which an individual is gregarious, assertive, and sociable, versus reserved, timid, and quiet. **Openness to experience** concerns the degree to which an individual is creative, curious, and cultured, versus practical with narrow interests. **Agreeableness** concerns the degree to which an individual is cooperative, warm, and agreeable, versus cold, disagreeable, and antagonistic. **Conscientiousness** concerns the degree to which an individual is hard-working, organized, dependable, and persevering, versus lazy, disorganized, and unreliable. Research conducted over the past decade shows that these are valid predictors of performance, but their validities differ depending on the nature of the job and the type of criteria. Conscientiousness has been shown to be the most generalizable predictor, with an average validity of .31. Validities tend to be highest when theory and job analysis information are used explicitly to select personality measures.[62]

At this point you are probably asking yourself about the relationship of the Big Five to integrity tests. Integrity tests have been found to measure mostly conscientiousness, but also some components of agreeableness and emotional stability.[63] That is why their validities tend to be higher than those of individual Big Five characteristics alone.

The Issue of Faking.   Can't applicants distort their responses in ways they believe will make a positive impression on the employer? The answer is yes.[64] However, do job applicants actually distort their responses? The manual for the Hogan Personnel Selection Series states, "the base rate of faking during the job application process is virtually non-existent."[65] As a result of this belief, many of the latest personality inventories designed to measure the five-factor model of personality do not include a measure of response distortion.[66] While *moderate* distortion may reduce predictive-related validities slightly, compared to validities obtained with job incumbents,[67] response distortion can have a dramatic effect on who is hired, even though it has no detectable effect on predictive validity.[68] On top of that, coaching can improve scores.[69] To control the effects of faking one strategy is to perform statistical corrections, but there is disagreement among experts about the best approach for doing that.[70] A more practical strategy is to warn job applicants in advance that distortion can and will be detected, that verification procedures exist, and that there will be a consequence for such distortion. Possible consequences might vary from elimination from the selection process to verification in a background check or oral interview. A review of eight studies that investigated the effects of such warnings found that in all eight warnings reduced the amount of intentional distortion in self-report instruments, relative to situations where no such warnings were given.[71]

Projective Measures

Projective measures present an individual with ambiguous stimuli (primarily visual) and allow him or her to respond in an open-ended fashion (Figure 7–4), for example, by telling a story regarding what is happening in the picture. Based on how the individual structures the situation through the story he or she tells, an examiner (usually a clinical psychologist) makes inferences concerning the individual's personality structure.

Sample projective stimulus. Candidates are told to look at the picture briefly and then to write the story it suggests. Stories are scored in terms of the key themes expressed.

Basically, the difference between an objective and a projective test is this: in an objective test, the test taker tries to guess what the examiner is thinking; in a projective test, the examiner tries to guess what the test taker is thinking.[72]

Although early research showed projective measures not to be accurate predictors of management success,[73] they can provide useful results when the examinee's responses are related to motivation to manage (e.g., achievement motivation, willingness to accept a leadership role).[74] Moreover, measures of intelligence are unrelated to scores on projective tests. So a combination of both types of instruments can provide a fuller picture of individual "can-do" (intelligence) and "will-do" (motivational) factors than can either one used alone.

Measures of Leadership Ability

At first glance, one might suspect that measures of leadership ability are highly predictive of managerial success since they appear to tap a critical management job requirement directly. Scales designed to measure two key aspects of leadership behavior, consideration and initiating structure, have been developed and used in many situations. **Consideration** reflects management actions oriented toward developing mutual trust, respect for subordinates' ideas, and consideration of their feelings. **Initiating structure**, on the other hand, reflects the extent to which an individual defines and structures her or his role and the roles of her or his subordinates toward accomplishing tasks.

Unfortunately, questionnaires designed to measure consideration and initiating structure have been inaccurate predictors of success in management.[75]

This is not to imply that leadership is unimportant in managerial jobs. Rather, it may be that the majority of such jobs are designed to encourage and reward managing (doing things right) rather than leading (doing the right things).

Personal-History Data

Based on the assumption that one of the best predictors of what a person will do in the future is what he or she has done in the past, biographical information has been used widely and successfully as one basis for staffing decisions. Table 7–1 shows its average validity to be a very respectable .35. As with any other method, careful, competent research is necessary if "biodata" are to prove genuinely useful as predictors of job success.[76] For example, items that are more objective and verifiable are less likely to be faked.[77] The payoff is that biodata can add significant explanatory power over and above "Big Five" personality dimensions and also general mental ability.[78] Here is another example of this kind of effort.

Many professionals resist taking preemployment tests, arguing "My record speaks for itself." The accomplishment record inventory, a biodata instrument, lets those records speak systematically.[79] Job candidates describe their accomplishments, in writing, in each job dimension that job analysis shows to be essential (e.g., for attorneys, technical knowledge, research and investigation, and assertive advocacy). Raters then use scales developed (by incumbents) for each dimension to evaluate the accomplishments. Research with five types of jobs (attorneys, librarians, economists, research analysts, and supervisors) yielded validities ranging from .22 to .45 and no adverse impact against protected groups.[80] The approach is legally defensible, results oriented, and highly job related, and it elicits unique, job-relevant information from each person. Not surprisingly, therefore, it is getting lots of attention.

Employment Interviews

Employment interviewing is a difficult mental and social task. Managing a smooth social exchange while instantaneously processing information about a job candidate makes interviewing uniquely difficult among all managerial tasks.[81] Researchers have been studying the employment interview for more than 60 years for two purposes: (1) to determine the reliability (consistency) and validity (accuracy) of employment decisions based on assessments derived from interviews, and (2) to discover the various psychological factors that influence interviewer judgments. Hundreds of research articles on these issues have been published, along with periodic reviews of the "state of the art" of interviewing research and practice.[82] Recent research leads to the following recommendations[83]:

1. Base interview questions on a job analysis.
2. Ask the same general questions of each candidate. That is, use a structured interview.
3. Use detailed rating scales, with behavioral descriptions to illustrate scale points.
4. Take detailed notes that focus on behavioral information about candidates.[84]
5. Use multiple interviewers.
6. Provide extensive training on interviewing.
7. Do not discuss candidates or answers between interviews.

8. Use statistical weights for each dimension, as well as an overall judgment of suitability, to combine information.[85]

The validity of the preemployment interview will be reduced to the extent that interviewers' decisions are overly influenced by such factors as first impressions, personal feelings about the kinds of characteristics that lead to success on the job, and contrast effects, among other nonobjective factors. **Contrast effects** describe a tendency among interviewers to evaluate a current candidate's interview performance relative to those that immediately preceded it. If a first candidate received a very positive evaluation and a second candidate is just "average," interviewers tend to evaluate the second candidate more negatively than is deserved. The second candidate's performance is "contrasted" to that of the first.

Employers are likely to achieve nonbiased hiring decisions if they concentrate on shaping interviewer behavior.[86] One way to do that is to establish a specific system for conducting the employment interview. Building on the suggestions made earlier, here are some things to consider in setting up such a system[87]:

- To know what to look for in applicants, focus only on the competencies necessary for the job. Be sure to distinguish between entry-level and full-performance competencies.[88]
- Screen résumés and application forms by focusing on (1) key words that match job requirements, (2) quantifiers and qualifiers that show whether applicants have these requirements, and (3) skills that might transfer from previous jobs to the new job.
- Develop interview questions that are strictly based on the job analysis results; use "open-ended" questions (those that cannot be answered with a simple yes or no response); and use questions relevant to the individual's ability to perform, motivation to do a good job, and overall "fit" with the firm.
- Consider asking "What would you do if...?" questions. Such questions compose the situational interview, which is based on the assumption that a person's expressed behavioral intentions are related to subsequent behavior. In the situational interview, candidates are asked to describe how they think they would respond in certain job-related situations. Alternatively, in an experienced-based interview they are asked to provide detailed accounts of actual situations. For example, instead of asking "How would you reprimand an employee?" the interviewer might say, "Give me a specific example of a time you had to reprimand an employee. What action did you take, and what was the result?" Answers tend to be remarkably consistent with actual (subsequent) job behavior.[89] The empirically observed validities for both types of interviews, uncorrected for statistical artifacts, vary from about .22 to .28.[90]
- Conduct the interview in a relaxed physical setting. Begin by putting the applicant at ease with simple questions and general information about the organization and the position being filled. Throughout, note all nonverbal cues, such as lack of eye contact and facial expressions, as possible indicators of the candidate's interest in and ability to do the job.
- To evaluate applicants, develop a form containing a list of competencies weighted for overall importance to the job, and evaluate each applicant relative to each competency.

A systematic interview developed along these lines will minimize the uncertainty so inherent in decision making that is based predominantly on "gut feeling." It also will contribute additional explanatory power over and above cognitive ability and measures of conscientiousness,[91] and it will reduce differences in evaluation scores among minorities and nonminorities.[92] Table 7–2 shows some examples of proper and improper interview questions, along with several examples of "situational"-type questions.

Peer Assessment

In the typical peer assessment procedure, raters are asked to predict how well a peer will do if placed in a leadership or managerial role. Such information can be enlightening, since peers evaluate managerial behavior from a different perspective than do managers themselves. Actually, the term **peer assessment** is a general term denoting three basic methods that members of a well-defined

Table 7–2

SOME EXAMPLES OF PROPER AND IMPROPER QUESTIONS IN EMPLOYMENT INTERVIEWS

Issue	Proper	Improper
Criminal history	Have you ever been convicted of a violation of a law?	Have you ever been arrested?
Marital status	None	Are you married? Do you prefer Ms., Miss, or Mrs.? What does your spouse do for a living?
National origin	None	Where were you born? Where were your parents born?
Disability	None	Do you have any disabilities or handicaps? Do you have any health problems?
Sexual orientation	None	Whom do you live with? Do you ever intend to marry?
Citizenship status	Do you have a legal right to work in the United States?	Are you a U.S. citizen? Are you an alien?
Situational questions (Assumption: Job analysis has shown such questions to be job-related.)	How do you plan to keep up with current developments in your field? How do you measure your customers' satisfaction with your product or services? If you were a product, how would you position yourself?	

group use in judging each other's performance: **Peer nomination** requires each group member to designate a certain number of group members as highest or lowest on a performance dimension. **Peer rating** requires each group member to rate the performance of every group member. **Peer ranking** requires each group member to rank the performance of all other members from best to worst.

Reviews of more than 50 studies found all three methods of peer assessment to be reliable, valid, and free from bias.[93] Peer assessments do predict job advancement.[94] However, since implicitly they require people to consider privileged information about their coworkers, it is essential that peers be thoroughly involved in the planning and design of the peer assessment method to be used.

Work-Sample Tests

Work-sample tests, or situational tests, are standardized measures of behavior whose primary objective is to assess the ability to do rather than the ability to know. They may be motor, involving physical manipulation of things (e.g., trade tests for carpenters, plumbers, or electricians), or verbal, involving problem situations that are primarily language oriented or people oriented (e.g., situational tests for supervisory jobs).[95] Since work samples are miniature replicas of actual job requirements, they are difficult to fake, and they are unlikely to lead to charges of discrimination or invasion of privacy. Recent research indicates that they produce smaller minority/nonminority group differences in performance, along with modest losses in predictive validity.[96] However, since the content of the test reflects the essential content of the job, the tests do have content-oriented evidence of validity.[97] Their use in one study of 263 applicants for city government jobs led to a reduction of turnover from 40 percent to less than 3 percent in the 9 to 26 months following their introduction. The reduction in turnover saved the city more than $875,000 in 2001 dollars.[98] Nevertheless, since each candidate must be tested individually, work-sample tests are probably not cost effective when large numbers of people must be evaluated.

Two types of situational tests are used to evaluate and select managers: group exercises, in which participants are placed in a situation in which the successful completion of a task requires interaction among the participants, and individual exercises, in which participants complete a task independently. The following sections consider three of the most popular situational tests: the leaderless group discussion, the in-basket test, and the business game.

Leaderless Group Discussion (LGD).   The LGD is simple and has been used for decades. A group of participants is given a job-related topic and is asked simply to carry on a discussion about it for a period of time. No one is appointed leader, nor is anyone told where to sit. Instead of using a rectangular table (with a "head" at each end), a circular table is often used so that each position carries equal weight. Observers rate the performance of each participant.

For example, IBM uses an LGD in which each participant is required to make a 5-minute oral presentation of a candidate for promotion and then subsequently defend her or his candidate in a group discussion with five other participants. All roles are well defined and structured. Seven characteristics are rated, each on a 5-point scale of effectiveness: aggressiveness, persuasiveness or selling ability, oral communication, self-confidence, resistance to stress, energy level, and interpersonal contact.[99]

LGD ratings have forecast managerial performance accurately in virtually all the functional areas of business.[100] Previous LGD experience appears to have little effect on present LGD performance, although prior training clearly does.[101] Individuals in one study who received a 15-minute briefing on the history, development, rating instruments, and research relative to the LGD were rated significantly higher than untrained individuals. To control for this, all those with prior training in LGD should be put into the same groups.

In-Basket Test.   A situational test designed to simulate important aspects of a position, the in-basket tests an individual's ability to work independently. In general, it takes the following form:

> It consists of the letters, memoranda, notes of incoming telephone calls, and other materials that have supposedly collected in the in-basket of an administrative officer. The subject who takes the test is given appropriate background information concerning the school, business, military unit, or whatever institution is involved. He is told that he is the new incumbent of the administrative position and that he is to deal with the material in the in-basket. The background information is sufficiently detailed that the subject can reasonably be expected to take action on many of the problems presented by the in-basket documents. The subject is instructed that he is not to play a role, he is not to pretend to be someone else. He is to bring to the new job his own background of knowledge and experience, his own personality, and he is to deal with the problems as though he were really the incumbent of the administrative position. He is not to say what he would do; he is actually to write letters and memoranda, prepare agenda for meetings, make notes and reminders for himself, as though he were actually on the job.[102]

Some sample in-basket items are shown in Figure 7–5.

Although the situation is relatively unstructured, each candidate faces the same complex set of materials. At the conclusion of the in-basket test, each candidate leaves behind a packet full of notes, memos, letters, etc., that provide a record of his or her behavior. The test is then scored by describing (if the purpose is development) or evaluating (if the purpose is selection for promotion) what the candidate did in terms of such dimensions as self-confidence, organizational and planning abilities, written communications, decision making, risk taking, and administrative abilities. The dimensions to be evaluated are identified through job analysis prior to designing or selecting the exercise. The major advantages of the in-basket, therefore, are its flexibility (it can be designed to fit many different types of situations, and modes of administration, such as via computer[103]), and the fact that it permits direct observation of individual behavior within the context of a job-relevant, standardized problem situation.

More than 25 years of research on the in-basket indicate that it validly forecasts subsequent job behavior and promotion.[104] Moreover, since performance on the LGD is not strongly related to performance on the in-basket, in combination the two are potentially powerful predictors of managerial success.

Business Games.   The business game is a situational test, a living case in which candidates play themselves, not an assigned role, and are evaluated within a group. Like in-baskets, business games are available for a wide variety of executive activities, from marketing to capital asset management. They may be simple (focusing on very specific activities) or complex models of complete

Figure 7–4

Sample in-basket items.

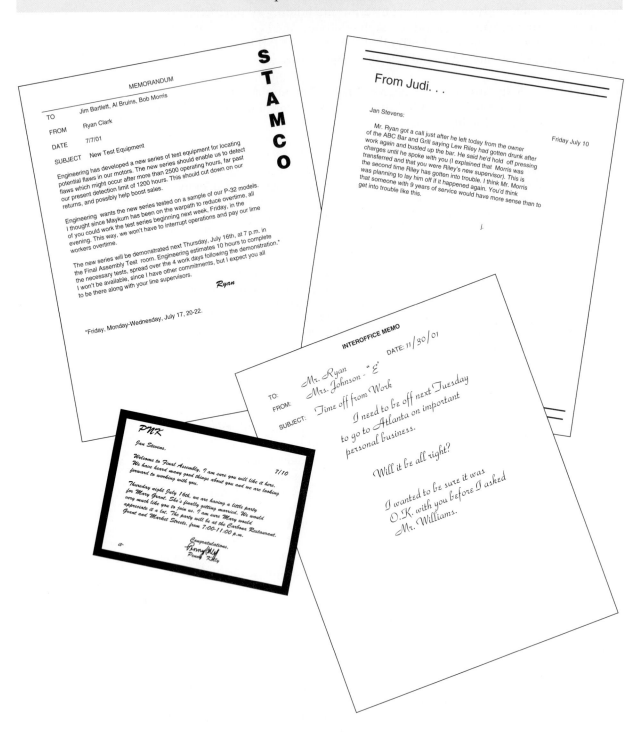

S T A M C O

MEMORANDUM

TO   Jim Bartlett, Al Bruins, Bob Morris

FROM   Ryan Clark

DATE   7/7/01

SUBJECT   New Test Equipment

Engineering has developed a new series of test equipment for locating potential flaws in our motors. The new series should enable us to detect flaws which might occur after more than 2500 operating hours, far past our present detection limit of 1200 hours. This should cut down on our returns, and possibly help boost sales.

Engineering wants the new series tested on a sample of our P-32 models. I thought since Maykum has been on the warpath to reduce overtime, all of you could work the test series beginning next week, Friday, in the evening. This way, we won't have to interrupt operations and pay our lime workers overtime.

The new series will be demonstrated next Thursday, July 16th, at 7 p.m. in the Final Assembly Test room. Engineering estimates 10 hours to complete the necessary tests, spread over the 4 work days following the demonstration.* I won't be available, since I have other commitments, but I expect you all to be there along with your line supervisors.

                                              Ryan

*Friday, Monday-Wednesday, July 17, 20-22.

From Judi. . .

Jan Stevens:

                                              Friday July 10

Mr. Ryan got a call just after he left today from the owner of the ABC Bar and Grill saying Lew Riley had gotten drunk after work again and busted up the bar. He said he'd hold off pressing charges until he spoke up the bar. He said he'd hold off pressing transferred and that you were Riley's new supervisor). This is the second time Riley has gotten into trouble. I think Mr. Morris was planning to lay him off if it happened again. You'd think that someone with 9 years of service would have more sense than to get into trouble like this.

                              j.

INTEROFFICE MEMO

                              DATE: 11/30/01

TO: *Mr. Ryan*

FROM: *Mrs. Johnson - "E"*

SUBJECT: *Time off from Work*

I need to be off next Tuesday to go to Atlanta on important personal business.

Will it be all right?

I wanted to be sure it was O.K. with you before I asked Mr. Williams.

PNK

Jan Stevens,

                              7/10

Welcome to Final Assembly. I am sure you will like it here. We have heard many good things about you and we are looking forward to working with you.

Thursday night July 16th, we are having a little party for Mary Grant. She's finally getting married. We would very much like you to join us. I am sure Mary would appreciate it a lot. The party will be at the Carbona Restaurant, Grant and Market Streets, from 7:00-11:00 p.m.

Congratulations,
Penny Riley

DOWNTOWN KEY–WANIS CLUB
Box 8003
Midville, Indiana

December 1, 2001

Mr. Sam Ryan, Superintendent
Midville Youth and Adult Development Center
Midville, Indiana

Dear Mr. Ryan:

We would like very much to have you speak at our luncheon meeting on Thursday, January 8th, at 12:30 p.m. at the Midville Hotel. Perhaps you could use the topic "The Extent of the Problem of Drug Abuse and Crime." The programs at our luncheon meetings usually run from 30-45 minutes.

We sincerely hope that you will be able to be with us on the 8th. Please let me know at the address shown above (or at telephone number 822-0136). If your schedule will not permit your accepting this invitation, perhaps one of your staff could present this program.

Yours truly,

Jack Williams

J.W. ("Jack") Williams
Program Chairman

2310 Lakewood Drive
Midville, Indiana
November 24, 2001

Mr. Sam Ryan
Midville Youth and Adult Development Center
Midville, Indiana

Dear Mr. Ryan:

The Youth Fellowship of Greenbriar Church would like to come to the Center and put on a Christmas Party for the people there. We would provide refreshments, presents for everybody, decorations and all the rest.

Would you please let me know if this is possible. If it is, our committee will come out and talk to you about the plans. My phone number is 823-9322.

Sincerely,

Cindy Fuller

Cindy Fuller
President, Greenbriar
Youth Fellowship

*Bill —
How does this
sound to you?
S-R 11/25/01*

MR. RYAN...
THE LAST TIME WE HAD A
CHURCH GROUP PUT ON A PARTY
OUT HERE WAS BEFORE YOU
CAME. THINGS WERE O.K.
UNTIL THE HOUSEPARENTS
TOOK A COFFEE BREAK. WHILE
THEY WERE GONE, IT GOT
COMPLETELY OUT OF HAND.
WE COULD HAVE
PROBLEMS.
BILL 11/28/2001

MIDVILLE APPLIANCE AND HARDWARE STORE
149 Peabody Street
Midville, Indiana

November 28, 2001

Mr. Sam Ryan
Superintendent
Midville Youth and Adult
Development Center
Midville, Indiana

Dear Mr. Ryan:

As you know, my store is located between your rehabilitation center and Midville Vocational and Technical School. During the past several months we have had several cases of shoplifting from our store, and the police haven't been able to do anything about it. Also, your people have been observed acting funny, with a dazed look on their faces, as though they are on drugs.

I initially was a supporter of the rehabilitation center being in this neighborhood. However, I am about to change my mind, and I can assure you that my position on the zoning commission carries a lot of weight in this community.

I would appreciate hearing from you within the next week. Otherwise, I will be forced to take appropriate measures to ensure protection of my store and this community.

Sincerely,

Arch Turkey

Arch Turkey

---

memo

7/3/2001   from Charlie Vernon

Bob:
We've had an 80% increase in rejects this week on our 38B model and most of them have been a result of poor armature wiring. Isn't that McGrady's operation? This doesn't help our production index, you know.

organizational systems. They may be computer-based or manually-operated, rigidly programmed or flexible.[105] They will probably be used more frequently for training purposes, given the continued development and availability of personal computers and simulation software—for example, stock market simulations and battle simulations for military academies.

COMPANY EXAMPLE   ## IBM'S MANUFACTURING PROBLEM

In this exercise, six participants must work together as a group to operate a manufacturing company. They must purchase raw materials, manufacture a product, and sell it in the market. Included in the exercise are a product forecast and specific prices (which fluctuate during the exercise) for raw materials and completed products. No preassigned roles are given to the participants, but each one is rated in terms of aggressiveness, persuasiveness or selling ability, resistance to stress, energy level, interpersonal contact, administrative ability, and risk taking. In one IBM study, performance on the manufacturing problem accurately forecast changes in position level for 94 middle managers 3 years later.[106] When the in-basket score was added as an additional predictor, the forecast was even more accurate.

Business games have several advantages. One, they compress time; events that might not actually occur for months or years are made to occur in a matter of hours. Two, the games are interesting because of their realism, their competitive nature, and the immediacy and objectivity of their feedback. Three, such games promote increased understanding of complex interrelationships among organizational units.

Business games also have drawbacks. One, in the context of training, some participants may become so engrossed in "beating the system" that they fail to grasp the underlying management principles being taught. Two, creative approaches to solving problems presented by the game may be stifled, particularly if the highly innovative manager is penalized financially during the game for her or his unorthodox strategies.[107]

Assessment Centers

The assessment center approach was first used by German military psychologists during World War II to select officers. They felt that paper-and-pencil tests took too narrow a view of human nature; therefore, they chose to observe each candidate's behavior in a complex situation to develop a broader appraisal of his or her reactions. Borrowing from this work and that of the War Office Selection Board of the British army during the early 1940s, the U.S. Office of Strategic Services used the method to select spies during World War II. Each candidate had to develop a cover story that would hide her or his identity during the assessment. Testing for the ability to maintain cover was crucial, and ingenious situational tests were designed to seduce candidates into breaking cover.[108]

After World War II many military psychologists and officers joined private companies, where they started small-scale assessment centers. In 1956, AT&T

was the first to use the method as the basis of a large-scale study of managerial progress and career development. As a result of extensive research conducted over 25 years, AT&T found that managerial skills and abilities are best measured by the following procedures[109]:

1. **Administrative skills.** Performance on the in-basket test.
2. **Interpersonal skills.** LGD, manufacturing problem.
3. **Intellectual ability.** Paper-and-pencil ability tests.
4. **Stability of performance.** In-basket, LGD, manufacturing problem.
5. **Work-oriented motivation.** Projective tests, interviews, simulations.
6. **Career orientation.** Projective tests, interviews, personality inventories.
7. **Dependency on others.** Projective tests.

Assessment centers do more than just test people. The **assessment center** method is a process that evaluates a candidate's potential for management based on three sources: (1) multiple assessment techniques, such as situational tests, tests of mental abilities, and interest inventories; (2) standardized methods of making inferences from such techniques, because assessors are trained to distinguish between effective and ineffective behaviors by the candidates; and (3) pooled judgments from multiple assessors to rate each candidate's behavior.

Today, assessment centers take many different forms, for they are used in a wide variety of settings and for a variety of purposes. Thousands of organizations in countries around the world are now using the assessment center method, and more are doing so every year. In addition to evaluating and selecting managers, the method is being used to train and upgrade management skills, to encourage creativity among research and engineering professionals, to resolve interpersonal and interdepartmental conflicts, to assist individuals in career planning, to train managers in performance appraisal, and to provide information for workforce planning and organization design.

The assessment center method offers great flexibility. The specific content and design of a center can be tailored to the characteristics of the job in question. For example, when used for management selection, the assessment center method should be designed to predict how a person would behave in the next-higher-level management job. By relating each candidate's overall performance on the assessment center exercises to such indicators as the management level subsequently achieved two (or more) years later or current salary, researchers have shown that the predictions for each candidate are very accurate. An accurate reading of each candidate's behavior before the promotion decision is made can help avoid potentially costly selection errors (erroneous acceptances as well as erroneous rejections).

As a specific example of the flexibility of the assessment center method in using multiple assessment techniques, consider the following six types of exercises used to help select U.S. Army recruiters[110]:

- **Structured interview.** Assessors ask a series of questions targeted at the subject's level of achievement motivation, potential for being a "self-starter," and commitment to the Army.
- **Cold calls.** The subject has an opportunity to learn a little about three prospects and must phone each of them for the purpose of getting them to

come into the office. Assessor role players have well-defined characters (prospects) to portray.

- **Interviews**. Two of the three cold-call prospects agree to come in for an interview. The subject's job is to follow up on what was learned in the cold-call conversations and to begin promoting Army enlistment to these people. A third walk-in prospect also appears for an interview with the subject.
- **Interview with concerned parent**. The subject is asked to prepare for and conduct an interview with the father of one of the prospects that he or she interviewed previously.
- **Five-minute speech about the Army**. The subject prepares a short talk about an Army career and delivers it to the rest of the group and to the assessors.
- **In-basket**. The subject is given an in-basket filled with notes, phone messages, and letters on which he or she must take some action.

A third feature of the assessment center method is assessor training. Assessors are typically line managers two or more levels above the candidates, trained (from 2 days to several weeks depending on the complexity of the center) in interviewing techniques, behavior observation, and in developing a common frame of reference with which to assess candidates.[111] In addition, assessors usually go through the exercises as participants before rating others. This experience, plus the development of a consensus by assessors on effective versus ineffective responses by candidates to the situations presented, enables the assessors to standardize their interpretations of each candidate's behavior. Standardization ensures that each candidate will be assessed fairly, that is, in terms of the same "yardstick."

Instead of professional psychologists, line managers are often used as assessors for several reasons:

1. They are thoroughly familiar with the jobs for which candidates are being assessed.
2. Their involvement in the assessment process contributes to its acceptance by participants as well as by line managers.
3. Participation by line managers is a developmental experience for them and may contribute to the identification of areas in which they need improvement themselves.[112]
4. Assessors can be more objective in evaluating candidate performance since they usually do not know the candidates personally.[113]

Despite these potential advantages, cumulative evidence across assessment center studies indicates that professional psychologists who are trained to interpret behaviors in the assessment center relative to the requirements of specific jobs provide more valid assessment center ratings than do managers.[114]

In order to rate each candidate's behavior, organizations pool the judgments of multiple assessors. The advantage of pooling is that no candidate is subject to ratings from only one assessor. Since judgments from more than one source tend to be more reliable and valid, pooling enhances the overall accuracy of the judgments made. Each candidate is usually evaluated by a different assessor on each exercise. Although assessors make their judgments independently, the judgments must be combined into an overall rating on each dimension of interest. A summary report is then prepared and shared with each candidate.

These features of the assessment center method—flexibility of form and content, the use of multiple assessment techniques, standardized methods of interpreting behavior, and pooled assessor judgments—account for the successful track record of this approach over the past five decades. It has consistently demonstrated high validity, with correlations between assessment center performance and later job performance as a manager sometimes reaching the .50s and .60s.[115] Both minorities and nonminorities, and both men and women, acknowledge that the method provides them a fair opportunity to demonstrate what they are capable of doing in a management job.[116]

In terms of its bottom-line impact, two studies have shown that assessment centers are cost effective, even though the per-candidate cost may vary from as little as $50 to more than $2,000. Using the general utility equation (Equation 7–1 in the appendix to this chapter, on page 277), both studies have demonstrated that the assessment center method should not be measured against the cost of implementing it, but rather against the cost (in lost sales and declining productivity) of promoting the wrong person into a management job.[117] In a first-level management job, the gain in improved job performance as a result of promoting people via the assessment center method is about $4,500 per year (in 2001 dollars). However, if the average tenure of first-level managers is, say, 5 years, the gain per person is about $22,500 (in 2001 dollars).

Despite its advantages, the method is not without potential problems. These include[118]:

- Adoption of the assessment center method without carefully analyzing the need for it and without adequate preparations to use it wisely.
- Blind acceptance of assessment data without considering other information on candidates, such as past and current performance.
- The tendency to rate only general "exercise effectiveness," rather than performance relative to individual behavioral dimensions (e.g., by using a behavioral checklist), as the number of dimensions exceeds the ability of assessors to evaluate each dimension individually.
- Lack of control over the information generated during assessment: for example, "leaking" assessment ratings to operating managers.
- Failure to evaluate the utility of the program in terms of dollar benefits relative to costs.
- Inadequate feedback to participants.

Here is an interesting finding: ratings of management potential made after a review of employee files correlated significantly (.46) with assessment ratings, suggesting that assessment might to some extent duplicate a much simpler and less costly process.[119] This conclusion held true for predictions made regarding each candidate's progress in management 1 and 8 years after assessment.[120] However, when the rating of management potential was added to the assessment center prediction, the validity of the two together (.58) was higher than that of either one alone. What does the assessment center prediction add? Not much, if we are simply trying to predict each candidate's rate and level of advancement. But if we are trying to predict performance in management—that is, to clarify and evaluate the promotion system in an organization—assessment centers can be of considerable help, even if they serve only to capture the promotion policy of the organization.[121]

International Application: The Japanese Approach To Staffing

Soon after Toyota announced that it would build an auto assembly plant in Kentucky, some 90,000 job applications poured in for the 2,700 production jobs and 300 office jobs available. To narrow the field, Toyota uses common tests to an uncommon degree. Even someone applying for the lowest-paying job on the shop floor goes through at least 14 hours of testing, administered on Toyota's behalf by state employment offices and Kentucky State University.

Rigorous testing is also standard procedure for the U.S. auto plants of Mazda Motor Corporation; for a joint venture of Isuzu Motors, Ltd., and Fuji Heavy Industries, Ltd.; and for Diamond-Star Motors Corporation, a Mitsubishi operation.

Initial tests cover reading and mathematics, manual dexterity, "job fitness," and, for skilled trades, technical knowledge. "Job fitness" is actually an attitude measure in which applicants are asked whether they agree or disagree with 100 different statements. Here are two examples: "It's important for workers to work past quitting time to get the job done when necessary" and "Management will take advantage of employees whenever possible."

Next come workplace simulations. Groups of applicants are assigned such problems as ranking the features of a hypothetical auto according to how well the market would accept them. As the job seekers discuss the options, trained assessors record their observations. Later they pool their findings in order to assess each candidate. Other problems focus on manufacturing and making repairs—though not of autos, since Toyota is interested in aptitude more than experience.

There are also mock production lines, where applicants assemble tubes or circuit boards. The objective is to identify applicants who can keep to a fast pace, endure tedious repetition, and yet stay alert. The tube-assembly procedure is intentionally flawed, and applicants are asked how they would improve it.

Only 1 applicant in 20 makes it to an interview, which is conducted by a panel representing various Toyota departments. By then, says an HRM staffer, "we're going to know more about these people than perhaps any company has ever known about people." The final steps are a physical examination and a drug test.

For all the testing being done by the Japanese auto-makers, there are some that use other methods. Honda, for example, uses few tests at its Marysville, Ohio, plant. Instead it puts every potential hire through three interviews. And Nissan Motor Co., which has been operating in Smyrna, Tennessee, since the early 1980s, prefers to give probable hires at least 40 hours of "preemployment" training—without pay. The training is intended partly as a final check on whether the company and those in training are really right for each other.[122]

Choosing the Right Predictor

Determining the right predictor depends on the following:

- **The nature of the job.**
- **An estimate of the validity of the predictor** in terms of the size of the correlation coefficient that summarizes the strength of the relationship between applicants' scores on the predictor and their corresponding scores on some measure of performance.
- **The selection ratio**, or percentage of applicants selected.
- **The cost of the predictor.**

To the extent that job performance is multidimensional (as indicated in job analysis results), multiple predictors, each focused on critical competencies, might be used. Other things being equal, the predictors with the highest estimated validities should be used; they will tend to minimize the number of erroneous acceptances and rejections, and they will tend to maximize workforce productivity. Table 7–1 summarizes the accumulated validity evidence for a number of potential predictors.

It is important to take into account the **selection ratio** (the percentage of applicants hired) in evaluating the overall usefulness of any predictor, regardless of its validity. On the one hand, low selection ratios mean that more applicants must be evaluated; on the other hand, low selection ratios also mean that only the "cream" of the applicant crop will be selected. Hence predictors with lower validity may be used when the selection ratio is low since it is necessary only to distinguish the very best qualified from everyone else.

Finally, the cost of selection is a consideration, but not a major one. Of course, if two predictors are roughly equal in estimated validity, then use the less costly procedure. However, the trade-off between cost and validity should almost always be resolved in favor of validity. Choose the more valid procedure, because the major concern is not the cost of the procedure, but rather the cost of a mistake if the wrong candidate is selected or promoted. In management jobs, such mistakes are likely to be particularly costly.[123]

ORGANIZATIONAL CULTURE—KEY TO STAFFING "FIT"

Human Resource Management in Action: Conclusion

There is an old maxim about industry: It's a numbers game and a people business. The fundamental business proposition at Southwest Airlines is that its people come first. As CEO Herb Kelleher commented,

> It used to be a business conundrum: Who comes first? The employees, customers, or shareholders? That's never been an issue to me. The employees come first. If they're happy, satisfied, dedicated, and energetic, they'll take real good care of the customers. When the customers are happy, they come back. And that makes the shareholders happy.

Southwest lets its best customers get involved in the preemployment interviews for flight attendants. The entire process focuses on a positive attitude and teamwork. Peers play active roles in the hiring of peers; for example, pilots hire other pilots, baggage handlers other baggage handlers. In one case Southwest pilots turned down a top pilot who worked for another major airline and did stunt work for movie studios. Even though he was a great pilot, he made the mistake of being rude to a Southwest receptionist. Teamwork also is critical. If applicants say "I" too much in the interview, they don't get hired. To be sure, Southwest's record of 28 consecutive years of profitable operations is not all due to the company's culture, but its culture is a major reason outsiders want to join the company, and seasoned veterans want to remain.

Other companies are trying to define or change their cultures, and it is difficult. Time Warner, the entertainment giant, was known just a few years ago as a hotbed of internal strife and turf wars. Financial stability and well-performing businesses changed that. Concerned about his legacy, CEO Gerald Levin set out to define and institutionalize a set of corporate values. More than 1,000 executives participated in intensive two-day programs to define and disseminate "core values and guiding principles." Words like "diversity," "respect" and "integrity" emerged from these sessions. While the values program initially was something of a tough sell to senior managers, Time Warner officials stress that a key reason for implementing the program was to attract young people with strong ideals in a competitive job market. Time Warner has 67,000 employees. Time will tell whether Levin's initiative is successful.

Meanwhile, at Ford Motor Company, with more than 300,000 employees, former CEO Jacques Nasser tried to change the culture, to remake its basic values in a relatively short time. His objective was to transform an Old Economy auto manufacturer into a nimble, Net-savvy, consumer powerhouse. In a bid to shake up the culture, Nasser chose outsiders rather than Ford veterans for powerful management posts. He flattened Ford's bureaucracy, giving more autonomy to regional executives, and shook up senior managers by tying their bonuses to gains in customer service. Gone were the days of automatic promotions and seniority. Employees now have to earn their promotions based on merit. Not surprisingly, there was a backlash against the pace and intensity of many of these initiatives. According to experts, getting the rest of the company to buy into such changes is the hardest challenge. This is why so many efforts to change organizational cultures fail. Blending organizational cultures, such as when companies merge or are acquired, is an even greater challenge. Yet from a staffing perspective, the ability to articulate the culture, to live it every day, and to make it real for applicants and for current employees, is a key feature of the decisions of successful applicants to join, and for seasoned veterans to stay and to compete for promotions.

SUMMARY

In staffing an organization or an organizational unit, it is important to consider its developmental stage—embryonic, high growth, mature, or aging—in order to align staffing decisions with business strategy. It also is important to communicate an organization's culture, since research shows that applicants will consider this information to choose among jobs if it is available to them. In order to use selection techniques meaningfully, however, it is necessary to specify the kinds of competencies that are necessary for success.

Organizations commonly screen applicants through recommendations and reference checks, information on application forms, and employment interviews. In addition, some firms use written ability or integrity tests, work-sample tests, drug tests, polygraph examinations, or handwriting analysis. In each case, it is important to pay careful attention to the reliability and validity of the information obtained. **Reliability** refers to the consistency or stability of scores over time, across different samples of items, or across different raters or judges. **Validity** refers to the job-relatedness of a measure—that is, the strength of the relationship between scores from the measure and some indicator or rating of actual job performance.

In the context of managerial selection, numerous techniques are available, but the research literature indicates that the most effective ones have been mental ability tests, personality and interest inventories, peer assessments, personal history data, and situational tests. Projective techniques and leadership ability

IMPACT OF STAFFING DECISIONS ON PRODUCTIVITY, QUALITY OF WORK LIFE, AND THE BOTTOM LINE

Some companies avoid validating their screening and selection procedures because they think validation is too costly—and its benefits are too elusive. Alternatively, scare tactics ("Validate or else lose in court") have not encouraged widespread validation efforts. However, a large body of research has shown that the dollar gains in productivity associated with the use of valid selection and promotion procedures far outweigh the cost of those procedures.[124] Think about that. If people who score high (low) on selection procedures also do well (poorly) on their jobs, high scores suggest a close "fit" between individual capabilities and organizational needs. Low scores, on the other hand, suggest a poor fit. In both cases, productivity, quality of work life, and the bottom line stand to gain from the use of valid selection procedures. Thus a study of firms in the service and financial industries reported correlations ranging from .71 to .86 between the use of progressive staffing practices (e.g., validation studies, use of structured interviews, biodata, and mental ability tests) and measures of organizational performance over a 5-year period (annual profit, profit growth, sales growth, and overall performance).[125]

tests have been less effective. The use of situational tests, such as the leaderless group discussion, the in-basket, and the business game, lies at the heart of the assessment center method. Key advantages of the method are its high validity, fair evaluation of each candidate's ability, and flexibility of form and content. Other features include the use of multiple assessment techniques, assessor training, and pooled assessor judgments in rating each candidate's behavior.

Recent research indicates, at least for ability tests, that a test that accurately forecasts performance on a particular job in one situation will also forecast performance on the same job in other situations. Hence it may not be necessary to conduct a new validity study each time a predictor is used. Research has also demonstrated that the dollar benefits to an organization that uses valid selection procedures may be substantial. In choosing the right predictors for a given situation, an employer should pay careful attention to four factors: the nature of the job, the estimated validity of the predictor or predictors, the selection ratio, and the cost of the predictor or predictors. Doing so can pay handsome dividends to organizations and employees alike.

DISCUSSION QUESTIONS

7–1. Your boss asks you how she can improve the accuracy of preemployment interviews. What would you tell her?

7–2. Why are reliability and validity key considerations for all assessment methods?

7–3. How does business strategy affect management selection?

7–4. "At lower levels, managers do basically the same things regardless of functional specialty." Do you agree or disagree with this statement, and why?

7–5. As jobs become more team-oriented, assessment centers will be used more often for nonmanagement jobs. Do you agree or disagree?

IMPLICATIONS FOR MANAGEMENT PRACTICE

The research evidence is clear: Valid selection procedures can produce substantial economic gains for organizations. The implication for policymakers also is clear:

- Select the highest-caliber managers and lower-level employees, for they are the ones most likely to profit from development programs.
- Do not assume that a large investment in training can transform marginally competent performers into innovative, motivated top performers.
- A wide variety of screening and selection procedures is available. It is your responsi-

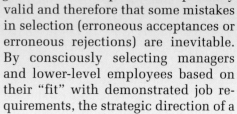

bility to ask "tough" questions of staff specialists about the reliability, job-relatedness, and validity of each one proposed for use.

- Recognize that no one predictor is perfectly valid and therefore that some mistakes in selection (erroneous acceptances or erroneous rejections) are inevitable. By consciously selecting managers and lower-level employees based on their "fit" with demonstrated job requirements, the strategic direction of a business, and organizational culture, you will minimize mistakes and make optimum choices.

KEY TERMS

organizational culture

reliability

validity

weighted application blanks

negligent hiring

tests

inventories

shrinkage

integrity tests

validity generalization

personality

neuroticism

extraversion

openness to experience

agreeableness

conscientiousness

projective measures

consideration

initiating structure

contrast effects

peer assessment

peer nomination

peer rating

peer ranking

work-sample tests

assessment center

selection ratio

APPLYING YOUR KNOWLEDGE

Exercise 7–1   *An In-Basket and an LGD for Selecting Managers*

There are several means by which an organization can attempt to determine the right choices in the managerial selection process. An approach that is growing rapidly in popularity is to attempt to assess what a managerial candidate can *do*, rather than what he or she *knows*.

Various kinds of work samples or situational tests can be used to assess what a candidate can do. In this exercise, you will have an opportunity to see how two of the most valid managerial work samples—in-baskets and leaderless group discussions (LGDs)—operate. An attractive feature of this combination of predictors is that while both are valid, the scores on each do not correlate highly with each other. This suggests that in-baskets and LGDs tap different, but important, subsets of the managerial performance domain.

PART A: IN-BASKET EXERCISE

An in-basket exercise is designed to assess a candidate's problem-solving, decision-making, and administrative skills. Further, because all responses are written ones, the exercise can also assess written communication ability.

An in-basket consists of a set of letters, notes, memos, and telephone messages to which a candidate must respond. To give you a sense of how an in-basket operates, a sample set of such stimuli is provided below. The set is similar to the one in the text, except that for ease of administration, all items are stated in memorandum form.

Procedure

You are to assume that you have just been appointed director of human resources at Ace Manufacturing Company and that your name is George Ryan. The president of the firm is Arnold ("Arnie") Ace. You were to replace the current HR director, John Armstrong, in 2 weeks, when he was scheduled to be transferred to Hong Kong. However, a family emergency in South Africa has required that John leave the country immediately and you must fill in for him as best as you can. You have taken an alternate flight on an important business trip to Washington, D.C., and have stopped over in Lompoc, where Ace's headquarters is located. It is Saturday morning and no one else is available in the office. You must resume your flight to Washington within an hour.

Read through the items in your in-basket, decide what to do with each item, and record your decision on a separate sheet of paper. If any decisions require writing a letter or memo, you are to draft the response in the space provided. You are not to role-play how you think someone else might behave in this situation. Rather, you are to behave exactly as you yourself would in each situation.

Item 1

MEMO TO: John Armstrong, HR Director
FROM: Jackie Williams, Downtown Business Club
SUBJECT: Speaking engagement next week

Thanks again for your willingness to speak to our Business Club next week. As you know, this group represents a good cross section of the Lompoc business community as well as a number of Ace's best customers. We are all looking forward to what you have to say regarding the relationship between strategic planning and human resource information systems.

Item 2

MEMO TO: Mr. Ryan
FROM: Judy [secretary to the director of human resources]
SUBJECT: Tom Tipster's employment status

Just after Mr. Armstrong left yesterday, we received a call from the owner of Stockman's Bar and Grill saying that Tom Tipster had gotten drunk in the middle of the day again and busted up the bar. He said he'd hold off pressing charges until he talked to you (I explained that you were Mr. Armstrong's replacement). This is the third time that Mr. Tipster has gotten in trouble over his drinking problem. I think Mr. Armstrong was planning to fire him if he had another problem like this. You'd think that someone with 17 years of service at Ace would have more sense than to get into trouble like this—especially with 7 kids at home to feed!

Item 3

MEMO TO: John
FROM: Arnie
SUBJECT: EEO Report

Where is that EEO report you promised me? There's no way I want to face the investigators from Denver Wednesday without it!

Item 4

MEMO TO: John Armstrong
FROM: Lisa Buller, Administrator of Training Programs
SUBJECT: Time off

I need to take next Thursday off to fly to San Francisco on important personal business. Will this be OK?

Item 5

MEMO TO: Mr. John Armstrong
FROM: Arch Turkey
SUBJECT: Thefts

As you know, my store is located between your downtown office extension and that of Deuce's. During the past several months we have had several cases of shoplifting from our store, and the police haven't been able to do anything about it. Further, several custodians from your facility have been observed acting funny (with dazed looks on their faces) and wandering around outside my store looking in. I think that your people may be responsible for the recent shoplifting losses I have suffered. I would appreciate hearing from you within the next week. Otherwise, I will be forced to take appropriate measures to ensure protection of my store.

Item 6

MEMO TO: John
FROM: Alice Calmers, Director of Manufacturing
SUBJECT: Thursday's training program

I finally got everything rearranged for that training program on Thursday. You can't imagine how difficult it is to try to rearrange the schedules of 15 very busy supervisors to attend anything at the same time. I certainly hope that Lisa's presentation is going to be worth all this juggling of schedules!

Item 7

MEMO TO: John Armstrong
FROM: Ralph Herzberg, Manager of Customer Relations
SUBJECT: New training program

We have a serious problem in the customer relations department. It is quite common for a large number of calls to come in all at once. When this happens, the customer relations contact employee is supposed to take the customer's phone number and get back to him or her within an hour. We've found in the past that this is a reasonable target since, after a big rush of calls, things usually settle down for a while. But when we check up on the contact employees, we find that they get back to the customer within an hour only about one-third of the time. Sometimes they don't get back to the customer until the next day! I sent a memo to all contact employees about a month ago reminding them of the importance of prompt responses on their parts, but it did very little good. We need a training program from your department to improve this critical performance area. Can we get together early next week?

Responses

On a separate sheet of paper, provide your responses to the in-basket items.

Item 1: Speaking engagement next week.
Item 2: Tom Tipster's employment status.
Item 3: EEO Report.
Item 4: Time off.
Item 5: Thefts.
Item 6: Thursday's training program.
Item 7: New training program.

PART B: LEADERLESS GROUP DISCUSSION (LGD)

Unlike the in-basket exercise, a leaderless group discussion exercise involves groups of managerial candidates working together on a job-related problem. The problem is usually designed to be as realistic as possible, and it is often tackled in groups of five or six candidates. No one in the group is appointed leader, nor is anyone told where to sit or how to act. Candidates are instructed simply to solve the problem to the best of their ability in the time allotted.

The LGD is used to assess such managerial traits and skills as aggressiveness, interpersonal skills, persuasive ability, oral communication skills, self-confidence, energy level, and resistance to stress.

Procedure

The problem that follows is typical of those in an LGD. However, to conserve time, we have simplified it somewhat. Read the statement of the problem and then, working in groups of five or six students, arrive at a consensus regarding the solution to the problem. When finished, be prepared to discuss the kinds of management skills exhibited by students in your group.

BONUS ALLOCATION PROBLEM

Your organization has recently instituted an incentive bonus in an attempt to stimulate and reward key employee behaviors. The company has budgeted $60,000 for this purpose, to be spent every 6 months. You have been appointed to a committee charged with the responsibility of determining the allocation of bonus funds to deserving employees over the previous 6-month period. A total of 25 employees were recommended by their supervisors. Decisions have already been made on 20 of them, and $48,000 of the original sum has been expended. Your task today is to decide on the size of the bonuses (if any) to be received by the remaining five employees. Summaries of the qualifications for the five employees are presented below:

Virginia Dewey.
Head custodian. Fifteen years with the firm. High school diploma. Twenty-two years of relevant job experience. Manages a flawless custodial staff with low turnover and few union grievances. Present salary below average in most recent salary survey. Supports a family of six. Overlooked for salary increase last year.

Alfred Newman.
Accounting clerk. 3 years with the firm. 2-year college degree. 3 years of relevant work experience. Performs well under pressure of deadlines. Present salary is average in recent salary survey. Is known to be looking for other jobs.

Augusta Nie.
Manager of corporate data analysis. 7 years with the firm. Master's degree in computer science. 14 years of relevant work experience. Has developed the data analysis department into one of the most efficient in the company. Present salary is above average in recent salary survey. Has leadership potential and may be offered jobs from other firms. Difficult to replace good data processing personnel.

Barry Barngrover.
Machinist. Eleven years with the firm. High school diploma. Eleven years of relevant job experience. Is the top performer in the milling machine department, and exhibits a positive company attitude. Present salary is average in a recent salary survey. Is single and seems to have all the money he needs to support his chosen lifestyle.

Harvey Slack.
Personnel administrator. 1 year with the firm. College degree from prestigious Ivy League school. 3 years of relevant work experience. Very knowledgeable in subject matter, but has trouble getting along with older coworkers. Present salary is above average in a recent salary survey. His mentor is the firm's vice president for human resources, who is said to be grooming Harvey for the VP position. Has received several offers from other firms recently.

TECHNICAL APPENDIX

The Estimation of Reliability

A quantitative estimate of the reliability of each measure used as a basis for employment decisions is important for two reasons: (1) if any measure is challenged legally, reliability estimates are important in establishing a defense, and (2) a measurement procedure cannot be any more valid (accurate) than it is reliable (consistent and stable). To estimate reliability, compute a coefficient of correlation (a measure of the degree of relationship between two variables) between two sets of scores obtained independently. As an example, consider the sets of scores shown in Table 7–3.

Table 7–3 shows two sets of scores obtained from two forms of the same test. The resulting correlation coefficient is called a parallel forms reliability estimate. By the way, the correlation coefficient for the two sets of scores shown in Table 7–3 is .93, a very strong relationship. (The word "test" is used in the broad sense here to include any physical or psychological measurement instrument, technique, or procedure.) However, the scores in Table 7–3 could just as easily have been obtained from two administrations of the same test at two different times (test-retest reliability) or from independent ratings of the same test by two different scorers (inter-rater reliability).

Finally, in situations where it is not practical to use any of the preceding procedures and where a test can be administered only once, use a procedure known as split-half reliability. With this procedure, split a test statistically into

Table 7–3

TWO SETS OF HYPOTHETICAL SCORES FOR THE SAME INDIVIDUALS ON FORM A AND FORM B OF A MATHEMATICAL APTITUDE TEST

Person no.	Form A	Form B
1	75	82
2	85	84
3	72	77
4	96	90
5	65	68
6	81	82
7	93	95
8	59	52
9	67	60
10	87	89

The coefficient of correlation between these sets of scores is .93. It is computed from the following formula:

$$r = \sum Z_x Z_y / N$$

where r = the correlation coefficient

$\sum$ = sum of

Z_x = the standard score on form A, where $Z = x$, each person's raw score on form A, minus $\bar{x}$, the mean score on form A, divided by the standard deviation of form A scores

Z_y = the standard score on form B

N = the number of persons in the sample (10 in this case)

two halves (e.g., odd items and even items) after it has been given, thereby generating two scores for each individual. In effect, therefore, one creates two sets of scores (so-called parallel forms) from the same test for each individual. Then correlate scores on the two "half-tests." However, since reliability increases as we sample larger and larger portions of a particular area of knowledge, skill, or ability, and since we have cut the length of the original test in half, the correlation between the two half tests underestimates the true reliability of the total test. Fortunately, formulas are available to correct such underestimates.

Validation Strategies

Although a number of procedures are available for evaluating evidence of validity, three of the best-known strategies are construct-oriented, content-oriented, and criterion-related. The three differ in terms of the conclusions and inferences that may be drawn, but they are interrelated logically and also in terms of the operations used to measure them.

Evaluation of *construct-oriented evidence of validity* begins by formulating hypotheses about the characteristics of those with high scores on a particular measurement procedure, in contrast to those with low scores. For example, we might hypothesize that sales managers will score significantly higher on the managerial interests scale of the California Psychological Inventory (CPI) than will pharmacy students (in fact, they do), and that they will also be more decisive and apt to take risks as well. The hypotheses form a tentative theory about the nature of the psychological construct, or trait, that the CPI is believed to be measuring. These hypotheses may then be used to predict how people at different score levels on the CPI will behave on other tests or in other situations during their careers. Construct validation is not accomplished in a single study. It requires that evidence be accumulated from different sources to determine the meaning of the test scores in terms of how people actually behave. It is a logical as well as an empirical process.

Content-oriented evidence of validity is also a judgmental, rational process. It requires an answer to the following question: *Is the content of the measurement procedure a fair, representative sample of the content of the job it is supposed to represent?* Such judgments can be made rather easily by job incumbents, supervisors, or other job experts when job knowledge or work-sample tests are used (e.g., typing tests and tests for electricians, plumbers, and computer programmers). However, content-oriented evidence becomes less appropriate as the behaviors in question become less observable and more abstract (e.g., the ability to draw conclusions from a written sample of material). In addition, since such judgments are not expressed in quantitative terms, it is difficult to justify ranking applicants in terms of predicted job performance, and it is difficult to estimate directly the dollar benefits to the firm from using such a procedure. To overcome these problems, we need a criterion-related validity strategy.

The term *criterion-related evidence of validity* calls attention to the fact that the chief concern is with the relationship between predictor (the selection procedure or procedures used) and criterion (job performance) scores, not with predictor scores per se. Indeed, the content of the predictor measure is relatively unimportant, for it serves only as a vehicle to predict actual job performance.

There are two strategies of criterion-related validation: *concurrent* and *predictive*. A *concurrent strategy* is used to measure job incumbents. Job performance (criterion) measures for this group are already available; so immediately after administering a selection measure to this group, it is possible to compute a correlation coefficient between predictor scores and criterion scores (over all individuals in the group). A procedure identical to that shown in Table 7–3 is used. If the selection measure is valid, those employees with the highest (or lowest) job performance scores should also score highest (or lowest) on the selection measure. In short, if the selection measure is valid, there should exist a systematic relationship between scores on that measure and job performance. The higher the test score, the better the job performance (and vice versa).

When a *predictive strategy* is used, the procedure is identical, except that we measure job candidates. We use the same methods that currently are used to select employees, and simply add the new selection procedure to the overall process. However, we select candidates without using the results of the new procedure. At a later date (e.g., 6 months to a year), when it becomes possible to develop a meaningful measure of job performance for each new hire, scores on the new selection procedure are correlated with job performance scores. We then assess the strength of the predictor-criterion relationship in terms of the size of the correlation coefficient.

Estimating the Economic Benefits of Selection Programs

If we assume that n workers are hired during a given year and that the average job tenure of those workers is t years, the dollar increase in productivity can be determined from Equation 7–1, below. Admittedly, this is a "cookbook recipe," but the formula was derived more than 50 years ago and is well established in applied psychology[126]:

$$\Delta U = ntr_{xy}SD_y\bar{Z}_x \qquad (7\text{–}1)$$

where ΔU = increase in productivity in dollars
  n = number of persons hired
  t = average job tenure in years of those hired
  r_{xy} = the validity coefficient representing the correlation between the predictor and job performance in the applicant population
  SD_y = the standard deviation of job performance in dollars (roughly 40 percent of annual wage)[127]
  $\bar{Z}_x$ = the average predictor score of those selected in the applicant population, expressed in terms of standard scores

When Equation 7–1 was used to estimate the dollar gains in productivity associated with use of the Programmer Aptitude Test (PAT) to select computer programmers for federal government jobs, given that an average of 618 programmers per year are selected, each with an average job tenure of 9.69 years, the payoff per selectee was $64,725 over his or her tenure on the job. This represents a per-year productivity gain of $6679 for each new programmer.[128] Clearly, the dollar gains in increased productivity associated with the use of valid selection procedures (the estimated true validity of the PAT is .76) are not trivial. Indeed, in a globally competitive environment, businesses need to take advantage of every possible strategy for improving productivity. The widespread use of valid selection and promotion procedures should be a priority consideration in this effort.

Valid selection and promotion procedures also benefit applicants in several ways. One is that a more accurate matching of applicant knowledge, skills, ability, and other characteristics to job requirements helps enhance the likelihood of successful performance. This, in turn, helps workers feel better about their jobs and adjust to changes in them, as they are doing the kinds of things they do best. Moreover, since we know that there is a positive spillover effect between job satisfaction and life satisfaction, the accurate matching of people and jobs will also foster an improved quality of life, not just an improved quality of work life, for all concerned.

REFERENCES

1. Snow, C. C., & Snell, S. A. (1993). Staffing as strategy. In N. Schmitt & W. C. Borman (eds.), *Personnel selection in organizations.* San Francisco: Jossey-Bass, pp. 448–478. See also Smith, E. C. (1982). Strategic business planning and human resources: Part I. *Personnel Journal, 61,* 606–610.
2. Van Vianen, A. E. M. (2000). Person-organization fit: The match between newcomers' and recruiters' preferences for organizational cultures. *Personnel Psychology, 53,* 113–149. See also Schneider, B., Smith, D. B., Taylor, S., & Fleenor, J. (1998). Personality and organizations: A test of the homogeneity of personality hypothesis. *Journal of Applied Psychology, 83,* 462–470. See also Schneider, B. (1987). The people make the place. *Personnel Psychology, 40,* 437–453.
3. Tetenbaum, T. (1999, Autumn). Beating the odds of merger & acquisition failure. *Organizational Dynamics,* 22–36.
4. Martin, J. (2001). *Organizational culture.* Thousand Oaks, CA: Sage. See also Schein, E. H. (1985). *Organizational culture and leadership.* San Francisco: Jossey-Bass.
5. Van Vianen, op. cit. See also Power, D. J., & Aldag, R. J. (1985). Soelberg's job search and choice model: A clarification, review, and critique. *Academy of Management Review, 10,* 48–58.
6. Kristof-Brown, A. L. (2000). Perceived applicant fit: Distinguishing between recruiters' perceptions of person-job and person-organization fit. *Personnel Psychology, 53,* 643–671.
7. Snow & Snell, op. cit.
8. Sheridan, J. E. (1992). Organizational culture and employee retention. *Academy of Management Journal, 35,* 1036–1056.
9. Hunter, J. E., Schmidt, F. L., & Judiesch, M. K. (1990). Individual differences in output variability as a function of job complexity. *Journal of Applied Psychology, 75,* 28–42.
10. Messick, S. (1995). Validity of psychological assessment. *American Psychologist, 50,* 741–749.
11. Schmitt, N., & Landy, F. J. (1993). The concept of validity. In N. Schmitt & W. C. Borman (eds.), *Personnel selection in organizations.* San Francisco: Jossey-Bass, pp. 275–309.
12. *Principles for the validation and use of personnel selection procedures* (3d ed., 1987). College Park, MD: Society of Industrial-Organizational Psychology. Author.
13. American Educational Research Association, American Psychological Association, National Council on Measurement in Education (1999). *Standards for educational and psychological testing.* Washington, DC: American Educational Research Association.

14. Uniform guidelines on employee selection procedures (1978). *Federal Register*, *43*, 38290–38315.

15. Lowell, R. S., & DeLoach, J. A. (1982). Equal employment opportunity: Are you overlooking the application form? *Personnel*, *59*(4), 49–55. See also Miller, E. C. (1980). An EEO examination of employment applications. *Personnel Administrator*, *25*(3), 63–69, 81.

16. Bahnsen, E. (1996, Nov.). Questions to ask, and not ask, job applicants. *HR News*, pp. 10, 11. See also Boas, K. M. (1996, Summer). Ask an expert. *Business Briefs*, *15*, pp. 1, 2.

17. Klimoski, R. J. (1993). Predictor constructs and their measurement. In N. Schmitt & W. C. Borman (eds.), *Personnel selection in organizations.* San Francisco: Jossey-Bass, pp. 99–134. See also Hunter, J. E., & Hunter, R. F. (1984). Validity and utility of alternative predictors of job performance. *Psychological Bulletin*, *96*, 72–98.

18. Lawrence, D. G., Salsburg, B. L., Dawson, J. G., & Fasman, Z. D. (1982). Design and use of weighted application blanks. *Personnel Administrator*, *27*(3), 47–53, 101.

19. Cappelli, P. (2001, March). Making the most of on-line recruiting. *Harvard Business Review*, 139–146.

20. Labor letter (1987, June 30). *The Wall Street Journal*, p. 1.

21. McCormick, E. J., & Ilgen, D. R. (1985). *Industrial psychology* (8th ed.). Englewood Cliffs, NJ: Prentice-Hall.

22. Knouse, S. B. (1987). An attribution theory approach to the letter of recommendation. *International Journal of Management*, *4*(1), 5–13.

23. LoPresto, R. L., Mitcham, D. E., & Ripley, D. E. (1993). *Reference checking handbook* (rev. ed.). Alexandria, VA: Society for Human Resource Management. See also Munchus, G. (1992, June). Check references for safer selection. *HRMagazine*, 75–77.

24. Click, J. (1995, July). SHRM survey highlights dilemmas of references checks. *HR News*, p. 13.

25. Job references: Handle with care (1987, Mar. 9). *BusinessWeek*, p. 124.

26. Rigdon, J. E. (1992, June 17). Deceptive résumés can be door openers but can become an employee's undoing. *The Wall Street Journal*, pp. B1; B7. See also LoPresto et al., op. cit.

27. Reliable references are getting difficult to find (1993, Feb. 23). *The Wall Street Journal*, p. A1.

28. Weiner, T. (1993, May 16). Firms tighten reference policies. *The Denver Post*, p. 5G. See also Reference preference: Employers button lips (1990, Jan. 4). *The Wall Street Journal*, p. B1. See also Revenge of the fired (1987, Feb. 16). *Newsweek*, pp. 46, 47.

29. Ryan, A. M., & Lasek, M. (1991). Negligent hiring and defamation: Areas of liability related to pre-employment inquiries. *Personnel Psychology*, *44*, 293–319.

30. Jackson, S., & Loftin, A. (2000, Jan.). Proactive practices avoid negligent hiring claims. *HR News*, 12.

31. Arnold, D. W. (1996, Feb.). Providing references. *HR News*, 16.

32. Bahls, J. E. (1998, Feb.). Drugs in the workplace. *HRMagazine*, 81–87.

33. Maltby, L. (1998, March). Another view: Drug testing may not be worth the cost. *HRMagazine*, pp. 112, 114. See also Morgan, J. P. (1989, Aug. 20). Employee drug tests are unreliable and intrusive. *Hospitals*, p. 42. See also Bogdanich, W. (1987, Feb. 2). False negative: Medical labs, trusted as largely error-free, are far from infallible. *The Wall Street Journal*, pp. 1, 14.

34. Normand, J., Salyards, S., and Mahoney, J. (1990). An evaluation of pre-employment drug testing. *Journal of Applied Psychology*, *75*, 629–639.

35. Harris, M. M., and Heft, L. L. (1993). Preemployment urinalysis drug testing: A critical review of psychometric and legal issues and effects on applicants. *Human Resource Management Review*, *3*, 271–291.

36. Bahls, J. E. (1998, March). Dealing with drugs: Keep it legal. *HRMagazine*, pp. 104–116. See also Stone, D. L., & Kotch, D. A. (1989). Individuals' attitudes toward

organizational drug testing policies and practices. *Journal of Applied Psychology*, *74*, 518–521.

37. Levy, L. (1979). Handwriting and hiring. *Dun's Review, 113*, 72–79.
38. Gorman, C. (1989, Jan. 23). Honestly, can we trust you? *Time*, p. 44. See also McCarthy, M. J. (1988, Aug. 25). Handwriting analysis as personnel tool. *The Wall Street Journal*, p. B1.
39. Rafaeli, A., & Klimoski, R. J. (1983). Predicting sales success through handwriting analysis: An evaluation of the effects of training and handwriting sample content. *Journal of Applied Psychology, 68*, 212–217.
40. Schmidt, F. L., & Hunter, J. E. (1998). The validity and utility of selection methods in personnel psychology: Practical and theoretical implications of 85 years of research findings. *Psychological Bulletin, 124*, 262–274. See also Neter, E., & Ben-Shakhar, G. (1989). The predictive validity of graphological inferences: A meta-analytic approach. *Personality and Individual Differences, 10*, 737–745. See also Ben-Shakhar, G., Bar-Hillel, M., Bilu, Y., Ben-Abba, E., & Flug, A. (1986). Can graphology predict occupational success? Two empirical studies and some methodological ruminations. *Journal of Applied Psychology, 71*, 645–653.
41. Kleinmutz, B. (1985, July–Aug.). Lie detectors fail the truth test. *Harvard Business Review, 63*, 36–42. See also Patrick, C. J., & Iacono, W. G. (1989). Psychopathy, threat, and polygraph test accuracy. *Journal of Applied Psychology, 74*, 347–355. See also Saxe, L., Dougherty, D., & Cross, T. (1985). The validity of polygraph testing. *American Psychologist, 40*, 355–356.
42. Shaffer, D. J., & Schmidt, R. A. (1999, Sept.–Oct.). Personality testing in employment. *Legal Report*, pp. 1–5.
43. Gorman, op. cit.
44. Susser, P. A. (1986). Update on polygraphs and employment. *Personnel Administrator, 31*(2), pp. 28, 32.
45. Conner, C. (1992, Dec. 5). Shoplifting, theft losses decline but U.S. retailers still vigilant. *The Denver Post*, p. 4.
46. Shaffer & Schmidt, op. cit.
47. Crime and punishment (2001, June). *Money*, p. 24.
48. Yandrick, R. M. (1995, Nov.). Employers turn to psychological tests to predict applicants' work behavior. *HR News, 2*, 13.
49. Camara, W. J., & Schneider, D. L. (1994). Integrity tests: Facts and unresolved issues. *American Psychologist, 49*(2), 112–119. See also Sackett, P. R., Burris, L. R., & Callahan, C. (1989). Integrity testing for personnel selection: An update. *Personnel Psychology, 42*, 491–529.
50. Schmidt & Hunter, op. cit. See also Ones, D. S., Viswesvaran, C., & Schmidt, F. L. (1993). Comprehensive meta-analysis of integrity test validities: Findings and implications for personnel selection and theories of job performance. *Journal of Applied Psychology* (monograph), *78*, 679–703.
51. Schmidt, F. L, Viswesvaran, V., & Ones, D. S. (1997). Validity of integrity tests for predicting drug and alcohol abuse: A meta-analysis. In Bukoski, W. J. (ed.), *Meta-analysis of drug abuse prevention programs*. NIDA Research Monograph 170. Washington, DC: U.S. Department of Health and Human Services, pp. 69–95.
52. Schmidt & Hunter, op. cit.
53. Lilienfeld, S. O., Alliger, G., & Mitchell, K. (1995). Why integrity testing remains controversial. *American Psychologist, 50*, 457–458.
54. Cunningham, M. R., Wong, D. T., & Barbee, A. P. (1994). Self-presentation dynamics on overt integrity tests: Experimental studies of the Reid Report. *Journal of Applied Psychology, 79*, 643–658.
55. See, for example, *www.careerharmony.com*.
56. Richman-Hirsch, W. L., Olson-Buchanan, J. B., & Drasgow, F. (2000). Examining the impact of administration medium on examinee perceptions and attitudes. *Journal of Applied Psychology, 85*, 880–887.

57. Donovan, M. A., Drasgow, F., & Probst, T. M. (2000). Does computerizing paper-and-pencil job attitude scales make a difference? New IRT analyses offer insight. *Journal of Applied Psychology, 85*, 305–313. See also Burke, M. J. (1993). Computerized psychological testing: Impacts on measuring predictor constructs and future job behavior. In N. Schmitt & W. C. Borman (eds.), *Personnel selection in organizations*. San Francisco: Jossey-Bass, pp. 203–239.

58. Goldstein, H. W., Yusko, K. P., Braverman, E. P., Smith, D. B., & Chung, B. (1998). The role of cognitive ability in the subgroup differences and incremental validity of assessment center exercises. *Personnel Psychology, 51*, 357–374. See also Ghiselli, E. E. (1973). The validity of aptitude tests in personnel selection. *Personnel Psychology, 26*, 461–467. See also Klimoski, R., & Brickner, M. (1987). Why do assessment centers work? The puzzle of assessment center validity. *Personnel Psychology, 40*, 243–260. See also Lord, R. G., DeVader, C. L., & Alliger, G. M. (1986). A meta-analysis of the relationship between personality traits and leadership perceptions: An application of validity generalization procedures. *Journal of Applied Psychology, 71*, 402–410.

59. Grimsley, G., & Jarrett, H. F. (1975). The relation of past managerial achievement to test measures obtained in the employment situation: Methodology and results—II. *Personnel Psychology, 28*, 215–231. See also Korman, A. K. (1968). The prediction of managerial performance: A review. *Personnel Psychology, 21*, 295–322. See also Kraut, A. I. (1969). Intellectual ability and promotional success among high-level managers. *Personnel Psychology, 22*, 281–290.

60. Murphy, K. R. (2000). Impact of assessments of validity generalization and situational specificity on the science and practice of personnel selection. *International Journal of Selection and Assessment, 8*(4), 194–206. See also Schmidt, F. L. (1992). What do data really mean? *American Psychologist, 47*, 1173–1181. See also Schmidt, F. L., Pearlman, K., Hunter, J. E., & Hirsch, H. R. (1985). Forty questions about validity generalization and meta-analysis. *Personnel Psychology, 38*, 697–798.

61. Smith, D. B., Hanges, P. J., & Dickson, M. W. (2001). Personnel selection and the five-factor model: Reexamining the effects of applicant's frame of reference. *Journal of Applied Psychology, 86*, 304–315. See also Hough, L. M., & Schneider, R. J. (1996). Personality traits, taxonomies, and applications in organizations. In K. R. Murphy (ed.), *Individual differences and behavior in organizations*. San Francisco: Jossey-Bass, pp. 31–88. See also Salgado, J. F. (1997). The five-factor model of personality and job performance in the European Community. *Journal of Applied Psychology, 82*, 30–43.

62. Hogan, J., & Holland, B. (2000, April). Updating personality measures as predictors of job performance: Theory, meta-analysis, and bandwidth. Paper presented at the fifteenth annual meeting of the Society for Industrial and Organizational Psychology, New Orleans, LA. See also McManus, M. A., & Kelly, M. L. (1999). Personality measures and biodata: Evidence regarding their incremental predictive value in the life insurance industry. *Personnel Psychology, 52*, 137–148. See also Mount, M. K., & Barrick, M. R. (1995). The Big-Five personality dimensions: Implications for research and practice in human resource management. *Research in Personnel and Human Resource Management, 13*, 153–200. See also Tett, R. P., Jackson, D. N., & Rothstein, M. (1991). Personality measures as predictors of job performance: A meta-analytic review. *Personnel Psychology, 44*, 703–742.

63. Ones, D. S. (1993). The construct validity of integrity tests. Unpublished doctoral dissertation, University of Iowa, Iowa City, IA.

64. McFarland, L. A., & Ryan, A. M. (2000). Variance in faking across noncognitive measures. *Journal of Applied Psychology, 85*, 812–821. See also Rosse, J. G., Stecher, M. D., Miller, J. L., & Levin, R. A. (1998). The impact of response distortion on preemployment personality testing and hiring decisions. *Journal of Applied Psychology, 83*, 634–644. See also Christiansen, N. D., Goffin, R. D., Johnston,

N. G., & Rothstein, M. G. (1994). Correcting the 16PF for faking: Effects on criterion-related validity and individual hiring decisions. *Personnel Psychology, 47,* 847–860.

65. Hogan, J., & Hogan, R. (1986). *Hogan Personnel Selection Series manual.* Minneapolis, MN: National Computer Systems.

66. Rosse et al., op cit.

67. Hough, L. M. (1998). Effects of intentional distortion in personality measurement and evaluation of suggested palliatives. *Human Performance, 11,* 209–244. See also Hough, L. M. (1997). The millennium for personality psychology: New horizons or good old daze. *Applied Psychology: An International Review, 47,* 233–261. See also Hough, L. M., Eaton, N. K., Dunnette, M. D., Kamp, J. D., & McCloy, R. A. (1990). Criterion-related validities of personality constructs and the effect of response distortion on those validities. *Journal of Applied Psychology Monograph, 71,* 581–595.

68. Rosse et al., op. cit.

69. Zickar, M. J., & Robie, C. (1999). Modeling faking good on personality items: An item-level analysis. *Journal of Applied Psychology, 84,* 551–563. See also Alliger, G. M., Lilienfeld, S. O., & Mitchell, K. E. (1996). The susceptibility of overt and covert integrity tests to coaching and faking. *Psychological Science, 11,* 32–39.

70. Ellingson, J. E., Sackett, P. R., & Hough, L. M. (1999). Social desirability corrections in personality measurement: Issues of applicant comparison and construct validity. *Journal of Applied Psychology, 84,* 155–166. See also Rosse et al., op. cit.

71. Hough, 1998, op. cit.

72. Kelly, G. A. (1958). The theory and technique of assessment. *Annual Review of Psychology, 9,* 323–352.

73. Kinslinger, H. J. (1966). Application of projective techniques in personnel psychology since 1940. *Psychological Bulletin, 66,* 134–150.

74. Hogan, R. T. (1991). Personality and personality measurement. In M. D. Dunnette & L. M. Hough (eds.), *Handbook of industrial and organizational psychology* (vol. 2). Palo Alto, CA: Consulting Psychologists Press, pp. 873–919.

75. Kerr, S., & Schriesheim, C. (1974). Consideration, initiating structure, and organizational criteria—an update of Korman's 1966 review. *Personnel Psychology, 27,* 555–568. See also Schriesheim, C., House, R. A., & Kerr, S. (1976). Leader initiating structure: A reconciliation of discrepant research results and some empirical tests. *Organizational Behavior and Human Performance, 15,* 297–321.

76. Carlson, K. D., Scullen, S. E., Schmidt, F. L., Rothstein, H., & Erwin, F. (1999). Generalizable biographical data validity can be achieved without multi-organizational development and keying. *Personnel Psychology, 52,* 731–755. See also Kluger, A. N., Reilly, R. R., & Russell, C. J. (1991). Faking biodata tests: Are option-keyed instruments more resistant? *Journal of Applied Psychology, 76,* 889–896.

77. Becker, T. E., & Colquitt, A. L. (1992). Potential versus actual faking of a biodata form: An analysis along several dimensions of item type. *Personnel Psychology, 45,* 389–406.

78. Mount, M. K., Witt, L. A., & Barrick, M. R. (2000). Incremental validity of empirically keyed biodata scales over GMA and the five-factor personality constructs. *Personnel Psychology, 53,* 299–323.

79. Hough, L. M. (1984). Development and evaluation of the "accomplishment record" method of selecting and promoting professionals. *Journal of Applied Psychology, 69,* 135–146.

80. Hough, L. M. (1985, Nov.). *The accomplishment record method of selecting, promoting, and appraising professionals.* Paper presented at the Conference on Selection Guidelines, Testing, and the EEOC: An Update. Berkeley: University of California, Institute for Industrial Relations.

81. Burnett, J. R., & Motowidlo, S. J. (1998). Relations between different sources of information in the structured selection interview. *Personnel Psychology, 51,* 963–983.

See also Hakel, M. D. (1989). Merit-based selection: Measuring the person for the job. In W. F. Cascio (ed.), *Human resource planning, employment, and placement.* Washington, DC: Bureau of National Affairs, pp. 2-135–2-158.

82. Moscoso, S. (2000). Selection interviews: A review of validity evidence, adverse impact, and applicant reactions. *International Journal of Selection and Assessment, 8* (4), 237–247. See also Schmidt & Hunter, op. cit. See also Conway, J. M., Jako, R. A., & Goodman, D. F. (1995). A meta-analysis of interrater and internal consistency reliability of selection interviews. *Journal of Applied Psychology, 80,* 565–579. See also McDaniel, M. A., Whetzel, D. L., Schmidt, F. L., & Maurer, S. (1994). The validity of employment interviews: A comprehensive review and meta-analysis. *Journal of Applied Psychology, 79,* 599–616. See also Bulkeley, W. (1994, Aug. 22). Replaced by technology: Job interviews. *The Wall Street Journal,* pp. B1, B5.

83. Campion, M. A., Palmer, D. K., & Campion, J. E. (1997). A review of structure in the selection interview. *Personnel Psychology, 50,* 655–702.

84. Burnett, J. R., Fan, C., Motowidlo, S., J., & DeGroot, T. (1998). Interview notes and validity. *Personnel Psychology, 51,* 375–396.

85. Ganzach, Y., Kluger., A. N., & Klayman, N. (2000). Making decisions from an interview: Expert measurement and mechanical combination. *Personnel Psychology, 53,* 1–20.

86. Dipboye, R. L. & Gaugler, B. B. (1993). Cognitive and behavioral processes in the selection interview. In N. Schmitt & W. C. Borman (eds.), *Personnel selection in organizations* (pp. 135–170). San Francisco: Jossey-Bass. See also Phillips, A. P., & Dipboye, R. L. (1989). Correlational tests of prediction from a process model of the interview. *Journal of Applied Psychology, 74,* 41–52.

87. Campion et al., op. cit.

88. Shippmann, J. S., Ash, R. A., Battista, M., Carr, L., Eyde, L. D., Hesketh, B., Kehoe, J., Pearlman, K., Prien, E. P., & Sanchez, J. I. (2000). The practice of competency modeling. *Personnel Psychology, 53,* 703–740.

89. Dipboye & Gaugler, op. cit. See also Weekley, J. A., & Gier, J. A. (1987). Reliability and validity of the situational interview for a sales position. *Journal of Applied Psychology, 72,* 484–487.

90. Motowidlo, S. J., Carter, G. W., Dunnette, M. D., Tippins, N., Werner, S., Burnett, J. R., & Vaughan, M. J. (1992). Studies of the structured behavioral interview. *Journal of Applied Psychology, 77,* 571–587.

91. Cortina, J. M., Goldstein, N. B., Payne, S. C., Davison, H. K., & Gilliland, S. (2000). The incremental validity of interview scores over and above cognitive ability and conscientiousness scores. *Personnel Psychology, 53,* 325–351.

92. Huffcutt, A. I., & Roth, P. L. (1998). Racial group differences in employment interview evaluations. *Journal of Applied Psychology, 83,* 179–189.

93. Schmidt & Hunter, op. cit. See also Schmitt, N., Gooding, R. Z., Noe, R. A., & Kirsch, M. (1984). Meta-analysis of validity studies published between 1964 and 1982 and the investigation of study characteristics. *Personnel Psychology, 37,* 407–422.

94. Shore, T. H., Shore, L. M., & Thornton, G. C., III. (1992). Construct validity of self- and peer evaluations of performance dimensions in an assessment center. *Journal of Applied Psychology, 77,* 42–54.

95. Asher, J. J., & Sciarrino, J. A. (1974). Realistic work sample tests: A review. *Personnel Psychology, 27,* 519–533.

96. Schmitt, N., & Mills, A. E. (2001). Traditional tests and job simulations: Minority and majority performance and test validities. *Journal of Applied Psychology, 86,* 451–458.

97. Callinan, M., & Robertson, I. T. (2000). Work sample testing. *International Journal of Selection and Assessment, 8*(4), 248–260.

98. Cascio, W. F., & Phillips, N. (1979). Performance testing: A rose among thorns? *Personnel Psychology, 32,* 751–766.

99. Wollowick, H. B., & McNamara, W. J. (1969). Relationship of the components of an assessment center to management success. *Journal of Applied Psychology, 53,* 348–352.

100. Bass, B. M. (1954). The leaderless group discussion. *Psychological Bulletin, 51,* 465–492. See also Tziner, A., & Dolan, S. (1982). Validity of an assessment center for identifying future female officers in the military. *Journal of Applied Psychology, 67,* 728–736.

101. Kurecka, P. M., Austin, J. M., Jr., Johnson, W., & Mendoza, J. L. (1982). Full and errant coaching effects on assigned role leaderless group discussion performance. *Personnel Psychology, 35,* 805–812. See also Petty, M. M. (1974). A multivariate analysis of the effects of experience and training upon performance in a leaderless group discussion. *Personnel Psychology, 27,* 271–282.

102. Fredericksen, N. (1962). Factors in in-basket performance. *Psychological Monographs, 76*(22, whole no. 541), 1.

103. Drasgow (1995, July). *Computer versus paper and pencil assessment.* Washington, DC. Personnel Testing Council of Metropolitan Washington.

104. See for example, Brass, G. J., & Oldham, G. R. (1976). Validating an in-basket test using an alternative set of leadership scoring dimensions. *Journal of Applied Psychology, 61,* 652–657. See also Tziner & Dolan, op. cit.

105. Goldstein, I. L. (1993). *Training in organizations: Needs assessment, development, and evaluation* (3d ed.). Monterey, CA: Brooks/Cole.

106. Wollowick & McNamara, op. cit.

107. Wexley, K. N., & Latham, G. P. (1991). *Developing and training human resources in organizations* (2d ed.). Glenview, IL: Scott, Foresman.

108. McKinnon, D. W. (1975). Assessment centers then and now. *Assessment and Development, 2,* 8–9. See also Office of Strategic Services (OSS) Assessment Staff (1948). *Assessment of men.* New York: Rinehart.

109. Bray, D. W. (1976). The assessment center method. In R. L. Craig (ed.), *Training and development handbook* (2d ed.). NY: McGraw-Hill, pp. 17-1–17-15.

110. Borman, W. C. (1982). Validity of behavioral assessment for predicting military recruiter performance. *Journal of Applied Psychology, 67,* 3–9. See also Pulakos, E. D., Borman, W. C., & Hough, L. M. (1988). Test validation for scientific understanding: Two demonstrations of an approach to studying predictor-criterion linkages. *Personnel Psychology, 41,* 703–716.

111. Lievens, F. (2001). Assessor training strategies and their effects on accuracy, interrater reliability, and discriminant validity. *Journal of Applied Psychology, 86,* 255–264.

112. Lorenzo, R. V. (1984). Effects of assessorship on managers' proficiency in acquiring, evaluating, and communicating information about people. *Personnel Psychology, 37,* 617–634.

113. Byham, W. C. (1970). Assessment centers for spotting future managers. *Harvard Business Review, 48,* 150–160.

114. Gaugler, B. B., Rosenthal, D. B., Thornton, G. C., III, & Bentson, C. (1987). Meta-analysis of assessment center validity. *Journal of Applied Psychology, 72,* 493–511.

115. Ibid. See also Howard, A. (1974). An assessment of assessment centers. *Academy of Management Journal, 17,* 115–134. See also Klimoski & Brickner, op. cit.

116. Thornton, G. C., III, & Byham, W. C. (1982). *Assessment centers and managerial performance.* New York: Academic Press. See also Huck, J. R., & Bray, D. W. (1976). Management assessment center evaluations and subsequent job performance of white and black females. *Personnel Psychology, 29,* 13–30.

117. Cascio, W. F., & Ramos, R. A. (1986). Development and application of a new method for assessing job performance in behavioral/economic terms. *Journal of Applied Psychology, 71,* 20–28. See also Cascio, W. F., & Silbey, V. (1979). Utility of the assessment center as a selection device. *Journal of Applied Psychology, 64,* 107–118.

118. Klimoski, op. cit. See also Gaugler, B. B., & Thornton, G. C., III (1989). Number of assessment center dimensions as a determinant of assessor accuracy. *Journal of Applied Psychology, 74,* 611–618. See also Reilly, R. R., Henry, S., & Smither, J. W. (1990). An examination of the effects of using behavior checklists on the construct validity of assessment center dimensions. *Journal of Applied Psychology, 43,* 71–84.

119. Hinrichs, J. R. (1969). Comparison of "real life" assessments of management potential with situational exercises, paper-and-pencil ability tests, and personality inventories. *Journal of Applied Psychology, 53,* 425–433.

120. Hinrichs, J. R. (1978). An eight-year follow-up of a management assessment center. *Journal of Applied Psychology, 63,* 596–601.

121. Ibid.

122. Koenig, R. (1987, Dec. 1). Exacting employer: Toyota takes pains, and time, filling jobs at its Kentucky plant. *The Wall Street Journal,* pp. 1, 31.

123. Cascio & Ramos, op. cit.

124. Cascio, W. F. (2000). *Costing human resources: The financial impact of behavior in organizations* (4th ed.). Cincinnati, OH: South-Western College Publishing. See also Schmidt & Hunter, op. cit. See also Boudreau, J. W. (1991). Utility analysis for decisions in human resource management. In M. D. Dunnette & L. M. Hough (eds.), *Handbook of industrial and organizational psychology* (vol. 2). Palo Alto, CA: Consulting Psychologists Press, pp. 621–745.

125. Terpstra, D. E., & Rozell, E. J. (1993). The relationship of staffing practices to organizational-level measures of performance. *Personnel Psychology, 46,* 27–48.

126. Cascio, op. cit. See also Boudreau, op. cit.

127. Hunter, J. E., & Schmidt, F. L. (1983). Quantifying the effects of psychological interventions on employee job performance and workforce productivity. *American Psychologist, 38,* 473–478.

128. Schmidt, F. L., Hunter, J. E., McKenzie, R., & Muldrow, T. (1979). The impact of valid selection procedures on workforce productivity. *Journal of Applied Psychology, 64,* 609–626.

DEVELOPMENT

Once employees are on board, their personal growth and development over time become a major concern. Change is a fact of organizational life, and to cope with it effectively, planned programs of employee training, development, and career management are essential. We address these issues in Chapters 8 through 10. Chapter 8 examines what is known about training and developing management and nonmanagement employees. Chapter 9 is concerned with performance management—particularly with the design, implementation, and evaluation of such systems. Finally, Chapter 10 considers the many issues involved in managing careers—from the perspective of individuals at different career stages and from the perspective of organizational staffing decisions. The overall objective of Part 3 is to establish a framework for managing the development process of employees as their careers in organizations unfold.

8. WORKPLACE TRAINING

9. PERFORMANCE MANAGEMENT

10. MANAGING CAREERS

WORKPLACE TRAINING

8

Questions This Chapter Will Help Managers Answer

1. Why should firms expect to expand their training outlays and their menu of choices for employees at all levels?
2. What kind of evidence is necessary to justify investments in training programs?
3. What are the key issues that should be addressed in the design, conduct, and evaluation of training programs?
4. Why should we invest time and money on new employee orientation? Is there a payoff?
5. How should new-employee orientation be managed for maximum positive impact?

E-LEARNING HELPS SMALL ORGANIZATIONS ACT LIKE BIG ONES*

Companies like Cambridge Technology Partners, a consulting concern, are moving to Internet training at warp speed. When a new CEO decided to explore web-based training, he brought in DigitalThink, an Internet start-up that offers Net-training technology, to digitize "E-Commerce Fundamentals" and "New Economy Fundamentals," two courses he believed were crucial for all the firm's 4,400 employees. Each course takes about 10 hours. As the CEO noted, "To train the entire company the old way would take a year. Now it takes us less than a quarter. When you're moving at Internet speed, that's important."

Before we go any further, let's take a moment to define some terms. E-learning is instruction that is delivered electronically. Almost anything that teaches a skill or conveys information in an organized fashion online can be considered e-learning. Such programs are administered through what are called learning management systems (LMSs). E-learning includes asynchronous—meaning it is not delivered to the same user at the same time—text-based courses, job aids, educational games, and video and audio segments, as well as synchronous media like video-conferencing and chat rooms. How does one access e-learning? There are two main ways to deliver it: through a company intranet, or through learning portals on the Internet. Learning portals are like online libraries. They offer courses on a wide variety of topics, from computer software tutorials, such as courses on spreadsheets, to time management and customer-service training.

Online learning is projected to boom in the near future. Of the more than $60 billion a year that corporations now spend on training, about 20 percent is spent on e-learning, and 80 percent on traditional classroom instruction. However, by 2003 that figure is expected to shift to 40 percent for online learning, and 60 percent for traditional classroom instruction. What's driving the trend? Both demand and supply forces are operating. On the demand side, rapid obsolescence of knowledge and training makes learning and relearning essential if workers are to keep up with the latest developments in their fields. In addition, there is a growing demand for just-in-time training delivery, coupled with demand for cost-effective ways to meet the learning needs of a globally distributed workforce. Finally, there is demand for flexible access to lifelong learning. On the supply side, Internet access is becoming standard at work and at home, and advances in digital technologies now enable training designers to create interactive, media-rich content. In addition, increasing bandwidth and better delivery platforms make e-learning more attractive. Finally, there is a growing selection of high-quality e-learning products and services. Features like these allow small companies, like Broadwing, Inc., a Cincinnati-based telecommunications firm, to offer a safety course delivered over the Internet. They also led the Greater Seattle Chamber of Commerce to create an online learning center for its 2,200 members—most of which have fewer than 100 employees. Online learning

*Sources: K. Tyler, E-learning: Not just for e-normous companies anymore, *HRMagazine,* pp. 82–88, May 2001; S. Shellenbarger, July 11, 2001; New training methods allow jobs to intrude further into off hours, *The Wall Street Journal,* p. B1, K. G. Brown, Using computers to deliver training: Which employees learn and why? *Personnel Psychology, 54,* 271–296, 2001; Log on for company training, *BusinessWeek,* p. 140, Jan. 10, 2000; E-learning strategies for executive education and corporate training, *Fortune,* p. S10, Apr. 10, 2001.

also permits large firms, such as General Motors, to reach more than 175,000 employees at 7,500 dealerships in less than a week, using interactive distance learning (IDL) technology. IDL will let employees view a live course, beamed in by satellite, and ask questions of the instructor, without leaving their dealerships. That will slash travel time and costs, and improve quality, because GM can select its best instructors to teach each course.

Classroom courses are not going away, and e-learning does have its drawbacks, as we shall see in the conclusion to this case, but one thing is certain: E-learning is changing corporate training forever.

Challenges

1. What are some of the key advantages of e-learning?
2. Are some types of material or course work better suited than others to e-learning?
3. What disadvantages or opportunity costs can you identify with e-learning?

Traditionally, lower-level employees were "trained," while higher-level employees were "developed." This distinction, focusing on the learning of hands-on skills versus interpersonal and decision-making skills, has become too blurry in practice to be useful. Throughout the remainder of this chapter, therefore, we will use the terms training and development interchangeably. In the United States, as in many other countries, training is big business, and the first half of this chapter examines some current issues in the design, conduct, and evaluation of training programs.

Change, growth, and sometimes displacement are facts of modem organizational life. In 2001, almost 2 million Americans lost their jobs through layoffs and restructuring. That total was higher by far than any year since 1993.[1] As those laid off found new jobs, they discovered what all new employees do: one has to "relearn the ropes" in the new job setting. Orientation training, the subject of the second part of this chapter, can ease that process considerably, with positive results both for the new employee and for the company. Trends such as leased employees, disposable managers, and free-agent workers will make orientation even more important in the future. Let's begin by defining training, and considering some emerging trends in this area.

EMPLOYEE TRAINING

What Is Training?

Training consists of planned programs designed to improve performance at the individual, group, and/or organizational levels. Improved performance, in turn, implies that there have been measurable changes in knowledge, skills, attitudes, and/or social behavior.

When we examine the training enterprise as a whole, it is clear that training issues can be addressed from at least two perspectives. At the structural level, one can examine issues such as the following: the aggregate level of expenditures by the various providers of training (e.g., federal, state, and local governments, educational institutions, private-sector businesses), the degree of cooperation among the providers, incentives (or lack of incentives) for providing training, who gets training, and the economic impact of training. These are macro-level concerns.

At the micro level, one may choose to examine issues such as the following: what types of training seem to yield positive outcomes for organizations and trainees (i.e., what "works"); how to determine whether training is needed and, if so, what type of training best fits the needs that have been identified; how to structure the delivery of training programs; and how to evaluate the outcomes of training efforts.

Unfortunately, organizations sometimes place too much emphasis on the techniques and methods of training and not enough on first defining what the employee should learn in relation to desired job behaviors. In addition, fewer than half of all organizations even try to measure the value of training, and fewer still calculate the return in monetary terms. This is true even of sales training, which would seem easy to measure. Just 11 percent of companies attempt to assess the payoffs of training on sales.[2]

In this section, we will do two things: (1) discuss several structural issues at the macro level, and (2) illustrate research-based findings that might lead to improvements in the design, delivery, and evaluation of training systems. Before we do so, however, let's consider some important training trends.

Training Trends

Both economic and demographic trends suggest radical changes in the composition of the workforce of the 21st century.[3] Other factors that affect the number, types, and requirements of available jobs include automation; continuing worker displacement as a function of mergers, acquisitions, and downsizing; and the shift from manufacturing to service jobs.[4] In 2001, for example, 87 percent of U.S. employees worked in service-based industries.[5]

These issues suggest five reasons why the time and money budgeted for training will increase during the next decade[6]:

1. The number of unskilled and undereducated youth who will be needed for entry-level jobs, and the need to train currently underutilized groups of racial and ethnic minorities, women, and older workers. This is the **social challenge.**
2. Increasingly sophisticated technological systems that will impose training and retraining requirements on the existing workforce. This is the **high-performance work systems challenge.**
3. Ongoing needs to meet the product and service needs of customers. This is the **quality challenge.**
4. The need, as more firms move to employee involvement and teams in the workplace, for team members to learn behaviors such as asking for ideas, offering help without being asked, listening and feedback skills, and recognizing and considering the ideas of others.[7] This is the **interpersonal challenge.**

5. Training needs stimulated by the expansion of many firms into global markets. Such needs involve the training of local nationals, as well as preparing employees from the home country to work in foreign markets. This is the **global challenge.**

Former Labor Secretary Robert Reich described the challenge clearly: "If we have an adequately educated and trained workforce and a state-of-the-art infrastructure linking them together and with the rest of the world, then global capital will come here to create good jobs. If we don't, the only way global capital will be invested here is if we promise low wages."[8]

Indeed, as the demands of the information age spread, companies are coming to regard training expenses as no less a part of their capital costs than plants and equipment. The Center for Workforce Development estimates that U.S. companies spend between $30 billion and $50 billion per year on formal training, but that 70 percent of all workplace learning is actually informal.[9] Indeed, since 1995 the time spent in training by the average large-company employee has risen about 25 percent.[10] At the individual-firm level, Merck, one of the world's largest pharmaceutical companies, is exemplary.

In an effort to build flexibility into its manufacturing operations, Merck has retooled several plants to be able to ramp up production of new products rapidly and to gear down production of old ones just as quickly. Flexible stainless steel tubes connect chemical-reaction chambers to one another, and they also link the chambers with giant holding tanks, centrifuges, and dryers. The tubes conduct different compounds through the different production processes they require. As demand for specific pharmaceuticals rises and falls, the tubes can be reconnected to make different ones. As you might suspect, considerable training is necessary for plant employees. Each one undergoes an average of 86 hours of training each year to learn how to operate the machines that put together so many different kinds of pills and packages.[11]

Retraining, too, can pay off. A study by the Work in America Institute found that retraining current workers for new jobs is more cost-effective than firing them and hiring new ones—not to mention the difference that retraining makes to employee morale.[12] Intel illustrates this approach nicely.

COMPANY EXAMPLE   ## REDEPLOYMENT AT INTEL[13]

Intel, the company that invented the microchip, and whose average product life-cycle is just *2.5* years, has avoided major layoffs through a strong in-house redeployment policy. Every employee receives a brochure entitled, "Owning Your Own Employability," and is afforded tools and resources to take advantage of the redeployment option. A redeployment event occurs when there is a business downturn or lack of a need for a particular skill. It does not replace performance management, as Intel's Marile Robinson, corporate manager of redeployment, points out: "It's not meant to shift around people with poor skills, poor performers, or those with behavioral problems."[14] To qualify, a full-time employee must have two consecutive years of performance reviews that "meet requirements."

Should an employee become eligible for redeployment, he or she is given options, tools, and resources. The company has five employee development centers offering self-assessment tools, career counseling, educational opportunities, and job listings within Intel. Job skills have been redefined to encourage people to find new places within the company, and temporary assignments (as many as two assignments for a total of 12 months) and up to $8,000 of training are provided to prepare them for new positions. Funds are also available for relocation. The entire process is managed through a system that provides centralized tracking and reporting of all redeployment activity.

The ranks of Intel employees are filled with those who have made successful transitions from shop floor to sales and public relations positions, or from obsolete technology divisions to high-margin technology centers within the company. If none of this works, the company pays for outplacement assistance for affected employees. Redeployment is a continuing challenge at Intel because the company's competitive strategy is to stay ahead of its rivals by making its products obsolete!

Intel redeploys approximately 80 percent of the affected workers. Thousands of employees have taken advantage of this option, just in the decade of the 1990s. In addition to being good for employees and their families, the policy is a strong deterrent to litigation based on allegations of wrongful discharge. It is a sound employee relations tool.

Structural Issues in the Delivery of Training

Despite compelling arguments for training, at least nine structural issues must be addressed if training systems are to reach their full potential. Here are some problems often identified at the macro level[15]:

1. **Corporate commitment is lacking and uneven.** Most companies spend nothing at all on training. Those that do tend to concentrate on managers, technicians, and professionals, not rank-and-file workers. Fortunately, this is changing, for as a result of the rapid pace of introduction of new technology, combined with new approaches to organization design and production management, many companies simply cannot afford to overlook training.[16] Workers have to learn three kinds of new skills: (1) the ability to use the new technology, (2) the ability to maintain it, and (3) the ability to diagnose system problems.[17] In an increasingly competitive marketplace, the ability to implement rapid changes in products and technologies is often a key requirement to preserve the competitive edge.

2. **Aggregate expenditures by business on training are inadequate.** Thus the American Society for Training and Development urges business to increase training expenditures to at least 2 percent of their annual payrolls on training—up from the current U.S. industry average of 1.2 percent. Leading companies invest much more: General Electric (4.6 percent of payroll), U.S. Robotics (4.2 percent), Motorola (4 percent), Texas Instruments (3 percent).[18]

3. **Businesses complain that schools award degrees, but they are no guarantee that graduates have mastered skills.** As a result, business must spend large amounts of money to retrain workers in basic skills. In a recent survey, companies reported that, on average, 34.1 percent of

applicants lack functional workplace literacy—the ability to read instructions, write reports, or do arithmetic at a level adequate to perform common workplace tasks. However, only about 6.5 percent of the companies provide remedial training in these basic skills.[19]

4. **Poaching trained workers is a major problem for U.S. businesses, and provides a strong disincentive for training.** Unlike Germany, where local business groups pressure companies not to steal each other's employees, there is no such system in the United States.[20] Despite this problem, business may have no choice but to train. As Gary Tooker, CEO of Motorola, says, "If knowledge is becoming antiquated at a faster rate, we have no choice but to spend on education."[21] This has profound consequences for "selling" senior managers on the value of training in the United States.

5. **Despite the rhetoric about training being viewed as an investment, current accounting rules require that it be treated as an expense.** Business might spend more on training if accounting rules were revised. Unlike investments in plant and equipment, which show up on the books as an asset, training expenditures are seen merely as expenses to be deducted in the year in which they are incurred.[22]

6. **Government is not providing enough funds for retraining to help workers displaced as a result of downsizing or the defense contraction.** This issue is difficult to address objectively, for what is "enough"? It's not just a problem in the United States. Throughout the industrialized world government leaders are focusing on one of the most corrosive, dangerous trends of the new millenium: the inability of modern economies to ease the transitions that the young, the poor, and older workers must make to keep up with rapid technological changes in the workplace.[23]

7. **Businesses, with help from the government, need to focus on the 70 percent of non–college graduates who enter the U.S. workforce.** At most, 30 percent of the future workforce will need a college degree. Marriott International, Inc. focuses on the remainder. It targets welfare recipients for its 6-week Pathways to Independence program that teaches business basics, such as showing up on time, and life lessons, such as self-esteem and personal financial management. Marriott works with federally-funded local organizations to split the $5,500-per-person costs. Over 600 Pathways graduates now work at Marriott as housekeepers, laundry workers, dishwashers, and other hourly jobs. Their 13 percent annual turnover rate is far below the company's national average.[24]

8. **Employers and schools must develop closer ties.** Schools are often seen as not responsive to labor market demands. Business is seen as not communicating its demands to schools. Fortunately, this is changing. Sematech, the semiconductor industry association, is working with Maricopa Community Colleges in Phoenix to develop a national curriculum for training entry-level manufacturing technicians. Aegon US, an insurer in Cedar Rapids, Iowa, built a $10 million corporate data center at Kirkwood Community College to be shared by company employees and college students.[25] The International Application on the next page shows how the Germans do it.

9. **Organized labor can help.** Unions have developed first-rate apprenticeship programs in a number of crafts. Now they are getting involved in "soft-skills" training as well. In San Francisco, 12 unionized hotels agreed,

INTERNATIONAL APPLICATION
In Germany Apprenticeship Training + College = Job Success

Young adults in Germany who opt for apprenticeship training before entering college tend make a smoother transition into the job market than those who do not. A recent survey by Hochshule Information Systems in Hanover found that 80 percent of those with the combined training find a full-time job as compared to 74 percent of youths with only a college education. Among new college students in Germany, 62 percent of young men and 50 percent of young women are former apprentices. Prior apprenticeship training also pays off when one has to find a new job. Thus, nearly 50 percent of those with apprenticeship training had no problem finding new employment when they lost their jobs, as compared to 38 percent of those with only a college degree.[26]

as part of a contract with the Hotel Employees and Restaurant Employees International Union, to a $3 million training program designed to teach problem-solving, communication, and conflict-resolution skills. The training program is being designed by the union and the hotels.[27]

CHARACTERISTICS OF EFFECTIVE TRAINING PRACTICE

One survey of corporate training and development practices found that four characteristics seemed to distinguish companies with the most effective training practices.[28]

- Top management is committed to training and development[29]; training is part of the corporate culture. This is especially true of leading companies such as Disney, Marriott, Hewlett-Packard, and Xerox.
- Training is tied to business strategy and objectives and is linked to bottom-line results. More on this shortly.
- A comprehensive, systematic approach to training exists; training and retraining are done at all levels on a continuous, ongoing basis.
- There is a commitment to invest the necessary resources, to provide sufficient time and money for training.

The Training Paradox

Some businesses, small and large, shy away from training because they think that by upgrading the skills of the workforce their employees will be more marketable to competitors. That is true. However, it also constitutes an interesting paradox that affects both employee and employer. That is, if an employee takes charge of her own employability by keeping her skills updated and varied so she can work for anyone, she also builds more security with her current employer—assuming the company values highly skilled, motivated employees. As

Hewlett-Packard's director of education noted, "What's going to entice them away? Money? Maybe you can buy them for a short time, but what keeps people excited is growing and learning."[30]

At the same time, if a company provides lots of training and learning opportunities, it is more likely to retain workers because it creates an interesting and challenging environment. As the general manager of London-based Marks & Spencer noted: "Train them to the point where you may lose them, and then you won't lose them."[31] This is the **training paradox:** Increasing an individual's employability outside the company simultaneously increases his or her job security and desire to stay with the current employer.

How Does Training Relate to Competitive Strategies?

This means that firms use to compete for business in the marketplace and to gain competitive advantage are known as competitive strategies.[32] A key objective of any training program, therefore, is to tie workplace training to business targets. Motorola is especially adept at this. For instance, it will set a goal to reduce product-development cycle time (i.e., to increase speed), then create a course on how to do it. This is not learning for its own sake: Trainers drill students in specific tasks until they get them right, whether it's operating a tool or being more persuasive with customers.[33] While the potential returns from well-conducted training programs are hefty, considerable planning and evaluation are necessary in order to realize these returns. The remainder of this chapter examines some key issues that managers need to consider. Let us begin by examining the broad phases that compose training systems.

ASSESSING TRAINING NEEDS AND DESIGNING TRAINING PROGRAMS

One way to keep in mind the phases of training is to portray them graphically, in the form of a model that illustrates the interaction among the phases. One such model is shown in Figure 8–1.

The **assessment phase** (or planning phase) serves as a foundation for the entire training effort. As Figure 8–1 shows, both the **training and development phase** and the **evaluation phase** depend on inputs from assessment. The purpose of the assessment phase is to define what it is the employee should learn in relation to desired job behaviors. If this phase is not carefully done, the training program as a whole will have little chance of achieving what it is intended to do.

Assuming that managers specify the objectives of the training program carefully, the next task is to design the environment in which to achieve those objectives. This is the purpose of the training phase. Choose methods and techniques carefully and deliver them systematically in a supportive, encouraging environment, based on sound principles of learning. More on this later.

Finally, if both the assessment phase and the training and development phase have been done competently, evaluation should present few problems. Evaluation is a twofold process that involves (1) establishing indicators of success in training, as well as on the job, and (2) determining exactly what job-related changes have occurred as a result of the training. Evaluation must

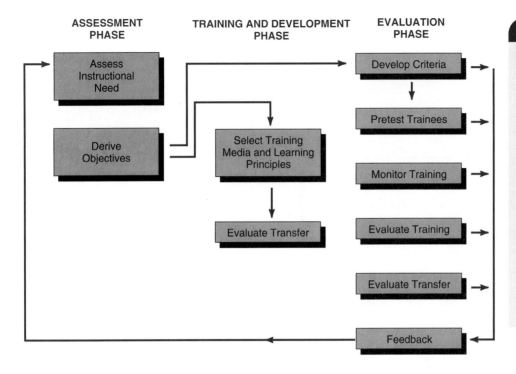

ASSESSMENT PHASE — TRAINING AND DEVELOPMENT PHASE — EVALUATION PHASE

Assess Instructional Need

Derive Objectives

Select Training Media and Learning Principles

Evaluate Transfer

Develop Criteria

Pretest Trainees

Monitor Training

Evaluate Training

Evaluate Transfer

Feedback

Figure 8–1

A general systems model of the training and development process. Note how information developed during the evaluation phase provides feedback, and therefore new input, to the assessment phase. This initiates a new cycle of assessment, training and development, and evaluation.

provide a continuous stream of feedback that can be used to reassess training needs, thereby creating input for the next stage of employee development.

Now that we have a broad overview of the training process, let us consider the elements of Figure 8–1 in greater detail.

Assessing Training Needs

There are three levels of analysis for determining the needs that training can fulfill[34]:

- **Organization analysis** focuses on identifying where within the organization training is needed.
- **Operations analysis** attempts to identify the content of training—what an employee must do in order to perform competently.
- **Individual analysis** determines how well each employee is performing the tasks that make up his or her job.

Training needs might surface in any one of these three broad areas, but in asking productive questions regarding training needs, managers often find that an "integrative model" such as that shown in Figure 8–2 is helpful.

At a general level, it is important to analyze training needs against the backdrop of organizational objectives and strategies. Unless you do this, you may waste time and money on training programs that do not advance the cause of the company.[35] **Preemployment training programs** (PET) are prime examples of close alignment between organizational needs and training curricula. PET programs are industry-specific, community-based coalitions. Member companies contribute time, money, and expertise to designing training,

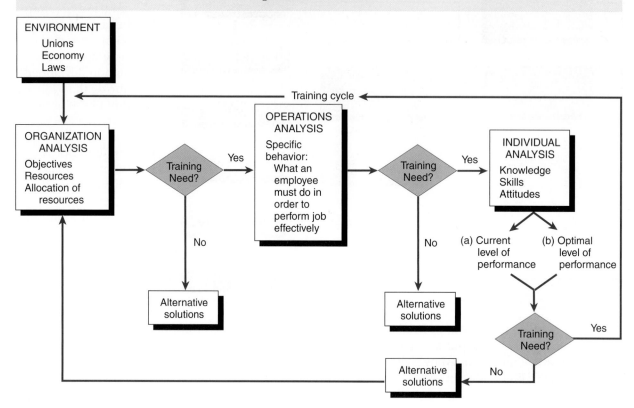

Figure 8–2

Training needs assessment model.

and they also contribute employees to teach courses. Such programs can be found in the aviation industry (Clarksburg, West Virginia), in manufacturing technology (Licking County, Ohio), in polymer chemistry (Parkerburg, Ohio), and in customer service (Knox County, Ohio).[36]

It is essential to analyze the organization's external environment and internal climate. Trends in the strategic priorities of a business, judicial decisions, civil rights laws, union activity, productivity, accidents, turnover, absenteeism, and on-the-job employee behavior will provide relevant information at this level. The important question then becomes "Will training produce changes in employee behavior that will contribute to our organization's goals?"

In summary, the critical first step is to relate training needs to the achievement of organizational goals. If you cannot make that connection, the training is probably unnecessary. However, if a training need does surface at the organizational level, an operations analysis is the next step.

Operations analysis requires a careful examination of the work to be performed after training. It involves (1) a systematic collection of information that describes how work is done, so that (2) standards of performance for that work can be determined; (3) how tasks are to be performed to meet the standards; and (4) the competencies necessary for effective task performance. Job analyses, performance appraisals, interviews (with jobholders, supervisors, and higher management), and analyses of operating problems (quality control, downtime reports, and customer complaints) all provide important inputs to the analysis of training needs.

Finally, there is **individual analysis.** At this level, training needs may be defined in terms of the following general idea: The difference between desired performance and actual performance is the individual's training need. Performance standards, identified in the operations analysis phase, constitute desired performance. Each employee's actual performance can be compared to standards that represent desired performance by using information such as the following: individual performance data; diagnostic ratings of employees by their supervisors, peers, or customers; records of performance kept by workers in diary form; attitude surveys; interviews; or tests (job knowledge, work sample, or situational). A gap between actual and desired performance may be filled by training.

However, assessing the needs for training does not end here. To evaluate the results of training and to assess what training is needed in the future, it is important to analyze needs regularly and at all three levels.

- At the organizational level, senior managers who set the organization's goals should analyze needs.
- At the operations level, the managers (or teams) who specify how the organization's goals are going to be achieved should analyze needs.
- At the individual level, the managers and workers who do the work to achieve those goals should analyze needs, keeping in mind that performance is a function both of ability (hence, training) and motivation (a worker who wants to perform well).

FROM NEEDS ANALYSIS TO TRAINING TO RESULTS! COMPANY EXAMPLE

At Pacific Bell, installers were uncertain about whether and how much they could charge for work on noncompany equipment and wiring, so they were billing very little. The company, in turn, seeing little revenue generated by the labor-hours spent, had stopped marketing the technicians' services.

A team of internal consultants—a company manager, a representative of the International Brotherhood of Electrical Workers, and a representative of the Communications Workers of America—recognized this problem and tried to solve it by involving a cross section of interested parties. The new task force agreed on two goals: increasing revenues and increasing job security.

A subcommittee of two task developers and two technicians developed a training program designed to teach installers how and what to charge, and also why they should keep accurate records: to increase their job security. The committee agreed to measure the revenues generated by time and materials charging so that these revenues could be weighed against labor costs in layoff decisions.

The training consisted of two 6-hour days and was presented by technicians to about 400 installers throughout Washington state and Oregon. In addition to the course, the task force identified a need for a hot line that technicians could call when they were bidding for a job. The line was set up, and one of the course instructors was promoted to a management position for answering calls.

RESULTS

The results of the training and hot line were phenomenal, as shown by the pattern of revenues from work on noncompany equipment. In January, prior to the training course, the installers had billed for $1,020 (in 2001 dollars). In April, when half the workers had completed the training, they billed for $36,000 in outside work. By the following February, billings for customized work and charges reached $311,000. Total revenues over the 14-month period were about $2.4 million (in 2001 dollars), or nearly twice the task force's projection of $1.4 million.

In light of these results, the company now markets the installers' services aggressively. For example, if an installation crew drives by a construction site on their way from another job, they stop and bid on the work. The hot line receives about 50 calls per day from systems technicians, installers, the business office, and customers.

The efforts of the task force increased company revenues, as well as the job security of the installers. Demand for their services grew with increased bidding on jobs, and more installers were added, providing union members in other job titles with opportunities for promotions or transfers into this work group. Future layoffs are unlikely, since the savings in labor costs must be weighed against the revenues generated by the installers.[37] Careful assessment of the need for training, coupled with the delivery of a training program that met targeted needs, produced results that startled management, the union, and the installation technicians. Everybody won!

After training needs have been identified, the next step is to structure the training environment for maximum learning. Careful attention to the fundamental principles of learning will enhance this process.

Principles of Learning

To promote efficient learning, long-term retention, and application of the skills or factual information learned in training to the job situation, training programs should incorporate principles of learning developed over the past century. Which principles should one consider? It depends on whether the trainees are learning skills (e.g., drafting) or factual material (e.g., principles of life insurance).[38]

To be most effective, *skill learning* should include four essential ingredients: (1) goal setting, (2) behavior modeling, (3) practice, and (4) feedback. However, when the focus is on *learning facts,* the sequence should change slightly: namely, (1) goal setting, (2) meaningfulness of material, (3) practice, and (4) feedback. Let's consider each of these in greater detail.

Motivating the Trainee: Goal Setting. A person who wants to develop herself or himself will do so; a person who wants to be developed rarely is. This statement illustrates the role that motivation plays in training—to learn, you must want to learn. While cognitive ability does predict training outcomes, so also does motivation. What determines motivation to succeed in training? Both personal and contextual factors are important. At the level of the individual, the personality characteristics of conscientiousness (striving for excellence, having high performance standards, setting challenging personal goals) and internal locus of control (belief that one controls his or her own fate) are important determinants of motivation to learn. At the level of the organization, the climate in which the trainee functions, coupled with the support he or she receives from supervisor and peers, is also critical.[39]

Perhaps the most effective way to raise a trainee's motivation is by setting goals. More than 500 studies have demonstrated goal setting's proven track record of success in improving employee performance in a variety of settings and cultures.[40] On average, goal setting leads to a 10 percent improvement in productivity, and it works best with tasks of low complexity.[41]

Goal theory is founded on the premise that an individual's conscious goals or intentions regulate her or his behavior.[42] Research indicates that once an individual accepts a goal, and is committed to achieving it, difficult but attainable goals result in higher levels of performance than do easy goals or even a generalized goal such as "do your best."[43] These findings have three important implications for motivating trainees:

1. Make the objectives of the training program clear at the outset.
2. Set goals that are challenging and difficult enough that the trainees can derive personal satisfaction from achieving them, but not so difficult that they are perceived as impossible to reach.

PYGMALION IN ACTION: MANAGERS GET THE KIND OF PERFORMANCE THEY EXPECT

To test the Pygmalion effect and to examine the impact of instructors' prior expectations about trainees on the instructors' subsequent style of leadership toward the trainees, a field experiment was conducted at a military training base.[44] In a 15-week combat command course, trainees were matched on aptitude and assigned randomly to one of three experimental groups. Each group corresponded to a particular level of expectation that was communicated to the instructors: high, average, or no prespecified level of expectation (due to insufficient information). Four days before the trainees arrived at the base, and prior to any acquaintance between instructors and trainees, the instructors were assembled and given a score (known as command potential, or CP) for each trainee that represented the trainee's potential to command others. The instructors were told that the CP score had been developed on the basis of psychological test scores, data from a previous course on leadership, and ratings by previous

commanders. The instructors were also told that course grades predict CP in 95 percent of the cases. The instructors were then given a list of the trainees assigned to them, along with their CPs, and asked to copy each trainee's CP into his or her personal record. The instructors were also requested to learn their trainees' names and their CPs before the beginning of the course.

The Pygmalion hypothesis that the instructor's prior expectation influences the trainee's performance was confirmed. Trainees of whom instructors expected better performance scored significantly higher on objective achievement tests, exhibited more positive attitudes, and were perceived as better leaders. In fact, the prior expectations of the instructors explained 73 percent of the variability in the trainees' performance, 66 percent in their attitudes, and 28 percent in leadership. The lesson to be learned from these results is unmistakable: Trainers (and managers) get the kind of performance they expect.

3. Supplement the ultimate goal of "finishing the program" with subgoals during training, such as trainer evaluations, work-sample tests, and periodic quizzes. As trainees clear each hurdle successfully, their confidence about attaining the ultimate goal increases.

While goal setting clearly affects trainees' motivation, so also do the expectations of the trainer. In fact, expectations have a way of becoming self-fulfilling prophecies, so that the higher the expectations, the better the trainees perform. Conversely, the lower the expectations, the worse the trainees perform. This phenomenon of the self-fulfilling prophecy is known as the **Pygmalion effect.** Legend has it that Pygmalion, a king of Cyprus, sculpted an ivory statue of a maiden named Galatea. Pygmalion fell in love with the statue, and, at his prayer, Aphrodite, the goddess of love and beauty, gave it life. Pygmalion's fondest wish—his expectation—came true.

Behavior Modeling. Much of what we learn is acquired by observing others. We will imitate other people's actions when they lead to desirable outcomes (e.g., promotions, increased sales, or more accurate tennis serves). The models' actions serve as a cue as to what constitutes appropriate behavior.[45] A model is someone who is seen as competent, powerful, and friendly and has high status within an organization. We try to identify with this model because her or his behavior is seen as desirable and appropriate. **Behavior modeling** tends to increase when the model is rewarded for behavior and when the rewards (e.g., influence, pay) are things the imitator would like to have. In the context of training (or coaching or teaching), we attempt to maximize trainees' identification with a model. For us to do this well, research suggests the following:

1. The model should be similar to the observer in age, gender, and race. If the observer sees little similarity between himself or herself and the model, it is unlikely that he or she will imitate the model's behaviors.
2. Portray the behaviors to be modeled clearly and in detail. To focus the trainees' attention on specific behaviors to imitate, provide them with a list of key behaviors to attend to when observing the model and allow them to express the behaviors in language that is most comfortable for them. For example, when one group of supervisors was being taught how to "coach" employees, the supervisors received a list of the following key behaviors[46]: (1) focus on the problem, not on the person; (2) ask for the employees' suggestions, and get their ideas on how to solve the problem; (3) listen openly; (4) agree on the steps that each of you will take to solve the problem; and (5) plan a specific follow-up date.
3. Rank the behaviors to be modeled in a sequence from least to most difficult, and be sure the trainees observe lots of repetitions of the behaviors being modeled.
4. Finally, have several models portray the behaviors, not just one.[47]

Research continues to demonstrate the effectiveness of behavior modeling over other approaches to training.[48] It is particularly appropriate for teaching interpersonal and computer skills.[49] To a large extent, this is because behavior modeling overcomes one of the shortcomings of earlier approaches to training: telling instead of showing.

Meaningfulness of the Material.   It's easier to learn and remember factual material when it is meaningful. **Meaningful material** is rich in associations for the trainees and is therefore easily understood by them. To structure material to maximize its meaningfulness:

1. Provide trainees with an overview of the material to be presented during the training. Seeing the overall picture helps trainees understand how each unit of the program fits together and how it contributes to the overall training objectives.[50]
2. Present the material by using examples, terms, and concepts that are familiar to the trainees in order to clarify and reinforce key learning points. Such a strategy is essential when training the hard-core unemployed.[51]
3. As complex intellectual skills are invariably made up of simpler ones, teach the simpler skills before the complex ones.[52] This is true whether one is teaching accounting, computer programming, or X-ray technology.

Practice (Makes Perfect).   Anyone learning a new skill or acquiring factual knowledge must have an opportunity to practice what he or she is learning.[53] Practice has three aspects: active practice, overlearning, and the length of the practice session. Let's consider each of these.

- **Active practice.** During the early stages of learning, the trainer should be available to oversee the trainee's practice directly. If the trainee begins to "get off the track," the inappropriate behaviors can be corrected immediately, before they become ingrained in the trainee's behavior. This is why low instructor–trainee (or teacher–pupil) ratios are so desirable. It also explains why so many people opt for private lessons when trying to learn or master a sport such as tennis, golf, skiing, or horseback riding.
- **Overlearning.** When trainees are given the opportunity to practice far beyond the point where they have performed a task correctly several times, the task becomes "second nature" and is "overlearned." For some tasks, **overlearning** is critical.[54] This is true of any task that must be performed infrequently and under great stress: for example, attempting to kick a winning field goal with only seconds left in a football game. It is less important in types of work where an individual practices his or her skills on a daily basis (e.g., auto mechanics, electronics technicians, assemblers).
- **Length of the practice session.** Suppose you have only 1 week to memorize the lines of a play, and during that week, you have only 12 hours available to practice. What practice schedule will produce the greatest improvement? Should you practice 2 hours a day for 6 days, should you practice for 6 hours each of the final 2 days before the deadline, or should you adopt some other schedule? The two extremes represent **distributed practice** (which implies rest intervals between sessions) and **massed practice** (in which the practice sessions are crowded together). Although there are exceptions, most of the research evidence on this question indicates that for the same amount of practice, learning is better when practice is distributed rather than massed.[55] This is especially true for learning simple motor tasks that involve very brief rest periods. It is less true for tasks of high complexity, such as those often found in organizational training settings. Under those circumstances, longer rest periods appear to be more beneficial for learning.[56]

Constructive feedback facilitates learning and supports a trainee's desire to perform well.

Feedback.   This is a form of information about one's attempts to improve. **Feedback** is essential both for learning and for trainee motivation.[57] The emphasis should be on when and how the trainee has done something correctly, for example, "You did a good job on that report you turned in yesterday—it was brief and went right to the heart of the issues." It is also important to emphasize that feedback affects group, as well as individual, performance.[58] For example, application of performance-based feedback in a small fast-food store over a 1-year period led to a 15 percent decrease in food costs and a 193 percent increase in profits.[59]

To have the greatest impact, provide feedback as soon as possible after the trainee demonstrates good performance. It need not be instantaneous, but there should be no confusion regarding exactly what the trainee did and the trainer's reaction to it. Feedback need not always be positive, but keep in mind that the most powerful rewards are likely to be those provided by the trainee's immediate supervisor. In fact, if the supervisor does not reinforce what is learned in training, the training will be transferred ineffectively to the job—if at all.

Transfer of Training

Transfer of training refers to the extent to which competencies learned in training can be applied on the job. Transfer may be positive (i.e., it enhances job performance), negative (i.e., it hampers job performance), or neutral. Long-term training or retraining probably includes segments that contain all three of these conditions. Training that results in negative transfer is costly in two ways—the cost of the training (which proved to be useless) and the cost of hampered performance.

Action learning, in which participants learn through experience and application, is an excellent vehicle for facilitating positive transfer from learning to doing.[60] Vulcan Materials Company, the largest producer of construction aggregates in the United States, used action learning to develop the next generation of senior executives. It wanted the executives to feel comfortable working in partnership with the peers from other divisions, and to be able to balance a sense of what was best for the enterprise with what was best for their own divisions.[61] The company example below is an overview of Vulcan's strategy for encouraging positive transfer from training to application.

ACTION LEARNING AT VULCAN MATERIALS COMPANY

At Vulcan, action learning helps focus attention on the important concept of "transfer of training."[62] All training activities are designed with a built-in compatibility between what managers are expected to learn and what they are expected to do on their jobs. Here is how the process works.

Following organizational and individual assessments of training needs, Vulcan offered a 3-day workshop followed by two 1-day follow-up sessions (phases II and III). The first two days of the workshop were designed to build trust, to provide a deeper understanding of group dynamics, and to give the participants an opportunity to get to know each other. On the third day, participants were divided into action-learning project teams. Each team was given a project that was strategically important to the firm, and that required cross-divisional cooperation. For example:

- Identifying best practices in the divisions, and developing a process for sharing them across divisions.
- Looking at a product that cut across all seven divisions to explore ways to increase efficiency and reduce redundancies.
- Improving customer satisfaction—identifying what customers want, how to measure and monitor their satisfaction, and how to build better customer responsiveness into Vulcan's system.

The teams then "went home" to work on their strategies for about 8 weeks.

Phase II was a "midterm review." A seminar faculty member visited each team to review its progress on the assignment and provided detailed feedback on how well the team was progressing. Sometimes teams made major changes at this point as they recognized, for example, that their analysis was not thorough enough.

Over the following 8 weeks, phase III of the program, each team prepared its final presentation —delivered to Vulcan's executive committee. After each team presented its strategy, the committee provided constructive comments and criticisms. Task forces subsequently worked to implement each team's recommendations, and they receive follow-up coaching to help them do so.

At the end of the process, an evaluation was completed that included qualitative as well as quantitative measures. Fully 89 percent of the participants reported observing increased cross divisional cooperation *in other participants' day-to-day behaviors* as a result of the action-learning process. Not only did the process change people's behaviors, but it also changed the company's systems and processes. As a result, Vulcan now has a group of high-potential managers who are skilled; who enjoy working across divisions; who are not likely to leave; and who are likely to create a common, cooperative culture across the firm.

Team Training

Up to this point, we have been discussing training and development as an individual enterprise. Yet today there is an increasing emphasis on *team* performance. Cross-functional teams, intact or virtual, are common features of many organizations. A **team** is a group of individuals who are working together toward a common goal. It is this common goal that really defines a team, and if team members have opposite or conflicting goals, the efficiency of the total unit is likely to suffer. For example, consider the effects on a basketball team when one of the players always tries to score, regardless of the team's situation.

There is a core set of skills that characterizes effective teamwork. These include adaptability, shared awareness of situations, performance monitoring and feedback, leadership or team management, interpersonal skills, coordination, communication, and decision-making skills. Attitudinal skills that characterize effective teamwork include beliefs about the importance of teamwork skills, belief in placing the team's goals above those of individual members, mutual trust, and shared vision.[63] When teams work effectively, there is more stability in their performance than that of individuals, at least over the short term.[64] In fact, high-performing teams include the following components[65]:

- A clear sense of direction.
- Talented members.
- Clear and enticing responsibilities.
- Reasonable and efficient operating procedures.
- Constructive interpersonal relationships.
- Active reinforcement systems.
- Constructive relationships with other teams and key organizational players who are not members.

Training can modify and enhance each of these. Moreover, research has revealed two broad principles regarding the composition and management of teams. One, the overall performance of a team strongly depends on the individual expertise of its members.[66] Thus individual training and development are still important. But individual training is only a partial solution, for interactions among team members must also be addressed. This interaction is what makes team training unique—it always uses some form of simulation or real-life practice, and it always focuses on the interaction of team members, equipment, and work procedures.[67] For example, Subaru-Isuzu uses a manufacturing simulation in which individuals role play team members of a small-parts assembly firm. Jobs are self-assigned within teams, and team members make their own decisions about planning and allocating resources.[68]

Two, managers of effective work groups tend to monitor the performance of their team members regularly, and they provide frequent feedback to them.[69] In fact, as much as 35 percent of variability in team performance can be explained by the frequency of use of monitors and consequences. Incorporating these findings into the training of team members and their managers should lead to better overall team performance.

Selecting Training Methods

New training methods appear every year. While some are well founded in learning theory or models of behavior change (e.g., behavior modeling), others result more from technological than from theoretical developments (e.g., presentation software, use of animation and sound, and computer-based business games).

Training methods can be classified in three ways: information presentation, techniques, simulation methods, and on-the-job training methods.[70]

- **Information presentation techniques** include lectures, conferences, correspondence courses, videos, distance learning, behavior modeling and systematic observation, programmed instruction, intelligent tutoring,[71] sensitivity training, and **organization development**—systematic, long-range programs of organizational improvement.
- **Simulation methods** include the case method, role playing, interactive simulations for virtual teams, virtual reality, the in-basket technique, and business games.
- **On-the-job training methods** include orientation training, apprenticeships, on-the-job training, near-the-job training (using identical equipment but away from the job itself), job rotation, committee assignments (or junior executive boards), understudy assignments, on-the-job coaching, and performance appraisal.

In the context of developing interpersonal skills, training methods are typically chosen to achieve one or more of three objectives:

- Promoting self-insight and environmental awareness—that is, an understanding of how one's actions affect others and how one is viewed by others. For example, at Parfums Stern, employees act out customer-salesperson roles to acquire a better understanding of customers' emotions. Wendy's International videotapes customers with disabilities; in one video a blind person asks that change be counted out loud. Meridian Bancorp has workers walk with seeds in their shoes to simulate older customers' corns and calluses.[72]
- Improving the ability of managers and lower-level employees to make decisions and to solve job-related problems in a constructive fashion.
- Maximizing the desire to perform well.

To choose the training method (or combination of methods) that best fits a given situation, first *define carefully what you wish to teach.* This is the purpose of the needs assessment phase. Only then can you choose a method that best fits these requirements. To be useful, the method should meet the minimal conditions needed for effective learning to take place; that is, the training method should:

- Motivate the trainee to improve his or her performance.
- Clearly illustrate desired skills.
- Allow the trainee to participate actively.
- Provide an opportunity to practice.
- Provide timely feedback on the trainee's performance.
- Provide some means for reinforcement while the trainee learns.
- Be structured from simple to complex tasks.
- Be adaptable to specific problems.
- Encourage positive transfer from the training to the job.

EVALUATING TRAINING PROGRAMS

To evaluate training, you must systematically document the outcomes of the training in terms of how trainees actually behave on the job and in terms of the

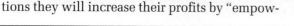

ETHICAL DILEMMA
Diversity Training—Fad or Here to Stay?

Diversity training is flourishing at the highest reaches of U.S. business. American Airlines, Coca-Cola, Procter & Gamble, and *The New York Times* are all engaged in one form or another of diversity training. All are built on the assumption that "Understanding breeds better relationships."[73] Fair enough. However, some diversity consultants promise corporations they will increase their profits by "empowering their whole workforce." How would one support that claim? To some, the preferred solution to the problems of measurement and description is to declare them irrelevant and proceed on faith alone.[74] Is this ethically justifiable in light of the principles of sound training practice—needs assessment, careful specification of objectives, and then evaluation of training in terms of the original objectives?

relevance of that behavior to the objectives of the organization.[75] To assess the utility or value of training, we seek answers to questions such as the following:

1. Have trainees achieved a specific level of skill, knowledge, or performance?
2. Did change occur?
3. Is the change due to training?
4. Is the change positively related to the achievement of organizational goals?
5. Will similar changes occur with new participants in the same training program?[76]

In evaluating training programs, it is possible to measure change in terms of four levels of rigor:[77]

- **Reaction.** How do the participants feel about the training program?
- **Learning.** To what extent have the trainees learned what was taught?
- **Behavior.** What on-the-job changes in behavior have occurred because of attendance at the training program?
- **Results.** To what extent has training produced cost-related behavioral outcomes (e.g., productivity or quality improvements, reductions in turnover or accidents)?

Since measures of reaction and learning are concerned with outcomes of the training program per se, they are referred to as **internal criteria.** Measures of behavior and results indicate the impact of training on the job environment; they are referred to as **external criteria.**

Measures of reaction typically focus on participants' feelings about the subject and the speaker, suggested improvements in the program, and the extent to which participants feel that the training will help them do their jobs better. Assess trainee learning, which may focus on changing knowledge, skills, attitudes, or motivation, by giving a paper-and-pencil or performance test. Note, however, that there is a very weak relationship between the reactions of trainees and measures of their actual learning or skill acquisition.[78]

Assessing changes in on-the-job behavior is more difficult than measuring reaction or learning because factors other than the training program (e.g., lengthened job experience, outside economic events, changes in supervision or performance incentives) may also improve performance. To rule out these rival hypotheses, it is essential to design a plan for evaluation that includes *before* and *after* measurement of the trained group's performance relative to that of one or more untrained control groups. (However, when it is relatively costly to bring participants to an evaluation and administration costs are particularly high, after-only measurement of trained and untrained groups is best.[79]) To rule out alternative explanations for the changes that occurred, match members of the untrained control group as closely as possible to those in the trained group. Table 8–1 shows a standard design for such a study. If the outcomes of the training are positive, the untrained control group at time 1 may become the trained group at a later time. It is important to note that the post-training appraisal of performance should not be done sooner than 3 months (or more) following training, so that the trainees have an opportunity to put into practice what they have learned.

Table 8–1		
A TYPICAL BEFORE-AFTER DESIGN FOR ASSESSING TRAINING OUTCOMES		
	Trained group	**Untrained group**
Pretest	Yes	Yes
Training	Yes	No
Posttest	Yes	Yes

Finally, the impact of training on organizational results is the most significant, but most difficult, effect to demonstrate. *Measures of results are the bottom line of training success.* Exciting developments in this area have come from recent research showing how the general utility equation (equation 7–1 on page 277) can be modified to reflect the dollar value of improved job performance resulting from training.[80] Utility formulas are now available for evaluating the dollar value of a single training program compared to a control group, a training program readministered periodically (e.g., annually), and a comparison between two or more different training programs.

EXECUTIVE COACHING: DOES IT PAY OFF?[81]

COMPANY EXAMPLE

External coaches are often used to help talented executives who are in trouble because of behavioral or style deficiencies, or to help them lead critical transitions, such as having to lead a major change effort.[82] Manchester International, a global purveyor of executive-coaching services, recently surveyed its customers on what they had gotten out of Manchester's programs. Bear in mind that the results came from *customers,* not the firm itself. The respondents were executives from large (mostly Fortune 1,000) companies who had participated either in "change-oriented" coaching, aimed at improving certain behaviors or skills, or

"growth-oriented" coaching, designed to sharpen overall job performance. The programs lasted from 6 months to a year. About 60 percent of the executives were ages 40 to 49—a prime age bracket for career retooling. Half held positions of vice president or higher, and a third earned $200,000 or more per year.

Asked for a conservative estimate of the monetary payoff from the coaching they got, these managers described an average return of more than $100,000, or about six times what the coaching had cost their companies. Almost 3 in 10 (28 percent) claimed that they had learned enough to boost quantifiable job performance—whether in sales, productivity, or profits—by $500,000 to $1 million since they took the training. They also reported better relationships with direct reports (77 percent), bosses (71 percent), peers (63 percent), and clients (37 percent), and cited a marked increase in job satisfaction (61 percent) and "organizational commitment" (44 percent), meaning they had become less likely to quit than they were before.

While these payoffs sound wonderful, remember that they are self-reports, not the result of experimental research that used a control group or before-and-after measurement of outcomes. In addition, not all coaches are equally proficient in what they do. Consider asking prospective coaches questions such as the ones listed below. Experienced coaches should have good answers to each of them.

- Whom have you worked with?
- What types of organizations, jobs, and levels have you dealt with?
- What processes do you build in to ensure that you get results?
- What kind of assessment will we go through to focus on the right things for me?
- What is your approach to helping me learn new things?
- How can we know we have achieved what we set out to achieve?
- Who would you turn down, and why?[83]

An often-neglected part of the training enterprise is the orientation of new employees to the company and its culture. Since most turnover occurs during the first few months on the job (at Marriott, 40 percent of new employees who leave do so during the first three months.[84]), failure to provide a thorough orientation can be a very expensive mistake.[85] Let us consider what progressive companies are doing in this area.

NEW EMPLOYEE ORIENTATION: AN OVERVIEW

One definition of **orientation** is "familiarization with and adaptation to a situation or an environment." While 8 out of every 10 organizations in the United States that have more than 50 employees provide orientation, the time and effort devoted to its design, conduct, and evaluation are woefully inadequate. In practice, orientation is often just a superficial indoctrination into company philosophy, policies, and rules; sometimes it includes the presentation of an employee handbook and a quick tour of the office or plant. This can be costly. Here is why.

In one way, a displaced worker from the factory who is hired into another environment is similar to a new college graduate. Upon starting a new job, both will face a kind of "culture shock." As they are exposed for the first time to a new organizational culture, both find that the new job is not quite what they imagined it to be. In fact, coming to work at a new company is not unlike visiting a foreign country. Either you are told about the local customs, or else you learn them on your own by a process of trial and error. An effective orientation program can help lessen the impact of this shock. But there must be more, such as a period of **socialization,** or learning to function as a contributing member of the corporate "family." New employee orientation facilitates socialization. The payoff? Higher levels of commitment to the organization, along with a deeper understanding of its goals, values, history, and people.[86]

The cost of hiring, training, and orienting a new person is far higher than most of us realize. For example, Merck & Co., the pharmaceutical giant, found that, depending on the job, turnover costs 1.5 to 2.5 times the annual salary paid for the job.[87] Moreover, since the turnover rate among new college hires can be as great as 50 percent during the first 12 months, such costs can be considerable.

A new employee's experiences during the initial period with an organization can have a major impact on his or her career. A new hire stands on the "boundary" of the organization—certainly no longer an outsider but not yet embraced by those within. There is great stress. The new hire wants to reduce this stress by becoming incorporated into the "interior" as quickly as possible. Consequently, during this period an employee is more receptive to cues from the organizational environment than she or he is ever likely to be again. Such cues to proper behavior may come from a variety of sources; for example:

- Official literature of the organization.
- Examples set by senior people.
- Formal instructions given by senior people.
- Examples given by peers.
- Rewards and punishments that flow from the employee's efforts.
- Responses to the employee's ideas.
- Degree of challenge in the assignments the employee receives.

Special problems may arise for a new employee whose young life has been spent mainly in an educational setting. As she approaches her first job, the recent graduate may feel motivated entirely by personal creativity. She is information-rich but experience-poor, eager to apply her knowledge to new processes and problems. Unfortunately, there are conditions that may stifle this creative urge. During her undergraduate days, the new employee exercised direct control over her work. Now she faces regular hours, greater restrictions, possibly a less pleasant environment, and a need to work through other people—often finding that most of the work is mundane and unchallenging. In short, three typical problems face the new employee:

1. **Problems in entering a group.** The new employee asks herself whether she will (a) be acceptable to the other group members, (b) be liked, and (c) be safe—that is, whether she will be free from physical and psychological harm. These issues must be resolved before she can feel comfortable and productive in the new situation.
2. **Naive expectations.** Organizations find it much easier to communicate factual information about pay and benefits, vacations, and company policies than information about employee norms (rules or guides to acceptable behavior), company attitudes, or "what it really takes to get ahead around here." Simple fairness suggests that employees ought to be told

about these intangibles. The bonus is that being up front and honest with job candidates produces positive results. As we saw in Chapter 6, the research on realistic job previews (RJPs) indicates that job acceptance rates will likely be lower for those who receive an RJP, but job survival rates will be higher.[88]

3. **First-job environment.** Does the new environment help or hinder the new employee trying to climb aboard? Can peers be counted on to socialize the new employee to desired job standards? How and why was the first job assignment chosen? Is it clear to the new employee what she or he can expect to get out of it?

The first year with an organization is the critical period during which an employee will or will not learn to become a high performer. The careful matching of company and employee expectations during this period can result in positive job attitudes and high standards, which then can be reinforced in new and more demanding jobs.

PLANNING, PACKAGING, AND EVALUATING AN ORIENTATION PROGRAM

Typically some time will elapse between the acceptance of a job and the actual start date. Some companies use this time to begin the orientation process. Latitude Communications actually sends out business cards to potential employees prior to their acceptance.[89] One West Coast company mails correspondence to the new employee's home, indicating how happy it is that the new employee will be joining the company's team. It also sends the employee handbook, along with information about the geographical area, as well as major, ongoing projects in the department where the new employee will be working. The company then follows up with a personal call to answer any new or outstanding questions that the new employee may have. Last, it calls the new employee the day before he or she is scheduled to begin work. This all occurs *before* the employee actually reports![90] By this time, the new employee probably feels extremely welcome and will be quite comfortable during the first day on the job.

At a broad level, new employees need specific information in three major areas:

- Company standards, expectations, norms, traditions, and policies.
- Social behavior, such as approved conduct, the work climate, and getting to know fellow workers and supervisors.
- Technical aspects of the job.

Keep in mind that the most common reasons for firing new hires are absenteeism and failure to adapt to the work environment. Fewer than 10 percent of employees are dismissed because of difficulties in learning how to perform their jobs.[91] These results suggest two levels of orientation: company and departmental. There will be some matters of general interest and importance to all new employees, regardless of department, and there will also be matters relevant only to each department. The human resources (HR) department should have overall responsibility for program planning and follow-up (subject to top-management review and approval), but the specific responsibilities of the HR department and the immediate supervisor should be made very clear to avoid duplication or omission of important information.

Be sure to avoid these approaches to orientation[92]:

- **An emphasis on paperwork.** After completing forms required by the HR department, the new employee is given a cursory welcome. Then the employee is directed to his or her immediate supervisor. The likely result: The employee does not feel like part of the company. In contrast, Hewlett-Packard sends out company forms to be completed *prior* to the first day on the job. That way the new employee can spend the first day meeting people and adjusting to the company's culture and work environment.[93]
- **A sketchy overview of the basics.** A quick, superficial orientation, and the new employee is immediately put to work—sink or swim.
- **Mickey Mouse assignments.** The new employee's first tasks are insignificant duties, supposedly intended to teach the job "from the ground up."
- **Suffocation.** Giving too much information too fast is a well-intentioned but disastrous approach, causing the new employee to feel overwhelmed and "suffocated."

We know from other companies' mistakes what works and what does not. For example, consider how the Marriott Corporation handles new employee orientation.

ORIENTATION AT MARRIOTT HOTELS

COMPANY EXAMPLE

At Marriott, all new recruits attend an 8-hour initial training session, the highlight of which is an elegant lunch, served by hotel veterans. To guide them through the next 90 days, each associate is assigned a mentor, known as a "buddy." Every member of the entering class attends refresher courses after the first and second months. Finally, once the new hires reach day 90, the hotel treats the whole class of them to a banquet.

As you can see, Marriott puts less emphasis on policies and procedures and more on emotion. Why? Because the company recognizes that excellent service is more than just a transaction. It is an experience, one that ought to satisfy the employee as well as the customer. As one observer noted, "You can't expect your employees to delight your customers unless you as an employer delight your employees."[94]

Orientation Follow-Up

The worst mistake a company can make is to ignore the new employee after orientation. Almost as bad is an informal open-door policy: "Come see me sometime if you have any questions." Many new employees are simply not assertive enough to seek out the supervisor or HR representative—more than likely, they fear looking "dumb." What is needed is formal and systematic orientation follow-up: for example, National Semiconductor uses focus groups of randomly selected new employees to find out what they like and don't like.[95] It found that many of the topics covered during orientation need to be explained briefly again, once the employee has had the opportunity to experience them firsthand. This is natural and understandable in view of the blizzard of information that often is communicated during orientation. In completing the orientation follow-up, review a checklist of items covered with each new employee or small group of employees to ensure that all items were in fact covered. Then make sure that the completed checklist is signed by the supervisor, the HR representative, and the new employee.

Evaluation of the Orientation Program

At least once a year, review the orientation program to determine whether it is meeting its objectives and to identify future improvements. To improve orientation, you need candid, comprehensive feedback from everyone involved in the program. There are several ways to provide this kind of feedback: through roundtable discussions with new employees after their first year on the job, through in-depth interviews with randomly selected employees and supervisors, and through questionnaires for mass coverage of all recent hires. Now let's consider one company's approach to the overall orientation process.

COMPANY EXAMPLE　　**NEW-EMPLOYEE ORIENTATION AT CORNING, INC.[96]**

Corning, like many other firms, faced a difficult problem: New people were getting the red-carpet treatment while being recruited, but once they started work, it was often a different story—a letdown. Often their first day on the job was disorganized and confusing, and sometimes this continued for weeks. One new employee said, "You're planting the seeds of turnover right at the beginning."

Managers at Corning realized that they needed a better way to help new employees make the transition to their new company and community. Corning needed a better way to help these new people get off on the right foot—to learn the how-tos, the wheres, and the whys, and to learn about the company's culture and its philosophies. And the company had to ensure the same support for newly hired secretaries in a district office, sales representatives working out of their homes, or engineers in a plant.

THE CORNING ORIENTATION SYSTEM AND HOW IT WORKS

Three features distinguish the Corning approach from others:

1. It is an orientation process, not a program.
2. It is based on guided self-learning. New people have responsibility for their own learning.
3. It is long-term (15–18 months), and it is in depth.

The new person learns with help and information from:

- The immediate supervisor, who has guidelines and checklists.
- Colleagues, whom the new person interviews before starting regular assignments.
- Attendance at multiple seminars conducted during the first 6 months.
- Answers to questions in a workbook for new employees.

Figure 8-3 provides an overview of how the system works.

OBJECTIVES OF THE PROGRAM

Corning set four objectives, each aimed at improving productivity. The first was to reduce voluntary turnover in the first 3 years of employment by 17 percent. The second was to shorten by 17 percent the time it takes a new person to learn the job. The third was to foster a uniform understanding among employees about the company: its objectives, its principles, its strategies, and what the company expects of its people. The fourth was to build a positive attitude toward the company and its surrounding communities.

Material distribution. As soon as possible after a hiring decision is made, orientation material is distributed:
- The new person's supervisor gets a pamphlet entitled *A Guide for Supervisors*.
- The new person gets an orientation plan.

The prearrival period. During this period, the supervisor maintains contact with the new person, helps with housing problems, designs the job, makes a preliminary MBO (management by objectives) list after discussing this with the new person, gets the office ready, notifies the organization that this has been done, and sets the interview schedule.

The 1st day. On this important day, new employees have breakfast with their supervisors, go through processing in the personnel department, attend a *Corning and You* seminar, have lunch with the seminar leader, read the workbook for new employees, are given a tour of the building, and are introduced to coworkers.

The 1st week. During this week, the new employee (1) has one-to-one interviews with the supervisors, coworkers, and specialists; (2) learns the how-tos, wheres, and whys connected with the job; (3) answers questions in the workbook; (4) gets settled in the community; and (5) participates with the supervisor in firming up the MBO plan.

The 2nd week. The new person begins regular assignments.

The 3rd and 4th weeks. The new person attends a community seminar and an employee benefits seminar (a spouse or guest may be invited).

The 2nd through 5th months. During this period, assignments are intensified and new people have biweekly progress reviews with their supervisors, attend six 2-hour seminars and intervals (on quality and productivity, technology, performance management and salaried compensation plans, financial and strategic management, employee relations and EEO, and social change), answer workbook questions about each seminar, and review answers with their supervisor.

The 6th month. The new employee completes the workbook questions, reviews the MBO list with the supervisor, participates in a performance review with the supervisor, receives a certification of completion for Phase I orientation, and makes plans for Phase II orientation.

The 7th through 15th months. This period features Phase II orientation: division orientation, function orientation, education programs, MBO reviews, performance reviews, and salary reviews.

Figure 8–3

Timetable of events in the Corning, Inc., orientation system.

MEASURING RESULTS

After 2 years, voluntary turnover among new hires was reduced by 69 percent—far greater than the 17 percent expected after 3 years. Corning also anticipates a major payback on its investment in the orientation system: an 8:1 benefit-cost ratio in the first year and a 14:1 ratio annually thereafter. These computations are shown in Figure 8–4.

LESSONS LEARNED

On the basis of the 2 years it took to develop the system, Corning's subsequent experience with it, and the recent experiences of many other companies, we offer the following considerations to guide the process of orienting new employees. They apply to any type of organization, large or small, and to any function or level of job[97]:

1. The impressions formed by new employees within their first 60 to 90 days on a job are lasting.

Figure 8–4

Calculation of benefits and costs in the Corning, Inc., orientation program.
(*Note:* "M" denotes thousands.)

A. Benefit Estimate:

A 17 percent decrease in the number of voluntary separations among those with 3 years or fewer of service:	$ 852M
A decrease in the time required to learn the job —from 6 months to 5 months	489M
	TOTAL $1,341M

B. Cost Estimate

	First Year Only	Ongoing Annual
Materials and salaries of developers, instructors, administrators	$171M	$95M

C. Benefit/Cost Ratio:

First year: $1,341M : 171M = 8 : 1
Ongoing annual: $1,341M : 95M = 14 : 1

The following formula was used to estimate productivity gains per year.

Improved Retention Rate:

Number of voluntary separations (3 or fewer years' service)	X	17% expected decrease with orientation	X	$30M investment in new hire	=	Annual productivity gain

Shorten Learning Curve from 6 Months to 5 Months:

1 month average base salary x 65%	X	Number of new hires per year	=	Annual productivity gain

2. Day 1 is crucial—new employees remember it for years. It must be managed well.

3. New employees are interested in learning about the total organization—and how they and their unit fit into the "big picture." This is just as important as is specific information about the new employee's own job and department. For example, new employees at Corning go through an Intranet scavenger hunt that requires them to use information learned during orientation and to demonstrate that they are comfortable with using the company's Intranet system.

4. Give new employees major responsibility for their own orientation, through guided self-learning, but with direction and support. For example, AT&T has its orientation program on CD-ROM so that employees can self-pace their learning.[98]

5. Avoid information overload—provide information in reasonable amounts.

6. Recognize that community, social, and family adjustment is a critical aspect of orientation for new employees.

7. Make the immediate supervisor ultimately responsible for the success of the orientation process.

8. Thorough orientation is a "must" for productivity improvement. It is a vital part of the total management system—and therefore the foundation of any effort to improve employee productivity.

In summary, the results of Corning's research are exciting and provocative. They suggest that we should be at least as concerned with preparing the new employee for the social context of his or her job and for coping with the insecurities and frustrations of a new learning situation as with the development of the technical skills necessary for job performance.

E-LEARNING HELPS SMALL ORGANIZATIONS ACT LIKE BIG ONES

Human Resource Management in Action: Conclusion

Technical as well as personal concerns may limit the growth of e-learning. Perhaps the biggest technical obstacle to more widespread use is bandwidth. High-speed, dedicated Internet connections are still a luxury for many people. When employees are parked in front of a standard dial-up connection, downloading a course's sound, video, and detailed color photographs takes way too long. Under those circumstances, interest wanes, as does motivation.

Personal concerns are another potential obstacle. Following classroom training, it is not unusual for employees to state emphatically that the best part of the learning experience was the network of personal relationships they developed in the course of their training. That kind of camaraderie doesn't form as easily with e-learning. Moreover, unless firms reserve time for learning on company time, employees have to find time on their own. While some people may relish the opportunity to squeeze in a little training via a computer or CD at home, on a plane, or in a hotel room, others may regard after-hours training as an unwarranted intrusion on their personal time. This raises an interesting question. If a company does not provide time for training during regular working hours, is it

IMPACT OF TRAINING AND DEVELOPMENT ON PRODUCTIVITY, QUALITY OF WORK LIFE, AND THE BOTTOM LINE

Does training "work"? One investigation reported the following returns on investment (ROI) for various types of training: 5:1 (behavior modification), 4.8:1 (customer service), 13.7:1 (team training), 15:1 (role of the manager), and 21:1 (sales training).[99] At a more general level, the literature on training evaluation shows that while the potential returns from well-conducted training programs can be substantial, there is often considerable variability in the effectiveness with which any given training method or content area is implemented.[100] As we have seen, considerable planning (through needs analysis) and follow-up program evaluation efforts are necessary in order to realize these returns. Given the pace of change in modern society and technology, retraining is imperative to enable individuals to compete for or retain their jobs and to enable organizations to compete in the marketplace. In recruiting and retaining a diverse workforce, for example, a recent WetFeet.com study reported that "opportunities for training and career development" was the number 1 feature that candidates demand.[101] Continual investments in training and learning are therefore essential, as they have such direct impacts on the productivity of organizations and on the quality of work life of those who work in them.

---

arbitrarily extending the workday? Some firms, like GlaxoSmithKline, urge managers to provide time for training during the workday. Other employers provide tools to help employees carve training time out of their workdays. Cisco Systems gives employees police tape to stretch across their cubicle doors. Others hand out signs saying "learning in progress." As learning becomes more a part of every job, and of day-to-day life—more companies will develop policies on these issues.

Suppose you are considering offering an e-learning course to your employees. Experts say that it is critical to test-drive each potential course from the vendor. Experience the course. See how easy it is to navigate the site, how fast it loads, and whether it provides quality take-home information. Are all elements of the course integrated? Is technical support available 24 hours a day, 7 days a week? An online course won't be of much use if employees can't access it or can't get help with it anytime they want. Inadequate support equals frustrated learners.

Start with a pilot group and test out the product. If your firm has limited funds, ask for a free tryout. Train several people for free before investing further. Solicit feedback, and then entice other employees to try it out. How? By promoting it in new employee orientation programs or encouraging managers to list it as a goal in performance reviews.

A final issue is this. Who profits most from e-learning? A recent study found considerable variability in the amount of time participants spent on each module and the time they spent practicing what was taught. Not surprisingly, employees who learned most from this type of learning environment were those who completed more of the practice opportunities made available and took more time to complete the experience.

IMPLICATIONS FOR MANAGEMENT PRACTICE

One of the greatest fears of managers and lower-level employees is obsolescence. Perhaps the **Paul principle** expresses this phenomenon most aptly: Over time, people become uneducated, and therefore incompetent, to perform at a level they once performed at adequately.[102] Training is an important antidote to obsolescence, but it is important to be realistic about what training can and cannot accomplish.

?

1. Training cannot solve all kinds of performance problems. In some cases, transfer, job redesign, changes in selection or reward systems, or discipline may be more appropriate.
2. Since productivity (the value of outputs per unit of labor) is a characteristic of a system, such as a firm or an industry, and not of an individual, changes in individual or team performance are only one possible cause of changes in productivity.[103]

3. As a manager, you need to ask yourself three key questions:
- "Do we have an actual or a potential performance problem for which training is the answer?"
- "Have we defined what is to be learned and what the content of training should be before we choose a particular training method or technique?"
- "What kind of evaluation procedure will we use to determine if the benefits of the training outweigh its costs?"

SUMMARY

The pace of change in our society is forcing both employed and displaced workers continually to acquire new knowledge and skills. In most organizations, therefore, lifelong training is essential. To be maximally effective, training programs should follow a three-phase sequence: needs assessment, implementation, and evaluation. First, define clearly what is to be learned before choosing a particular method or technique. To define what is to be learned, a continuous cycle of organization analysis, operations analysis, and analysis of the training needs of employees is necessary.

Then relate training needs to the achievement of broader organizational goals and ensure that they are consistent with management's perceptions of strategy and tactics. Beyond these fundamental concerns, principles of learning—goal setting, behavior modeling, meaningfulness of material, practice, feedback, and transfer of training—are essential considerations in the design of any training program. Choose a particular technique according to the degree to which it fits identified needs and incorporates the learning principles.

In evaluating training programs, we measure change in terms of four categories: reaction, learning, behavior, and results. Measures of the impact of training on organizational results are the bottom line of training success. Fortunately, advances in utility analysis now make evaluations possible in terms of dollar benefits and dollar costs.

One of the most neglected areas of training is new employee orientation. Clearly, a new employee's initial experience with a firm can have a major effect on his or her later career. To maximize the impact of orientation, it is important to recognize that new employees need specific information in three major areas: (1) company standards, traditions, and policies; (2) social behavior; and (3) technical aspects of the job. This suggests two levels of orientation: company, conducted by an HR representative, and departmental, conducted by the immediate supervisor. An orientation follow-up is essential (e.g., after 1 week by the supervisor and after 1 month by an HR representative) to ensure proper quality control plus continual improvement.

DISCUSSION QUESTIONS

8–1. Would you be able to recognize a sound training program if you saw one? What features would you look for?

8–2. How does goal setting affect trainee learning and motivation?

8–3. Outline an evaluation procedure for a training program designed to teach sales principles and strategies.

8–4. Why do organizations so frequently overlook new employee orientation?

8–5. Think back to your first day on the most recent job you have held. What could the organization have done to hasten your socialization and your adjustment to the job?

KEY TERMS

training

social challenge

high-performance work systems challenge

quality challenge

interpersonal challenge

global challenge

training paradox

assessment phase

training and development phase

evaluation phase

preemployment training programs

operations analysis

individual analysis

goal theory

Pygmalion effect

behavior modeling

meaningful material

overlearning

distributed practice

massed practice

feedback

transfer of training

action learning

team

organization development

internal criteria

external criteria

orientation

socialization

Paul principle

APPLYING YOUR KNOWLEDGE

Case 8–2.1   ***Evaluating Training at Hutchinson Inc.***

Hutchinson Inc. is a large insurance brokerage firm operating out of Seattle, Washington. The company was founded in 1922 by John Hutchinson, Sr., grandfather of the current president. Hutchinson offers a complete line of insurance services for both individuals and business firms. As is true with other insurance companies, Hutchinson emphasizes sales. In fact, over half of all corporate employees are involved in sales to some degree.

Because the sales activity is so important to Hutchinson, the company spends a considerable amount of time, effort, and money in sales training. Its training director, Tom Jordan, is constantly on the lookout for new training techniques that can improve sales and profits. He recently uncovered one that he had never heard of before, but which seemed to have some promise. He immediately scheduled a meeting with his boss, Cathy Archer, vice president for human resources at Hutchinson, to discuss the possibility of sending some salespeople to this new training course.

Cathy: Come in Tom. What's this I hear about a new sales training course?

Tom: Well, as you know Cathy, I always try to keep up to date on the latest in training techniques so that we can remain competitive. I got a flyer yesterday in the mail announcing a new approach to sales training. The course is offered by a guy named Bagwan Shri Lansig. Apparently, the course involves flying trainees off to a secluded spot in the mountains of Oregon where they undergo a week of intensive training, personal growth exercises, synchronized chanting, and transcendental meditation. The brochure is brimming with personal testimonials from "million-dollar" salespeople who claim to have been helped immeasurably by the training. I already have 10 people in mind to send to the training session next month, but before I speak with them, I thought I'd run it by you.

Cathy: How much does it cost?

Tom: It's not bad. Only $3,500 per person. And there's a 10 percent discount if we send more than five people.

Cathy: I don't know Tom. That sounds a little steep to me. Besides, John has been bugging me again about the results of our last training effort. He wants to know whether all the money we're spending on sales training is really paying off. As you know, sales and profits are down this quarter, and John is looking for places to cut corners. I'm afraid that if we can't demonstrate a payoff somehow for our training courses, he is going to pull the rug out from under us.

Tom: But we evaluate all our training programs! The last one got rave reviews from all the participants. Remember how they said that they hardly had time to enjoy Hawaii because they were so busy learning about proper closing techniques?

Cathy: That's true, Tom. But John wants more proof than just the reactions of the salespeople. He wants something more tangible. Now before we buy into any more sales training programs, I want you to develop a plan for evaluation of the training effort.

Questions

1. What is meant by the statement that training is extremely "faddish"?
2. How can Hutchinson Inc. avoid becoming a victim of the faddishness of the training business?
3. Develop a detailed training evaluation strategy that Tom can present to Cathy, which would provide evidence of the effectiveness of a particular training technique.

REFERENCES

1. Retrieved from the World Wide Web at www.CBS.Marketwatch.com on January 22, 2002.
2. Stewart, T. A. (2001, Apr. 2). Mystified by training? Here are some clues. *Fortune,* p. 184.

3. U.S. Bureau of Labor Statistics, Employment Projections, 1998–2008. See *www.stats.bls.gov.*

4. Uchitelle, L, & Kleinfield, N. R. (1996, Mar. 3). On the battlefields of business, millions of casualties. *The New York Times,* pp. 1, 14–17.

5. U.S. Bureau of Labor Statistics, op. cit.

6. Noe, R. A. (1999) *Employee training and development.* Burr Ridge, IL: McGraw-Hill Irwin. See also Thayer, P. W. (1997). A rapidly changing world: Some implications for training systems in the year 2001 and beyond. In Quinones, M. A., & Ehrenstein, A. (eds.), *Training for a rapidly changing workplace.* Washington, DC: American Psychological Association, pp. 15–30. See also Goldstein, I. L., & Gilliam, P. (1990). Training system issues in the year 2000. *American Psychologist, 45,* 134–143.

7. Huszczo, G. E. (1996). *Tools for team excellence.* Palo Alto, CA: Davies-Black.

8. Reich, R., quoted in Greenhouse, S. (1992, Feb. 9). Attention America! Snap out of it! *The New York Times,* pp. 1F, 8F.

9. Stewart, op. cit.

10. Shellenbarger, S. (2001, July 11). New training methods allow jobs to intrude further into off hours. *The Wall Street Journal,* p. B1.

11. Harris, G. (2000, Feb. 9). Cold turkey: How Merck intends to ride out a wave of patent expirations. *The Wall Street Journal,* pp. A1, A8.

12. Brody, M. (1987, June 8). Helping workers to work smarter. *Fortune,* pp. 86–88.

13. Cascio, W. F. (1995, May). *Guide to responsible restructuring.* Washington, DC: U.S. Department of Labor, Office of the American Workplace.

14. Robinson, M., quoted in Stuller, J. (1993, June). Why not "inplacement"? *Training,* p. 40.

15. Cascio, W. F. (1993, Nov.). *Public investments in training: Perspectives on macro-level structural issues and micro-level delivery systems.* Philadelphia: University of Pennsylvania, National Center on the Educational Quality of the Workforce.

16. Overman, S. (2001, May). PET projects: Train before you hire. *HRMagazine,* pp. 66–74. See also Gerbman, R. V. (2000, Feb.). Corporate universities 101. *HRMagazine,* pp. 101–106. See also Rouzer, P. A. (2000, June). May I help you? A more complex customer service relationship demands superior training. *HRMagazine,* pp. 140–146. See also The new factory worker (1996, Sept. 30). *BusinessWeek,* pp. 59–68.

17. Hodson, R., Hooks, G., & Rieble, S. (1992). Customized training in the workplace. *Work and Occupations, 19*(3), 272–292.

18. Gerbman, op. cit. See also Motorola: Training for the millennium (1994, Mar. 28). *BusinessWeek,* pp. 158–162.

19. *2001 AMA Survey on Workplace Testing: Basic skills, job skills, psychological measurement* (2001). New York: American Management Association.

20. Salwen, K. G. (1993, Apr.19). The cutting edge: German-owned maker of power tools finds job training pays off. *The Wall Street Journal,* pp. A1, A7.

21. Toker, G., quoted in Motorola: Training for the millenium, op. cit., p. 158.

22. Labor letter (1991, Oct. 22). *The Wall Street Journal,* p. A1.

23. Backlash: Behind the anxiety over globalization (2000, Apr. 24). *BusinessWeek,* pp. 38–43, 202. See also Risen, J. (1994, Mar. 17). Nations struggle to retrain workers as times change. *Los Angeles Times,* p. A9.

24. Low-wage lesson (1996, Nov. 11). *BusinessWeek,* pp. 108–116.

25. Overman, op. cit. See also Your local campus: Training ground zero (1996, Sept. 30). *BusinessWeek,* p. 68.

26. Apprenticeship training and college combine for success in Germany (1996, Mar.): *Manpower Argus,* no. 330, p. 8.

27. Low-wage lessons, op. cit.

28. Sirota, Alper, & Pfau, Inc. (1989). *Report to respondents: Survey of views toward corporate education and training practices.* New York: Author.

29. Rodgers, R., Hunter, J. E., & Rogers, D. L. (1993). Influence of top management commitment on management program success. *Journal of Applied Psychology, 78,* 151–155.

30. Davis, in Filipczak, B. (1995, Jan.). You're on your own: Training, employability, and the new employment contract. *Training,* pp. 29–36.

31. General manager, Marks & Spencer (2000, March). London Business School, Career Creativity conference. London, England.

32. Porter, M. E. (1985). *Competitive advantage.* New York: Free Press.

33. Motorola: Training for the millennium, op. cit.

34. Noe, op. cit. See also Goldstein, I. L. (1991). Training in work organizations. In M. D. Dunnette & L. M. Hough (eds.), *Handbook of industrial and organizational psychology.* Palo Alto, CA: Consulting Psychologists Press, pp. 507–619. See also Ostroff, C., & Ford, J. K. (1989). Assessing training needs: Critical levels of analysis. In I. L. Goldstein (ed.), *Training and development in organizations.* San Francisco: Jossey-Bass, pp. 25–62.

35. Moore, M. L., & Dutton, P. (1978). Training needs analysis: Review and critique. *Academy of Management Review, 3,* 532–454.

36. Overman, op. cit.

37. Hilton, M. (1987). Union and management: A strong case for cooperation. *Training and Development Journal, 41*(1), 54–55.

38. Wexley, K. N., & Latham, G. P. (1991). *Developing and training human resources in organizations.* New York: Harper Collins.

39. Colquitt, J. A., LePine, J. A., & Noe, R. A. (2000). Toward an integrative theory of training motivation: A meta-analytic path analysis of 20 years of research. *Journal of Applied Psychology, 85,* 678–707.

40. Ludwig, T. D., & Geller, E. S. (1997). Assigned versus participative goal setting and response generalization: Managing injury control among professional pizza deliverers. *Journal of Applied Psychology, 82,* 253–261. See also Locke, E. A., & Latham, G. P. (1990). *A theory of goal setting and task performance.* Englewood Cliffs, NJ: Prentice Hall. See also Matsui, T., Kakuyama, T., & Onglatco, M. L. U. (1987). Effects of goals and feedback on performance in groups. *Journal of Applied Psychology, 72,* 407–415. See also Mento, A. J., Steel, R. P., & Karren, R. J. (1987). A meta-analytic study of the effects of goal setting on performance: 1966–1984. *Organizational Behavior and Human Decision Processes, 39,* 52–83.

41. Wood, R. E., Mento, A. J., & Locke, E. A. (1987). Task complexity as a moderator of goal effects: A meta-analysis. *Journal of Applied Psychology, 72,* 416–425.

42. Locke, E. A. (1968). Toward a theory of task motivation and incentives. *Organizational Behavior and Human Performance, 3,* 157–189.

43. Klein, H. J., Wesson, M. J., Hollenbeck, J. R., & Alge, B. J. (1999). Goal commitment and the goal-setting process: Conceptual clarification and empirical synthesis. *Journal of Applied Psychology, 84,* 885–896. See also Locke, E. A., Latham, G. P., & Erez, M. (1988). The determinants of goal commitment. *Academy of Management Review, 13,* 23–39.

44. Eden, D., & Shani, A. B. (1982). Pygmalion goes to boot camp: Expectancy, leadership, and trainee performance. *Journal of Applied Psychology, 67,* 194–199.

45. Bandura, A. (1986). *Social foundations of thought and action: A social cognitive theory.* Englewood Cliffs, NJ: Prentice-Hall.

46. Hogan, P. M., Hakel, M. D., & Decker, P. J. (1986). Effects of trainee-generated versus trainer-provided rule codes on generalization in behavior-modeling training. *Journal of Applied Psychology, 71,* 469–473.

47. Goldstein, A. P., & Sorcher, M. (1974). *Changing supervisor behavior.* New York: Pergamon Press. See also Latham, G. P., & Saari, L. M. (1979). The application of social learning theory to training supervisors through behavior modeling. *Journal of Applied Psychology, 64,* 239–246.

48. Cascio (1993), op. cit. See also Baldwin, T. T. (1992). Effects of alternative modeling strategies on outcomes of interpersonal-skills training. *Journal of Applied Psychology, 77,* 147–154.

49. Simon, S. J., & Werner, J. M. (1996). Computer training through behavior modeling, self-paced, and instructional approaches: A field experiment. *Journal of Applied Psychology, 81,* 648–659.

50. Wexley & Latham, op. cit.

51. Low-wage lessons, op. cit. See also Gray, I., & Borecki, T. B. (1970). Training programs for the hard-core: What the trainer has to learn. *Personnel, 47,* 23–29.

52. Gist, M. E. (1997). Training design and pedagogy: Implications for skill acquisition, maintenance, and generalization. In Quinones, M. A., & Ehrenstein, A. (eds.), *Training for a rapidly changing workplace. Washington, DC:* American Psychological Association, pp. 201–222. See also Gagné R. M. (1977). *The conditions of learning.* New York: Holt, Rinehart, & Winston.

53. Ehrenstein, A., Walker, B. N., Czerwinski, M., & Feldman, E. M. (1997). Some fundamentals of training and transfer: Practice benefits are not automatic. In Quinones, M. A., & Ebrenstein, A. (eds.), *Training for a rapidly changing workplace.* Washington, DC: American Psychological Association, pp. 119–147.

54. Driskell, J. E., Willis, R. P., & Copper, C. (1992). Effect of overlearning on retention. *Journal of Applied Psychology, 77,* 615–622.

55. Goldstein, I. L. (1993*). Training in organizations: Needs assessment, development, and evaluation* (3d ed.). Monterey, CA: Brooks/Cole. See also Tyler, K. (2000, May). Hold on to what you've learned. *HRMagazine,* pp. 94–102.

56. Donovan, J. J., & Radosevich, D. J. (1999). A meta-analytic review of the distribution of practice effect: Now you see it, now you don't. *Journal of Applied Psychology, 84,* 795–805.

57. Latham, G. P. (1989). Behavioral approaches to the training and learning process. In I. L. Goldstein (ed.), *Training and development in organizations.* San Francisco: Jossey-Bass, pp. 256–295.

58. Pritchard, R. D., Jones, S.D., Roth, P. L., Steubing, K. K., & Ekeberg, S. E. (1988). Effects of group feedback, goal setting, and incentives on organizational productivity. *Journal of Applied Psychology, 73,* 337–358.

59. Florin-Thuma, B. C., & Boudreau, J. W. (1987). Performance feedback utility in a small organization: Effects on organizational outcomes and managerial decision processes. *Personnel Psychology, 40,* 693–713.

60. Stewart, op. cit.

61. Houston, W. (2000, Apr.). The impact of executive education on Vulcan's culture. In W. F. Cascio (chair), *Executive education as a vehicle for organizational change.* Symposium presented at the annual conference of the Society for Industrial and Organizational Psychology, New Orleans, LA, Apr. 2000.

62. See also Seitchik, M. (2000, Apr.). A practitioner's model for using executive education as a change intervention. In Cascio (Apr. 2000), op. cit.

63. Salas, E., & Cannon-Bowers, J. A. (1997). Methods, tools, and strategies for team training. In Quinones, M. A., & Ehrenstein, A. (eds.), *Training for a rapidly changing workplace.* Washington, DC: American Psychological Association, pp. 249–279. See also Cannon-Bowers, J. A., Tannenbaum, S. I., Salas, E., & Volpe, C. E. (1995). Defining competencies and establishing team training requirements. In R. A. Guzzo & E. Salas (eds.), *Team effectiveness and decision making in organizations.* San Francisco: Jossey-Bass, pp. 333–380.

64. Landis, R. S. (2001). A note on the stability of team performance. *Journal of Applied Psychology, 86,* 446–450.

65. Huszczo, op. cit.

66. Ganster, D. C., Williams, S., & Poppler, P. (1991). Does training in problem solving improve the quality of group decisions? *Journal of Applied Psychology, 76,* 479–483.

67. Salas & Cannon-Bowers, op. cit. See also Bass, B. M. (1980). Team productivity and individual member competence. *Small Group Behavior, 11,* 431–504.

68. Wellins, R. S., Byham, W. C., & Wilson, J. M. (1991). *Empowered teams.* San Francisco: Jossey-Bass.

69. Jose, J. R. (2001). Evaluating team performance. In M. J. Fleming and J. B. Wilson (eds.), *Effective HR measurement techniques.* Alexandria, VA: Society for Human Resource Management, pp. 107–112. See also Komaki, J. L., Desselles, J. L., & Bowman, E. D. (1989). Definitely not a breeze: Extending an operant model of supervision to teams. *Journal of Applied Psychology, 74,* 522–529.

70. Campbell, J. P., Dunnette, M. D., Lawler, E. E., & Weick, K. E. (1970). *Managerial behavior, performance, and effectiveness.* New York: McGraw-Hill.

71. Steele-Johnson, D., & Hyde, B. G. (1997). Advanced technologies in training: Intelligent tutoring systems and virtual reality. In Quinones, M. A., & Ehrenstein; A. (eds.), *Training for a rapidly changing workplace.* Washington, DC: American Psychological Association, pp. 225–248.

72. Labor letter (1990, May 8). *The Wall Street Journal,* p. A1.

73. Lee, M. (1993, Sept. 2). Diversity training grows at small firms. *The Wall Street Journal,* p. B2.

74. MacDonald, H. (1993, July 5). The diversity industry. *The New Republic,* pp. 22–25.

75. Noe, op. cit. See also Kraiger, K., Ford, J. K., & Salas, E. (1993). Application of cognitive, skill-based, and affective theories of learning outcomes to new methods of training evaluation. *Journal of Applied Psychology* (monograph), *78,* 311–328.

76. Sackett, P. R., & Mullen, E. J. (1993). Beyond formal experimental design: Towards an expanded view of the training evaluation process. *Personnel Psychology, 46,* 613–627. See also Goldstein, op. cit.

77. Kirkpatrick, D. L. (1996). Evaluation. In R. L. Craig (ed.), *The ASTD Training and Development Handbook* (2nd ed.) New York: McGraw-Hill, pp. 294–312.

78. Colquitt et al. (2000), op. cit.

79. Arvey, R. D., Maxwell, S. E., & Salas, E. (1992). The relative power of training evaluation designs under different cost configurations. *Journal of Applied Psychology, 77,* 155–160.

80. Cascio, W. F. (2000). *Costing human resources: The financial impact of behavior in organizations* (4th ed.). Cincinnati, OH: South-Western College Publishing. See also Cascio, W. F. (1989). Using utility analysis to assess training outcomes. In I. L. Goldstein (ed.), *Training and development in organizations.* San Francisco: Jossey-Bass, pp. 63–88.

81. Fisher, A. (2001, Feb 19). Executive coaching—with returns a CFO could love. *Fortune,* p.250.

82. Graddick, M. M. & Lane, P. (1998). Evaluating executive performance. In J. W. Smither (ed.), *Performance appraisal: State of the art in practice.* San Francisco: Jossey-Bass, pp. 370–403.

83. Tyler, K. (2000, June). Scoring big in the workplace. *HRMagazine,* pp. 96–106.

84. Henkoff, R. (1994, Oct. 3). Finding, training, and keeping the best service workers. *Fortune,* pp. 110–122.

85. Garvey, C. (2001, June). The whirlwind of a new job. *HRMagazine,* pp. 111–118.

86. Klein, H. J., & Weaver, N. A. (2000). The effectiveness of an organizational-level orientation training program in the socialization of new hires. *Personnel Psychology, 53,* 47–66.

87. Solomon, J. (1988, Dec.29). Companies try measuring cost savings from new types of corporate benefits. *The Wall Street Journal,* p. B1.

88. Phillips, J. M. (1998). Effects of realistic job previews on multiple organizational outcomes: A meta-analysis. *Academy of Management Journal, 41,* 673–690.

89. Ballon, M. (1998). Roll out the red carpet for new hires. *Inc., 20*(8), p. 105.

90. Lindo, D. K. (1999, Aug.). New employee orientation is your job! *Supervision, 60*(8), pp. 6–10.

91. Cappelli, P. (1995). Is the "skills gap" really about attitudes? *California Management Review,* 37 108–124.

92. St. John, W. D. (1980, May). The complete employee orientation program. *Personnel Journal,* pp. 373–378.

93. Garvey, op. cit.

94. Henkoff, op. cit.

95. Starcke, A. M. (1996). Building a better orientation program. *HRMagazine, 41*(11), 108–114.

96. Garvey, op. cit. See also Welcome to the jungle: Companies revamp new-employee orientations (1998, Oct. 13). *The Wall Street Journal,* p. A1. See also McGarrell, E. J., Jr. (1984). An orientation system that builds productivity. *Personnel Administrator, 29*(10), 75–85.

97. Ibid. See also Garvey, op. cit., and Starcke, op. cit.

98. Finney, M. I. (1996, October). Employee orientation programs can help introduce success. *HR News,* p. 2.

99. Philips, J. J. (1996, Feb.). ROI: The search for best practices. *Training and Development,* p. 45.

100. Cascio (1993), op. cit.

101. Thaler-Carter, R. E. (2001, June). Diversify your recruitment advertising. *HRMagazine,* pp. 92–100.

102. Armer, P. (1970). The individual: His privacy, self-image, and obsolescence. *Proceedings of the meeting of the panel on science and technology, 11th "Science and Astronautics."* Washington, DC: U.S. Government Printing Office.

103. Campbell, J. P. (1988). Training design for performance improvement. In J. P. Campbell & R. J. Campbell (eds.), *Productivity in organizations.* San Francisco: Jossey-Bass, pp. 177–215.

9 PERFORMANCE MANAGEMENT

Questions This Chapter Will Help Managers Answer

1. What steps can I, as a manager, take to make the performance management process more relevant and more acceptable to those who will be affected by it?
2. How can we best fit our approach to performance management with the strategic direction of our department and business?
3. Should managers and nonmanagers be appraised from multiple perspectives—for example, by those above, by those below, by coequals, and by customers?
4. What strategy should we use to train raters at all levels in the mechanics of performance management and in the art of giving feedback?
5. What would an effective performance management process look like?

PERFORMANCE REVIEWS: PERILOUS CURVES AHEAD*

In companies across the country, from General Electric to Hewlett-Packard, forced ranking systems (also known as forced distributions or "rank and yank")—in which all employees are ranked against one another and grades are distributed along some sort of bell-shaped curve—are creating a firestorm of controversy. In the past 15 months employees have filed class-action lawsuits against Microsoft and Conoco as well as Ford, claiming that the companies discriminate in assigning grades. In each case a different group of disaffected employees is bringing the charges: older workers at Ford, African-Americans and women at Microsoft, U.S. citizens at Conoco.

Here's how some companies assign grades. A common approach is to divide employees into six categories: superior (5 percent of employees), excellent (30 percent), strong (30 percent), satisfactory (20 percent), needs improvement, and issues (combined, 15 percent). Ford, which last year gave 10 percent of employees A's, 80 percent B's, and 10 percent C's (the lowest grade), will give only 5 percent C's this year. General Electric divides employees into top (20 percent), middle (80 percent), and bottom (10 percent) categories. Hewlett-Packard uses a 1:5 scale, with 15 percent of employees getting a 5 (the top grade) and 5 percent getting a 1. The percentage of employees getting 2, 3, and 4 varies. Finally, Microsoft ranks employees from 1 to 5. Most fall between 2.5 and 4.5.

Such systems have been around for decades, but thanks to a slowing economy and an increased focus on pay for performance, a quarter of the Fortune 500 by one estimate, have instituted such forced rankings or gotten tougher with their existing systems. For example, last fall Hewlett-Packard decreed that a full 5 percent of its workforce would receive HP's lowest grade, rather than the fuzzy 0 to 5 percent of years past.

Of course, one reason that employees are up in arms about forced rankings is that they suspect—often correctly—that the rankings are a way for companies to rationalize firings more easily. In his last message to GE shareholders, former CEO Jack Welch said, "Not removing the bottom 10 percent . . . is not only a management failure but false kindness as well. This year Sun Microsystems will use a forced-ranking system to identify its worst-performing 10 percent, who will be given 90 days to shape up, find another job inside Sun, or ship out.

In the conclusion to this case we will examine some of the arguments for and against the use of forced rankings, but in the meantime, what do you think?

Challenges

1. Do you support the use of forced rankings or not?
2. If the criteria used to determine an employee's rank are more qualitative than quantitative, does this undermine the forced-ranking system?
3. Suppose all the members of a team are superstars. Can forced ranking deal with that situation?

---

*Source: Adapted from M. Boyle, Performance reviews: Perilous curves ahead, *Fortune,* pp. 187–188, May 28, 2001.

The chapter opening vignette reveals just how complex performance management can be, for it includes both developmental (feedback) and administrative (pay, promotions) issues, as well as both technical aspects (design of an appraisal system) and interpersonal aspects (appraisal interviews). This chapter's objective is to present a balanced view of the performance management process, considering both its technical and its interpersonal aspects. Let's begin by examining the nature of this process.

MANAGING FOR MAXIMUM PERFORMANCE[1]

Consider following situations:

- The athlete searching for a coach who really understands her.
- The student waiting to see his guidance counselor at school.
- The worker who has just begun working for a new boss.
- A self-managing work team and a supervisor about to meet to discuss objectives for the next quarter.

What do these situations all have in common? The need to manage performance effectively—at the level of either the individual or the work team. Think of performance management as a kind of compass—one that indicates actual direction as well as desired direction. Like a compass, the job of the manager (or athletic coach or school guidance counselor) is to indicate where the individual or team is now, and to help focus attention and effort on the desired direction.

Unfortunately, the concept of **performance management** means something very specific, and much too narrow, to many managers. They tend to equate it with **performance appraisal**—an exercise they typically do once a year to identify and discuss job-relevant strengths and weaknesses of individuals or work teams. This is a mistake! Would it surprise you to learn that employees often react to appraisal interviews in the following ways?

- Employees are often less certain about where they stand *after* the appraisal interview than before it.
- Employees tend to evaluate their supervisors less favorably after the interview than before it.
- Employees often report that few constructive actions or significant improvements resulted from appraisal interviews.
- Employees feel that the authoritarian "tell and sell" approach, so common in appraisal interviews, is completely out of step with today's emphases on empowerment and workplace democracy.

In fact, a recent international survey of 8,000 employees and managers revealed that fully one-third of employees reported that their manager provided little or no assistance in improving their performance, and that they had never had a formal discussion with their manager regarding their overall performance! Conversely, more than 90 percent said that they would welcome the opportunity to have a real dialogue about their performance and to discuss their potential for progress. Senior executives in the same survey said that having such an open and honest dialogue is one of the most difficult things they are required to do. Perhaps that is why so many of them fail to do it.[2]

These are discouraging findings that certainly run counter to what we know about performance management. And what do we know about this concept? We know that performance management is part of a continuous process of improvement over time, that it demands daily, not annual, attention. Think of it this way. Why is the weekend tennis player (the "player") willing to pay handsomely for private lessons? So that he or she can have a professional who understands and can demonstrate what good performance looks like, observe the player's performance, make an appraisal of it, and then provide real-time feedback to build sound habits and eliminate unsound ones. Subsequent lessons stay focused on the overall objective (a smooth, accurate serve, for example), while recalling information about performance that builds on the foundation of earlier lessons. That's managing for maximum performance.

So what is the role of performance appraisal in the overall performance management process? Performance appraisal is a necessary, but far from sufficient, part of performance management. Managers who are committed to moving from a performance appraisal orientation to one of performance management tell us that the first step is probably the hardest, for it involves a break with tradition. Typically, appraisal is done annually or, in some firms, quarterly. *Performance management requires a willingness and a commitment to focus on improving performance at the level of the individual or team every day.* A compass provides instantaneous, real-time information that describes the difference between one's current and desired course. To practice sound performance management, managers must do the same thing—provide timely feedback about performance, while constantly focusing everyone's attention on the ultimate objective (e.g., world-class customer service).

At a general level, the broad process of performance management requires that you do three things well:

1. Define performance.
2. Facilitate performance.
3. Encourage performance.

Let's explore each of these ideas briefly.

Define Performance. A manager who creates a **performance definition** ensures that individual employees or teams know what is expected of them, and that they stay focused on effective performance.[3] How does the manager do this? By paying careful attention to three key elements: *goals, measures,* and *assessment.*

Goal setting has a proven track record of success in improving performance in a variety of settings and cultures.[4] How does it improve performance? Studies show that goals direct attention to the specific performance in question (e.g., percentage of satisfied customers), they mobilize effort to accomplish higher levels of performance, and they foster persistence for higher levels of performance.[5] The practical implications of this work are clear: Set specific, challenging goals, for this clarifies precisely what is expected and leads to high levels of performance.[6] On average, studies show, you can expect to improve productivity 10 percent by using goal setting.[7]

The mere presence of goals is not sufficient. Managers must also be able to *measure* the extent to which goals have been accomplished. Goals such as "make the company successful" are too vague to be useful. Measures such as the number of defective parts produced per million or the average time to respond to a customer's inquiry are much more tangible.

In defining performance, the third requirement is *assessment.* Here is where performance appraisal comes in. Regular assessment of progress toward goals focuses the attention and efforts of an employee or a team. If a manager takes the time to identify measurable goals but then fails to assess progress toward them, he's asking for trouble. To define performance properly, therefore, you must do three things well: Set goals, decide how to measure accomplishment, and provide regular assessments of progress. Doing this will leave no doubt in the minds of your people what is expected of them, how it will be measured, and where they stand at any given point in time. There should be no surprises in the performance management process—and regular appraisals help ensure that there won't be.

Facilitate Performance.   Managers who are committed to managing for maximum performance recognize that one of their major responsibilities is provide **performance facilitation**—that is, to eliminate roadblocks to successful performance.[8] Another is to provide adequate resources to get a job done right and on time, and a third is to pay careful attention to selecting employees.

What are some examples of *obstacles* that can inhibit maximum performance? Consider just a few: outdated or poorly-maintained equipment, delays in receiving supplies, inefficient design of work spaces, and ineffective work methods. Employees are well aware of these, and they are only too willing to identify them—if managers will only ask for their input. Then it's the manager's job to eliminate these obstacles.

Having eliminated roadblocks to successful performance, the next step is to *provide adequate resources*—capital resources, material resources, or human resources. After all, if employees lack the tools to reach the challenging goals they have set, they will become frustrated and disenchanted. Indeed, one observer has gone so far as to say "It's immoral not to give people tools to meet tough goals."[9] Conversely, employees really appreciate it when their employer provides everything they need to perform well. Not surprisingly, they usually do perform well under those circumstances.

A final aspect of performance facilitation is the *careful selection of employees.* After all, the last thing any manager wants is to have people who are ill suited to their jobs (e.g., by temperament or training), because this often leads to overstaffing, excessive labor costs, and reduced productivity. In leading companies, even top managers often get involved in selecting new employees. Microsoft, with over 15,000 employees, hires software writers "like we're a ten-person company hiring an 11th," with CEO Bill Gates enticing senior engineers, and requiring even experienced software developers to go through 5 or 6 hours of intense interviews.[10] If you're truly committed to managing for maximum performance, you pay attention to all the details—all the factors that might affect performance—and leave nothing to chance. That doesn't mean that you are constantly looking over everyone's shoulder. On the contrary, it implies greater self-management, more autonomy, and lots of opportunities to experiment, take risks, and be entrepreneurial.

Encourage Performance. The last area of management responsibility in a coordinated approach to performance management is **performance encouragement.** To encourage performance, especially repeated good performance, it's important to do three more things well: *(1) provide a sufficient amount of rewards that employees really value (2) in a timely and (3) fair manner.*

Don't bother offering rewards that nobody cares about, such as gift certificates to see a fortune teller. On the contrary, begin by asking your people what's most important to them—for example, pay, benefits, free time, merchandise, or special privileges. Then consider tailoring your awards program so that employees or teams can choose from a menu of similarly valued options.

Next, *provide rewards in a timely manner,* soon after major accomplishments. For example, North American Tool & Die, Inc., a metal-stamping plant in San Leandro, California, provides monthly cash awards for creativity. In one instance, an employee earned $500 for installing an oil-recycling machine. The company uses large amounts of oil in 55-gallon drums to lubricate its giant metal-stamping machinery. One employee purchased a $900 oil-recycling machine to filter the dirty oil so that it could be reused. The machine paid for itself in one month, and the company avoided potential toxic-waste problems associated with disposal of the dirty oil. The employee received the reward within 2 weeks after the recycling machine began to operate. This is important, for if there is an excessive delay between effective performance and receipt of the reward, then the reward loses its potential to motivate subsequent high performance.

- Finally, provide rewards in a manner that employees consider *fair.* Fairness is a subjective concept, but it can be enhanced by adhering to four important practices[11]:
  1. **Voice.** Collect employee input through surveys or interviews.
  2. **Consistency.** Ensure that all employees are treated consistently when seeking input and communicating about the process for administering rewards.
  3. **Relevance.** As noted earlier, include rewards that employees really care about.
  4. **Communication.** Explain clearly the rules and logic of the rewards process.

Not surprisingly, employees often behave very responsibly when they are asked in advance for their opinions about what is fair. Indeed, it only seems fair to ask them!

In summary, managing for maximum performance requires that you do three things well: Define performance, facilitate performance, and encourage performance. The role of the manager, like that of a compass, is to provide orientation, direction, and feedback. These ideas are shown graphically in Figure 9–1.

PURPOSES OF PERFORMANCE APPRAISAL SYSTEMS

As we have seen, performance appraisal plays an important part in the overall process of performance management. Hence it is important that we examine it in some detail. Performance appraisal has many facets. It is an exercise in

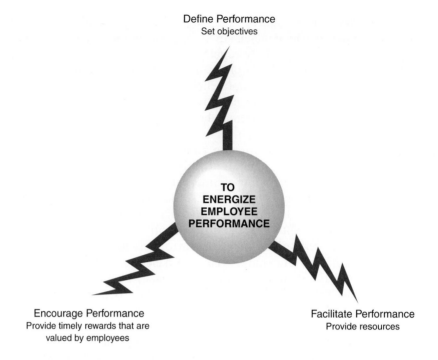

Figure 9–1

Elements of a performance management system.

observation and judgment, it is a feedback process, and it is an organizational intervention. It is a measurement process as well as an intensely emotional process. Above all, it is an inexact, human process. Not surprisingly, therefore, it is judged effective in less than 10 percent of the organizations that use it.[12] In view of such widespread dissatisfaction, why do appraisals continue to be used? What purposes do they serve?

In general, appraisal serves a twofold purpose: (1) to improve employees' work performance by helping them realize and use their full potential in carrying out their firms' missions, and (2) to provide information to employees and managers for use in making work-related decisions. More specifically, appraisals serve the following purposes:

1. **Appraisals provide legal and formal organizational justification for employment decisions** to promote outstanding performers; to weed out marginal or low performers; to train, transfer, or discipline others; to justify merit increases (or no increases); and as one basis for reducing the size of the workforce. In short, appraisal serves as a key input for administering a formal organizational reward and punishment system.
2. **Appraisals are used as criteria in test validation.** That is, test results are correlated with appraisal results to evaluate the hypothesis that test scores predict job performance.[13] However, if appraisals are not done carefully, or if considerations other than performance influence appraisal results, the appraisals cannot be used legitimately for any purpose.
3. **Appraisals provide feedback to employees** and thereby serve as vehicles for personal and career development.
4. **Appraisals can help establish objectives for training programs** once the development needs of employees are identified.

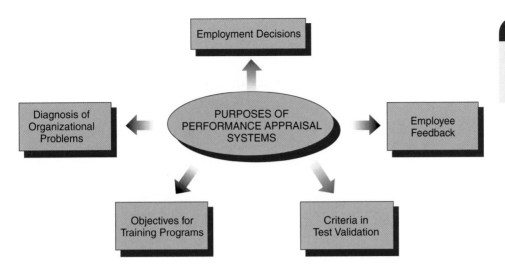

Figure 9–2

Purposes of performance appraisal systems.

5. **Appraisals can help diagnose organizational problems** as a result of the proper specifications of performance levels. They do so by identifying training needs and the knowledge, abilities, skills, and other characteristics to consider in hiring, and they also provide a basis for distinguishing between effective and ineffective performers. Appraisal therefore represents the beginning of a process, rather than an end product.[14] These ideas are shown graphically in Figure 9–2.

Despite their shortcomings, appraisals continue to be used widely, especially as a basis for tying pay to performance.[15] To attempt to avoid these shortcomings by doing away with appraisals is no solution, for whenever people interact in organized settings, appraisals will be made—formally or informally. The real challenge, then, is to identify the appraisal techniques and practices that (1) are most likely to achieve a particular objective and (2) are least vulnerable to the obstacles listed above. Let us begin by considering some of the fundamental requirements that determine whether a performance appraisal system will succeed or fail.

ETHICAL DILEMMAS IN PERFORMANCE APPRAISAL

Performance appraisal actually encompasses two distinct processes: observation and judgment. Managers must observe performance, certainly a representative sample of an employee's performance, if they are to be competent to judge its effectiveness.[16] Yet some managers assign performance ratings on the basis of small (and perhaps unrepresentative) samples of their subordinates' work. Others assign ratings based only on the subordinate's most recent work. Is this ethical? Further, is it ethical to assign performance ratings (either good or bad) that differ from what a manager knows a subordinate deserves?

Requirements of Effective Appraisal Systems

Legally and scientifically, the key requirements of any appraisal system are relevance, sensitivity, and reliability. In the context of ongoing operations, the key requirements are acceptability and practicality.[17] Let's consider each of these.

Relevance

Relevance implies that there are (1) clear links between the performance standards for a particular job and an organization's goals and (2) clear links between the critical job elements identified through a job analysis and the dimensions to be rated on an appraisal form. In short, relevance is determined by answering the question "What really makes the difference between success and failure on a particular job, and according to whom?" The answer to the latter question is simple: the customer. Customers may be internal (e.g., your immediate boss, workers in another department) or external (those who buy your company's products or services). In all cases, it is important to pay attention to the things that the customer believes are important (e.g., on-time delivery, zero defects, information to solve business problems).

Performance standards translate job requirements into levels of acceptable or unacceptable employee behavior. They play a critical role in the job analysis–performance appraisal linkage, as Figure 9–3 indicates. Job analysis identifies *what* is to be done. Performance standards specify *how well* work is to be done. Such standards may be quantitative (e.g., time, errors) or qualitative (e.g., quality of work; ability to analyze, say, market research data or a machine malfunction).

Relevance also implies the periodic maintenance and updating of job analyses, performance standards, and appraisal systems. Should the system be challenged in court, relevance will be a fundamental consideration in the arguments presented by both sides.

Sensitivity

Sensitivity implies that a performance appraisal system is capable of distinguishing effective from ineffective performers. If it is not, and the best employees are rated no differently from the worst employees, then the appraisal system cannot be used for any administrative purpose, it certainly will not help employees to develop, and it will undermine the motivation of both supervisors ("pointless paperwork") and subordinates.

A major concern here is the purpose of the rating. One study found that raters process identical sets of performance appraisal information differently, depending on whether a merit pay raise, a recommendation for further devel-

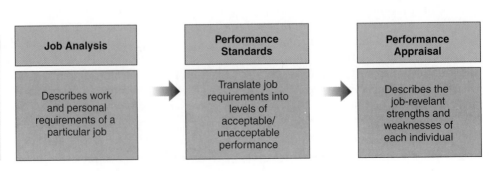

Figure 9–3

Relationship of performance standards to job analysis and performance appraisal.

Job Analysis	Performance Standards	Performance Appraisal
Describes work and personal requirements of a particular job	Translate job requirements into levels of acceptable/ unacceptable performance	Describes the job-revelant strengths and weaknesses of each individual

opment, or the retention of a probationary employee is involved.[18] These results highlight the conflict between appraisals made for administrative purposes and those made for employee development. Appraisal systems designed for administrative purposes demand performance information about differences *between* individuals, while systems designed to promote employee growth demand information about differences *within* individuals. The two different types of information are not interchangeable in terms of purposes, and that is why performance management systems designed to meet both purposes are more complex and costly.

Reliability

A third requirement of sound appraisal systems is **reliability.** In this context, "reliability" refers to consistency of judgment. For any given employee, appraisals made by raters working independently of one another should agree closely. In practice, ratings made by supervisors tend to be more reliable than those made by peers.[19] Certainly raters with different perspectives (e.g., supervisors, peers, subordinates) may see the same individual's job performance very differently.[20] To provide reliable data, each rater must have an adequate opportunity to observe what the employee has done and the conditions under which he or she has done it; otherwise, unreliability may be confused with unfamiliarity.

Note that throughout this discussion there has been no mention of the validity or accuracy of appraisal judgments. This is because we really do not know what "truth" is in performance appraisal. However, by making appraisal systems relevant, sensitive, and reliable—by satisfying the scientific and legal requirements for workable appraisal systems—we can assume that the resulting judgments are valid as well.

Acceptability

In practice, **acceptability** is the most important requirement of all, for it is true that HR programs must have the support of those who will use them, or else human ingenuity will be used to thwart them. Unfortunately, many organizations have not put much effort into garnering the front-end support and participation of those who will use the appraisal system. We know this in theory, but practice is another matter. Experts say that appraisal systems often don't work because most were designed primarily by HR specialists with limited input from managers and even less input from the employees.[21] Is it any surprise, then, that something designed to be helpful is hated like a root canal? Conversely, evidence indicates that appraisal systems that are acceptable to those who will be affected by them lead to more favorable reactions to the process and actually increase trust for top management.[22]

Smart managers enlist the active support and cooperation of subordinates or teams by making explicit exactly what aspects of job performance they will be evaluated on. As we have seen, performance definition is the first step in performance management. Only after managers and subordinates or team members define performance clearly can we hope for the kind of acceptability and commitment that is so sorely needed in performance appraisal.

Practicality

Practicality implies that appraisal instruments are easy for managers and employees to understand and use. The importance of this was brought home forcefully to me in the course of mediating a conflict between a county's Metropolitan Transit Authority (MTA) and its HR unit. Here's what happened:

COMPANY EXAMPLE   ## PRACTICAL PERFORMANCE APPRAISAL FOR BUS DRIVERS

The conflict erupted over the HR unit's *imposition* of a new appraisal system on all county departments regardless of each department's need for the new system. MTA had developed an appraisal system jointly with its union 5 years earlier, and it was working fine. In brief, each MTA supervisor (high school–educated) was responsible for about 30 subordinates (a total of 890 bus drivers who were also high school–educated or less). The "old" appraisal system was based on a checklist of infractions (e.g., reporting late for work, being charged with a preventable traffic accident), each of which carried a specified number of points. Appraisals were done quarterly, with each driver assigned 100 points at the beginning of each quarter. A driver's quarterly appraisal was simply the number of points remaining after all penalty points had been deducted during the quarter. Her or his annual appraisal (used as a basis for decisions regarding merit pay, promotions, and special assignments) was simply the average of the four quarterly ratings. Both supervisors and subordinates liked the old system because it was understandable and practical, and also because it had been shown to be workable over a 5-year period.

The new appraisal system required MTA supervisors to write quarterly narrative reports on each of their 30-odd subordinates. The HR unit had made no effort to determine the ratio of supervisors to subordinates in the various departments. Not surprisingly, therefore, objections to the new system surfaced almost immediately. MTA supervisors had neither the time nor the inclination to write quarterly narratives on each of their subordinates. The new system was highly impractical. Furthermore, the old appraisal system was working fine and was endorsed by MTA management, employees, and their union. MTA managers therefore refused to adopt the new system. To dramatize their point, they developed a single, long, detailed narrative on an outstanding bus driver. Then they made 890 copies of the narrative (one for each driver), placed a different driver's name at the top of each "appraisal," and sent the 2-foot-high stack of "appraisals" to the HR unit. MTA made its point. After considerable haggling by both sides, the HR unit backed down and allowed MTA to continue to use its old (but acceptable and eminently practical) appraisal system. That system was not perfect (e.g., drivers could only lose points for poor performance, not earn points for good performance), but it illustrates how strongly the parties in the appraisal process will fight for a system that they find acceptable.

In a broader context, we are concerned with developing employment-decision systems. From this perspective, relevance, sensitivity, and reliability are simply technical components of a system designed to make decisions about employees. As we have seen, just as much attention needs to be paid to ensuring the acceptability and practicality of appraisal systems. These are the five basic requirements of performance appraisal systems, and none of them can be ignored. However, since some degree of error is inevitable in all employment decisions, the crucial question to be answered in regard to each appraisal system is whether its use results in less human, social, and organizational cost than is currently paid for these errors. The answers to that question can result only in a wiser, fuller utilization of our human resources.

PERFORMANCE APPRAISAL

There is a rich body of case law on performance appraisal, and multiple reviews of it reached similar conclusions.[23] To avoid legal difficulties, consider taking the following steps:

1. Conduct a job analysis to determine the characteristics necessary for successful job performance.
2. Incorporate these characteristics into a rating instrument. This may be done by tying rating instruments to specific job behaviors (e.g., BARS, see page 345), but the courts routinely accept less sophisticated approaches, such as simple graphic rating scales. Regardless of the method used, provide written standards to all raters.
3. Provide written instructions and train supervisors to use the rating instrument properly, including how to apply performance standards when making judgments. The uniform application of standards is very important. The vast majority of cases lost by organizations have involved evidence that subjective standards were applied unevenly to members of protected groups versus all other employees.
4. Establish a system to detect potentially discriminatory effects or abuses of the appraisal process.
5. Include formal appeal mechanisms, coupled with higher-level review of appraisals.
6. Document the appraisals and the reason for any termination decisions. This information may prove decisive in court. Credibility is enhanced by documented appraisal ratings that describe specific examples of poor performance based on personal knowledge.[24]
7. Provide some form of performance counseling or corrective guidance to assist poor performers.

Here is a good example of step 6. In *Stone v. Xerox* the organization had a fairly elaborate procedure for assisting poor performers.[25] Stone was employed as a sales representative and in fewer than 6 months had been given several written reprimands concerning customer complaints about his selling methods and failure to develop adequate written selling proposals. As a result, he was placed on a 1-month performance improvement program designed to correct these deficiencies. This program was extended 30 days at Stone's request. When his performance still did not improve, he was placed on probation and told that failure to improve substantially would result in termination. Stone's performance continued to be substandard, and he was discharged at the end of the probationary period. When he sued Xerox, he lost.

Certainly, the type of evidence required to defend performance ratings is linked to the *purposes* for which the ratings are made. For example, if appraisal of past performance is to be used as a predictor of future performance (i.e., promotions), evidence must show (1) that the ratings of past performance are, in fact, valid and (2) that the ratings of past performance are statistically related to *future* performance in another job.[26] At the very least, this latter step should include job analysis results indicating the extent to which the requirements of the lower- and higher-level jobs overlap. Finally, to assess adverse impact, organizations should keep accurate records of who is eligible for and interested in promotion. These two factors, *eligibility* and *interest,* define the **applicant group.**

In summary, it is not difficult to offer prescriptions for scientifically sound, court-proof appraisal systems, but as we have seen, implementing them requires diligent attention by organizations, plus a commitment to making them work. In developing a performance appraisal system, the most basic requirement is to determine what you want the system to accomplish. This requires a strategy for the management of performance.

The Strategic Dimension of Performance Appraisal

In the study of work motivation, a fairly well established principle is that the things that get rewarded get done. At least one author has termed this "The greatest management principle in the world."[27] So a fundamental issue for managers is "What kind of behavior do I want to encourage in my subordinates?" If employees are rewarded for generating short-term results, they will generate short-term results. If they are rewarded (e.g., through progressively higher commissions or bonuses) for generating repeat business or for reaching quality standards over long periods of time, then they will do those things.

Managers therefore have choices. They can emphasize short- or long-term objectives in the appraisal process, or some combination of the two. Short-term objectives emphasize such things as bottom-line results for the current quarter. Long-term objectives emphasize such things as increasing market share and securing repeat business from customers. To be most useful, however, the strategic management of performance must be linked to the strategies an organization (or strategic business unit) uses to gain competitive advantage—for example, innovation, speed, quality enhancement, or cost control.[28]

Some appraisal systems that are popular in the United States, such as management by objectives (MBO), are less popular in other parts of the world, such as Japan and France. MBO focuses primarily on results, rather than on how the results were accomplished. Typically it has a short-term focus, although this need not always be the case.

In Japan, greater emphasis is placed on the psychological and behavioral sides of performance appraisal than on objective outcomes. Thus an employee will be rated in terms of the effort he or she puts into a job, on integrity, loyalty, and cooperative spirit, and on how well he or she serves the customer. Short-term results tend to be much less important than long-term personal development, the establishment and maintenance of long-term relationships with customers (that is, behaviors), and increasing market share.[29]

Once managers decide what they want the appraisal system to accomplish, their next question is, "What's the best method of performance appraisal, which technique should I use?" As in so many other areas of HR management, there is no simple answer. The following section considers some alternative methods, along with their strengths and weaknesses. Since readers of this book are more likely to be users of appraisal systems than developers of them, the following will focus most on describing and illustrating them. For more detailed information, consult the references at the end of the chapter.

ALTERNATIVE METHODS OF APPRAISING EMPLOYEE PERFORMANCE

Many regard rating methods or formats as the central issue in performance appraisal; this, however, is not the case.[30] Broader issues must also be considered—such as *trust* in the appraisal system; the *attitudes* of managers and employees; the *purpose, frequency,* and *source* of appraisal data; and rater *training.* Viewed in this light, rating formats play only a supporting role in the overall appraisal process.

Many rating formats—**behavior-oriented rating methods** focus on employee behaviors, either by comparing the performance of employees to that of other employees—**relative rating systems**—or by evaluating each employee in terms of performance standards without reference to others—**absolute rating systems.** Other rating formats place primary emphasis on what an employee produces—**results-oriented rating systems;** dollar volume of sales, number of units produced, and number of interceptions during a football season are examples. Management by objectives and work planning and review use this results-oriented approach.

Evidence indicates that ratings (that is, judgments about performance) are not strongly related to results.[31] Why? Ratings depend heavily on the mental processes of the rater. Because these processes are complex, there may be errors of judgment in the ratings. Conversely, results depend heavily on conditions that may be outside the control of the individual worker, such as the availability of supplies or the contributions of others. Thus most measures of results provide only partial coverage of the overall domain of job performance. With these considerations in mind, let's examine the behavior- and results-oriented systems more fully.

Behavior-Oriented Rating Methods

Narrative Essay
The simplest type of absolute rating system is the narrative essay, in which a rater describes, in writing, an employee's strengths, weaknesses, and potential, together with suggestions for improvement. This approach assumes that a candid statement from a rater who is knowledgeable about an employee's performance is just as valid as more formal and more complicated rating methods. The MTA bus driver case presented earlier illustrated this approach.

If essays are done well, they can provide detailed feedback to subordinates regarding their performance. On the other hand, comparisons across individuals, groups, or departments are almost impossible since different essays touch on different aspects of each subordinate's performance. This makes it difficult to use essay information for employment decisions since subordinates are not

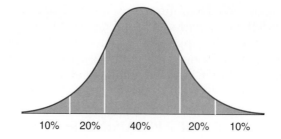

10%   20%   40%   20%   10%

compared objectively and ranked relative to one another. Methods that compare employees to one another are more useful for this purpose.

Ranking

Simple ranking requires only that a rater order all employees from highest to lowest, from "best" employee to "worst" employee. **Alternation ranking** requires that a rater initially list all employees on a sheet of paper. From this list he or she first chooses the best employee (No. 1), then the worst employee (No. n), then the second best (No. 2), then the second worst (No. $n - 1$), and so forth, alternating from the top to the bottom of the list until all employees have been ranked.

Paired Comparisons

Use of **paired comparisons** is a more systematic method for comparing employees to one another. Here each employee is compared with every other employee, usually in terms of an overall category such as "present value to the organization." The rater's task is simply to choose the "better" of each pair, and each employee's rank is determined by counting the number of times she or he was rated superior. However, since these comparisons are made on an overall basis (that is, "Who is better?") and not in terms of specific job behaviors or outcomes, they may be subject to legal challenge.[32] On the other hand, methods that compare employees to one another are useful for generating initial rankings for purposes of salary administration.

Forced Distribution

Another method of comparing employees to one another is **forced distribution.** As the chapter-opening vignette noted, the overall distribution of ratings is forced into a normal, or bell-shaped, curve under the assumption that a relatively small portion of employees is truly outstanding, a relatively small portion is unsatisfactory, and everybody else falls in between. Figure 9–4 illustrates this method, assuming that five rating categories are used.

Forced distribution does eliminate clustering almost all employees at the top of the distribution (rater **leniency**), at the bottom of the distribution (rater **severity**), or in the middle **(central tendency).** However, it can foster a great deal of employee resentment if an entire group of employees *as a group* is either superior or substandard. It is most useful when a large number of employees must be rated and there is more than one rater. Who tends to be most lenient? One study found that individuals who score high in agreeableness (trustful, sympathetic, cooperative, and polite) tend to be most lenient, while those who score high in conscientiousness (strive for excellence, high performance standards, set difficult goals) tend to be least lenient.[33]

Figure 9–5

A portion of a summed rating scale. The rater simply checks the response category that best describes the teacher's behavior. Response categories vary in scale value from 5 points (Strongly Agree) to 1 point (Strongly Disagree). A total score is computed by summing the points associated with each item.

	Strongly Agree	Agree	Neutral	Disagree	Strongly Disagree
The teacher was well prepared.					
The teacher used understandable language.					
The teacher made me think.					
The teacher's feedback on students' work aided learning.					
The teacher knew his or her field well.					

Behavioral Checklist

Here the rater is provided with a series of statements that describe job-related behavior. His or her task is simply to "check" which of the statements, or the extent to which each statement, describes the employee. In this approach raters are not so much evaluators as reporters whose task is to describe job behavior. Moreover, descriptive ratings are likely to be more reliable than evaluative (good-bad) ratings.[34] In one such method, the **Likert method** of **summed ratings,** a declarative statement (e.g., "She or he follows up on customer complaints") is followed by several response categories, such as "always," "very often," "fairly often," "occasionally," and "never." The rater checks the response category that he or she thinks best describes the employee. Each category is weighted, for example, from 5 ("always") to 1 ("never") if the statement describes desirable behavior. To derive an overall numerical rating (or score) for each employee, one simply *sums* the weights of the responses that were checked for each item. Figure 9–5 shows a portion of a summed rating scale for appraising teacher performance.

Critical Incidents

Critical incidents are brief anecdotal reports by supervisors of things employees do that are particularly effective or ineffective in accomplishing parts of their jobs. They focus on behaviors, not traits. For example, a store manager in a retail computer store observed Mr. Wang, a salesperson, do the following:

> Mr. Wang encouraged the customer to try our new word processing package by having the customer sit down at the computer and write a letter. The finished product was full of typographical and spelling errors, each of which was highlighted for the customer when Mr. Wang applied a "spelling checker" to the written material. As a result, Mr. Wang sold the customer the word processing program plus a typing tutor and a spelling checker program.

Such anecdotes force attention onto the ways in which situations determine job behavior and also on ways of doing the job successfully that may be

Figure 9–6

A portion of a graphic rating scale.

Rating Factors	Level of Performance				
	Unsatisfactory	Conditional	Satisfactory	Above Satisfactory	Outstanding
Attendance					
Appearance					
Dependability					
Quality of work					
Quantity of work					
Relationship with people					
Job knowledge					

unique to the person described. Hence they can provide the basis for training programs. Critical incidents also lend themselves nicely to appraisal interviews because supervisors can focus on actual job behaviors rather than on vaguely defined traits. They are judging performance, not personality. On the other hand, supervisors may find that recording incidents for their subordinates on a daily or even a weekly basis is burdensome. Moreover, incidents alone do not permit comparisons across individuals or departments. Graphic rating scales may overcome this problem.

Graphic Rating Scales

Many organizations use graphic rating scales.[35] Figure 9–6 shows a portion of one such scale. Many different forms of graphic rating scales exist. In terms of the amount of structure provided, the scales differ in three ways:

1. The degree to which the meaning of the response categories is defined (in Figure 9–6, what does "conditional" mean?).
2. The degree to which the individual who is interpreting the ratings (e.g., a higher-level reviewing official) can tell clearly what response was intended.
3. The degree to which the performance dimensions are defined for the rater (in Figure 9–6, for example, what does "dependability" mean?).

Graphic rating scales may not yield the depth of essays or critical incidents, but they are less time consuming to develop and administer. They also allow results to be expressed in quantitative terms, they consider more than one performance dimension, and, since the scales are standardized, they facilitate comparisons across employees. Graphic rating scales have come under frequent attack, but when compared to more sophisticated forced-choice scales, the graphic scales have proved just as reliable and valid and are more acceptable to raters.[36]

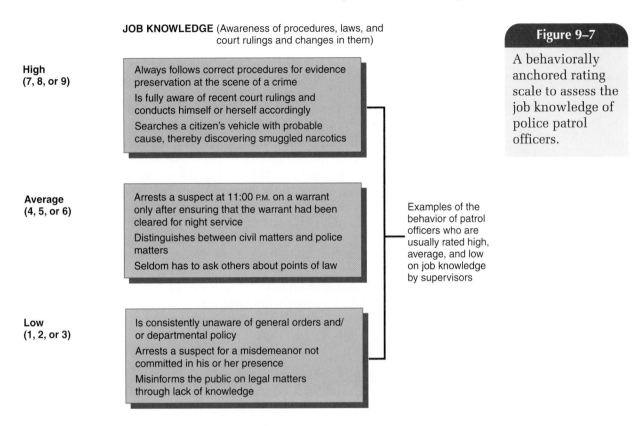

JOB KNOWLEDGE (Awareness of procedures, laws, and court rulings and changes in them)

High
(7, 8, or 9)

Always follows correct procedures for evidence preservation at the scene of a crime

Is fully aware of recent court rulings and conducts himself or herself accordingly

Searches a citizen's vehicle with probable cause, thereby discovering smuggled narcotics

Average
(4, 5, or 6)

Arrests a suspect at 11:00 P.M. on a warrant only after ensuring that the warrant had been cleared for night service

Distinguishes between civil matters and police matters

Seldom has to ask others about points of law

Low
(1, 2, or 3)

Is consistently unaware of general orders and/or departmental policy

Arrests a suspect for a misdemeanor not committed in his or her presence

Misinforms the public on legal matters through lack of knowledge

Examples of the behavior of patrol officers who are usually rated high, average, and low on job knowledge by supervisors

Figure 9–7

A behaviorally anchored rating scale to assess the job knowledge of police patrol officers.

Behaviorally Anchored Rating Scales

A variation of the simple graphic rating scale is **behaviorally anchored rating scales (BARS).** The major advantage of BARS is that they define the dimensions to be rated in behavioral terms and use critical incidents to describe various levels of performance. BARS therefore provide a common frame of reference for raters. An example of the job knowledge portion of a BARS for police patrol officers is shown in Figure 9–7. BARS require considerable effort to develop,[37] yet there is little research evidence to support the superiority of BARS over other types of rating systems.[38] Nevertheless, the participative process required to develop them provides information that is useful for other organizational purposes, such as communicating clearly to employees exactly what "good performance" means in the context of their jobs.

Results-Oriented Rating Methods

Management by Objectives

Management by objectives (MBO) is a well-known process of managing that relies on goal-setting to establish objectives for the organization as a whole, for each department, for each manager within each department, and for each employee. MBO is not a measure of employee behavior; rather, it is a measure of each employee's contribution to the success of the organization.[39]

To establish objectives, the key people involved should do three things: (1) meet to *agree on the major objectives* for a given period of time (e.g., every year, every 6 months, or quarterly), (2) *develop plans* for how and when the objectives will be accomplished, and (3) *agree on the yardsticks* for determining whether the objectives have been met. Progress reviews are held regularly until the end of the period for which the objectives were established. At that time, those who established objectives at each level in the organization meet to evaluate the results and to agree on the objectives for the next period.[40]

The Air Force Research Laboratory, which employs 3,200 scientists and engineers, applied a slightly different twist to traditional MBO. It assumes that all staff members are performing well, and it evaluates them on the contribution their particular jobs make to the mission of the organization. The lab encourages the scientists and engineers to take on as much responsibility as they can handle. Naturally they gravitate to the toughest jobs they can perform competently, and their pay is based on the value of those jobs to the lab.[41]

To some, MBO is a complete system of planning and control and a complete philosophy of management.[42] In theory, MBO promotes success in each employee because, as each employee succeeds, so do that employee's manager, the department, and the organization; but this is true only to the extent that the individual, departmental, and organizational goals are compatible.[43] Very few applications of MBO have actually adopted a formal **"cascading process"** to ensure such a linkage. An effective MBO system takes from 3 to 5 years to implement, and since relatively few firms are willing to make that kind of commitment, it is not surprising that MBO systems often fail.[44]

Work Planning and Review

Work planning and review is similar to MBO; however, it places greater emphasis on the periodic review of work plans by both supervisor and subordinate in order to identify goals attained, problems encountered, and the need for training.[45] This approach has long been used by Corning, Inc. Table 9–1 presents a summary of the appraisal methods we have just discussed.

When Should Each Technique Be Used?

You have just read about a number of alternative appraisal formats, each with its own advantages and disadvantages. At this point you are probably asking yourself, "What's the bottom line? I know that no method is perfect, but what should I do?" First, remember that the rating format is not as important as the relevance and acceptability of the rating system. Second, here is some advice based on systematic comparisons among the various methods.

An extensive review of the research literature that relates the various rating methods to indicators of performance appraisal effectiveness found no clear "winner."[46] However, the researchers were able to provide several "if . . . then" propositions and general statements based on their study. Among these are:

- If the objective is to compare employees across raters for important employment decisions (e.g., promotion, merit pay), don't use MBO and work planning and review. They are not based on a standardized rating scheme for all employees.
- If you use a BARS, also make diary keeping a part of the process. This will improve the accuracy of the ratings, and it also will help supervisors distinguish between effective and ineffective employees.

Table 9–1

A SNAPSHOT OF THE ADVANTAGES AND DISADVANTAGES OF ALTERNATIVE APPRAISAL METHODS

Behavior-oriented methods

Narrative essay. Good for individual feedback and development, but difficult to make comparisons across employees.

Ranking and paired comparisons. Good for making comparisons across employees, but provides little basis for individual feedback and development.

Forced distribution. Forces raters to make distinctions among employees but may be unfair and inaccurate if a group of employees, as a group, is either very effective or ineffective.

Behavioral checklist. Easy to use, provides a direct link between job analysis and performance appraisal, can be numerically scored, and facilitates comparisons across employees. However, the meaning of response categories may be interpreted differently by different raters.

Critical incidents. Focuses directly on job behaviors, emphasizes what employees did that was effective or ineffective, but can be very time-consuming to develop.

Graphic rating scales (including BARS). Easy to use, very helpful for providing feedback for individual development, and facilitate comparisons across employees. BARS are very time-consuming to develop, but dimensions and scale points are defined clearly. Graphic rating scales often do not define dimensions or scale points clearly.

Results-oriented methods

Management by objectives. Focuses on results and on identifying each employee's contribution to the success of the unit or organization. However, MBO is generally short-term-oriented, provides few insights into employee behavior, and does not facilitate comparison across employees.

Work planning and review. In contrast to MBO, emphasizes process over outcomes. Requires frequent supervisor-subordinate review of work plans. Is time consuming to implement properly and does not facilitate comparisons across employees.

- If objective performance data are available, MBO is the best strategy to use. Work planning and review is not as effective as MBO under these circumstances.
- In general, the appraisal methods that are best in a broad, organizational sense—BARS and MBO—are the most difficult to use and maintain. Recognize, however, that no rating method is foolproof.
- Methods that focus on describing, rather than evaluating, behavior (e.g., BARS, summed rating scales) produce results that are the most interpretable across raters. They help remove the effects of individual differences in raters.[47]
- No rating method has been an unqualified success when used as a basis for merit pay or promotional decisions.

■ When certain statistical corrections are made, the correlations between scores on alternative rating formats are very high. Hence all the formats measure essentially the same thing.

Which techniques are most popular? A survey of 324 organizations in southern California found that among larger organizations 51 percent use rating scales of some sort, 23 percent use essays, 17 percent use MBO, and 9 percent use all other forms of appraisal systems, which included behavioral checklists, forced choice, and rankings.[48]

WHO SHOULD EVALUATE PERFORMANCE?

The most fundamental requirement for any rater is that he or she has an adequate opportunity to observe the ratee's job performance over a reasonable period of time (e.g., 6 months). This suggests several possible raters.

The Immediate Supervisor. If appraisal is done at all, it will probably be done by this person.[49] She or he is probably most familiar with the individual's performance and, in most jobs, has had the best opportunity to observe actual job performance. Furthermore, the immediate supervisor is probably the person best able to relate the individual's performance to what the department and organization are trying to accomplish. Since she or he also is responsible for reward (and punishment) decisions, and for managing the overall performance management process,[50] it is not surprising that feedback from supervisors is more highly related to performance than that from any other source.[51]

Peers. In some jobs, such as outside sales, the immediate supervisor may observe a subordinate's actual job performance only rarely (and indirectly, through written reports). In other environments, such as self-managed work teams, there is no "supervisor." Sometimes objective indicators, such as number of units sold, can provide useful performance-related information, but in other circumstances the judgment of peers is even better. Peers can provide a perspective on performance that is different from that of immediate supervisors. Thus a member of a cross-functional team may be in a better position to rate another team member than that team member's immediate supervisor. However, to reduce potential friendship bias while simultaneously increasing the feedback value of the information provided, it is important to specify exactly what the peers are to evaluate[52]—for example, "the quality of her help on technical problems."

Another approach is to require input from a number of colleagues. Thus, at Harley-Davidson, salaried workers have five colleagues critique their work. They are "accountability partners."[53] Evidence from a recent study that used peer appraisals to provide developmental feedback found that features such as prompting appraisers for both negative and positive feedback, pooling feedback from multiple appraisers, and face-to-face discussions increased the reliability, validity, and user acceptance of the feedback. Such feedback had an immediate, positive impact on perceptions of open communication, motivation to perform well, the viability of the group, and member relationships. In addition, the beneficial effects of the feedback last longest if the feedback is conducted before the group is engaged in executing a project, yet not so far in advance that the project is not yet a priority.[54]

Subordinates. Appraisal by subordinates can be a useful input to the immediate supervisor's development.[55] Subordinates know firsthand the extent to which the supervisor *actually* delegates, how well he or she communicates, the type of leadership style he or she is most comfortable with, and the extent to which he or she plans and organizes. However, ratings by subordinates tend to have less impact on supervisors with more cynical attitudes toward organizational change than those who are less cynical, perhaps because those who are more cynical are less likely to take action based on the upward feedback they receive.[56]

Longitudinal research shows that managers who met with their direct reports to discuss their upward feedback improved more than other managers. Further, managers improved more in years when they discussed the previous year's feedback with their direct reports than in years when they did not. This is important because it demonstrates that what managers do with upward feedback is related to its benefits.[57]

Should subordinate ratings be anonymous? Managers want to know who said what, but subordinates prefer to remain anonymous to avoid retribution. To address these concerns, collect and combine the ratings in such a manner that a manager's overall rating is not distorted by an extremely divergent opinion.[58] Like peer assessments, they provide only one piece of the appraisal puzzle, although evidence indicates that ratings provided by peers and subordinates are comparable, for they reflect the same underlying dimensions.[59]

Self-appraisal. There are several arguments to recommend wider use of self-appraisals. The opportunity to participate in the performance appraisal process, particularly if appraisal is combined with goal setting, improves the ratee's motivation and reduces her or his defensiveness during the appraisal interview.[60] On the other hand, self-appraisals tend to be more lenient, less variable, and more biased, and to show less agreement with the judgments of others.[61] In terms of performance, effectiveness is highest under two conditions: When ratings from both self- and others are high, or when self-ratings are substantially lower than ratings from others (severe underestimation). Effectiveness is lowest for overestimators when self-ratings are moderate and

Customers are often able to rate important aspects of the performance of employees in front-line customer contact positions.

subordinate ratings are low.[62] Since U.S. employees tend to give themselves higher marks than their supervisors do (conflicting findings have been found with mainland Chinese and Taiwanese employees),[63] self-appraisals are probably more appropriate for counseling and development than for employment decisions.

Customers Served.   In some situations the "consumers" of an individual's or organization's services can provide a unique perspective on job performance. Examples abound: subscribers to a cable television service, bank customers, clients of a brokerage house, and citizens of a local police or fire-protection district. Although the customers' objectives cannot be expected to correspond completely to the organization's objectives, the information that customers provide can serve as useful input for employment decisions, such as those regarding promotion, transfer, and need for training. It can also be used to assess the impact of training or as a basis for self-development. At General Electric, for example, the customers of senior managers are interviewed formally and regularly as part of the managers' appraisal process. Their evaluations are important in appraisal, but at the same time they also build commitment, because customers are giving time and information to help GE.[64]

Computers.   As noted earlier, employees spend a lot of time unsupervised by their bosses. Now technology has made continuous supervision possible—and very real for millions of workers. What sort of technology? Computer software that monitors employee performance.

USING COMPUTERS TO MONITOR JOB PERFORMANCE

To proponents, it is a great new application of technology to improve productivity. To critics, it represents the ultimate intrusion of Big Brother into the workplace. For several million workers today, being monitored on the job by a computer is a fact of life.[65]

Computers measure quantifiable tasks performed by secretaries, factory and postal workers, and grocery and airline reservation sales agents. For example, major airlines regularly monitor the time reservation sales agents spend on each call. Until now, lower-level jobs have been affected most directly by computer monitoring. But as software becomes more sophisticated, even engineers, accountants, and doctors are expected to face electronic scrutiny.

Critics feel that overzealous employers will get carried away with information gathering and overstep the boundary between work performance and privacy. Moreover, being watched every second can be stressful, thereby stifling worker creativity, initiative, and morale.

Not everyone views monitoring as a modern-day version of *Modern Times*, the Charlie Chaplin movie in which the hapless hero is tyrannized by automation. At the Third National Bank of Nashville, for example, encoding clerks can earn up to 25 percent more than their base pay if their output is high—and they like this system.

To be sure, monitoring itself is neither good nor bad; how managers use it determines its acceptance in the workplace. Practices such as giving employees access to data collected on them, establishing procedures for challenging erroneous records, and training supervisors to base actions and decisions on actual observation of employees, not just on computer-generated records, can alleviate the fears of employees.[66] At American Express, for example, monitored employees are given feedback about their performance every 2 weeks.

Managers who impose monitoring standards without asking employees what is reasonable may be surprised at the responses of employees. Tactics can include work station operators who pound the space bar or hold down the underlining bar while chatting, and telephone operators who hang up on customers with complicated problems. The lesson, perhaps, is that even the most sophisticated technology can be thwarted by human beings who feel they are being pushed beyond acceptable limits.[67]

MultiRater or 360-Degree Feedback

A recent survey revealed that about one-third of U.S. organizations now use input from managers, subordinates, peers, and customers to provide a perspective on performance from all angles (360 degrees), and that many more intend to do so in the future.[68] There are at least four reasons why such an approach is valuable[69]:

1. It includes observations from different perspectives, and perhaps includes different aspects of performance that capture the complexities of an individual's performance in multiple roles.
2. Feedback from multiple sources may reinforce feedback from the boss, thereby making it harder to discount the viewpoint of that single person.
3. Discrepancies between self-ratings and those received from others may create an awareness of one's needs for development, and motivate individuals to improve their performance in order to reduce or eliminate such discrepancies.
4. At least some senior managers believe that if they can improve leadership among their organization's leaders, ultimately that will benefit the bottom line.

What does the research literature on 360-degree feedback tell us? Evidence indicates that ratings from these different sources generally do not agree closely with each other. Thus one study found that the correlations among ratings made by self, peer, supervisor, and subordinate raters ranged from a high of .79 (supervisor-peer) to a low of .14 (subordinate-self).[70] However, evidence also indicates that ratings from the different sources are comparable, for they reflect the same underlying dimensions of performance.[71]

Suppose that, in designing a **360-degree feedback** program for the purpose of providing feedback for development, you were asked which of the following five factors would have the greatest influence on performance ratings: the ratee's general level of performance, the ratee's performance on specific dimensions of performance, the rater's personal biases, the rater's perspective (self, subordinate, peer, or boss), and random error. Results from two large data sets of managers who received developmental ratings on three performance dimensions from seven raters (two bosses, two peers, two subordinates, and self) found the following[72]:

1. The rater's overall biases had the strongest influence on performance ratings for all combinations of rater perspective and performance dimensions. For peer and subordinate ratings, and for self-ratings, the effect of overall bias was stronger than that of all other factors combined.
2. Ratings from bosses captured more of the ratee's actual job performance, and contained less personal bias, than did ratings from any other perspective. Although true or actual performance levels were unknown, this finding does suggest that the validity of ratings from bosses was higher than that from other perspectives.
3. The ratee's actual performance accounted for only about 20–25 percent of the variability in performance ratings when averaged across dimensions, perspectives, and instruments.
4. Both bosses and subordinates assessed different aspects of ratee performance from their unique perspectives. While peer ratings did contain considerable amounts of performance variability, they did not capture anything unique to that perspective.

To overcome these potential problems, decision makers need to be aware of the personal biases of raters and attempt to control their effects. To do this, consider taking the following steps[73]:

- Make sure appraisal has a single, clear purpose—development. Tell employees if ratings are being used for decision making.
- Train all raters to understand the overall process as well as in how to complete forms and avoid common rating errors. UPS, for example, explains the 360-degree feedback process, and discusses how data will be used. Recognize, however, that no amount of training is going to be of any help if the organizational climate is politically charged and trust is low.[74]
- Seek a variety of types of information about performance, possibly including objective measures or ratings made by multiple individuals, and make raters accountable to upper-level review. It is not necessary to have all raters evaluate the employee in all areas.
- Help employees interpret and react to the ratings, perhaps with the help of a personal coach, include goal setting, and implement the 360-degree process regularly, so that the employee can track improvements over time.
- Continue to use multirater systems, and take the time to evaluate their effectiveness.[75]

In addition to these steps, make it clear who owns the 360-degree reports—is it the individual, the manager, or the HR function? Emphasize business results (work outputs), and include feedback on individual characteristics in the context of how they help to achieve or detract from the business results. Finally, the written report should contain the following elements: a summary that integrates the main themes from the scores (assuming quantitative results are part of the process) and the respondents' comments. Consider sorting the respondents' comments into categories.[76]

Careful attention to these action steps is an integral component of performance management. Another important consideration is the timing and frequency of performance appraisal.

WHEN AND HOW OFTEN SHOULD APPRAISAL BE DONE?

Traditionally, formal appraisal is done once, or at best twice, a year. Research, however, has indicated that once or twice a year is far too infrequent.[77] Unless he or she keeps a diary, considerable difficulties face a rater who is asked to remember what several employees did over the previous 6 or 12 months. This is why firms such as Western Digital, Southern California Gas, and Fluor add frequent, informal "progress" reviews between the annual ones.[78]

Research indicates that if a rater is asked to assess an employee's performance over a 6- to 12-month period, biased ratings may result, especially if information has been stored in the rater's memory according to irrelevant, over-simplistic, or otherwise faulty categories.[79] Unfortunately, faulty categorization seems to be the rule more often than the exception.

For example, consider the impact of prior expectations on ratings.[80] Supervisors of tellers at a large West Coast bank provided predictions about the future job performance of their new tellers. Six months later they rated the job performance of each teller. The result? Inconsistencies between prior expectations and later performance clearly affected the judgments of the raters. Thus when a teller's actual performance disappointed or exceeded a supervisor's prior expectations about that performance, ratings were lower than warranted by actual performance. The lesson to be learned is that it is unwise to assume that raters are faulty, but motivationally neutral, observers of on-the-job behavior.

More and more companies are realizing that once-a-year reviews don't work very well. Many now require managers to review employees formally at least twice a year, and to talk with them informally even more often about how they are doing. At Sibson & Company, a management consulting firm, employees get formal reviews every 6 months or at the end of each project.[81] Such an approach has merit because the appraisals are likely to provide more accurate inputs to employment decisions, and they have the additional advantage of sending clear messages to employees about where they stand. There should be no "surprises" in appraisals, and one way to ensure this is to do them frequently. A study of 437 companies by Hewitt Associates may provide some incentive to do so. Companies with year-round performance management systems (as opposed to once-a-year performance appraisal systems or no systems) outperformed competitors without such systems on every financial and productivity measure used in the study, including profits, cash flow, and stock market performance.[82]

PERFORMANCE APPRAISAL AND TOTAL QUALITY MANAGEMENT

Total quality management (TQM) emphasizes the continuous improvement of products and processes to ensure long-term customer satisfaction. Its group problem-solving focus encourages employee empowerment by using the job-related expertise and ingenuity of the workforce. Cross-functional teams develop solutions to complex problems, often shortening the time taken to design, develop, or produce products and services. Since a team may not include a representative of management, the dividing line between labor and management often becomes blurred in practice, as workers themselves begin to solve organizational problems. Thus adoption of TQM generally requires cultural change within the organization as management reexamines its past methods and practices in light of the demands of the new philosophy.[83]

If the "father of TQM," W. Edwards Deming, had his way, appraisal systems that tie individual performance to salary adjustments would be eliminated. In his view, such systems hinder teamwork, create fear and mistrust, and discourage risk-taking behavior, thereby stifling innovation. Worse yet, Deming has argued, most appraisal systems are based on the faulty assumption that individuals have significant control over their own performance—that is, that most individuals can improve if they choose to do so by putting forth the necessary effort.[84]

Here is the basis for his argument. Everything done in an organization is done within the framework of one or more systems (e.g., accounting, purchasing, production, sales). The systems provide limits on the activities of machines, processes, employees, and even managers. In a well-designed system, it will be nearly impossible to do a job improperly. Conversely, a poor system can thwart the best efforts of the best employee. If the system itself prevents good work (e.g., outdated technology that makes it impossible to meet current quality standards), performance appraisal cannot serve its intended purpose of differentiating among individuals for purposes of salary adjustments. Further, since employees (and most lower-level managers as well) have little opportunity to change those systems, they may become frustrated and demoralized.

What's the bottom line in all of this? As a basis for implementing a "pay-for-performance" philosophy, performance appraisal is a meaningful tool only if workers have significant control over the variables that affect their individual performance.[85] If not, then it is true, as Deming has argued, that appraisals measure only random statistical variation within a particular system.

How Performance Appraisals Can Incorporate Key Elements of TQM

Organizations need not sacrifice their performance-appraisal programs on the altar of total quality management. Here are three suggestions for harmonizing these two processes.[86]

1. **Let customer expectations generate individual or team performance expectations.** Start by identifying customer expectations by product or service. Customers may be internal or external. Then individuals or teams can begin to assess their performance against those expectations. Using this baseline of achievement, individuals, teams, and managers can develop continuous improvement targets. Comparing actual performance against expected performance helps avoid detrimental intrateam competition, because individuals or teams are compared against their own benchmarks, rather than against the accomplishments of others.

2. **Include results expectations that identify actions to meet or exceed those expectations.** Employee (or team) and supervisor together consider these customer expectations in conjunction with the business plan and begin to establish priorities for improvement opportunities.

INTERNATIONAL APPLICATION
Impact of National Culture on Peformance Appraisals

Western expatriate managers are often surprised to learn that their management practices have unintended consequences when applied in non-Western cultures. To illustrate such differences, consider the results of a study of Taiwanese and U.S. business students that examined preferences for various performance appraisal practices.[87]

Compared to Americans, Taiwanese students indicated the following:

- Less support for performance appraisal as practiced in Western cultures.
- More focus on group rather than individual performance.
- Greater willingness to consider nonperformance factors (e.g., off-the-job behaviors, age) as criteria in appraisal.

- Less willingness to attribute performance levels to the skills and efforts of particular individuals.
- Less open and direct relations between supervisor and subordinate.
- An expectation of closer supervisory styles.

These results suggest that U.S. managers will need to modify the performance appraisal process that is familiar to them when working with Taiwanese subordinates in order to make it more consistent with Taiwanese values and culture. Such a process recognizes the importance of groups as well as individuals in the organization and honors the criteria of cooperation, loyalty, and attitudes toward superiors, as well as individual goal accomplishment.

---

3. **Include behavioral skills that make a real difference in achieving quality performance and total customer satisfaction.** For example, effective customer service requires "attention to detail," "initiative," and "listening skills." These continuous-improvement skills are as important to total quality as are results-oriented targets.

When performance expectations focus on process improvements as well as on the behavioral skills needed to provide a product or service, total quality, excellent customer service, and appraisal of individual or team performance become "the way we do business."

APPRAISAL ERRORS AND RATER-TRAINING STRATEGIES

The use of ratings assumes that the human observer is reasonably objective and accurate. As we have seen, raters' memories are quite fallible, and raters subscribe to their own sets of likes, dislikes, and expectations about people, expectations that may or may not be valid.[88] These biases produce rating errors, or deviations between the "true" rating an employee deserves and the actual rating assigned.[89] We discussed some of the most common types of rating errors previously: leniency, severity, and central tendency. Three other types are halo, contrast, and recency errors.

1. **Halo error** is not as common as is commonly believed.[90] Raters who commit this error assign their ratings on the basis of global (good or bad) impressions of ratees. An employee is rated either high or low on many aspects of job performance because the rater knows (or thinks she or he knows) that the employee is high or low on some specific aspect. In practice, halo is probably due to situational factors or to the interaction of a rater and a situation (e.g., a supervisor who has limited opportunity to observe her subordinates because they are in the field dealing with customers).[91] Thus halo is probably a better indicator of how raters process cognitive information than it is as a measure of rating validity or accuracy.[92]

2. **Contrast error** results when a rater compares several employees to one another rather than to an objective standard of performance.[93] If, say, the first two workers are unsatisfactory while the third is average, the third worker may well be rated outstanding because in contrast to the first two, her or his "average" level of job performance is magnified. Likewise, "average" performance could be downgraded unfairly if the first few workers are outstanding. In both cases, the "average" worker receives a biased rating.

3. **Recency error** results when a rater assigns his or her ratings on the basis of the employee's most recent performance. It is most likely to occur when appraisals are done only after long periods. Here is how one manager described the dilemma of the recency error: "Many of us have trouble rating for the entire year. If one of my people has a stellar three months prior to the review . . . [I] don't want to do anything that impedes that person's momentum and progress."[94] Of course, if the subordinate's performance peaks 3 months prior to appraisal *every year,* that suggests a different problem!

Traditionally, rater training has focused on teaching raters to eliminate errors. Unfortunately, such programs usually have only short-term effects. Worse yet, training raters to reduce errors may actually reduce the accuracy of the ratings![95] What can be done? First, rater training should emphasize how to observe behavior more accurately, not "how to" or "how not to" rate. Such an appraisal might proceed as follows[96]:

1. Show participants a video of an employee performing his or her job.
2. Ask participants to evaluate the employee on the video using rating scales that the trainer provides.
3. Place each participant's ratings on a flip chart.
4. The trainer leads a discussion among participants about the differences between ratings and reasons for them.
5. Ask the raters to reach a consensus regarding performance standards and relative levels of effective or ineffective behavior.
6. Show the video again.
7. Have the participants reassign ratings, this time on the basis of specific examples of behavior that each rater records.
8. Evaluate the ratings relative to the earlier consensus judgments of participants.
9. Provide specific feedback to each participant.

Second, encourage raters to become actively involved in the training process, because, in general, the more actively involved raters become, the better the outcome.[97] Third, encourage raters to discuss the performance dimensions on which they will be rating *before* they observe and evaluate the performance of others. Fourth, give them the opportunity to practice rating a sample of job performance. Finally, provide them with "true" (or expert) ratings to which they can compare their own ratings. Rater training is clearly worth the effort, and research indicates that the kind of approach advocated here is especially effective in improving the meaningfulness and usefulness of the performance appraisal process.[98]

SECRETS OF EFFECTIVE PERFORMANCE FEEDBACK INTERVIEWS

The use of performance feedback, at least in terms of company policies on the subject, is widespread. Most companies require that appraisal results be discussed with employees.[101] As is well known, however, the existence of a policy is no guarantee that it will be implemented, or implemented effectively. Consider just two examples. First, we know that feedback is most effective when it is given immediately following the behavior in question.[102] How effective can feedback be if it is given only once a year during an appraisal interview?

Second, for more than two decades we have known that when managers use a problem-solving approach, subordinates express a stronger motivation to improve performance than when other approaches are used.[103] Yet evidence indicates that most organizations still use a "tell-and-sell" approach in which a manager completes an appraisal independently, shows it to the subordinate, justifies the rating, discusses what must be done to improve performance, and then asks for the subordinate's reaction and sign-off on the appraisal.[104] Are the negative reactions of subordinates really that surprising?

IMPACT OF PERFORMANCE MANAGEMENT ON PRODUCTIVITY, QUALITY OF WORK LIFE, AND THE BOTTOM LINE

Performance management is fundamentally a feedback process. And research indicates that feedback may result in increases in performance varying from 10 to 30 percent.[99] That is a fairly inexpensive way to improve productivity; but, to work effectively, feedback programs require sustained commitment. The challenge for managers, then, is to provide feedback regularly to all their employees.

From an employee's perspective, lack of regular feedback about performance detracts from his or her quality of work life. Most people want to improve their performance on the job, to receive constructive suggestions regarding areas they need to work on, and to be commended for things that they do well. The cost of failure to provide such feedback may result in the loss of key professional employees, the continued poor performance of employees who are not meeting performance standards, and a loss of commitment by all employees. In sum, the myth that employees know how they are doing without adequate feedback from management can be an expensive fantasy.[100]

If organizations really are serious about fostering improved job performance as a result of performance feedback interviews, the kinds of activities shown in Table 9–2 are essential before, during, and after the interview. Let's briefly examine each of these important activities.

Communicate Frequently. Research on the appraisal interview at General Electric indicated clearly that once-a-year performance appraisals are of questionable value and that coaching should be a day-to-day activity[105]—particularly with poor performers or new employees.[106] Feedback has maximum impact when it is given as close as possible to the action. If a subordinate behaves effectively (ineffectively), tell him or her immediately. Don't file incidents away so that they can be discussed in 6 to 9 months.

Research strongly supports this view. Thus one study found that communication of performance feedback in an interview is most effective when the subordinate already has relatively accurate perceptions of her or his performance before the session.[107]

Get Training in Performance Feedback and Appraisal Interviewing. As we noted earlier, train raters to observe behavior more accurately and fairly. Focus on managerial characteristics that are difficult to rate and on characteristics that people think are easy to rate but which generally result in disagreements. Such

Table 9–2

SUPERVISORY ACTIVITIES BEFORE, DURING, AND AFTER PERFORMANCE FEEDBACK INTERVIEWS

Before

Communicate frequently with subordinates about their performance.
Get training in performance appraisal interviewing.
Plan to use a problem-solving approach rather than "tell-and-sell."
Encourage subordinates to prepare for performance feedback interviews.

During

Encourage subordinates to participate.
Judge performance, not personality and mannerisms.
Be specific.
Be an active listener.
Avoid destructive criticism.
Set mutually agreeable goals for future improvements.

After

Communicate frequently with subordinates about their performance.
Periodically assess progress toward goals.
Make organizational rewards contingent on performance.

factors include risk taking and development of subordinates.[108] Use a problem-solving, rather than a "tell-and-sell," approach, as noted earlier.

Encourage Subordinates to Prepare. Research conducted across a variety of organizations has yielded consistent results. Subordinates who spend more time prior to performance feedback interviews analyzing their job responsibilities and duties, problems they encounter on the job, and the quality of their performance are more likely to be satisfied with the performance management process, more likely to be motivated to improve their performance, and more likely actually to improve.[109]

Encourage Participation. A perception of ownership—a feeling by the subordinate that his or her ideas are genuinely welcomed by the manager—is related strongly to subordinates' satisfaction with the appraisal interview, the appraisal system, motivation to improve performance, and the perceived fairness of the system.[110] Participation provides an opportunity for employee voice in performance appraisal. It encourages the belief that the interview was a fair process, that it was a constructive activity, that some current job problems were cleared up, and that future goals were set.[111]

Judge Performance, Not Personality. In addition to the potential legal liability of dwelling on personality rather than on job performance, supervisors are far less likely to change a subordinate's personality than they are his or her job performance. Maintain the problem-solving, job-related focus established earlier, for evidence indicates that supervisory support enhances employees' motivation to improve.[112]

Be Specific, and Be an Active Listener. By being candid and specific, the supervisor offers clear feedback to the subordinate concerning past actions. She or he also demonstrates knowledge of the subordinate's level of performance and job duties. By being an active listener, the supervisor demonstrates genuine interest in the subordinate's ideas. **Active listening** requires that you do five things well: (1) Take the time to listen—hold all phone calls and do not allow interruptions. (2) Communicate verbally and nonverbally (e.g., by maintaining eye contact) that you genuinely want to help. (3) As the subordinate begins to tell his or her side of the story, do not interrupt and do not argue. (4) Watch for verbal as well as nonverbal cues regarding the subordinate's agreement or disagreement with your message. (5) Summarize what was said and what was agreed to. Specific feedback and active listening are essential to subordinates' perceptions of the fairness and accuracy of the process.[113]

Avoid Destructive Criticism. **Destructive criticism** is general in nature, frequently delivered in a biting, sarcastic tone, and often attributes poor performance to internal causes (e.g., lack of motivation or ability). It leads to three predictable consequences. (1) It produces negative feelings among recipients and can initiate or intensify conflict; (2) it reduces the preference of individuals for handling future disagreements with the giver of the feedback in a conciliatory manner (e.g., compromise, collaboration); and (3) it has negative effects on self-set goals and on feelings of self-confidence.[114] Needless to say, this is one type of communication to avoid.

Set Mutually Agreeable Goals.   How does goal setting work to improve performance? Studies demonstrate that goals direct attention to the specific performance in question, that they mobilize effort to accomplish higher levels of performance, and that they foster persistence for higher levels of performance.[115] The practical implications of this work are clear: set specific, challenging goals, for this clarifies for the subordinate precisely what is expected and leads to high levels of performance. We cannot change the past, but interviews that include goal setting and specific feedback can affect future job performance.

Continue to Communicate, and Assess Progress toward Goals Regularly.   Periodic tracking of progress toward goals has three advantages: (1) it helps keep behavior on target, (2) it provides a better understanding of the reasons behind a given level of performance, and (3) it enhances the subordinate's commitment to perform effectively. All of this helps to improve supervisor-subordinate work relationships. Improving supervisor-subordinate work relationships, in turn, has positive effects on performance.[116]

Make Organizational Rewards Contingent on Performance.   Research results are clear-cut on this point. If subordinates see a link between appraisal results and employment decisions regarding issues like merit pay and promotion, they are more likely to prepare for performance feedback interviews, to participate actively in them, and to be satisfied with the overall performance management system.[117] Furthermore, managers who base employment decisions on the results of appraisals are likely to overcome their subordinates' negative perceptions of the appraisal process.

Human Resource Management in Action: Conclusion

PERFORMANCE REVIEWS: PERILOUS CURVES AHEAD

Proponents of forced rankings argue that they facilitate budgeting and guard against spineless managers who are too afraid to jettison poor performers. Forced rankings, the thinking goes, force managers to be honest with workers about how they are doing.

Critics say they compel managers to penalize a good but not great employee who's part of a superstar team. Conversely, a mediocre employee on a struggling unit can come out looking great. Most companies guard against this problem by refraining from rigidly applying the distribution to smaller teams—but this means the spread has to be made up somewhere else. The result: Different managers spend hours haggling with one another to meet the overall distribution requirements. According to one middle manager at Microsoft, this horse-trading process can be frustrating and time-consuming. While the company says it does not require managers to assign a certain percentage of employees to each level, the middle manager says there is unspoken pressure to do so.

Another area of contention is the ranking criteria. In contrast to objective criteria, such as sales revenue generated or errorfree products produced, many organizations use fuzzy, qualitative criteria to evaluate employees. While there is no doubt that teamwork and communication skills are vital, they are tough to measure. After all, one manager's team player is another's yes-person. Indeed a

IMPLICATIONS FOR MANAGEMENT PRACTICE

Throughout this chapter we have emphasized the difficulty of implementing and sustaining performance-management systems. A basic issue for every manager is "What's in it for me?" If organizations are serious about improving the performance-management process, top management must consider the following policy changes:

- Make "quality of performance feedback to subordinates" and "development of subor-

dinates" integral parts of every manager's job description.

- Tie rewards to effective performance in these areas.
- Recognize that performance management and appraisal is a dialogue involving people and data; both political and interpersonal issues are involved. No appraisal method is perfect, but with management commitment and employee "buy-in," performance management can be a very useful and powerful tool.

---

senior manager at one large firm admits that the company's ranking criteria are "very subjective," adding, "There aren't easy labels for what type of person someone is."

So is this spate of new forced-ranking systems an anomaly or a taste of things to come? One employment lawyer predicts a lot of litigation surrounding this issue. Managers had better get ready.

SUMMARY

Performance management requires a willingness and a commitment to focus on improving performance at the level of the individual or team *every day*. Like a compass, an ongoing performance management system provides instantaneous, real-time information that describes the difference between one's current and desired course. To practice sound performance management, managers must do the same thing—provide timely feedback about performance, while constantly focusing everyone's attention on the ultimate objective (e.g., world-class customer service).

At a general level, the broad process of performance management requires that you do three things well. Define performance (through goals, measures, and assessments), facilitate performance (by identifying obstacles to good performance and providing resources to accomplish objectives) and encourage performance (by providing timely rewards that people care about in a sufficient amount, and fairly).

Performance appraisal (the systematic description of the job-relevant strengths and weaknesses of an individual or a team), is a necessary, but not sufficient, part of the performance-management process. It serves two major purposes in organizations: (1) to improve the job performance of employees, and (2) to provide information to employees and managers for use in making decisions. In practice, many PA systems fail because they do not satisfy one or more of the following requirements: relevance, sensitivity, reliability, acceptability, and practicality. The failure is frequently accompanied by legal challenge to the system based on its adverse impact against one or more protected groups.

Performance appraisal is done once or twice a year in most organizations, but research indicates that this is far too infrequent. Do it upon the completion of projects or upon the achievement of important milestones. The specific rating method used depends on the purpose for which the appraisal is intended. Thus comparisons among employees are most appropriate for generating rankings for salary administration purposes, while MBO, work planning and review, and narrative essays are least appropriate for this purpose. For purposes of employee development, critical incidents or behaviorally anchored rating scales are most appropriate. Finally, the rating methods that focus on describing rather than evaluating behavior (e.g., BARS, behavioral checklists) are the most interpretable across raters.

Rater judgments are subject to various types of biases: leniency, severity, central tendency, and halo, contrast, and recency errors. To improve the reliability and validity of ratings, however, train raters to observe behavior more accurately rather than on showing them "how to" or "how not to" rate. To improve the value of performance feedback interviews, communicate frequently with subordinates; encourage them to prepare and to participate in the process; judge performance, not personality; be specific, avoid destructive criticism; set goals; assess progress toward goals regularly; and make rewards contingent on performance.

DISCUSSION QUESTIONS

9–1. What would an effective performance management system look like?

9–2. Working in small groups, develop a performance management system for a cashier in a neighborhood grocery with little technology but lots of personal touch.

9–3. The chief counsel for a large corporation comes to you for advice. She wants to know what makes a firm's appraisal system legally vulnerable. What would you tell her?

9–4. How can we overcome employee defensiveness in performance feedback interviews?

9–5. Can discussions of employee job performance be separated from salary considerations? If so, how?

KEY TERMS

performance management	practicality
performance appraisal	applicant group
performance definition	behavior-oriented rating methods
performance facilitation	relative rating systems
performance encouragement	absolute rating systems
relevance	results-oriented rating systems
performance standards	simple ranking
sensitivity	alternation ranking
reliability	paired comparisons
acceptability	forced distribution

leniency

severity

central tendency

Likert method

summed ratings

critical incidents

graphic rating scales

behaviorally anchored rating scales
  (BARS)

management by objectives (MBO)

cascading process

work planning and review

360-degree feedback

total quality management

halo error

contrast error

recency error

active listening

destructive criticism

APPLYING YOUR KNOWLEDGE

Problems in Appraisal at Peak Power   Case 9–1

Peak Power, a medium-size hydroelectric power plant near Seattle, Washington, has been having difficulty with its performance appraisal system. The plant's present appraisal system has been in existence for about 10 years and was designed by the head of administrative operations, a clerk who had been promoted into the position without any professional training in human resource management. Presently, all operating employees are evaluated once a year by their supervisors, using the following form:

PEAK POWER PERFORMANCE APPRAISAL FORM

General Instructions: This form is to be completed in triplicate, and all entries should be typewritten or printed in ink. After the employee's performance has been evaluated by the supervisor and reviewed by higher-level supervision, the employee will be informed of his or her performance rating and will sign all copies of the form indicating that he or she has been so informed. The employee's signature does not necessarily indicate that he or she agrees with the ratings given. Send one completed form to the human resources office, and allow the employee to keep a copy for his or her files. The other copy is the supervisor's.

Complete the form by marking "X" in the appropriate locations below.

Performance dimension	Excellent	Above average	Average	Below average	Poor
Quantity of work					
Quality of work					
Dependability					
Initiative					
Cooperativeness					
Leadership potential					

"Excellent" is worth 5 points, "Above average" is worth 4 points, "Average" is worth 3 points, "Below average" is worth 2 points, and "Poor" is worth 1 point. Determine the employee's overall evaluation by summing the appropriate number of points from each of the six dimension scores above, and write the total here: _____ .

Supervisor's signature _____

Employee's signature _____

Ratings from each year are maintained in employee files in the HR department. If promotions come up, the cumulative ratings are considered at that time. Further, ratings are supposed to be used as a check when raises are given. In practice, little use is made of the ratings, either for determination of promotions or for salary decisions. Employee feelings about the appraisal system range from indifference to outright hostility. A small, informal survey 2 years ago determined that supervisors spent on average about 3 minutes filling out the form, and less than 10 minutes discussing it with employees.

Recent problems in other areas of HR management at the plant and the fear of potential lawsuits led Peak's president to consider hiring an experienced HR professional to upgrade all HR systems. You are being interviewed for the job, and have just been presented with the above information.

Questions

1. The president asks you for your general evaluation of this appraisal system. What is your response?
2. The president asks you for some suggestions for ways in which the present system can be improved. How do you respond?
3. If you should be selected for this position, outline some steps you would take to ensure that a new performance management system will be accepted by its users.

REFERENCES

1. Cascio, W. F. (1996, Sept.). Managing for maximum performance. *HRMonthly* (Australia), pp. 10–13.
2. Pickett, L. (2001, Jan.). The annual fiasco. ARDTO Asia-Pacific HRD Center, Melbourne, Australia.
3. Bernardin, H. J., Hagan, C. M., Kane, J. S., & Villanova, P. (1998). Effective performance management. In J. W. Smither (ed.), *Performance appraisal: State of the art in practice.* San Francisco: Jossey-Bass, pp. 3–48.
4. Matsui, T., Kakuyama, T., & Onglatco, M. L. T. (1987). Effects of goals and feedback on performance in groups. *Journal of Applied Psychology, 72,* 407–415.
5. Tubbs, M. E. (1986). Goal setting: A meta-analytic examination of the empirical evidence. *Journal of Applied Psychology, 71,* 474–483.
6. Knight, D., Durham, C. C., & Locke, E. A. (2001). The relationship of team goals, incentives, and efficacy to strategic risk, tactical implementation, and performance. *Academy of Management Journal, 44,* 326–338.
7. Wood, R. E., Mento, A. J., & Locke, E. A. (1987). Task complexity as a moderator of goal effects: A meta-analysis. *Journal of Applied Psychology, 72,* 416–425.
8. Grensing-Pophal, L. (2001, Mar.). Motivate managers to review performance. *HRMagazine,* pp. 44–48.
9. Kerr, S., in Sherman S. (1995, Nov. 13). Stretch goals: The dark side of asking for miracles. *Fortune,* p. 31
10. Deutschman, A. (1994, Oct. 17) The managing wisdom of high-tech superstars. *Fortune,* pp. 197–205.

11. Gilliland, S. W., & Langdon, J. C. (1998). Creating performance management systems that promote perceptions of fairness. In J. W. Smither (ed.), *Performance appraisal: State of the art in practice.* San Francisco: Jossey-Bass, pp. 209–243.

12. Grensing-Pophal, op. cit. See also Schellhardt, T. D. (1996, Nov. 19). Annual agony: It's time to evaluate your work, and all involved are groaning. *The Wall Street Journal,* pp. A1, A5.

13. Cascio, W. F. (1998). Applied psychology in human resource management (5th ed.). Englewood Cliffs, NJ: Prentice-Hall.

14. Jacobs, R., Kafry, D., & Zedeck, S. (1980). Expectations of behaviorally anchored rating scales. *Personnel Psychology, 33,* 595–640.

15. Arvey, R. D., & Murphy, K. R. (1998). Performance evaluation in work settings. *Annual Review of Psychology, 49,* 141–168. See also Schellhardt, op. cit.

16. Moser, K., Schuler, H., & Funke, U. (1999). The moderating effect of raters' opportunities to observe ratees' job performance on the validity of an assessment center. *International Journal of Selection and Assessment, 7*(3), 355–367. See also Arvey & Murphy, op. cit. See also Ilgen, D. R., Barnes-Farrell, J. L., & McKellin, D. B. (1993). Performance appraisal process research in the 1980s: What has it contributed to appraisals in use? *Organizational Behavior and Human Decision Processes, 54,* 321–368.

17. Cascio, W. F. (1982). Scientific, legal, and operational imperatives of workable performance appraisal systems. *Public Personnel Management, 11,* 367–375.

18. Zedeck, S., & Cascio, W. F. (1982). Performance appraisal decisions as a function of rater training and purpose of the appraisal. *Journal of Applied Psychology, 67,* 752–758.

19. Viswesvaran, C., Ones, D. S., & Schmidt, F. L. (1996). Comparative analysis of the reliability of job performance ratings. *Journal of Applied Psychology, 81,* 557–574.

20. Borman, W. C. (1991). Job behavior, performance, and effectiveness. In M. D. Dunnette & L. M. Hough (eds.), *Handbook of industrial and organizational psychology* (vol. 2). Palo Alto, CA: Consulting Psychologists Press, pp. 271–326.

21. Schellhardt, op. cit.

22. Mayer, R. C., & Davis, J. H. (1999). The effect of the performance appraisal system on trust for management: A field quasi-experiment. *Journal of Applied Psychology, 84,* 123–136. See also Taylor, M. S., Masterson, S. S., Renard, M. K., & Tracy, K. B. (1998). Managers' reactions to procedurally just performance management systems. *Academy of Management Journal, 41,* 568–579.

23. For a comprehensive review, see Malos, S. B. (1998). Current legal issues in performance appraisal. In J. W. Smither (ed.), *Performance appraisal: State of the art in practice.* San Francisco: Jossey-Bass, pp. 49–94.

24. *Paquin v. Federal National Mortgage Association* (1996, July 31). Civil Action No. 94-1261 SSH.

25. *Stone v. Xerox* (1982). 685 F. 2d 1387 (11th Cir.).

26. *United States v. City of Chicago* (1978). 573 F. 2d 416 (7th Cir.).

27. LeBoeuf, M. (1987). *The greatest management principle in the world.* New York: Berkley Publishing Co.

28. Marentette, D. (2000). *Performance management systems: A vital key to retention.* Minneapolis, MN: Personnel Decisions International.

29. Cascio, W. F., & Serapio, M. G., Jr. (1991, Winter). Human resource systems in an international alliance: The undoing of a done deal? *Organizational Dynamics* 63–74. See also Schneider, S. C. (1988). National versus corporate culture: Implications for human resource management. *Human Resource Management, 27,* 231–246.

30. Guion, R. M. (1986). Personnel evaluation. In R. A. Berk (ed.), *Performance assessment.* Baltimore: Johns Hopkins University Press, pp. 345–360. Bernardin, H. J., & Beatty, R. W. (1984). *Performance appraisal: Assessing human behavior at work.* Boston: Kent.

31. Murphy, K. R., & Cleveland, J. N. (1991). *Performance appraisal: An organizational perspective.* Boston: Allyn & Bacon. See also Heneman, R. L. (1986). The relationship

between supervisory ratings and results-oriented measures of performance: A meta-analysis. *Personnel Psychology, 39,* 811–826.

32. Cascio, W. F., & Barnardin, H. J. (1981). Implications of performance appraisal litigation for personnel decisions. *Personnel Psychology, 34,* 211–226.

33. Bernardin, H. J., Cooke, D. K., & Villanova, P. (2000). Conscientiousness and agreeableness as predictors of rating leniency. *Journal of Applied Psychology, 85,* 232–234.

34. Stockford, L., & Bissell, H. W. (1949). Factors involved in establishing a merit rating scale. *Personnel, 26,* 94–116.

35. Landy, F. J., & Rastegary, H. (1988). Criteria for selection. In M. Smith & I. Robertson (eds.), *Advances in personnel selection and assessment.* New York: Wiley, pp. 68–115.

36. Cascio (1998), op. cit.

37. Bernardin, H. J., & Smith, P. C. (1981). A clarification of some issues regarding the development and use of behaviorally anchored rating scales. *Journal of Applied Psychology, 66,* 458–463.

38. Borman, W. C. (1991). Job behavior, performance, and effectiveness. In M. D. Dunnette & L. M. Hough (eds.), *Handbook of industrial and organizational psychology* (vol. 2). Palo Alto, CA: Consulting Psychologists Press, pp. 271–326.

39. Campbell, J. P., Dunnette, M. D., Lawler, E. E., & Weick, K. E. (1970). *Managerial behavior, performance, and effectiveness.* New York: McGraw-Hill.

40. McConkie, M. L. (1979). A clarification of the goal-setting and appraisal process in MBO. *Academy of Management Review, 4,* 29–40.

41. Grote, D. (2000, Jan.–Feb.). Performance appraisal reappraised. *Harvard Business Review,* p. 21.

42. Albrecht, K. (1978). *Successful management by objectives: An action manual.* Englewood Cliffs, NJ: Prentice-Hall. See also Odiorne, G. S. (1965). *Management by objectives: A system of managerial leadership.* Belmont, CA: Fearon.

43. Barton, R. F. (1981). An MCDM approach for resolving goal conflict in MBO. *Academy of Management Review, 6,* 231–241.

44. Kondrasuk, J. N. (1981). Studies in MBO effectiveness. *Academy of Management Review, 6,* 419–430.

45. Meyer, H. H., Kay, E., & French, J. R. P. (1965). Split roles in performance appraisal. *Harvard Business Review, 43,* 123–129.

46. Bernardin & Beatty, op. cit.

47. Hartel, C. E. J. (1993). Rating format research revisited: Format effectiveness and acceptability depend on rater characteristics. *Journal of Applied Psychology, 78,* 212–217.

48. Locher, A. H., & Teel, K. S. (1988, Sept.). Appraisal trends. *Personnel Journal,* pp. 139–145.

49. *Performance management survey* (2000). Alexandria, VA: Society for Human Resource Management.

50. Ghorpade, J., & Chen, M. M. (1995). Creating quality-driven performance appraisal systems. *Academy of Management Executive, 9*(1), 32–39.

51. Becker, T. E., & Klimoski, R. J. (1989). A field study of the relationship between the organizational feedback environment and performance. *Personnel Psychology, 42,* 353–358.

52. McEvoy, G. M., & Buller, P. F. (1987). User acceptance of peer appraisals in an industrial setting. *Personnel Psychology, 40,* 785–787.

53. Lancaster, H. (1998, Dec. 1). Performance reviews: Some bosses try a fresh approach. *The Wall Street Journal,* p. B1. Labor Letter. (1990, Oct. 16). *The Wall Street Journal,* p. A1.

54. Druskat, V. U., & Wolff, S. B. (1999). Effects and timing of developmental peer appraisals in self-managing work groups. *Journal of Applied Psychology, 84,* 58–74.

55. Reilly, R. R., Smither, J. W., & Vasilopoulos, N. L. (1996). A longitudinal study of upward feedback. *Personnel Psychology, 49,* 599–612. See also Smither, J. W., London, M., Vasilopoulos, N. L., Reilly, R. R., Milisap, R., & Salvemini, N. (1995). An examination of the effects of an upward feedback program over time. *Personnel Psychology, 48,* 1–34.

56. Atwater, L. E., Waldman, D. A., Atwater, D., & Cartier, P. (2000). An upward feedback field experiment: Supervisors' cynicism, reactions, and commitment to subordinates. *Personnel Psychology, 53,* 297.

57. Walker, A. G., & Smither, J. W. (1999). A five-year study of upward feedback: What managers do with their results matters. *Personnel Psychology, 52,* 393–423.

58. Antonioni, D. (1994). The effects of feedback accountability on upward appraisal ratings. *Personnel Psychology, 47,* 249–256.

59. Maurer, T. J., Raju, N. S., & Collins, W. C. (1998). Peer and subordinate performance appraisal measurement equivalence. *Journal of Applied Psychology, 83,* 693–702.

60. Campbell, D. J., & Lee, C. (1988). Self-appraisal in performance evaluation: Development versus evaluation. *Academy of Management Review, 13,* 302–314.

61. Cheung, G. W. (1999). Multifaceted conceptions of self-other ratings disagreement. *Personnel Psychology, 52,* 1–36. See also Fox, S., & Dinur, Y. (1988). Validity of self-assessment: A field evaluation. *Personnel Psychology, 41,* 581–592. See also Harris, M., & Schaubroeck, J. (1988). A meta-analysis of self-supervisory, self-peer, and peer-supervisory ratings. *Personnel Psychology, 41,* 43–62.

62. Atwater, L. E., Ostroff, C., Yammarino, F. J., & Fleenor, J. W. (1998). Self-other agreement: Does it really matter? *Personnel Psychology, 51,* 577–598.

63. Yu, J., & Murphy, K. R. (1993). Modesty bias in self-ratings of performance: A test of the cultural relativity hypothesis. *Personnel Psychology, 46,* 357–363. But see also Farh, J. L., Dobbins, G. H., & Cheng, B. S. (1991). Cultural relativity in action: A comparison of self-ratings made by Chinese and U.S. workers. *Personnel Psychology, 44,* 129–147.

64. Ulrich, D. (1989, Summer). Tie the corporate knot: Gaining complete customer commitment. *Sloan Management Review, 10*(4), 19–27, 63.

65. Piller, C. (1993, July). Privacy in peril. *Macworld,* pp. 124–130. See also Brophy, B. (1986, Sept. 29). New technology, high anxiety. *U.S. News & World Report,* pp. 54, 55.

66. Nebeker, D. M., & Tatum, C. B. (1993). The effects of computer monitoring, standards, and rewards on work performance and stress. *Journal of Applied Social Psychology, 28,* 508–534. See also Chalykoff, J., & Kochan, T. A. (1989). Computer-aided monitoring: Its influence on employee job satisfaction and turnover. *Personnel Psychology, 42,* 807–834.

67. Brophy, op. cit.

68. *Performance management survey,* op. cit.

69. Waldman, D., & Atwater, L. E. (1998). *The power of 360-degree feedback: How to leverage performance evaluations for top productivity.* Houston, TX: Gulf Publishing. See also Borman, W. C. (1997). 360-degree ratings: An analysis of assumptions and a research agenda for assessing their validity. *Human Resource Management Review, 7,* 299–315.

70. Conway, J. M., & Huffcutt, A. I. (1997). Psychometric properties of multisource performance ratings: A meta-analysis of subordinate, supervisor, peer, and self-ratings. *Human Performance, 10,* 331–360.

71. Facteua, J. D., & Craig, S. B. (2001). Are performance appraisal ratings from different rating sources comparable? *Journal of Applied Psychology, 86,* 215–227.

72. Scullen, S. E., Mount, M. K., & Goff, M. (2000). Understanding the latent structure of performance ratings. *Journal of Applied Psychology, 85,* 956–970.

73. DeNisi, A. S., & Kluger, A. N. (2000). Feedback effectiveness: Can 360-degree appraisals be improved? *Academy of Management Executive, 14*(1), 129–139.

74. Ghorpade, J. (2000). Managing the five paradoxes of 360-degree feedback. *Academy of Management Executive, 14*(1), 140–150. See also Waldinan, D. A., Atwater, L. E., & Antonioni, D. (1998). Has 360-degree feedback gone amok? *Academy of Management Executive, 12*(2), 86–94.

75. Kozlowski, S. W. J., Chao, G. T., & Morrison, R. F. (1998). Games raters play. In J. W. Smither (ed.) *Performance appraisal: State of the art in practice.* San Francisco: Jossey-Bass, pp. 163–205. See also Mount, M. K., Judge, T. A., Scullen, S. E., Sytsma, M. R., & Hezlett, S. A. (1998). Trait, rater, and level effects in 360-degree performance ratings. *Personnel Psychology, 51,* 557–576.

76. Parmenter, D. (1999, Dec.). Implementing 360-degree feedback. *Human Resources* (New Zealand), pp. 18–19.

77. Schellhardt, op. cit. See also Meyer et al., op. cit.

78. Labor letter, op. cit.

79. Mount, M. K., & Thompson, D. E. (1987). Cognitive categorization and quality of performance ratings. *Journal of Applied Psychology, 72,* 240–246.

80. Hogan, E. A. (1987). Effects of prior expectations on performance ratings: A longitudinal study. *Academy of Management Journal, 30,* 354–368.

81. Schellhardt, op. cit.

82. Campbell, R. B., & Garfinkel, L. M. (1996, June). Strategies for success in measuring performance. *HRMagazine,* 99–104.

83. Wiedman, T. G. (1993, Oct.) Performance appraisal in a total quality management environment. *The Industrial-Organizational Psychologist, 31*(2), pp. 64–66.

84. Deming, W. E. (1986). *Out of the crisis.* Cambridge, MA: MIT Center for Advanced Engineering Study.

85. Wiedman, op. cit.

86. Total quality and performance appraisal. (1992, Oct.). *Bulletin.* Denver: Mountain States Employers Council, Inc., p. 5.

87. McEvoy, G. M., & Cascio, W. F. (1990). The United States and Taiwan: Two different cultures look at performance appraisal. *Research in Personnel and Human Resources Management* (Suppl. 2), pp. 201–219.

88. Varma, A., DeNisi, A., & Peters, L. M. (1996). Interpersonal affect and performance appraisal: A field study. *Personnel Psychology, 49,* 341–360.

89. Hogan, op. cit.

90. Murphy, K. R., Jako, R. A., & Anhalt, R. L. (1993). Nature and consequences of halo error: A critical analysis. *Journal of Applied Psychology, 78,* 218–225.

91. Murphy, K. R., & Anhalt, R. L. (1992). Is halo error a property of the rater, ratees, or the specific behavior observed? *Journal of Applied Psychology, 77,* 494–500.

92. Balzer, W. K., & Sulsky, L. M. (1992). Halo and performance appraisal research: A critical examination. *Journal of Applied Psychology, 77,* 975–985.

93. Sumer, H. C., & Knight, P. A. (1996). Assimilation and contrast effects in performance ratings: Effects of rating the previous performance on rating subsequent performance. *Journal of Applied Psychology, 81,* 436–442. See also Maurer, T. J., Palmer, J. K., & Ashe, D. K. (1993). Diaries, checklists, evaluations, and contrast effects in the measurement of behavior. *Journal of Applied Psychology, 78,* 226–231.

94. Longenecker, C. O., Sims, H. P., Jr., & Gioia, D. A. (1987). Behind the mask: The politics of employee appraisal. *Academy of Management Executive, 1,* 183–193.

95. Murphy, K. R., & Balzer, W. K. (1989). Rater errors and rating accuracy. *Journal of Applied Psychology, 74,* 619–624. See also Smith, D. E. (1986). Training programs for performance appraisal: A review. *Academy of Management Review, 11,* 22–40.

96. Pulakos, E. D. (1986). The development of training programs to increase accuracy with different rating tasks. *Organizational Behavior and Human Decision Processes, 38,* 76–91. See also Latham, G. P., Wexley, K. N., & Pursell, E. D. (1975). Training managers to minimize rating errors in the observation of behavior. *Journal of Applied Psychology, 60,* 550–555.

97. Smith, op. cit.

98. Sanchez, J. I., & DeLaTorre, P. (1996). A second look at the relationship between rating and behavioral accuracy in performance appraisal. *Journal of Applied Psychology, 81,* 3–10. See also Day, D. V., & Sulsky, L. M. (1995). Effects of frame-of-reference training and information configuration on memory organization and rating accuracy. *Journal of Applied Psychology, 80,* 159–167.

99. Landy, F. J., Farr, J. L., & Jacobs, R. R. (1982). Utility concepts in performance measurement. *Organizational Behavior and Human Performance, 30,* 15–40.

100. Joinson, C. (1996, August). Re-creating the indifferent employee. *HRMagazine,* pp. 77–80. See also Darling, M. J. (1994, November). Coaching people through difficult times. *HRMagazine,* pp. 70–73.

101. Schellhardt, op. cit.

102. Murphy & Cleveland, op. cit.

103. Wexley, K. N., Singh, V. P., & Yukl, G. A. (1973). Subordinate participation in three types of appraisal interviews. *Journal of Applied Psychology, 58,* 54–57.

104. Schellhardt, op. cit. See also Wexley, K. N. (1986). Appraisal interview. In R. A. Berk (ed.), *Performance assessment.* Baltimore: Johns Hopkins University Press, pp. 167–185.

105. Meyer et al., op. cit.

106. Cederblom, D. (1982). The performance appraisal interview: A review, implications, and suggestions. *Academy of Management Review, 7,* 219–227.

107. Ilgen, D. R., Mitchell, T. R., & Frederickson, J. W. (1981). Poor performers: Supervisors' and subordinates' responses. *Organizational Behavior and Human Performance, 27,* 386–410.

108. Wohlers, A. J., & London, M. (1989). Ratings of managerial characteristics: Evaluation, difficulty, co-worker agreement, and self-awareness. *Personnel Psychology, 42,* 235–261.

109. Cawley, B. D., Keeping, L. M., & Levy, P. E. (1998). Participation in the performance appraisal process and employee reactions: A meta-analytic review of field investigations. *Journal of Applied Psychology, 83,* 615–633.

110. Ibid.

111. Dulebohn, J. H., & Ferris, G. R. (1999). The role of influence tactics in perceptions of performance evaluations' fairness. *Academy of Management Journal, 42,* 288–303. See also Nathan, B. R., Mohrman, A. M., Jr., & Milliman, J. (1991). Interpersonal relations as a context for the effects of appraisal interviews on performance and satisfaction: A longitudinal study. *Academy of Management Journal, 34*(2), 352–369.

112. Dorfman, P. W., Stephan, W. G., & Loveland, J. (1986). Performance appraisal behaviors: Supervisor perceptions and subordinate reactions. *Personnel Psychology, 39,* 579–597.

113. Landy, F. J., Barnes-Farrell, J., & Cleveland, J. N. (1980). Perceived fairness and accuracy of performance evaluation: A follow-up. *Journal of Applied Psychology, 65,* 355–356.

114. Baron, R. A. (1988). Negative effects of destructive criticism: Impact on conflict, self-efficacy, and task performance. *Journal of Applied Psychology, 73,* 199–207.

115. Locke, E. A., & Latham, G. P. (1990). *A theory of goal setting and task performance.* Englewood Cliffs, NJ: Prentice-Hall. See also Tubbs, M. E. (1986). Goal setting: A meta-analytic examination of the empirical evidence. *Journal of Applied Psychology, 71,* 474–483.

116. Judge, T. A., & Ferris, G. R. (1993). Social context of performance evaluation decisions. *Academy of Management Journal, 36,* 80–105.

117. Burke, R. S., Weitzel, W., & Weir, T. (1978). Characteristics of effective employee performance review and development interviews: Replication and extension. *Personnel Psychology, 31,* 903–919.

MANAGING CAREERS

10

Questions This Chapter Will Help Managers Answer

1. What strategies might be used to help employees "self-manage" their careers?
2. What can supervisors do to improve their management of dual-career couples?
3. Why are the characteristics and environment of an employee's first job so important?
4. What steps can managers take to do a better job of responding to the special needs of workers in their early, middle, and late career stages?
5. How can layoffs be handled in the most humane way?

SELF-RELIANCE: KEY TO CAREER MANAGEMENT FOR THE 21ST CENTURY*

Consider this stark fact: In today's corporate environment, you are ever more likely to crash into the ranks of the unemployed with no safety net, and it could happen over and over again. Moreover, candor about career issues is in short supply at many companies these days. Bottom line: Career survival is up to you—not the company. Consider yourself to be self-employed, responsible for your own career development, CEO of You, Inc. This new approach is based on an underlying assumption that would have been considered heresy 10 or 20 years ago in the paternalistic, "We'll take care of you" environments of many companies—the assumption that self-reliance is the key to career management in the 21st century.

In the past, many companies assumed responsibility for the career paths and growth of their employees. The company determined to what position, and at what speed, people would advance. That approach worked reasonably well in the corporate climate of the last three decades. However, the corporate disruptions of the last decade have rendered this approach to employee career development largely unworkable.

Acquisitions, divestitures, rapid growth, and downsizing have left many companies unable to deliver on the implicit career promises made to their employees. Organizations find themselves in the painful position of having to renege on career mobility opportunities their employees had come to expect. In extreme cases, employees who expected career growth no longer even have jobs!

Increasingly, corporations have come to realize that they cannot win if they take total responsibility for the career development of their employees. No matter what happens, employees often blame top management or "the company" for their lack of career growth.

One company changed its approach to career growth as a result of pressure from its professional workforce. Employees felt suffocated by 20-plus years of management's determining people's career progress for them. Task teams worked with top management to develop career self-management training for employees and career counseling skills for managers. The resulting increases in employee productivity, enhanced morale, and decreased turnover of key employees have more than justified the new approach to employee career management.

Characteristics of the New Approach

Although the primary and final responsibility for career development rests with each employee, the company has complementary responsibilities. The

---

*For more information on the new approach to career self-management, see W. F. Cascio, The changing world of work: preparing yourself for the road ahead, in J. M. Kummerow (ed.), *New directions in career planning and the workplace,* Palo Alto, CA, Davies-Black, 2000, pp. 3–31. See also J. A. Waterman, Informed opportunism: Career and life planning for the new millennium, in J. M. Kummerow (ed.), *New directions in career planning and the workplace,* Palo Alto, CA, Davies-Black, 2000, pp. 163–196. See also W. J. Morin, You are absolutely, positively on your own, *Fortune,* Dec. 9, 2000, p. 222. See also D. T. Hall, Protean careers of the 21st century, *Academy of Management Executive, 10*(4), 1996, pp. 8–16. See also E. H. Schein, Career anchors revisited: Implications for career development in the 21st century, *Academy of Management Executive, 10*(4), 1996, pp. 80–88.

company is responsible for communicating to employees where it wants to go and how it plans to get there (the corporate strategy), providing employees with as much information about the business as possible, and responding to the career initiatives of employees with candid, complete information. One of the most important contributions a company can make to each employee's development is to provide him or her with honest performance feedback about current job performance. Employees, in turn, are responsible for knowing what their skills and capabilities are and what assistance they need from their employers, asking for that assistance, and preparing themselves to assume new responsibilities. Career self-reliance, or career resilience, as it is sometimes called, does not mean free agency. Rather, each individual needs to become an "informed opportunist," combining accurate information with a flexible, opportunistic approach to his or her career.

This approach to career management can be summed up as follows: Assign employees the responsibility for managing their own careers, and then provide the support they need to do it. This support takes different forms in different companies but usually contains several core components—as we will see in the conclusion to this vignette, at the end of the chapter.

Challenges

1. Should employees be responsible for their own career development?
2. Is the new approach to corporate career management likely to be a passing fad, or is it here to stay?
3. What kinds of support mechanisms are necessary to make career self-management work?

As the chapter opening vignette demonstrates, corporate career management has come a long way in the last several decades. This chapter presents a number of topics that have sparked this reevaluation. We will consider the impact of mergers, acquisitions, and downsizing on corporate loyalty, the impact of dual-career couples on the career management process, and the major issues that workers and managers must deal with during the early, middle, and late career stages of the adult life cycle. Finally, we will examine alternative patterns of career change: promotions, demotions, lateral transfers, relocations, layoffs, and retirements. Career management has many facets, both for the individual and for the organization. The chapter opening vignette emphasized that in the new concept of career management the company and the employee are partners in career development. This chapter emphasizes that theme. Let's begin by attempting to define the word "career."

TOWARD A DEFINITION OF "CAREER"

In everyday parlance, the word career is used in a number of different ways. People speak of "pursuing a career"; "career-planning" workshops are common; colleges and universities hold "career days" during which they publicize jobs in different fields and assist individuals through "career counseling." A person may be characterized as a "career" woman or man who shops in a store that specializes in "career clothing." Likewise, a person may be characterized as a "career military officer." We may overhear a person say, "That movie 'made' his career" (i.e., it enhanced his reputation) or in a derogatory tone, after a subordinate has insulted the CEO, "She can kiss her career good-bye" (i.e., she has tarnished her reputation). Finally, an angry supervisor may remark to her dawdling subordinate, "Watney, are you going to make a career out of changing that lightbulb?"

As these examples illustrate, the word "**career**" can be viewed from a number of different perspectives. From one perspective *a career is a sequence of positions occupied by a person during the course of a lifetime.* This is the *objective* career. From another perspective, though, *a career consists of a sense of where one is going in one's work life.* This is the *subjective* career, and it is held together by a self-concept that consists of (1) perceived talents and abilities, (2) basic values, and (3) career motives and needs.[1] Both of these perspectives, objective and subjective, focus on the individual. Both assume that people have some degree of control over their destinies and that they can manipulate opportunities in order to maximize the success and satisfaction derived from their careers.[2] They assume further that HR activities should recognize career stages and assist employees with the development tasks they face at each stage. Career planning is important because the consequences of career success or failure are linked closely to each individual's self-concept, identity, and satisfaction with career and life.

Given the downsizing mentality that has characterized most large organizations over the past decade, career development and planning have been deemphasized in some firms as employees wondered whether they would even have jobs, much less careers. Companies that ignore career issues are mistaken if they think those issues will somehow go away. They won't. Here are some reasons[3]:

1. Rising concerns for quality of work life and for personal life planning.
2. Pressures to expand workforce diversity throughout all levels of an organization.[4]
3. Rising educational levels and occupational aspirations, coupled with
4. Slow economic growth and reduced opportunities for advancement.

PROACTIVE CAREER MANAGEMENT

A career is not something that should be left to chance; instead, in the evolving world of work it should be shaped and managed more by the individual than by the organization.[5] Traditionally, careers tended to evolve in the context of one or two firms and to progress in linear stages, as one moved upward through the hierarchy of positions in an organization. Today, given the disruptions caused by downsizing, restructuring, technological advancements, and global competition, careers span multiple organizations and are distinctly nonlinear. They are *boundaryless,* and tend to be characterized by features such as the following[6]:

- Portable knowledge, skills, and abilities across multiple firms.
- Personal identification with meaningful work.
- On-the-job action learning.
- Development of multiple networks of associates and peer-learning relationships.
- Responsibility for managing one's own career.

The concept of a boundaryless career raises an interesting question—namely, what is the meaning of "career success"?

Toward a Definition of "Career Success"

The tradition-oriented "organization man" of the 1950s had a clear definition of success and a stable model for achieving it. However, massive changes in the business environment have forced employees at all levels to explore alternative models of **career success,** and they are confronted with a variety of possibilities.[7] Is it occupational success? Job satisfaction? Growth and development of skills? Successful movement through various life stages? Traditionally, career development and success have been defined in terms of occupational advancement, which is clear and easy to measure. Today, however, it seems appropriate to consider a new model, as more careers tend to be cyclical in nature. That is, they involve periodic cycles of skill apprenticeship, mastery, and reskilling. Lateral, rather than upward movement, often constitutes career development, and cross-functional experience is essential to multiskilling and continued employability. Late careers increasingly are defined in terms of phased retirement.[8] In this new world, the ultimate goal is *psychological success,* the feeling of pride and personal accomplishment that comes from achieving one's most important goals in life, be they achievement, family happiness, inner peace, or something else.[9] The following section examines career management in more detail; by way of background to this, let's consider the adult life-cycle stages.

Adult Life-Cycle Stages

For years, researchers have attempted to identify the major developmental tasks that employees face during their working lives and to organize these tasks into broader career stages (such as early, middle, and late career). Although a number of models have been proposed, very little research has tested their accuracy. Moreover, there is little, if any, agreement about whether career stages are linked to age or not. Most theorists give age ranges for each stage, but these vary widely. Consequently, it may make more sense to think in terms of career stages linked to time. This would allow a "career clock" to begin at different points for different individuals, based on their backgrounds and experiences.[10]

Such an approach allows for differences in the number of distinct stages through which individuals may pass, the overlapping tasks and issues they may face at each stage, and the role of transition periods between stages. The lesson for managers is that all models of adult life-cycle stages should be viewed as broad guidelines rather than as exact representations of reality.

MERGERS, ACQUISITIONS, RESTRUCTURINGS, AND THE DEMISE OF CORPORATE LOYALTY

Worldwide, more than 287,000 mergers and acquisitions took place between 1990 and 2000 among both large and small companies.[11] In general, after a buyout, the merged company eliminates staff duplications and unprofitable divisions. Restructuring, including downsizing, often leads to similar effects—diminished loyalty from employees. In the wave of takeovers, mergers, downsizings, and layoffs, thousands of workers have discovered that years of service mean little to a struggling management or a new corporate parent. This leads to a rise in stress and a decrease in satisfaction, commitment, intentions to stay, and perceptions of an organization's trustworthiness, honesty, and caring about its employees.[12]

Companies counter that today's competitive business environment makes it difficult to protect workers. Understandably, organizations are streamlining in order to become more competitive by cutting labor costs and to become more flexible in their response to the demands of the marketplace. But the rising disaffection of workers at all levels has profound implications for employers.

U.S. companies now lose half their employees every four years, half their customers in 5 years, and half their investors in fewer than 12 months.[13] Among workers 25 to 34, average time on the job was 3 years in 2000, and just 13 months in information technology.[14] Furthermore, employee turnover is expensive. It costs as much as $100,000 (in 2001 dollars) in the case of a middle manager, and 3 to 5 times annual salary for a CEO.[15] The average worker goes through about nine jobs by age 32, and 10 percent of the American workforce actually switches occupations every year![16] Yet there is hope, as companies like Monsanto, United Technologies, and Xerox recognize an opportunity to create value in the midst of such turmoil. How? By understanding that they can only retain loyal customers with a base of loyal employees.[17] Decreasing defection rates of customers, employees, and investors can lead to substantial growth, profits, and lasting value. That's a win-win for all concerned.

CAREER MANAGEMENT: INDIVIDUALS FOCUSING ON THEMSELVES

In thinking about career management, it is important to emphasize the increasingly *temporary* relationships between individuals and organizations. Said a victim of three corporate downsizings in four years: "A job is just an opportunity to learn new skills that you can then peddle elsewhere in the marketplace."[18] While such a view might appear cynical to some, the fact is that responsibility for career development ultimately belongs to each individual. Unfortunately, few individuals are technically prepared (and willing) to handle this assignment. This is not surprising, for very few college programs specifically address the problems of managing one's own career. However, as long as it remains difficult for organizations to match the career expectations of their employees (a later section of this chapter shows actual corporate examples of this), one option for employees will be to switch organizations. Guidelines for doing this fall into the following three major categories.[19]

Selecting a Field of Employment and an Employer

1. You cannot manage your career unless you have a macro, long-range objective. The first step, therefore, is to think in terms of where you ultimately want to be, recognizing, of course, that your career goals will change over time.

2. View every potential employer and position in terms of your long-range career goal. That is, ask yourself: How well does this job serve to position me in terms of my ultimate objective? For example, if you aspire to reach senior management by the year 2010, consider the extent to which your current job helps you develop a global orientation, develop public speaking skills, practice the "bring out the best in people" leadership style, and learn to manage cultural diversity. These are now, and will continue to be, key requirements for such senior positions.[20]

3. Accept short-term trade-offs for long-term benefits. Certain lateral moves or low-paying jobs can provide extremely valuable training opportunities or career contacts.

4. Consider carefully whether to accept highly specialized jobs or isolated job assignments that might restrict or impede your visibility and career development.

Knowing Where You Are

1. Always be aware of opportunities available to you in your current position—for instance, training programs that might further your career development.

2. Carefully and honestly assess your current performance. How do you see yourself, and how do you think higher management sees your performance? Ask yourself, "Am I in the right job? Are my skills of real value to my organization? What other positions might fit my needs and skills well?"[21]

3. Try to recognize when you and your organization have outlived your utility for each other. This is not an admission of failure but rather an honest reflection of the fact that there is little more the organization can do for you and, in turn, that your contribution to the organization has reached a point of diminishing returns.

Here are five important symptoms: You're not excited by what you are doing, advancement is blocked, your organization is poorly managed and is losing market share, you feel you are not adequately rewarded for your work, or you are not fulfilling your dreams.[22]

Planning Your Exit

1. Try to leave at your convenience, not the organization's. To do this, you must do two things well: (a) know when it is time to leave (as before), and (b) since downsizing can come at any time, establish networking relationships while you still have a job.

2. Leave your current organization on good terms and not under questionable circumstances.

3. Don't leave your current job until you've landed another one, for it's easier to find a new job when you're currently employed. Like bank loans, jobs often go to people who don't seem to need them.[23]

The Role of the Organization

Up to this point it may sound as though managing your career is all one-sided. This is not true; the organization should be a proactive force in this process. To do so, organizations must think and plan in terms of shorter employment relationships. This can be done, as it often is in professional sports, through fixed-term employment contracts with options for renegotiation and extension.

A second strategy for organizations is to invest adequate time and energy in job design and equipment. Given that mobility among workers is expected to increase, careful attention to these elements will make it easier to make replacements fully productive as soon as possible. How does the self-management of careers work in practice? If Hewlett-Packard's experience is any indication, we can expect to see more of it in the future.

HEWLETT-PACKARD HELPS EMPLOYEES SELF-MANAGE THEIR CAREERS

COMPANY EXAMPLE

A 3-month course in personal career management **(career self-management)** was developed at Hewlett-Packard's Colorado Springs Division based on two methods: self-assessment and subsequent application of findings to the workplace to chart a career path for each employee.[24]

The idea of self-assessment as the first step toward **career planning** is certainly not new. Self-help books have flooded the market for years. However, books by themselves lack a critical ingredient for success: the emotional support of a group setting in which momentum and motivation can be shared and maintained. Make no mistake about it, self-assessment can be a grueling process.

Hewlett-Packard uses six devices to generate data for self-assessment (based on earlier work for a second-year Harvard MBA course in career development). These include:

- **A written self-interview.** Participants are given 11 questions to answer about themselves. They are also asked to provide facts about their lives (people, places, events) and to discuss the future and the transitions they have made. This autobiographical sketch provides core data for the subsequent analysis.
- **Strong Vocational Interest Inventory.** Participants complete this 325-item instrument to determine their preferences about occupations, academic subjects, types of people, and so forth. An interest profile is developed for each individual by comparing her or his responses to those of successful people in a wide range of occupations.
- **Allport-Vernon-Lindzey Study of Values.** Each participant makes 45 choices among competing values in order to measure the relative strength of theoretical, economic, aesthetic, social, political, and religious values.

- **24-hour diaries.** Participants log their activities during one workday and also during one nonworkday. This information is used to confirm, or occasionally to contradict, information from the other sources.
- **Interviews with two "significant others."** Each participant asks two people of importance (friends, a spouse, relatives, coworkers, or others) questions about himself or herself. The two interviews are tape-recorded.
- **Lifestyle representations.** Participants depict their lifestyles using words, photos, drawings, or whatever else they choose.

A key ingredient in this program is its emphasis on an inductive approach. That is, the program begins by generating new data about each participant, rather than by starting with generalizations and deducing from them more specific information about each person. The process proceeds from the specific to the general (inductive), rather than from the general to the specific (deductive). Participants slowly recognize generalizations or themes within the large amounts of information they have produced. They come to tentative conclusions about these themes, first in each device individually and then in all the workshop's instruments as a whole, by analyzing the data they have collected.

Following the self-assessment, department managers interview subordinates to learn about their career objectives. They record these objectives and describe the people and positions currently in their departments. This information is then available for senior management to use in devising an overall HR plan, defining the skills required, and including a timetable. When data on the company's future needs are matched against each employee's career objectives, department managers can help employees chart a career course in the company (e.g., through training or additional job experience). Career development objectives for each employee are incorporated into performance objectives for future performance appraisals. The department head monitors the employee's career progress as part of the review process, and she or he is responsible for offering all possible support.

Results of the Career Self-Management Program

Senior managers at Hewlett-Packard found that after the workshops they had far more flexibility in moving employees than previously. The company was able either to give employees reasons to stay where they were, to develop a new path for them in the company, or to help them move out. Significantly, the Colorado Springs Division's overall turnover rate was unchanged in the year following the workshops. At an estimated replacement cost for a departing middle manager of 1.5 times annual salary, this was a welcome finding.

Within 6 months after the course, 37 percent of the participants had advanced to new jobs within the company, while 40 percent planned moves within the following 6 months. Of those who advanced, 74 percent credited the program for playing a significant part in their job change. The workshops also promoted workforce diversity since the sessions were open to all employees who expressed an interest in career development.

Perhaps the most persuasive reason for helping employees manage their own careers is the need to remain competitive. Although it might seem like a contradiction, such efforts can enhance a company's stability by developing more purposeful, self-assured employees. As noted earlier, today's employees are more difficult to manage. Companies that recognize the need to provide employees with satisfying opportunities will have the decided advantage of a loyal and industrious workforce.

One of the most challenging career management problems organizations face today is that of the dual-career couple. Let's examine this issue in detail.

Dual-Career Couples: Problems and Opportunities

Today, families in which both parents are working have become the majority among married couples with children.[25] In fact, dual-career couples now compose 45 percent of the workforce.[26] Dual-career couples face the problems of managing work and family responsibilities. Furthermore, it appears that there may be an interaction effect that compounds the problems and stresses of each separate career.[27] This implies that, by itself, career planning and development may be meaningless unless an employee's role as a family member also is considered, particularly when this role conflicts with work activities.[28] What can be done?

Research indicates that if dual-career couples are to manage their family responsibilities successfully, they (and their managers) must be flexible; they must be mutually committed to both careers; and they must develop the competencies to manage their careers through planning, goal setting, and problem solving.[29]

From an organizational perspective, successful management of the dual-career couple includes flexible work schedules and company-supported child care. It also includes customized career paths that include elements such as the ability to turn down advancement and be offered it again in the future, the ability to move laterally for development, the ability to turn down relocation and be asked again in the future, and the ability to specialize in one area of the organization.[30] Evidence across a wide array of industries indicates that some firms are more responsive to work-family issues than others. Firms are more likely to offer such benefits when work and family issues are prominent and important to senior HR executives and when the executives believe that failure to offer the benefits will detract from the ability of the organization to perform well in the marketplace.[31]

BOTTOM-LINE BENEFITS FOR FAMILY-FRIENDLY COMPANIES[32]   COMPANY EXAMPLE

Companies that truly "get it" actually go farther and integrate family-support mechanisms into the business itself. Thus Hewlett-Packard requires that every business unit identify work-family issues and propose an action plan as part of its annual business review. A Ford Foundation study found that successful solutions involved rethinking work processes, rather than finding ways to make people's lives fit the work. Thus when Xerox's Dallas customer-administration center handed over responsibility for scheduling shifts to workers themselves, it saw an overnight drop in absenteeism, followed by a rise in productivity. First Tennessee National Corporation found that supervisors rated by their subordinates as supportive of work-family balance retained employees twice as long as the bank average, and kept 7 percent more retail customers. Higher retention rates, according to the company, contributed to a 55 percent profit gain

over 2 years, to $106 million. At a broader level, results from a national sample of 527 U.S. firms revealed that organizations with more extensive work-family practices have higher levels of organizational performance (relative to other firms doing the same kind of work), market performance, and profit-sales growth. Bottom line: Work-family strategies haven't just hit the corporate mainstream—they've become a competitive advantage.

For all the talk about family-friendly policies, however, only about 25 percent of large employers actually provide on-site or near-site child-care programs.[33] Yet demand for the service has never been greater. Families nationwide pay an average of about 7.5 percent of their annual pretax income for child care.[34] Here are some reasons why employer-supported child care will continue to grow:

- Dual-career couples now compose a preponderance of the workforce.
- There has been a significant rise in the number of single parents, over half of whom use child-care facilities.[35]
- More and more, career-oriented women are arranging their lives to include motherhood and professional goals.

Employer-sponsored dependent care is no longer limited just to on-site or near-site child-care centers, however. The concept has expanded to include elder care, intergenerational care, sick-child care, and programs for school-age children (before and after school, as well as holiday programs). Other variations include centers located in office and industrial parks for use by all tenants, and centers sponsored by networks of businesses.[36]

Data from a national random sample indicate that *providing family benefits promotes a dedicated, loyal workforce among people who benefit directly from the policies, as well as from those who do not.*[37] However, the lesson from two other studies is clear: Don't expect that a day-care center or a flexible schedule will keep women managers from leaving corporations. They may be quite willing to throw corporate loyalty to the wind if they aren't getting adequate opportunities for career growth and job satisfaction.[38]

Managing dual-career couples, from an individual as well as from an organizational perspective, is difficult. But if current conditions are any indication of long-term trends, we can be quite sure of one thing: This "problem" is not going to go away.

CAREER MANAGEMENT: ORGANIZATIONS FOCUSING ON INDIVIDUALS

In this section we will examine current organizational practices used to manage workers at various stages of their careers. Let's begin by considering organizational entry.

Organizational Entry

Once a person has entered the workforce, the next stage is to enter a specific organization, to settle down, and to begin establishing a career there. **Organiza-**

tional entry refers to the process of "moving inside," or becoming more involved in a particular organization.[39] To do this well, a process known as socialization is essential. **Socialization** refers to the mutual adaptation of the new employee and the new employer to one another. Learning organizational policies, norms, traditions, and values is an important part of the process. Getting to know one's peers, supervisor, and subordinates is, too. All this enhances the newcomer's commitment, job satisfaction, job performance, and desire for personal control.[40] Since most turnover occurs early in a person's tenure with an organization, programs that accelerate socialization will tend also to reduce early turnover (i.e., at entry) and therefore reduce a company's overall turnover rate. Two of the most effective methods for doing this are realistic job previews (see Chapter 6) and new-employee orientation (see Chapter 8). A third is "mentoring."

Mentoring

A **mentor** is a teacher, an advisor, a sponsor, and a confidant.[41] He or she should be bright and well seasoned enough to understand the dynamics of power and politics in the organization, and should also be willing to share this knowledge with one or more new hires. Indeed, to overcome the potential problems associated with one-on-one, male-female mentoring relationships, some firms have established "quad squads" that consist of a mentor plus three new hires: a male, a female, and one other member of a protected group. Bank of America is typical. It assigns mentors to three or four promising young executives for a year at a time. There are also benefits for the mentor. For example, just being chosen as a mentor, according to one 35-year-old female branch bank manager, boosted her self-esteem. This is a central goal of any mentoring effort.

Organizations should actively promote such relationships, either formally or informally, and should provide sufficient time for mentors and new hires (or promising young executives) to meet on a regularly scheduled basis, at least initially. Evidence indicates that a new employee's satisfaction with the mentoring relationship has a greater impact on job and career attitudes than whether the mentoring is formal or informal.[42] Conversely, bad mentoring may be destructive, and worse than no mentoring at all.[43]

The mentor's role is to be a "culture carrier," to teach new hires "the ropes," to provide candid feedback on how they are being perceived by others, and to serve as a confidential "sounding board" for dealing with work-related problems. If successful, mentor relationships can help reduce the inflated expectations that newcomers often have about organizations; can relieve the stress experienced by all new hires; and, best of all, can improve the newcomer's chances for survival and growth in the organization.[44]

General Electric uses **reverse mentoring,** in which older managers meet with younger subordinates to learn about the Internet and electronic commerce (e-commerce). They learn to navigate the Internet and to critique their own Web sites as well as those of competitors. They discuss the articles and books they've been given for homework, and they barrage their subordinates with questions. It's a win-win situation for both parties. One 27-year-old mentor said the sessions made her more comfortable in dealing with her 54-year-old boss. "I can teach him things. . . . I know things he doesn't know." At the same time, she gets to observe firsthand the skills a manager needs to run a big operation, such as the ability to communicate with lots of different people.[45]

ETHICAL DILEMMA
Bringing Mentors and Protégés Together

Research has revealed that informal mentorships (spontaneous relationships that occur without involvement from the organization) lead to more positive career outcomes than do formal mentorships (programs that are managed and sanctioned by the organization).[46] Random assignment of protégès to mentors is like a blind date—there is only a small

chance that the match will be successful. On the other hand, not all new hires are willing or able actively to seek out opportunities to work with a mentor. For those that do not, is it ethically acceptable to assign them randomly to mentors, or to let them "sink or swim"? How would you advise an organization faced with this dilemma to proceed?

Early Career: The Impact of the First Job

Many studies of early careers focus on the first jobs to which new employees are assigned. The positive impact of initial job challenge upon later career success and retention has been found many times in a wide variety of settings. Among engineers, challenging early work assignments were related to strong initial performance as well as to the maintenance of competence and performance throughout the engineer's career.[47] In other words, challenging initial job assignments are an antidote to career obsolescence.

The characteristics of the first supervisor are also critical. He or she must be personally secure; unthreatened by the new subordinate's training, ambition, and energy; and able to communicate company norms and values.[48] Beyond that, the supervisor should ideally be able to play the roles of coach, feedback provider, trainer, role model, and protector in an accepting, esteem-building manner.

One other variable affects the likelihood of obtaining a high-level job later in one's career: *initial aspirations.*[49] Employees should be encouraged to "aim high" because, in general, higher aspirations lead to higher performance. Parents, teachers, employers, and friends should therefore avoid discouraging so-called impractical aspirations.

Many 20- and 30-somethings, who cut their professional teeth at a time when the possibilities seemed endless and the Internet the path to instant riches, have had to reassess their priorities as dot.coms turned into dot.bombs. Dreams of stock options at 27 and retirement at 32, if only you worked hard enough and sacrificed all things personal, led to big disappointments in the ensuing shakeout. According to a psychologist who specializes in work-life issues, it's as if a segment of today's young adults came of age too fast and lost something en route. The pattern for human development usually includes acquiring skills related to personal intimacy, time management, and exploration of culture alongside professional growth. But because many Internet entrepreneurs averaged 70- to 80-hour weeks, everything but work got put on hold. Said one such entrepreneur, "The peer pressure in Silicon Valley is to have no life. It was almost as if you were purely in execution mode, with no time to reflect or think if this was the right trajectory for me."

The silver lining to such angst is that by reassessing their priorities so early in life, this generation could ultimately lead far more balanced lives than their parents did. Not only do many boast extraordinary work experience, but they are developing a maturity far beyond their years.[50]

IMPACT OF THE FIRST JOB ON LATER CAREER SUCCESS

COMPANY EXAMPLE

For more than 20 years researchers generally accepted the view that unless an individual has a challenging first job and receives quick, early promotions, the entire career will suffer. This is a "tournament" model of upward mobility. It assumes that everyone has an equal chance in the early contests but that the losers are not eligible for later contests, at least not those of the major tournament. An alternative model is called "signaling" theory. It suggests three cues ("signals") that those responsible for promotion may use: (1) prior history of promotions (a signal of ability), (2) functional-area background, and (3) number of different jobs held.

A study of the patterns of early upward mobility for 180 employees of an oil company over an 11-year period are enlightening.[51] The company's very detailed job classification systems and actual salary grades served as measures of career attainment. The results generally did not support the tournament model of career mobility, because the losers—those passed over in the early periods— were later able to move up quickly. Rather, the results were more analogous to a horse race: Position out of the gate had relatively little effect in comparison to position entering the home stretch.

Different mobility patterns for administration and technical personnel helped to explain why the pattern of the early years did not always persist. Those who started early in administrative positions began to move up early but also plateaued early. A technical background meant a longer wait before upward movement, followed by relatively rapid promotion. The number of different positions held also predicted higher attainment.

In summary, one's past position, functional background, and number of different jobs all seem to act as signals to those making decisions about promotions. All were related strongly to career attainment. Together they accounted for more than 60 percent of the variability in promotions.

MANAGING MEN AND WOMEN IN MIDCAREER

To a large extent, middle age is still a mystery. Myths about psychological landmarks of midlife, such as the "empty-nest syndrome," the "midlife crisis," and the menopausal "change of life" have little scientific basis.[52] Nevertheless, the following issues may arise at some point between the ages of 35 and 55[53]:

- An awareness of advancing age and an awareness of death.
- An awareness of bodily changes related to aging.
- Knowing how many career goals have been or will be attained.
- A search for new life goals.
- A marked change in family relationships.

- A change in work relationships (one is now more of a "coach" than a novice or "rookie").
- A growing sense of obsolescence at work (as Satchel Paige once said, "Never look back; someone may be gaining on you").
- A feeling of decreased job mobility and increased concern for job security.[54]

One's career is a major consideration during this period. If a person has been in the same job for 10 years or more (sometimes less), he or she must face the facts of corporate politics, changing job requirements, possibilities of promotion, demotion, or job loss altogether. The fact of the matter is, over the next decade promotions will slow down markedly as middle-level managers are put into "holding patterns."

While career success traditionally has been defined in terms of upward mobility, more and more leading corporations are encouraging employees to step off the fast track and convincing them that they can find rewards and happiness in lateral mobility. In lectures and newsletters, the companies are trying to convince employees that "plateauing" is a fact of life, not a measure of personal failure, and that success depends on lateral integration of the business. Does such a move make sense? Yes, if it puts a **plateaued worker** into a core business, gives that person closer contact with customers, or teaches new skills that will increase marketability (both inside and outside one's present company) in case the person is fired.[55] Companies that are moving this way are still a minority, but they include such giants as Monsanto, Motorola, BellSouth, General Electric (GE), and RJR Nabisco.

Others note that, while there are fewer middle managers at medium and large companies as a result of the reductions in layers of managers during the corporate restructurings of the last decade, their jobs are more important. Middle managers now focus less on supervision and more on decision making.[56] However, for those who simply cannot accept lateral mobility, there is still hope. From 1998 to 2008, according to the Bureau of Labor Statistics, many firms will face shortages of managers with leadership and technical knowledge (such as engineers with MBA degrees) and those with expertise in management and computer matters.[57]

What can a middle-aged man or woman do? The rapid growth of technology and the accelerating development of new knowledge require that a person in midlife make some sort of *change* for her or his own survival. A 30-year-old might make the statement "I can afford to change jobs or careers a couple of more times before I have to settle down." A 50-year-old faces the possibility that there is only one chance left for change, and that now may be the time to take it.[58]

Not everyone who goes through this period in life is destined to experience problems, but everyone does go through the transition, and some are better equipped to cope than are others. Evidence now indicates that the older people are, the more control they feel in their work, finances, and marriages, but the less control they feel over health, children, and sex.[59] Life planning and career planning exercises are available that encourage employees to face up to feelings of restlessness and insecurity, to reexamine their values and life goals, and to set new ones or to recommit themselves to old ones.

One strategy is to *train midcareer employees to develop younger employees* (i.e., to serve as coaches or mentors). Both parties can win under such an arrangement. The midcareer employee keeps himself or herself fresh, energetic, and up to date, while the younger employee learns to see the "big picture" and to profit from the experience of the older employee. An important psychological need at midcareer is to build something lasting, something that will be a permanent contribution to one's organization or profession. The development of a future generation of leaders could be a significant, lasting, and highly satisfying contribution.

Another strategy for coping with midcareer problems is to *deal with or prevent obsolescence.* To deal with the problem, some firms send their employees to seminars, workshops, university courses, and other forms of "retooling." A better solution is to prevent obsolescence from occurring in the first place. Research with engineers indicated that this can be done through challenging initial jobs; periodic changes in assignments, projects, or jobs; work climates that contain frequent, relevant communications; rewards that are closely tied to performance; and participative styles of leadership.[60] Furthermore, three personal characteristics tend to be associated with low obsolescence: high intellectual ability, high self-motivation, and personal flexibility (lack of rigidity).

STRATEGIES FOR COPING WITH "PLATEAUED" WORKERS[61]

COMPANY EXAMPLE

ChevronTexaco, General Motors, and Chicago's Continental Bank are encouraging employees to move across departmental lines on a horizontal basis since restructuring has made vertical promotions less frequent. In banking, for example, someone from auditing might switch to commercial training; someone from systems research and development might move into international development. The inflexible HRM policies of the past are rapidly fading to accommodate present and future problems. Another strategy is to create dual technical and management ladders. New "technical executive" positions are equal to management jobs in title and dollars. For example, Continental Bank has created senior lending positions and positions for accounting and systems specialists that are equivalent to senior managerial posts in those departments.

An alternative way to placate people who do not move up is to pay them more for jobs well done. For years, companies that rely heavily for growth on creative people—scientists, engineers, writers, artists—have provided incentives for them to stay on. Companies are now offering such incentives to a broader spectrum. For example, at Monsanto, favored scientists can now climb a university-like track of associate fellow, fellow, senior fellow, distinguished fellow. The company has 130 fellows, and they earn from about $90,000 a year to over $150,000 (in 2001 dollars).

At General Electric, employees who are "plateaued" (either organizationally, through a lack of available promotions, or personally, through lack of ability or desire) are sometimes assigned to task forces or study teams. These employees have not been promoted in a technical sense, but at least they have gotten a new assignment, a fresh perspective, and a change in their daily work.

Finally, Prudential Life Insurance Company rotates managers to improve their performance. Rockwell International uses task forces, where possible, to "recharge" managers so they do not feel a loss of self-worth if they do not move up as fast as they think they should.

Many older workers have valuable skills that contribute significantly to organizations and society.

Actually, there may be a bright side to all of this. Because of increased competition for fewer jobs, the *quality* of middle managers should increase. Those unwilling to wait for promotions in large corporations may become entrepreneurs and start their own businesses. Others may simply accept the status quo, readjust their life and career goals, and attempt to satisfy their needs for achievement, recognition, and personal growth off the job. Research at AT&T supports this proposition. By the time managers were interviewed after 20 years on the job, most had long ago given up their early dreams, and many could not even remember how high they had aspired in the first place. At least on the surface, most had accepted their career plateaus and adjusted to them. Midlife was indeed a crisis to some of the managers, but not to the majority.[62]

It is possible to move through the middle years of life without reevaluation of one's goals and life. But it is probably healthier to develop a new or revised "game plan" during this period.

Managing the Older Worker

"Work is life" is a phrase philosophers throughout the ages have emphasized. Today, advances in health and medicine make it possible for the average male to live for more than 72 years and for the average female to live for more than 79 years.[63] Longevity increased by 27 years in the 20th century. The result: an army of healthy, over-65, unemployed adults. Legally, the elimination of mandatory retirement at any age has made this issue even more significant. As managers, what can we expect in terms of demographic trends?

In a nutshell, we can expect fewer younger workers, and more older workers. The Census Bureau predicts that the number of workers aged 25–34 will drop by 8.8 percent between 1996 and 2006. Meanwhile, the number of workers aged 55–64 will increase 54 percent over the same time period.[64] Figure 10–1 graphically illustrates these trends over a 40-year period. In short, the baby boom of the postwar period will become the "rocking-chair boom" of the early 21st century.

Myths versus Facts about Older Workers

Age stereotypes are an unfortunate impediment to the continued growth and development of workers over the age of 55. Here are some common myths about age, along with the facts:

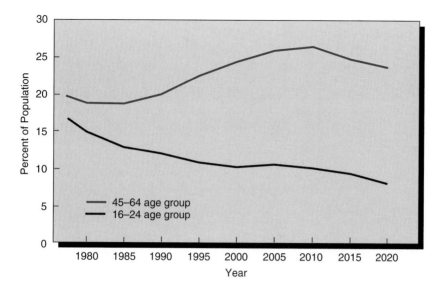

Figure 10–1

Population distribution by age group, ages 16–24 and 45–65.
(*Source:* U.S. Bureau of the Census, "Projections of the Population of the United States, by Age, Sex, and Race: 1983 to 2080," *Current Population Reports,* Series P-25, No. 952, May 1984).

Myth. Older workers are less productive than younger workers.

Fact. Cumulative research evidence on almost 39,000 individuals indicates that in both professional and nonprofessional jobs, age and job performance are generally unrelated.[65] The relationship of aging to the ability to function and the implication of aging for job performance are complex. Overwhelming evidence contradicts simple notions that rate of decline is tied in some linear or direct fashion to chronological age. Rather, the effects of aging on performance can be characterized by stability and growth, as well as decline, with large individual differences in the timing and amount of change in the ability to function.[66]

Myth. It costs more to prepare older workers for a job.

Fact. Studies show that mental abilities, such as verbal, numerical, and reasoning skills, remain stable into the seventies.[67]

Myth. Older workers are absent more often because of age-related infirmities and above-average rates of illness.

Fact. Cumulative research has found that older workers tend to be absent less frequently, at least in nonillness situations, but the duration of the absences that do take place tends to be longer.[68]

Myth. Older workers have an unacceptably high rate of accidents on the job.

Fact. According to a study by the Department of Health and Human Services, persons aged 55 and over had only 9.7 percent of all workplace injuries, even though they made up 13.6 percent of the workforce at the time of the study.[69] The data are even more compelling when only healthy workers are considered (i.e., as a result of a thorough medical screening). Among healthy workers aged 23–75, age was not associated with increased accidents and illnesses at work.[70] One might argue that this is because older workers have more experience on a job. But regardless of length of experience, the younger the employee, the higher the accident rate (see Chapter 15).

Myth.   Older workers do not get along well with other employees.

Fact.   Owners of small and large businesses alike agree that older employees bring stability and relate well. Indeed, over-55 workers, because of their sense of responsibility and their consistent job performance, make positive role models for younger workers.[71]

Myth.   The cost of employee benefits outweighs any other possible benefits from hiring older workers.

Fact.   True, when older people get sick, the illness is often chronic and requires repeated doctor's visits and hospitalization. However, the costs of health care for an older worker are lower than those for a younger, married worker with several children.[72]

Myth.   Older people are inflexible about the type of work they will perform.

Fact.   A study of job candidates by Right Associates, placement counselors, found that 55 percent of those under age 50, but 63 percent of those aged 50–59 and 78 percent of those over age 60, changed industries. Many older workers saw difficulties in being rehired by their old industries.

Myth.   Older people do not function well if constantly interrupted.

Fact.   Neither do younger people.

Implications of the Aging Workforce for HRM

Certainly not all older workers are model employees, just as not all older workers fit traditional stereotypes. What are the implications of this growing group of able-bodied individuals for human resource management?

We know what the future labor market will look like in general terms: Both the demand for and the supply of older workers will continue to expand. To capitalize on these trends, one approach is to recruit workers from among those individuals who would otherwise retire. *Make the job more attractive than retirement, and keep the employee who would otherwise need replacing.*[73] As the following example illustrates, some companies are doing exactly this.

COMPANY EXAMPLE   **UNRETIREES**

Travelers Corporation is one of a growing number of companies that are finding their own retirees to be a valuable source of experienced, dependable, and motivated help. The retirees meet seasonal or sporadic employment needs for the company, and the company gets a tax break. The retirees fill a variety of jobs, including typist, data-entry operator, systems analyst, underwriter, and accountant. Working a maximum of 40 hours per month, retirees are paid at the midpoint of the salary range for their job classifications. If they work more than half a standard workweek, they risk losing their pension benefits. Nevertheless, retirees generally like the program, for it keeps them in better physical, mental, and financial shape than full-time retirement does.[74]

With a smaller cohort of young workers entering the workforce, other companies are also seeking workers who once would have been considered "over the hill." Deloitte Consulting launched a Senior Leaders Program to allow high-talent executives to redesign their jobs rather than lose them to early retirement. Both Monsanto and Prudential use retirees as temporary workers to do everything from sophisticated technical jobs to answering phones. GE Information Services hires retired engineers to service older systems that are still in use.[75]

A second approach is to *survey the needs of older workers and, where feasible, adjust HRM practices and policies to accommodate these needs:*

1. Keep records on why employees retire and on why they continue to work.[76]
2. Implement flexible work patterns and options. For example, older workers might work on Mondays and Fridays and on days before and after holidays, when so many other employees fail to show up.
3. Where possible, redesign jobs to match the physical capabilities of the aging worker.
4. At a broader level, develop career paths that consider the physical capabilities of workers at various stages of their careers.[77]
5. Provide opportunities for retraining in technical and managerial skills. Particularly with older workers, it is important to provide a nonthreatening training environment that does not emphasize speed and does not expose the older learner to unfavorable comparisons with younger learners. Encourage self-confidence by allowing older workers to master a skill-development task; by making sure they observe similarly aged models who are performing well; and by offering verbal assurances, ample time, and privacy.[78]
6. Examine the suitability of performance appraisal systems as bases for employment decisions affecting older workers. To avoid age discrimination suits, be able to provide documented evidence of ineffective job performance.
7. Despite the encouraging findings presented earlier, in the section "Myths versus Facts about Older Workers," research has indicated no overall improvement in attitudes toward older workers over a 40-year period.[79] The characteristics employers consider most desirable in employees—flexibility, adaptability to change, and capacity and willingness to exercise independent judgment—are not commonly associated with older workers.[80]

For their part, older workers say their biggest problem is discrimination by would-be employers who underestimate their skills. They say they must convince supervisors and coworkers, not to mention some customers, that they're not stubborn, persnickety, or feeble.[81] To change this trend, workers and managers alike need to know the facts about older workers, so that they do not continue to espouse myths.

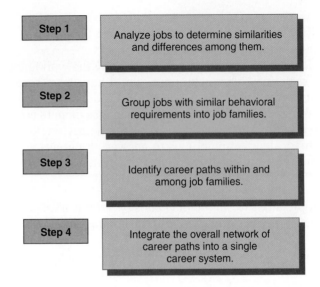

Figure 10–2

Development of a career system composed of individual career paths.

Step 1 — Analyze jobs to determine similarities and differences among them.

Step 2 — Group jobs with similar behavioral requirements into job families.

Step 3 — Identify career paths within and among job families.

Step 4 — Integrate the overall network of career paths into a single career system.

CAREER MANAGEMENT: ORGANIZATIONS FOCUSING ON THEIR OWN MAINTENANCE AND GROWTH

Ultimately, it is top management's responsibility to develop and implement a cost-effective career planning program. The program must fit the nature of the business, its competitive employment practices, and the current (or desired) organizational structure. This process is complex because organizational career management combines areas that previously have been regarded as individual issues: performance appraisal, development, transfer, and promotion. Before coaching and counseling take place, however, it is important to identify characteristic career paths that employees tend to follow.

Career paths represent logical and possible sequences of positions that could be held, based on an analysis of what people actually do in an organization.[82] Career paths should:

- Represent real progression possibilities, whether lateral or upward, without implied "normal" rates of progress or forced specialization in a technical area.
- Be tentative and responsive to changes in job content, work priorities, organizational patterns, and management needs.
- Be flexible, taking into consideration the compensating qualities of a particular employee, managers, subordinates, or others who influence the way that work is performed.
- Specify the skills, knowledge, and other attributes required to perform effectively at each position along the paths and specify how they can be acquired. (If specifications are limited to educational credentials, age, and experience, some capable performers may be excluded from career opportunities.)

Data derived from HRM research are needed to define career paths in this manner. Behaviorally based job analyses (see Chapter 5) that can be expressed in quantitative terms are well suited to this task since they focus directly on

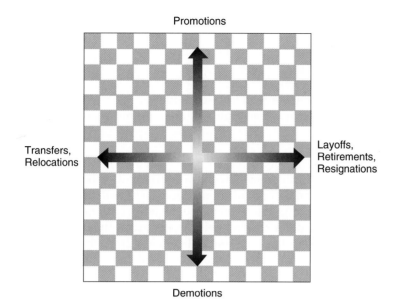

Promotions

Transfers, Relocations

Layoffs, Retirements, Resignations

Demotions

Figure 10–3

As in chess, people can make a variety of internal moves in an organization.

what people must do effectively in each job. Clusters or families of jobs requiring similar patterns of behavior can then be identified.

The next task is to identify career paths within and among the job families and to integrate the overall network of these paths into a single career system. The process is shown graphically in Figure 10–2.

Federal guidelines on employee selection require a job-related basis for all employment decisions. Career paths based on job analyses of employee behaviors provide a documented, defensible basis for organizational career management and a strong reference point for individual career planning and development activities.

In practice, organizational career management systems sometimes fail for the following reasons: (1) employees believe that supervisors do not care about their career development, (2) neither the employee nor the organization is fully aware of the employee's needs and organizational constraints, and (3) career plans are developed without regard for the support systems necessary to fulfill the plans.[83] The following section gives examples of several companies that avoided these pitfalls.

Internal Staffing Decisions: Patterns of Career Change

From the organization's point of view, there are four broad types of internal moves: up, down, over, and out (Figure 10–3). These moves correspond to promotions (up); demotions (down); transfers and relocations (over); and layoffs, retirements, and resignations (out). Technically, dismissals also fall into the last category, but we will consider them in the context of disciplinary actions and procedural justice. Briefly, let's consider each of these patterns of movement.

Promotions

Promoted employees usually assume greater responsibility and authority in return for higher pay, benefits, and privileges. Psychologically, **promotions** help satisfy employees' needs for security, belonging, and personal growth. Promotions are important organizational decisions that should receive the same careful attention as any other employment decision. They are more likely to be successful to the extent that firms:

1. Conduct an extensive search for candidates.
2. Make standardized, clearly understandable information available on all candidates.[84]

Organizations must continue to live with those who are bypassed for promotion. Research indicates that these individuals often feel they have not been treated fairly, their commitment decreases, and their absenteeism increases. Conversely, promoted individuals tend to increase their commitment.[85] To minimize defensive behavior, it is critical that the procedures used for promotion decisions (e.g., assessment centers plus performance appraisals) be acceptable, valid, and fair to the unsuccessful candidates. Further, emphasize the greater merits of the promoted candidates, relative to those who were not promoted.

In unionized situations, the collective bargaining contract will determine the relative importance given to seniority and ability in promotion decisions. Management tends to emphasize ability, while unions favor seniority. Although practices vary considerably from firm to firm, a compromise is usually reached through which promotions are determined by a formula, such as promoting the employee with the greatest seniority *if* ability and experience are equal. However, if one candidate is clearly a superior performer relative to others, many contracts will permit promotion on this basis regardless of seniority.

A further issue concerns promotion from within versus outside the organization. Many firms, such as Delta Air Lines, have strict promotion-from-within policies. However, there are situations in which high-level jobs or newly created jobs require talents that are just not available in-house. Under these circumstances, even the most rigid promotion-from-within policy must yield to a search for outside candidates.

COMPANY EXAMPLE   ## UP-OR-OUT PROMOTIONS IN PROFESSIONAL SERVICE FIRMS[86]

Professional Service Firms (PSFs) are involved in a variety of activities, from consulting, law, civil engineering, and architecture to software production. They trade mainly on the knowledge of their human capital—employees and producer-owners—to develop and deliver solutions to client problems. The usual ownership form of the PSF is the partnership, and a key decision for the existing owners is promotion to partner. This has implications for the reputation of the firm, as well as its future direction.

Conventionally, PSFs use up-or-out promotion policies, excluding from permanent tenure all except those offered partnership. If employees fail to obtain promotion within a certain time period, they are expected to quit or are dismissed. The attraction of up-or-out for the owners of the firm is that it creates a strong incentive for aspiring juniors to perform, reducing supervision or monitoring costs. It also leaves career paths inside the firm relatively clear by exiting those not elected to the top jobs, thereby helping to attract ambitious entrants who do not want to be stuck in a promotion logjam. However, up-or-out also involves losing talented and knowledgeable staff in whom the firm will have invested not only formal training (and possibly signing bonuses), but also the time and effort associated with mentoring and developing them.

In general, the more that firms value their knowledge base and see it as a source of competitive advantage, or where the knowledge loss represents a competitive threat, the greater the costs of losing that knowledge that exiting unsuccessful candidates take with them through up-or-out. In such cases, firms may adapt by creating permanent career positions. There are costs to this strategy as well, in the form of the need for higher-powered incentives linked to the performance of the firm for those in permanent career positions below the level of partner (to reduce the risk of shirking or loafing) and higher compensation to attract and retain good-quality staff. What's the bottom line in all of this? Where firms perceive their knowledge base as distinctive and a source of competitive advantage, a promotion system like up-or-out may be less appropriate. Where the knowledge is codified and publicly available (as in public accounting firms), firms are more likely to retain up-or-out.

Demotions

Employee **demotions** usually involve a cut in pay, status, privilege, or opportunity. They occur infrequently since they tend to be accompanied by problems of employee apathy, depression, and inefficiency that can undermine the morale of a work group. For these reasons, many managers prefer to discharge or to move employees laterally rather than demote them. In either case, careful planning, documentation, and concern for the employee should precede such moves.

What causes a demotion? The cause could be a disciplinary action, the inability of an employee to handle the requirements of a higher-level job, health problems, or changing interests (e.g., a desire to move from production to sales). Demotions also may result from structural changes, as one-time managers are recast into project leaders, technical specialists, or internal consultants by companies in the throes of reorganization. In many cases, demotion is mutually satisfactory to the organization and to the affected employee.[87]

Transfers and Relocations

Who is most likely to be transferred? A survey by the Employee Relocation Council found that the prototypical transferee is a married 37-year-old male with children. Female workers are less likely to be transferred, although this situation is changing.[88] Reduced mobility, like leave of absence, tends to retard women's salary progression relative to that of similarly situated men.[89]

With respect to relocations, senior management sometimes faces resistance from employees for family reasons, although in 2001 the number 1 reason was high housing costs in the new area.[90] The effect of a move on a family can be profound.[91] For the employee, relocation often means increased prestige and income.

However, the costs of moving and the complications resulting from upsetting routines, loss of friends, and changing schools and jobs are borne by the family. Uprooted families often suffer from loss of credentials as well. They do not enjoy the built-in status that awaits the employee at the new job; they must start from scratch. Wives may become more dependent on their husbands for social contacts (or vice versa, depending on who is transferred). Women now account for about 25 percent of corporate moves, up from 5 percent in 1980. Currently, about a third of transferees are female, and one in four trailing spouses is male. Do such moves work out? ExxonMobil Corporation finds that a man generally will follow his wife only if she earns at least 25 percent to 40 percent a year more than he does.[92]

There is one bright side to all of this, however. Research has shown that transfers produce little short-term impact on the mental or physical health of children.[93]

Transferred employees who are promoted estimate that it will take them a full 9 months to get up to speed in their new posts. Lateral transfers take an average of 7.8 months. However, the actual time taken to reach competency varies with (1) the degree of similarity between the old and new jobs and (2) the amount of support from peers and superiors at the new job.[94]

To reduce this "downtime," companies are taking some unusual steps. Thus Sprint Corp. spends up to $4,000 to replace a relocated spouse's income for 60 days. That has helped transferees to return to full productivity in about 3 months; it had taken 6. Marriott Corporation installed a computerized job-posting system that tracks its managerial vacancies nationwide. Both employees and their trailing spouses can apply for the openings.[95] As an overall strategy on relocation, some companies have developed frequency standards whereby no manager can be relocated more than once in 2 years or three times in 10 years. Another firm has set up one-stop rotational programs at its larger facilities to replace what used to be four stints of 6 months each at different plants over a 2-year training period.

The financial implications of relocation are another major consideration. In 1980, most relocation programs consisted of a few cost categories: house-hunting trips, the shipment of household goods, temporary living expenses at the new location, and often 1 month's salary bonus to cover other incidentals. In the early 2000s, typical relocation expenses and services included all those offered in 1980 plus ongoing cost-of-living differentials; mortgage-interest differentials; home disposal and home-finding expenses; expenses to help defray losses on home sales; real estate commissions; home purchase expenses; home maintenance, repair, and refurbishing costs; equity loans; and, for renters, lease-breaking expenses. Employees on temporary assignments often receive home-property-management expenses. All of this adds up. According to the Employee Relocation Council, the average cost of moving a home-owning employee in 2001 was $57,279.[96]

Organizations are well aware of these social and financial problems and in many cases they are responding by providing improved support systems to make the process easier. These include special online relocation programs, intranets, house-hunting on the Internet, and electronic data interchange (EDI) that lets relocation professionals keep track of every detail of every move.[97]

Layoffs, Retirements, and Resignations
These all involve employees moving *out* of the organization.

Layoffs. How safe is my job? For many people, that is the issue of the early 21st century. It's becoming clear that corporate cutbacks were not an oddity of the 1990s but rather are likely to persist through this decade as well.[98]

Involuntary layoffs are never pleasant, and management policies must consider the impacts on those who leave, on those who stay, on the local community, and on the company. For laid-off workers, efforts should be directed toward a rapid, successful, and orderly career transition.[99] Emphasize outplacement programs that help laid-off employees deal with the psychological stages of career transition (anger, grief, depression, family stress), assess individual strengths and weaknesses, and develop support networks.[100]

How long does it take on average to find a new job? While it depends a great deal on the state of the economy and on the amount of effort put into the job search, a recent survey of 35- to 60-year-old job seekers showed that the older they were, the fewer interviews they got, and the longer it took them to find a job. How much longer? Compared to a 35- to 40-year-old job seeker, it took almost 25 percent longer for a 46- to 50-year-old, and 65 percent longer for a 50- to 60-year-old.[101]

Termination is a traumatic experience. Egos are shattered, and employees may become bitter and angry. Family problems may also occur because of the added emotional and financial strain.[102] For those who remain, it is important that they retain the highest level of loyalty, trust, teamwork, motivation, and productivity possible. This doesn't just happen—and unless there is a good deal of face-to-face, candid, open communication between senior management and "survivors," it probably won't.[103] Within the community, layoff policies should consider the company's reputation and image in addition to the impact of the layoff on the local economy and social services agencies. Although layoffs are intended to reduce costs, some costs may in fact increase. These include:

Direct costs	Indirect costs
Severance pay, pay in lieu of notice	Recruiting and employment cost of new hires
Accrued vacation and sick pay	Training and retraining
Supplemental unemployment benefits	Increase in unemployment tax rate
Outplacement	Potential charges of unfair discrimination
Pension and benefit payoffs	Low morale among remaining employees
Administrative processing costs	Heightened insecurity and reduced productivity

What are the options? One approach is to initiate a program of job sharing to perform the reduced workload. While no one is laid off, everyone's workweek and pay are reduced. This helps the company to reduce labor costs. In an area experiencing high unemployment, it may be better to have all employees share the "misery" rather than to lay off selected ones. Some of the benefits of job sharing are[104]:

- Twice as much talent and creativity is available.
- Benefits continue.
- Overtime is reduced.

IMPACT OF CAREER MANAGEMENT ON PRODUCTIVITY, QUALITY OF WORK LIFE, AND THE BOTTOM LINE

From first-job effects through midcareer transition to preretirement counseling, career management has a direct bearing on productivity, quality of work life, and the bottom line. It is precisely because organizations are sensitive to these concerns that career management activities have become as popular as they are. The saying "Organizations have many jobs, but individuals have only one career" is as true today as it ever was. While organizations find themselves in worldwide competition, most individuals are striving for achievement, recognition, personal growth,

?

variety, and inspiring colleagues.[108] In a world that is becoming more open, more interconnected, and boundaryless, attempting to seek balance, equilibrium, and stability may be counterproductive. Leave behind the notion that the amount of time and energy devoted to "work" needs to balance the time and energy devoted to "life." Instead, focus on enriching your overall quality of life. Reframing the issues in this way changes the focus from *work* to *life* and from *balance* to *quality*.[109] The payoff is obvious for individuals and their organizations.

- Workers retain a career orientation and the potential for upward mobility.
- It eliminates the need for training a temporary employee, for example, when one employee is sick or is on vacation, because the other can take over.

However, job sharing is not without its drawbacks[105]:

- There is a lack of job continuity.
- Supervision is inconsistent.
- Accountability is not centered in one person.
- Nonsalary expenses do not decrease, because many benefits are a function of the employee, not the amount of pay.
- When workers are represented by a union, seniority is bypassed, and senior workers may resist sharing jobs.[106]

However, when Motorola reviewed job sharing at its facilities in Arizona, it found that avoiding layoffs saved an average of more than $3,000 per employee—and $1.6 million in total (in 2001 dollars).[107]

Retirements.   For some employees, early retirement is a possible alternative to being laid off. Early retirement programs take many forms, but typically they involve partial pay stretched over several years along with extended benefits. Early retirement programs are intended to provide incentives to terminate; they are not intended to replace regular retirement benefits.[110] Any losses in pension resulting from early retirement are usually offset by attractive incentive payments.

What about the effects on those who remain? With respect to layoffs, generous benefits provided to victims tend to be associated with *lower* intentions to quit on the part of survivors. With an early retirement program, however, perceptions of overly generous benefits to early retirees tends to be associated

IMPLICATIONS FOR MANAGEMENT PRACTICE

To profit from current workforce trends, consider taking the following steps:

- Develop explicit policies to attract and retain dual-career couples.
- Plan for more effective use of "plateaued" workers as well as those who are in midcareer transitions.

- Educate other managers and workers in the facts about older workers; where possible, hire older workers for full-time or part-time work.
- Commit to broadening career opportunities for women and members of protected groups.

---

with *higher* intentions to quit on the part of ineligible employees who remain.[111] This is not the only downside risk associated with voluntary severance and early retirement programs. Both Kodak and IBM had lost skilled, senior-level employees in past cutbacks. To overcome that problem, the firms targeted subsequent programs to specific groups of employees, such as those in manufacturing and in some administrative jobs.[112] The keys to success are to *identify, before the incentives are offered, exactly which jobs are targeted for attrition and to understand the needs of the employees targeted to leave.*[113]

Since mandatory retirement at a specified age can no longer be required legally, most employees will choose their own times to retire. In 2000, 0.6 percent of all people in their 30s were retired, 5.4 percent of those in their 40s, 17.7 percent of those in their 50s, 65.1 percent of those in their 60s, and 83.5 percent of those in their 70s or older.[114]

Research indicates that both personal and situational factors affect retirement decisions. Personally, individuals with Type A behavior patterns (those who have a tendency to be hard-driving, aggressive, and impatient) are less likely to prefer to retire, while those with obsolete job skills, chronic health problems, and sufficient financial resources are more likely to retire. Situationally, employees are more likely to retire to the extent that they have reached their occupational goals, that their jobs have undesirable characteristics, that home life is seen as preferable to work life, and that there are attractive alternative (leisure) activities.[115]

While retirement is certainly attractive to some, many retirees are returning to the workforce. In fact, retirees are the fastest-growing part of the temporary workforce. Many are bored with retirement, have high energy levels, and can maintain flexible schedules.[116] Others need the money, and need health benefits to compensate for those they have lost. Many want in retirement what they don't currently have: *balance.* They want what aging experts now call a **blended life course**—an ongoing mix of work, leisure, and education.[117]

Resignations. The National Quit Rate—the percentage of people currently unemployed who left their jobs voluntarily—hit 14.7 percent in 2000, the highest level in 10 years.[118] While the incidence of voluntary resignations may have changed, the rules for how to do it have not. Employees who resign should avoid "burning bridges" behind them, leaving anger and resentment in their wake; instead, they should leave gracefully and responsibly, stressing the value of their experience in the company. After all, who knows? They may want to return to the very same employers subsequently, as happened in 2000–2001 when disaffected executives, both young and not so young, bolted from dot.com ventures that didn't work out.[119]

Human Resource Management in Action: Conclusion	## SELF-RELIANCE: KEY TO CAREER MANAGEMENT FOR THE 21ST CENTURY

Corporate career management programs often include one or more of the following support mechanisms:

Self-Assessment.   The goal of **self-assessment** is to help employees focus on appropriate career goals. For example, Career Architect is a deck of 67 skills cards that each employee sorts into three piles: greatest strengths, strengths, and weaknesses. The system, also available in software form, helps employees walk themselves through the difficult and sometimes emotional process of assessing their own skills—for example, dealing with new technology or working in teams. It is a process of identifying and calibrating one's professional aptitudes and capabilities and of identifying improvements that will enhance one's career growth. As we saw in the Hewlett-Packard example, that company has pioneered in offering self-assessment training to its employees at all levels.

Career Planning.   Verizon uses the results of Career Architect to chart the skills the company most needs for future business and to forge career development plans for its high-potential managers. Royal Insurance created a series of success profiles for important jobs using the cards.[120] The companies then teach employees how to plan their career growth once they have determined where they want to go. Employees learn what they need as well as how to "read" the corporate environment and to become "savvy" about how to get ahead in their own companies.

Supervisory Training.   Employees frequently turn first to their immediate supervisors for help with career management. At Sikorsky Aircraft, for example, supervisors are taught how to provide relevant information and to question the logic of each employee's career plans, but not to give specific career advice. Giving advice relieves the employee of responsibility for managing his or her own career.

Succession Planning.   Simply designating replacements for key managers and executives is no guarantee that those replacements will be ready when needed. Enlightened companies are adopting an approach to succession planning that is consistent with the concept of career self-management. They develop their employees broadly to prepare them for any of several positions that may become available. As business needs change, broadly developed people can be moved into positions that are critical to the success of the business.

While the concept of career self-management is appealing, research has revealed some significant cautions. One, don't make the programs mandatory. Two, don't offer the programs as a one-time opportunity that will not be repeated in the future. Three, provide opportunities for employees to practice their career self-management behaviors in the workplace. This may require new HR policies and new roles for supervisors.[121]

The practice of making career self-management part of the corporate culture has spread rapidly over the past several years. Companies are using this approach to build a significant competitive advantage. Given today's turbulent, sometimes convulsive corporate environments, plus workers who seek greater control over their own destinies, it may be the only approach that can succeed over the long term.

SUMMARY

A career is a sequence of positions occupied by a person during the course of a lifetime. Career planning is important because the consequences of career success or failure are closely linked to an individual's self-concept and identity, as well as with career and life satisfaction. This chapter has addressed career management from three perspectives. The first was that of individuals focusing on themselves: self-management of one's own career, establishment of career objectives, and dual-career couples. The second perspective was that of organizations focusing on individuals: that is, managing individuals during early career (organizational entry, impact of the first job); midcareer, including strategies for coping with midlife transitions and "plateaued" workers; and late-career (age 50 and over) stages. We considered the implications of each of these stages for human resource management in both large- and small-business settings. Finally, a third perspective was that of organizations focusing on their own maintenance and growth. This requires the development of career management systems based on career paths defined in terms of employee behaviors. It involves the management of patterns of career movement up, down, over, and out.

DISCUSSION QUESTIONS

10–1. Why is the design of one's first permanent job so important?

10–2. What practical steps can you suggest to minimize midcareer crises?

10–3. How can an organization avoid the problems associated with older workers clogging the career paths of younger workers?

10–4. Discuss the special problems faced by dual-career couples.

10–5. Working in small groups, develop a corporate policy that specifies how training, performance appraisal, and reward systems might integrate career planning considerations.

KEY TERMS

career	socialization
career success	mentor
career self-management	reverse mentoring
career planning	plateaued worker
organizational entry	career paths

promotions   blended life course
demotions   self-assessment

APPLYING YOUR KNOWLEDGE

Exercise 10-1   *Self-Assessment and Career Planning*

Awareness of both the job market and your own strengths, weaknesses, needs, and desires is required to make an effective career choice. This exercise focuses on the second part of the equation: personal traits, interests, needs, and aspirations as they relate to the choice of a career. Professionally developed interest inventories and personality tests can help in this diagnosis. They are usually available through college placement offices.

Following are three exercises designed to help you discover how your personal characteristics relate to your career choices. A sample self-assessment exercise is followed by an exercise providing guidelines for discussing and evaluating answers to the self-assessment questions. The final exercise provides additional ways to examine self-perceptions and interests.

A. Self-Assessment

An approach that has proved useful is that of answering a series of probing questions. A list of typical questions is provided below. Answer them as honestly as you can.

1. List five words that describe my personality well (not roles such as student, husband, daughter).
    a.
    b.
    c.
    d.
    e.
2. Who am I? List five statements that answer this question.
    a.
    b.
    c.
    d.
    e.
3. My best childhood memory is:
4. The single achievement in my life of which I am most proud is:
5. The type of people I like best are:
6. When I have 15 minutes to do anything I want, I most enjoy:
7. When I think about making changes, I feel:
8. My overriding goal in life is to:
9. My greatest strengths in the following work-related areas are (list specific strengths):
    a.   Intellectual abilities
    b.   Social skills
    c.   Leadership skills
    d.   Communication skills
10. My greatest weaknesses in the following work-related areas are (list specific weaknesses):
    a.   Intellectual abilities
    b.   Social skills
    c.   Leadership skills
    d.   Communication skills

11. Ranking values. Rank the following 16 values in terms of their importance to you (1 is most important, 2 is second most important, etc.).

    a. Family security
    b. Social recognition
    c. Salvation
    d. An exciting life
    e. A world of beauty
    f. Inner harmony
    g. Mature love
    h. Accomplishment
    i. A world at peace
    j. Self-respect
    k. True friendship
    l. Happiness
    m. Equality
    n. Wisdom
    o. Freedom
    p. Pleasure

12. Ranking job outcomes. Rank the following 14 job outcomes in terms of their importance to you (1 is most important, 2 is second most important, etc.).

    a. Status
    b. Money
    c. Security
    d. Variety
    e. Independence
    f. Power
    g. Challenge
    h. Travel
    i. Respect
    j. Flexible hours
    k. Working conditions
    l. Socially important work
    m. Self-actualization
    n. Achievement

13. Life line. Draw a line representing your life. Use peaks and valleys to represent positive and negative periods or events in your life. Mark an "X" where you are now; then project your life line out to the end. At the end of your life line, write the epitaph that you think will best summarize your life's work.

B. Discussion and Career Planning

The class should now divide into groups of two (dyads). Each individual in turn should explain to the other what insights were gained about himself or herself from answering the questions in part A. Then the dyads should discuss appropriate career options based on the answers. Finally, using the insights and information gained from the responses to the questions and from the discussions, each student should answer the following questions individually.

1. What are my three major career strengths?
2. What characteristics of jobs are most important to me?
3. What occupations, jobs, and types of organizations seem most suitable for me?
4. What career goals should I set for myself, both long-term and short-term?
5. What steps should I take, and by when should I take them, to accomplish these goals?

Further Exploration of Self-Perceptions and Interests

1. It is frequently helpful in career planning to get others' perspectives on you to compare with your self-perceptions. One way to do this involves interviewing one or two people who know you very well, such as a parent, spouse, or best friend. Ask them the same questions you asked yourself in Part A of this exercise. Then compare their responses with your own. What are the similarities and differences? What explains the differences?

2. Another way to get a different perspective beyond your own is to take an interest inventory. Such questionnaires typically assess your career interests according to some underlying model of careers and compare your responses with those of individuals in a variety of career fields. Your career development office on campus should be able to administer an instrument such as the Strong Vocational Interest Inventory or the Kuder Preference Scale.

3. It is also sometimes useful to keep a 24-hour diary. For one full schoolday, keep track of how you spend your time. Then repeat the process for a weekend day or

some other day when you do no schoolwork. What did you learn about how you like to spend your time? What does this indicate about your interests?

REFERENCES

1. Schein, E. H. (1996). Career anchors revisited: Implications for career development in the 21st century. *Academy of Management Executives, 10*(4), 80–88.
2. Greenhaus, J. H. (1987). *Career management.* Chicago: Dryden.
3. Sullivan, S. E. (1999). The changing nature of careers: A review and research agenda. *Journal of Management, 25,* 457–484. Hall, D. T. (1996). Protean careers of the 21st century. *Academy of Management Executive, 10*(4), 8–16. See also Nicholson, N. (1996). Career systems in crisis: Change and opportunity in the information age. *Academy of Management Executive, 10*(4), 40–51.
4. Lublin, J. S. (1996, Nov. 22). Texaco case causes a stir in boardrooms. *The Wall Street Journal,* pp. B1, B2.
5. Andy Grove on navigating your career (1999, Mar. 29). *Fortune,* pp. 187–192. See also Hall, D. T., & Mirvis, P. H. (1995). Careers as lifelong learning. In A. Howard (ed.), *The changing nature of work.* San Francisco: Jossey-Bass, pp. 323–361.
6. Sullivan, op. cit. See also Arthur, M. B., & Rousseau, D. M. (1996). The boundaryless career as a new employment principle. In M. G. Arthur & D. M. Rousseau (eds.), *The boundaryless career.* NY: Oxford University Press, pp. 3–20.
7. Rousseau, D. M., & Wade-Benzoni, K. A. (1995). Changing individual-organizational attachments. In A. Howard (ed.), *The changing nature of work.* San Francisco: Jossey-Bass, pp. 290–322.
8. Wang, P. (2000, Nov.). Is this retirement? *Money,* pp. 101–108. See also Hall & Mirvis, op. cit.
9. Hall, op. cit.
10. Milkovich, G. T., & Anderson, J. C. (1982). Career planning and development systems. In K. M. Rowland & G. R. Ferris (eds.), *Personnel management,* Boston: Allyn & Bacon, pp. 364–389.
11. Schmidt, J. A. (ed.) (2001). *Making mergers work: The strategic importance of people.* Alexandria, VA: Towers Perrin/Society for Human Resource Management.
12. Kleinfeld, N. R. (1996, Mar. 4). The company as family no more. *The New York Times,* pp. A1, A8–A11. See also Gutknecht, J. E., & Keys, J. B. (1993). Mergers, acquisitions, and takeovers: Maintaining morale of survivors and protecting employees. *Academy of Management Executive, 7*(3), 26–36. See also Schweiger, D. M., & DeNisi, A. S. (1991). Communication with employees following a merger: A longitudinal field experiment. *Academy of Management Journal, 34,* 110–135.
13. Reichheld, F. F. (1996). *The loyalty effect.* Boston: Harvard Business School Press.
14. Daniels, C., & Vinzant, C. (2000, Feb. 7). The joy of quitting. *Fortune,* pp. 199–202.
15. Dalton, D. R., Daily, C. M., & Kesner, I. F. (1993). Executive severance agreements: Benefit or burglary? *Academy of Management Executive, 7*(4), 69–76.
16. Daniels & Vinzant, op. cit. See also Henkoff, R. (1996, Jan. 15). So, you want to change your job. *Fortune,* pp. 52–56.
17. Reichheld, 1996, op. cit. See also White, J. B., & Lublin, J. S. (1996, Sep. 27). Some companies try to rebuild loyalty. *The Wall Street Journal,* pp. B1, B2.
18. Working scared (1993, Apr. 17). *NBC News.*
19. Bolles, R. N. (2000). *The 2000 What color is your parachute?* Berkeley, CA: Ten-Speed Press. See also Andy Grove on navigating your career, op. cit. See also Henkoff, op. cit. See also Farnham, A. (1996, Jan. 15). Casting off: Three who did it right. *Fortune,* pp. 60–64.
20. Aburdene, P. (1990, Sep.). How to think like a CEO for the 1990s. *Working Woman,* pp. 134–137.

21. Waterman, J. A. (2000). Informed opportunism: Career and life planning for the new millennium. In J. M. Kummerow (ed.), *New directions in career planning and the workplace.* Palo Alto, CA: Davies-Black, pp. 163–196.

22. Fisher, A. (2001, Apr. 2). Surviving the downturn. *Fortune,* pp. 98–106. See also Petras, K., & Petras, R. (1989). *The only job book you'll ever need.* New York: Simon & Schuster.

23. Ibid. See also Andy Grove on navigating your career, op cit.

24. Wilhelm, W. R. (1983). Helping workers to self-manage their careers. *Personnel Administrator, 28*(8), 83–89.

25. Lewin, T. (2000, Oct. 24). Working parents: Two-income families now the norm. *The Denver Post,* pp. 1A, 15A.

26. Dual career couples exert influence (1998, Sept.–Oct.). *Workplace Visions,* p. 3.

27. Greenhaus, op. cit.

28. Balancing work and family (1996, Sept. 16). *Business Week,* pp. 74–80.

29. Dual career couples, op. cit. See also Work & family (1993, June 28). *BusinessWeek,* pp. 80–88.

30. Lublin, J. S. (2000, May 30). Working dads find family involvements can help out careers. *The Wall Street Journal,* p. B1.

31. Milliken, F. J., Martins, L. L., & Morgan, H. (1998). Explaining organizational responsiveness to work-family issues: The role of human resource executives as issue interpreters. *Academy of Management Journal, 41,* 580–592.

32. Perry-Smith, J. E., & Blum, T. C. (2000). Work-family human resource bundles and perceived organizational performance. *Academy of Management Journal, 43,* 1107–1117. See also Balancing work and family, op. cit.

33. Flynn, G. (1995, Oct.). Deciding how to provide dependent care isn't child's play. *Personnel Journal,* pp. 92–94.

34. Asinof, L. (1996, Dec. 12). The nanny facts. *The Wall Street Journal,* p. R26.

35. Lewin, T. (1992, Oct. 5). Rise in single parenthood is reshaping U.S. *The New York Times,* pp. B1, B6.

36. Ritter, B. (1996, Dec.). *Work-family conflicts.* Unpublished manuscript, Graduate School of Business, University of Colorado–Denver.

37. Grover, S. L., & Crooker, K. J. (1995). Who appreciates family-responsive human resource policies: The impact of family friendly policies on the organizational attachments of parents and non-parents. *Personnel Psychology, 48,* 271–288.

38. Trost, C. (1990, May 2). Women managers quit not for family but to advance their corporate climb. *The Wall Street Journal,* pp. B1, B8.

39. Breaugh, J. A. (1992). *Recruitment: Science and practice.* Boston: PWS-Kent.

40. Wannberg, C. R., & Kammeyer-Mueller, J. D. (2000). Predictors and outcomes of proactivity in the socialization process. *Journal of Applied Psychology, 85,* 373–385. See also Ashford, S. J., & Black, J. S. (1996). Proactivity during organizational entry: The role of desire for control. *Journal of Applied Psychology, 81,* 199–214.

41. Whitely, W., Dougherty, T. W., & Dreher, G. F. (1991). Relationship of career mentoring and socioeconomic origin to managers' and professionals' early career progress. *Academy of Management Journal, 34,* 331–351. See also Wilson, J. A., & Elman, N. S. (1990). Organizational benefits of mentoring. *Academy of Management Executive, 4*(4), 88–94.

42. Ragins, B. R., Cotton, J. L., & Miller, J. S. (2000). Marginal mentoring: The effects of type of mentor, quality of relationship, and program design on work and career attitudes. *Academy of Management Journal, 43,* 1177–1194. See also Young, A. M., & Perrewe, P. L. (2000). What did you expect? An examination of career-related support and social support among mentors and protègès. *Journal of Management, 26,* 611–632.

43. Scandura, T. A. (1998). Dysfunctional mentoring relationships and outcomes. *Journal of Management, 24,* 449–467.

44. Dreher, G. F., & Cox, T. H., Jr. (1996). Race, gender, and opportunity: A study of compensation attainment and the establishment of mentoring relationships. *Journal of Applied Psychology, 81,* 297–308. See also Whitely et al., op. cit.

45. Murray, M. (2000, Feb. 15). GE mentoring program turns underlings into teachers of the web. *The Wall Street Journal,* pp. B1, B18.

46. Ragins, B. R., & Cotton, J. L. (1999). Mentor functions and outcomes: A comparison of men and women in formal and informal mentoring relationships. *Journal of Applied Psychology, 84,* 529–550. See also Chao, G. T., Walz, P. M., & Gardner, P. D. (1992). Formal and informal mentorships: A comparison of mentoring functions and contrast with non-mentored counterparts. *Personnel Psychology, 45,* 619–636.

47. Northrup, H. R., & Malin, M. E. (1986). *Personnel policies for engineers and scientists.* Philadelphia: Industrial Research Unit, Wharton School, University of Pennsylvania.

48. Schein, E. H. (1978). *Career dynamics: Matching individual and organizational needs.* Reading, MA: Addison-Wesley.

49. Raelin, J. A. (1983). First-job effects on career development. *Personnel Administrator, 28*(8), 71–76, 92.

50. Bounds, W. (2000, Nov. 15). The *really* early midlife crisis. *The Wall Street Journal,* pp. B1, B4.

51. Forbes, J. B. (1987). Early intraorganizational mobility: Patterns and influences. *Academy of Management Journal, 30,* 110–125.

52. Azar, B. (1996, Nov.). Project explores landscape of midlife. *Monitor,* p. 26.

53. Bell, J. E. (1982, Aug.). Mid-life transition in career men. *AMA Management Digest,* pp. 8–10.

54. Bennett, A. (1990, Sept. 11). A white-collar guide to job security. *The Wall Street Journal,* pp. B1, B12.

55. Lublin, J. S. (1993, Aug. 4). Strategic sliding: Lateral moves aren't always a mistake. *The Wall Street Journal,* p. B1. Rigdon, J. E. (1993, Dec. 1). You're not all alone if there's a mentor just a keyboard away. *The Wall Street Journal,* p. B1.

56. Floyd, S. W., & Woolridge, B. (1996). *The strategic middle manager.* San Francisco: Jossey-Bass.

57. *Occupational outlook handbook* (June, 2001). Table 3C, The 10 occupations with the largest job growth, 1998–2008. *www.bls.gov.*

58. Bell, op. cit.

59. Azar, op. cit.

60. Northrup & Malin, op. cit.

61. London, M. (1996). Redeployment and continuous learning in the 21st century: Hard lessons and positive examples from the downsizing era. *Academy of Management Executive, 10*(4), pp. 67–79. See also Fierman, J. (1993, Sept. 6). Beating the midlife career crisis, *Fortune,* pp. 52–60. See also Ference, T. P., Stoner, J. A., & Warren, E. K. (1977). Managing the career plateau. *Academy of Management Review, 2,* 602–612. See also Labor letter (1991, Feb. 19). *The Wall Street Journal,* p. A1.

62. Howard, A., & Bray, D. W. (1982, Mar. 21). AT&T: The hopes of middle managers. *The New York Times,* p. F1.

63. *The aging workforce* (1995). Washington, DC: American Association of Retired Persons.

64. Brain drain (1999, Sept. 20). *BusinessWeek,* pp. 111–126.

65. McEvoy, G. M., & Cascio, W. F. (1989). Cumulative evidence of the relationship between employee age and job performance. *Journal of Applied Psychology, 74,* 11–20.

66. Czaja, S. J. (1995, Spring). Aging and work performance. *Review of Public Personnel Administration,* 46–61. See also Sterns, H. L., & Miklos, S. M. (1995). The aging worker in a changing environment: Organizational and individual issues. *Journal of Vocational Behavior, 47,* 248–268. See also Landy, F. J., et. al. (1992, Jan.). Alternatives to chronological age in determining standards of suitability for public safety jobs. Report submitted to the U.S. Equal Employment Opportunity Commission, Washington, DC.

67. Cascio, W. F. (1996). Is age a proxy for declines in performance among workers over age 65? Working Paper 96-09, Graduate School of Business, University of Colorado–Denver.

68. U.S. survey challenges myths about older workers in the workplace (1999, Apr.). *Manpower Argus,* p. 8. See also Martocchio, J. J. (1989). Age-related differences in employee absenteeism: A meta-analysis. *Psychology and Aging, 4,* 410–414. See also Berkowitz, M. (1988). Functioning ability and job performance as workers age. In Borus, M. E., Parnes, H. S., Sandell, S. H., & Seidman, B. (eds.), *The older worker.* Madison, WI: Industrial Relations Research Association, pp. 87–114.

69. Bureau of National Affairs (1987). Older Americans in the workforce: Challenges and solutions. *Labor Relations Week, 1*(27), 1–237.

70. Farrimond, T. (1989). Accident and illness rates for younger and older workers when employment is based on medical examination. *Psychological Reports, 65,* 556–558.

71. Brotherton, P. (2000, Mar.–Apr.). Tapping into an older workforce. *Mosaics, 6*(2), 1, 4. See also American Association of Retired Persons (1993). *America's changing work force.* Washington, DC: Author.

72. New study cracks myth about the costs of older workers (1995). *Working Age, 11*(4), pp. 2, 3. See also Bureau of National Affairs, op. cit.

73. Brain drain, op. cit. See also *The aging workforce,* op. cit.

74. Wang, op. cit. See also Solomon, J., & Fuchsberg, G. (1990, Jan. 26). Great number of older Americans seem ready to work, *The Wall Street Journal,* p. B1.

75. Brain drain, op. cit.

76. Lefkovich, J. L. (1992). Older workers: Why and how to capitalize on their powers. *Employment Relations Today, 19*(1), 63–79.

77. Paul R. J., & Townsend, J. B. (1993). Managing the older worker—Don't just rinse away the gray. *Academy of Management Executive, 7*(3), 67–74. See also Labich, K. (1993, Mar. 8). The new unemployed. *Fortune,* pp. 40–49.

78. Maurer, T. J. (2001). Career-relevant learning and development, worker age, and beliefs about self-efficacy for development. *Journal of Management, 27,* 123–140. See also Few companies pursue strategies that would better use older workers (2000, May–June). *Working Age,* pp. 2–4. See also Simon, R. (1996, July), "Too damn old." *Money,* pp. 118–126.

79. Ibid. See also Bird, C. P., & Fisher, T. D. (1986). Thirty years later: Attitudes toward the employment of older workers. *Journal of Applied Psychology, 71,* 315–317.

80. New study cracks myth about the costs of older workers, op. cit.

81. Gardenswartz, L. & Rowe, A. (2000, Mar.–Apr.) How do we address conflict between employees because of age differences? *Mosaics, 6*(2), 3, 6. See also Leger, D. E. (2000, May 29). Help! I'm the new boss. *Fortune,* pp. 281–284.

82. Walker, J. W. (1992). *Human resource strategy.* New York: McGraw-Hill.

83. Quaintance, M. K. (1989). *Internal placement and career management.* In W. F. Cascio (ed.), Human resource planning, employment, and placement. Washington DC: Bureau of National Affairs, pp. 2-200 to 2-235.

84. Stumpf, S. A., & London, M. (1981). Management promotions: Individual and organizational factors influencing the decision process. *Academy of Management Review, 6,* 539–549.

85. Schwarzwald, J., Koslowsky, M. & Shalit, B. (1992). A field study of employees' attitudes and behaviors after promotion decisions. *Journal of Applied Psychology, 77,* 511–514.

86. Morris, T. (2000). Promotion policies and knowledge bases in the professional service firm. In M. Peiperl, M. Arthur, R. Coffee, and T. Morris (eds.), *Career frontiers.* Oxford, UK: Oxford University Press, pp. 138–152.

87. Lancaster, H. (1996, Nov. 19). A demotion does not have to mean the end of a fulfilling career. *The Wall Street Journal,* p. B1.

88. Auerbach, J. (1996, Apr. 5). Executive relocations–and hassles—increase. *The Wall Street Journal,* p. B8.

89. Judiesch, M. K., & Lyness, K. S. (1999). Left behind? The impact of leaves of absence on managers' career success. *Academy of Management Journal, 42,* 641–651. See also Stroh, L. K., Brett, J. M., & Reilly, A. H. (1992). All the right stuff: A comparison of female and male managers' career progression. *Journal of Applied Psychology, 77,* 251–260.

90. Albus, S. M. (2001, July). *2001 transfer volume and cost survey.* Washington, DC: Employee Relocation Council.

91. Grensing-Pophal, L. (2000, May). Think about the children. *HRMagazine,* pp. 133–142.

92. Lublin, J. S. (1993, Apr. 13). Husbands in limbo. *The Wall Street Journal,* pp. A1; A8.

93. Labor letter (1989, Nov. 17). *The Wall Street Journal,* p. A1.

94. Pinder, C. C., & Schroeder, K. G. (1987). Time to proficiency following job transfers. *Academy of Management Journal, 30,* 336–353.

95. Lublin (1993, Apr. 13), op. cit.

96. Albus, op. cit.

97. Mumma, J. S. (1996, Oct.). New technologies speed relocation process. *HRMagazine,* pp. 55–60.

98. Morris, J. R., Cascio, W. F., & Young, C. E. (1999, Winter). Downsizing after all these years: Questions and answers about who did it, how many did it, and who benefited from it. *Organizational Dynamics,* pp. 78–87. See also M. K. Gowing, J. D. Kraft, & J. C. Quick (eds.) (1998). *The new organizational reality: Downsizing, restructuring, and revitalization.* Washington, DC: American Psychological Association.

99. Grant, M., & Kraft, J. D. (1998). Results-based career transition and revitalization at the U.S. Office of Personnel Management. In Gowing et. al., op., pp. 143–163. See also Bragg, R. (1996, Mar. 5). Big holes where the dignity used to be. *The New York Times,* pp. 1, 8–10.

100. Knowdell, R. L., Branstead, E., & Moravec, M. (1994). *From downsizing to recovery.* Palo Alto, CA: Consulting Psychologists Press. See also Collarelli, S. M., & Beehr, T. A. (1993). Selection out: Firings, layoffs, and retirement. In N. Schmitt & W. C. Borman (eds.), *Personnel selection in organizations.* San Francisco: Jossey-Bass, pp. 341–384. See also Sweet, D. H. (1989). Outplacement. In W. F. Cascio (ed.), *Human resource planning, employment, and placement.* Washington, DC: Bureau of National Affairs, pp. 2-236–2-261.

101. The job-huntin' blues (1998, Dec. 14). *BusinessWeek,* p. 8.

102. Leana, C. R. (1996, Apr. 14). Why downsizing won't work. *Chicago Tribune Magazine,* pp. 15–18.

103. Noer, D. (1998). Layoff survivor sickness: What it is and what to do about it. In M. K. Gowing, J. D. Kraft, & J. C. Quick (eds.), *The new organizational reality: Downsizing, restructuring, and revitalization.* Washington, DC: American Psychological Association, pp. 207–220.

104. Sheley, E. (1996, Jan.). Job-sharing offers unique challenges. *HRMagazine,* pp. 46–49.

105. Solomon, C. M. (1994, Sept.). Job-sharing: One job, double headache? *Personnel Journal,* pp. 88–93.

106. Noble, K. B. (1988, Mar. 15). Union experiment provokes a fight. *The New York Times,* pp. A1, B20.

107. Labor letter (1986, Apr. 1). *The Wall Street Journal,* p. A1.

108. Where the next generation wants to work (1999, Oct. 11). *Fortune,* p. 322.

109. Collard, B., & Gelatt, H. B. (2000). Beyond balance to life quality. In J. M. Kummerow (ed.), *New directions in career planning and the workplace.* Palo Alto, CA: Davies-Black, pp. 197–225.

110. Damato, K. (1995, Apr. 14). Retire with the biggest pension check you can get. *The Wall Street Journal,* p. C1.

111. Mollica, K. A., & DeWitt, R. L. (2000). When others retire early: What about me? *Academy of Management Journal, 43,* 1068–1075.

112. Take the money and run—or take your chances (1993, Aug. 16). *BusinessWeek,* pp. 28, 29.

113. Hymowitz, C. (2001, July 24). Using layoffs to battle downturns often costs more than it saves. *The Wall Street Journal,* p. B1.

114. Clifford, L. (2000, Oct.). Getting over the hump before you're over the hill. *Money,* pp. 140–148.

115. Kim, S., & Feldman, D. C. (1998). Healthy, wealthy, or wise: Predicting actual acceptances of early retirement incentives at three points in time. *Personnel Psychology, 51,* 623–642. See also Greene, M. S. (1992). *Retirement: A new beginning.* St. John's, Newfoundland, Canada: Jesperson Press.

116. Andrews, E. S. (1992). Expanding opportunities for older workers. *Journal of Labor Research, 13*(1), 55–65.

117. Morris, B. (1996, Aug. 19). The future of retirement. *Fortune,* pp. 86–94.

118. Daniels & Vinzant, op. cit.

119. Give me that old-time economy (2000, Apr. 24). *BusinessWeek,* pp. 99–104.

120. Lancaster, H. (1995, Aug. 29). Professionals try new way to assess and develop skills. *The Wall Street Journal,* p. B1.

121. Kossek, E. E., Roberts, K., Fisher, S., & Demarr, B. (1998). Career self-management: A quasi-experimental assessment of the effects of a training intervention. *Personnel Psychology, 51,* 935–962.

COMPENSATION

Compensation, which includes direct cash payments, indirect payments in the form of employee benefits, and incentives to motivate employees to strive for higher levels of productivity, is a critical component of the employment relationship. Compensation is affected by forces as diverse as labor market factors, collective bargaining, government legislation, and top management's philosophy regarding pay and benefits. This is a dynamic area, and Chapters 11 and 12 present the latest developments in compensation theory and examples of company practices. Chapter 11 is a nontechnical introduction to the subject of pay and incentive systems, while Chapter 12 focuses on employee benefits. You will find that the material in both chapters has direct implications for sound management practice.

11. PAY AND INCENTIVE SYSTEMS

12. INDIRECT COMPENSATION: EMPLOYEE BENEFIT PLANS

PAY AND INCENTIVE SYSTEMS

11

Questions This Chapter Will Help Managers Answer

1. How can we tie compensation strategy to general business strategy?
2. What economic and legal factors should be considered in establishing pay levels for different jobs?
3. What is the best way to develop pay systems that are understandable, workable, and acceptable to employees at all levels?
4. How can we tie incentives to individual, team, or organizationwide performance?
5. In implementing a pay-for-performance system, what key traps must I avoid to make the system work as planned?

THE TRUST GAP*

Over the years, few topics have generated as much controversy as executive compensation. CEOs say, "We're a team; we're all in this together." But employees look at the difference between their pay and the CEO's. They see top management's perks—oak dining rooms and heated garages—versus cafeterias for lower-level workers and parking spaces a half-mile from the plant. And they wonder, "Is this togetherness?" As the disparity in pay widens (some heads of major U.S. companies receive compensation that is more than 500 times higher than the pay of the average American), the wonder grows. Hourly workers and supervisors indeed agree that "we're all in this together," but what we're in turns out to be a frame of mind that mistrusts senior management's intentions, doubts its competence, and resents its self-congratulatory pay. Indeed, the widening gulf has ignited a political firestorm and raised the specter of social turmoil.

Study after study, involving hundreds of companies and thousands of workers, has found evidence of a **trust gap**—and it is growing. Indeed, the attitudes of middle managers and professionals toward the workplace are becoming more like those of hourly workers, historically the most disaffected group.

As an example, consider that over a 5-year period, the number 1 earners got pay packages that averaged $274 million. Yet, far from delivering the superb results that employees and investors might have expected from the world's highest-priced managers, four of the five companies were marginal to horrible performers. They are Walt Disney, Cendant, Computer Associates, and Apple Computer. At a broader level, fully 62 percent of companies that posted negative returns in 1999 actually increased the overall compensation of their CEOs!

Between 1990 and 2000, for example, the median increase in CEO pay among the largest companies in 13 different industries exceeded 500 percent. Over the same time period, both the Consumer Price Index (CPI) and the minimum wage increased 36 percent, and the average hourly wage of autoworkers increased 37 percent, but the average pay of a tenured New York City teacher increased only 20 percent.

To be sure, much of the trust gap can be traced to inconsistencies between what management says and what it does—between saying "People are our most important asset" and in the next breath ordering layoffs, or between sloganeering about quality while continuing to evaluate workers by how many pieces they push out the door.

The result is a world in which top management thinks it's sending crucial messages but employees never hear a word. Thus a recent survey found that 82 percent of Fortune 500 executives believe their corporate strategy is understood by everyone who needs to know. Unfortunately, less than a third of employees in the same companies say management provides clear goals and direction.

Confidence in top management's competence is collapsing. The days when top management could say, "Trust us; this is for your own good" are over.

Sources: G. Colvin, The great CEO pay heist, *Fortune,* June 25, 2001, pp. 64–84. A. Lewis, Corporate execs flying high on alternate plane, *The Denver Post,* p. 1L, Aug. 13, 2001, CEO pay: The more things change . . . , *BusinessWeek,* Oct. 16, 2000, pp. 106–108. T. A. Stewart, Can even heroes get paid too much? *Fortune,* June 8, 1998, pp. 289, 290. A. Farnham, The trust gap, *Fortune,* Dec. 4, 1989, pp. 56–78.

Employees have seen that if the company embarks on a new strategic tack and it doesn't work, employees are the ones who lose their jobs—not management.

While competence may be hard to judge, pay is known, and to the penny. The rate of increase in top management's pay split from workers' in 1979 and has rocketed upward ever since. CEOs who make 200 times the average hourly worker's pay are no longer rare. European and Japanese CEOs, who seldom earn more than 15 times the employee average, look on in amazement. Said one observer, "The gap is widening beyond what the guy at the bottom can even understand. There's very little common ground left in terms of the experience of the average worker and the CEO."

While most U.S. workers are willing to accept substantial differentials in pay between corporate highs and lows and acknowledge that the highs should receive their just rewards, more and more of the lows—and the middles—are asking "Just how just is just?"

Challenges

1. To many people, a deep-seated sense of unfairness lies at the heart of the trust gap. How might perceptions of unfairness develop?
2. What are some of the predictable consequences of a trust gap?
3. Can you suggest alternative strategies for reducing the trust gap?

The chapter-opening vignette illustrates important changes in the current thinking about pay: Levels of pay will always be evaluated by employees in terms of "fairness," and unless pay systems are acceptable to those affected by them, they will breed mistrust and lack of commitment. Pay policies and practices are critically important, for they affect every single employee, from the janitor to the CEO. This chapter begins by exploring four major questions: (1) What economic and legal factors determine pay levels within a firm? (2) How do firms tie compensation strategy to general business strategy? (3) How do firms develop systematic pay structures that reflect different levels of pay for different jobs? (4) What key policy issues in pay planning and administration must managers address? These "challenges" are shown graphically in Figure 11–1.

Michael Eisner (on the right), CEO of Disney, is one of the highest-paid CEOs in the United States.

We will then consider what is known about incentives at the individual, team, and organizationwide levels. As an educated worker or manager, it is important that you become knowledgeable about these important issues. This chapter will help you develop that knowledge base.

CHANGING PHILOSOPHIES REGARDING PAY SYSTEMS

Today there is a continuing move away from policies of "salary entitlement," in which inflation or seniority, not performance, were the driving forces behind pay increases. Pay for performance is the new mantra. Managers are asking, "What have you done for me lately?" Current performance is what counts, and every year performance standards are raised. In this atmosphere, we are seeing three major changes in company philosophies concerning pay and benefits:

1. Increased willingness to reduce the size of the workforce and to restrict pay to control the costs of wages, salaries, and benefits.
2. Less concern with pay position relative to that of competitors and more concern with what the company can afford.
3. Implementation of programs to encourage and reward performance—thereby making pay more variable. In fact, a recent study revealed that this is one of the most critical compensation issues facing large companies today.[1]

We will consider each of these changes, as well as other material in this and the following chapter, from the perspective of the line manager, not from that of the technical compensation specialist.

Cost-Containment Actions

Given that wage and salary payments constitute about 60 percent of the costs of non-financial corporations, employers have an obvious interest in controlling them.[2] To do so, they are attempting to contain staff sizes, payrolls, and benefits costs. Some of the cutbacks are only temporary, such as pay freezes and postponements of raises. Other changes are meant to be permanent: firing executives

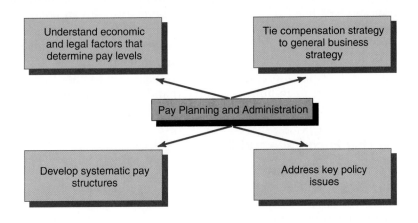

Figure 11–1

Four key challenges in planning and administering a pay system.

Figure 11-2

Percentage of companies offering some form of variable pay, 1990–2000.

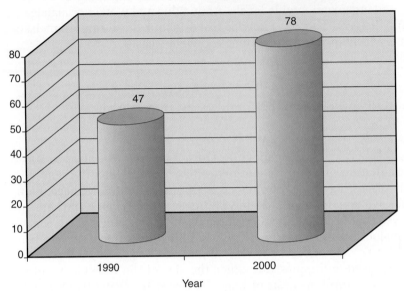

Percent of Companies Offering Some Form of Variable Pay

or offering them early retirement; asking employees to work longer hours, to take fewer days off, and to shorten their vacations; reducing the coverage of medical plans or asking employees to pay part of the cost; trimming expense accounts, with bans on first-class travel and restrictions on phone calls and entertainment. If such a strategy is to work, however, CEOs will first need to demonstrate to employees at all levels, by means of tangible actions, that they are serious about closing the "trust gap" (see chapter-opening vignette).

Paying What the Company Can Afford

To cover its labor costs and other expenses, a company must earn sufficient revenues through the sales of its products or services. It follows, then, that an employer's ability to pay is constrained by its ability to compete. The nature of the product or service markets affects a firm's external competitiveness and the pay level it sets.[3]

Key factors in the product and service markets are the degree of competition among producers (e.g., fast-food outlets) and the level of demand for the products or services (e.g., the number of customers in a given area). Both of these affect the ability of a firm to change the prices of its products or services. If an employer cannot change prices without suffering a loss of revenues due to decreased sales, that employer's ability to raise the level of pay is constrained. If the employer does pay more, it has two options: to try to pass the increased costs on to consumers or to hold prices fixed and allocate a greater portion of revenues to cover labor costs.[4]

Programs That Encourage and Reward Performance

Firms are continuing to relocate to areas where organized labor is weak and pay rates are low. They are developing pay plans that channel more dollars into incentive awards and fewer into fixed salaries. Entrepreneurs in start-up, high-risk organizations, salespeople, piecework factory workers, and rock stars have long lived with erratic incomes.[5] People in other jobs are used to fairly fixed paychecks that grow a bit every year. It is a bedrock of the U.S. compensation system, but it is gradually being nudged aside by programs that put more pay at risk.[6] These programs are being linked to profit and productivity gains— usually a moving, ever-rising target.

Such variable-pay systems almost guarantee cost control. In many new plans any productivity gains are shared 25 percent by the employees and 75 percent by the company. If business takes off, more pay goes to workers. If it doesn't, the company is not locked into high fixed costs of labor. In the United States, 78 percent of large and medium-size companies now offer some kind of variable pay—such as profit sharing and bonus awards—up from 47 percent in 1990 (see Figure 11–2).[7] Later in this chapter we will discuss more fully the pay-for-performance theme and how it can be put into effect.

INTERNATIONAL APPLICATION
Tying Pay to Performance in the United States and Japan[8]

In an effort to hold down labor costs, thousands of U.S. companies are changing the way they increase workers' pay. Instead of the traditional annual increase, millions of workers in industries as diverse as supermarkets and aircraft manufacturing are receiving cash bonuses. For most workers, the plans mean less money. The bonuses take many names: "profit sharing" at Abbott Laboratories and Hewlett-Packard, "gain sharing" at Mack Trucks and Panhandle Eastern Corporation, and "lump-sum payments" at Boeing. All have two elements in common: (1) they can vary with the company's fortunes, and (2) they are not permanent. Because the bonuses are not folded into base pay (as merit increases are), there is no compounding effect over time. They are simply provided on top of a constant base level of pay. This means that both wages and benefits rise more slowly than if the base level of pay were rising each year. The result: a flattening of wages nationally.

Fully 78 percent of Fortune 1000 companies offer bonuses to exempt employees, and 45 percent offer them to nonexempt employees. How have unions reacted? In the view of the AFL-CIO, "Where there is justification for belt-tightening, then profit sharing is not an unreasonable means of passing on earnings when times improve.[9]

"Flexible pay"—tied mostly to profitability

and promising better job security, but not guaranteeing it—is at the heart of the evolving bonus system. Employees are being asked to share the risks of the new global marketplace. How large must the rewards be? MIT economist Martin Weitzman estimates that over the long run the proper bonus level is 20 to 25 percent of total compensation, because that would give workers a pay increase equal to the rate of inflation plus productivity gains. But in the United States most bonus payments have been averaging about 10 percent of a worker's base pay annually. Conversely, the Japanese currently pay many workers a bonus that represents about 25 percent of base pay. For workers in both nations, a significant amount of their pay is "at risk."

Have such plans generated greater productivity in the U.S. manufacturing sector in recent years? Maybe, but an equally plausible explanation is that the gains were due to automation, to company efforts to give workers more of a say in how they do their jobs, and to workers' fear that if they did not improve their productivity, their plants would become uncompetitive and be closed. In short, the jury is still out on the productivity impact of bonus systems, but evidence does indicate that bonus satisfaction is a separate and distinct component of overall pay satisfaction.[10]

The previous example focused on the *outcomes* of bonus decisions. However, the *process* is also important. To a large extent the relative emphasis managers place on performance versus relationships varies with cultural factors. Thus, when making bonus decisions, Chinese managers tend to place less emphasis on employees' work performance than do American managers. However, when making decisions about nonmonetary recognition of employees, Chinese managers tend to place more emphasis on employees' relationships with coworkers and managers than do their American counterparts. Finally, Chinese managers tend to give larger bonuses to employees with greater personal needs, while American managers tend not to take personal needs into consideration in making bonus decisions.[11]

COMPONENTS AND OBJECTIVES OF ORGANIZATIONAL REWARD SYSTEMS

At a broad level, an **organizational reward system** includes anything an employee values and desires that an employer is able and willing to offer in exchange for employee contributions. The employer provides **compensation** for those contributions. More specifically, the reward system includes both financial and nonfinancial rewards. Financial rewards include direct payments (e.g., salary) plus indirect payments in the form of employee benefits (see Chapter 12). Nonfinancial rewards include everything in a work environment that enhances a worker's sense of self-respect and sense of being esteemed by others (e.g., work environments that are physically, socially, and mentally healthful; opportunities for training and personal development; effective supervision; recognition). These ideas are shown graphically in Figure 11–3.

Figure 11–3

Organizational reward systems include financial as well as nonfinancial components.

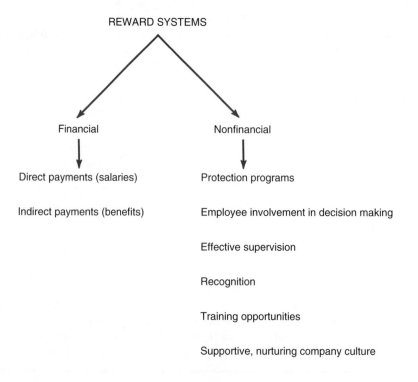

REWARD SYSTEMS

Financial

Nonfinancial

Direct payments (salaries)

Indirect payments (benefits)

Protection programs

Employee involvement in decision making

Effective supervision

Recognition

Training opportunities

Supportive, nurturing company culture

While money is obviously a powerful tool to capture the minds and hearts of workers and to maximize their productivity, don't underestimate the impact of nonfinancial rewards. As an example, consider Wilton Connor Packaging Inc. in Charlotte, North Carolina. In addition to offering on-site laundry service, it has a handyman on staff who does free, minor household repairs for employees while they're at work—thus cutting down on excuses for missing work. If there's a major problem—say a toilet that needs to be replaced—the handyman orders it from Home Depot and charges it to the company's account there. The employee repays the company a few dollars a month.

"We have virtually no turnover, we have no quality problems, we have very few supervisors," asserts Wilton Connor, the company's chief executive. "Those are the hard-nosed business reasons for doing these things."[12] Companies are doing these things because they don't have much choice. Giving their workers more ease and freedom is simple enlightened self-interest. As one executive noted, "The demand for brains is higher than it's ever been." Satisfying this demand will require radical rethinking of employment practices that have served organizations reasonably well in the past.[13]

Rewards bridge the gap between organizational objectives and individual expectations and aspirations. To be effective, organizational reward systems should provide four things: (1) a sufficient level of rewards to fulfill basic needs, (2) equity with the external labor market, (3) equity within the organization, and (4) treatment of each member of the organization in terms of his or her individual needs.[14] More broadly, pay systems are designed to attract, retain, and motivate (ARM) employees. In this ARM concept, much of the design of compensation systems involves working out trade-offs among more or less seriously conflicting objectives.[15]

Perhaps the most important objective of any pay system is fairness, or equity. Equity can be assessed on at least three dimensions:

1. **Internal equity.** In terms of the relative worth of individual jobs to an organization, are pay rates fair?
2. **External equity.** Are the wages paid by an organization "fair" in terms of competitive market rates outside the organization?
3. **Individual equity.** Is each individual's pay "fair" relative to that of other individuals doing the same or similar jobs?

Researchers have proposed several bases for determining equitable payment for work.[16] They have three points in common:

1. Each assumes that employees perceive a fair return for what they contribute to their jobs.
2. All include the concept of social comparison, whereby employees determine what their equitable return should be after comparing their inputs (e.g., skills, education, effort) and outcomes (e.g., pay, promotion, job status) with those of their peers or coworkers (comparison persons).
3. The theories assume that employees who perceive themselves to be in an inequitable situation will seek to reduce that inequity. They may do so by mentally distorting their inputs or outcomes, by directly altering their inputs or outcomes, or by leaving the organization.

Ethical Dilemma
Should Board Members Who Set CEO Pay Be Independent?

At Citizens Utilities, based in Stamford, Connecticut, the firm's chief executive officer received $21.6 million in pay. That's about $26 from each of more than 800,000 Citizens customers in 13 states who get their electricity, water, and gas from the company. All three of the board of directors members who negotiated the CEO's employment contract had close ties to the company. One of them made more than $500,000 in consulting fees. The second benefited from legal work at Citizens. The third received 7,271 stock options in a cellular-phone subsidiary of Citizens that sold stock, netting him a $123,000 paper profit.[19] Now, however, powerful institutional investors and money managers are demanding that such cozy relationships be disclosed, because, to quote former Supreme Court Justice Louis D. Brandeis, "Sunlight is the best disinfectant."[20] At Citizens Utilities, the board members' actions were legal, but were they ethical? Whose interests should be considered in matters such as these?

Reviews of both laboratory and field tests of equity theory are quite consistent: Individuals tend to follow the equity norm and to use it as a basis for distributing rewards. They report inequitable conditions as distressing, although there may be individual differences in sensitivity to equity.[17]

A final objective is **balance**—the relative size of pay differentials among different segments of the workforce. If pay systems are to accomplish the objectives set for them, ultimately they must be perceived as adequate and equitable. For example, there should be a balance in pay relationships between supervisors and the highest-paid subordinates reporting to them. According to the public accounting firm Coopers & Lybrand, among companies judged to be well managed, this differential is generally 15 percent.[18] As the chapter-opening vignette illustrates, ratios of 200:1 (or greater) between the highest- and lowest-paid employees are generally regarded as out of balance.

STRATEGIC INTEGRATION OF COMPENSATION PLANS AND BUSINESS PLANS

Unfortunately, the rationale behind many compensation programs is "Two-thirds of our competitors do it" or "That's corporate policy." Compensation plans need to be tied to an organization's strategic mission and should take their direction from that mission. They must support the general business strategy—for instance, innovation or cost leadership.[21] Further, evidence now shows that inferior performance by a firm is associated with a lack of fit between its pay policy and its business strategy.[22] From a managerial perspective, therefore, the most fundamental question is: What do you want your pay system to accomplish?

As an example, consider Dial Corporation, the big consumer-products maker. Over the 3-year period 1997–1999 the company eliminated merit raises for its 1400 nonunion staffers. Instead they became eligible for annual cash bonuses, which primarily reflect three measures of corporate financial performance—net revenue growth, operating margin, and asset turnover. These measures reflect business strategies of cost-leadership and differentiation (setting oneself apart from the competition). Potential bonuses (up to 14 percent of base pay) rose as merit raises were phased out.[23]

This approach to managing compensation and business strategies dictates that actual levels of compensation should not be strictly a matter of what is being paid in the marketplace. Instead, compensation levels derive from an assessment of what must be paid to attract and retain the right people, what the organization can afford, and what will be required to meet the organization's strategic goals. The idea is to align the interests of managers and employees.

When compensation is viewed from a strategic perspective, therefore, firms do the following:

1. They recognize compensation as a pivotal control and incentive mechanism that can be used flexibly by management to attain business objectives.
2. They make the pay system an integral part of strategy formulation.
3. They integrate pay considerations into strategic decision-making processes, such as those that involve planning and control.
4. They view the firm's performance as the ultimate criterion of the success of strategic pay decisions and operational compensation programs.[24]

DETERMINANTS OF PAY STRUCTURE AND LEVEL

In the simplest terms, marginal revenue product theory in labor economics holds that the value of a person's labor is what someone is willing to pay for it.[25] In practice, a number of factors interact to determine wage levels. Some of the most influential of these are labor market conditions, legislation, collective bargaining, management attitudes, and an organization's ability to pay. Let us examine each of these.

Labor Market Conditions

As noted in Chapter 6, whether a labor market is "tight" or "loose" has a major impact on wage structures and levels. Thus, if the demand for certain skills is high, while the supply is low (a "tight" market), there tends to be an increase in the price paid for these skills. Conversely, if the supply of labor is plentiful, relative to the demand for it, wages tend to decrease. As an example, consider Jordan Machine Company.

SMALL BUSINESS CONTENDS WITH TIGHT LABOR MARKETS   COMPANY EXAMPLE

Jordan Machine Company of Birmingham, Alabama, has never worked so hard to find so few employees. "We've turned over barrels and drums and searched just about everywhere we can think," says Jerry Edwards, chief executive officer. The company needs skilled machinists to help manufacture molds for everything from fishing lures to submarine hatch covers.

Despite his efforts—including offers of high pay, full health benefits, and a company-sponsored savings program—Mr. Edwards estimated that his company lost more than half a million dollars last year, simply because it couldn't find enough workers to meet the demand for new orders.

Jordan Machine Company is not alone, as companies, high-tech and low-tech alike, simply cannot find workers. Thus in a recent survey, the International Franchise Association found that 95 percent of its members ranked labor as their biggest challenge. The labor shortage has emerged as the number 1 headache for franchisees. In some cases it is curbing growth and expansion possibilities, and in others it is forcing operators to shut down early for lack of staff.[26] Such tight labor markets have predictable effects on wages. In Birmingham, for example, wages have risen 24 percent since 1990, compared to 19 percent for the United States as a whole.[27]

Another labor market phenomenon that causes substantial differences in pay rates, even among people who work in the same field and are of similar age and education, is the payment of wage premiums by some employers to attract the best talent available, and to enhance productivity in order to offset any increase in labor costs. This is known as the "efficiency wage hypothesis" in labor economics, and it has received considerable support among economic researchers.[28] The forces discussed thus far affect pay levels to a considerable extent. So also does government legislation.

Legislation

As in other areas, legislation related to pay plays a vital role in determining internal organization practices. Although we cannot analyze all the relevant laws here, Table 11–1 presents a summary of the coverage, major provisions, and federal agencies charged with administering four major federal wage-hour laws. Wage-hour laws set limits on minimum wages to be paid and maximum hours to be worked.

Of the four laws shown in Table 11–1, the Fair Labor Standards Act (FLSA) affects almost every organization in the United States. It is the source of the terms "exempt employees" (exempt from the overtime provisions of the law) and "nonexempt employees." It established the first national minimum wage (25 cents an hour) in 1938; subsequent changes in the minimum wage and in national policy on equal pay for equal work for both sexes (the Equal Pay Act of 1963) were passed as amendments to this law.

There are many loopholes in FLSA minimum-wage coverage.[29] Certain workers, including casual babysitters and most farm workers, are excluded, as are employees of small businesses and firms not engaged in interstate commerce. State minimum-wage laws are intended to cover these workers. At the same time, if a state's minimum is higher than the federal minimum, the state minimum applies. For example, while the federal minimum wage was $5.15 per hour in 2001, California's was $6.75. More than 50 cities and counties also require contractors to pay a "living wage," which in generally more than federal or state minimums. Effective in 2002, Santa Monica, California, will require the city and its contractors, plus businesses in the downtown and beach areas, to pay workers $12.25 an hour, or $10.50 an hour if they provide health benefits. While opponents argue that such laws will force some businesses to close, at least some academic research suggests that living wage laws do more good than harm. They have imposed little, if any, cost upon the cities that have passed them, they have led to few job losses, and they have lifted many families out of poverty.[30]

Table 11–1

FOUR MAJOR FEDERAL WAGE-HOUR LAWS

	Scope of coverage	Major provisions	Administrative agency
Fair Labor Standards Act (FLSA) of 1938 (as amended)	Employers involved in interstate commerce with two or more employees and annual revenues greater than $500,000. Exemption from overtime provisions for managers, supervisors, executives, outside salespersons, and professional workers.	Minimum wage of $5.15 per hour for covered employees (as of September 1997); time-and-a-half pay for over 40 hours per week; restrictions by occupation or industry on the employment of persons under 18; prohibits wage differentials based exclusively on sex—equal pay for equal work. No extra pay required for weekends, vacations, holidays, or severance.	Wage and Hour Division of the Employment Standards Administration, U.S. Department of Labor
Davis-Bacon Act (1931)	Federal contractors involved in the construction or repair of federal buildings and public works with a contract value over $2,000.	Employees on the project must be paid prevailing community wage rates for the type of employment used. Overtime of time and a half for more than 40 hours per week. Three-year blacklisting of contractors who violate this act.	Comptroller General and Wage and Hour Division
Walsh-Healy Act (1936)	Federal contractors manufacturing or supplying materials, articles, or equipment to the federal government with a value exceeding $10,000 annually.	Same as Davis-Bacon. Under the Defense Authorization Act of 1986, overtime is required only for hours worked in excess of 40 per week, not 8 per day, as previously.	Same as FLSA
McNamara-O'Hara Service Contract Act (1965)	Federal contractors who provide services to the federal government with a value in excess of $2,500.	Same as Davis-Bacon.	Same as Davis-Bacon

An important feature of the FLSA is its provision regarding the employment of young workers. On school days, 14- and 15-year-olds are allowed to work no more than 3 hours (no more than 8 hours on nonschool days), or a total of 18 hours a week when school is in session. They may work 40-hour weeks during the summer and during school vacations, but they may not work outside the hours of 7 A.M. to 7 P.M. (or 9 P.M. from June 1 to Labor Day). Both federal and state laws allow 16- and 17-year-olds to work any hours but forbid them to work in hazardous occupations, such as driving or working with power-driven meat slicers.

The remaining three laws shown in Table 11–1 apply only to organizations that do business with the federal government in the form of construction or by supplying goods and services.

Collective Bargaining

Another major influence on wages in unionized as well as non-unionized firms is collective bargaining. Nonunionized firms are affected by collective bargaining agreements made elsewhere since they must compete with unionized firms for the services and loyalties of workers. Collective bargaining affects two key factors: (1) the level of wages, and (2) the behavior of workers in relevant labor markets. In an open, competitive market, workers tend to gravitate toward higher-paying jobs. To the extent that nonunionized firms fail to match the wages of unionized firms, they may have difficulty attracting and keeping workers. Furthermore, benefits negotiated under union agreements have had the effect of increasing the "package" of benefits in firms that have attempted to avoid unionization. In addition to wages and benefits, collective bargaining is also used to negotiate procedures for administering pay, procedures for resolving grievances regarding compensation decisions, and methods used to determine the relative worth of jobs.[31]

Managerial Attitudes and an Organization's Ability to Pay

These factors have a major impact on wage structures and levels. Earlier we noted that an organization's ability to pay depends, to a large extent, on the competitive dynamics it faces in its product or service markets. Therefore, regardless of its espoused competitive position on wages, an organization's ability to pay ultimately will be a key factor that limits actual wages.

This is not to downplay the role of management philosophy and attitudes on pay. On the contrary, management's desire to maintain or to improve morale, to attract high-caliber employees, to reduce turnover, and to improve employees' standard of living also affect wages, as does the relative importance of a given position to a firm.[32] A safety engineer is more important to a chemical company than to a bank. Wage structures tend to vary across firms to the extent that managers view any given position as more or less critical to their firms. Thus compensation administration reflects management judgment to a considerable degree. Ultimately, top management renders judgments regarding the overall competitive pay position of the firm (above-market, at-market, or below-market rates), factors to be considered in determining job worth, and the relative weight to be given seniority and performance in pay decisions. Such judgments are key determinants of the structure and level of wages.[33]

AN OVERVIEW OF PAY SYSTEM MECHANICS

The procedures described below for developing pay systems help those involved in the development process to apply their judgments in a systematic manner. The hallmarks of success in compensation management, as in other areas, are understandability, workability, and acceptability. The broad objective in developing pay systems is to assign a monetary value to each job in the organization (a base rate) and an orderly procedure for increasing the base rate (e.g., based on merit, inflation, or some combination of the two). To develop such a system, we need four basic tools:

1. Updated job descriptions.
2. A job evaluation method (i.e., one that will rank jobs in terms of their overall worth to the organization).
3. Pay surveys.
4. A pay structure.

Figure 11–4 presents an overview of this process.

Job descriptions are key tools in the design of pay systems, for they serve two purposes:

1. They identify important characteristics of each job so that the relative worth of jobs can be determined.

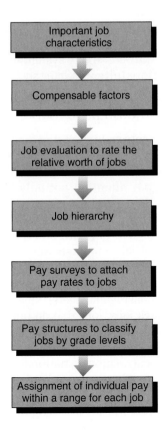

Figure 11–4

Traditional job-based compensation model.

2. From them we can identify, define, and weight **compensable factors** (common job characteristics that an organization is willing to pay for, such as skill, effort, responsibility, and working conditions).

Once this has been done, the next step is to rate the worth of all jobs using a predetermined system.

A number of **job evaluation** methods have been developed since the 1920s, and many, if not most, of them are still used. They all have the same final objective—ranking jobs in terms of their relative worth to the organization so that an equitable rate of pay can be determined for each job. Moreover, they all yield similar results.[34]

For example, in the point-factor method of job evaluation, each job is analyzed and defined in terms of the compensable factors an organization has agreed to adopt. Points are assigned to each level (or degree) of a compensable factor, such as responsibility. The total points assigned to each job across each compensable factor are then summed. A hierarchy of job worth is therefore defined when jobs are rank-ordered from highest-point total to lowest-point total.

Job evaluation is used widely, but not universally, among firms. One reason is that several policy issues must be resolved first. These include[35]:

- Does management perceive meaningful differences among jobs?
- Is it possible to identify and operationalize meaningful criteria for distinguishing among jobs?
- Will job evaluation result in meaningful distinctions in the eyes of employees?
- Are jobs stable, and will they remain stable in the future?
- Is job evaluation consistent with the organization's goals and strategies? For example, if the goal is to ensure maximum flexibility among job assignments, a knowledge- or skill-based pay system may be most appropriate. We will address that topic more fully in a later section.

Linking Internal Pay Relationships to Market Data

In the point-factor method of job evaluation, the next task is to translate the point totals into a pay structure. Two key components of this process are identifying and surveying pay rates in relevant labor markets. This can often be a complex task since employers must pay attention not only to labor markets but also to product markets.[36] Pay practices must be designed not only to attract and retain employees, but also to ensure that labor costs (as part of the overall costs of production) do not become excessive in relation to those of competing employers.

The definition of relevant labor markets requires two key decisions: which jobs to survey and which markets are relevant for each job. Jobs selected for a survey are generally characterized by stable tasks and stable job specifications (e.g., computer programmers, purchasing managers). Jobs with these characteristics are known as "key" or **benchmark jobs.** Jobs that do not meet these criteria, but that are characterized by high turnover or are difficult to fill, should also be included.

As we noted earlier, the definition of **relevant labor markets** should consider geographical boundaries (local, regional, national, or international) as well as product-market competitors. Such an approach might begin with product-market competitors as the initial market, followed by adjustments downward (e.g., from national to regional markets) on the basis of geographical considerations.

Once target populations and relevant markets have been identified, the next task is to obtain survey data. Surveys are available from a variety of sources, including the federal government (Bureau of Labor Statistics), employers' associations, trade and professional associations, users of a given job evaluation system (e.g., the Hay Group's point-factor system), and compensation consulting firms.

WHAT ARE YOU WORTH?   COMPANY EXAMPLE

In a world where information is power, salary negotiations have long been greatly imbalanced. The Internet, however, is leveling the playing field, as a growing number of Web sites offer salary surveys, job listings with specified pay levels, and even customized compensation analyses.[37] For example, America's Career InfoNet (*www.acinet.org*) provides access to wage data compiled by the Bureau of Labor Statistics. However, Salary.com is arguably the most popular provider of salary comparisons. It averages 13.4 million page views in a 6-month period! Salary.com provides detailed geographic information and matching job descriptions for 1,200 positions. The primary tool used by Salary.com is the Salary Wizard, which allows users to enter a job title and zip code, and receive a median salary number as well as a range from 25 percent of the median through 75 percent of the median.

The Salary Wizard is based on Salary.com's analysis of several different data sources, which the company's team of compensation specialists aggregates into a database and then uses to power the Wizard. If you prefer to see data presented by industry, try Career-Journal.com, from *The Wall Street Journal.* In about 50 categories, there are 2 to 10 articles about compensation in a field, and 4 to 10 salary tables, depending on the industry.[38] Go to these sites and compare the kinds of information presented in each one. Do they provide information on which employers are included and which are not? Where do their data come from? Answering questions like these can help to judge the credibility of the data. Credible data, in turn, can help you do a better job of negotiating compensation in a new job—or trying to improve your pay at your current one. How much more should you expect when switching jobs? While the average is about 12–14 percent more than you are currently making, if a company really wants you, and the hiring manager knows you are in demand elsewhere, you can reasonably expect an offer of 20 percent more than your current salary. For someone with other offers who is the absolute right fit for a given job, however, the jump could be as high as 50 percent. What's the moral of this story? The better the fit, the more wiggle room you have.[39]

Managers should be aware of two potential problems with pay survey data.[40] The most serious is the assurance of an accurate job match. If only a "thumbnail sketch" (i.e., a very brief description) is used to characterize a job, there is always the possibility of legitimate misunderstanding among survey respondents. To deal with this, some surveys ask respondents if their salary data for a job are direct matches, or somewhat higher or lower than those described (and therefore worthy of more or less pay).

A second problem has resulted from the explosion of "at-risk" forms of pay, some of which are based on individual performance and some on the profitability of an organization. As we noted earlier, base pay is becoming a smaller part of the total compensation package for a broad range of employees. This makes it difficult to determine the actual pay of job incumbents, and can make survey results difficult to interpret. For example, how does one compare salary figures that include only base pay or direct cash payouts with "at-risk" pay that may take the form of a lump-sum bonus, additional time off with pay, or an employee stock-ownership plan? Despite these potential problems, all indications are that pay surveys will continue to be used widely.

The end result is often a chart, as in Figure 11–5, that relates current wage rates to the total points assigned to each job. For each point total, a trend line is fitted to indicate the average relationship between points assigned to the benchmark jobs and the hourly wages paid for those jobs. Once a midpoint trend line is fitted, two others are also drawn: (1) a trend line that represents the minimum rate of pay for each point total and (2) a trend line that represents the maximum rate of pay for each point total.[41]

Developing a Pay Structure

The final step in attaching dollar values to jobs using the point method is to establish pay grades, or ranges, characterized by a point spread from mini-

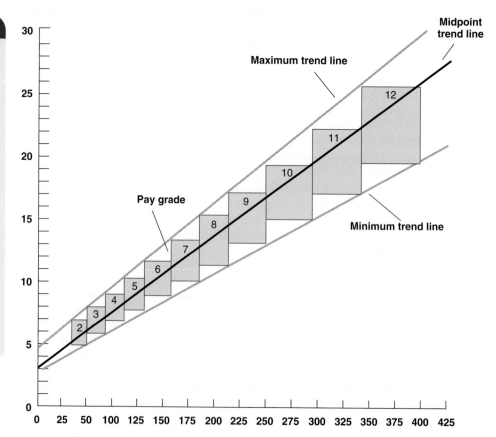

Figure 11–5

Chart relating hourly wage rates to the total points assigned to each job. Three trend lines are shown—minimum, midpoint, and maximum—as well as 11 pay grades. Within each pay grade there is a 30 percent spread from minimum to maximum and a 50 percent overlap from one pay grade to the next.

mum to maximum for each grade. Starting wages are given by the trend line that represents the minimum rate of pay for each pay grade, while the highest wages that can be earned within a grade are given by the trend line that represents the maximum rate of pay. The pay structure is described numerically in Table 11–2.

For example, consider the job of "administrative clerk." Let's assume that the job evaluation committee arrived at a total allocation of 142 points across all compensable factors. The job therefore falls into pay grade 6. Starting pay is $13.12 per hour, with a maximum pay rate of $17.06 per hour.

The actual development of a pay structure is a complex process, but there are certain rules of thumb to follow:

- Jobs of the same general value should be clustered into the same pay grade.
- Jobs that clearly differ in value should be in different pay grades.
- There should be a smooth progression of point groupings.
- The new system should fit realistically into the existing allocation of pay within a company.
- The pay grades should conform reasonably well to pay patterns in the relevant labor markets.[42]

Once such a pay structure is in place, the determination of each individual's pay (based on experience, seniority, and performance) becomes a more systematic, orderly procedure. A compensation planning worksheet, such as that shown in Figure 11–6, can be very useful to managers confronted with these weighty decisions.

Table 11–2

ILLUSTRATIVE PAY STRUCTURE SHOWING PAY GRADES, THE SPREAD OF POINTS WITHIN GRADES, THE MIDPOINT OF EACH PAY GRADE, AND THE MINIMUM AND MAXIMUM RATES OF PAY PER GRADE

Grade	Point spread	Midpoint	Minimum rate of pay	Maximum rate of pay
2	62– 75	68	$ 7.50	$ 9.75
3	76– 91	83	8.63	11.21
4	92–110	101	9.92	12.90
5	111–132	121	11.41	14.83
6	133–157	145	13.12	17.06
7	158–186	172	15.09	19.62
8	187–219	203	17.35	22.56
9	220–257	238	19.95	25.94
10	258–300	279	22.95	29.83
11	301–350	325	26.39	34.31
12	351–407	379	30.35	34.45

Figure 11–6

Sample annual compensation planning worksheet.

ANNUAL COMPENSATION PLANNING WORKSHEET															

ORG. UNIT _____

MGR. OR SUPV. _____

EMPLOYEE NAME	JOB TITLE	LAST SALARY ADJUSTMENT				CURRENT SALARY	RANGE MINIMUM	RANGE MIDPOINT	RANGE MAXIMUM	PERFORMANCE APPRAISAL	FORECAST SALARY ADJUSTMENT (If Any)				
		Amt.	%	Date	Type*						Amt.	%	Date	New Salary	Inter-val

*Code for "Type"
1—Promotion
2—Merit

PREPARED BY _____

Alternatives to Pay Systems Based on Job Evaluation

There are at least two such alternatives. These are market-based pay and skill- or knowledge-based pay, also referred to as competency-based pay.

Market-Based Pay

The **market-based pay** system uses a direct market-pricing approach for all of a firm's jobs. This type of pay structure is feasible if all jobs are benchmark jobs and direct matches can be found in the market. Pay surveys can then be used to determine the market prices of the jobs in question. This type of pay system may be used in entrepreneurial start-up firms, research and development units, sales organizations, and for very senior jobs.[43] Larger firms with more diverse jobs, however, may have to rely on market pricing only for benchmark jobs and use job evaluation in order to price nonbenchmark jobs.

Competency-Based Pay

Under a **competency-based pay** system, workers are paid not on the basis of the job they currently are doing but rather on the basis of the number of jobs they are capable of doing, that is, on the basis of their skills or on their depth of knowledge, both of which are termed "competencies." Skill-based plans are usually applied to so-called blue-collar work, and competencies to so-called white-collar work. The distinctions are not hard and fast. They can focus on depth (specialists in corporate law, finance, or welding and hydraulic maintenance) or breadth (generalists with knowledge in all phases of operations including marketing, manufacturing, finance, and HR).[44] In a world of slimmed-down big companies and agile small ones, the last thing any manager wants to hear from an employee is "It's not my job." To see how such a system might work in practice, let's consider Polaroid.

COMPETENCY-BASED PAY AT POLAROID CORPORATION[45]   **COMPANY EXAMPLE**

Polaroid initiated a companywide, competency-based pay system in 1990. Polaroid employees are encouraged to form work teams and to redesign their work functions in order to make them more efficient, according to Richard G. Terry, compensation manager at Polaroid, which is based in Cambridge, Mass. Although Polaroid's system includes everyone from the mailroom clerk to the chief executive officer, it has been more effective in the manufacturing part of the business.

Polaroid's manufacturing employees have learned skills in a number of different areas, rather than focusing on a single job. In addition, the work teams have picked up some of the responsibilities of supervisors, such as scheduling assignments and overtime. Employees who have succeeded at the new jobs have received more money. "Their pay has gone beyond what was traditionally the top," Mr. Terry said.

The focus of Polaroid's white-collar employees has been on learning new technologies. But here, the process has not worked as smoothly. Part of the problem is that skills, or competencies, are not so easy to measure in managerial jobs, but this will not stop companies from attempting to apply this scheme to their white-collar workforces. "Slowly, but surely, we're becoming a skill-based society where your market value is tied to what you can do and what your skill set is. In this new world, where skills and knowledge are what really count, it doesn't make sense to treat people as jobholders. It makes sense to treat them as people with specific skills, and to pay them for those skills."

In such a "learning environment," the more workers learn, the more they earn." Competency-based plans become increasingly expensive as the majority of employees become certified at the highest pay levels. As a result, the employer may have an average wage higher than competitors who use conventional job evaluation. Unless the increased flexibility permits leaner staffing, the employer may also experience higher labor costs. This is what caused Motorola and TRW to abandon their plans after just a few years.[46] Is there any impact on productivity, quality, or labor costs? A 37-month study in a component-assembly plant found a 58 percent improvement in productivity, a 16 percent reduction on the cost of labor per part, and an 82 percent reduction in scrap compared to a similar facility that did not use skill-based pay.[47] Another study linked the ease of communication and understanding of skill-based plans to employees' general perceptions of being treated fairly by the employer.[48] Not surprisingly, there is growing interest in this approach.

Companies view competency-based pay plans as a way to develop the critical behaviors and abilities employees need to achieve specific business results. By linking compensation directly to individual contributions that make a difference to the organization, a company can maintain the highest caliber of workers, regardless of their particular specialty or role. Such plans also provide a mechanism for cross-training employees to ensure that people in different functional areas have the behavioral or technical skills to take on additional responsibilities as needed.[49] Competency-based pay systems work best when the following conditions exist[50]:

1. A supportive HRM philosophy underpins all employment activities. Such a philosophy is characterized by mutual trust and the conviction that employees have the ability and motivation to perform well.
2. HRM programs such as profit sharing, participative management, empowerment, and job enrichment complement the competency-based pay system.
3. Technology and organization structure change frequently.
4. Employee exchanges (i.e., assignment, rotation) are common.
5. There are opportunities to learn new skills.
6. Employee turnover is relatively high.
7. Workers value teamwork and the opportunity to participate.

In summary, if compensation systems are to be used strategically, it is important that management (1) understand clearly what types of behavior it wants the compensation system to reinforce, (2) recognize that compensation systems are integral components of planning and control, and (3) view the firm's performance as the ultimate criterion of the success of strategic pay decisions and operational compensation programs.

Now let us consider some key policy issues.

POLICY ISSUES IN PAY PLANNING AND ADMINISTRATION

Pay Secrecy

The extent to which information on pay is public or private is a basic issue that needs to be addressed by management. Pay secrecy is a difficult policy to maintain, particularly as so much pay-related information is now available on the Web. Anyone with access to the Internet can find out fairly easily what a position is worth in the job market. In the United States, the pay of senior executives is disclosed in annual reports. However, this is not the case in Europe. Continental Europe still has a way to go before it matches the United States and the United Kingdom in disclosing executive pay. Spain and Italy, for example, have no reporting requirements. Under current German law, companies lump together the pay of all management-board members. However, France, Switzerland, and especially Ireland are beginning the lift the veil of secrecy that shrouds the compensation of executives in these countries.[51]

Openness versus secrecy is not an either/or phenomenon. Rather, it is a matter of degree. For example, organizations may choose to disclose one or more of the following: (1) the work- and business-related rationale on which the system is based, (2) pay ranges, (3) pay increase schedules, and (4) the availability of pay-related data from the compensation department.[52] Posting salary ranges, experts contend, is a public show of trust in employees. It demonstrates that the employer values them and will help them to advance.[53] However, there is also a downside to pay openness:

1. It forces managers to defend their pay decisions and practices publicly. Since the process is inherently subjective, there is no guarantee that satisfactory answers will ever be found that can please all concerned parties.
2. The cost of a mistaken pay decision escalates, since all the system's inconsistencies and weaknesses become visible once the cloak of secrecy is lifted.
3. Open pay might induce some managers to reduce differences in pay among subordinates in order to avoid conflict and the need to explain such differences to disappointed employees.[54]

In general, open-pay systems tend to work best under the following circumstances: individual or team performance can be measured objectively, performance measures can be developed for all the important aspects of a job, and effort and performance are related closely over a relatively short time span.

The Effect of Inflation

All organizations must make some allowance for inflation in their salary programs. Given an inflation rate of 5 percent, for example, the firm that fails to increase its salary ranges at all over a 2-year period will be 10 percent behind its competitors. Needless to say, it becomes difficult to recruit new employees under these circumstances, and it becomes difficult to motivate present employees to remain and, if they do remain, to produce.

How do firms cope? Automatic pay raises for nonunion employees have almost disappeared at most major concerns. Average increases for salaried employees dropped to 4.2 percent in 2000, while variable pay rose to an average of 16 percent.[55] As we have seen, companies such as Dial, Corning, DuPont, Merck, and America West Airlines are tying pay more to performance in an attempt to make the costs of labor more variable and less fixed. At Dial, for example, "Employees have gotten merit increases irrespective of company performance. . . . We can't afford to go on doing business through [that] kind of pay program."[56] More and more companies, large and small, feel the same way.

Pay Compression

Pay compression is related to the general problem of inflation. It is a narrowing of the ratios of pay between jobs or pay grades in a firm's pay structure.[57] Pay compression exists in many forms, including (1) higher starting salaries for new hires, which lead long-term employees to see only a slight difference between their current pay and that of new hires; (2) hourly pay increases for unionized employees that exceed those of salaried and nonunion employees; (3) recruitment of new college graduates for management or professional jobs at salaries above those of current jobholders; and (4) excessive overtime payments to some employees or payment of different overtime rates (e.g., time and a half for some, double time for others). Failure of organizations to address compression issues may cause long-serving employees to rethink their commitment to a company they think does not value or reward loyalty. Their frustration can also show up in the form of lower productivity, reluctance to work overtime, and unwillingness to cooperate with higher-paid new recruits.[58] However, first-line supervisors, unlike middle managers, may actually benefit from pay inflation among nonmanagement employees since companies generally maintain a differential between the supervisors' pay and that of their highest-paid subordinates. As we noted earlier, these differentials average 15 percent.[59]

One solution to the problem of pay compression is to institute equity adjustments; that is, to give increases in pay to employees to maintain differences in job worth between their jobs and those of others. Some companies provide for equity adjustments through a constantly changing pay scale. Thus Aluminum Company of America (ALCOA) surveys its competitors' pay every 3 months and adjusts its pay rates accordingly. ALCOA strives to maintain at least a 20 percent differential between employees and their supervisors.[60]

Another approach is to grant sign-on bonuses to new hires in order to offer a competitive total compensation package, especially to those with scarce skills. Since bonuses do not increase base salaries, the structure of differences in pay between new hires and experienced employees does not change. Alternatively, some firms provide benefits that increase gradually to more senior employees. Thus, although the difference between the direct pay of this group and that of their shorter-service coworkers may be slim, senior employees have a distinct advantage when the entire compensation package is considered.

Overtime as a cause of compression can be dealt with in two ways. First, it can be rotated among employees so that all share overtime equally. However, in situations where this kind of arrangement is not feasible, firms might consider establishing an overtime pay policy for management employees; for example, a supervisor may be paid an overtime rate after he or she works a minimum number of overtime hours. Such a practice does not violate the Fair Labor Standards Act, for under the law overtime pay is not required for exempt jobs,[61] although it may be adopted voluntarily, as it is at some public-accounting firms.

Pay compression is certainly a difficult problem—but not so difficult that it cannot be managed. Indeed, it must be managed if companies are to achieve their goal of providing pay that is perceived as fair.

Pay Raises

Coping with inflation is the biggest hurdle to overcome in a pay-for-performance plan. On the other hand, the only measure of a raise is how much it exceeds the increase in the cost of living: the 12.4 percent inflation of 1980 more than wiped out the average raise. However, the average 4.2 percent increase that white-collar workers received in 2000 matched inflation and therefore maintained the purchasing power of their dollars.[62]

The simplest, most effective method for dealing with inflation in a merit-pay system is to increase salary ranges. By raising salary ranges (e.g., based on a survey of average increases in starting salaries for the coming year) without giving general increases, a firm can maintain competitive hiring rates and at the

Figure 11–7

Sample merit
guide chart.

EMPLOYEE PERFORMANCE	PERCENT INCREASE				
Distinguished	14%	12%	11%	10%	9%
Commendable	11%	10%	9%	8%	Ceiling
Competent	9%	8%	7%	Ceiling	
Adequate	5%	0	Ceiling		
Provisional	0	Ceiling			
Salary (as % of midpoint) is:	80% → 88% → 96% → 104% → 112% → 120%				

same time maintain the merit concept surrounding salary increases. Since a raise in minimum pay for each salary range creates an employee group that falls below the new minimum, it is necessary to raise these employees to the new minimum. Such adjustments technically violate the merit philosophy, but the advantages gained by keeping employees in the salary range and at a rate that is sufficient to retain them clearly outweigh the disadvantages.[63]

The size of the merit increase for a given level of performance should decrease as the employee moves farther up the salary range. Merit guide charts provide a means for doing this. Guide charts identify (1) an employee's current performance rating and (2) his or her location in a pay grade. The intersection of these two dimensions identifies a percentage of pay increase based on the performance level and location of the employee in the pay grade. Figure 11–7 shows an example of such a chart. The rationale for the merit guide chart approach is that a person at the top of the range is already making more than the "going rate" for that job. Hence she or he should have to demonstrate more than satisfactory performance in order to continue moving farther above the going rate. Performance incentives, one-time awards that must be reearned each year, allow employees to supplement their income. To this topic we now turn.

PERFORMANCE INCENTIVES

Over the past decade, incentive awards that once were reserved for upper management have boomed in popularity. A recent survey by Federal Reserve regional banks found that nearly 90 percent of companies offer some form of variable-pay incentives to nonexecutive employees.[64] The incentives need not only be in cash. Thus MasterCard International replaced cash bonuses for its employees with hotel, show-ticket, and other gift certificates.[65] Evidence indicates that incentives work.[66] A quantitative review of 39 studies containing 47 relationships revealed that financial incentives were not related to performance quality, but were related fairly strongly (correlation of .34) to performance quantity.[67]

There are many different approaches to performance incentives. Since each has different consequences, each needs special treatment.[68] One way to classify them is according to the level of performance targeted—individual, team, or total organization. Within these broad categories, literally hundreds of different approaches for relating pay to performance exist. In this chapter we will consider the three categories described above, beginning with merit pay for individuals—both executives and lower-level workers. First, however, let's consider some fundamental requirements of all incentive programs.

REQUIREMENTS OF EFFECTIVE INCENTIVE SYSTEMS

At the outset it is important to distinguish merit systems from incentive systems. Both are designed to motivate employees to improve their job performance. Most commonly, merit systems are applied to exempt employees in the form of permanent increases to their base pay. The goal is to tie pay increases to each employee's level of job performance. Incentives (e.g., sales commissions, profit sharing) are one-time supplements to base pay. They are also awarded on the basis of job performance, and they are applied to broader segments of the labor force, including nonexempt and unionized employees.

Properly designed incentive programs work because they are based on two well-accepted psychological principles: (1) increased motivation improves performance, and (2) recognition is a major factor in motivation.[69] Unfortunately, however, many incentive programs are improperly designed, and they do not work. They violate one or more of the following rules (shown graphically in Figure 11–8):

- **Be simple.** The rules of the system should be brief, clear, and understandable.

Figure 11–8

Requirements of effective incentive systems.

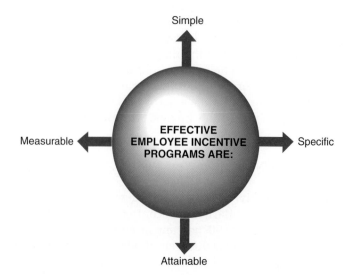

- **Be specific.** It is not sufficient to say, "Produce more," or "Stop accidents." Employees need to know precisely what they are expected to do.
- **Be attainable.** Every employee should have a reasonable chance to gain something.
- **Be measurable.** Measurable objectives are the foundation on which incentive plans are built. Program dollars will be wasted (and program evaluation hampered) if specific accomplishments cannot be related to dollars spent.

MERIT-PAY SYSTEMS

Surveys show that about 90 percent of U.S. employers use merit-pay increases.[70] Unfortunately, many of the plans don't work. Here are some reasons why[71]:

1. **The incentive value of the reward offered is too low.** Give someone a $5,000 raise and she keeps $250 a month after taxes. The "stakes," after taxes, are nominal.[72]
2. **The link between performance and rewards is weak.** If performance is measured annually on a one-dimensional scale, employees will remain unclear about just what is being rewarded. In addition, the timing of a merit-pay award may have little or no correlation with the timing of desirable behaviors.[73] If such conditions prevail, and cannot be fixed, then don't use financial incentives.
3. **Supervisors often resist performance appraisal.** Few supervisors are trained in the art of giving feedback accurately, comfortably, and with a minimum likelihood of creating other problems (see Chapter 8). As a result, many are afraid to make distinctions among workers—and they do not. When the best performers receive rewards that are no higher than the worst performers, motivation plummets.
4. **Union contracts influence pay-for-performance decisions within and between organizations.** Failure to match union wages over a 3- or 4-year period (especially during periods of high inflation) invites dissension and turnover among nonunion employees.
5. **The "annuity" problem.** As past "merit payments" are incorporated into an individual's base salary, the payments form an annuity (a sum of money received at regular intervals) and allow formerly productive individuals to slack off for several years and still earn high pay—an effect called the **annuity problem.** The annuity feature also leads to another problem: topping out. After a long period in a job, individuals often reach the top of the pay range for their jobs. As a result, pay no longer serves as a motivator, because it cannot increase as a result of performance.[74]

These reasons are shown graphically in Figure 11–9.

Barriers Can Be Overcome

Lincoln Electric, a Cleveland-based manufacturer of welding machines and motors, boasts a productivity rate more than double that of other manufacturers in its industry. It follows two cardinal rules:

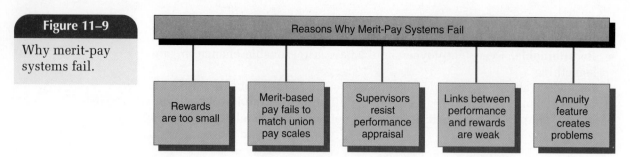

Figure 11–9

Why merit-pay
systems fail.

1.   Pay employees for productivity, and only for productivity.
2.   Promote employees for productivity, and only for productivity.[75]

Furthermore, research on the effect of merit-pay practices on performance in white-collar jobs indicates that not all merit reward systems are equal. Those that tie performance more closely to rewards are likely to generate higher levels of performance, particularly after a year or two. In addition, merit systems that incorporate a wide range of possible increases tend to generate higher levels of job performance after 1 year. Some typical ranges used in successful merit systems are: Digital Equipment, 0 to 30 percent; Xerox, 0 to 13 percent; and Westinghouse, 0 to 19 percent.[76]

GUIDELINES FOR EFFECTIVE MERIT-PAY SYSTEMS

Those affected by the merit-pay system must support it if it is to work as designed. This is in addition to the requirements for incentive programs shown in Figure 11–8. From the very inception of a merit-pay system, it is important that employees feel a sense of "ownership" of the system. To do this, consider implementing a merit-pay system on a step-by-step basis (for example, over a 2-year period), coupled with continued review and revision. Here are five steps to follow:

1.   **Establish high standards of performance.** Low expectations tend to be self-fulfilling prophecies. In the world of sports, successful coaches such as Lombardi, Wooden, and Shula have demanded excellence. Excellence rarely results from expectations of mediocrity.
2.   **Develop accurate performance appraisal systems.** Focus on job-specific, results-oriented criteria (outcomes) as well as on employees' behavior (processes).
3.   **Train supervisors in the mechanics of performance appraisal and in the art of giving feedback to subordinates.** Train them to manage ineffective performance constructively.
4.   **Tie rewards closely to performance.** For example, use semiannual performance appraisals as bases for merit increases (or no increases).
5.   **Use a wide range of increases.** Make pay increases meaningful.

Merit-pay systems can work, but they need to follow these guidelines if they are to work effectively. Figure 11–10 depicts these guidelines graphically.

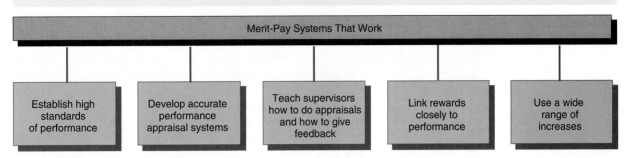

Figure 11–10

Guidelines for effective merit-pay systems.

Merit-Pay Systems That Work

| Establish high standards of performance | Develop accurate performance appraisal systems | Teach supervisors how to do appraisals and how to give feedback | Link rewards closely to performance | Use a wide range of increases |

INCENTIVES FOR EXECUTIVES

"It took me a long while to learn that people do what you pay them to do, not what you ask them to do," says Hicks Waldron, former chairman and CEO of Avon Products, Inc.[77]

Companies with a history of outperforming their rivals, regardless of industry or economic climate, have two common characteristics: (1) a long-term, strategic view of their executives, and (2) stability in their executive groups.[78] It makes sense, therefore, to develop integrated plans for total executive compensation so that rewards are based on achieving the company's long-term strategic goals. This may require a rebalancing of the elements of executive reward systems: base salary, annual (short-term) incentives, and long-term incentives.

Regardless of the exact form of rebalancing, base salaries (considerably more than $1 million a year for CEOs of the largest American corporations[79]) will continue to be the center point of executive compensation. This is because they generally serve as an index for benefit values. Objectives for short- and long-term incentives frequently are defined as a percentage of base salary. However, incentives are likely to become more long- than short-term oriented. Here's why:

1. Annual, or short-term, incentive plans encourage the efficient use of existing assets. They are usually based on indicators of corporate performance, such as net income, total dividends paid, or some specific return on investment (i.e., net profit divided by net assets). Most such bonuses are paid immediately in cash, with CEOs receiving an average of 48 percent of their base pay, senior management 35 percent, and middle management 22 percent.[80]

2. Long-term plans encourage the development of new processes, plants, and products that open new markets and restore old ones. Hence long-term performance encompasses qualitative progress as well as quantitative accomplishments. Long-term incentive plans are designed to reward strategic gains rather than short-term contributions to profits. They are as common in owner-controlled firms (where at least 5 percent of outstanding stock is held by an individual or organization not involved in the actual management of a company) as they are in management-controlled firms (where no individual or organization controls more than 5 percent

of the stock).[81] This is the kind of view we should be encouraging among executives, for it relates consistently to company success.

In the face of widespread criticism of executive pay practices, some firms are rethinking the way they reward top executives.[82] Take stock options, for example. Executives are granted the right to buy the company's stock sometime in the future at a fixed price, usually the price on the day the options are granted. Options are popular because they allow issuing companies to contend that the executives won't benefit unless the shareholders do. However, even enthusiasts can't prove that options motivate executives to perform better. Critics contend that stock options reward executives not just for their own performance, but for a booming stock market. To a large extent, they are right, for as much as 70 percent of the change in a company's stock price depends only on changes in the overall market.[83] In response, companies such as Transamerica, Colgate-Palmolive, and Ecolab now grant stock options not at the market price but at some higher price. These are known as **premium-price options.**[84] Thus executives will profit only after the stock has risen substantially. Take Monsanto, for example.

COMPANY EXAMPLE ## PREMIUM-PRICE OPTIONS AT MONSANTO

At Monsanto, CEO Robert Shapiro and 31 other executives receive options to purchase stock at prices that *ascend* over time. Before their options are "in the money" they must increase the stock price by 50 percent between 1998 and 2003. Since Shapiro and the other executives have to pay for their options, they must raise the share price even higher (an average of 10.5 percent per year) before they can start cashing in. The company allowed them to plow as much as half their salaries into options over the first 2 years of the plan. All elected to participate. Monsanto is now being run as though its managers have a stake in it, because they really do have a stake in it. If Shapiro and his top executives are right about the company's future prospects, they will be richly rewarded. If not, and the market drops and stays depressed, their options will be underwater and the company will have to find some other way to motivate them to stay on.[85]

INCENTIVES FOR LOWER-LEVEL EMPLOYEES

As noted earlier in this chapter, a common practice is to supplement employees' pay with increments related to improvements in job performance. Most such plans have a "baseline," or normal, work standard; performance above this standard is rewarded. The baseline should be high enough so that employees are not given extra rewards for what is really just a normal day's work. On the other hand, the baseline should not be so high that it is impossible to earn additional pay.

It is more difficult to specify work standards in some jobs than in others. At the top management level, for instance, what constitutes a "normal" day's output? As one moves down the organizational hierarchy, however, jobs can be defined more clearly, and shorter-run goals and targets can be established.

Setting Workload Standards

All incentive systems depend on **workload standards.** The standards provide a relatively objective definition of the job, they give employees targets to shoot for, and they make it easier for supervisors to assign work equitably. Make no mistake about it, though, effective performance is often hard to define. For example, when a Corning group set up a trial program to reward workers for improving their efficiency, a team struggled to figure out "What's a meaningful thing to measure? What's reasonable?" The measures finally settled on included safety, quality, shipping efficiency, and forecast accuracy.[86] Once workload standards are set, employees have an opportunity to earn more than their base salaries, often as much as 20 to 25 percent more. In short, they have an incentive to work both harder and smarter.

In setting workload standards for production work, the ideal job (ideal only in terms of the ability to measure performance, not in terms of improving work motivation or job satisfaction) should (1) be highly repetitive; (2) have a short job cycle; and (3) produce a clear, measurable output. However, before explicit workload standards can be set, management must do the following:

- Describe the job by means of job analysis.
- Decide how the job is to be done—do a **motion study.**
- Decide how fast the job should be done—do a **time study.**

The standards themselves will vary, of course, according to the *type* of product or service (e.g., a hospital, a factory, a cable television company), the *method of service delivery,* the degree to which service can be *quantified,* and *organizational needs,* including legal and social pressures. In fact, the many different forms of incentive plans for lower-level employees really differ only along two dimensions:

1. How premium rates are determined.
2. How the extra payments are made.

To be sure, incentives oriented toward individuals are becoming less popular as work increasingly becomes interdependent in nature. Nevertheless, individual incentives remain popular in some industries, particularly manufacturing. Lincoln Electric is a prime example.

INDIVIDUAL INCENTIVES AT LINCOLN ELECTRIC[87]

COMPANY EXAMPLE

From its earliest years, 100-year-old Lincoln Electric Company of Cleveland, Ohio, has charted a unique path in worker-management relations, featuring high wages, guaranteed employment, few supervisors, a lucrative bonus-incentive system, and piecework compensation. The company is the world's largest maker of arc-welding equipment; it has 3,400 U.S. employees, 23 plants in 17 countries, and no unions. Among the innovative management practices that set Lincoln apart are these:

- Guaranteed employment for all full-time workers with more than 2 years' service, and no mandatory retirement. No worker has been laid off since 1948, and turnover is less than 4 percent for those with more than 180 days on the job.
- High wages (an average of $35,000), including a substantial annual bonus (up to 100 percent of base pay) based on the company's profits. Wages at Lincoln ($16.54 an hour) are roughly equivalent to wages for similar work elsewhere in the Cleveland area ($14.25), but the bonuses the company pays make its compensation substantially higher. For example, in 1995 the average worker at Lincoln earned a bonus of 56 percent of his or her base pay, for total earnings of almost $54,000. (The most hard-driving workers made over $100,000.) Lincoln has never had a strike and has not missed a bonus payment since the system was instituted in 1934. Individual bonuses are set by a formula that judges workers on five dimensions: quality, output, dependability, ideas, and cooperation. The ratings determine how much of the total corporate bonus pool each worker will get, on top of his or her hourly wage.
- Piecework—more than half of Lincoln's workers are paid according to what they produce, rather than an hourly or weekly wage. If a worker is sick, he or she does not get paid.
- Promotion is almost exclusively from within, according to merit, not seniority.
- Few supervisors, with a supervisor-worker ratio of 1:100, far lower than in much of the industry. Each employee is supposed to be a self-managing entrepreneur, and each is accountable for the quality of his or her own work.
- No break periods, and mandatory overtime. Workers must work overtime, if ordered to, during peak production periods and must agree to change jobs to meet production schedules or to maintain the company's guaranteed employment program.

While the company insists on individual initiative—and pays according to individual effort—it works diligently to foster the notion of teamwork. It did this long before the Japanese became known for emphasizing such concepts. If a worker is overly competitive with fellow employees, he or she is rated poorly in terms of cooperation and team play on his or her semiannual rating reports. Thus that worker's bonus will be smaller. Says one company official: "This is not an easy style to manage; it takes a lot of time and a willingness to work with people."

Union Attitudes

A unionized employer may establish an incentive system, but it will be subject to negotiation through collective bargaining. Unions may also wish to participate in the day-to-day management of the incentive system, and management ought to consider that demand seriously. Employees often fear that management will manipulate the system to the disadvantage of employees. Joint participation helps reassure employees that the plan is fair.

Union attitudes toward incentives vary with the type of incentive offered. Unions tend to oppose individual piece-rate systems because they pit worker against worker and can create unfavorable intergroup conflict. However, unions tend to support organizationwide systems, such as profit sharing, because of the extra earnings they provide to their members.[88] In one experiment, for example, an electric utility instituted a division-level incentive plan in one division but not in others. The incentive payout was based on equal percentage shares based on salary. Relative to a control division, the one operating under the incentive plan performed significantly better in reducing unit cost, budget performance, and on 9 of 10 other objective indicators. Nevertheless, union employees helped kill the plan for two reasons: (1) negative reactions from union members in other divisions who did not operate under the incentive plan; and (2) a preference for equal dollar shares, rather than equal percentage shares, because the earnings of bargaining-unit employees were lower, on average, than those of managers and staff employees.[89]

TEAM INCENTIVES

To provide broader motivation than is furnished by incentive plans geared to individual employees, several other approaches have been tried. Their aim is twofold: to increase productivity and to improve morale by giving employees a feeling of participation in and identification with the company. Team or work-group incentives are one such plan.

Team incentives provide an opportunity for each team member to receive a bonus based on the output of the team as a whole. Teams may be as small as 4 to 7 employees or as large as 35 to 40 employees. Team incentives are most appropriate when jobs are highly interrelated. In fact, highly interrelated jobs are the wave of the future and, in many cases, the wave of the present. In the past, relatively few firms used team incentives. In the future, they will need to be more creative in using team performance appraisal and team incentives.[90] Here's an example of one firm's efforts to do so.

TEAM INCENTIVES IN A SMALL BUSINESS[91]   COMPANY EXAMPLE

XEL, a manufacturer of electronic equipment for the telecommunications industry, uses a three-tier incentive compensation plan to complement its use of self-managed work teams: a lump-sum profit-sharing plan, a pay-for-skills program, and a team-based variable-pay system. For the team-based pay system, XEL sets aside a percentage of its total payroll, and payouts are determined by team rankings. A team's ranking is based on three criteria: ratings by internal and external customers, achievement of quarterly team objectives, and management input recognizing special circumstances.

In this system, members on the same team do not all receive the same payout, since the final payout is adjusted to reflect peer evaluations. For example, if the overall merit-pay budget is 5 percent of payroll, the top-ranked team might get 8 percent, a mid-ranked team 5%, and a bottom-ranked team nothing. Further, within the top team there may be a spread of 5–10 percent among individual members' ratings. The major benefit of such a system: Team deficiencies get quick attention.

Team incentives have the following advantages:

1. They make it possible to reward workers who provide essential services to line workers (so-called indirect labor), yet who are paid only their regular

base pay. These employees do things like transport supplies and materials, maintain equipment, or inspect work output.

2.   They encourage cooperation, not competition, among workers.

On the other hand, team incentives also have disadvantages, which are as follows:

1.   Fear that management will cut rates (or employees) if employees produce too much.
2.   Competition between teams.
3.   Inability of workers to see their individual contributions to the output of the team. If they do not see the link between their individual effort and increased rewards, they will not be motivated to produce more.

Recent large-scale research with work groups has revealed the critical relationship between employees' understanding of the work-group incentive plan and their perceptions of the fairness of that plan. Managers should ensure that all members of work groups understand how pay plan goals are established, the goals themselves, how the plan goals are evaluated, and how the payouts are determined.[92] To overcome some of the first two disadvantages of team incentives, many firms have introduced organizationwide incentives.

ORGANIZATIONWIDE INCENTIVES

In this our final section, we consider three broad classes of organizationwide incentives: profit-sharing, gain-sharing, and employee stock-ownership plans. As we shall see, each is different in its objectives and implementation.

Profit Sharing

In the United States, **profit sharing** is the most common method companies use to provide retirement income for their employees. Firms use it for one or more of the following reasons: to provide a group incentive for increased productivity, to institute a flexible reward structure that reflects a company's actual economic position, to enhance employees' security and identification with the company, to attract and retain workers more easily, and/or to educate individuals about the factors that underlie business success and the capitalistic system.[93]

Employees receive a bonus that is normally based on some percentage (e.g., 10 to 30 percent) of the company's profits beyond some minimum level. Does profit sharing improve productivity? One review of 27 econometric studies found that profit sharing was positively related to productivity in better than 9 of every 10 instances. Productivity was generally 3 to 5 percent higher in firms with profit-sharing plans than in those without plans.[94]

A most ambitious profit-sharing program was started by DuPont for nearly all its 20,000 managers and employees in the fibers business in the United States. Under the plan, employees could earn up to 12 percent of their base pay if the business exceeds its profit goals, but they could also lose part of their original increase if the profit goals aren't met.[95] Two years later, when it appeared that workers would lose as much as 4 percent of their base pay as a result of poor sales in the fibers unit, discontent among workers was so high that DuPont canceled the plan.[96] Although there were many reasons for the plan's failure, two of the most telling were (1) the fact that employees felt powerless to influence profits, and (2) employee resentment over loopholes for high-level managers in the fibers unit, who were still able to benefit from DuPont's companywide bonus program. That program is geared to the company's total profits, not just to the profits of the fibers unit.

This case illustrates the two-sided nature of profit sharing. On the one hand, compensation costs become more variable, since a company pays only if it makes a profit. On the other hand, from the employee's perspective, benefits and pensions are insecure. While profit sharing can stimulate innovation and creativity, the actual success of such plans depends on the stability and security of the overall work environment, on the company's overall HR management policy and on the state of labor-management relations.[97] This is even more true of gain-sharing plans.

Gain Sharing

Gain sharing is a formal reward system that has existed in a variety of forms for more than 50 years. Sometimes known as the Scanlon plan, the Rucker plan, or Improshare (improved productivity through sharing), gain sharing comprises three elements[98]:

1. A philosophy of cooperation.
2. An involvement system.
3. A financial bonus.

The philosophy of cooperation refers to an organizational climate characterized by high levels of trust, two-way communication, participation, and harmonious industrial relations. The involvement system refers to the structure and process for improving organizational productivity. Typically, it is a broad-based suggestion system implemented by an employee-staffed committee structure that usually reaches all areas of the organization. Sometimes this structure involves work teams, but usually it is simply an employee-based suggestion system. The employees involved develop and implement ideas related to productivity. The third component, the financial bonus, is determined by a calculation that measures the difference between expected and actual costs during a bonus period.

The three components mutually reinforce one another.[99] High levels of cooperation lead to information sharing, which in turn leads to employee involvement, which leads to new behaviors, such as offering suggestions to improve organizational productivity. This increase in productivity then results in a financial bonus (based on the amount of the productivity increase), which rewards and reinforces the philosophy of cooperation.

It is important to distinguish gain sharing from profit sharing. The two approaches differ in three important ways[100]:

1. Gain sharing is based on a measure of productivity. Profit sharing is based on a global profitability measure.

2. Gain sharing, productivity measurement, and bonus payments are frequent events, distributed monthly or quarterly, in contrast to the annual measures and rewards of profit-sharing plans.

3. Gain-sharing plans are current distribution plans, in contrast to most profit-sharing plans, which have deferred payments. Hence gain-sharing plans are true incentive plans rather than employee benefits. As such, they are more directly related to individual behavior and therefore can motivate worker productivity.

When gain-sharing plans such as the Scanlon plan work, they work well. For example, consider a 17-year evaluation of such a plan in a manufacturing operation, DeSoto, Inc., of Garland, Texas. The bonus formula, which measures labor productivity, revealed that average bonuses ranged from 2.5 percent to more than 22 percent, with an overall average of 9.6 percent. Moreover, over the 17-year period of the study, output (as measured by gallons of paint) increased by 78 percent.[101] Nevertheless, in the 50 years since the inception of gain sharing, it has been abandoned by firms about as often as it has been retained. Here are some reasons:

1. Generally, it does not work well in piecework operations.
2. Some firms are uncomfortable about bringing unions into business planning.
3. Some managers may feel they are giving up their prerogatives.[102]

Neither the size of a company nor the type of technology it employs seems to be related to Scanlon plan success. However, employee (and union) participation in the design of the plan, positive managerial attitudes, the number of years a company has had a Scanlon plan, favorable and realistic employee attitudes, and involvement by a high-level executive are strongly related to the success of a Scanlon plan.[103] To develop an organizationwide incentive plan that has a chance to survive, let alone succeed, careful, in-depth planning must precede implementation. It is true of all incentive plans, though, that *none will work well except in a climate of trustworthy labor-management relations and sound human resource management practices.*

Employee Stock Ownership Plans

Employee stock ownership plans (ESOPs) have become popular in both large and small companies in the United States (e.g., Pepsico, Lincoln Electric, DuPont, Coca-Cola) as they have in Western Europe, some countries in Central Europe, and China.[104] About 10,000 U.S. firms now share ownership with 10 million employees. Employees own an average of 13 percent of the stock at 562 public companies. However, they have board seats at fewer than a dozen of them, and most of those are unionized.[105] Employee ownership can be found in every industry, in every size firm, and in every part of the country.[106] The goal is to increase employee involvement in the organization, and it is hoped that this will influence performance.[107]

Generally, ESOPs are established for any of the following reasons:

■ As a means of tax-favored, company-financed transfer of ownership from a departing owner to a firm's employees. This is often done in small firms with closely held stock.[108]

IMPACT OF PAY AND INCENTIVES ON PRODUCTIVITY, QUALITY OF WORK LIFE, AND THE BOTTOM LINE

High salary levels alone do not ensure a productive, motivated workforce. This is evident in the auto industry, where wages are among the highest in the country, yet quality problems and high absenteeism persist. A critical factor, then, is not *how much* a company pays its workers but, more importantly, *how the pay system is designed, communicated, and managed.*[110] Excessively high labor costs can bankrupt a company.[111] This is especially likely if, to cover its labor costs, the company cannot price its products competitively. If that happens, productivity and profits both suffer directly, and the quality of work life suffers indirectly. Conversely, when the interests of employees and their organizations are aligned, then employees are likely to engage in behavior that goes above and beyond the call of duty (such as helping others accomplish their goals), that is not recognized by the formal reward system, and that contributes to organizational effectiveness.[112] This improves both quality of work life and productivity. What's the bottom line? When sensible policies on pay and incentives are established using the principles discussed in this chapter, everybody wins: the company, the employees, and employees' families as well.

- As a way of borrowing money relatively inexpensively. A firm borrows money from a bank using its stock as collateral, places the stock in an employee stock ownership trust, and, as the loan is repaid, distributes the stock at no cost to employees. Companies can deduct the principal as well as interest on the amount borrowed, and lenders pay taxes on only 50 percent of their income from ESOP loans.
- To fulfill a philosophical belief in employee ownership. For example, at 22,000-employee Science Applications International Corp., a $2.1 billion high-tech research and engineering concern, founder J. Robert Beyster began giving employees stock in the company every time they landed a new contract. That was 27 years ago, and he has never stopped. Beyster attributes much of the company's growth not to management skills or to an overarching strategy, but to his ownership philosophy. He says, "Employee-ownership really did it. Who has a better right to own the company than the people who make it worth something?" So far that has proved to be a winning formula.[109]
- As an additional employee benefit.

Do ESOPs improve employee motivation and satisfaction? Longitudinal research spanning 45 case studies found that stock ownership alone does not make employees work harder or enjoy their day-to-day work more.[113] However, certain features of ESOPs do promote an increase in employee willingness to participate in company decisions. Companies that take advantage of that willingness can harness employees' energy and creativity.[114] In particular:

1. ESOP satisfaction tends to be highest in companies where (a) the company makes relatively large annual contributions to the plan; (b) management is committed to employee ownership and is willing to share power and decision-making authority with employees, and (c) there are

extensive company communications about the ESOP, the company's current performance, and its future plans.[115]

2. Employees tend to be most satisfied with stock ownership when the company established its ESOP for employee-centered reasons (management was committed to employee ownership) rather than for strategic or financial reasons (e.g., as an antitakeover device or to gain tax savings).

3. Satisfaction breeds satisfaction. That is, the same individual-level and ESOP characteristics that lead to ESOP satisfaction also lead (somewhat less strongly) to organizational commitment.

How does employee stock ownership affect economic performance? When the above three conditions are met, employee-owned firms have been 150 percent as profitable, have had twice the productivity growth, and have generated three times more new jobs than their competitors. High-tech companies that share ownership widely grow two to four times as fast as those that do not. Publicly held companies that are at least 10 percent employee-owned outperform 62 to 75 percent of their competitors, depending on the measure used.[116] On an aggregate level, between 1979 and 1992, a portfolio of companies that were at least 10 percent employee-owned would have produced an annualized return of 27.17 percent, against 16.54 percent for Standard & Poor's 500-stock index.[117]

While such data do not prove that employee stock ownership causes success (it may be that successful firms are more likely to make employees part owners), they do suggest that if implemented properly, such plans can improve employee attitudes and economic productivity. Nevertheless, ESOPs are not riskfree to employees. ESOPs are not insured, and if a company goes bankrupt, its stock may be worthless.

IMPLICATIONS FOR MANAGEMENT PRACTICE

In thinking about pay and incentives, expect to see three trends continue:

1. The movement to performance-based pay plans, in which workers put more of their pay "at risk" in return for potentially higher rewards. Recognize, however, that organizations facing higher risks place less emphasis on short-term incentives than do other organizations. To compensate for such uncertainty, they tend to rely more on higher base pay.[118]

2. The movement toward the use of teamwide or organizationwide incentive plans at all levels.

3. Use of a wide range of pay increases, in an effort to make distinctions in performance as meaningful as possible.

In the wave of restructurings and reengineerings that continue to unfold, research has found that the jobs of employees who remain may well impose greater demands on them in the form of know-how, problem solving, and accountability.[119] Be prepared to reevaluate those jobs, and, if justified, to adjust compensation accordingly.

THE TRUST GAP

What steps can companies take to sew corporate top and bottom back together? Here are seven suggestions. One, start with the obvious. Tie the financial interests of high- and low-level workers closer together by making exposure to risks *and* rewards more equitable. Thus, when NUCOR, a steel company in Charlotte, North Carolina, went through tough times, President Ken Iverson took a 60 percent cut in pay. Said a compensation consultant, "How often do you see that? . . . It makes a real difference if employees see that their CEO is willing to take it in the shorts along with them"[120] Likewise, after a prolonged market slide, Charles Schwab Corporation cut the salaries of its co-CEOs by 50 percent in 2001. The cuts were extended indefinitely as the slide deepened. The firm also cut the salaries of other officers, though not as deeply, from 5–20 percent, in an effort to make employee layoffs a last resort. Although some layoffs did become necessary, Schwab pays anyone rehired within 18 months a bonus of $7,500.[121]

Two, consider instituting profit sharing, a Scanlon plan, gain sharing, or some other program that lets employees profit from their efforts. Make sure, however, that incentive pay is linked to performance over which the beneficiaries have control.

Three, rethink perquisites. Now that perks come under taxable income, they just don't have the same appeal to executives as they used to. Yet they still have at least the same downside with the rank and file.

Four, look at the office layout with an eye toward equity. In Sweden, for example, same-size offices are the norm. When an American visitor asked his Swedish corporate hosts how they could give the same amount of space to a secretary as to an engineer, they said, "How can we hire a secretary and expect her to be committed to our company, when, by the size of the office we give her, we tell her she's a second-class citizen?"[122]

Five, make sure your door is really open. If that means meeting with employees at unorthodox times, such as when their shifts end, then do it. Not a single one of the CEOs interviewed by *Fortune* could recall employees ever abusing an open-door policy. The lesson is clear for managers at all levels: Employees don't walk through your door unless they have to.

Six, if you don't survey employee attitudes now, start. What you find can help identify problems before they become crises. Share findings, and be sure employees know how subsequent decisions may be related to them. Don't worry about raising expectations too high. As one executive commented, "Employees by and large are reasonable people. They understand you can't do everything they want. As long as they know their views are being considered and they get some feedback from you to that effect, you will be meeting their expectations."[123]

Seven, explain things—personally. While one study found that 97 percent of CEOs believe that communicating with employees has a positive impact on job satisfaction and 79 percent think it benefits the bottom line, only 22 percent do it weekly or more often.

There is no doubt that these seven steps can help close the trust gap that exists in so many U.S. organizations today. On the other hand, virtually all experts cite one important qualification: It is suicidal to start down this road unless you are absolutely sincere.

SUMMARY

Contemporary pay systems (outside the entertainment and professional sports fields) are characterized by cost containment, pay, and benefit levels commensurate with what a company can afford, and by programs that encourage and reward performance.

Generally speaking, pay systems are designed to attract, retain, and motivate employees; to achieve internal, external, and individual equity; and to maintain a balance in relationships between direct and indirect forms of compensation and between the pay rates of supervisory and nonsupervisory employees. Pay systems need to be tied to the strategic mission of an organization, and they should take their direction from that strategic mission. However, actual wage levels depend on labor market conditions, legislation, collective bargaining, management attitudes, and an organization's ability to pay. Our broad objective in developing pay systems is to assign a monetary value to each job or skill set in the organization (a base rate) and to establish an orderly procedure for increasing the base rate. To develop a job-based system, we need four basic tools: job analyses and job descriptions, a job evaluation plan, pay surveys, and a pay structure. In addition, the following pay policy issues are important: pay secrecy versus openness, the effect of inflation on pay systems, pay compression, and pay raises.

In terms of incentive plans, the most effective ones are simple, specific, attainable, and measurable. Consider merit pay, for example. Merit pay works best when these guidelines are followed: (1) establish high standards of performance, (2) develop appraisal systems that focus on job-specific, results-oriented criteria; (3) train supervisors in the mechanics of performance appraisal and in the art of giving constructive feedback; (4) tie rewards closely to performance; and (5) provide a wide range of possible pay increases.

Long-term incentives, mostly in the form of stock options, are becoming a larger proportion of the executives' pay package. Finally, there is a wide variety of individual, group, and organizationwide incentive plans (e.g., profit sharing, gain sharing, employee stock-ownership plans) with different impacts on employee motivation and economic outcomes. Blending fixed versus variable pay in a manner that is understandable and acceptable to employees will present a management challenge for years to come.

DISCUSSION QUESTIONS

11–1. What steps can a company take to integrate its compensation system with its general business strategy?

11–2. What can companies do to ensure internal, external, and individual equity for all employees?

11–3. Discuss the advantages and disadvantages of competency or skill-based pay systems.

11–4. How has "strategic thinking" affected executive incentives?

11–5. If you were implementing an employee stock-ownership plan, what key factors would you consider?

KEY TERMS

trust gap	market-based pay
organizational reward system	competency-based pay
compensation	pay compression
internal equity	annuity problem
external equity	premium-price options
individual equity	workload standards
balance	motion study
job descriptions	time study
compensable factors	profit sharing
job evaluation	gain sharing
benchmark jobs	employee stock ownership plans
relevant labor markets	

APPLYING YOUR KNOWLEDGE

Compensation and Incentive Pay at Shaver, Inc.   *Case 11–1*

"I don't understand it. We're a successful company that pays well, and we have a reputation to uphold. Now you tell me that last year most of the raises employees got were *not* given on the basis of performance. How can that be?" So asked Shaver, Inc.'s chief executive officer (CEO) Phyllis Johnstone. Mike Mercer, Shaver, Inc.'s vice president for human resources, fumbled for an answer. "Well, we've got a darn good compensation system. The problem is simply that managers don't know how to use it effectively."

This exchange of views prompted Mike Mercer to return to his office and think about the journey that he and his Salary Review Task Force had begun several years ago. This task force, which involved employees from virtually every division at Shaver, Inc., had reviewed the earlier compensation system and had instituted a series of changes designed to make the system more effective. But apparently the changes had not been very successful, and Mike Mercer was on the horns of a dilemma.

Company Background

Shaver, Inc., a manufacturer of all kinds of wood and steel tables for business and industry, was headquartered in Eugene, Oregon. Its roots date back to 1907, when founder Jason Bishop started up a new business near a saw mill on the outskirts of Eugene and developed a uniquely crafted writing table for bookkeepers. The business initially was family owned and remained relatively small until the 1940s. By then, however, outside investors had begun to take an interest in the quality of workmanship that was demonstrated by the Bishop family, and they purchased the business and began to expand its operations both domestically and overseas. The organization was incorporated in 1952 and continued to expand rapidly throughout the 1950s and 1960s. Today, Shaver manufactures and markets more than 40 varieties of tables and is the leader in the western United States in this particular business.

Shaver, Inc. enjoys a reputation for excellent management practice and has been written up in numerous business magazines over the years. It consistently receives high ratings for product innovation, return on stockholder investment, product quality, and financial acumen. It also receives high marks for its ability to attract, develop, and retain talented employees.

Shaver has also traditionally been a very profitable organization, which is what attracted the initial investor interest in the 1940s. Until 1999, Shaver had always outperformed its competitors in terms of return on investment for its shareholders. For instance, in 1997, Shaver's return on assets averaged 15 percent, while its largest competitor's in the same year averaged only 11 percent. However, in 1999 the situation began to change. Shaver's traditional lead over its competitors deteriorated, possibly due to changes in organizational structure or to a set of disappointments in new product innovations in the marketplace. But CEO Phyllis Johnstone was not convinced that only factors such as these were to blame for some of Shaver's problems. She was concerned that perhaps employee motivation was deteriorating as well, and her impressions of the salary and compensation system did not provide her with any comfort in this regard.

Compensation Policy at Shaver, Inc.

Shaver employs about 16,000 people, roughly half of whom are hourly manufacturing or clerical employees. The other half are salaried exempt employees, including salespeople, engineers, technicians, supervisors and managers, and others. Compensation for the 8,000 exempt salaried employees at Shaver has historically ranked among the top 33 percent of midsize U.S. corporations. These progressive HR policies and pay practices have contributed to inordinately high levels of employee commitment and loyalty, as characterized by historically low voluntary turnover rates (averaging less than 2 percent of the workforce per year).

As with other companies, the salary determination process at Shaver was built upon the annual performance review. Shaver's existing performance appraisal process had been designed and developed by Mike Mercer's Salary Review Task Force in 1998. Under this plan, supervisors rated employees on a scale from 1 to 5, with 5 designating exceptional performance and 1 indicating unacceptable performance. Plus and minus ratings were allowed, with the exception that no one with a 5 could earn a plus and no one with a 1 could earn a minus. Thus, managers could choose from 13 different rating categories in assigning an overall performance evaluation for a particular employee (5, 5−, 4+, 4, 4−, etc.).

Salaries for the 8,000 exempt employees at Shaver were based on a combination of job characteristics and merit. The job characteristics were measured using "Hay points." Hay points were determined by evaluating each position at Shaver in terms of the three Hay factors—know-how, problem solving, and accountability. For each job, numerical scores were assigned to each of the three factors according to guide charts provided by Hay Associates. The guide charts revealed what was meant by "know-how" or one of the other compensable factors. Each compensable factor was broken down in terms of more specific building blocks to make the process as objective as possible. The total number of Hay points for each position in the organization was calculated by summing the points given on each of the three compensable factors. At Shaver, Inc., Hay points were then converted to a "a control point" (which equated roughly to an average monthly salary) using a "salary line formula." For example, in 2000, the salary line formula was as follows: Control point = $1,462 + $3.23 X (where X = number of Hay points).

With this formula, an employee with 550 Hay points had a 2001 control point of $3,238 per month. At Shaver, the employee's actual salary could range from 80 percent to 125 percent of the control point. Actual salary as a percentage of the control point is called the employee's **compa-ratio.** For example, an employee with 550 Hay points and a compa-ratio of 110 would have a 2001 monthly salary of $3,562. On the other hand, an employee with 550 Hay points and a compa-ratio of 80 would have a 2001 monthly salary of $2,591. Each employee's compa-ratio goes down whenever the salary line formula is moved upward, and goes up each time he or she gets a merit salary increase.

Shaver, Inc. has always prided itself on being an organization that pays above-average salaries. It sets its salary line formula so that employees with compa-ratios of 100 earn approximately 10 percent more than the average compensation in other medium-size organizations. This means that a Shaver employee in a position with 550 Hay points would earn roughly 10 percent more than a similarly situated employee with 550 Hay points at another organization, assuming that both had similar compa-ratios. In order to guarantee that Shaver is paying about 10 percent above market, it takes part in a variety of salary surveys each year. In these surveys, it sends its salary data in and receives reports back from the surveying organization showing how its salaries compare with those of other organizations.

The salary line formula is revised annually on July 1, the beginning of Shaver's fiscal year. The salary line formula is adjusted upward so that control points for particular positions approximate 10 percent above the market salary goal that Shaver sets for itself. However, the salaries themselves are not automatically adjusted when the salary line formula changes. Instead, individual compa-ratios decline every July 1st when control points are increased.

Merit-Pay Increases

Salary revisions themselves are linked to both control-point increases and performance appraisal ratings through guidelines established by Mike Mercer's HR management department. Theoretically, employees with higher performance appraisal ratings should get larger pay increases, and raises for a given performance rating should be smaller for employees with higher compa-ratios. For example, the salary increase for an employee receiving a performance rating of 4 might be in the 5–7 percent range if his or her compa-ratio is 90, but only in the 3–5 percent range if his or her compa-ratio is 110.

Employees who achieve compa-ratios considerably above 100 over an extended period of time are generally viewed as the star performers at Shaver, Inc. This level of sustained performance suggests that the individual is a clear candidate for promotion. In addition, since salaries are rarely decreased, compa-ratios may be above 100 in the short run for employees who are not performing particularly well and, therefore, not actually candidates for promotion.

The maximum obtainable compa-ratio is 125. Thus, salaries are effectively capped at 125 percent of the control point, and employees near the cap can receive up to, but cannot surpass, the cap during each annual merit-salary increase. In practice, however, only a few employees achieve and maintain compa-ratios exceeding 115. One reason is that the salary line formula is adjusted prior to salary revisions each year. Therefore, even employees hitting the cap in a particular year will likely be well below the cap after the salary line changes on July 1. The second reason that few employees maintain a salary close to 125 percent of the control point is that those with high compa-ratios are frequently promoted once they attain that level of salary. Since it takes time to learn the skills necessary in a new position, the starting compa-ratio for a newly promoted employee is almost always lower than his or her final compa-ratio in the previous position. For example, in 2000 the average starting compa-ratio for all employees promoted into positions with 500 Hay points was 85.

Performance Appraisal at Shaver

Back in 1999 when Mike Mercer and his Salary Review Task Force had looked into the problems associated with compensation and the performance appraisal system, they had discovered through interviews that there was general agreement that rewards for excellent performance were inadequate. Outstanding performers were getting salary increases that were in many cases only marginally better than those given to average and below-average performers. And in many cases, outstanding performance was not even being identified through the appraisal system.

The Salary Review Task Force had redesigned the appraisal system so that it looked like the one described earlier in the case, and this revision had been implemented in 1998. It was the hope of the task force that this redesigned system would help overcome some of the problems that were uncovered during the interviews. According to Mike Mercer, "One thing that really hit home for us was the negative feeling of some of our best performers concerning the reward system here at Shaver. The key issue seemed to be the appraisal system itself and it simply had to be dealt with."

The problem was that everyone seemed to have different ideas about how to restructure the performance appraisal system. The Salary Review Task Force got a variety of opinions, mostly negative, about the existing appraisal system. Many pointed out that managers were afraid to give experienced people ratings below 8 (the old system had been based on a 11-point rating scale). They also pointed out that it was very difficult to get a rating of 10. In many cases the supervisor had never received a rating of 10 and was not about to give that rating to a subordinate. Some other quotes that were representative of problems uncovered included:

"What's the use of working hard? You still get the same rating everyone else does, and you still get the same 4 percent salary increase. It's demoralizing and demotivating."

"Sharlene has been in that job for 11 years and hasn't done anything extraordinary for the last 8. But do you think my boss would give her a 7? No way! If he did, he'd spend the next year listening to Sharlene complain about her rating."

"How can I evaluate my direct reports fairly and objectively when the other managers are giving all their people 8s? A 7 simply isn't acceptable. The system would be okay if everyone played by the same rules, but they don't."

"It's getting to the point where many of the best people are going to leave Shaver unless they get the right kinds of rewards. Now, who do you want to do the walking? Your best people or your worst?"

2000 RATING DISTRIBUTION AND AVERAGE PAY INCREASE UNDER THE 1998 PERFORMANCE APPRAISAL AND SALARY ADMINISTRATION PROGRAM

2000 rating	Number of employees	Percentage distribution	Average 2000 pay increase		
			Compa-ratio 80–94	Compa-ratio 95–109	Compa-ratio 110–125
5	16	0.2			
5–	49	0.6	9.3%	8.7%	6.5%
4+	1,421	17.6			
4	2,447	30.4	6.5	5.5	4.8
4–	1,471	18.3			
3+	1,394	17.3			
3	876	10.9	5.9	4.8	4.1
3–	281	3.5			
2+	63	0.8			
2	27	0.3	4.4	1.9	0.1
2–	1				
1+	1				
1	4				

It was with these problems in mind that the Salary Review Task Force undertook the redesign of the performance appraisal system in 1999. The recent results of appraisal ratings distribution and salary increases in 2001 for all salaried exempt employees are presented in the following table. It was the information in this table that

Mike Mercer presented to Phyllis Johnstone that created the incident described at the beginning of the case.

Questions

1. What are the problems with Shaver, Inc.'s present performance appraisal and salary review program?
2. What changes would you recommend in Shaver, Inc.'s performance appraisal and salary review system?
3. Discuss the rationale for and relative advantages of each of the changes you recommend.

REFERENCES

1. Unstable pay becomes ever more common. (1995, Dec. 4). T*he Wall Street Journal,* p. A1.
2. Mahoney, T. A. (1989). Employment compensation planning and strategy. In L. R. Gomez-Mejia (ed.), *Compensation and benefits.* Washington, DC: Bureau of National Affairs, pp. 3-1–3-28.
3. Milkovich, G. T., & Newman, J. M. (2002). *Compensation* (7th ed.). Burr Ridge, IL: McGraw-Hill/Irwin.
4. Ibid.
5. Stroh, L. K., Brett, J. M., Baumann, J. P., & Reilly, A. H. (1996). Agency theory and variable pay compensation strategies. *Academy of Management Journal, 39,* 751–767.
6. Show you the money? It's with variable pay (2000, Nov. 16). *BusinessWeek,* p. 8. See also Koretz, G. (1999, Dec. 13). A safety valve for wages? Variable pay's rewards—and risks. *BusinessWeek,* p. 32.
7. Fisher, A. (2000, June 26). Boosting your pay and finding your passion. *Fortune,* p. 340.
8. Buck survey: Pay raises to remain flat in 1999 (1998, Nov. 27). *ACA Newsline.* See also Nelson, E. (1995, Sept.. 29). Gas company's gain-sharing plan turns employees into cost-cutting vigilantes. *The Wall Street Journal,* pp. B1, B4. See also Uchitelle, L. (1987, June 26). Bonuses replace wage raises and workers are the losers. *The New York Times,* pp. A1, D3.
9. Ibid., p. D3.
10. Sturman, M. C., & Short, J. C. (2000). Lump-sum bonus satisfaction: Testing the construct validity of a new pay satisfaction dimension. *Personnel Psychology, 53,* 673–700.
11. Zhou, J., & Martocchio, J. J. (2001). Chinese and American managers' compensation award decisions: A comparative policy-capturing study. *Personnel Psychology, 54,* 115–145.
12. Dolan, K. A. (1996, Nov. 18). When money isn't enough. *Forbes,* pp. 164–170.
13. Ibid., p. 166.
14. Lawler, E. E., III (1989). Pay for performance: A strategic analysis. In Gomez-Mejia, op. cit., pp. 3-136–3-181. See also Lawler, E. E., III (1977). Reward systems. In J. R. Hackman & J. L. Suttle, *Improving life at work: Behavioral science approaches to organizational change* (pp. 163–226). Santa Monica, CA: Goodyear.
15. Foulkes, F. K., & Livernash, E. R. (1989). *Human resources management: Cases and text* (2d ed.). Englewood Cliffs, NJ: Prentice-Hall.
16. Thierry, H. (1992). Pay and payment systems. In J. F. Hartley & S. M. Stephenson (eds.), *Managing employment relations.* Oxford: Basil Blackwell, pp. 136–160. See

also Sweeney, P. D., McFarlin, D. B., & Inderrieden, E. J. (1990). Using relative deprivation theory to explain satisfaction with income and pay level: A multistudy examination. *Academy of Management Journal, 33,* 423–436.

17. Huseman, R. C., Hatfield, J. D., & Miles, E. W. (1987). A new perspective on equity theory: The equity sensitivity construct. *Academy of Management Review, 12,* 222–234.

18. Labor letter (1990, Oct. 2). *The Wall Street Journal,* p. A1.

19. Cowan, A. L. (1993, May 21). At what point is pay too high? *The New York Times,* pp. D1, D2.

20. The best and worst boards. (1996, Nov. 25). *BusinessWeek,* p. 94.

21. Grossman, W., & Hoskisson, R. E. (1998). CEO pay at the crossroads of Wall Street and Main: Toward the strategic design of executive compensation. *Academy of Management Executive, 12* (1), 43–57. See also Gomez-Mejia, L. R., & Balkin, D. B. (1992). *Compensation, organizational strategy, and firm performance.* Cincinnati, OH: South-Western College Publishing.

22. Grossman & Hoskisson, op. cit. See also Montemayor, E. (1996). Congruence between pay policy and competitive strategy in high-performing firms. *Journal of Management, 22,* 889–908.

23. Lublin, J. S. (1997, Jan. 7). Don't count on that merit raise this year. *The Wall Street Journal,* pp. B1, B6.

24. Grossman & Hoskisson, op. cit. See also Gomez-Mejia & Balkin, op. cit.

25. Milkovich & Newman, op. cit.

26. Morse, D. (2000, Aug. 22). Labor shortage has franchisees hustling for workers. *The Wall Street Journal,* p. B2.

27. Jaffe, G. (1997, Jan. 15). South's growth rate hits speed bump. *The Wall Street Journal,* p. A2.

28. Klaas, B. S., & Ullman, J. C. (1995). Sticky wages revisited: Organizational responses to a declining market-clearing wage. *Academy of Management Review, 20,* 281–310. See also Cappelli, P., & Chauvin, K. (1991). An interplant test of the efficiency wage hypothesis. *Quarterly Journal of Economics, 106,* 769–794. See also Holzer, H. J. (1990). Wages, employer costs, and employee performance in the firm. *Industrial and Labor Relations Review, 43,* 147S–164S.

29. Ormiston, K. A. (1988, May 10). States know best what labor's worth. *The Wall Street Journal,* p. 38.

30. Gentile, G. (2001, July 28). Wealthy city insists on living wage. *The Miami Herald,* p. 3C. See also What's so bad about a living wage? (2000, Sept. 4). *BusinessWeek,* pp. 68, 70.

31. Mills, D. Q. (1994). *Labor-management relations* (5th ed.). New York: McGraw-Hill.

32. Pfeffer, J., & Davis-Blake, A. (1987). Understanding organizational wage structures: A resource dependence approach. *Academy of Management Journal, 30,* 437–455.

33. Klaas, B. (1999). Containing compensation costs: Why firms differ in their willingness to reduce pay. *Journal of Management, 25,* 829–850.

34. Gomez, L. R., Page, R. C., & Tornow, W. W. (1982). A comparison of the practical utility of traditional, statistical, and hybrid job evaluation approaches. *Academy of Management Journal, 25,* 790–809.

35. Milkovich & Newman, op. cit. See also Gerhart, B., & Milkovich, G. T. (1992). Employee compensation: Research and practice. In M. D. Dunnette & L. M. Hough (eds.), *Handbook of industrial and organizational psychology.* Palo Alto, CA: Consulting Psychologists Press, pp. 481–569.

36. Rynes, S. L., & Milkovich, G. T. (1986). Wage surveys: Dispelling some myths about the "market wage." *Personnel Psychology, 39,* 71–90.

37. Geary, L. H., & Kirwan, R. (2000, Sept.). Get paid more! The top salary sites. *Money,* pp. 109–118. See also Lublin, J. S. (1999, July 22). Web transforms art of negotiating raises. *The Wall Street Journal,* pp. B1, B16.

38. Wellner, A. S. (2001, May). Salaries in site. *HRMagazine,* pp. 89–96.

39. Fisher, A. (2001, Apr. 30). Being lowballed on salary? How to eke out more bucks. *Fortune*, p. 192.

40. Fay, C. H. (1989). External pay relationships. In Gomez-Mejia, op. cit. pp. 3-70–3-100.

41. Wallace, M. J., Jr., & Fay, C. H. (1988). *Compensation theory and practice* (2d ed.). Boston: PWS-Kent.

42. Sibson, R. E. (1991). *Compensation* (5th ed.). New York: American Management Association.

43. Colvin, G. (2001, June 25). The great CEO pay heist. *Fortune*, pp. 64–84. Lavelle, L. (2001, Mar. 26). The artificial sweetener in CEO pay. *BusinessWeek*, pp. 102, 104. See also Balkin, D. B., & Logan, J. W. (1988). Reward policies that support entrepreneurship. *Compensation and Benefits Review, 20*(1), 18–25.

44. Milkovich & Newman, op. cit.

45. Rowland, M. (1993, June 6). It's what you can do that counts. *The New York Times*, p. F17.

46. Southall, D., & Newman, J. (2000). *Skill-based pay development.* Buffalo, NY: HR Foundations, Inc.

47. Murray, B., & Gerhart, B. (1998). An empirical analysis of a skill-based pay program and plant performance outcomes. *Academy of Management Journal, 41*, 68–78.

48. Lee, C., Law, K. S., & Bobko, P. (1999). The importance of justice perceptions on pay effectiveness: A two-year study of a skill-based pay plan. *Journal of Management, 25* (6), 851–873.

49. Grib, G., & O'Donnell, S. (1995, July). Pay plans that reward employee achievement. *HRMagazine*, pp. 49, 50. See also Leonard, B. (1995, Feb.). Creating opportunities to excel. *HRMagazine*, pp. 47–51.

50. Gomez-Mejia & Balkin, op. cit.

51. Olson, E. (2001, May 19). A spotlight on Swiss executives. *International Herald Tribune*, p. 11. See also Woodruff, D. (2000, Sept. 11). A vanishing European taboo: Disclosing executive pay. *The Wall Street Journal*, p. A28.

52. Milkovich & Newman, op. cit.

53. Rouzer, P. A. (2000, Aug.). Adding salary ranges to internal postings. *HRMagazine*, pp. 107–114.

54. Markels, A., & Berton, L. (1996, Apr. 11). Something to talk about. *The Wall Street Journal Supplement*, p. R10. See also Gomez-Mejia & Balkin, op. cit.

55. Fisher, op. cit.

56. Casner, in Lublin, op. cit., p. B1.

57. Gomez-Mejia & Balkin, op. cit.

58. Dreazen, Y. (2000, July 25). Morale problem: When recruits earn more. *The Wall Street Journal*, pp. B1, B10.

59. Labor letter, op. cit. See also Kanter, R. M. (1987, Mar.–Apr.). The attack on pay. *Harvard Business Review*, pp. 60–67.

60. Bergmann, T. J., Hills, F. S., & Priefert, L. (1983, 2d quarter). Pay compression: Causes, results, and possible solutions. *Compensation Review, 6*, 17–26.

61. Revenge of the "managers." (2001, Mar. 12). *BusinessWeek*, pp. 60, 62. See also Zacharay, G. P. (1996, June 24). Shortchanged: Many firms refuse to pay for overtime, employees complain. *The Wall Street Journal*, pp. A1, A6.

62. Fisher, op. cit.

63. Schwartz, J. D. (1982, February). Maintaining merit compensation in a high-inflation economy. *Personnel Journal*, pp. 147–152.

64. A safety valve for wages? op. cit.

65. Many employers seek to replace cash bonuses with other work incentives (2000, Apr. 4). *The Wall Street Journal*, p. A1. See also Good job! (1998, Dec. 5). *BusinessWeek*, p. 14.

66. Banker, R. D., Lee, S. Y., Potter, G., & Srinivasan, D. (1996). Contextual analysis of performance impacts of outcome-based incentive compensation. *Academy of*

Management Journal, 39, 920–948. See also Kaufman, R. T. (1992). The effects of improshare on productivity. *Industrial and Labor Relations Review, 45,* 311–322.

67. Jenkins, G. D., Jr., Mitra, A., Gupta, N., & Shaw, J. D. (1998). Are financial incentives related to performance? A meta-analytic review of empirical research. *Journal of Applied Psychology, 83,* 777–787.

68. Lawler, E. E., III (1989). Pay for performance: A strategic analysis. In Gomez-Mejia, op. cit., pp. 3-136–3-181.

69. Rethinking rewards (1993, Nov.–Dec.). *Harvard Business Review,* pp. 37–49.

70. Milkovich & Newman, op. cit. See also Bennett, A. (1991, Sept. 10). Paying workers to meet goals spreads, but gauging performance proves tough. *The Wall Street Journal,* pp. B1, B2.

71. Waldman, S., & Roberts, B. (1988, Nov. 14). Grading "merit pay." *Newsweek,* pp. 45, 46.

72. Dolan, op. cit.

73. Rollins, T. (1987, June). Pay for performance: The pros and cons. *Personnel Journal,* pp. 104–107.

74. Lawler, op. cit.

75. A model incentive plan gets caught in a vise. (1996, Jan. 22). *BusinessWeek,* pp. 89, 92. See also Wiley, C. (1993, Aug.). Incentive plan pushes production. *Personnel Journal,* pp. 86–91.

76. Kopelman, R. E., & Reinharth, L. (1982, 4th quarter). Research results; The effect of merit-pay practices on white-collar performance. *Compensation Review, 5,* 30–40.

77. Bennett, A. (1991, Apr. 17). The hot seat: Talking to the people responsible for setting pay. *The Wall Street Journal,* p. R3.

78. Meyer, P. (1983). Executive compensation must promote long-term commitment. *Personnel Administrator, 28*(5), 37–42.

79. Lavelle, L., op. cit.

80. Kanter, op. cit.

81. Gomez-Mejia, L. R., Tosi, H., & Hinkin, T. (1987). Managerial control, performance, and executive compensation. *Academy of Management Journal, 30,* 51–70.

82. Lublin, J. S. (2001, Apr. 12). Hedging their bets. *The Wall Street Journal,* pp. R1, R4. See also Lowenstein, R. (1996, Apr. 4). Renegade firms redefine executive pay. *The Wall Street Journal,* p. B1.

83. Bennett, A. (1992, Mar. 11). Taking stock: Big firms rely more on options but fail to end pay criticism. *The Wall Street Journal,* pp. A1, A8.

84. Tully, S. (1998, June 8). Raising the bar. *Fortune,* pp. 272–278. See also Share the wealth with the workforce. (1996, Apr. 22). *BusinessWeek,* p. 158.

85. Silverman, R. E. (2001, Apr. 12). Breathing underwater: Companies look for ways to help workers stuck with worthless stock options. *The Wall Street Journal,* p. R8. See also Simon, R., & Dugan, I. J. (2001, June 4). Options overdose. *The Wall Street Journal,* pp. C1, C17. See also Coy, P. (1999, Dec. 13). The drawbacks of stock-option fever. *BusinessWeek,* p. 204.

86. Bennett, op. cit.

87. A model incentive plan gets caught in a vise (1996, Jan. 22). *BusinessWeek,* pp. 89, 92. See also Wiley, C. (1993, Aug.). Incentive plan pushes production. *Personnel Journal,* pp. 86–91. See also Serrin, W. (1984, Jan. 15). The way that works at Lincoln. *The New York Times,* p. D1.

88. M. Smith, Director of Hose Manufacturing, and T. Cecil, Manufacturing Supervisor, Gates Rubber Company, Denver. Personal interviews, Dec., 1996.

89. Petty, M. M., Singleton, B., & Connell, D. W. (1992). An experimental evaluation of an organizational incentive plan in the electric utility industry. *Journal of Applied Psychology, 77,* 427–436.

90. Norman, C. A., & Zawacki, R. A. (1991, Sept.). Team appraisals—team approach. *Personnel Journal,* pp. 101–104. See also Rowland, M. (1992, Feb. 9). Pay for quality, by the group. *The New York Times,* p. D6.

91. Sheudan, J. H. (1996, Mar. 4). Yes: To team incentives. *Industry Week,* p. 63.

92. Dulebohn, J. H., & Martocchio, J. J. (1998). Employee perceptions of the fairness of work group incentive plans. *Journal of Management, 24,* 469–488.

93. Schroeder, M. (1988, Nov. 7). Watching the bottom line instead of the clock. *BusinessWeek,* pp. 134, 136. See also Florkowski, G. W. (1987). The organizational impact of profit sharing. *Academy of Management Review, 12,* 622–636.

94. Banerjee, N. (1994, Apr. 12). Rebounding earnings stir old debate on productivity's tie to profit-sharing. *The Wall Street Journal,* pp. A2, A12. See also U.S. Department of Labor (1993, Aug.). *High performance work practices and firm performance.* Washington, DC: Author.

95. Hays, L. (1988, Dec. 5). All eyes on DuPont's incentive-pay plan. *The Wall Street Journal,* p. B1.

96. Koenig, R. (1990, Oct. 25). DuPont plan linking pay to fibers profit unravels. *The Wall Street Journal,* pp. B1, B5.

97. Colvin, G. (1998, Aug. 17). What money makes you do. *Fortune,* pp. 213, 214.

98. Collins, D., Hatcher, L., & Ross, T. L. (1993). The decision to implement gainsharing: Role of work climate, expected outcomes, and union status. *Personnel Psychology, 46,* 77–104. See also Graham-Moore, B., & Ross, T. L. (1990). Understanding gainsharing. In B. Graham-Moore & T. L. Ross (eds.), *Gainsharing.* Washington, DC: Bureau of National Affairs, pp. 3–18.

99. Graham-Moore & Ross, op. cit.

100. Hammer, T. H. (1988). New developments in profit sharing, gainsharing, and employee ownership. In J. P. Campbell & R. J. Campbell (eds.), *Productivity in organizations.* San Francisco: Jossey-Bass, pp. 328–366.

101. Graham-Moore, B. (1990). Seventeen years of experience with the Scanlon plan: DeSoto revisited. In B. Graham-Moore & T. L. Ross (eds.), *Gainsharing.* Washington, DC: Bureau of National Affairs, pp. 139–173.

102. Tyler, L. S., & Fisher, B. (1983). The Scanlon concept: A philosophy as much as a system. *Personnel Administrator, 29*(7), 33–37. See also Moore, B., & Ross, T. (1978). *The Scanlon way to improved productivity.* New York: Wiley.

103. Kim, D. (1999). Determinants of the survival of gainsharing programs. *Industrial and Labor Relations Review, 53* (1), 21–42. See also White, J. K. (1979). The Scanlon plan: Causes and consequences of success. *Academy of Management Journal, 22,* 292–312.

104. IOMA (1999, Jan.). Another pan of stock option plans. *IOMA's Pay for Performance Report,* p. 11. See also Becker, G. S. (1989, Oct. 23). ESOPs aren't the magic key to anything. *BusinessWeek,* p. 20.

105. Why ESOP deals have slowed to a crawl. (1996, Mar. 18). *BusinessWeek,* pp. 101, 102.

106. Jones, D., & Schmitt, J. (1993, Dec. 20). UAL plan may put industry in new hands. *USA Today,* pp. 1B, 2B.

107. Milkovich & Newman, op. cit.

108. ESOPs offer way to sell stakes in small firms (1988, May 3). *The Wall Street Journal,* p. 33.

109. Happy fallout down at the nuke lab (1996, Oct. 7). *BusinessWeek,* p. 42.

110. Stajkovic, A. D., & Luthans, F. (2001). Differential effects of incentive motivators on work performance. *Academy of Management Journal, 44* (3), 580–590.

111. Northwest's sigh of relief has rivals groaning (1993, July 26). *BusinessWeek,* p. 84.

112. Deckop, J. R., Mangel, R., & Cirka, C. (1999). Getting more than you pay for: Organizational citizenship behavior and pay-for-performance plans. *Academy of Management Journal, 42,* 420–428.

113. Klein, K. J., & Hall, R. J. (1988). Correlates of employee satisfaction with stock ownership: Who likes an ESOP most? *Journal of Applied Psychology, 73,* 630–638. See also Klein, K. J. (1987). Employee stock ownership and employee attitudes: A test of three models. *Journal of Applied Psychology, 72,* 319–332. See also Rosen, C., Klein, K. J., & Young, K. M. (1986). When employees share the profits. *Psychology Today, 20,* 30–36.

114. IOMA, op. cit.

115. Labich, K. (1996, Oct. 14). When workers really count. *Fortune,* pp. 212–214. See also United we own: Employee ownership is working at the airline. Can it travel? (1996, Mar. 18). *BusinessWeek,* pp. 96–100.

116. Rosen et al., op. cit.

117. White, J. A. (1992, Feb. 13). When employees own big stake, it's a buy signal for investors. *The Wall Street Journal,* pp. C1, C9.

118. Bloom, M., & Milkovich, G. T. (1998). Relationships among risk, incentive pay, and organizational performance. *Academy of Management Journal, 41,* 283–297.

119. Tullar, W. L. (1998). Compensation consequences of reengineering. *Journal of Applied Psychology, 83,* 975–980.

120. Farnham, op. cit., p. 66.

121. Moore, B. L. (2001, Apr. 12). No, thanks. CEOs who give up part of their pay? What's that all about? *The Wall Street Journal,* p. R4.

122. Farnham, op. cit.

123. Ibid., p. 70.

12

INDIRECT COMPENSATION:

EMPLOYEE BENEFIT PLANS

Questions This Chapter Will Help Managers Answer

1. What strategic considerations should guide the design of benefits programs?
2. What options are available to help a business control the rapid escalation of health care costs?
3. Should companies offer a uniform "package" of benefits, or should they move to a flexible plan that allows employees to choose the benefits that are most meaningful to them, up to a certain dollar amount?
4. What cost-effective benefits options are available to a small business?
5. In view of the considerable sums of money that are spent each year on employee benefits, what is the best way to communicate this information to employees?

THE NEW WORLD OF EMPLOYEE BENEFITS*

In the early 1990s, experts predicted that benefits packages would become ever more generous as companies competed for a shrinking pool of workers. Today, that forecast seems as outdated as the notion that computers would create a paperless society. Struggling to deal with benefits costs that seem to rise relentlessly, many firms are eliminating benefits or asking employees to pay more for them. Plans that allow employees to choose among alternative benefits choices, so-called flexible benefits, force employees to make trade-offs—and profoundly affect how they think about security, company loyalty, and employment itself. It wasn't always this way.

In the past, major corporations offered their employees a wide array of company-paid insurance and retirement benefits. Corporations decided what was best for their employees. Now, however, most employers are not only changing the range of benefit choices they offer, but also changing the basic structure of their benefits.

Economics and demographics are driving these changes. Economically, most employers realize that the traditional blanket approach to benefits—total coverage for everyone—would subject them to unbearable expense. Benefits are no longer the "fringe" of compensation. Today they often compose 30 percent or more of wages. As a result of unending increases in the price of medical care, for example, health care expenses now consume an average of 56 percent of pretax profits of U.S. corporations. Increasing life expectancy has made pensions more costly as well. The combination of increased longevity, rising health care costs, and an accounting standard that requires firms to report the cost of future retiree health care benefits on their balance sheets—thereby reducing profits—has led employers to rethink their entire approach to employee benefits dramatically.

Demographically the United States now has a much more diverse workforce than it has had in the past. As a result, the "one-size-fits-all" approach to employee benefits doesn't work. Employees who have working spouses covered by health insurance have different insurance needs from those who are sole breadwinners. Single parents and childless couples place very different priorities on child care benefits. So rather than attempt to fashion a single approach that suits all of these interests, many employers determine a sum they'll spend on each employee, establish a menu of benefits, and then let each employee choose the benefits he or she wants or needs. At the same time such plans allow employers to trim benefits merely by raising the prices of the various options on the benefits menu. Such "life-cycle benefits plans" represent the next generation of full-blown flexible benefits.

These changes reflect more than demographic diversity, however. A fundamental change in philosophy is taking place as employees are forced to take more responsibility. Part of this is a movement toward employee self-management. Indeed, the new approach might well be described as one of "sharing costs, sharing risks."

---

*Sources: America's best company benefits, *Money,* Sept. 2000, pp. 103–108; E. P. Gunn, How to maximize your pension payout. *Fortune,* Oct. 28, 1996, p. 233; B. Leonard, Perks give way to life-cycle benefits plans, *HRMagazine,* Mar. 1995, pp. 45–48.

Challenges

1. Do you think companies should provide a broader menu of "exotic" benefits (e.g., veterinary care, dietary counseling) or improve the menu of "core" benefits (e.g., health care, insurance, pensions)? Why?
2. How might one's preference for various benefits change as one grows older or as one's family situation changes?

Benefits currently account for almost 40 percent of the total compensation costs for each employee. Yesterday's "fringes" have become today's (expected) benefits and services. Here are some reasons why benefits have grown:

- The imposition of wage ceilings during World War II forced organizations to offer more benefits in place of wage increases to attract, retain, and motivate employees.
- The interest by unions in bargaining over benefits has grown, particularly since employers are pushing for more cost-sharing by employees.[1]
- The tax treatment of benefits makes them preferable to wages. Many benefits remain nontaxable to the employee and are deductible by the employer. With other benefits, taxes are deferred. Hence employees' disposable income increases since they are receiving benefits and services that they would otherwise have to purchase with after-tax dollars.
- Granting benefits (in a nonunionized firm) or bargaining over them (in a unionized firm) confers an aura of social responsibility on employers; they are "taking care" of their employees. This is important, for evidence indicates that employees retain a strong sense of entitlement to benefits.[2]

STRATEGIC CONSIDERATIONS IN THE DESIGN OF BENEFITS PROGRAMS

As is the case with compensation systems in general, managers need to think carefully about what they wish to accomplish by means of their benefits programs. On average, firms spend over $15,000 in benefits for each worker on the payroll.[3] General Motors, for example, spends about $1200 for every car it builds in the United States, $700 more than it spends on the car's steel, just to provide health benefits to active and retired workers.[4] It's no exaggeration to say that for most firms, benefits represent substantial annual expenditures, for they compose fully 28 percent of the overall costs of doing business.[5] In order to leverage the impact of these expenditures, managers should be prepared to answer questions such as the following:

- Are the type and level of our benefits coverage consistent with our long-term strategic business plans?

- Given the characteristics of our workforce, are we meeting the needs of our employees?
- What legal requirements must we satisfy in the benefits we offer?
- Are our benefits competitive in cost, structure, and value to employees and their dependents?
- Is our benefits package consistent with the key objectives of our total compensation strategy, namely, adequacy, equity, cost control, and balance?

In the following sections, we will discuss each of these points.

Long-Term Strategic Business Plans

Such plans outline the basic directions in which an organization wishes to move in the next 3 to 5 years. One strategic issue that should influence the design of benefits is an organization's stage of development. For example, a start-up venture probably will offer low base pay and benefits but high incentives; a mature firm with well-established products and substantial market share will probably offer much more generous pay and benefits combined with moderate incentives.

Other strategic considerations include the projected rate of employment growth or downsizing, geographic redeployment, acquisitions, and expected changes in profitability.[6] Each of these conditions suggests a change in the optimum "mix" of benefits in order to be most consistent with an organization's business plans.

IBM'S NEW PRODUCT—EMPLOYEE BENEFITS[7]

COMPANY EXAMPLE

Like most other companies, IBM has been looking for cost-effective ways to cut its annual cost of employee benefits (more than $1 billion per year). It found one that is consistent with its long-term business plan to make each of its independent units a profit center. Guess what IBM did. It spun off its huge human resources (HR) operation into a separate company called Workforce Solutions, which is now saving IBM more than $45 million annually in the form of reduced staffing, consolidation of offices, and use of new technology, such as automated telephones. In fact, the overall HR staff has shrunk by about a third, to 1,500 employees. The spin-off provides customized services to each of IBM's 13 independent business units. Before, IBM took a one-size-fits-all approach to benefits. In addition, Workforce Solutions also handles business for other companies, such as the National Geographic Society, capitalizing on IBM's reputation for excellence and lots of practical experience in the benefits area. Each IBM unit is free to choose its own provider of benefits and HR functions. As a result, Workforce Solutions has to compete for that business. Its success shows that marketing internal operations to outsiders can turn benefits departments from drains on the bottom line to profit centers in their own right.

Diversity in the Workforce Means Diversity in Benefits Preferences

Young employees who are just starting out are likely to be more concerned with direct pay (e.g., for a house purchase) than with a generous pension program. Older workers may desire the reverse. Unionized workers may prefer a uniform benefits package, while single parents, older workers, or workers with disabilities may place heavy emphasis on flexible work schedules. Employers that hire large numbers of temporary or part-time workers may offer entirely different benefits to these groups. Among temporary employees, while 56 percent receive holiday pay, 46 percent skills training, and 22 percent performance bonuses, only 8 percent get health care benefits.[8]

Legal Requirements

The government plays a central role in the design of any benefits package. While controlling the cost of benefits is a major concern of employers, the social and economic welfare of citizens is the major concern of government.[9] As examples of such concern, consider the four income-maintenance laws shown in Table 12–1.

Income-maintenance laws were enacted to provide employees and their families with income security in case of death, disability, unemployment, or retirement. At a broad level, government tax policy has had, and will continue to have, a major impact on the design of benefits programs. Two principles have had the greatest impact on benefits.[10] One is the **doctrine of constructive receipt,** which holds that an individual must pay taxes on benefits that have monetary value when the individual receives them. The other principle is the **antidiscrimination rule,** which holds that employers can obtain tax advantages only for those benefits that do not discriminate in favor of highly compensated employees. Such an employee is one who owns at least 5 percent of company stock or partnership rights, is a company officer earning more than $45,000 a year, or earns more than $50,000 a year and has income in the top 20 percent of the general workforce. These dollar amounts are adjusted periodically.

These two tax-policy principles define the conditions for the preferential tax treatment of benefits. Together they hold that if benefits discriminate in favor of highly paid or "key" employees, both the employer and the employee receiving those benefits may have to pay taxes on the benefits when they are transferred.

Social Security, which accounts for $1 of every $5 spent by the federal government, has had, and will continue to have, an effect on the growth, development, and design of employee benefits. National health policy increasingly is shifting costs to the private sector and emphasizing cost containment; such pressures will intensify. Finally, national policy on unfair discrimination, particularly through the civil rights laws, has caused firms to reexamine their benefits policies.

Competitiveness of the Benefits Offered

The issue of benefits-program competitiveness is much more complicated than that of salary competitiveness.[11] In the case of salary, both employees and

Table 12–1

FOUR MAJOR INCOME-MAINTENANCE LAWS

Law	Scope of coverage	Funding	Benefits	Administrative agency
Social Security Act (1935)	Full coverage for retirees, dependent survivors, and disabled persons insured by 40 quarters of payroll taxes on their past earnings or earnings of heads of households. Federal government employees hired prior to January 1, 1984, and railroad workers are excluded.	For 2002, payroll tax of 7.65% for employees and 7.65% for employers on the first $84,900 in earnings. Self-employed persons pay 15.3% of this wage base. Of the 7.65%, 6.2% is allocated for retirement, survivors, and disability insurance, and 1.45% for Medicare. The Omnibus Budget Reconciliation Act of 1993 extended the 1.45% Medicare payroll tax to all wages and self-employment income.	Full *retirement payments* after age 65, or at reduced rates after 62, to worker and spouse. Size of payment depends on past earnings. *Survivor benefits* for the or family of a deceased worker retiree. At age 65 a widow or widower receives the full age 65 pension granted to the deceased. A widow or widower of any age with dependent children under 16, and each unmarried child under 18, receives a 75% benefit check. *Disability benefits* to totally disabled workers, after a 5-month waiting period, as well as to their spouses and children. *Health insurance* for persons over 65 (Medicare). All benefits are adjusted upward whenever the consumer price index (CPI) increases more than 3% in a calendar year and trust funds are at a specified level. Otherwise the adjustment is based on the lower of the CPI increase or the increase in average national wages (1983 amendments).	Social Security Administration
Federal Unemployment Tax Act (1935)	All employees except some state and local government workers, domestic and farm workers, railroad workers, and some nonprofit employees.	Payroll tax of at least 3.4% of first $7,000 of earnings paid by employer. (Employees also taxed in Alaska, Alabama, and New Jersey.) States may raise both the percentage and base earnings taxed through legislation. Employer contributions may be reduced if state experience ratings for them are low.	Benefits average roughly 50% of average weekly earnings and are available for up to 26 weeks. Those eligible for benefits have been employed for some specified minimum period and have lost their jobs through no fault of their own. Most states exclude strikers. During periods of high unemployment, benefits may be extended for up to 52 weeks.	U.S. Bureau of Employment Security, U.S. Training and Employment Service, and the several state employment security commissions

continues on page 466

Table 12–1 (cont.)

FOUR MAJOR INCOME-MAINTENANCE LAWS

Law	Scope of coverage	Funding	Benefits	Administrative agency
Workers' compensation (state laws)	Generally, employees of nonagricultural, private-sector firms are entitled to benefits for work-related accidents and illnesses leading to temporary or permanent disabilities.	One of the following options, depending on state law: self-insurance, insurance through a private carrier, or payroll-based payments to a state insurance system. Premiums depend on the riskiness of the occupation and the experience rating of the insured.	Benefits average about two-thirds of an employee's weekly wage and continue for the term of the disability. Supplemental payments are made for medical care and rehabilitative services. In case of a fatal accident, survivor benefits are payable.	Various state commissions
Employee Retirement Income Security Act (ERISA) (1974)	Private-sector employees over age 21 enrolled in noncontributory (100% employer-paid) retirement plans who have 1 year's service	Employer contributions.	The 1986 Tax Reform Act authorizes several formulas to provide vesting of retirement benefits after a certain length of service (5–7 years). Once an employee is "vested," receipt of the pension is not contingent on future service. Authorizes tax free transfer of vested benefits to another employer or to an individual retirement account ("portability") if a vested employee changes jobs and if the present employer agrees. Employers must fund plans on an actuarially sound basis. Pension trustees ("fiduciaries") must make prudent investments. Employers may insure vested benefits through the federal Pension Benefit Guaranty Corporation.	Department of Labor, Internal Revenue Service, Pension Benefit Guaranty Corporation

management focus on the same item: direct pay (fixed plus variable). However, in determining the competitiveness of benefits, senior management tends to focus mainly on cost, while employees are more interested in value. The two may conflict. Thus employees' perceptions of the value of their benefits as competitive may lead to excessive costs, in the view of top management. On the other hand, achieving cost competitiveness provides no assurance that employees will perceive the benefits program as valuable to them.

HOW NIKE MATCHES PEOPLE WITH BENEFITS[12]   COMPANY EXAMPLE

To attract and retain skilled workers, Nike enlists current employees to help enrich its benefits offerings. It starts by probing workers' fears, needs, and desires in focus groups and surveys, in which employees often express worries about not being able to buy a house, send their children to college, or care for elderly parents. Then Nike asks employee teams to design new benefits packages that offer more choices without raising costs. Some of the choices the teams come up with include company-matching funds for college tuition, subsidies for child care or elder care, paid time off for family leave, group discounts on auto or home insurance, discounted mortgages, legal services, and financial planning advice.

Many of the new offerings are relatively cheap for the company. To contain costs further, Nike gives employees incentives to make health-benefits trade-offs, such as pledging to stop smoking or using company-chosen physician networks. By tailoring its benefits to those that employees really need and care deeply about, Nike is maximizing the return on its "benefits bucks."

Total Compensation Strategy

The broad objective of the design of compensation programs (that is, direct as well as indirect compensation) is to integrate salary and benefits into a package that will encourage the achievement of an organization's goals. For example, while a generous pension plan may help retain employees, it probably does little to motivate them to perform on a day-to-day basis. This is because the length of time between performance and reward is too great. On the other hand, a generous severance package offered to targeted segments of the employee population may facilitate an organization's objective of downsizing to a specified staffing level. In all cases, considerations of adequacy, equity, cost control, and balance should guide decision making in the context of a total compensation strategy.

With these considerations in mind, let us now examine some key components of the benefits package.

COMPONENTS OF THE BENEFITS PACKAGE

There are many ways to classify benefits, but we will follow the classification scheme used by the U.S. Chamber of Commerce. According to this system, benefits fall into three categories: security and health, payments for time not worked, and employee services. Within each of these categories there is a bewildering array of options. The following discussions consider only the most popular options and cover only those that have not been mentioned previously.

Cost.   How much do benefits cost? In its 2001 benefits survey, the Society for Human Resource Management found that across organizations of all sizes in a variety of industries, the average percentage of salary reflecting the total cost of benefits was 30 percent, with a range of 27–34 percent as a function of organizational size. Medium-sized companies with 501 to 1,000 employees offered the lowest percentage of benefits, while companies with 2,501 to 5,000 employees offered the largest percentage of benefits.[13] Thus for a company that pays an average salary of $45,000 per year, its average cost of benefits *per employee* is $13,500.

Security and Health Benefits

These include:

- Life insurance.
- Workers' compensation.
- Disability insurance.
- Hospitalization, surgical, and maternity coverage.
- Health maintenance organizations (HMOs).
- Other medical coverage.
- Sick leave.
- Pension plans.
- Social Security.
- Unemployment insurance.
- Supplemental unemployment insurance.
- Severance pay.

Insurance is the basic building block of almost all benefits packages, for it protects employees against income loss caused by death, accident, or ill-health. Most organizations provide group coverage for their employees. The plans may be **contributory** (in which employees share in the cost of the premiums) or **noncontributory** (in which the employer pays the full cost of the premiums).

It used to be that when a worker switched jobs, he or she lost health insurance coverage. The worker had to "go naked" for months until coverage began at a new employer. No longer. Under the Consolidated Omnibus Budget Reconciliation Act (COBRA) of 1986, companies with at least 20 employees must make medical coverage available at group insurance rates for as long as 18 months after the employee leaves—whether the worker left voluntarily, retired, or was dismissed. The law also provides that, following a worker's death or divorce, the employee's family has the right to buy group-rate health insurance for as long as 3 years. Employers who do not comply can be sued and denied corporate tax deductions related to health benefits.[14]

However, since some corporate medical plans do not cover preexisting conditions, some employees have found that when they changed jobs (and health plans), their benefits were reduced sharply. To alleviate that problem, Congress passed the Health Insurance Portability and Accountability Act (HIPAA) in 1997. In general, HIPAA includes the following provisions:

1. Limits exclusions for preexisting conditions to 12 months.
2. If employees don't enroll as soon as they become eligible, employers may impose exclusions for preexisting conditions of up to 18 months.
3. Companies must reduce the 12-month cap by 1 month for each month of prior continuous coverage. Thus if an employee has had prior continuous

coverage for more than 12 months, the new employer may not claim any exclusion for preexisting conditions.

4. If there is a break in coverage of more than 63 days, employers need not count prior continuous coverage before that time against the 12-month cap.[15]

With this in mind, let us consider the major forms of security and health benefits commonly provided to employees.

Group Life Insurance

This type of insurance is usually **yearly renewable term insurance;** that is, each employee is insured 1 year at a time. The actual amounts of coverage vary, but typical group term life insurance coverage is one to two times the employee's annual salary. This amount provides a reasonable financial cushion to the surviving spouse during the difficult transition to a different way of life. Thus a manager making $60,000 per year may have a group term-life policy with a face value of $120,000 or $150,000. Keep in mind, however, that the more expenses and dependents you have, the more life insurance you will need.[16] To discourage turnover, almost all companies cancel this benefit if an employee terminates.

Life insurance has been heavily affected by **flexible benefits** programs. Typically such programs provide a core of basic life coverage (e.g., $25,000) and then permit employees to choose greater coverage (e.g., in increments of $10,000 to $25,000) as part of their optional package.[17] Employees purchase the additional insurance through payroll deductions.[18]

Workers' Compensation

Workers' compensation programs provide payments to workers who are injured on the job, or who contract a work-related illness. The payments cover three areas: payments to replace lost wages, medical treatment and rehabilitation costs, and retraining to perform a different type of work (if necessary). As shown in Table 12–1, these payments vary by state. Disability benefits, which have been extended to cover stress (in four states) and occupational disease, tend to be highest in states where organized labor is strong.[19] With regard to stress, most states require some bodily injury manifestation of stress—that is, mental-physical, or where some specific and defined event occurred.[20]

A state's industrial structure also plays a big part in setting disability insurance rates. Thus serious injuries are more common and costly among Oregon loggers and Michigan machinists than among assembly-line workers in a Texas semiconductor plant. Sometimes the costs can get out of hand, especially for small businesses. Consider Bartow, Florida, construction contractor Jean Stinson. Her company's liability insurance costs—of which workers' compensation is the biggest part—jumped 187 percent in 1 year, to $250,000. When she raised her bids to recoup the higher costs, customers put their projects on hold.[21] Trends such as these have prompted high-cost states, such as California, Florida, Michigan, and Maine, to lower workers' compensation premiums so that they can continue to attract and retain businesses in their states.

COMPANY EXAMPLE   ## CONTROLLING THE COSTS OF WORKERS' COMPENSATION

Workers' compensation costs employers some $52 billion a year, and it is a major cost of doing business.[22] Some of the driving forces behind these costs are higher medical costs, the increasing involvement of attorneys, and widespread fraud. According to *The New York Times,* 20 percent or more of claims may involve cheating.[23] What are states and companies doing to control costs?

California set up a fund, financed by employers, that pays for special teams to go after fraud. Job-injury claims declined to 8.4 per 100 workers, from nearly 10 per 100 workers 2 years earlier. Connecticut no longer awards disability benefits for mental or psychological disorders unless they are the result of an injury. It has eliminated cost-of-living adjustments on disability benefits, and has cut some benefits by a third. Insurance premiums in the state have fallen 24 percent in the last 2 years.

Finally, workers' compensation insurers are forming alliances with managed care providers in order to take advantage of case-management methods and volume discounting. At Coca-Cola Bottling Co. of New York, the company paid an average of $3,164 in workers' compensation claims, when it turned to managed care and addressed longstanding safety issues in its plants. Six years later its average claim was $1,257—a 60 percent reduction.[24]

Is there an underlying theme in these approaches? Yes, and it's simple: Aggressive management of workplace safety issues pays dividends for workers and for their employers as well.

At present, all 50 states have workers' compensation laws. While specific terms and levels of coverage vary by state, all state laws share the following features[25]:

- All job-related injuries and illnesses are covered.
- Coverage is provided regardless of who caused the injury or illness (i.e., regardless of who was "at fault").
- Payments are usually made through an insurance program financed by employer-paid premiums.
- A worker's loss is usually not covered fully by the insurance program. Most cash payments are at least two-thirds of the worker's weekly wage, but, together with disability benefits from Social Security, the payments may not exceed 80 percent of the worker's weekly wage.
- Workers' compensation programs protect employees, dependents, and survivors against income loss resulting from total disability, partial disability, or death; medical expenses; and rehabilitation expenses.

Disability Insurance

Disability insurance coverage provides a supplemental, one-time payment when death is accidental, and it provides a range of benefits when employees are disabled—that is, when they can't perform the "main functions" of their occupations.[26] **Long-term disability** (LTD) plans cover employees who are disabled 6 months or longer, usually at no more than 60 percent of their base pay, until they begin receiving pension benefits.

Disability leaves for those in their 20s to 50s rose throughout the 1980s and 1990s, coinciding with significant rises in the incidence of obesity, diabetes, and asthma. These illnesses can cause disability among those most severely afflicted. Disability leaves cost companies between 8 and 20 percent of payroll annually.[27] The company example below shows what progressive firms are doing to control these costs.

HOW CANADIAN IMPERIAL BANK OF COMMERCE (CIBC) CONTROLS DISABILITY COSTS[28]

COMPANY EXAMPLE

To control disability-leave costs, CIBC turned to **disability management** programs that emphasize a partnership between the physician, the employee, the manager, and the HR representative, known as a "facilitator." The physician's role is to specify what the employee can and cannot do. Ongoing discussions between the employee and manager, assisted by the facilitator, determine what tasks an employee is actually capable of doing—the opposite of traditional disability management, which focuses on what the employee cannot do. This approach balances flexibility in meeting individual needs with consistency and fairness.

Does disability management work? At CIBC, the average duration for short-term disability dropped by 32 percent in the first 9 months of the program. In addition, the firm's long-term disability insurance carrier reported that employees on LTD were back to work 38 percent faster than the average for LTD claimants in general.

Although disability benefits traditionally were divided into salary continuation, short-term disability, and long-term disability, combined "disability-management" programs now merge all three. Doing so allows for a single claim-application process and uniform case management. An employee whose short-term illness turns into a lengthy disability doesn't have to reapply for benefits or start over with a new case manager; the process is uniform and seamless, regardless of the length of the disability.

Another developing trend is toward integrating disability coverage with workers' compensation, and, eventually, with group health care. Under this scenario, patients would be treated under the same health care delivery system, regardless of whether they became ill or were injured at work or on their own time. This concept—called **managed health** or "total health and productivity management," is still in its infancy but holds great potential.[29]

Hospitalization, Surgical, and Maternity Coverage

These are essential benefits for most working Americans. Self-insurance is out of the question since the costs incurred by one serious, prolonged illness could easily wipe out a lifetime of savings and assets and place a family in debt for years to come. The U.S. health insurance system is based primarily on group coverage provided by employers. At a general level, the system is characterized by statistics such as the following[30]:

- Most Americans have health insurance and receive excellent care. Except for the poor, especially in inner cities, Americans are healthier than ever.

- Those over age 65 are covered by Medicare, but fewer than half of those living below the poverty line are covered by Medicaid. About 45 million Americans have no health insurance.[31]
- Contrary to popular belief, most of the uninsured are jobholders—part-timers and per-day workers—the working poor. Nearly one-third of workers in companies with 25 or fewer employees are uninsured.
- Insurance rates have climbed faster for small businesses than for large ones.
- Whether employed or not, younger people, as well as African-American and Hispanic people, are most likely to lack health insurance. Americans with chronic diseases or a history of serious illness have trouble obtaining affordable insurance.
- Figures on the number of uninsured people understate the extent of vulnerability. Over a recent 28-month period, one in four Americans spent at least a month without health insurance.
- Polls indicate that most Americans are pleased with their doctors and hospitals. Yet there is widespread anxiety about the reliability of the system. Medical costs rose an average of 10.5 percent from 1999 to 2000, and 12 percent in 2001. This far exceeded the levels of overall inflation in those years.[32] Figure 12–1 shows the annual increase in health care costs from 1988 through 2001. Recent increases have hit small businesses hardest, as Figure 12–2 on page 475 illustrates.

Since employers pay most of the nation's health care premiums, over time such increases may make them less competitive in global markets. Rising premiums cut into profits by increasing operating costs. To put this into perspective, let us return to an example we cited earlier, namely, that General Motors spends $1,200 per car to provide health benefits to its active and retired workers in the United States. Overall, General Motors spent nearly $4 billion on health care costs in 2000, of which prescription drug costs alone totaled $1 billion.[33] Chrysler spends $700 a car, and Ford $510. Both have fewer retirees than GM does. However, those outlays compare with as little as $100 per car for the U.S. factories of foreign automakers, which have younger, healthier workers and hardly any retirees.[34] Competitiveness issues arising from health-care costs are particularly acute at companies with the following three characteristics:

Figure 12–1

Annual increase in health care costs for public and private employers, 1988–2001.
Source: What comes after managed care? *BusinessWeek,* Oct. 23, 2000, p. 152.

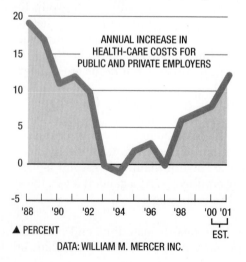

ANNUAL INCREASE IN HEALTH-CARE COSTS FOR PUBLIC AND PRIVATE EMPLOYERS

▲ PERCENT

DATA: WILLIAM M. MERCER INC.

1. Their workforces are composed largely of people in their 40s and 50s, who require more health care than younger workers do.
2. Their health plans cover a much larger number of retired workers than do those of newer companies, like computer or airline concerns.
3. They make products that must compete on world markets.[35]

Why is this happening? What's driving these increases in the cost of health care? In addition to population changes, general inflation, and excess medical inflation (including administrative costs that add millions to the country's health-care spending[36]), other factors are costly new drugs and rising prescription volumes, plus the cost of new technology.

It is true that drugs are the fastest-growing part of health-care spending, but it is not true that costs are soaring. Increased usage of drugs, not price hikes, cause much of that increase. In 1999, for example, U.S. prescription-drug spending rose 19 percent, but just 4 percent of that was traceable to price increases. Compared to other things we spend money on, the costs of prescriptions are not so bad. American consumers spend, on average, 64 cents a day on prescriptions, as compared to 91 cents on alcohol, 92 cents on electricity, and $1.05 on car repairs.[37]

When it comes to health-care technology, the United States relies far more heavily on it than do other advanced nations. On a per capita basis, for example, the United States has four times as many diagnostic imaging machines (magnetic resonance imaging) as Germany and eight times as many as Canada. U.S. doctors perform open-heart surgery 2.6 times as often as Canadian doctors and 4.4 times as often as German doctors. When it comes to the use of "smart" machines to perform medical tests, one expert noted: "There's no way to shut it off. The doctors crave it, it's reassuring, and patients crave it."[38] On top of that, hospitals often push to buy the latest machines in order to retain their competitive status as full-service, modern health care centers.

Cost-Containment Strategies

Strategies to contain the high costs of health care are taking center stage in the boardroom as well as in the health care industry itself. Here are some measures that firms have taken to gain tighter management control over the cost of health care:

1. **Band together with other companies to form a "purchasing coalition" to negotiate better rates with insurers.** Coalitions have become key cost-control devices for small businesses, and about 75 such coalitions exist today, according to the National Business Coalition on Health.[39]
2. **Deal with hospitals and insurers as with any other suppliers.** Begin by providing benefits information online. Companies are using the Net and their intranet sites to give employees access to medical treatment information as well as sophisticated comparisons of benefit-plan options. Pacific Business Group on Health (a consortium of large San Francisco companies like ChevronTexaco, Bechtel, and Safeway) ranks providers by quality as well as cost on its Web site. Ford Motor Company started distributing a ranking of hospitals on quality and costs to Detroit-area employees in hopes of steering them to the most responsive providers.[40] Soon employees may have enough information to comparison shop for

health care, much the same way they now buy a car. It's a win-win situation for employees and their companies. Employees gain control, and companies slash their administrative costs.[41]

3. **Induce employees to choose reduced medical coverage voluntarily through flexible benefit plans** (more on this shortly).

4. **Negotiate directly with doctors.** In Minneapolis, 26 of the area's biggest employers, including 3M, Honeywell, Dayton Hudson, and Pillsbury formed a consortium to bypass insurers and contract directly with providers. Doctors are free to charge, organize, and operate as they choose. Greedy or cavalier doctors will suffer though, because the employers make sure the patients know which ones are overpriced or deliver poor service. This concept is known as **direct contracting.** It is free-market economics, and it has been missing for a long time in the health-care industry.[42]

5. **Require preadmission certification,** that is, doctor's clearance for the treatment desired for the employee before he or she enters the hospital. If the medical staff gives additional treatment or tests, refuse to pay bills unless doctors can confirm that a deviation from the original plan was necessary. For example, Merrill Lynch pays doctors to review other doctors' medical-procedure recommendations.[43]

These strategies have been termed **managed care,** and large insurers such as Aetna, Cigna, and Prudential offer managed care. Fully 85 percent of Americans with health insurance belong to some kind of managed care plan.[44] Managed care relies on a "gatekeeper" system of cost controls. The **gatekeeper** is a primary-care physician who monitors the medical history and care of each employee and his or her family. The doctor orders testing, makes referrals to specialists, and recommends hospitalization, surgery, or outpatient care, as appropriate. To make this approach pay off, insurers like Cigna must deliver high-quality medical care and still keep a tight lid on medical expenses. Managed care may take a variety of forms. In our next section we discuss one of the most popular, the health maintenance organization (HMO).

HMOs

An **HMO** is an organized system of health care that assures the delivery of services to employees who enroll voluntarily under a prepayment plan. The emphasis is on preventive medicine, that is, maintaining the health of each employee. Legally, HMOs are authorized under the HMO Act of 1973.

The objective of HMOs is to control health-care costs by keeping people out of the hospital. It was quite successful in the early 1990s in doing so. In fact, as Figure 12–1 shows, health-care costs actually lagged overall inflation in 1994, but the gains have not lasted. Here are five reasons why[45]:

1. Much of the progress came from eliminating unnecessary procedures and hospitalizations—a one-time savings.
2. At the same time, an explosion of new medical technologies and drug treatments has jacked up prices again.
3. The population has also aged, further spiking expenses.
4. Hospitals and doctors have refused to accept reduced reimbursement rates.
5. Employees have rebelled against managed-care limits on doctors and procedures.

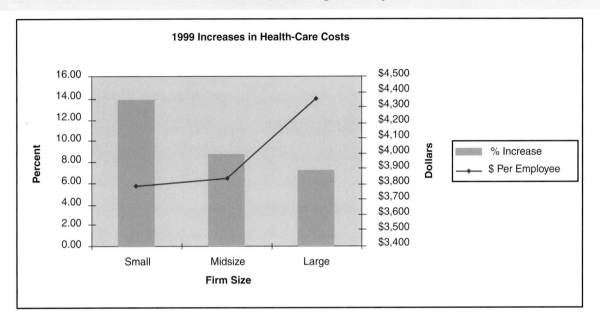

Figure 12–2

Recent increases in health care costs have hit small companies hardest.
Source: Adapted from J. H. Prager. Smaller firms see biggest jump in health-care costs,
The Wall Street Journal, Aug. 29, 2000, p. B2.

These factors have led to a growing realization that the managed-care revolution seems to have run its course.

To overcome some employees' complaints about the lack of freedom to choose their doctors in an HMO, some firms offer a **point-of-service plan** (POS plan). Such a plan offers patients a choice every time they seek medical care. They can use the plan's network of doctors and hospitals and pay no deductibles, with only a $10 copayment for office visits, as with a traditional HMO; or they can see a physician outside the network and pay 30–40 percent of the total cost, just as in traditional health coverage.[46] Table 12–2 presents a summary of alternative types of managed-care plans, HMOs, preferred-provider organizations, and POS plans.

Recent evidence indicates that employees who are provided a choice are continuing to move away from the more stringent HMO and POS plans, toward preferred-provider organizations (PPOs), even though PPOs are more expensive on a monthly basis. Apparently employees are willing to pay more for freedom of choice.[47]

In the extreme, a few companies are giving workers the money they would have contributed to their health-insurance premiums, and letting them make their own decisions about coverage. Forces driving the trend include the backlash against managed care, the popularity of company-sponsored savings plans that let employees decide how to invest their money, and the rise of websites that help consumers make decisions. While the practice is controversial, experts see only a gradual transition to greater consumer control—perhaps over the next decade—as policy makers, the market, and employees themselves get used to the idea.[48]

Table 12–2

THE ABCs OF MANAGED CARE

Plan	How it works	What you pay	Benefits
Health maintenance organization (HMO)	A specified group of doctors and hospitals provide the care. A gatekeeper must approve all services before they are performed.	There is no deductible. The nominal fees generally range from nothing to $15 a visit depending on the service performed.	Virtually all services are covered, including preventive care. Out-of-pocket costs tend to be lower than for any other managed-care plan.
Preferred-provider organization (PPO)	In-network care comes from a specified group of physicians and hospitals. Patients can pay extra to get care from outside the network. There generally is no gatekeeper.	The typical yearly family deductible is $400. The plan pays 80% to 100% for what is done within the network, but only 50% to 70% for services rendered outside it.	Preventive services may be covered. There are lower deductibles and copayments for in-network care than for out-of-network care.
Point-of-service (POS) plan	POSs combine the features of HMOs and PPOs. Patients can get care in or out of the network, but there is an in-network gatekeeper who must approve all services.	In addition to a deductible, there is a flat $5 to $15 fee for in-network care, and patients pay 20% to 50% of the bills for care they get outside the network.	Preventive services are generally covered. And there are low out-of-pocket costs for the care patients get in the network.

Other Medical Coverage

Medical coverage in areas such as drug abuse, alcoholism, and mental illness is decreasing. Big insurers often limit coverage for most psychiatric benefits to just two years for all ailments for the lifetime of an insured individual. The benefits can be used all at once or broken up over a period of time.[49] As for dental care, dental HMOs, PPOs, and indemnity (traditional fee-for-service plans) are growing fast. As with medical HMOs, a dental plan is usually paid a set annual fee per employee (usually about 10–15 percent of the amounts paid for medical benefits). Dental coverage is a standard inclusion for 96 percent of U.S. employers. Fully 71 percent offer their employees some form of vision-care insurance as well.[50]

Sick-Leave Programs

These programs provide short-term insurance to workers against loss of wages due to short-term illness. In 2001, 76 percent of U.S. firms offered paid sick leave benefits.[51] However, in many firms such well-intentioned programs have often *added* to labor costs because of abuse by employees and because of the widespread perception that sick leave is a right and that if it is not used, it will be lost ("use it or lose it"). From the employer's perspective, such unscheduled absences cost between 8 and 20 percent of payroll annually. As we noted earlier, some firms are turning to "managed-disability" programs to control these costs.[52] Others, like Garden Valley Telephone Co. of Minnesota, have taken a different tack. This company reduced discretionary sick-leave time from 12 days to 5. Unused benefits at year-end are paid to employees at their current wage rates. Extended sick-leave benefits (8–12 weeks, based on years of service) are available after a 5-day waiting period. Over a 10-year period, paid absences decreased by 22,000 hours.[53]

Pensions

A **pension** is a sum of money paid at regular intervals to an employee (or to his or her dependents) who has retired from a company and is eligible to receive such benefits. Before World War II, private pensions were rare. However, two developments in the late 1940s stimulated their growth: (1) clarification of the tax treatment of employer contributions and (2) the 1948 Inland Steel case, in which the National Labor Relations Board ruled that pensions were subject to compulsory collective bargaining.[54]

For a time there were no standards and little regulation, which led to abuses in funding many pension plans and to the denial of pension benefits to employees who had worked many years. Perhaps the most notorious example of this occurred in 1963, when Studebaker closed its South Bend, Indiana, car factory and stopped payments to the seriously underfunded plan that covered the workers. Only those already retired or on the verge of retirement received the pension benefits they expected. Others got only a fraction—or nothing.[55]

Incidents like these led to the passage of the Employee Retirement Income Security Act (ERISA; see Table 12–1) in 1974. Despite increased regulation, ERISA has generally been beneficial. In 1960, only 9 percent of retirees received a private pension. In 1993, about 30 percent did, and by 2004, 88 percent will.[56]

Money set aside by employers to cover pension obligations has become the nation's largest source of capital.[57] Pension funds hold 26 percent of the company equity and 15 percent of the taxable bonds in the U.S. economy, for a total of $2.5 trillion.[58] That's roughly $8,000 for every man, woman, and child in the United States! This is an enormous force in the nation's (and the world's) capital markets.

Pension-fund managers tend to invest for the long term, and the big corporate pension funds (95 percent of pension fund assets are covered by 5 percent of the plans) have less than 1 percent of their assets invested in leveraged buyouts or high-risk, high-yield junk bonds.[59]

In general, the financial health of most private pension plans is good.[60] However, to assure that covered workers will receive their accrued benefits even if their companies fail, ERISA created the Pension Benefit Guaranty Corporation (PBGC). This agency acts as an insurance company, collecting annual premiums from companies with defined-benefit plans that spell out specific payments upon retirement. A company can still walk away from its obligation to pay pension benefits to employees entitled to receive them, but it must then hand over up to 30 percent of its net worth to the PBGC for distribution to the affected employees.

The PBGC insures the pensions of 43 million U.S. workers.[61] Typically it takes over about 100 underfunded plans a year, and it currently oversees almost 38,000 pension plans.[62] If a company terminates its pension plan, the PBGC guarantees the payment of vested benefits to employees up to a maximum amount set by law. In 2001 that maximum amount was $40,704.[63]

Despite these protections, the consequences of pension-plan termination can still be devastating to some pensioners. Executives whose accrued benefits are bigger than the PBGC's guaranteed limits can see their monthly checks shrivel. Employees who haven't worked at a company long enough (typically 5 years[64]) to be *vested,* that is, whose receipt of pension benefits does not depend on future service, aren't entitled to any benefits—so they wind up having to get by with less to support them than they had planned. Nevertheless, as a matter of social policy, it is important that, as retirees, most workers end up getting nearly all that is promised to them—and they do.

How Pension Plans Work.   Contributions to pension funds are typically managed by trustees or outside financial institutions, frequently insurance companies. As an incentive for employers to begin and maintain such plans, the government defers taxes on the pension contributions and their earnings. Retirees pay taxes on the money as they receive it.

Traditionally, most big corporate plans have been **defined-benefit plans,** under which an employer promises to pay a retiree a stated pension, often expressed as a percentage of preretirement pay. In 2001, 46 percent of companies offered them.[65] The most common formula is 1.5 percent of average salary over the last 5 years prior to retirement ("final average pay") times the number of years employed. In determining final average pay, the company may use base pay alone or base pay plus bonuses and other compensation. An example of a monthly pension for a worker earning final average pay of $50,000 a year, as a function of years of service, is shown in Figure 12–3. When combined with Social Security benefits, that percentage is often about 50 percent of final average pay.[66] The company then pays into the fund each year whatever is needed to cover expected benefit payments.

A second type of pension plan, popular either as a support to an existing defined-benefit plan or as a stand-alone retirement-savings vehicle, is called a **defined-contribution plan.** Fully 70 percent of U.S. employers offered some form of such a plan in 2001.[67] Examples include stock bonuses, savings plans, profit sharing, and various kinds of employee stock-ownership plans. Brief descriptions of five types of such plans are shown in Table 12–3.

Figure 12–3

Monthly pension for a worker whose final average pay is $50,000 per year.

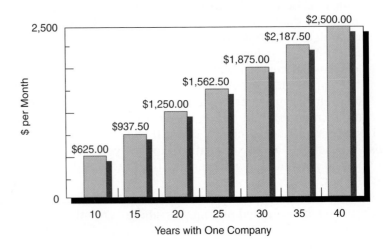

Defined-contribution plans fix a rate for employer contributions to the fund. Future benefits depend on how fast the fund grows. Such plans therefore favor young employees who are just beginning their careers (because they contribute for many years). Defined-benefit plans favor older, long-service workers.

Defined-contribution plans have great appeal for employers because a company will never owe more than what was contributed. However, since the amount of benefits received depends on the investment performance of the monies contributed, employees cannot be sure of the size of their retirement checks. In fact, regardless of whether a plan is a defined-benefit or a defined-contribution plan, employees will not know what the purchasing power of their pension checks will be, because the inflation rate is variable.

A third type of pension plan is known as a **cash-balance plan,** offered by 36 percent of large employers.[68] Under it, everyone gets the same, steady annual credit toward an eventual pension, adding to his or her pension account "cash balance." Employers contribute a percentage of an employee's pay, typically 4 percent. The balance earns an interest credit, usually around 5 percent. It is portable when the employee leaves, but cash-balance plans do not vest any sooner than traditional pension plans (5 years). So if a 4-year employee leaves, he or she gets nothing.[69]

Table 12–3

FIVE TYPES OF DEFINED-CONTRIBUTION PENSION PLANS

- **Profit-sharing plan.** The company puts a designated amount of its profits into each employee's account and then invests the money. ESOPs are a form of profit sharing.

- **ESOP.** An employee stock-ownership plan pays off in company stock. Each employee gets shares of company stock that are deposited into a retirement account. Dividends from the stock are then added to the account.

- **401(k) plan.** A program in which an employee can deduct up to $10,500 of his or her income (in 2001, rising to $15,000 in 2006) from taxes and place the money into a personal retirement account. Many employers add matching funds, and the combined sums grow tax-free until they are withdrawn, usually at retirement.

- **Money-purchase plan.** The employer contributes a set percentage of each employee's salary, up to 25 percent of net income, or $40,000 (whichever is less), to each employee's account. Employees must be vested to be eligible to receive funds. Withdrawals after age $59\frac{1}{2}$ are taxed at ordinary income tax rates.

- **Simplified employee pension (SEP).** Under SEP, a small-business employer can contribute up to the lesser of 100 percent of an employee's salary or $40,000. The employee is vested immediately for the amount paid into the account. The employee cannot withdraw any funds before age $59\frac{1}{2}$ without penalty.

Source: Contribution limits in the various plans are based on: What the tax cut means to you, *Money,* Aug. 2001, pp. 90–96.

For the young, 4 percent of pay each year is more than what they were accruing under a defined benefit plan. But for those nearing retirement the amount is far less. So an older employee who is switched into a cash-balance system can find his or her eventual pension reduced by 20 to 50 percent, and in rare cases, even more. Employers are aware of this effect on older workers, so they often offer features to soften the blow. They may agree to contribute somewhat more than the standard 4 percent for older employees, or else provide a **grandfather clause** to allow older employees to remain in the old plan.[70]

At a broader level, empirical research shows that employees differ in their preferences for various features of defined benefit, defined contribution, and cash-balance plans. Allowing employees choices to choose plans that are consistent with their personal characteristics and needs should lead to greater satisfaction with the plans, and also serve as an effective tool in attracting and retaining employees.[71]

Just as the practice of awarding large bonuses to some executives as their companies were laying off workers aroused a deep sense of injustice among members of the public, similar sentiments now apply to the pension plans of many large employers. Why? Because they have been cutting back on pension payouts in many subtle ways, while at the same time boosting payouts for senior executives.[72] Consider just one example. Leo Mullin, chief executive officer of Delta Air Lines, was awarded 22 years of service in 1998, when he had been at the company only 10 months.[73] As an employee of the company, would this help close the trust gap?

COMPANY EXAMPLE   **RETIREMENT BENEFITS AND SMALL BUSINESS[74]**

Only 46 percent of full-time employees of small businesses have a retirement plan, compared with 79 percent of those who work for large companies. The most common reason small employers cite is cost. Fortunately, there are alternatives that need not cost owners a bundle. One of these is a simplified version of the well-known 401(k) plan. For an annual administrative fee of $700 plus $10 per participant in excess of 10, the 401(k) Association of Langhorne, Pennsylvania, will administer a simple starter plan for businesses with fewer than 25 employees. Participants receive performance statements quarterly, and they direct how their contributions are invested. Although employees may invest in only three mutual funds from within a mutual fund family, and there are no provisions for loans or hardship withdrawals, these features keep administrative costs down. As the business grows larger, or as employees amass larger sums of money in their savings plans, the firm may gravitate to a full-featured 401(k).

Pension Reforms That Benefit Women.   These reforms were incorporated into the Retirement Equity Act of 1984. Corporate pension plans must now include younger workers and permit longer breaks in service. Women typically start work at a younger age than do men, and they are more likely to stop working for several years in order to have and care for children. However, since the new rules apply to both sexes, men also will accrue larger benefits. There are five major changes under the act[75]:

1. As of January 1, 1985, pension plans must include all employees 21 or older (down from 25). This provision extended pension coverage to an additional 600,000 women and 500,000 men.
2. Employers must use 18 rather than 22 as the starting age for counting years of service. For example, consider an employee who works at a firm that requires five years of service to be fully "vested." If the employee is hired at age 19, he or she can join a plan at 21 and can be fully vested by age 24.
3. Employees may have breaks in service of as long as 5 years before losing credit for prior years of work. In addition, a year of maternity or paternity leave cannot be considered a break in service.
4. Pension benefits may now be considered a joint asset in divorce settlements. State courts can award part of an individual's pension to the ex-spouse.
5. Employers must provide survivor benefits to spouses of fully vested employees who die before reaching the minimum retirement age.

Social Security

Table 12–1 outlined provisions for this program. Social Security is an income-maintenance program, not a pension program. It is the nation's best defense against poverty for the elderly, and it has worked well. Without it, according to one study, the poverty rate among the elderly would have jumped from about 15 to 50 percent.[76] Table 12–4 shows maximum and average Social Security benefits for 2001.

Table 12–4

SOCIAL SECURITY BENEFITS—MONTHLY

Maximum monthly benefit for a person retiring in 2002 at age 65	$1,660
Average benefit for:	
All retired workers	$874
Retired couples	$1,454
Young widows with two eligible children	$1,764
Disabled worker, spouse, and one or more children	$1,360

Current Social Security beneficiaries are benefiting from the massive surplus accumulated throughout the 1990s as baby boomers hit their peak earning potential. In 2000, that surplus was $167 billion.[77] However, keep in mind that Social Security is a pay-as-you-go system. Payroll taxes earned by current workers are distributed to pay benefits for those who are already retired. Right now there are more than 3 workers for every retiree in our society, but by 2015 there will only be 2.7, and by 2030 there will only be about 2 workers per retiree.[78] In addition, people are living substantially longer—by 2020 the life expectancy for 65-year-old men and women will be 81.5 and 85 years, respectively.

While the system will be solvent through the year 2030, at that time, given the large number of retirements by baby boomers, Social Security taxes will cover only 75 percent of promised benefits.[79] To meet such long-term funding

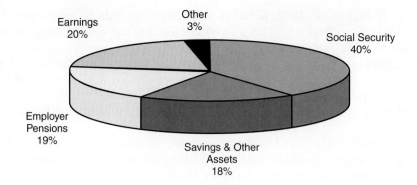

Figure 12–4

Where retirees get their income. (*Source:* Apfel, K. S., Commissioner of Social Security. 1998, July 22. New Directions in Retirement Income: Social Security, Pensions, and Personal Savings. Testimony before the U.S. Senate Committee on Finance.)

needs, the system will have to be reformed soon—by raising payroll taxes or retirement ages, cutting benefits, or by investing a portion of the current surplus in the stock market.[80]

This last alternative raises several vexing policy arguments[81]:

- Should workers' retirement be built on government guarantees or the economy's health?
- Should the government own one-sixth of the stock market?
- Should Washington expose workers' retirement funds to market fluctuations?

Keep in mind, however, that Social Security was never intended to cover 100 percent of retirement expenses. For a worker earning $60,000 a year, for example, experts estimate that he or she will need about 75 percent of that in retirement. Social Security will replace about 40 percent of preretirement income; pensions and personal savings will have to make up the rest. How does this compare to the actual distribution of retirees' income?

Figure 12–4 shows the distribution of retirees' income, on average. Almost 60 percent comes from Social Security plus pensions; the rest comes primarily from personal savings and current earnings in retirement. By contrast, the percentage of final salary that Social Security replaces depends on the actual final salary of the retiree. For a worker whose final salary is $50,000, Social Security replaces 45 percent in the United States, 75 percent in Italy, 74 percent in Portugal, 63 percent in Spain, 51 percent in France, 43 percent in Germany, 31 percent in the Netherlands, 21 percent in Ireland, and just 14 percent in the United Kingdom.[82]

Unemployment Insurance

Although 97 percent of the workforce is covered by federal and state unemployment-insurance laws, each worker must meet eligibility requirements in order to receive benefits. That is, an unemployed worker (1) must be able and available to work and be actively seeking work; (2) must not have refused suitable employment; (3) must not be unemployed because of a labor dispute (except in Rhode Island and New York); (4) must not have left a job voluntarily; (5) must not have been terminated for gross misconduct; and (6) must have been employed previously in a covered industry or occupation, earning a designated minimum amount for a specific minimum amount of time. Many claims are disallowed for failure to satisfy one or more of these requirements.

INTERNATIONAL APPLICATION
Social Security in Other Countries

Many countries outside the United States have adopted pension programs that combine Social Security with private retirement accounts. In Britain, for example, workers can opt out of part of the state pension system by applying up to 44 percent of their Social Security tax to their own private individual investment accounts. Japan, Finland, Sweden, France, and Switzerland have similar programs. In these countries, the Social Security component of the pension system remains on a pay-as-you-go basis in which current tax receipts are used to pay for both current benefits and other government programs.

In contrast, Chile's retirement system is 100 percent privatized, with a mandatory 10 percent of employees' pay going into individual accounts. Australia is moving to a privatization plan that calls for 9 percent of workers' pay to go into private retirement accounts, up from 6 percent previously. The employer chooses a menu of investment options that employees can use to allocate their retirement savings.

Singapore uses a payroll tax to fund retirement, but it works like a private pension system. The revenues are invested in individually owned accounts; unlike U.S. Social Security taxes, they are tax deductible and not subject to income taxes.

Employees can withdraw money from their retirement funds to purchase housing, and, as a result, 80 percent of Singapore's citizens own their own residences. If an employee is dissatisfied with the return earned by the public fund, he or she can transfer the account to investments in the Singapore stock market or other approved vehicles. The asset balance in a Singaporean's retirement fund passes to his or her beneficiaries upon death. Among the countries that have systems similar to Singapore's are India, Kenya, Malaysia, Zambia, and Indonesia.[83]

As of 2000, states have the option to use state unemployment compensation resources to make partial wage replacement available to parents who leave employment after the birth or adoption of a child. This rule, published by the Department of Labor, creates a new exemption to the requirement that recipients of unemployment funds be able and available to work.[84]

Every unemployed worker's benefits are "charged" against one or more companies. The more money paid out on behalf of a firm, the higher is the unemployment insurance rate for that firm.

The tax in most states amounts to 6.2 percent of the first $7,000 earned by each worker. The state receives 5.4 percent of this 6.2 percent, and the remainder goes to the federal government. However, the tax rate may fall to 0 percent in some states for employers who have had no recent claims by former employees, and it may rise to 10 percent for organizations with large numbers of layoffs. Benefit levels have generally not kept up with inflation. They average about 36 percent of what workers were earning at their last jobs.[85] Recognizing this problem, some states have begun to increase the levels of benefits that they pay.

Supplemental Unemployment Insurance
This type of insurance is common in the auto, steel, rubber, flat glass, and farm equipment industries. Employers contribute to a special fund for this purpose.

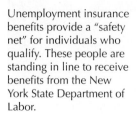

Unemployment insurance benefits provide a "safety net" for individuals who qualify. These people are standing in line to receive benefits from the New York State Department of Labor.

Initially, the primary purpose of such plans was to replace employees' pay during seasonal layoffs, but the provisions also apply in the case of permanent layoffs. Such plans, when combined with unemployment compensation, usually replace nearly all after-tax base wages for 6 months, with extensions under certain conditions. Only 8 percent of employees are covered by supplemental unemployment insurance plans, but many others are protected by some form of severance pay. Both types of arrangements are covered by ERISA, and this point has been affirmed by the Supreme Court.[86]

Severance Pay

Such pay is not legally required, and, because of unemployment compensation, many firms do not offer it. This is especially true of dot.com companies that went bankrupt in 2000 and 2001.[87] However, severance pay has been used extensively by some firms that are downsizing in order to provide a smooth outflow of employees.[88] This is a good example of the strategic use of compensation. Thus Philadelphia Electric Co. gave an extra 9 months' severance pay to 1859 older workers who agreed to stagger their early retirements over a 2-year period. Roughly 17 percent of the workforce took advantage of the offer.[89] Said an executive of the firm: "If we lost all of them at once, we couldn't keep our electricity going."

Length of service, organization level, and the cause of the termination are key factors that affect the size of severance agreements. Most lower-level employees receive 1 week of pay for each year they work for a company, with a minimum of 1 to 2 months. Middle managers can expect 1–2 weeks of pay for each year of service, with a minimum of 3–4 months, while executives normally receive 1–4 weeks of severance pay per year of service, with a minimum of 6 months to one year.[90] Chief executive officers with management contracts may receive 2–3 years of salary in the event of a takeover.[91] Besides wages, today's severance packages may also include outplacement counseling, extended health coverage, loans of computers or other equipment, free retraining courses, and sometimes a bargain deal on a company car.[92]

Payments for Time Not Worked

Included in this category are such benefits as the following:

Vacations	Personal excused absences
Holidays	Grievances and negotiations
Reporting time	Sabbatical leaves

Suppose you could take as much vacation time as you like? Sound crazy? Think about your own experience. On your last vacation did you do no work at all? Or did you listen to your voice mail, check your email, and spend further time responding to messages and maybe participating in one or two phone meetings? The reality in the Infotech Age is that, for huge numbers of workers, the concept of a vacation—as an entitlement or an imposed restriction—is not realistic.[93] Suppose instead that you had no allotted vacation time? When you go on vacation is up to you, something to be worked out with your goals and your coworkers in mind? Microsoft recently decided that high-level executives would get to take vacation as needed, with no time limit imposed. Do you think people would abuse this freedom? Or would they recognize that they are responsible for most decisions that affect their job performance, and that decisions about vacation time fall into that general category? What do you think?

SABBATICAL LEAVES AT WELLS FARGO

COMPANY EXAMPLE

Wells Fargo Bank in San Francisco offers both 3- and 6-month paid leaves. A selection committee receives about 40 proposals per year, most of which it rejects. The committee uses two criteria in its decisions: (1) It must fit the sabbaticals into a budget; highly paid employees deplete the budget faster than lower-paid employees. (2) The committee looks for projects that really require a full-time commitment. Those that an employee could do while working full or part time are less likely to be chosen. Some employees work with persons with disabilities, others do alcohol and drug counseling, and still others do preretirement counseling. Employees want such a program, and society needs them.

Only about 5 percent of large employers in the United States currently offer sabbaticals.[95] While companies of all sizes offer unpaid leave with job security on an informal basis, sabbaticals are most popular at law firms, computer firms, and consulting companies, where burnout is often a problem.

Employee Services

A broad group of benefits falls into the employee services category. Employees qualify for them purely by virtue of their membership in the organization, and not because of merit. Some examples are:

Tuition aid.	Thrift and short-term savings plans.
Credit unions.	Stock-purchase plans.
Auto insurance.	Fitness and wellness programs.
Food service.	Moving and transfer allowances.
Company car.	Transportation and parking.

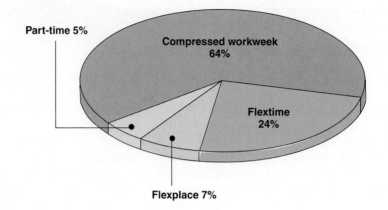

Figure 12–5

Distribution of requests for flexible work arrangements. (*Source:* S. Shellenbarger, The keys to successful flexibility, *The Wall Street Journal,* Jan. 13, 1994, p. B1.)

Part-time 5%

Compressed workweek 64%

Flextime 24%

Flexplace 7%

Career clothing.	Merchandise purchasing.
Legal services.	Christmas bonuses.
Counseling.	Service and seniority awards.
Child adoption.	Umbrella liability coverage.
Child care.	Social activities.
Elder care.	Referral awards.
Gift matching.	Purchase of used equipment.
Charter flights.	Family leaves.
Domestic partner benefits.	Flexible work arrangements.

National survey data now indicate that people are more attached and more committed to organizations that offer family-friendly policies, than to those that do not, regardless of the extent to which they benefit personally from the policies.[96] Benefits that define family-friendly firms include on-site child care, subsidized child care on-site and off-site, child adoption, elder care, flexible work schedules, and the ability to convert sick days into personal days off that employees can use to care for a sick child or family member. For example, Figure 12–5 shows the distribution of requests for flexible work arrangements.

Once viewed as an expense with little return, such policies are now endorsed by a growing number of executives as an investment that pays dividends in morale, productivity, and ability to attract and retain top-notch talent. DuPont is typical. It estimated that it received a 637 percent return on its family-friendly spending. The payback came from improved performance, employee retention, reduced stress, and reduced absenteeism.[97] Said an executive at DuPont: "If we don't have programs that will encourage our people to stay, then somebody else is going to invent the next breakthrough product."[98]

Domestic partner benefits are voluntarily offered by employers to an employee's unmarried partner, whether of the same or opposite sex. Firms such as General Motors, Ford, Daimler Chrysler, Boeing, Citigroup, General Mills, Goldman Sachs, and Texas Instruments offer such benefits, as do about 16 percent of U.S. firms.[99] They do so to be fair to all employees, regardless of their sexual orientation and marital status, and because of the competition and diversity that characterize today's labor markets.

Ethical Dilemma
To Accept or Not to Accept Gifts?

Nearly 9 out of every 10 companies surveyed by the Bureau of National Affairs limit employees' abilities to accept gifts from clients and outside business contacts. They do so to avoid even the appearance of a conflict of interest. At PriceWaterhouse Coopers, such gifts may not exceed $50 in value, while policies at Aetna, 3M, and Motorola do not set specific limits, thus leaving the appropriateness to the judgment of the recipient.

However, even as companies broadcast their policies to the rank and file, some top executives may be participating in golf tournaments, sitting in stadium skyboxes, and riding chartered jets courtesy of clients and suppliers. Said one observer: "People have come to look on these things as perquisites—untaxed compensation that you get when you're in the right job."[100] Is this a double standard? Is it a conflict of interest? If your answer to these questions is "yes," develop a policy that takes into account the interest of all parties and that, in your view, is ethical and just.

BENEFITS ADMINISTRATION

Benefits and Equal Employment Opportunity

Equal employment opportunity requirements also affect the administration of benefits. Consider as examples health care coverage and pensions. The Age Discrimination in Employment Act has eliminated mandatory retirement at any age. It also requires employers to provide for employees over the age of 70 the same group health insurance coverage that they offer to younger employees. Medicare payments are limited to what Medicare would have paid for in the absence of a group health plan and to the actual charge for the services. This is another example of government **cost shifting** to the private sector.

As we noted in Chapter 3, the Older Workers Benefit Protection Act of 1990 restored age-discrimination protection to employee benefits. Early retirement offers are now legal if they are offered at least 45 days prior to the decision, and, if they are accepted, employees are given 7 days to revoke them. Employers were also granted some flexibility in plant closings to offset retiree health benefits or pension sweeteners against severance pay. That is, an employer is entitled to deny severance pay if an employee is eligible for retiree health benefits.

With regard to pensions, the IRS considers a plan *discriminatory* unless the employer's contribution for the benefit of lower-paid employees covered by the plan is comparable to contributions for the benefit of higher-paid employees. An example of this is the 401(k) salary-reduction plan described briefly in Table 12–3. The plan permits significant savings out of pretax compensation, produces higher take-home pay, and results in lower Social Security taxes. The catch: *The plan has to be available to everyone in any company that implements it.* Maximum employee contributions each year ($10,500 in 2001, rising

Table 12–5

EMPLOYEE BENEFITS: THE FORGOTTEN EXTRAS

Listed below are the benefits for the average full-time employee of Sun, Inc. (annual salary $42,000*).

Benefit	Who pays	Sun's annual cost	Percentage of base earnings	What the employee receives
Health, dental, and life insurance	Sun and employee	$ 3,364.20	8.01	Comprehensive health and dental plus life insurance equivalent to the employee's salary
Holidays	Sun	2,100.00	5.00	13 paid holidays
Annual leave (vacation)	Sun	1,617.00	3.85	10 days of vacation per year (additional days starting with sixth year of service)
Sick days	Sun	1,936.20	4.61	12 days annually
Company retirement	Sun	3,360.00	8.00	Vested after 5 years of service
Social Security	Sun and employee	3,213.00	7.65	Retirement and disability benefits as provided by law
Workers' compensation and unemployment insurance	Sun	420	1.00	Compensation if injured on duty and if eligible; income while seeking employment
Total		$16,010.40 or $7.70 per hour	38.12	

*The dollar amount and percentages will differ slightly depending upon the employee's salary. If an employee's annual salary is less than $42,000, the percentage of base pay will be greater. If the employee's salary is greater than $42,000, the percentage will be less but the dollar amount will be greater. Benefit costs to Sun, Inc., on behalf of 5480 employees are almost $88,000,000 per year.

to $15,000 in 2006) are based on average company participation. Thus poor participation by lower-paid employees curbs the ability of the higher paid to make full use of the 401(k).[101]

Costing Benefits

Despite the high cost of benefits, many employees take them for granted. A major reason for this is that employers have failed to do in-depth cost analyses of their benefit programs and thus have not communicated the value of their benefits programs to employees. Four approaches are used widely to express the costs of employee benefits and services. Although each has value individually, a combination of all four often enhances their impact on employees. The four methods are[102]:

- **Annual cost of benefits for all employees.** Valuable for developing budgets and for describing the total cost of the benefits program.
- **Cost per employee per year.** The total annual cost of each benefits program divided by the number of employees participating in it.
- **Percentage of payroll.** The total annual cost divided by total annual payroll (this figure is valuable in comparing benefits costs across organizations).

- **Cents per hour.** The total annual cost of benefits divided by the total number of hours worked by all employees during the year.

Table 12–5 presents a company example of actual benefits costs for a fictitious firm named Sun, Inc. The table includes all four methods of costing benefits. Can you find an example of each?

Cafeteria, or Flexible, Benefits

The theory underlying **cafeteria benefits** is simple: Instead of all workers at a company getting the same benefits, each worker can pick and choose among alternative options, "cafeteria style." Thus the elderly bachelor might pass up maternity coverage for additional pension contributions. The mother whose children are covered under her husband's health insurance may choose legal and auto insurance instead.

The typical plan works like this: Workers are offered a package of benefits that includes "basic" and "optional" items. Basics might include modest medical coverage, life insurance equal to a year's salary, vacation time based on length of service, and some retirement pay. But then employees can use "flexible credits" to choose among such additional benefits as full medical coverage, dental and eye care, more vacation time, additional disability income, and higher company payments to the retirement fund. Nationwide, about 50 percent of large firms have flexible-benefit plans.[103] They were devised largely in response to the rise in the number of two-income families. When working spouses both have conventional plans, their basic benefits, such as health and life insurance, tend to overlap. Couples rarely can use both plans fully. But if at least one spouse is covered by a "flex" plan, the couple can add benefits, such as child care, prepaid legal fees, and dental coverage, that it might otherwise have to buy on its own. Two studies have now examined employees' satisfaction with their benefits and understanding of them both before and after the introduction of a flexible benefits plan. Both found substantial improvements in satisfaction and understanding after the plan was implemented.[104]

There are advantages for employers as well. Under conventional plans, employers risked alienating employees if they cut benefits, regardless of increases in the costs of coverage. Flexible plans allow them to pass some of the increases on to workers more easily. Instead of providing employees a set package of benefits, the employer says, "Based on your $40,000 annual salary, I promise you $12,000 to spend any way you want." If health care costs soar, the employee—not the employer—decides whether to pay more or to take less coverage.

There's help for employees even under these circumstances if they work for firms that sponsor **flexible spending accounts** (about 70 percent of all large firms). Employees can save for expenses such as additional health insurance or day care with pretax dollars, up to a specified amount (e.g., in a dependent-care spending account, up to $5,000 for child or elder care). As a result, it's a win-win situation for both employer and employee.[105]

To realize these potential advantages, major communications efforts are needed to help employees understand their benefits fully. Since employees have more choices, they often experience anxiety about making the "right" choices. In addition, they need benefits information on a continuing basis to ensure that their choices continue to support their changing needs. Careful

IMPACT OF BENEFITS ON PRODUCTIVITY, QUALITY OF WORK LIFE, AND THE BOTTOM LINE

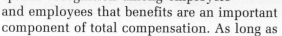

Generally speaking, employee benefits do not enhance productivity. Their major impact is on attraction and retention (although there is little research on this issue) and on improving the quality of life for employees and their dependents. Today there is widespread recognition among employers and employees that benefits are an important component of total compensation. As long as employees perceive that their total compensation is equitable and that their benefits options are priced fairly, benefits programs can achieve the strategic objectives set for them. The challenge for executives will be to maintain control over the costs of benefits while providing genuine value to employees in the benefits offered. If they can do this, everybody wins.

attention to communication can enhance recruitment efforts, help cut turnover, and make employees more aware of their total package of benefits.

Communicating the Benefits

Try to make a list of good reasons why any company should not make a deliberate effort to market its benefits package effectively. It will be a short list. Generally speaking, there are four broad objectives in communicating benefits:

1. To make employees *aware* of them. This can be done by reminding them of their coverages periodically and of how to apply for benefits when needed.
2. To help employees *understand* the benefits information they receive in order to take full advantage of the plans.
3. To make employees confident that they can *trust* the information they receive.
4. To convince present and future employees of the *worth* or value of the benefits package. After all, it's their "hidden paycheck."[106]

Major employers such as Allied Signal and AT&T successfully incorporate strategic graphic design when presenting benefits and compensation information to their employees.[107] They provide their employees "the benefits information you need, when you need it." Company-based Intranets, with ready access by all employees to personalized benefits information, make "HR on the desktop" a reality for these and other firms, at a cost that is as much as 99 percent cheaper than conventional means of presentation.[108]

As an example, IBM employees use an interactive question-and-answer tool called Plan Finder on the company's Intranet to weigh the merits of different benefits and criteria, such as cost, coverage, customer service, or performance. The tool sorts through dozens of different health plans offered by the company, uses data and choices supplied by the employee, and then returns views of preferred plans, ranked and graphed. Plan Finder allows employees to model the information that is most important to them in order to make better benefits selections. It's no surprise then, that 80 percent of employees now enroll via the Intranet system, saving IBM $1 million per year in costs associated with the delivery of benefits information. The *Electronic Signatures in Global and National Commerce Act,* enacted in 2000, generally gives electronic signatures the same legal standing as ink-on-paper signatures—a fact that probably will enable companies to place more transactions online.[109]

THE NEW WORLD OF EMPLOYEE BENEFITS

Human Resource Management in Action: Conclusion

In this new world of sharing costs and sharing risks, there are four major areas that change has affected most profoundly: health insurance, programs to promote healthy lifestyles, retirement programs, and employee savings programs.

Health Insurance. No more blank checks. Both employers and insurers are taking an aggressive role in shifting from reimbursement plans (in which employees or medical providers receive direct payments for medical expenses) to a managed-care approach (e.g., health-maintenance organizations). Fully 85 percent of all workers were in managed-care programs in 2000, up sharply from 49 percent four years earlier.[110] At the same time, firms as varied as IBM, Harley Davidson, Charles Schwab, Walt Disney, and Microsoft have extended medical benefits to same-sex couples. In an effort to recruit and retain the best talent in their industries, they offer the same compensation and benefits to people doing the same work.[111]

Keeping Employees Healthier. One of the most important themes in employee benefits is now prevention: limiting health-care claims by keeping employees and their families healthier. The Travelers Insurance Companies thoroughly studied its own programs in this area and found that the funds it spent on health promotion helped it save $7.8 million in employee benefits costs. That's a savings of $3.40 for every dollar spent. The biggest payoffs came from education programs, including efforts to discourage smoking and drinking and to encourage healthier diets.

Some companies have added new benefits, even as they eliminated others. Johnson & Johnson and Hewlett-Packard began paying for routine checkups and tests for infants, while AT&T launched a prenatal care program.

Retirement Programs—Sharing the Risk. More employers are now shifting to defined-contribution pension plans, in which the employee shares the investment risk. In return, however, employees have a larger voice in choosing how the funds will be invested. They also have greater "portability"—due largely to the meteoric growth of 401(k) plans.[112] Nine out of 10 companies that offer 401(k) plans provide a partial matching (up to $5,000 a year or more) of employees' savings, and nearly 80 percent of those eligible participate in them. Such plans provide a true incentive to save because they are easily funded through payroll deductions. Meanwhile, as we have seen, companies like IBM, BankAmerica, and Enron are developing "cash-balance" plans that combine elements of defined-benefit and defined-contribution plans. The most progressive companies allow workers to choose the type of plan that best fits their individual circumstances.[113]

Expanding the 401(k) Concept. To many observers, the kind of sharing and choice embodied in 401(k) plans is the wave of the future in employee benefits. Companies want plans that give employees choices to suit their needs, incentives to conserve funds, and risks to share with the company. For example, it is possible that the 401(k) concept of individual and corporate partnership will be expanded to assist in saving for long-term medical care.

Of one thing we can be sure, however. During the next decade the number of choices available to employees seems likely to expand and become more complicated. Advice on how to make informed choices will itself become an increasingly popular employee benefit.

SUMMARY

Managers need to think carefully about what they wish to accomplish by means of their benefits programs. At a cost of about 40 percent of base pay for every employee on the payroll, benefits represent substantial annual expenditures. Factors such as the following are important strategic considerations in the design of benefits programs: the long-term plans of a business, its stage of development, its projected rate of growth or downsizing, characteristics of its workforce, legal requirements, the competitiveness of its overall benefits "package," and its total compensation strategy.

There are three major components of the benefits "package": security and health, payments for time not worked, and employee services. Despite the high cost of benefits, many employees take them for granted. A major reason for this is that employers have not done in-depth cost analyses or communicated the value of their benefits programs. This is a multimillion-dollar oversight. Certainly the counseling that must accompany the implementation of a flexible-benefits program, coupled with the use of computer-based expert systems and decision-support systems, can do much to alleviate this problem.

IMPLICATIONS FOR MANAGEMENT PRACTICE

As you think about the design and implementation of employee benefits plans, consider three practical issues:

?

1. What are you trying to accomplish by means of the benefits package? Ensure that the benefits offered are consistent with the strategic objectives of the unit or organization as a whole.

2. Take the time to learn about alternative benefits arrangements. Doing so can save large amounts of money.

3. Develop an effective strategy for communicating benefits regularly to all employees.

DISCUSSION QUESTIONS

12–1. What should a company do over the short and long term to maximize the use and value of its benefits choices to employees?

12–2. Should employees have more or less control over how their company-sponsored retirement funds are invested?

12–3. In terms of the "attract-retain-motivate" philosophy, how do benefits affect employee behavior?

12–4. What can firms do to control health care costs?

12–5. Your company has just developed a new, company-sponsored savings plan for employees. Develop a strategy to publicize the program and to encourage employees to participate in it.

KEY TERMS

doctrine of constructive receipt

antidiscrimination rule

contributory plans

noncontributory plans

yearly renewable term insurance

flexible benefits

workers' compensation programs

long-term disability

disability management

managed health

direct contracting

managed care

gatekeeper

HMO

point-of-service plan

pension

defined-benefit plan

defined-contribution plan

cash-balance plan

grandfather clause

cost shifting

cafeteria benefits

flexible spending accounts

APPLYING YOUR KNOWLEDGE

Reducing Health Care Costs   *Case 12–1*

In the Spring of 2000, Ron McGee, vice president of group insurance and labor relations at Polson Corporation, delivered the bad news to top management. Medical insurance premiums for the following fiscal year were expected to increase approximately 40 percent, up dramatically from the 8 percent increase of the previous year. Future cost projections were equally grim. It was estimated that by 2004, the company's $355 million annual health care bill would increase to a staggering $613 million.

Polson is a large high-technology automotive and electronics products company that employs about 70,000 people in the United States. It decided not to tinker with traditional remedies to escalating health-care costs, such as increasing deductibles and shifting larger copayments to employees. Instead, it turned to managed health care. It did so by contracting with Whitefish Corporation, a large employee-benefits company specializing in such managed health-care plans.

A task force was formed in 2000 under the direction of Ron McGee. The task force included HR executives from the corporate office of Polson in Morristown, New Jersey.

This group was given the challenge of developing a custom-designed program that would hold down health-care premium costs to a reasonable level. The group decided that the new program would be built on the following foundation:

1. The insurance carrier, Whitefish Corporation, would be a partner in the program and would carry a financial risk, not merely be an administrator that paid the bills as they came in.
2. The insurance carrier would use its buying power to establish a network of highly qualified primary-care physicians and specialists throughout the United States, coinciding with the company's primary locations.
3. The insurance carrier would guarantee a high level of quality care to be provided to Polson's employees.
4. Unlike other health-maintenance organization plans, under the new Polson Plan employees would be able to switch from managed care to a traditional indemnity plan at will, but would pay extra for exercising this option.

"We sought to change the way health care was delivered to our employees," says Al Gesler, corporate director of HR for Polson. "The net result was a hybrid program, taking into account the best features of HMOs and indemnity plans and combining that with a partnership arrangement between Whitefish, Polson, and its employees." Whitefish was chosen because it was a large and experienced insurance carrier and had a health-care network in place across the United States that pretty well coincided with major locations where Polson had operations.

In March 2001, Polson signed a 3-year agreement with Whitefish for a managed-care program that was called "The Health Care Connection." This plan covered medical, dental, vision, and hearing care, as well as prescription medications. It also included a well-care program covering such items as an annual physical exam and pre-natal care. An important feature of the plan was that Whitefish guaranteed annual premium increases of less than 10 percent during each of the 3 contract years on the managed-care side of the program. No similar guarantee was provided on the indemnity side. The actual figure would depend on the number of employees using the indemnity portion of the program.

"We wanted a very strong gatekeeper system," says McGee. "For our employees to take advantage of the extremely comprehensive benefits found on the in-network side of The Health Care Connection program, as well as the modest $15 copayment feature, they had to agree to choose a primary-care physician from within the closed panel and visit specialists in hospitals only when referred by their primary-care physicians. That was the trade-off." For employees who stayed in the network, the costs were modest: a $15 copayment per office visit and $10 per prescription. Employees who chose to go outside the network could switch to the indemnity side of the plan at any time for any particular illness or injury, with no restrictions. Those who did this, however, paid an annual deductible equal to 1 percent of their annual salaries and then were subject to an 80/20 copayment split (in other words, employees paid 20 percent of the medical care costs after the deductible was met).

"The basic concept behind managed care is just that, managing it," says McGee. "By staying in the network, everyone saves money. We felt this was a major effort aimed at limiting unnecessary care."

For its part, Whitefish is responsible for guaranteeing the quality of the managed-care side of the network. It is responsible for using its buying power to ensure that hospitals in the plan attract an adequate supply of high-quality physicians. It also means continual monitoring of employee usage of different types of medical care through "utilization studies."

Questions

1. How should Polson communicate its new health benefits plan to employees?
2. What results in terms of cost reduction do you anticipate Polson will achieve through the implementation of its new health-care program?
3. What additional follow-up should the benefits administration people at Polson take now that the program has been in effect for several years?
4. To what extent do you believe managed health-care plans such as those at Polson are the wave of the future for health-benefits plans in major American corporations?

REFERENCES

1. Bennet, J. (1993, Sept. 5). Auto talks hang on health costs, but workers are loath to chip in. *The New York Times*, pp. 1, 8–10.
2. Leonard, B. (1995, Mar.). Perks give way to life-cycle benefits plans. *HRMagazine*, pp. 45–48.
3. Benefits costs (1996, Apr.). *MSEC Bulletin*. Denver: Mountain States Employers Council, Inc.
4. Blumenstein, R. (1996, Dec. 9). Seeking a cure: Auto makers attack high health-care bills with a new approach. *The Wall Street Journal*, pp. A1, A4.
5. Trouble ahead in the battle to contain labor costs (1997, Feb. 10). *BusinessWeek*, p. 29.
6. McCaffery, R. M. (1989). Employee benefits and services. In L. R. Gomez-Mejia (ed.), *Compensation and benefits*. Washington, DC: Bureau of National Affairs, pp. 3-101–3-135.
7. Smart, T. (1993, May 10). IBM has a new product: Employee benefits. *Business-Week*, p. 58.
8. Rubis, L. (1995, Jan.). Benefits boost appeal of temporary work. *HRMagazine*, pp. 54–58.
9. Ledvinka, J., & Scarpello, V. G. (1991). *Federal regulation of personnel and human resource management* (2d ed.). Boston: PWS-Kent.
10. Ibid.
11. McCaffery, op. cit.
12. Shellenbarger, S. (1993, Dec. 17). Firms try to match people with benefits. *The Wall Street Journal*, p. B1.
13. Society for Human Resource Management (2001). *2001 benefits survey*. Alexandria, VA: Author.
14. Peers, A. (1987, June 29). Firms now must offer health insurance to some ex-workers —but at what price? *The Wall Street Journal*, p. 29.
15. Williams, P. II. (1996, Oct.). Law enhances portability of health benefits. *HRNews*, pp. 4, 5. See also Jeffrey, N. A. (1996, Aug. 30). Healthy switch: New law eases job-hops, sometimes. *The Wall Street Journal*, p. C1.
16. Do I have enough life insurance? (2001, Sept.). *Money*, pp. 92, 94.
17. McCaffery, R. M. (1992). *Employee benefit programs: A total compensation perspective* (2d ed.). Boston: PWS-Kent.
18. Leonard, op. cit.
19. Say, does workers' comp cover wretched excess? (1991, July 22). *BusinessWeek*, p. 23.
20. Atkinson, W. (2000, July). Is workers' comp changing? *HRMagazine*, pp. 50–61.
21. Marsh, B. (1991, Dec. 31). Rising worker compensation costs worry small firms. *The Wall Street Journal*, p. B2.

22. National Academy of Social Insurance. *www.nasi.org*. Retrieved Aug. 9, 2001.

23. Kerr, P. (1991, Dec. 29). Vast amount of fraud discovered in workers' compensation system. *The New York Times*, pp. 1, 14.

24. First aid for workers' comp (1996, Mar. 18). *BusinessWeek*, p. 106. See also Crackdown on job-injury costs: New workers' compensation rules have double edge. (1995, Mar. 16). *The New York Times*, pp. D1, D7. See also Evangelista-Uhl, G. A. (1995, June). Avoid the workers' comp crunch. *HRMagazine*, pp. 95–99. See also Fefer, M. D. (1994, Oct. 3). Taking control of your workers' comp costs. *Fortune*, pp. 131–136.

25. McCaffery (1992), op. cit.

26. Gutner, T. (2001, June 4). What if suddenly you can't work? *BusinessWeek*, p. 106. See also There when you need it: Disability coverage (1996, Oct.). *USAA Magazine*, p. 5.

27. The young and the disabled (2001, June 4). *BusinessWeek*, p. 30. See also King, D. (1996, Oct.). A comprehensive approach to disability management. *HRMagazine*, pp. 97–102.

28. Lawrence, L. (2000, Dec.). Disability management partnerships save time, money. *HR News*, pp. 11, 17.

29. Ibid.

30. Prager, J. H. (2000, Aug. 29). Smaller firms see biggest jump in health-care costs. *The Wall Street Journal*, p. B2. See also Health plans feel the boom. (2000, Oct. 2). *BusinessWeek*, p. 40. See also Kuttner, R. (1995, Aug. 7). The lethal side effects of managed care. *BusinessWeek*, p. 166. See also Lewin, T. (1991, Apr. 28). High medical costs affect broad areas of daily life. *The New York Times*, pp. 1, 28–32.

31. Freudenheim, M. (2000, Sept. 6). Health premiums soaring. *The Denver Post*, pp. 1A, 19A.

32. What comes after managed care? (2000, Oct. 23). *BusinessWeek*, pp. 149, 152. See also Barrette, D. L. (2000, Nov.). Survey finds employers offering additional health care choices. *HR News*, pp. 10, 22.

33. What comes after managed care? op. cit.

34. Blumenstein, op. cit.

35. Gentry, C. (2000, May 23). Doctor yes: How is Merrill Lynch limiting health costs? By expanding benefits. *The Wall Street Journal*, pp. A1, A6. See also Uchitelle, L. (1991, May 1). Insurance as a job benefit shows signs of overwork. *The New York Times*, pp. A1, D23.

36. What comes after managed care? op. cit. See also Stodghill, R. (1997, Jan. 13). Minnesota's HMO-ectomy. *BusinessWeek*, p. 115.

37. O'Reilly, B. (2001, July 23). There's still gold in them thar pills. *Fortune*, pp. 58–70.

38. A crisis of medical success (1993, Mar. 15). *BusinessWeek*, pp. 78–80. See also Pollack, A. (1991, Apr. 29). Medical technology "arms race" adds billions to the nation's bills. *The New York Times*, pp. A1, B8–B10.

39. What comes after managed care? op. cit.

40. Blumenstein, op. cit.

41. What comes after managed care? op. cit.

42. "Reilly, B. (1998, Feb. 16). Taking on the HMOs. *Fortune*, pp. 96–104.

43. Gentry, op. cit.

44. Winslow, R. (1998, Jan. 20). Health-care inflation kept in check last year. *The Wall Street Journal*, p. B1.

45. What comes after managed care? op. cit.

46. Jeffrey, N. A. (1996, Dec. 2). Bills and costs lurk within HMO options. *The Wall Street Journal*, pp. C1; C19.

47. Barrette, op. cit.

48. Winslow, R., & Gentry, C. (2000, Feb. 8). Medical vouchers. Health benefits trend: Give workers money, let them buy a plan. *The Wall Street Journal*, pp. A1, A12.

49. Stressed out over stress benefits? (1997, Feb. 10). *BusinessWeek,* p. 132.
50. Society for Human Resource Management, op. cit. See also Barrette, op. cit.
51. Society for Human Resource Management, op. cit.
52. King, op. cit.
53. Howe, R. C. (1995, Mar.). Rx for an ailing sick-leave plan. *HRMagazine,* pp. 67–69.
54. Widder, P. (1982, May 31). Individuals gain more control over their pensions. *The Denver Post,* pp. 1C, 8C.
55. Colvin, G. (1982, Oct. 4). How sick companies are endangering the pension system. *Fortune,* pp. 72–78.
56. Topolnicki, D. M. (1993, Nov.). Beat the five threats to your retirement. *Money,* pp. 66–73. See also Widder, op. cit.
57. White, J. A. (1990, Mar. 20). Pension funds try to retire idea that they are villians. *The Wall Street Journal,* pp. C1, C8.
58. The smart 401(k) (1995, July 3). *BusinessWeek,* pp. 58–62. See also Salwen, K. G., & Scism, L. (1993, Dec. 14). Corporate pensions face proxy rules. *The Wall Street Journal,* pp. C1, C6.
59. Raabe, S. (2000, Aug. 13). Aggressive tactics boost pension plan. *The Denver Post,* pp. 1M, 11M. See also White, op. cit.
60. Work week (1997, Jan. 14). *The Wall Street Journal,* p. A1.
61. *www.pbgc.org.* Accessed Aug. 9, 2001.
62. O'Connell, V. (1996, Aug. 8). Smith Corona acts to end pension plans; move would reduce benefits to many. *The Wall Street Journal,* pp. A2, A4.
63. *www.pbgc.org,* op. cit.
64. Schultz, E. E. (1999, Dec. 16). Young and vestless. *The Wall Street Journal,* pp. A1, A8.
65. Society for Human Resource Management, op. cit.
66. Schultz, E. E. (2001, June 20a). Big send-off: As firms pare pensions for most, they boost those for executives. *The Wall Street Journal,* pp. A1, A8.
67. Society for Human Resource Management, op. cit.
68. America's best company benefits (2000, Sept.). *Money,* pp. 103–108.
69. Schultz (1999, Dec. 16), op. cit.
70. Schultz (2001, June 20a). op. cit. See also Schultz, E. E., & Rundle, R. L. (1999, Sept. 23). Utility's pension plan allowing choice offers contrast to the bitterness at IBM. *The Wall Street Journal,* pp. C1, C21. See also Schultz, E. E. & Mcdonald, E. (1998, Dec. 4). Retirement wrinkle: Employers win big with a pension shift; employees often lose. *The Wall Street Journal,* pp. A1, A6.
71. Dulebohn, J. H., Murray, B., & Sun, M. (2000). Selection among employer-sponsored pension plans: The role of individual differences. *Personnel Psychology, 53,* 405–432.
72. Schultz, E. E. (2001, June 20b). Companies reduce 401(k) contributions. *The Wall Street Journal,* pp. C1, C19. See also Schultz (2001, June 20a)., op. cit. See also Schultz, E. E. (2000, July 27). Pension cuts 101: Companies find host of subtle ways to pare pension payouts. *The Wall Street Journal,* pp. A1, A6.
73. Schultz (2001, June 20a), op. cit.
74. De Lisser, E. (2000, May 30). Many small firms are unaware of pension-plan options. *The Wall Street Journal,* p. B2. See also Smaller firms lack 401(k)s (1998, Feb. 23). *USA Today,* p. 1B. See also Zall, M. (1995, July). Retirement benefits small employers can afford. *HRMagazine,* pp. 53–56.
75. Pension reform has something for everyone (1984, Aug. 27). *U.S. News & World Report,* p. 67.
76. Social Security is more secure (2000, June 26). *BusinessWeek,* p. 34.
77. Milkovich, G. T., & Newman, J. M. (2001). *Compensation* (7th ed.). Burr Ridge, IL: McGraw-Hill/Irwin. See also Richards, P. (1997, Winter). Social Security: Will it be there? *Stages,* pp. 5–9.

78. Apfel, K. S. (1998, July 22). New directions in retirement income: Social Security, pensions, and personal savings. Testimony before the U.S. Senate Committee on Finance.

79. Social Security: Safer than you think (2000, July 3). *BusinessWeek*, p. 168. See also Coy, P. (1998, Nov. 30). Social Security: Let it be. *BusinessWeek*, pp. 34, 35.

80. Carter, M. N., & Shipman, W. G. (1996). *Saving Social Security's dream.* Washington, DC: Regnery Publishing.

81. Tyson, L. D. (2000, June 26). Social Security is working just fine, thank you. *BusinessWeek*, p. 32.

82. Winestock, G. (2000, Oct. 30). Social Security reform rocks the world. *The Wall Street Journal*, p. A21, A24.

83. Shoven, J. (1996, Aug.). Should Social Security be privatized? *USAA Financial Spectrum*, pp. 1–3. See also Roberts, P. C. (1990, Feb. 1). Let workers own their own retirement funds . . . that's how it's done in other countries. *The Wall Street Journal*, p. A21. See also Riley, B. (1996, Oct. 29). All work and no pension. *Financial Times*, p. 12.

84. Hewitt and Associates (2000, June 19). Unemployment insurance funds for parental leave. Washington Status Reports. *was.hewitt.com/hewitt/resource/wsr/index.htm.* Retrieved Aug. 9, 2001.

85. Social Security Bulletin. (2000). *Annual Statistical Supplement.* Washington, DC: Author.

86. McCaffery (1992), op. cit.

87. Dunham, K. J. (2000, Oct. 17). When dot-coms cut the cord: Laid-off Internet workers cite shabby treatment as they are shown door. *The Wall Street Journal*, pp. B1, B16.

88. Hirschman, C. (2001, Apr.). The kindest cut. *HRMagazine*, pp. 49–53. See also Capell, P. (1996, Feb. 26). Take the money and run. *The Wall Street Journal*, pp. R1, R11.

89. Lublin, J. S. (1991, Apr. 1). Bosses alter early-retirement windows to be less coercive—and less generous. *The Wall Street Journal*, pp. B1, B7.

90. Hirschman, op. cit.

91. Koudsi, S. (2000, May 29). Why CEOs are paid so much to beat it. *Fortune*, pp. 34, 35. See also Binkley, C., & Lublin, J. S. (1998, Feb. 12). ITT brass to get "golden bungee" in takeover. *The Wall Street Journal*, pp. B1, B6.

92. Ibid.

93. Colvin, G. (2000, May 15). Endless summer? *Fortune*, p. 88.

94. Sheley, E. (1996, Mar.). Why give employees sabbaticals? To reward, relax, and recharge. *HRMagazine*, pp. 58–70. See also Tannenbaum, J. A. (1981, May 6). Paid public-service leaves buoy workers, but return to old jobs can be wrenching. *The Wall Street Journal*, p. 29. See also Axel, H. (1992). *Company sabbatical policies.* NY: Conference Board.

95. Society for Human Resource Management, op. cit.

96. Shellenbarger, S. (2000, Oct. 18). Employees who care for elders find help in special collaboration. *The Wall Street Journal*, p. B1. See also Dunking, A. (2000, Feb. 21). Adopting? You deserve benefits too. *BusinessWeek*, p. 160. See also Woodward, N. H. (2000, Dec.). Benefiting from adoption. *HRMagazine*, pp. 119–126. See also Grover, S. L., & Crooker, K. J. (1995). Who appreciates family responsive human resource policies: The impact of family-friendly policies on the organizational attachment of parents and non-parents. *Personnel Psychology, 48,* 271–288.

97. Leib, J. (1997, Feb. 16). Family-friendly nets bottom-line gains. *The Denver Post*, pp. 1J, 19J.

98. Gardner, J., in Sheley, E. (1996, Feb.). Flexible work options: Beyond 9 to 5. *HRMagazine*, p. 53.

99. Society for Human Resource Management, op. cit. See also Gender-neutral benefits (2000, May 15). *BusinessWeek,* p. 14. See also Shirouzu, N. (2000, June 9). Gay couples to get benefits at auto makers. *The Wall Street Journal,* pp. A3, A6.

100. Jacobs, D. L. (1993, Dec. 5). The rules for giving, and for giving back. *The New York Times,* p. 25.

101. Reiner, E. L. (2001, Aug. 13). Playing the new tax laws. *Fortune,* p. 90. See also The smart 401(k), op. cit.

102. McCaffery (1992), op. cit.

103. Society for Human Resource Management, op. cit.

104. Sturman, M. C., Hannon, J. M., & Milkovich, G. T. (1996). Computerized decision aids for flexible-benefits decisions: The effects of an expert system and decision-support system on employee intentions and satisfaction with benefits. *Personnel Psychology, 49,* 883–908. See also Barber, A. E., Dunham, R. B., & Formisano, R. A. (1992). The impact of flexible benefits on employee satisfaction: A field study. *Personnel Psychology, 45,* 55–75.

105. Society for Human Resource Management, op. cit.

106. Geutal, H. G. (2001, Aug.). HR & the Internet age: The brave new world of eHR. Paper presented at the SHRM Foundation Thought Leaders Conference, Washington, DC. See also Markowich, M. M. (1992, Oct.). 25 ways to save a bundle. *HRMagazine,* pp. 48–57.

107. Smith, H. C. (2000, Jan.). Get your message across with graphics. *HRMagazine,* pp. 84–88.

108. Wells, S. J. (2001, Feb.) Communicating benefits information online. *HRMagazine,* pp. 69–76. See also Geutal, op. cit.

109. Wells, op. cit.

110. Winslow, op. cit.

111. Gender-neutral benefits, op. cit. See also Gay rights, corporate style (1996, Oct. 7). *BusinessWeek,* p. 170.

112. What the tax cut means to you (2001, Aug.). *Money,* pp. 90–96. See also How to take your 401(k) on the road (1995, June 5). *BusinessWeek,* p. 132.

113. Dulebohn et al., op. cit. See also McLean, B. (1996, Oct. 28). The latest twist: Cash-balance plans. *Fortune,* p. 234.

LABOR-MANAGEMENT ACCOMMODATION

Harmonious working relations between labor and management are critical to organizations. Traditionally the two parties have assumed a win-lose, adversarial posture toward each other. This must change if U.S. firms are to remain competitive in the international marketplace. Part 5 is entitled "Labor-Management Accommodation" to emphasize a general theme: To achieve long-term success, labor and management must learn to accommodate one another's needs, rather than repudiate them. By doing so, management and labor can achieve two goals at once: increasing productivity and improving the quality of work life. In the current climate of wants and needs, there is no alternative.

The focus of Chapter 13 is on union representation and collective bargaining. Chapter 14 focuses on procedural justice, ethics, and concerns for privacy in employee relations. These are currently some of the most dominant issues in this field. As managers, you must develop and implement sound practices with respect to them. Chapters 13 and 14 will help you do that.

13

UNION REPRESENTATION AND COLLECTIVE BARGAINING

Questions This Chapter Will Help Managers Answer

1. How have changes in product and service markets affected the way labor and management relate to each other?
2. How should management respond to a union organizing campaign?
3. To what extent should labor-management cooperative efforts be encouraged?
4. What kinds of dispute-resolution mechanisms should be established in order to guarantee due process for all employees?

IMPROVING PRODUCTIVITY, QWL, AND PROFITS THROUGH LABOR-MANAGEMENT COOPERATION*

Many managers see unions as a major stumbling block to the implementation of workplace changes that are essential to increased competitiveness. To these managers, unions are a problem. To other managers, unions can be and should be part of the solution to problems of workplace competitiveness. Many union leaders and members, in turn, deeply distrust management's motives. They see "enhanced competitiveness" as thinly veiled code words for downsizing. Who is right? Is it possible for a well-established union to take a leadership role in workplace innovation and imaginative approaches to enhancing competitiveness?

Is it possible for management to allow creative approaches to more efficient operations without cutting workers as a result of the increases in efficiency? Conversely, many union leaders fear cooperative work systems, because they suspect that management's real intention is to circumvent lawfully designated unions.

Despite such potential problems, some employee-involvement plans have worked brilliantly. For example, the United Auto Workers (UAW) played a key role in the improvement of productivity and quality at Ford Motor Company during the early 1980s. Ford has improved its assembly-line productivity by 36 percent since 1980, at least in part because of its employee-involvement system. J. D. Power & Associates named three Ford plants as having the highest quality in North America. Is this just an isolated example, or are there other success stories?

Challenges

1. What are some key obstacles that stand in the way of true cooperation by labor and management?
2. Is labor-management cooperation just a short-term solution to economic problems, or can it become institutionalized into the very culture of an organization?
3. Will widespread labor-management cooperation lead to a loss of union power?

WHY DO EMPLOYEES JOIN UNIONS?

Beliefs about the effects of a union at a person's own workplace are critical determinants of intentions to vote for or against union representation.[1] Visualize this scenario: It's 7:30 on a cool December evening in Las Vegas, and 105 off-duty hotel maids, cooks, and bellhops are waiting for their monthly union

*Sources: J. Ball, G. Burkins, & G. L. White. Don't walk: Why labor unions have grown reluctant to use the "S" word. *The Wall Street Journal,* Dec. 16, 1999, pp. A1, A8. If Ford can do it, why can't GM? *BusinessWeek,* June 29, 1998, pp. 36, 37; A. Bernstein, Why America needs unions—but not the kind it has now, *BusinessWeek,* May 23, 1994, pp. 70–82; A. Bernstein, Now labor can be part of the solution, *BusinessWeek,* Mar. 1, 1993, p. 35.

meeting to start. It has been a long day working in the big casino hotels, but still the room buzzes with energy. One by one, a dozen or so members recount their success in recruiting, 2,700 new colleagues at the MGM Grand, the world's largest hotel. After a 3-year campaign of street demonstrations, mass arrests, and attacks on the company's HR practices, which helped oust a stridently antilabor CEO, MGM Grand recognized the union a year later without an election. Another group reports on the victory at New York, New York, a new hotel that agreed to the unionization of 900 workers.

Much of the credit for these successes lies with the spirited rank and file. Indeed, the day after the meetings, some members gathered—on their day off— to sign up recruits outside the New York, New York hiring office. Says Edelisa Wolf, an $11.25-an-hour waitress at the MGM Grand: "I spend a day a week volunteering for the union, because otherwise we would earn $7.50 an hour and no benefits."[2]

On the other hand, it is pure folly to assume that pro-union attitudes are based simply on expected economic gains; much deeper values are at stake.[3] As one author noted:

> If one talks to any worker long enough, and candidly enough, one discovers that his loyalty to the union is not simply economic. One may even be able to show him that, on a strictly cost-benefit analysis, measuring income lost from strikes, and jobs lost as a result of contract terms, the cumulative economic benefits are delusions. It won't matter. In the end, he will tell you, the union is the only institution that ensures and protects his "dignity" as a worker, that prevents him from losing his personal identity, and from being transformed into an infinitesimal unit in one huge and abstract "factor of production."[4]

This conclusion that values deeper than money are at stake was illustrated in the 11-year battle to organize workers at the J. P. Stevens plant in North Carolina. The organizing drive was much publicized—the award-winning movie *Norma Rae* was based on it—and the settlement was heralded widely as an historic breakthrough in a decades-old attempt to organize southern industry. Even though the wages at the unionized Stevens plant are not substantially higher now than at the company's nonunionized plants or than at other nonunion textile plants in the South, the wage level was never the biggest issue. The union contract has meant expanded benefits, a seniority system to protect workers when jobs are lost and to provide opportunities when jobs open, and a grievance procedure with access to binding arbitration. For the company, the settlement allowed it to put its past squabbles with the workers behind and to concentrate on battling foreign textile imports. Among union members, however, worker after worker echoes the same sentiment: the collective bargaining agreement has meant that they are treated with new dignity on the job.[5]

Managers who fail to treat workers with respect, or companies that view workers only as costs to be cut rather than as assets to be developed, *invite* collective action by employees to remedy these conditions. However, unions are not without sin either, and workers will vote against them to the extent that the unions are seen as unsympathetic to a company's need to remain viable, or if they feel unions abuse their power by calling strikes, or have fat-cat leaders who selfishly promote their own interests at the expense of the members' interests.[6]

Figure 13–1

Percentage of non-farm employees represented by unions between 1930 and 2000.
Sources: Bureau of the Census, *Historical Statistics of the United States, Colonial Times to 1970;* Bureau of Labor Statistics, *Handbook of Labor Statistics* Bulletin 2070, Dec. 1980; and Bureau of Labor Statistics, *Employment and Earnings,* Jan., various years, 1983–2001. Prepared by the AFL-CIO. Available at AFL-CIO, *www.AFLCIO.org,* accessed Aug., 15, 2001. *Note:* Bureau of Labor Statistics information before 1981 was compiled on a different basis from the present series and it is not necessarily comparable; data for 1981 and 1982 were imputed.

UNION MEMBERSHIP IN THE UNITED STATES

Union membership has shrunk from a high of 35 percent of the workforce in 1945 to 22 percent in 1980 to 13.5 percent in 2000. Unions still represent 16.3 million workers, but that's just one in every seven employees. Excluding public-sector membership, unions represented just 9 percent of private-sector employees in 2000.[7] Figure 13–1 shows the percentage of nonfarm employees represented by unions between 1930 and 2000.

Several economic and demographic forces favor a resurgence of unions. The same trends toward globalization and corporate downsizing that have sharply cut union membership have also created a new receptiveness for union organizers among surviving employees, who find themselves overworked and under excessive stress. And it is not just blue-collar workers who are organizing. Unions are championing issues important to mobile dot.commers (think teleworking), they are organizing employees across companies by job type (Web designers of the world, unite!), and they are looking for dot.commers in their natural habitats (online chats and pink-slip parties).[8] Further, while labor productivity has increased 20 percent since 1978, wage growth has been stagnant over the same time period. For example, after adjustment for inflation, the median income of full-time workers declined by 8.6 percent. The typical salaried worker got a 4 percent raise in 2000, while hourly workers averaged 3 percent.[9] To add insult to injury, the gap between the pay of executives at large firms has grown from 42 times the average income of U.S. workers in 1980 to 85 times in 1990, to a staggering 531 times in 2000.[10]

Finally, both women and other minority-group members, who are expected to continue entering the workforce at a high rate, tend to favor unions. Evidence indicates that women's participation is likely to be enhanced to the extent that there is greater representation of women in local union offices.[11] However, organized labor's biggest untapped strength is its 16.3 million members. If 5 percent of them volunteer a day a month, according to one calculation, labor's effective spending on recruitment would jump to $4 billion a year (assuming professional organizers cost a total of $75,000 a year). That would dwarf the estimated $1 billion employers spend annually to thwart unionization.[12]

Despite these factors, a large-scale resurgence of unions seems unlikely. Organized labor complains that U.S. labor laws favor employers,[13] but what complicates organizing efforts is that many in this new generation are white-collar workers—in fields as diverse as insurance information technology, and electronics. Their goals and desires are different from those of labor's traditional blue-collar stalwarts, who seemed to want little more than high wages and steady work. And because so many young workers are highly mobile (average job tenure for workers of all ages was just 3.5 years in 2000[14]), they might not be willing to support a 6-month unionization drive that might culminate in a strike to win a first contract. Finally, many young workers are taking jobs in the rapidly growing service sector—banking, computer programming, financial services—jobs that unions traditionally have not penetrated.

The very nature of high-tech industry also hampers organizing efforts. Many software designers and biotechnical engineers work for small, start-up companies that unions find difficult and expensive to organize. Among larger firms, such as Compaq Computer, which has no production unions, workers are often parts of flexible teams that change tasks from month to month and work closely with management. Such teamwork creates a sense of empowerment that can leave unions with little role to play. As one observer noted: "The new industries in the U.S. are evolving so rapidly that there is no stable craft pattern for a union to represent."[15]

Despite the drop-off in membership, unions are powerful social, political, and organizational forces. In the unionized firm, managers must deal with the union rather than directly with employees on many issues. Indeed, the "rules of the game" regarding wages, hours, and conditions of employment are described in a collective bargaining agreement (or contract) between management and labor. Although it need not always be so, adversarial "us" and "them" feelings are frequently an unfortunate by-product of this process.

Economic and working conditions in unionized firms directly affect those in nonunionized firms, as managers strive to provide competitive working conditions for their employees. Yet the nature of the internal and external environments of most U.S. firms differs dramatically in the late 1990s relative to that of earlier periods. This difference has lead to fundamental changes in labor-management relations, as we will see in the next section.

THE CHANGING NATURE OF INDUSTRIAL RELATIONS IN THE UNITED STATES

Fundamentally, labor-management relations are about power—who has it and how they use it. As we will see, both parties are finding that they achieve the best results when they share power rather than revert to a win-lose orientation.[16] In recent years, unions have lost power as a result of six interrelated factors: global competition, nonunion domestic competition, deregulation, the growth of service industries, corporate downsizing (which has depleted the membership of many unions), and the willingness of firms to move operations overseas. In today's world, firms face more competitive pressures than ever before. That competition arises from abroad (e.g., Toyota, Nissan, Hyundai,

Sanyo, Pohang, and third-world steelmakers); from domestic, nonunion operators (e.g., Nucor in steel); and from nonregulated new entities (e.g., dozens of new telecommunications companies).

The deregulation of many product markets created two key challenges to existing union relationships. First, it made market entry much easier, for example, in over-the-road trucking, airlines, and telecommunications. Second, under regulation, management had little incentive to cut labor costs, because high labor costs could be passed on to consumers; conversely, labor-cost savings could not be used to gain a competitive advantage in the product market. Under deregulation, however, even major airlines (which are almost entirely organized) found that low costs translated into low fares and a competitive advantage. As a result, all carriers need to match the lowest costs of their competitors by matching their labor contracts.[17]

These competitive pressures have forced business to develop the ability to shift rapidly, to cut costs, to innovate, to enter new markets, and to devise a flexible labor-force strategy. As managers seek to make the most cost-effective use of their human resources, the old "rules of the labor-management game" are changing.[18]

Traditionally, the power of unions to set industrywide wage levels and to relate these in "patterns" was based on the market power of strong domestic producers or industries sheltered by regulation. As employers lost their market power in the 1970s and 1980s, union wage dominance shrank and fragmented. One union segment had to compete with another and with nonunion labor both in the United States and abroad. Management's objective was (and is) to get labor costs per unit of output to a point below that of the competition at the product-line level. Out of this approach have come wage-level differences and, with them, the breakdown of pattern bargaining. As a result, even under union bargaining pressures, wages are now far more responsive to economic conditions at the industry and firm levels, and even at the product-line level, than they traditionally have been.[19]

The labor relations system that evolved during the 1940s and lasted until the early 1980s was institutionalized around the market power of the firm and around those unions that had come to represent large proportions, if not nearly all, of an industry's domestic workforce. The driving force for change in the new millennium has been business conditions in the firm. Those conditions have changed for good—and so must the U.S. industrial relations system. In order to put that system into better perspective, let us consider some of its fundamental features.

FUNDAMENTAL FEATURES OF THE U.S. INDUSTRIAL RELATIONS SYSTEM

Six distinctive features of the U.S. system, as compared to the systems prevalent in other countries, are as follows:[20]

1. **Exclusive representation.** One and only one union in a given job territory, selected by majority vote, this union has **exclusive representation.** However, multiple unions may represent different groups of employees who work for the same employer (e.g., pilots, flight attendants, and machinists

at an airline). This situation is in contrast to that existing in continental Europe, where affiliations by religious and ideological attachment exist in the same job territory.

2. **Collective agreements that embody a sharp distinction between negotiation of and interpretation of an agreement.** Most agreements are of fixed duration, often 2 or 3 years, and they result from legitimate, overt conflict that is confined to a negotiations period. They incorporate no-strike (by employees) and no-lockout (by employer) provisions during the term of the agreement, as well as interpretation of the agreement by private arbitrators or umpires. In contrast, the British system features open-ended, nonenforceable agreements.

3. **Decentralized collective bargaining,** largely due to the size of the United States, the diversity of its economic activity, and the historic role of product markets in shaping the contours of collective bargaining. By contract, in Sweden the government establishes wage rates, and in Australia, some wages are set by arbitration councils, and others by bargaining at the enterprise level.[21]

4. **Relatively high union dues and large union staffs** to negotiate and administer private, decentralized agreements, including grievance arbitration, to organize against massive employer opposition and to lobby before legislative and administrative tribunals.

5. **Opposition by both large and small employers to union organization,** in contrast to countries such as France and Germany. Such opposition has been modified in terms of the constraints placed on management only slightly by more than 50 years of legislation.

6. **The role of government** in the U.S. industrial relations system, as compared with other systems, such as those of Mexico and Australia. The U.S. government has been relatively passive in dispute resolution and highly legalistic both in administrative procedures and in the courts.[22] As regulation has expanded to cover health and safety, pension benefits, and equal employment opportunity, the litigious quality of relations has grown in many relationships.

Before we examine the U.S. system in greater detail, let's briefly consider its historical origins.

A BRIEF HISTORY OF U.S. LABOR RELATIONS

The labor movement has had a long, colorful, and turbulent history in the United States. It began with the Industrial Revolution of the 19th century. Economically the Industrial Revolution was a great boon to productive output and to capital accumulation by business owners. Not so for the average worker. Wages were generally low, and working conditions were often hazardous. Labor was considered a commodity to be bought and sold, and the prevailing political philosophy of laissez faire (leave things alone) resulted in little action by governments to protect the lot of workers.[23]Against this backdrop, it was inevitable that workers would organize collectively to improve their wages and working conditions.

The first overt union activity in the United States took place in 1794 when the Philadelphia shoemakers attempted to raise their wages, in reaction to a wage

INTERNATIONAL APPLICATION
COMPARING INDUSTRIAL RELATIONS (IR) SYSTEMS
AROUND THE WORLD

Direct comparisons among IR systems are almost impossible. Here are three reasons why:[24]

1. **The same concept may be interpreted differently in different industrial relations contexts.** For example, consider the concept of collective bargaining. In the United States it is understood to mean negotiations between a labor union local and management. In Sweden and Germany, however, the term refers to negotiation between an employers' organization and a trade union at the industry level.[25]

2. **The objectives of the bargaining process may differ in different countries.** For example, European unions view collective bargaining as a form of class struggle, but in the United States collective bargaining is viewed mainly in economic terms.

3. **No industrial relations system can be understood without an appreciation of its historical origins.** Such historical differences may be due to managerial strategies for labor relations in large companies, ideological divisions within the trade union movement, the influence of religious organizations on the development of trade unions, methods of union regulation by governments, or the mode of technology and industrial organization at critical stages of union development.[26]

cut by their employers. The employers sued the union, arguing that the combination of workers to raise their wages constituted an illegal conspiracy in restraint of trade. In 1806 a federal court ruled in favor of the employers, and fined the employees involved. Until this **conspiracy doctrine** was overturned in 1842 in the case of *Commonwealth of Massachusetts v. Hunt,* workers were discouraged from forming unions. In that case, the court ruled that labor unions were not criminal per se, for they could have honorable as well as destructive objectives. In short, a union's conduct will determine whether it is legal or illegal.[27]

Emergence of the American Federation of Labor. The American Federation of Labor (AFL) was organized in 1886 as a group of national craft unions. Some of these unions were: the Metal Workers, Carpenters, Cigar Makers, Iron Molders, Miners, Granite Cutters, Bakers, Furniture Workers, Tailors, and Typographers. It espoused no particular political philosophy or set of broad social goals, for its objectives were more pragmatic. It sought immediate benefits for its members in the companies where they were employed. In the words of Samuel Gompers, the AFL's first president, the goals of the AFL were: "More, more, more; now, now, now."[28]

Emergence of the Congress of Industrial Organization. A combination of factors in the 1930s made industrial unionism attractive:

1. The Great Depression, which engendered such general gloom and pessimism in the entire economic system that it inevitably increased the propensity of workers to join unions.

2. Passage of federal labor laws that made it easier to organize workers.
3. The emergence of rebel leaders within the AFL who wanted to organize unskilled workers into industrial unions.

In 1935 the rebels formed their own Congress of Industrial Organizations (CIO), and intended to work within the AFL. However, the issue of craft versus industrial unionism, together with power rivalries within the AFL, led to an open break. The CIO's strategy was to organize *all* the workers in a given plant or company, rather than to focus on certain crafts. It was quite successful, principally through the use of the **sit-down strike,** in which workers refused to leave the premises until employers met their demands for recognition. Even before the formal break between the AFL and the CIO in 1937, membership in CIO unions had reached 3.7 million, exceeding AFL membership by 300,000 workers.[29]

Merger of the AFL and the CIO.　By the early 1950s, both the AFL and the CIO realized they were sacrificing power and efficiency by fighting on two fronts simultaneously: against employers and against each other. In 1955 they merged into the AFL-CIO under the leadership of George Meany, new president of the AFL, and Walter Reuther, former head of the United Auto Workers (UAW) and new president of the CIO. In 1967, however, Meany and Reuther became bitter enemies when Reuther withdrew his United Auto Workers from the federation in a policy dispute. Meany became the first president of the AFL-CIO.

Integrity was Meany's hallmark, and he vigorously fought union corruption, most notably by expelling Jimmy Hoffa's Teamsters union from the AFL-CIO in 1957. Throughout his career, Meany said that the wages and working conditions of the laborer, not economic philosophy, were his primary concerns; but he elevated the labor movement beyond wages and hours to unprecedented standing in Washington, particularly with Democratic presidents. In fact, Meany played the game of power politics so well that, by 1979, when he retired, organized labor, in the words of a noted labor lawyer, "became a middle class movement of people earning $25,000, $30,000 a year, supplemented by federal benefits."[30] Things certainly were different when Meany first appeared on the national scene in 1934. Then there was no Social Security to provide for aging workers, and no National Labor Relations Act; public employee unions were unheard of; and the first national minimum wage—25 cents per hour for a 48-hour workweek—was still four years away.

Now let's jump to the present. In the sections below, we describe the unionization process under current labor law.

THE UNIONIZATION PROCESS

The Legal Basis

The Wagner Act, or *National Labor Relations Act,* of 1935 affirmed the right of all employees to engage in union activities, to organize, and to bargain collectively without interference or coercion from management. It also created the National Labor Relations Board (NLRB) to supervise representation elections and to investigate charges of unfair labor practices by management. The *Taft-*

Hartley Act of 1947 reaffirmed those rights and, in addition, specified unfair labor practices for both management and unions. The unfair labor practices are shown in Table 13–1. The act was later amended (by the *Landrum-Griffin Act* of 1959) to add the secondary boycott as an unfair labor practice. A **secondary boycott** occurs when a union appeals to firms or other unions to stop doing business with an employer who sells or handles a struck product.

Table 13–1

UNFAIR LABOR PRACTICES FOR MANAGEMENT AND UNIONS UNDER THE TAFT-HARLEY ACT OF 1947

Management

1. Interference with, coercion of, or restraint of employees in their right to organize.
2. Domination of, interference with, or illegal assistance of a labor organization.
3. Discrimination in employment because of union activities.
4. Discrimination because the employee has filed charges or given testimony under the act.
5. Refusal to bargain in good faith.
6. "Hot cargo" agreements: refusals to handle another employer's products because of that employer's relationship with the union.

Union

1. Restraint or coercion of employees who do not want to participate in union activities.
2. Any attempt to influence an employer to discriminate against an employee.
3. Refusal to bargain in good faith.
4. Excessive, discriminatory membership fees.
5. Make-work or featherbedding provisions in labor contracts that require employers to pay for services that are not performed.
6. Use of pickets to force an organization to bargain with a union, when the organization already has a lawfully recognized union.
7. "Hot cargo" agreements: that is, refusals to handle, use, sell, transport, or otherwise deal in another employer's products.

A so-called **free-speech clause** in the act specifies that management has the right to express its opinion about unions or unionism to employees, provided that it does not threaten or promise favors to employees to obtain anti-union actions. The Taft-Hartley Act covers most private-sector employers and nonmanagerial employees, except railroad and airline employees (they are covered under the *Railway Labor Act* of 1926). Federal government employees are covered by the *Civil Service Reform Act* of 1978. That act affirmed their right to organize and to bargain collectively over working conditions, established unfair labor practices for both management and unions, established the Federal Labor Relations Authority to administer the act, authorized the

Ethical Dilemma
Are Unfair Practices Unethical?

Are the unfair labor practices shown in Table 13–1 also unethical? Are there circumstances under which activities might be legal (e.g., cutting off health care benefits for striking workers), but at the same time also be unethical?

Federal Services Impasse Panel to take whatever action is necessary to resolve impasses in collective bargaining, and prohibited strikes in the public sector.

The Organizing Drive

There are three ways to kick off an organizing campaign: (1) Employees themselves may begin a campaign, (2) employees may request that a union begin one for them, or (3) in some instances, national and international unions may contact employees in organizations that have been targeted for organizing. In all three cases, employees are asked to sign **authorization cards** that designate the union as the employees' exclusive representative in bargaining with management.

Well-defined rules govern organizing activities:

1. Employee organizers may solicit fellow employees to sign authorization cards on company premises, but not during working time.
2. Outside organizers may not solicit on premises if a company has an existing policy of prohibiting all forms of solicitation, and if that policy has been enforced consistently.[31]
3. Management representatives may express their views about unions through speeches to employees on company premises. However, they are legally prohibited from interfering with an employee's freedom of choice concerning union membership.

The organizing drive usually continues until the union obtains signed authorization cards from 30 percent of the employees. At that point it can petition the National Labor Relations Board (NLRB) for a representation election. If the union secures authorization cards from more than 50 percent of the employees, however, it may ask management directly for the right to exclusive representation. This is known as a **card check**.[32] Usually the employer refuses, and then the union petitions the NLRB to conduct an election.

The Bargaining Unit

When the petition for election is received, the NLRB conducts a hearing to determine the appropriate (collective) **bargaining unit,** that is, the group of employees eligible to vote in the representation election. Sometimes labor and management agree jointly on the appropriate bargaining unit. When they do not, the NLRB must determine the unit. The NLRB is guided in its decision, especially if there is no previous history of bargaining between the parties, by a concept called **community of interest.** That is, the NLRB will define a unit that reflects the shared interests of the employees involved. Such elements include similar wages, hours, and working conditions; the physical proximity of employees to one another; common supervision; the amount of interchange of employees within the proposed unit; and the degree of integration of the employer's production process or operation.[33] Under the Taft-Hartley Act, however, professional employees cannot be forced into a bargaining unit with nonprofessionals without their majority consent.

The *size* of the bargaining unit is critical for both the union and the employer because it is strongly related to the outcome of the representation election. The larger the bargaining unit, the more difficult it is for the union to win. In fact, if a bargaining unit contains several hundred employees, the unit is almost invulnerable.[34]

The Election Campaign

Emotions on both sides run high during a representation-election campaign. However, management typically is unaware that a union campaign is under way until most or all of the cards have been signed. At that point, management has some tactical advantages over the union. It can use company time and premises to stress the positive aspects of the current situation, and it can emphasize the costs of unionization and the loss of individual freedom that may result from collective representation. Supervisors may hold information meetings to emphasize these antiunion themes. However, certain practices by management are prohibited by law, such as:

1. Physical interference, threats, or violent behavior toward union organizers.
2. Interference with employees involved with the organizing drive.
3. Discipline or discharge of employees for prounion activities.
4. Promises to provide or withhold future benefits depending on the outcome of the representation election.

These illegal activities are **TIPS**—that is, management may not *t*hreaten, *i*nterrogate, *p*romise, or *s*py.

Unions are also prohibited from unfair labor practices (see Table 13–1), such as coercing or threatening employees if they fail to join the union. In addition, the union can picket the employer *only* if (1) the employer is not currently unionized, (2) the petition for election has been filed with the NLRB in the past 30 days, and (3) a representation election has not been held during the previous year. Unions tend to emphasize three themes during organizing campaigns:

- The union's ability to help employees satisfy their economic and personal needs.
- The union's ability to ensure that workers are treated fairly.
- The union's ability to improve working conditions.[35]

The campaign tactics of management and the union are monitored by the NLRB. If the NLRB finds that either party engaged in unfair labor practices during the campaign, the election results may be invalidated and a new election conducted. However, a federal appeals court has ruled that the NLRB cannot force a company to bargain with a union that is not recognized by a majority of the workers, even if the company has made "outrageous" attempts to thwart unionization.[36] For example, in 2000, a NLRB study found that over a recent 5-year period, employers fired or otherwise punished more than 125,000 workers for supporting a union. In the 3–5 years that it took for fired workers to be reinstated, organizing drives often died.[37]

The Representation Election and Certification

If management and the union jointly agree on the size and composition of the bargaining unit, a representation election occurs shortly thereafter. However, if management does not agree, a long delay may ensue. Since such delays, sometimes more than 4 years, often erode rank-and-file union support, they work to management's advantage.[38] Not surprisingly, therefore, few organizations agree with unions on the size and composition of the bargaining unit.

When a date for the representation election is finally established, the NLRB conducts a **secret ballot election.** If the union receives a majority of the ballots *cast* (not a majority of votes from members of the bargaining unit), the union becomes certified as the **exclusive bargaining representative** of all employees in the unit. Once a representation election is held, regardless of the outcome, no further elections can be held in that bargaining unit for 1 year. The entire process is shown graphically in Figure 13–2.

The records of elections won and lost by unions and management have changed drastically since the 1950s. In the 1950s, unions won over 70 percent of representation elections. By the 1990s, that figure had slipped to less than half.[39] However, unions win 73 percent of elections when they use rank-and-file campaigns, versus just 27 percent when they rely on professional organizers.[40]

The Decertification of a Union

If a representation election results in union certification, the first thing many employers want to know is when and how they can *decertify* the union. Under NLRB rules, an incumbent union can be decertified if a majority of employees within the bargaining unit vote to rescind the union's status as their collective bargaining agent in another representation election conducted by the NLRB.[41]

Since **decertification of a union** is most likely to occur the first year or so after certification, unions will often insist on multiyear contracts. Once both parties agree to the terms and duration of the labor contract, the employer is obligated to recognize the union and to follow the provisions of the contract for the specified contract period.

In an important ruling in 2001, the NLRB held that an employer need only demonstrate a "reasonable, good-faith uncertainty" that union representation is still preferred by the majority of bargaining-unit employees in order to call for a decertification election. Evidence such as the following is necessary[42]:

Figure 13–2

Steps involved and decisions to be made in a union organizing campaign.

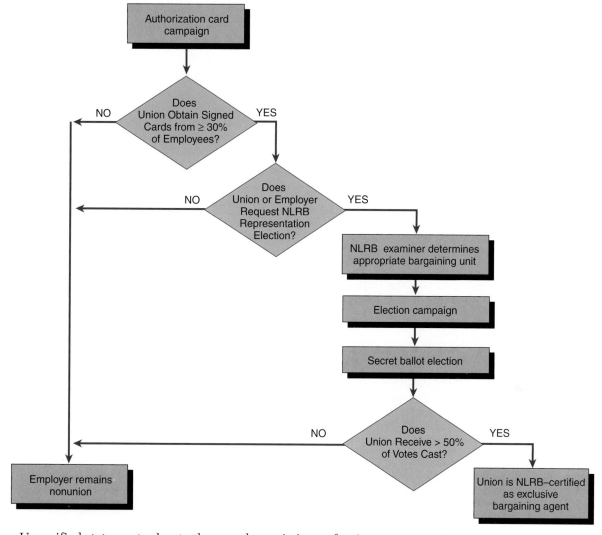

- Unverified statements about other employees' views of union representation.
- Employee statements expressing dissatisfaction with the union's performance.
- A majority of employees did not support the union during a strike.
- The union has become less and less active as a representative of employees.
- There was substantial turnover among employees subsequent to certification.
- The union has admitted a lack of majority support.

As with certification elections, the outcome is determined by a majority of the votes cast. Once a decertification election is held, a full year must elapse before another representation election can take place.

Once a union is legally certified as the exclusive bargaining agent for workers, the next task is to negotiate a contract that is mutually acceptable to management and labor. We examine this process in more detail below.

COLLECTIVE BARGAINING: CORNERSTONE OF AMERICAN LABOR RELATIONS

The Art of Negotiation

Negotiation is a two-party transaction whereby both parties intend to resolve a conflict.[43] What constitutes a "good" settlement? To be sure, the best outcome of negotiations occurs when both parties win. Sometimes negotiations fall short of this ideal. A really bad bargain is one in which both parties lose, yet this is a risk that is inherent in the process. Despite its limitations, abuses, and hazards, negotiation has become an indispensable process in free societies in general and in the U.S. labor movement in particular. The fact is that negotiation is the most effective device thus far invented for realizing common interests while compromising on conflicting interests.[44] Any practice that threatens the process of collective bargaining will be resisted vigorously by organized labor.

In general, there are two postures that the parties involved in bargaining might assume: win-lose and win-win. In win-lose bargaining, or **distributive bargaining,** the goals of the parties initially are irreconcilable—or at least they appear that way. Central to the conflict is the belief that there is a limited, controlled amount of key resources available—a "fixed pie" situation. Both parties may want to be the winner; both may want more than half of what is available.[45]

Evidence indicates that when one party adopts a distributive, contentious posture, the other party tends to reciprocate with contentious communications. To break the spiral of conflict, use mixed communications, that is, use both contentious and cooperative, problem-solving communications in one speaking turn. For example, a negotiator might threaten, "If you persist in these demands we'd prefer to see you in court, where we expect the judge to find in our favor." The other party might respond with the following mixed communication. "We are prepared to let a judge decide, but we think that we will both be better off if we reach an agreement based on interests. Tell me again what your software needs are."[46]

In contrast, in win-win bargaining, or **integrative bargaining,** the goals of the parties are not mutually exclusive. If one side pursues its goals, this does not prohibit the other side from achieving its own goals. One party's gain is not necessarily at the other party's expense. The fundamental structure of an integrative bargaining situation is that it is possible for both sides to achieve their objectives.[47] While the conflict initially may appear to be win-lose to the parties, discussion and mutual exploration usually will suggest win-win alternatives.

How do skilled negotiators actually behave? One study defined skilled negotiators in terms of three criteria: (1) they were rated as effective by both sides, (2) they had a "track record" of significant success, and (3) they had a low incidence of "implementation" failures. Of the 48 skilled negotiators studied, 17 were union representatives, 12 were management representatives, 10 were contract negotiators, and 9 were classified as "other." The behavior of this group was then compared with that of an "average" group over 102 negotiating sessions. The study examined negotiating behavior in six areas[48]:

- **Planning time.** There were no significant differences between the groups.
- **Exploration of options.** Skilled negotiators considered a wider range of outcomes or options for action (5.1 per issue) than average negotiators (2.6 per issue).

- **Common ground.** Skilled negotiators gave over 3 times as much attention to finding common-ground areas as did average negotiators.
- **Long-term versus short-term orientation.** The skilled group made twice as many comments of a long-term nature as did the average group.
- **Setting limits.** The average negotiators tended to plan their objectives around a fixed point (e.g., "We aim to settle at 81"). Skilled negotiators were much more likely to plan in terms of upper and lower limits—to think in terms of ranges.
- **Sequence and issue planning.** Average negotiators tended to link issues in sequence (A, then B, then C, then D), whereas skilled negotiators tended to view issues as independent and not linked by sequence. The advantage: flexibility.

Face-to-Face Negotiating Behavior

The same study also identified important differences between skilled and average negotiators in terms of their actual behavior toward each other.

- **Irritators.** Certain words and phrases that are commonly used during negotiations have negligible value in persuading the other party but do cause irritation. One of the most prevalent is "generous offer," used by a negotiator to describe his or her own proposal. Average negotiators used irritators more than 4 times as often as did skilled negotiators.
- **Counterproposals.** Frequently during bargaining, one party puts forward a proposal and the other party immediately counters. Skilled negotiators make immediate counterproposals significantly less frequently than do average negotiators.
- **Argument dilution.** If one party has five reasons for doing something, is this more persuasive than having only one reason? Apparently not. Skilled negotiators used an average of 1.8 reasons; average negotiators used 3.0.
- **Reviewing the negotiation.** Over two-thirds of the skilled negotiators claimed they always set aside some time after a negotiation to review it and to consider what they had learned. In contrast, just under half of average negotiators made the same claim.

Table 13–2

MAJOR SECTIONS OF A TYPICAL COLLECTIVE BARGAINING AGREEMENT

Unchallenged representation	Protection of employees
Employee rights	Continuous hours of work
Management rights	Recall pay
No strikes	Distribution of overtime
Compensation	Out-of-title work
Travel	No discrimination
Health insurance	Benefits guaranteed
Attendance and leave	Job classifications
Workers' compensation leave with pay	Promotional examinations
Payroll	Employee assistance program
Employee development and training	Employee orientation
Safety and health maintenance	Performance rating procedures
Layoff procedures	Day care centers
Joint labor-management committees	Discipline
Seniority	Grievance and arbitration procedures
Posting and bidding for job vacancies	Resignation
Employee benefit fund	Job abandonment
Workweek and workday	Duration of agreement

There is one important qualifier in any discussion of negotiation strategies. This is national culture. Evidence indicates that managers from the United States, Japan, and Germany use different strategies to negotiate conflict. Americans value individualism, egalitarianism, and multitasking. They try to integrate their interests with those of the other party. The German value for explicit contracting leads them to rely on independent, objective standards as a basis for resolving conflict. Finally, the Japanese value collectivism and hierarchy, and tend to resolve conflict by emphasizing status differences between the parties.[49] What is the bottom line in all this? If you want to become a win-win negotiator, be aware of the behaviors to imitate and those to avoid, and make an effort to understand the cultural norms that influence the behavior of the other party.[50]

Successful collective bargaining results in an agreement that is mutually acceptable both to labor and management. Table 13–2 shows some of the major sections of a typical agreement.

Unfortunately, contract negotiations sometimes fail because the parties are not able to reach a timely and mutually acceptable settlement of the issues—economic, noneconomic, or a combination of both. When this happens, the union may strike, management may shut down operations (a lockout), or both parties may appeal for third-party involvement. Let's examine these processes in some detail.

BARGAINING IMPASSES: STRIKES, LOCKOUTS, AND THIRD-PARTY INVOLVEMENT

Strikes

In every labor negotiation there exists the possibility of a strike. The right of employees to strike in support of their bargaining demands is protected by the Landrum-Griffin Act. However, there is no unqualified right to strike. A work stoppage by employees must be the result of a lawful labor dispute and must not be in violation of an existing agreement between management and the union. Strikers engaged in activities protected by law may not be discharged, but they may be replaced during the strike. Strikers engaged in activities that are not protected by law need not be rehired after the strike.[51]

Types of Strikes

As you might suspect by now, there are several different types of strikes. Let's consider the major types:

Unfair Labor Practice Strikes. Unfair labor practices by an employer can cause or prolong an **unfair labor practice strike.** Employees engaged in this type of strike are afforded the highest degree of protection under the act, and under most circumstances they are entitled to reinstatement once the strike ends. Management must exercise great caution in handling unfair labor practice strikes because the NLRB will become involved and company liability can be substantial.

Economic Strikes. Actions in which a union withdraws its labor in support of bargaining demands, including those for recognition or organization, are **economic strikes.** Economic strikers have limited rights to reinstatement.

Unprotected Strikes. These include all remaining types of work stoppages, both lawful and unlawful, such as sit-down strikes, strikes in violation of federal laws (e.g., the prohibition of strikes by employees of the federal government), slowdowns, wildcat strikes, and partial walkouts. Participants in **unprotected strikes** may be discharged by their employers.

Sympathy Strikes. These are refusals by employees of one bargaining unit to cross a picket line of a different bargaining unit (e.g., when more than one union is functioning at an employer's plant). Although the NLRB and the courts have recognized the right of the sympathy striker to stand in the shoes of the primary striker, the facts of any particular situation ultimately will determine the legal status of a **sympathy strike.**[52]

During a strike, certain rules of conduct apply to both parties; these are summarized in Table 13–3. In addition, certain special rules apply to management. *Management must not:*

■ Offer extra rewards to nonstrikers or attempt to withhold the "extras" from strikers once the strike has ended and some or all strikers are reinstated.

Table 13–3

RULES OF CONDUCT DURING A STRIKE

- People working in or having any business with the organization have a right to pass freely in and out.
- Pickets must not block a door, passageway, driveway, crosswalk, or other entrance or exit.
- Profanity on streets and sidewalks may be a violation of state law or local ordinances.
- Company officials, with the assistance of local law enforcement agents, should make every effort to permit individuals and vehicles to move in and out of the facility in a normal manner.
- Union officials or pickets have a right to talk to people going in or out. Intimidation, threats, and coercion are not permitted, either by verbal remarks or by physical action.
- The use of sound trucks may be regulated by state law or local ordinance with respect to noise level, location, and permit requirements.
- If acts of violence or trespassing occur on the premises, officials should file complaints or seek injunctions. If you are the object of violence, sign a warrant for the arrest of the person or persons causing the violence.
- Fighting, assault, battery, violence, threats, and intimidation are not permissible under the law. The carrying of knives, firearms, clubs and other dangerous weapons may be prohibited by state law or local ordinance.

- Threaten nonstrikers or strikers.
- Promise benefits to strikers in an attempt to end the strike or to undermine the union.
- Threaten employees with discharge for taking part in a lawful strike.
- Discharge nonstrikers who refuse to take over a striker's job.

COMPANY EXAMPLE   **WHY THERE ARE FEWER STRIKES IN THE AUTO INDUSTRY53**

The number of strikes involving 1,000 workers or more has been declining for more than 50 years (see Figure 13–3). To a large extent this is due to some major economic and social changes that are prompting even hard-nosed union leaders to reassess their tactics. At least three such changes are:

1. The old lines between labor and capital are being blurred as more workers own stock in their companies and share in company profits. Workers own 20 percent of the stock at Ford Motor Company, and 10 percent of the stock at General Motors. This means that workers' personal fortunes are dependent on factors such as profits, market share, and stock prices, not just on what the union can get at the bargaining table. This, in turn, has led union leaders and members to think and act more like owners, and less like cogs in the machine.

Number of work stoppages involving
1,000 workers or more

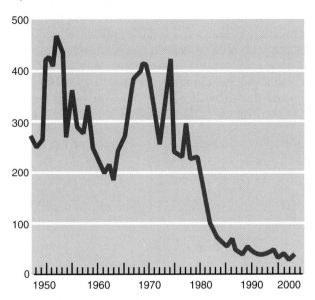

Figure 13–3

Number of work stoppages involving 1,000 employees or more. (*Source: Work stoppages involving 1,000 workers or more, 1947–2000*, Bureau of Labor Statistics, www.bls.gov, accessed Aug. 15, 2001.)

2. Technology and global markets make it easier than ever for big companies to displace highly paid but low-skilled workers—either through outsourcing or by relocating plants to cheaper, foreign sites, such as Mexico. If U.S. workers do go on strike, employers use replacement workers, thereby blunting the overall effectiveness of a strike.[54] Another reason for the drop in membership at the United Auto Workers is that much of the work traditionally done in automakers' own factories has been outsourced to suppliers' plants, which tend to be nonunion. While the number of production and skilled-trades jobs in U.S. auto-assembly plants has dropped by 90,000 in the past two decades, parts-making jobs have jumped by 40,000, according to the union.

3. A final reason for unions' reluctance to strike is the advent of foreign-owned auto plants in the United States which, like the supplier factories, usually aren't unionized. Many of the products built at these plants are gaining market share at the expense of UAW-built products.

Says former UAW president Douglas Fraser, "The reality is, unorganized workers feel that the strike is a very negative thing, and one of the reasons they don't join unions is fear of strikes."

When the Strike Is Over

The period of time immediately after a strike is critical, since an organization's problems are not over when the strike is settled. There is the problem of conflict between strikers and their replacements (if replacements were hired), and the reaccommodation of strikers to the workplace. After an economic strike is settled, the method of reinstatement is best protected by a written memorandum of agreement with the union that outlines the intended procedure. A key point of consideration in any strike aftermath is misconduct by some strikers. To refuse reinstatement for such strikers following an economic strike, management must be able to present evidence (e.g., photographs) to prove the misconduct.

The most important human aspect at the end of the strike is the restoration of harmonious working relations as soon as possible so that full operations can be resumed. A letter, a video, or a speech to employees welcoming them back to work can help this process along, as can meetings with supervisors indicating that no resentment or ill will is to be shown toward returning strikers. In practice, this may be difficult to do. However, keep these points in mind:

- Nothing is gained by allowing vindictiveness of any type in any echelon of management.
- The burden of maintaining healthy industrial relations now lies with the organization.
- There is always another negotiation ahead, and rancor has no place at any bargaining table.[55]

Lockouts

A **lockout** may occur when a collective bargaining agreement has expired. If an employer's purpose is to put economic pressure on a union to settle a contract on terms favorable to the employer, it is legal for the employer to lock out its employees.[56] It also is legal for a company to replace the locked-out workers with temporary replacements in order to continue operations during the lockout. However, the use of permanent replacements (without first consulting the union) is not permissible, according to the National Labor Relations Board, because such an action would completely destroy the bargaining unit and represent an unlawful withdrawal of recognition of a duly designated union.[57]

Third-Party Involvement

A **bargaining impasse** occurs when the parties are unable to move further toward settlement. However, because there is no clear formula to determine if or when an impasse in negotiations has been reached, litigation often ensues, and a judge must decide the issue.[58] In an effort to resolve the impasse, a neutral third party may become involved. In most private-sector negotiations, the parties have to agree voluntarily before any third-party involvement can be imposed on them. Because employees in the public sector are prohibited by law from striking, the use of third parties is more prevalent there.[59]

Three general types of third-party involvement are common: mediation, fact finding, and interest arbitration. Each becomes progressively more constraining on the freedom of the parties.

Mediation

Mediation is a process by which a neutral third party attempts to help the parties in dispute to reach a settlement of the issues that divide them. The neutral third party does not act as a judge to decide the resolution of the dispute (a process referred to as *arbitration*).[60] Rather, mediation involves persuading, opening communications, allowing readjustment and reassessment of bargaining stances, and making procedural suggestions (e.g., scheduling, conducting, and controlling meetings; establishing or extending deadlines).

Mediators have two restrictions on their power: (1) they are involved by invitation only, and (2) their advice lacks even so much as the umpire's option of throwing someone out of the game. However, mediation has some important advantages. It is a face-saving procedure in that each side can make concessions to the other without appearing weak. Disputants often see mediation procedures as fair, and this helps account for its 60 to 80 percent settlement rate.[61] Settlement rates tend to be higher when mediators are perceived by disputants as having high expertise.[62]

Fact Finding

Fact finding is a dispute-resolution mechanism that is commonly used in the public sector at the state- and local-government levels. In a fact-finding procedure, each party submits whatever information it believes is relevant to a resolution of the dispute. A neutral fact finder then makes a study of the evidence and prepares a report on the facts. This procedure is often useful where the parties disagree over the truthfulness of the information each is using.[63]

Actually, the term "fact finding" is a misnomer. This is because fact finders often proceed, with statutory authority, to render a public recommendation of a reasonable settlement. In this respect, fact finding is similar to mediation. However, neither fact finding nor mediation necessarily results in a contract between management and labor. Consequently, the parties often resort to arbitration of a dispute, either as a matter of law *(compulsory arbitration)* or by mutual agreement between union and management *(interest arbitration)*.

Interest Arbitration

Like fact finding, **interest arbitration** is used primarily in the public sector. However, arbitration differs considerably from mediation and fact finding. As one author noted: "While mediation assists the parties to reach their own settlement, arbitration hears the positions of both and decides on binding settlement terms. While fact finding would recommend a settlement, arbitration dictates it."[64]

Interest arbitration is controversial for at least two reasons. One, imposition of interest arbitration eliminates the need for the parties to settle on their own because if they reach an impasse, settlement by an outsider is certain.[65] Two, many municipal employers apparently feel that arbitrators have been too generous in the awards made to public-employee unions. As a result, some states now specify the factors arbitrators must consider in making awards. Some of these, such as comparable wage rates, are items favored by unions; others, such as productivity and the ability of the employer to pay, are items favored by management.[66]

DOES THE ADA OVERRIDE SENIORITY RIGHTS?

LEGALITIES

Does the requirement in the Americans with Disabilities Act for "reasonable accommodation" supersede collectively bargained seniority rights? A federal appeals court ruled on this issue in a recent case that involved an employee of Consolidated Rail Corporation who was diagnosed with epilepsy. Medical restrictions prevented him from returning to his night-time shift. So he sought to invoke a provision in the collective bargaining agreement that permitted an employee with a disability, upon written agreement of the employer and the union, to "bump" a more senior employee or to occupy a more senior position

and be immune from bumping by more senior employees. When the union refused to sign the agreement, the employee brought suit under the ADA.

The court rejected the employee's argument, finding that "collective-bargaining seniority rights have a pre-existing special status in the law and that Congress to date has shown no intent to alter this status by the duties created by the ADA."[67]

ADMINISTRATION OF THE COLLECTIVE-BARGAINING AGREEMENT

To many union and management officials, the real test of effective labor relations comes after the agreement is signed, that is, in its day-to-day administration. At that point, the major concern of the union is to obtain in practice the employee rights that management has granted on paper. The major concern of management is to establish its right to manage the business and to keep operations running.[68] A key consideration for both is the form of union security that governs conditions of employment.

Union-Security Clauses

Section 14b of the Taft-Hartley Act enables states to enact **right-to-work laws** that prohibit compulsory union membership (after a probationary period) as a condition of continued employment. Table 13–4 illustrates the forms that such **union-security clauses** can take and indicates that most of them are illegal in the 21 states that have passed right-to-work laws.

Table 13–4

FORMS OF UNION SECURITY AND THEIR LEGAL STATUS IN RIGHT-TO-WORK STATES.

	Legal	Illegal
Closed shop. An individual must join the union that represents employees in order to be considered for employment.		X
Union shop. As a condition of continued employment, an individual must join the union that represents employees after a probationary period (typically a minimum of 30 days.)		X
Preferential shop. Union members are given preference in hiring.		X
Agency shop. Employees need not join the union that represents them, but, in lieu of dues, they must pay a service charge for representation.		X
Maintenance of membership. An employee must remain a member of the union once he or she joins.		X
Checkoff. An employee may request that union dues be deducted from his or her pay and be sent directly to the union.	X	

Figure 13–4

Example of a formal grievance procedure in a unionized firm.

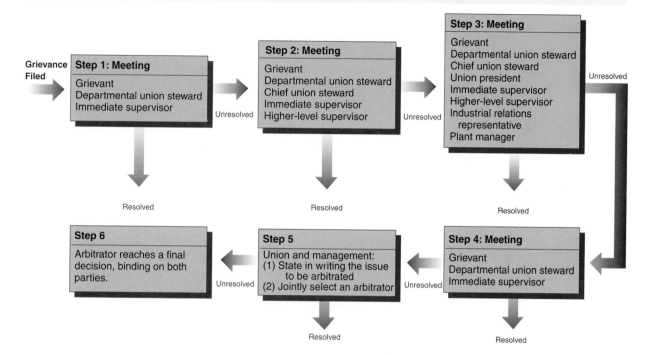

Grievance Procedures in the Unionized Firm

Occasionally during the life of a contract, disputes arise about the interpretation of the collective bargaining agreement, potential violations of federal or state law, violations of past practices or company rules, or violations of management's responsibility (e.g., to provide safe and healthy working conditions). In each instance, an aggrieved party may file a grievance. A **grievance** is an alleged violation of the rights of workers on the job.[69] A formal process known as a *grievance procedure* is then invoked to help the parties resolve the dispute. Grievance procedures are the keystone of industrial relations because of their ability to resolve disputed issues while work continues without litigation, strikes, or other radical dispute-resolution strategies.[70]

In addition to providing a formal mechanism for resolving disputes, the grievance procedure defines and narrows the nature of the complaint. Thus each grievance must be expressed in writing. The written grievance identifies the grievant, when the incident leading to the grievance occurred (it could, of course, be ongoing), and where the incident happened. The written statement also indicates why the complaint is considered a grievance and what the grievant thinks should be done about the matter.[71] A typical grievance procedure in a unionized firm works as shown in Figure 13–4. As the figure indicates, unresolved grievances proceed progressively to higher and higher levels of management and union representation, and culminate in voluntary, binding arbitration. Specific time limits for management's decision and the union's approval are normally imposed at each step, for example, 3 days for each party at step 1, 5 days for each party at steps 2 and 3, and 10 days for each party at step 4.

It also is important to note that many unions have a policy that up to step 3 of the procedure the grievance "belongs" to the employee. That is, the union will process a grievance through step 2 (and in some cases through step 3) at the grievant's request. However, if the grievance is not settled and reaches step 3, it becomes the union's grievance. At that point, the union will decide whether or not the grievance has merit and whether additional time and financial resources of the union should be spent in carrying it forward. Indeed, many local unions let the membership vote formally to decide whether to take a grievance to arbitration.[72] They do this for good reason: the grievance process is expensive. How expensive? In complex grievance cases that proceed all the way to arbitration (step 6 in Figure 13–4), the cost to the company or union may exceed $7,800 per grievance (in 2001 dollars).[73] The American Postal Workers Union allocates fully 20 percent of its members' dues to the costs of processing grievances.[74]

Resolving Grievances

The majority of grievances filed are resolved without resorting to **grievance arbitration.** Of these, unions and management each win about half the time. However, unions tend to win more grievances related to such issues as the denial of sick benefits, termination, transfer, suspension, and disciplinary memoranda. Ordinarily, the burden of proof in a grievance proceeding is on the union. Since fewer issues of interpretation are involved in the areas that unions usually win, this pattern of grievance resolution is not surprising.[75]

In summary, there are two key advantages to the grievance procedure. One, it ensures that the complaints and problems of workers can be heard, rather than simply allowed to fester. Two, grievance procedures provide formal mechanisms to ensure due process for all parties. Research indicates that employees who have access to such a system are more willing to continue working for their organizations after filing a grievance than are employees who do not have access to such a system.[76] On the other hand, the job performance of grievance filers is likely to be lower after they learn the outcome of their grievances.[77]

The process is not completely objective, however, in that factors other than merit sometimes determine the outcome of a grievance. Some of these factors include the cost of granting a grievance, the perceived need for management to placate disgruntled workers or to settle large numbers of grievances in order to expedite the negotiation process,[78] and the grievant's work history (good performance, long tenure, few disciplinary incidents).[79]

What is the role of the line manager in all this? To know and understand the collective bargaining contract, as well as federal and state labor laws. Above all, whether you agree or disagree with the terms of the contract, it is legally binding on both labor and management. Respect its provisions, and manage according to the spirit as well as the letter of the contract.

Does a High Number of Grievances Indicate Poor Labor Relations?

Conventional wisdom suggests that large numbers of grievances signal an unhealthy organizational climate. This is often the case, as indicated by the

126,000 grievances currently pending at the U.S. Postal Service. Postal workers file grievances to protest issues such as the elimination of paid wash-up time, the installation of monitoring equipment that tracks their movements, and changes to different work shifts. They also file grievances because they have few other ways to air their gripes. The massive number of grievances stifles productivity and innovation, and it is terribly expensive. Just keeping the grievance system going takes an army of 300 outside arbitrators and costs more than $200 million a year. That's about as much as the Postal Service lost at the end of fiscal year 2000![80]

On the other hand, a 6-year longitudinal study of grievances filed at a utility company in the western United States reached a different conclusion, namely, that a large number of grievances signals the presence of a friendly system that is easily accessible and time-efficient. At a minimum, it seems that high grievance rates do not invariably indicate poor labor relations.[81]

Grievance Arbitration

Grievance arbitration is used widely by management and labor to settle disputes arising out of and during the term of a labor contract.[82] Figure 13–4 shows that compulsory, binding arbitration is the final stage of the grievance process. It is also used as an alternative to a work stoppage, and it is used to ensure labor peace for the duration of a labor contract. Arbitrators may be chosen from a list of qualified people supplied by the American Arbitration Association or the Federal Mediation and Conciliation Service.

Arbitration hearings are quasi-judicial proceedings. Both parties may file prehearing briefs, along with lists of witnesses to be called. Witnesses are crossexamined, and documentary evidence may be introduced. However, arbitrators are not bound by the formal rules of evidence, as they would be in a court of law.

Following the hearing, the parties may each submit briefs to reiterate their positions, evidence supporting them, and proposed decisions. The arbitrator then considers the evidence, the contract clause in dispute, the powers granted the arbitrator under the labor agreement, and issues a decision. In the rare instances where a losing party refuses to honor the arbitrator's decision, the decision can be enforced by taking that party to federal court.[83]

Generally an arbitration award cannot be appealed in court simply because one party believes the arbitrator made a mistake in interpreting an agreement.[84] Courts have held that arbitrator awards are extensions of labor contracts, and court deference is the rule.[85]

We noted earlier that only 13.5 percent of U.S. workers belong to unions. To put this into perspective, let us consider rates of union membership in other countries. Then we will examine the two faces of workforce flexibility in the United States, as compared to the situation in other countries.

UNION MEMBERSHIP IN COUNTRIES OTHER THAN THE UNITED STATES

Union membership has fallen in many parts of the world, particularly in Eastern Europe after the collapse of communism. Trade union membership fell by 71 percent in Estonia and by more than 50 percent in the Czech Republic. In many former Eastern-bloc nations, union membership was virtually

Figure 13–5

Percentage of union members in various countries. *Sources: Japanese working life profile 2000: Labor statistics,* Japan Institute of Labor, Tokyo; Australian Bureau of Statistics (ABS), *Earnings, benefits, and union members,* cat. no. 6310, ABS, Canberra, 1999; Workers drift away from unions, BBC News, Nov. 22, 1997, *news.bbc.co.uk/hi/ english/business.*

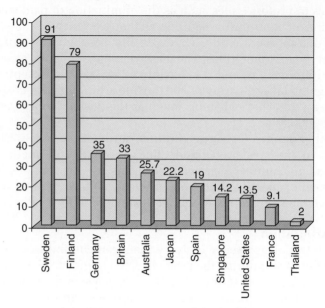

Percentage of Union Members in Eleven Countries

compulsory. Figure 13–5 shows current union membership as a percentage of the workforce in 11 countries. Union membership is highest in Sweden and Finland, and then drops off considerably in Western European countries: 35 percent in Germany, 33 percent in Britain, 19 percent in Spain, and 9.1 percent in France. Among Asian countries, unions represent 22.2 percent of the workforce in Japan, 14.2 in Singapore, and just 2 percent in Thailand. In Australia, 25.7 percent of the workforce belong to unions. Unions remain a powerful force in national labor policies, particularly with respect to layoffs.

HOW LAWS AND FOREIGN-OWNED FIRMS AFFECT LAYOFFS IN THE UNITED STATES[86]

For most of the last decade, many observers cited the flexibility of U.S. labor laws as a key factor in restoring the competitiveness of the U.S. economy and turning it into a veritable job-creation machine. However, as multinational firms scrambled to cut costs in response to a slowdown in the global economy, Americans discovered that the same flexibility that made the United States a preferred place to create jobs also makes it a cheap and easy place to cut them.

Foreign companies currently account for about 6 percent of the U.S. workforce, and an estimated 15 percent of manufacturing employees. Thus their behavior is now of more than trivial concern to Americans.

In contrast to the flexibility of U.S. labor laws, in Europe or Japan, laws, customs, or union contracts impose strict conditions on when workers can be laid off, and how part-time or contract workers can be used. They also prohibit the hiring of replacement workers during strikes. In France, layoffs are done not by seniority, but by which worker needs the job the most. In fact a recent French labor law doubles minimum severance packages and prevents compa-

nies from laying off workers unless "all other means" have been tried to preserve jobs, including alternative plans submitted by workers' councils at each
plant. If the company and councils cannot come to some agreement, a govern-
ment-approved mediator decides. In the United States, most of these issues are
left up to companies.

Consider the cost to Delphi Automotive to close three European plants in
2001. Local laws required Delphi to pay more than 1 year's total pay and benefits
to each worker. In the United States, by contrast, union contracts usually put the
cost noticeably lower, and labor laws do not require companies to pay severance
costs. For this reason, when job cuts become necessary, foreign-owned firms often choose to lay off American workers rather than home-country workers.

Consider these examples. After the bursting of the telecom bubble in 2001,
Alcatel, the French telecommunications company, eliminated 5,000 of its U.S.
positions, or slightly more than 1 in 4. However, it cut only about 1 in 17 of its
70,000 European workers. Of the 3,000 cuts in permanent and contract employment announced by Nokia, the Finnish maker of cellular telephones, half
were in the United States, despite the fact that only 20 percent of its employees
were in the U.S. DuPont Company, which recorded more than half its sales and
employees outside the United States in 2000, made 70 percent of its job cuts in
the United States.

One response is to change U.S. labor laws. Thus unions are lobbying hard
for prolabor legislation, for example, restrictions on the ability of U.S. firms
to shift operations to Mexico or Canada under the North American Free Trade
Agreement (NAFTA). With respect to autos and auto parts, for example,
NAFTA phases out tariffs, from 20 percent in 1994, before NAFTA was
passed, to 6 percent in 1998, to 0 percent in 2004. This has encouraged U.S.
automakers to move ever bigger chunks of their car and truck operations
to Mexico, and it has encouraged both local and foreign suppliers to invest

IMPACT OF UNION REPRESENTATION ON PRODUCTIVITY, QUALITY OF WORK LIFE, AND THE BOTTOM LINE

Is there a link between unionization and organizational performance? Unionization of a
workforce often increases control over wage
levels by giving monopoly power to the union
as the single seller of labor to an enterprise. It also creates a "voice" mechanism for employees by establishing
negotiated grievance procedures and
the right to bargain collectively.[89]

Economic studies generally show
that the existence of a grievance
process that acts as a check or balance on management's authority can enhance productivity.
One explanation for this is that higher produc-

tivity results from lower turnover, which in
turn enhances employees' knowledge of the
jobs they perform.[90]

If unions actually do raise productivity,
why do managers oppose them so vigorously? The answer lies in the impact unions have on corporate profits.
A number of studies support the argument that while unions may increase
productivity, the wage and benefit increases associated with unionization
(25 percent more than those of nonunion
workers) often exceed productivity gains.[91]

IMPLICATIONS FOR MANAGEMENT PRACTICE

Given current conditions in the economic environment, a distributive (win-lose) orientation toward labor is simply inefficient. Rather, view your employees as a source of potential competitive advantage. Treat them with dignity and respect, and they will respond in kind. As a cover of *Fast Company* magazine noted in 2001, "The best leaders know where all great companies start. (It's the people, stupid!)"[92]

millions of dollars in Mexico on technology to produce high-quality auto parts to supply the car makers. The net result is a loss of hundreds of thousands of American jobs.[87]

What is the lesson in all this? Said the chief European economist at Deutche Bank, "I guess it's a fair assumption that if companies located facilities in places with flexible labor rules, they could be expected to take advantage of that flexibility when the economy becomes soft."[88] In short, it is important to recognize that flexible labor rules have an upside as well as a downside.

Human Resource Management in Action: Conclusion

IMPROVING PRODUCTIVITY, QWL, AND PROFITS THROUGH LABOR-MANAGEMENT COOPERATION

Make no mistake about it: the recent popularity of cooperation stems largely from the sweeping changes in the economic environment that have occurred. Another reason is new technology—the Internet, factory automation, robotics, and more modern production systems. Cooperation offers a pragmatic approach to problems that threaten the survival of companies, the jobs and income security of their employees, and the institutional future of their unions.[93] Progressive unions are at the forefront of a revolutionary change in the way unions view cooperation with management. The unions are asking what kinds of improvements in productivity or quality the employer needs to stay competitive while paying union wages, and then they help the employer achieve its objectives.[94] As one union leader noted, "A trade unionist can't operate as trade unionists did in the past. The global economy has forced us to change."[95]

In Seattle, the Communications Workers of America teamed with Cisco Systems to build a lab to house Web-based programming classes. In fact the International Association of Machinists (IAM) is now marketing itself as a resource for employers. It runs week-long courses for plant managers and local union leaders on high-performance work systems in its Maryland school. The managers and union officers study side by side, learning everything from the history of high-performance systems to new accounting methods to measure them. The goal: to protect workers' jobs and pay by making their employers more competitive. Unions also want to win for employees more say over their work and how their companies are run.

In addition to training programs, progressive unions are working with management to raise productivity by agreeing to adopt teams and new work systems.[96] For example, following an IAM training module, union leaders and managers from manufacturing to marketing created team systems and joint decision-making councils at a 500-employee unit of Aluminum Company of America—which makes equipment for the packaging industry. Relations on the shop floor have improved dramatically, and efficiency gains are expected to follow.[97] Cooperative efforts such as these have produced big gains in efficiency at companies such as National Steel Corporation, Scott Paper Company, and LTV Corporation.

Institutionalizing cooperative relationships is no easy task. However, successful efforts have been characterized by features such as the following[98]:

- The reason for the cooperative effort remains strong.
- Benefits derived from the cooperation are distributed equitably.
- The union is perceived as instrumental in attaining program benefits.
- The program does not threaten management prerogatives.
- Management has refrained from subcontracting out bargaining-unit work.
- Union leaders continue to pursue member goals on traditional economic issues.

As we have seen, the business world has changed dramatically, largely due to changes in technology and global competition. If U.S. labor leaders let today's opportunities for labor-management cooperation slip by, they may not get another chance to be part of the solution to the continuing challenge to improve productivity, quality of work life, and profits.

SUMMARY

At a general level, the goal of unions is to improve economic and other conditions of employment. Although unions have been successful over the years in achieving these goals, more recently they have been confronted with challenges that have led to membership losses. Unions are trying to reverse that decline by organizing more workers.

Six features characterize the U.S. industrial relations system. These are: exclusive representation, collective agreements that embody a sharp distinction between negotiation of and interpretation of an agreement, decentralized collective bargaining, relatively high union dues and large union staffs, opposition by both large and small employers to union organization, and a government role that is relatively passive in dispute resolution and highly legalistic in administrative proceedings and in the courts.

The National Labor Relations Board, created by the Wagner Act, supervises union organizing campaigns and representation elections. If the union wins, it becomes the sole bargaining agent for employees. Collective bargaining is the cornerstone of the U.S. labor movement, and anything that threatens its continued viability will be resisted vigorously by organized labor.

Unfortunately, bargaining sometimes reaches an impasse, at which point the parties may resort to a strike (workers) or a lockout (management). Alternatively, the parties may request third-party intervention in the form of mediation, fact finding, or interest arbitration. In the public sector, such intervention is usually required.

Occasionally during the life of a contract, disputes arise about the interpretation of the collective bargaining agreement. Under these circumstances, an aggrieved party may file a grievance. A grievance is an alleged violation of the rights of workers on the job. A formal process known as a grievance procedure is then invoked to help the parties resolve the dispute. Compulsory, binding arbitration is the final stage of the grievance process. It is also used as an alternative to a work stoppage, and it is used to ensure labor peace for the duration of a labor contract.

U.S. labor laws, in contrast to those in other countries, provide great flexibility with respect to hiring and laying off workers. Many foreign-owned and domestic firms take advantage of that flexibility when the economy turns down. To counter such actions, unions have been lobbying hard for more legal protections against layoffs. Perhaps a more sensible approach, however, is for labor and management to cooperate in an effort to enhance the productivity and overall competitiveness of their enterprises. In the current climate of global competition and the migration of technology and capital across borders, this seems more appropriate than the old adversarial win-lose approach.

DISCUSSION QUESTIONS

13–1. Are the roles of labor and management inherently adversarial?
13–2. Discuss the rights and obligations of unions and management during a union organizing drive.
13–3. Discuss key differences in the behavior of successful versus average negotiators.
13–4. What are the key features of the U.S. industrial relations system?
13–5. Compare and contrast mediation, interest arbitration, and grievance arbitration.

KEY TERMS

exclusive representation	unfair labor practice strike
conspiracy doctrine	economic strike
sit-down strike	unprotected strike
secondary boycott	sympathy strike
free-speech clause	lockout
authorization cards	bargaining impasse
card check	mediation
bargaining unit	fact finding
community of interest	interest arbitration
secret ballot election	right-to-work laws
exclusive bargaining representative	union-security clauses
decertification	grievance
distributive bargaining	grievance arbitration
integrative bargaining	

APPLYING YOUR KNOWLEDGE

Contract Negotiations at Moulton Machine Shop   *Exercise 13–1*

Collective bargaining is the cornerstone of American labor relations. Face-to-face negotiations involving give-and-take on the part of both management and labor representatives are an inherent part of our present system. It is through these negotiations that both sides attempt to understand the positions of the other and attempt to persuade the other side of the fairness of their own demands.

The purpose of this exercise is for you to experience the collective bargaining process and to gain an awareness of the nature and complexity of labor negotiations.

Background Information

Moulton Machine Shop is a 60-year-old shop located near Lake Erie in Pennsylvania. The company manufactures a wide variety of made-to-order products, but its primary business is the repair of mechanical airplane parts and components, a business that it conducts on an international basis. The firm has developed a reputation for quality and timely work on difficult machining projects. The mostly blue-collar workforce at Moulton consists of about 200 workers who were organized 30 years ago by the International Machinists Union (IMU). The labor relations climate at Moulton has been fairly good over the last 20 years (after a rather stormy beginning), with no strikes in the last 9 years. In the past 2 years, however, the number of grievances has increased substantially.

Recent economic conditions have been difficult for Moulton. Over the past 5 years, increased competition from lower-priced foreign-based machine shops has pruned Moulton's profit margins. Overall, sales are down about 10 percent compared with projections made earlier in the year. Moulton's management believes that competition will intensify in the near future, creating even more problems for the firm. The union is aware of the financial situation at Moulton and is sympathetic, but has been very clear in its overtures to management that it intends to fight for an improved contract for its members because they have fallen behind equivalent workers in recent years.

CURRENT CONTRACT PROVISIONS	
Clause	**Current contract**
Wages	Average hourly wage is $13.66.
Benefits	Company-paid medical and life insurance.
Overtime	Time-and-a-half.
Layoffs	A 2-week notice is required to lay off any union member who has been at Moulton more than 2 months.
Vacations	2 weeks for all employees except those with over 20 years' service, who receive 3 weeks.
Holidays	Nine paid per year.
Sick leave	4 paid days per year unless verified by doctor, in which case, can be up to 10 days.
Length of contract	2 years.

Additional Information

1. Hourly wage rates for union members doing similar work elsewhere in the local vicinity average $14.30.
2. A $50 deductible dental insurance plan would cost about $45 per employee.
3. Overtime averaged 185 hours per employee last year.
4. Among competitors, the most frequent vacation, holiday, and sick-leave schedules are as follows: (a) 2 weeks' vacation for starters, 3 weeks after 10 years of service, and 4 weeks after 25 years; (b) 10 paid holidays per year; and (c) 6 paid sick-leave days per year (although there is a wide variation here, with a few firms having no paid sick leave at all).
5. Contract length at similar firms varies from 1 to 3 years.

Procedure

Divide the class into groups of three. Each group consists of a union negotiator, a management negotiator, and an observer. The instructor will provide a role statement for each negotiator. These role statements should not be shared with the other negotiator or with the observer. Each group's task is to negotiate a contract between Moulton Machine Shop and the IMU. Your instructor will tell you how much time you have available for this task. It is important that you settle this contract in the limited time available so that you can avert a costly strike.

As the negotiations proceed, observers should record significant events. (A sample observation form is depicted below.) When the negotiations end, observers will be asked to report the final agreed-upon contract provisions to the rest of the class and to describe the process by which the negotiations took place in each group.

CONTRACT NEGOTIATIONS OBSERVATION FORM	
Clause	**Final settlement**
Wages	_____
Benefits	_____
Overtime	_____
Layoffs	_____
Vacations	_____
Holidays	_____
Sick leave	_____
Length of contract	_____
Other provisions	_____

Questions

1. How do the negotiations begin? Which side talks the most in the beginning? Does each side have a clear understanding of the purpose of the negotiations?
2. What behaviors of the negotiators seem to either bring the parties closer together or drive them farther apart?
3. How does the climate of the negotiations change over time? Which side talks the most as the negotiations wear on? Do the parties agree more or less as time passes?
4. How do the negotiations end? Are the parties friendly with each other? Do they both seem committed to the final solution? Are future union-management relations likely to get better or worse as a result of this agreement?

REFERENCES

1. Deshpande, S. P., & Fiorito, J. (1989). Specific and general beliefs in union voting models. Academy of Management Journal, 32, 883–897.
2. Sweeney's blitz (1997, Feb. 17). BusinessWeek, pp. 56–62.
3. Greenwald, J. (1993, Dec. 6). A growing itch to fight. Time, pp. 34, 35. See also Ayres, B. D., Jr. (1989, Apr. 27). Coal miners' strike hits feelings that go deep. The New York Times, p. A16.
4. Kristol, I. (1978, Oct. 23). Understanding trade unionism. The Wall Street Journal, p. 28.
5. Serrin, W. (1985, Dec. 5). Union at Stevens, yes; upheaval, no. The New York Times, p. A18.
6. Whitford, D. (2001, July 23). Carpenter gives AFL-CIO labor pains. Fortune, pp. 44, 46. See also Tough love for labor (2000, Oct. 16). BusinessWeek, pp. 118, 120. See also Hoffa at halftime (2000, June 26). BusinessWeek, pp. 156–162. See also Kochan, T. A. (1979). How American workers view labor unions. Monthly Labor Review, 103(4), 23–31.
7. Union members summary (2001, Jan. 18). stats.bls.gov/newsrels.htm.
8. Daniels, C. (2001, Apr. 2). Watch for rallies in the valley. Fortune, p. 36.
9. www.AFLCIO.org. Accessed Aug. 15, 2001. See also Bernstein, A. (1996, Nov. 18). Bigger paychecks, yes. Better pay, no. BusinessWeek, p. 116.
10. Executive paywatch. www.aflcio.org. Accessed Aug. 15, 2001.
11. Mellor, S. (1995). Gender composition and gender representation in local unions: Relationships between women's participation in local office and women's participation in local activities. Journal of Applied Psychology, 80, 706–720.
12. Sweeney's blitz, op. cit.
13. Greenhouse, S. (2000, Oct. 24). Labor law hinders unions, leaders say. The Denver Post, p. 20A.
14. Employee tenure in 2000. www.stats.bls.gov/newsrels.htm. Accessed Aug. 15, 2001.
15. Greenwald, op. cit., p. 35. See also Jones, D. (1998, Aug. 10). In labor's drumbeat, an echo of glory days. USA Today, p. 3B.
16. Schuster, M. (1990). Union-management cooperation. In J. A. Fossum (ed.), Employee and labor relations. Washington, DC: Bureau of National Affairs, pp. 4-44–4-81.
17. Brooks, R., & Brannigan, M. (2001, Apr. 24). Delta's pact with pilots will be costly, bolstering higher industry expectations. The Wall Street Journal, pp. A3, A12. See also Brooker, K. (2001, May 28). The chairman of the Board looks back. Fortune, pp. 63–76. See also Will United's woes spread? (2000, Nov. 13). BusinessWeek, pp. 180–190.
18. Dreazen, Y. (2000, Aug. 15). Old labor tries to establish role in new economy. The Wall Street Journal, pp. B1, B10. See also Workers—and bosses—unite? (1999, Apr. 19). BusinessWeek, pp. 66–70. See also Labor relations at crossroads (1998, Sept. 6). The Denver Post, pp. 1L, 11L.
19. Dreazen, op. cit. See also Ball et al., op. cit.
20. Dunlop, J. T. (1988, May). Have the 1980's changed U.S. industrial relations? Monthly Labor Review, pp. 29–34.
21. Dabscheck, B. (2001). "A felt need for increased efficiency": Industrial relations at the end of the millennium. Asia Pacific Journal of Human Resources, 39(2), 4–30.
22. White House lends an ear to airlines in labor woes: Settlements between Delta, Northwest, and unions followed aggressive lobbying (2001, Apr. 24). The Wall Street Journal, p. A26.
23. Dulles, F. R. (1960). Labor in America: A history (2nd rev. ed.). New York: Crowell.
24. Dowling, P. J., Welch, D. E., & Schuler, R. S. (1999). International human resource management (3d ed.). Cincinnati, OH: Southwestern.
25. Rohwedder, C. (1999, Nov. 29). Paying dues: Once the big muscle of German industry, unions see it all sag. *The Wall Street Journal*, pp. A1, A16.

26. Poole, M. (1986). *Industrial relations: Origins and patterns of national diversity.* London: Routledge & Kegan Paul.

27. Commons, J. R., & Filmore, E. A. (eds.) (1958). *Labor conspiracy cases, 1806–1842.* vol. 3 of *A documentary history of American industrial society.* New York: Russell & Russell.

28. Dulles, op. cit.

29. Ibid.

30. Meany's legacy (1980, Jan. 13). *The Miami Herald,* p. 5E.

31. *NLRB v. Babcock & Wilcox* (1956). 105 U.S. 351.

32. Ball, J. (2000, Jan. 31). UAW's reception in Alabama Mercedes plant is sour. *The Wall Street Journal,* p. A15.

33. Mills, D. Q. (1994). Labor-management relations (5th ed.). New York: McGraw-Hill.

34. NLRB proposal on single units criticized (1996, Mar.). *HR News,* p. 2. See also Kilgour, J. G. (1983, Mar.–Apr.). Union organizing activity among white-collar employees. *Personnel,* pp. 18–27.

35. Tough love for labor, op. cit.

36. Wermiel, S. (1983, Nov. 16). NLRB can't force companies to bargain with minority unions, U.S. court rules. *The Wall Street Journal,* p. 12.

37. Greenhouse, op. cit.

38. Zachary, G. P. (1995, Nov. 17). Long litigation often holds up union victories. *The Wall Street Journal,* pp. B1, B15. See also Prosten, W. (1979). The rise in NLRB election delays: Measuring business's new resistance. *Monthly Labor Review, 103*(2), 39–41.

39. Unions holding fewer, winning more elections (1992, Dec.). *Mountain States Employers Council Bulletin,* p. 4.

40. Sweeney's blitz, op. cit.

41. McGolrick, S. (2001, May). NLRB revises standards for employers to withdraw union recognition. *HR News,* pp. 7, 22. See also Swann, J. P., Jr. (1983). The decertification of a union. *Personnel Administrator, 28* (1), 47–51.

42. McGolrick, op. cit.

43. Fisher, K., Ury, W., & Patton, B. (1991). *Getting to yes* (2d ed.). New York: Penguin.

44. Ibid.

45. Thompson, L. (1998). The mind and heart of the negotiator. Upper Saddle River, NJ: Prentice-Hall. See also Lewicki, R. J. (1997). *Negotiation* (3d ed.). Homewood, IL: McGraw-Hill Irwin.

46. Brett, J. M., Shapiro, D. L., & Lytle, A. L. (1998). Breaking the bonds of reciprocity in negotiations. *Academy of Management Journal, 41,* 410–424.

47. Ibid. See also Walton, R. E., & McKersie, R. B. (1965). *A behavioral theory of labor negotiations.* New York: McGraw-Hill.

48. Moran, R. T. (1987). *Getting your yen's worth: How to negotiate with Japan, Inc.* Houston: Gulf.

49. Tinsley, C. H. (2001). How negotiators get to yes: Predicting the constellation of strategies used across cultures to negotiate conflict. *Journal of Applied Psychology, 86,* 583–593.

50. Brett, J. M., & Okumura, T. (1998). Inter- and intra-cultural negotiation: U.S. and Japanese negotiators. *Academy of Management Journal, 41,* 495–510.

51. Ball, J., Burkins, G., & White, G. L. (1999, Dec. 16). Don't walk: Why labor unions have grown reluctant to use the "S" word. *The Wall Street Journal,* pp. A1, A8. See also American Society for Personnel Administration (1983). *Strike preparation manual* (rev. ed.). Berea, OH: Author.

52. Ibid.

53. Ball, Burkins, & White, op. cit. See also Why Mexico scares the UAW (1998, Aug. 3). *BusinessWeek,* pp. 37, 38. See also Up in arms, but down in clout (1998, Aug. 3). *BusinessWeek,* pp. 36, 37. See also Jones, op. cit.

54. Deals end bitter Detroit news fight (2000, Dec. 19). *The Denver Post,* p. 8A.

55. Grossman, R. J. (1998, Sept.). Trying to heal the wounds. *HRMagazine,* pp. 85–92. See also American Society for Personnel Administration, op. cit.

56. Mills, op. cit.

57. Ibid. See also A labor-management standoff of two years nears an end (2001, Aug. 1). *The Wall Street Journal,* p. A1.

58. Oviatt, C. R., Jr. (1995, Oct.). Case shows difficulty of declaring negotiating impasse. *HR News,* pp. 13, 16.

59. Fossum, J. A. (1999). *Labor relations: Development, structure, process* (7th ed.). Burr Ridge, IL: Irwin/McGraw-Hill.

60. Hirschman, C. (2001, July). Order in the hearing! *HRMagazine,* pp. 58–64. See also Ross, W. H., & Conlon, D. E. (2000). Hybrid forms of third-party dispute resolution: Theoretical implications of combining mediation and arbitration. *Academy of Management Review, 25,* 416–427.

61. Ross & Conlon, op. cit.

62. Arnold, J. A., & O'Connor, K. M. (1999). Ombudspersons or peers? The effect of third-party expertise and recommendations on negotiation. *Journal of Applied Psychology, 84,* 776–785.

63. Mills, op. cit

64. Fossum, op. cit.

65. Hirschman, op. cit.

66. Mills, op. cit.

67. Union contracts and the ADA (1996, Nov.–Dec.). *Mountain States Employers Council Bulletin,* p. 2.

68. Mills, op. cit.

69. Ibid.

70. Labig, C. E., & Greer, C. R. (1988). Grievance initiation: A literature survey and directions for future research. *Journal of Labor Research, 9,* 1–27.

71. Ibid.

72. Ibid.

73. Kotlowitz, A. (1987, Aug. 28). Labor's turn? *The Wall Street Journal,* pp. 1, 14. See also Kotlowitz, A. (1987, Apr. 1). Grievous work. *The Wall Street Journal,* pp. 1, 12.

74. Brooks, R. (2001, June 28). Mail disorder: Blizzard of grievances joins a sack of woes at U.S. Postal Service. *The Wall Street Journal,* pp. A1, A4.

75. Mesch, D. J., & Dalton, D. R. (1992). Unexpected consequences of improving workplace justice: A six-year time series assessment. *Academy of Management Journal, 35,* 1099–1114. See also Dalton, D. R., & Todor, W. D. (1981). Win, lose, draw: The grievance process in practice. *Personnel Administrator, 26* (3), 25–29.

76. Aryee, S., & Chay, Y. W. (2001). Workplace justice, citizenship behavior, and turnover intentions in a union context: Examining the mediating role of perceived union support and union instrumentality. *Journal of Applied Psychology, 86,* 154–160.

77. Olson-Buchanan, J. B. (1996). Voicing discontent: What happens to the grievance filer after the grievance? *Journal of Applied Psychology, 81,* 52–63.

78. Meyer, D., & Cooke, W. (1988). Economic and political factors in the resolution of formal grievances. *Industrial Relations, 27,* 318–335.

79. Klaas, B. S. (1989). Managerial decision-making about employee grievances: The impact of the grievant's work history. *Personnel Psychology, 42,* 53–68. See also Dalton, D. R., Todor, W. D., & Owen, C. L. (1987). Sex effects in workplace justice outcomes: A field assessment. *Journal of Applied Psychology,* 72, 156–159. See also Dalton, D. R., & Todor, W. D. (1985). Gender and workplace justice: A field assessment. *Personnel Psychology, 38,* 133–151.

80. Brooks, op. cit.

81. Mesch & Dalton, op. cit.

82. Hirschman, op. cit. See also Egler, T. D. (1995, July). The benefits and burdens of arbitration. *HRMagazine,* pp. 27–30.

83. Arbitrator overruled (1997, Feb.). *Bulletin,* p. 4. Denver: Mountain States Employers Council, Inc. See also Hill, M., Jr., & Sinicropi, A. V. (1980). *Evidence in arbitration.* Washington, DC: Bureau of National Affairs.

84. Egler, op. cit.

85. Labor letter (1989, Nov. 14). *The Wall Street Journal,* p. A1.

86. Pearlstein, S. (2001, Aug. 6). Foreign firms' layoffs hit home for U.S. workers. *The Washington Post,* pp. A1, A8.

87. Why Mexico scares the UAW, op. cit. See also Crutsinger, M. (1997, Feb. 24). Issue of broader NAFTA to focus on lost U.S. jobs. *The Denver Post,* p. 4A.

88. Schneider, S., quoted in Pearlstein, op. cit. p. A8.

89. Freeman, R. B., & Medoff, J. (1984). *What do unions do?* New York: Basic Books.

90. Kleiner, M. M. (1990). The role of industrial relations in industrial performance. In J. A. Fossum (ed.), *Employee and labor relations.* Washington, DC: Bureau of National Affairs, pp. 4-23–4-43.

91. Up in arms, but down in clout, op. cit. See also Labor's surprising reemergence (1997, Feb. 17). *BusinessWeek,* p. 110. See also Linneman, P. D., Wachter, M. L., & Carter, W. H. (1990). Evaluating the evidence on union employment and wages. *Industrial and Labor Relations Review, 44*(1), 34–53.

92. Cited in Hitt, M. (2001, Aug.). The human capital advantage in the new millennium. Paper presented at the Society for Human Resource Management Foundation, Thought Leaders Conference, Washington, DC.

93. Daniels, op. cit. See also Schuster, op. cit.

94. Daniels, op. cit. See also Look who's pushing productivity (1997, Apr. 7). *BusinessWeek,* pp. 72, 73, 75.

95. Schuh, P., cited in Ball, Burkins, & White, op. cit., p. A8.

96. Labor's surprising reemergence, op. cit.

97. Ibid.

98. Cooke, W. N. (1990). Factors influencing the effect of joint union-management programs on employee-supervisor relations. *Industrial and Labor Relations Review, 43,* 587–603. See also Schuster, op. cit.

14 PROCEDURAL JUSTICE AND ETHICS IN EMPLOYEE RELATIONS

Questions This Chapter Will Help Managers Answer

1. How can I ensure procedural justice in the resolution of conflicts between employees and managers?
2. How can I administer discipline without at the same time engendering resentment toward me or my company?
3. How do I fire people legally and humanely?
4. What should be the components of a fair information practice policy?
5. What is ethical decision making in employee relations? What steps or considerations are involved?

ALTERNATIVE DISPUTE RESOLUTION: GOOD FOR THE COMPANY, GOOD FOR EMPLOYEES?*

At the McGraw-Hill Companies in New York, word came down from chief executive Joseph Dionne: It was time to supplement the open-door policy with a formal, in-house ADR program. He told attorneys in the legal department to develop something that settled disputes quickly, something good for morale.

After 6 months of work with consultants, and meetings with employees and managers, as well as executives from Chemical Bank, Cigna, J. C. Penney, and the Brown & Root construction company—all of which have **alternative dispute resolution (ADR) programs**—McGraw-Hill unveiled its Fast and Impartial Resolution (FAIR) ADR program. The three-step program is voluntary, and starts with bringing in a supervisor or an HR representative to resolve a dispute. If that doesn't work, it moves to mediation with a third party. If mediation is fruitless, the third step is binding arbitration with a written decision. The company pays the costs of mediation and arbitration.

The FAIR program is typical of the programs many organizations are developing, as they move from informal fact-finding or open-door policies to formal, structured policies. Clearly such programs are beneficial to employers, for they save time and money. According to JAMS/Endispute, based in Irvine, California, it takes up to 6 weeks, from the time that company is contacted, to the time mediation actually begins. The parties spend an average of 12.5 hours in the process, and problems are resolved in up to 90 percent of cases. Says Douglas McDowell, general counsel for the Equal Employment Advisory Council, an employer association based in Washington with about 300 member companies: "We think mediation is a fairly safe way to go. . . . It allows the participants to meet with trained mediators, diffuse the acrimony, and come to a resolution in a voluntary agreement. Once settled, it's binding, which is enforceable." The Equal Employment Opportunity Commission has been promoting voluntary mediation of employment discrimination claims since mid-1999, although only 36 percent of employers agree to voluntary mediation, while 81 percent of charging parties do.

Houston-based Brown & Root has had about 1,100 ADR cases, with 17 going to arbitration. The cost of an arbitration has ranged from about $6,000 to $20,000, saving 50 percent to 80 percent on legal costs. Roughly 75 percent of the cases are resolved within 2 months, as opposed to several years in the courts. In Irvine, California, American Savings Bank's 2-year old, four-step program is enjoying similar success, reducing legal costs by more than 60 percent.

Challenges

1. What do you see as some key advantages and disadvantages of ADR programs?

Sources: M. M. Clark, Alternative dispute resolution goes mainstream, *HR News,* Aug. 2001, p. 5; M. M. Clark, Supreme Court supports arbitration agreements; *HR News,* May 2001, pp. 1, 20; J. Wetchler, Agreements to arbitrate, *HRMagazine,* Feb. 2000, pp. 127–134; L. C. Outwater, Alternative dispute resolution can save time and money for employees, employers, *HR News,* pp. 36, 37; P. Petesch, & J. Javits, Mediation's on—grab a spoon, *HRMagazine,* Apr. 2000, pp. 163–170; B. Bencivenga, Fair play in the ADR arena, *HRMagazine,* Jan. 1996, pp. 50–56.

2. Should an employee's agreement to binding arbitration be a condition of employment or a condition of continuing employment?
3. Working in small groups, identify characteristics that would make an ADR program fair both for employees and employers.

The chapter-opening vignette illustrates another facet of labor-management accommodation: the use of workplace due process to resolve disputes. It is another attempt to enhance the productivity and QWL of employees. Indeed, the broad theme of this chapter is "justice on the job." We will consider alternative methods for resolving disputes, such as nonunion grievance and arbitration procedures. We also examine discipline and termination in the employment context. Finally, we will examine the growing concern for employee privacy and ethical issues in these three areas: fair information practice in the Internet age, the assessment of job applicants and employees, and whistle-blowing. Let us begin by defining some important terms.

SOME DEFINITIONS

In this chapter we are concerned with three broad issues in the context of employee relations: (1) procedural justice, (2) due process, and (3) ethical decisions about behavior.

Employee relations includes all the practices that implement the philosophy and policy of an organization with respect to employment.[1]

Justice refers to the maintenance or administration of what is just, especially by the impartial adjustment of conflicting claims or the assignment of merited rewards or punishments.[2] It is one of the fundamental bases of cooperative action in organizations.[3]

Procedural justice focuses on the fairness of the procedures used to make decisions. Procedures are fair to the extent that they are consistent across persons and over time, free from bias, based on accurate information, correctable, and based on prevailing moral and ethical standards.[4]

Distributive justice focuses on the fairness of the outcomes of decisions, for example, in the allocation of bonuses or merit pay, or in making reasonable accommodations for employees with disabilities.[5]

Due process in legal proceedings provides individuals with rights such as the following: prior notice of prohibited conduct; timely procedures adhered to at each step of the procedure; notice of the charges or issues prior to a hearing; impartial judges or hearing officers; representation by counsel; opportunity to confront and to cross-examine adverse witnesses and evidence, as well as to present proof in one's own defense; notice of decision; and protection from retaliation for using a complaint procedure in a legitimate manner. These are constitutional due-process rights. They protect individual rights with respect to state, municipal, and federal government processes. However, they normally do not apply to work situations. Hence, employee rights to due process are based on a collective bargaining agreement, on legislative protections, or on procedures provided unilaterally by an employer.[6]

Ethical decisions about behavior concern one's conformity to moral standards or to the standards of conduct of a given profession or group. Ethical decisions about behavior take account not only of one's own interests, but also equally of the interests of those affected by the decision.[7]

WHY ADDRESS PROCEDURAL JUSTICE?

In the wake of decisions that affect them, such as those involving pay, promotions, or assignments, employees often ask, "Was that fair?" Judgments about the fairness or equity of procedures used to make decisions, that is, procedural justice, are rooted in the perceptions of employees. Strong research evidence indicates that such perceptions lead to important consequences, such as employee behavior and attitudes.[8] In short, the judgments of employees about procedural justice matter. Perceptions of fairness are especially important in the context of HR management, for example, in the hiring process, with respect to drug testing, and in performance management, compensation, and layoffs.

Procedurally fair treatment has been demonstrated to result in reduced stress[9] and increased performance, job satisfaction, commitment to an organization, trust, and **organizational citizenship behaviors** (discretionary behaviors performed outside of one's formal role that help other employees perform their jobs or that show support for and conscientiousness toward the organization).[10] These include behaviors such as the following:

- Volunteering to carry out activities that are not formally a part of one's job.
- Persisting with extra enthusiasm or effort when necessary to complete one's own tasks successfully.
- Helping and cooperating with others.
- Following organizational rules and procedures, even when they are personally inconvenient.
- Endorsing, supporting, and defending organizational objectives.[11]

Procedural justice affects citizenship behaviors by influencing employees' perceptions of **organizational support,** the extent to which the organization values employees' general contributions and cares for their well being. In turn, this prompts employees to reciprocate with organizational citizenship behaviors.[12] These effects have been demonstrated to occur at the level of the work group as well as at the level of the individual.[13] In general, perceptions of procedural justice are most relevant and important to employees during times of significant organizational change. When employees experience change, their perceptions of fairness become especially potent factors that determine their attitudes and their behavior.[14] Since the only constant in organizations is change, considerations of procedural justice will always be relevant.

Components of Procedural Justice

Although there is disagreement in the professional literature about the number of components of the broad topic of organizational justice,[15] we consider procedural justice to have three components. The first of these is a *structural* component. Organizational policies and rules may provide lots of opportunities for employee input to decisions. This structural element of procedural justice is known as **employee voice,** and we will have more to say about it below.

Interactional justice is a second component. It refers to the quality of interpersonal treatment that employees receive in their everyday work. Treating others with dignity and respect is the positive side of interactional justice. Derogatory judgments, deception, invasion of privacy, inconsiderate or abusive actions, public criticism, and coercion represent the negative side of interactional justice.[16] Violating any of these elements of interactional justice leads to decreased perceptions of fair treatment. Evidence indicates that employee perceptions of interactional justice that stem from the quality of their relationships with their supervisors are positively related to their performance, citizenship behaviors directed toward their supervisors, and job satisfaction.[17]

Informational justice is the third component of procedural justice. It is expressed in terms of providing explanations or accounts for decisions made. Consider layoffs, for example. Evidence indicates that layoff survivors who were provided explanations for the layoffs, or who received advance notice of them, had more positive reactions to layoffs and higher commitment to the organization.[18] Survivors had the most negative reactions to layoffs when they identified with the victims and when they perceived the layoffs to be unfair.[19]

Think about your own experiences in times of change. Was the fairness of procedures important to you? Did your perceptions affect your attitudes toward your employer and your behavior at work? Did you wish you had more say in decisions that might affect you? This is the role of employee voice systems, and we consider it further in the next section.

PROCEDURAL JUSTICE IN ACTION: EMPLOYEE-VOICE SYSTEMS

For most organizations, the most important thing they can do to ensure procedural justice is to provide individuals and groups the capacity to be heard, a way to communicate their interests upward—a voice system. Voice systems serve four important functions:

1. They assure fair treatment to employees.
2. They provide a context in which unfair treatment can be appealed.
3. They help to improve the effectiveness of an organization.
4. They sustain employee loyalty and commitment.[20]

Here are some examples of voice systems that are commonly used:

- Grievance or internal complaint procedures, by which an employee can seek a formal, impartial review of an action that affects him or her.
- Ombudspersons, who may investigate claims of unfair treatment or act as intermediaries between an employee and senior management and recommend possible courses of action to the parties.[21]
- Open-door policies by which employees can approach senior managers with problems that they may not be willing to take to their immediate supervisor. A related mechanism, particularly appropriate when the immediate supervisor is the problem, is a skip-level policy, whereby an employee

may proceed directly to the next higher level of management above his or her supervisor.

- Participative management systems that encourage employee involvement in all aspects of organizational strategy and decision making.
- Committees or meetings that poll employee input on key problems and decisions.
- Senior-management visits, where employees can meet with senior company officials and openly ask questions about company strategy, policies, and practices or raise concerns about unfair treatment.
- Question-and-answer newsletters, in which employee questions and concerns submitted to a newsletter editor and investigated by that office are answered and openly reported to the organizational community.[22]
- Toll-free telephone numbers that employees can use anonymously to report waste, fraud, or abuse.

Characteristics of Effective Voice Systems

A thorough review of the literature on voice systems revealed five "core" characteristics of the most effective ones. These are shown in Table 14–1.

The first criterion is *elegance.* That is, the system should be simple to understand; it should apply to a broad range of issues, it should use an effective diagnostic framework; and, finally, those who manage the system should be able to respond definitively to the issues raised.

The second criterion is *accessibility.* Effective voice systems are easy to use, well-advertised, comprehensible, open processes. Information is publicized on how to file a complaint. Indeed, research has found that employees view this feature as a key attribute of an effective dispute-handling system.[23]

The third criterion of effective voice systems is *correctness,* that is, the system should provide the "right" answer to problems by being unbiased, thorough, and effective. The more correct a system, the more likely it is that (1) the complainant can provide relevant input about the problem, (2) the organization can investigate and call for more information if it needs it, (3) a system exists

Table 14–1

CORE CHARACTERISTICS OF EFFECTIVE VOICE SYSTEMS

Elegance—simple procedures, broad application, vested authority, good diagnostic system

Accessibility—easy to use, advertised, comprehensive, open process

Corrrectness—administered well, includes follow-up, self-redesigning, correctable outcomes

Responsiveness—timely, culturally-viable, tangible results, management commitment

Nonpunitiveness—appeal system, anonymity, no retaliation for using the system

Source: B. H. Sheppard, R. J. Lewicki, & J. W. Minton, *Organizational justice: The search for fairness in the workplace,* Lexington Books, New York, 1992, p. 149.

for classifying and coding information in order to determine the nature of the problem, (4) employees can appeal lower-level decisions, and (5) both procedures and outcomes make good sense to most employees.[24]

A fourth criterion is *responsiveness.* At the most basic level, responsive systems let individuals know that their input has been received. Thus IBM's "Speak Up" program requires the manager of the function in question to prepare a written response to the employee within 3 days or face severe sanctions. Responsive systems provide timely responses, are backed by management commitment, are designed to fit an organization's culture, provide tangible results, involve participants in the decision-making process, and give those who manage the system sufficient "clout" to ensure that it works effectively.

Finally, effective voice systems are *nonpunitive.* This is essential if employees are to trust the system. Individuals must be able to present problems, identify concerns, and challenge the organization in such a way that they are not punished for providing this input, even if the issues raised are sensitive and highly politicized. If the input concerns wrongdoing or malfeasance, the individual's identity must be protected so that direct or indirect retribution cannot occur. Employees as well as managers must be protected.[25]

INTERNATIONAL APPLICATION
Perceptions of Procedural Justice Across Cultures

Research seems to indicate that perceptions of procedural justice are similar across cultures, and that employee voice systems in particular are associated with judgments of fairness in different cultures. These findings are consistent across cultures as diverse as Argentina, the Dominican Republic, Mexico, Great Britain, the Netherlands, and United States.[26] Another study found that when employees had input (voice) in choosing the method of payment, this affected their judgments of the fairness (distributive justice) of the actual payments made. Both Russian and U.S. participants emphasized the need to base pay allocations on a standard of fairness rather than on equality or individual need.[27]

Individualism and collectivism also seem to influence judgments of procedural justice. Specifically, people in individualistic cultures such as the United States prefer to have higher levels of control over the processes used to make decisions, than do people in more collectivistic cultures, such as China. This may be due to the more confrontational orientation of people in individualistic cultures, in contrast to the orientation toward harmony in collectivistic cultures.[28]

Finally, in terms of the *effects* of perceptions of procedural justice, there may well be differences across cultures. Thus a study in Mexico found that distributive justice was more important than procedural justice was in predicting trust and citizenship behavior. The opposite result was found in the United States and India. In Germany, distributive justice was slightly stronger than procedural justice was in predicting trust. Collectively, the evidence indicates similarity across cultures in the predictors of judgments of justice, but differences in the consequences of procedural and distributive justice across cultures.[29]

Now that we have discussed the theory of procedural justice, let's examine how it can be applied in a number of areas of employee relations. We begin by examining nonunion grievance procedures.

GRIEVANCE PROCEDURES IN NONUNION COMPANIES: WORKPLACE DUE PROCESS

The grievance process has generally worked well in unionized settings, and this is why many companies have extended it as an option to their non-union employees. For example, Federal Express Corporation's "guaranteed fair-treatment process" lets employees appeal problems to a peer review board chosen by the worker involved and management. The board rules for employees about half the time. Bosses cannot appeal decisions, but employees can, to a panel of top executives up to and including the chairman of the board.[30] TWA employees take disputes to a panel comprised of an arbitrator, a representative from the HR staff, and another employee. One reason for the growing popularity of these programs is that they tend to reduce lawsuits. At Aetna Life & Casualty Co., for example, only one of the almost 300 complaints handled by Aetna's program has gone to litigation.[31]

Figure 14–1 illustrates how such a procedure works in one company. This procedure emphasizes the supervisor as a key figure in the resolution of grievances. As a second step, the employee is encouraged to see the department head, an HR representative, or any other member of management. Alternatively, the employee may proceed directly to the roundtable, a body of employee and

Figure 14–1

Example of a nonunion grievance procedure. This diagram indicates the possible routes a grievant may take to resolve a complaint. The regular procedural route is designed to resolve the grievance at the lowest possible level—the supervisor. However, if the grievant feels uncomfortable approaching the supervisor, the grievance may be presented directly to any level of management via the open-door policy or the roundtable. (*Source:* Reprinted from D. A. Drost & F. P. O'Brien, Are there grievances against your non-union grievance procedure? *Personnel Administrator, 28*(1), 1983, 37. Copyright 1983. Reprinted with permission from *HRMagazine* (formerly *Personnel Administrator*), published by the Society for Human Resource Management, Alexandria, VA.)

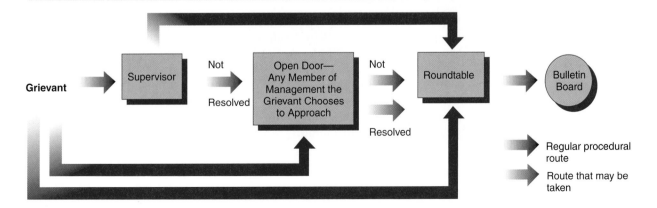

management representatives who meet biweekly to resolve grievances. Management immediately answers those questions that it can and researches those requiring an in-depth review. The minutes of roundtable meetings, plus the answers to the questions presented, are posted conspicuously on bulletin boards in work areas.[32]

To work effectively, a nonunion grievance procedure should meet three requirements:

1. All employees must know about the procedure and exactly how it operates.
2. They must believe that there will be no reprisals taken against them for using it.
3. Management must respond quickly and thoroughly to all grievances.[33]

Workplace due process is one of the fastest-developing trends in industry. In the coming decade, a majority of people-oriented firms are likely to adopt some form of internal complaint procedure. But how does one begin? Here are some key steps[34]:

1. **Create a standardized form for complaints.** This is a more uniform approach than a broad open-door policy. Explain where the form should be sent for centralized processing. Further, since it is a formal complaint, it should not be anonymous.
2. **Acknowledge in writing each complaint received.**
3. **Assign a trained investigator to gather facts and respond to the complainant.**
4. **The investigator should discuss possible actions with the manager who has the power to make a final decision.** The manager then shares the decision with the complainant.
5. **Provide a written report to the complainant.** The report should include a summary of the complaint, key facts uncovered during the investigation, and the outcome of the complaint.
6. **The investigator should document each part of the investigation.** Keep a copy at the centralized processing unit.
7. **Provide employees with an appeal process.**
8. **Make the due-process system visible.** At a minimum, the system should be described in the employee handbook and publicized by HR specialists. SmithKline Beecham goes even further. Periodically, it features its internal complaint procedure on closed-circuit television for all company employees.

The trend toward workplace due process represents an effort by companies to broaden employees' rights in disciplinary matters. A position paper at Control Data stated: "It is inherently difficult for the management power structure to concede to a system that allows review of its decision making. . . . But any concept of employee justice is incomplete without the presence of some mechanism to challenge the power system."[35] Due-process mechanisms build an open, trusting atmosphere, help deter union organizing, and stem the rising number of costly lawsuits claiming wrongful discharge and discrimination.

Discipline

Make no mistake about it: most employees want to conduct themselves in a manner acceptable to the company and to their fellow employees. Occasionally, problems of absenteeism, poor work performance, or rule violations arise. When informal conversations or coaching sessions fail to resolve these problems, formal disciplinary action is called for.

In a unionized firm, the "management rights" clause of the collective bargaining agreement typically retains for management the authority to impose reasonable rules for workplace conduct and to discipline employees for **just cause.** The concept of just cause requires an employer not only to produce persuasive evidence of an employee's liability or negligence, but also to provide the employee a fair hearing and to impose a penalty appropriate to the proven offense.[36] Unions rarely object to employee discipline, provided that (1) it is applied consistently, (2) the rules are publicized clearly, and (3) the rules are considered reasonable.

Discipline is indispensable to management control. Ideally, it should serve as a corrective mechanism to create and maintain a productive, responsive workforce.[37] Unfortunately, some managers go to great lengths to avoid using discipline. To some extent this is understandable, for discipline is one of the hardest HR actions to face. Managers may avoid imposing discipline because of (1) ignorance of organizational rules, (2) fear of formal grievances, or (3) fear of losing the friendship of employees.[38] Yet failure to administer discipline can result in implied acceptance or approval of the offense. Thereafter, problems may become more frequent or severe, and discipline becomes that much more difficult to administer.

As an alternative, some companies are experimenting with a technique called **positive discipline.** On its face, it sounds a lot like traditional discipline dressed up in euphemisms. It works as follows: Employees who commit offenses first get an oral "reminder" rather than a "reprimand." Then comes a written reminder, followed by a paid day off—called a "decision-making leave day" (a suspension, in traditional parlance). There is a homework assignment, namely, the employee has to write a letter to the supervisor explaining how he or she will fix the problem.[39] The paid day off is a one-shot chance at reform. The process is documented, and if the employee does not change, termination follows.

How has positive discipline worked? At Tampa Electric, which has used it for over 10 years, more employees have improved their job performance than have left the company. Says one power-station manager: "Before, we punished employees and treated them worse and worse and expected them to act better. I don't ever recall suspending someone who came back ready to change."[40] These arguments for not imposing punishment are persuasive. But evidence also indicates that discipline (that is, punishment) may be beneficial.[41] Consider that:

- Discipline may alert the marginal employee to his or her low performance and result in a change in behavior.
- Discipline may send a signal to other employees regarding expected levels of performance and standards of behavior.
- If the discipline is perceived as legitimate by other employees, it may increase motivation, morale, and performance.

In fact, statistical reanalyses of the original Hawthorne experiments suggest that managerial discipline was the major factor in increased rates of output.[42] Department managers in a retail store chain who used informal warnings, formal warnings, and dismissals more frequently than their peers had higher departmental performance ratings (in terms of annual cost and sales data and ratings by higher-level managers). This relationship held even when length of service was taken into account. More frequent use of sanctions was associated with improved performance. Why is this so?

The answer may lie in **social-learning theory.**[43] According to this theory, individuals in groups look to others to learn appropriate behaviors and attitudes. They learn them by modeling the behavior of others, by adopting standard operating procedures, and by following group norms. Individuals whose attitudes or behaviors violate these norms may cause problems. Tolerance of such behavior by the supervisor may threaten the group by causing feelings of uncertainty and unfairness. On the other hand, management actions that are seen as maintaining legitimate group standards may instill feelings of fairness and result in improved performance. Failure to invoke sanctions may lead to a loss of management control and unproductive employee behavior.[44] Finally, do not underestimate the *symbolic* value of disciplinary actions, especially since punitive behavior tends to make a lasting impression on employees.[45]

Progressive Discipline

Many firms, both unionized and nonunionized, follow a procedure of **progressive discipline** that proceeds from an oral warning to a written warning to a suspension to dismissal. If progressive discipline is to be effective, however, employers need to follow four rules. Specifically, the employee needs to (1) know what the problem is, (2) know what he or she must do to fix the problem, (3) have a reasonable period of time to fix the problem, and (4) understand the consequences of inaction.[46]

Is it possible to administer discipline without at the same time engendering resentment by the disciplined employee? The answer is yes, if managers follow what Douglas McGregor called the **red-hot-stove rule.** Discipline should be:

Immediate.   Just like touching a hot stove, where feedback is immediate, there should be no misunderstanding about why discipline was imposed. People are disciplined not because of who they are (personality) but because of what they did (behavior).

With Warning.   Small children know that if they touch a hot stove, they will be burned. Likewise, employees must know very clearly what the consequences of undesirable work behavior will be. They must be given adequate warning.

Consistent.   Every time a person touches a red-hot stove, he or she gets burned. Likewise, if discipline is to be perceived as fair, it must be administered consistently, given similar circumstances surrounding the undesirable behavior. Consistency among individual managers across the organization is essential, but evidence indicates (1) that line managers vary considerably in their attitudes about discipline,[47] and (2) that they tend to be less concerned with consistency than with satisfying immediate needs within their work units.[48]

Impersonal.   A hot stove is blind to who touches it. So also, managers cannot play favorites by disciplining subordinates they do not like while allowing the same behavior to go unpunished for those they do like.

A recent review of arbitration cases and case law suggests two other characteristics of a legally defensible progressive-discipline system: (1) *Allow an employee the opportunity to respond,* and (2) *allow employees a reasonable period of time to improve their performance.*[49]

Documenting Performance-Related Incidents

Documentation is a fact of organizational life for most managers. While such paperwork is never pleasant, it should conform to the following guidelines:

- Describe what led up to the incident—the problem and the setting. Is this a first offense or part of a pattern?
- Describe what actually happened, and be specific: that is, include names, dates, times, witnesses, and other pertinent facts.
- Describe what must be done to correct the situation, and by when.
- State the consequences of further violations.

Can you see the parallel with the four rules of progressive discipline described earlier? Conclude the warning by obtaining the employee's signature that he or she has read and understands the warning. A sample written warning is shown in Figure 14–2. Note how it includes each of the ingredients just described.

The Disciplinary Interview

Generally, such interviews are held for one of two reasons: (1) over issues of *workplace conduct,* such as attendance or punctuality, or (2) over issues of *job performance,* such as low productivity. They tend to be very legalistic. As an example, consider the following scenario.

You are a first-line supervisor at a unionized facility. You suspect that one of your subordinates, Steve Fox, has been distorting his time reports to misrepresent his daily starting time. While some of the evidence is sketchy, you know that Fox's time reports are false. Accompanied by an industrial-relations

---

Figure 14–2

Sample written warning of disciplinary action.

DATE: April 14, 2002

TO: J. Hartwig

FROM: D. Curtis

SUBJECT: Written Warning

On this date you were 30 minutes late to work with no justification for your tardiness. A similar offense occurred last Friday. At that time you were told that failure to report for work on schedule will not be condoned. I now find it necessary to tell you in writing that you must report to work on time. Failure to do so will result in your dismissal from employment. Please sign below that you have read and that you understand this warning.

[Name]   [Date]

representative, you decide to confront Fox directly in a disciplinary interview. However, before you can begin the meeting, Fox announces, "I'd appreciate it if a coworker of mine could be present during this meeting. If a coworker cannot be present, I refuse to participate." Your reaction to this startling request is to:

A. Ask Fox which coworker he desires and reconvene the meeting once the employee is present.

B. Deny his request and order him to participate or face immediate discipline for insubordination.

C. Terminate the meeting with no further discussion.

D. Ignore the request and proceed with the meeting, hoping that Fox will participate anyway.

E. Inform Fox that, as his supervisor, you are a coworker and attempt to proceed with the meeting.

Unless your reaction was A or C, you have probably committed a violation of the National Labor Relations Act.[50]

In *NLRB v. J. Weingarten, Inc.,* the Supreme Court ruled that a *union* employee has the right to demand that a union representative be present at an investigatory interview that the employee reasonably believes may result in disciplinary action.[51] And in *Epilepsy Foundation of Northeast Ohio* (July 20, 2000), the NLRB held that the *Weingarten* principle should be extended to nonunion employees as well. This decision was upheld by the U.S. Court of Appeals for the District of Columbia Circuit on November 2, 2001.[52] To summarize the Weingarten mandate:

1. The employee must *request* representation; the employer has no obligation to offer it voluntarily. If such a request is made, the employee representative may meet with the employee privately before the investigatory interview takes place.[53]

2. The employee must reasonably believe that the investigation may result in disciplinary action taken against him or her.

3. The employer is not obligated to carry on the interview or to justify its refusal to do so. The employer may simply cancel the interview and thus effectively disallow union or coworker representation.

4. The employer has no duty to bargain with any union representative during the interview, and the employee or union representative may not limit the employer's questioning.[54]

If the National Labor Relations Board determines that these rights were violated and that an employee subsequently was disciplined for conduct that was the subject of the unlawful interview, the board will issue a "make-whole" remedy. This may include (1) restitution of back pay, (2) an order expunging from the employee's employment records any notation of related discipline, or (3) a cease-and-desist order. To avoid these kinds of problems, top management must decide what company policy will be in such cases, communicate that policy to first-line supervisors, and give them clear, concise instructions regarding their responsibilities should an employee request representation at an investigatory interview.[55]

Having satisfied their legal burden, how should supervisors actually conduct the disciplinary interview? They must do *nine* things well:

1. Come to the interview with as many facts as possible. Check the employee's employment file for previous offenses as well as for evidence of exemplary behavior and performance.

2. Conduct the interview in a quiet, private place. "Praise in public, discipline in private" is a good rule to remember. Whether the employee's attitude is truculent or contrite, recognize that he or she will be apprehensive. In contrast to other interviews, where your first objective is to dispel any fears and help the person relax, a "light touch" is inappropriate here.

3. Avoid aggressive accusations. State the facts in a simple, straightforward way. Be sure that any fact you use is accurate, and never rely on hearsay, rumor, or unconfirmed guesswork.

4. Be sure that the employee understands the rule in question and the reason it exists.

5. Allow the employee to make a full defense, even if you think he or she has none. If any point the employee makes has merit, tell him or her so and take it into consideration in your final decision.

6. Stay cool and calm; treat the subordinate as an adult. Never use foul language or touch the subordinate. Such behaviors may be misinterpreted or grossly distorted at a later date.

7. If you made a mistake, be big enough to admit it.

8. Consider extenuating circumstances, and allow for honest mistakes on the part of the subordinate.

9. Even when corrective discipline is required, try to express confidence in the subordinate's worth as a person and ability to perform acceptably in the future. Rather than dwelling on the past, which you cannot change, focus on the future, which you can.

Employment-at-Will

For the 85 percent of U.S. workers who are not covered by a collective-bargaining agreement or an individual-employment contract, dismissal is an ever-present possibility.[56] **Employment-at-will** is created when an employee agrees to work for an employer but there is no specification of how long the parties expect the agreement to last. Under a century-old common law in the United States, employment relationships of indefinite duration can, in general, be terminated at the whim of either party.[57] Furthermore, under certain situations, successful victims of unjust dismissal can collect sizable punitive and compensatory damages from their former employers. Thus an analysis of 120 wrongful discharge cases that went to trial in California found that the average salary of fired employees was $36,254. Plaintiffs won 67.5 percent of their cases and were awarded an average of $646,855. About 40 percent of the awards were for punitive damages.[58] It's important to note, however, that initial jury awards, while frequently high, are almost always reduced after trial, according to a study by the Rand Institute for Civil Justice. Half of all damage awards in California, for example, are for less than $177,000.[59]

COMPANY EXAMPLE   **FIRED EMPLOYEE SHOWS CHARACTER DEFAMATION[60]**

A $15.6 million Texas jury verdict against Procter & Gamble Co. illustrates just how costly such suits can be. The case involved Don Hagler, a 41-year company employee who claimed P&G fired him after publicly accusing him of stealing a $35 company telephone. Mr. Hagler proved that the phone was his property and that P&G libeled him by posting notices accusing him of theft on 11 bulletin boards and on the plant's electronic-mail system. He testified that P&G used him as an example to stop a rash of thefts at the plant. After his firing, he applied for more than 100 jobs, only to be turned down when prospective employers learned why he had been fired by P&G. The state-court jury agreed with Mr. Hagler and awarded him $1.6 million in actual damages and $14 million in punitive damages.

In recent years, several important exceptions to the "at-will" doctrine have emerged. These exceptions provide important protections for workers. The first—and most important—is legislative. Federal laws limit an employer's right to terminate at-will employees for such reasons as age, race, sex, religion, national origin, union activity, reporting of unsafe working conditions, or disability.[61] However, employment-at-will is primarily a matter of state law.[62]

Such suits are now permitted in 46 states, and in many of them courts have shown a willingness to apply traditional causes of action—such as defamation, fraud, intentional infliction of emotional distress, and invasion of privacy—to this area of employment law.[63]

State courts have carved out three judicial exceptions. The first is a **public policy exception.** That is, an employee may not be fired because he or she refuses to commit an illegal act, such as perjury or price fixing. Employees in 43 states can sue if their dismissal violates a public policy.[64] Second, when an employer has promised not to terminate an employee except for unsatisfactory job performance or other good cause, the courts will insist that the employer carry out that promise. This includes **implied promises** (such as oral promises and implied covenants of good faith and fair dealing) as well as explicit ones.[65] For example, in *Fortune v. National Cash Register Company,* a salesperson (Mr. Fortune) was fired after he sold a large quantity of cash registers. Under the terms of his contract, Mr. Fortune would not receive a portion of his commission until the cash registers were delivered. He claimed he was fired before delivery was made to avoid payment of the full $92,000 commission on the order. The court held that terminating Mr. Fortune solely to deprive him of his commissions would breach the covenant of good faith implied in every contract.[66] In addition, courts in 34 states have found that informal assurances of job security can sometimes amount to an enforceable contract.[67]

The third exception allows employees to seek damages for outrageous acts related to termination, including character defamation (see the Company Example above). This includes so-called **retaliatory discharge** cases, in which a worker is fired for actions ranging from filing a workers' compensation claim to reporting safety violations to government agencies. The Supreme Court has ruled that where state law permits (as it does in 34 states), union as well as nonunion employees have the right to sue over their dismissals, even if they are covered by a collective bargaining contract that provides a grievance procedure and remedies.[68]

For some employers, however, relief is in sight. Since 1988, the California Supreme Court has disallowed thousands of lawsuits by employees seeking punitive damages for wrongful discharge.[69] On the other hand, courts in many states—notably Illinois, Massachusetts, Michigan, and New York—expressly permit punitive damages in certain instances.[70]

To avoid potential charges of unjust dismissal, managers should scrutinize each facet of the HR management system. They should look, for example, at the following:

Recruitment.   Beware of creating implicit or explicit contracts in recruitment advertisements. Ensure that no job duration is implied and that employment is not guaranteed or "permanent."

Interviewing.   Phrases intended to entice a candidate into accepting a position, such as "employment security," "lifelong relationship" with the company, "permanent" hiring, and so forth, can create future problems.

Employment Applications.   Include a statement that describes the rights of the at-will employee, as well as those of the employer. However, do not be so strident that you scare off applicants.

Handbooks and Manuals.   A major source of company policy statements regarding "permanent" employment and discharge for "just cause" is the employee handbook. According to a growing number of state laws, such handbook language constitutes an implied contract for employment. Courts have upheld an employer's prerogative to refrain from making any promises to employees regarding how a termination will be conducted or the conditions under which they may be fired. However, if an employer does make such a promise of job security, whether implied verbally or in writing in an employment document or employee handbook, the employer is bound by that promise.[71]

Performance Appraisals.   Include training and written instructions for all raters, and use systems that minimize subjectivity to the greatest extent possible. Give employees the right to read and comment on their appraisals, and require them to sign an acknowledgment that they have done so whether or not they agree with the contents of the appraisal.[72] Encourage managers to give "honest" appraisals; if an employee is not meeting minimum standards of performance, "tell it like it is" rather than leading the employee to believe that his or her performance is satisfactory. Document employee misconduct and poor performance, and provide a progressive disciplinary policy, thereby building a record establishing "good cause."[73]

Employment Contracts

Earlier we noted that employees with contracts (bargained collectively or individually) are not at-will employees. In fact, where a collective bargaining contract does exist, employers cannot enter into separate employment agreements with employees covered by that contract.[74] However, more and more executives, professionals, and even middle managers are demanding contracts. While getting a contract can be a wise career move, when is the proper time to ask for one—and how?

You should consider asking for a contract in any business where the competition for talent is intense, where ideas are at a premium, or when the conditions of your employment differ in unusual ways from a company's standard practices. A contract assures you of a job and a minimum salary for some period of time, usually 2 to 3 years, during which you agree not to quit. Other typical provisions include your title, compensation (salary, procedures for salary increases, bonuses), benefits, stock options, length of vacation, the circumstances under which you can be fired, and severance pay. However, with all these perks come a handful of restrictive covenants, or clauses, that basically limit your ability to work elsewhere. For example[75]:

- A *nonsolicitation* clause prohibits you from recruiting key clients or employees away from your former employer for a year or two.
- *"Payback"* clauses require that you not take another job until you have repaid the company any expenses incurred in your relocation and recruitment.
- Less common is a clause that mandates that the company must have an opportunity to *match* any employment offer that you get. If the employer matches a competing offer, you must remain.
- A *no-disclosure* clause prohibits you from divulging trade secrets or other proprietary information to outsiders during your employment at a company or after you leave.
- A *no-compete* clause bars you from working for a competitor for 6 months to 2 years. The clause is valid whether you are fired, your job is eliminated, or you leave voluntarily.

No-compete agreements are most common in such highly competitive industries as computers, pharmaceuticals, toys, biotechnology, and electronics. However, whether or not a contract has been signed, executives are still required to maintain all trade secrets with which their employers have entrusted them. This obligation, often called a **fiduciary duty of loyalty,** cannot keep the executive out of the job market, but it does provide the former employer with legal recourse if an executive joins a competitor and tells all. Indeed, this is precisely what McDonald's claimed when it succeeded in muzzling a former market researcher.[76]

COMPANY EXAMPLE   ## McLITIGATION

The former employee (we'll call him McEx) was an expert in market research. He quit to join a competitor a few years ago, taking with him a large batch of papers. McDonald's filed suit, alleging that he walked away with company secrets.

Before filing suit and within a few days of his leaving, McDonald's sent a letter to McEx warning him not to divulge any "confidential information" regarding activities such as marketing, advertising, training methods, profit margins, raw materials prices, selling prices, and operating procedures.

The letter further requested a meeting with McEx, during which he would be asked to return any written materials he had taken from McDonald's and

also to sign an agreement not to divulge any company trade secrets to his new employer.

When McEx declined to attend the meeting, McDonald's promptly filed suit in McEx's new home state. The company managed to win a temporary restraining order that McEx says effectively meant he could not perform any market research for his new employer. He was thereafter relegated to less important work.

Finally, about 6 months after the suit was filed, the case was settled out of court. McEx agreed not to use information gained on the job with McDonald's in his new job. But the issue had become academic. Disenchanted with his new nonjob and aware that his new employer was viewing him more as a problem than as an asset, McEx left his new job. He is now employed by another food chain, not involving fast-food restaurants. In short, companies are now playing hardball when it comes to the disclosure of trade secrets. For both parties, the stakes are high.

Another scenario was recently played out in front of a national audience when a key executive of Campbell" soup, who had signed a no-compete agreement, "jumped ship" to go to work for Campbell's main rival, H. J. Heinz Company. After weeks of acrimonious litigation, a settlement finally was reached. It included an agreement that the departing Campbell's executive would not be allowed to begin working for Heinz for several months, would keep a log of all contacts he had with Heinz employees once he did start working there, and would forfeit pension and other benefits from Campbell's. For its part, Heinz agreed to permit certain of its facilities to be inspected regularly to assure Campbell's that none of its trade secrets were being used.[77]

Companies say they need no-compete agreements now that growing numbers of acquisitions, bankruptcies, mergers, and layoffs regularly set loose employees with access to trade secrets and other sensitive information. Sometimes, however, judges find that the agreements go too far in restraining employees. In such cases they will modify terms to make them less restrictive (e.g., with respect to geographical boundaries or the length of time an employee is barred from competing).[78]

From the company's perspective, it is important to recognize that employment agreements are governed by state law. Thus a company with facilities in multiple states may have to contend with multiple interpretations of the same agreement. To avoid that, firms generally include a **choice-of-law provision,** which designates that the laws of a particular state will be used to interpret the contract. Finally, a contract should state that it reflects the entire agreement of the parties, and can only be amended in writing when signed by both parties. This provision prevents employee claims that the employer made oral promises or agreements that expanded his or her rights.[79]

Now back to the negotiation process for employment contracts. In dealing with a prospective employer, do not raise the issue of a contract until you have been offered a job and have thoroughly discussed the terms of your employment. How do you broach the subject? Calmly. Say, for example, "I'd appreciate a letter confirming these arrangements." If the employer asks why, you might point out that both of you are used to putting business agreements on paper and that it's to your mutual benefit to keep all these details straight.[80]

Here are some tips on how to negotiate an employment contract:

1. Keep the tone upbeat. Don't use the words "I" and "you"; talk about "we"— as though you're already aboard.
2. Decide beforehand on three or four "make-or-break" issues (e.g., salary, job assignment, location). These are your "need-to-haves." Also make a list of secondary issues, called "nice-to-haves" (e.g., company car, sign-on bonus).
3. Negotiate the entire package at one time. Don't keep coming back to nit-pick.
4. Be flexible (except on your make-or-break issues); let the company win on some things.

Once you receive the proposed contract, have an attorney review it before you sign. Remember: employment contracts are legally enforceable documents.

Termination

We discussed layoffs in Chapter 10. The focus here is on how to terminate employees for cause, typically for disciplinary reasons or for poor performance. Termination is one of the most difficult tasks a manager has to perform. As we learned in our discussion of employment-at-will, disgruntled former employees are winning about two-thirds of court cases contesting their dismissals. Clearly, there is room for improvement on the part of managers. For those fired, the perception of inequity, of procedural injustice, is often what drives them to court.

Termination is not an infrequent occurrence, since some 2 million workers in the United States are fired every year[81]—and this doesn't include large-scale layoff announcements, which totaled 1.96 million U.S. jobs in 2001.[82] With respect to layoffs, while the *Plant Closing Law* of 1988 requires employers of more than 100 workers to grant 60 days' written notice before closing a plant or before laying off more than one-third of a workforce in excess of 150 people, very few firms provide any training to supervisors on how to conduct terminations.[83]

While termination may be traumatic for the employee, it is often no less so for the boss. Faced with saying the words "Your services are no longer required," even the strongest person can get the "shakes," sleepless nights, and sweaty palms.[84] So how should termination be handled? Certainly not the way it was at one company that was trying to downsize. At 8:30 A.M. all employees were ordered to their offices. Between then and 10:30 A.M., like angels of death, managers accompanied by security guards knocked on the office doors; brusquely informed the affected employees that their services were no longer required; gave them boxes in which to place their personal articles; and asked them to leave the premises within 15 minutes, each accompanied by a security guard. . . . Is this procedural justice? Certainly not.

As an alternative, more humane procedure, companies should familiarize all supervisors with company policies and provide a termination checklist to use when conducting dismissals. One such checklist is shown in Figure 14–3.

Before deciding to dismiss an employee, managers should conduct a detailed review of all relevant facts, including the employee's side of the story. To ensure consistent treatment, the supervisor should also examine how similar cases have been handled in the past. Once the decision to terminate has been made, the termination interview should minimize the trauma for the affected employee. Prior to conducting such an interview, the supervisor should be prepared to answer three basic questions: Who? When? Where?

THE TERMINATION CHECKLIST

Documentation

_____ If the job is eliminated, gather supporting evidence of a company or department reduction in head-count.

_____ If poor performance is the reason, the file should contain copies of several successive poor appraisals that were transmitted to (and usually signed by) the candidate at the time they were prepared.

Clearances

_____ Who needs to approve the termination?

Prior Notices

_____ Safeguards to prevent leaks to the public
_____ Key staff members
_____ Board members
_____ Key customers
_____ Regulatory agency officers

Precautions for New Leaks

_____ Ignore the leak
_____ Advance the date of termination to immediate
_____ Delay the termination with no comment

Terms of Termination

_____ Resignation
_____ Transfer to special assignment
_____ Early retirement
_____ Outright termination

Legal Precautions

_____ Salary
_____ Bonuses
_____ Benefits
_____ Other obligations
_____ Scientists and inventors
_____ No-compete agreements

Public Announcements

_____ Should it be a standard press release?
_____ What should the content of the statement be?

Personal Considerations

_____ Medical data
_____ Significant dates
_____ Family circumstances
_____ Personal emotional state

Figure 14–3

The termination checklist. (*Source:* D. H. Sweet, Outplacement. In W. F. Cascio (ed.), *Human resource planning, employment, and placement,* Bureau of National Affairs, Washington, DC, 1989, pp. 246, 247.)

Who? The responsibility for terminating rests with the manager of the individual who is to be released. No one else has the credibility to convey this difficult message.

When? This decision may be crucial to the success of the termination process. First of all, consider personal situations—birthdays, anniversaries, family illnesses. Some experts caution that Friday is the worst day of the week for terminations because it leaves the employee with the entire weekend to brood before he or she can take any positive action.[85] On the other hand, this is less of a concern now that so many organizations are recruiting over the Web.

Where? Neutral territory—not the manager's or the employee's office. The firing manager should arrange a neutral location so that each party is easily able to leave after the interview.

Figure 14–3 (cont.)	

The Termination Interview

_____ Think through details.
_____ When? Not late on Friday.
_____ Who? It's the line manager's responsibility.
_____ Where? Best place is in a neutral area or the candidate's office.
_____ Outplacement consultant on hand?
_____ Termination letter prepared?

Orderly Transitions of Commitments

_____ Reassign internal assignments and projects.
_____ External activities to be reassigned:
   • Customer servicing
   • Convention or professional meetings
   • Speeches and public relations commitments
   • Civic and professional commitments
   • Club memberships
   • Board memberships, e.g., of subsidiaries

Regrouping the Staff

_____ Announcement to immediate colleagues and support staff
_____ What they are to be told
_____ Transfer of assignments
_____ References
_____ Reassurances

Termination Letters

_____ Written evidence to verify the termination
_____ Summary of important information the candidates may not have listened to, or remembered
_____ Brief and businesslike confirmation of the facts and the details
_____ Include:
   • Termination date
   • Severance or bridging pay allowance
   • Vacation pay
_____ Continuation of benefits:
   • Regular benefits
   • Special benefits, such as pension rights
_____ Job search support:
   • Logistical
   • Financial
   • Outplacement
   • Transfer of responsibilities
   • Continuation of responsibilities
   • Return of company property
   • Legal documents
   • Conditions of termination?

Source: Reprinted with permission from James J. Gallagher, chairman, J. J. Gallagher Associates, New York, N.Y.

Following these activities, the firing manager should follow five rules for the termination interview[86]:

1. **Present the situation in a clear, concise, and final manner.** Don't confuse the message to be delivered, and don't drag it out. "Tom, no doubt you are aware that the organization has eliminated some jobs, and one of them is yours." Remember: Spend only a few minutes, don't make excuses, don't bargain, and don't compromise. Get to the point quickly and succinctly. As one outplacement executive noted: "It's not cruel to cut clean."[87]

2. **Avoid debates or a rehash of the past.** Every employee has some redeeming features, so emphasize something positive about the employee, along with any deficiencies that may have contributed to the termination deci-

sion. Arguments about past performance may only compound bad feelings that already exist.

3. **Never talk down to the individual.** Be considerate and supportive, and allow the employee to maintain his or her dignity. Your objective should be to remove as much of the emotion and trauma as possible. Emphasize that it's a situation that isn't working and that the decision is made. It's a business decision—don't make excuses or apologies.

4. **Be empathetic but not compromising.** "I'm sorry that this has to happen, but the decisions are made. We are going to provide assistance to you [or to each of the people affected]."

5. **What's the next step?** "I'm going to give you this letter outlining the severance, benefit, and outplacement arrangements. I suggest you take the rest of the day off and plan on being here at 9 A.M. tomorrow to talk with the benefits people. Also, we have engaged a very successful outplacement firm, and I would like to introduce you to Fred Martin, who, if you wish, will be working with you through your transition."[88]

Be prepared for a variety of reactions from disbelief to silent acceptance to rage. The key is to remain calm and focus on helping the employee confront the reality of the situation. Maintain your distance and composure. It does no good to argue or to cry along with the employee.

After terminations or layoffs, the work attitudes and behaviors of remaining employees ("survivors") may suffer. If the layoff (or its management, or both) is perceived to be unjust—for example, if it is seen as a result of mismanagement, as opposed to external conditions—survivors are likely to feel angry.[89] In addition, they may feel guilty, thinking that they, rather than their laid-off coworkers, could have been dismissed just as easily. This layoff-induced stress, with its attendant feelings of anger, guilt, and job insecurity, can be reduced in two ways. One, provide extra social support (e.g., from coworkers and supervisors) to those survivors who are perceived as especially "at risk." Two, organizations that provide outplacement support to those who are dismissed enjoy, as a secondary benefit, reduced post-layoff stress among survivors.[90]

Finally, public disclosure of termination practices (e.g., in the case of layoffs) may actually help displaced employees, since it assures potential employers that economic factors—not individual shortcomings—caused the dismissals.[91] Having examined a very public issue, termination, let us now turn our attention to a related issue, employee privacy.

EMPLOYEE PRIVACY AND ETHICAL ISSUES

Privacy refers to the interest employees have in controlling the use that is made of their personal information and in being able to engage in behavior free from regulation or surveillance.[92] Attention centers on three main issues: the kind of information collected and retained about individuals, how this information is used, and the extent to which it can be disclosed to others. These issues often lead to **ethical dilemmas** for managers, that is, situations that have the potential to result in a breach of acceptable behavior.

But what is "acceptable" behavior? The difficulty lies in maintaining a proper balance between the common good and personal freedom, between the

Public computer networks provide access to vast amounts of information. Personal privacy is a major business and public policy issue.

legitimate business needs of an organization and a worker's feelings of dignity and worth.[93] Although we cannot prescribe the *content* of ethical behavior across all conceivable situations, we can prescribe *processes* that may lead to an acceptable (and temporary) consensus among interested parties regarding an ethical course of action. In the remainder of this chapter, we will examine several areas that pose potential ethical dilemmas for employers and privacy concerns for employees or job applicants. Let us begin by considering fair information practice policies.

Fair Information Practices in the Internet Age

The *Electronic Communications Privacy Act* of 1986 prohibits "outside" interception of electronic mail by a third party—the government, the police, or an individual—without proper authorization (such as a search warrant). Information sent on public networks, such as Hotmail and America On Line

(AOL), to which individuals and companies subscribe, is therefore protected. However, the law does not cover "inside" interception, for example, on a company's Intranet, and, in fact, no absolute privacy exists in a computer system, even for bosses.[94] Bosses may view employees on video monitors; tap their phones, e-mail, and network communications; and rummage through their computer files with or without employee knowledge or consent, 24 hours a day.[95] Bosses can tag along secretly when you're surfing the Internet, and they can even put video cameras in washrooms—though not in the stalls.[96] Among major U.S. companies, about 74 percent do some form of electronic monitoring of employees. Some 54 percent monitor Internet connections, 38 percent e-mail, 31 percent computer files, and 11.5 percent phone conversations.[97]

Why do employers monitor their employees? They are mostly worried about two things: their legal liability and employees' productivity. Companies monitor e-mail and Net activity to minimize their exposure to defamation, trade secret, and breach-of-contract lawsuits. They also worry about copyright infringement suits based on material employees download, including pictures, music files, and software. Their biggest concern, however, has to do with sexually explicit, racist, or other potentially offensive material that could lead to charges of a hostile work environment, as defined by harassment and discrimination laws. As an employee, how do you stay out of trouble? Consider adhering to the following practices in your personal conduct at work:

- Know your company's written policy. Ask your boss what constitutes "unreasonable" or "inappropriate" use.
- If you have any doubt about what personal Internet use your company allows, total abstinence is the best bet.
- Use your own e-mail account instead of your company's for personal correspondence at work.
- Limit personal surfing and e-mail to times clearly outside office hours.

Ethical Dilemma
When a Soon-to-Be-Laid-Off Employee Asks for Advice[98]

You are a manager of a division targeted for layoffs. You've seen the list of employees to be cut, but you've been asked to keep the information secret for 2 weeks. An employee on the list asks you whether he should be putting a down payment on his first home.

If you don't tell him, then he could be heading into a financial nightmare. If you do tell, you obviously break confidence with your company. Word may spread, panicking enough employees that you end up with a stampede to the exit door. The problem deepens if yours is a public company implementing layoffs because of a pending merger or acquisition that has yet to be announced. If the employee you tell acts on the information or passes it on to others who do, you might incur legal problems because of violated securities regulations. What would you do?

- When composing e-mail or downloading Internet information, ask yourself whether you would be willing to post it on your office door. If the answer is no, then don't proceed further.
- Remember this: When it comes to privacy in the workplace, you don't have any.[99]

Safeguards to protect personal privacy are more important than ever. Yet the results of a recent survey of top corporate managers of 300 businesses of all sizes and in a wide range of industries revealed some unsettling facts. Nearly half collect information on employees without informing them, 38 percent do not even tell them the types of records that are kept, and 44 percent don't explain how the records are used. Fully 70 percent disclose personal information to credit grantors without a subpoena or employee consent.[100] What should managers do? To establish a fair information practice policy, here are some general recommendations:

1. Set up guidelines and policies to protect information in the organization: types of data to be sought, methods of obtaining the data, retention and dissemination of information, employee or third-party access to information, release of information about former employees, and mishandling of information.
2. Inform employees of these information-handling policies.
3. Become thoroughly familiar with state and federal laws regarding privacy.
4. Establish a policy that states specifically that employees and prospective employees cannot waive their rights to privacy.
5. Establish a policy that any manager or nonmanager who violates these privacy principles will be subject to discipline or termination.[101]

Next, managers should articulate, communicate, and implement fair information practice policies by taking the following actions:[102]

1. Avoid fraudulent, secretive, or unfair means of collecting data. When possible, collect data directly from the individual concerned.
2. Do not maintain secret files on individuals. Inform them of what information is stored on them, the purpose for which it was collected, how it will be used, and how long it will be kept.
3. Collect only job-related information that is relevant for specific decisions.
4. Maintain records of individuals or organizations who have regular access or who request information on a need-to-know basis.
5. Periodically allow employees the right to inspect and update information stored on them.
6. Gain assurance that any information released to outside parties will be used only for the purposes set forth prior to its release.

Companies that have taken such measures, such as IBM, Bank of America, AT&T, Cummins Engine, Avis, and TRW report that they have not been overly costly, produced burdensome traffic in access demands, or reduced the general quality of their HR decisions. Furthermore, they receive strong employee approval for their policies when they ask about them on company attitude surveys. By matching words with deeds, companies such as these are weaving their concerns for employee privacy into the very fabric of their corporate cultures.

Assessment of Job Applicants and Employees

Decisions to hire, promote, train, or transfer are major events in individuals' careers. Frequently, such decisions are made with the aid of tests, interviews, situational exercises, performance appraisals, and other assessment techniques. Developers and users of these instruments must be concerned with questions of fairness, propriety, and individual rights, as well as with other ethical issues.

Developers, if they are members of professional associations such as the American Psychological Association, the Society for Human Resource Management, or the Academy of Management, are bound by the ethical standards put forth by those bodies. Managers who use assessment instruments are subject to other ethical principles, beyond the general concerns for accuracy and equality of opportunity. These include[103]:

- Guarding against invasion of privacy (e.g., with respect to biodata items, four areas seem to generate the greatest concern: self-incriminating items, items that require applicants to recall traumatic events, intimacy, and religion).[104]
- Guaranteeing confidentiality.
- Obtaining informed consent from employees and applicants before assessing them.
- Respecting employees' rights to know (e.g., regarding test content and the meaning, interpretation, and intended use of scores).
- Imposing time limitations on data (i.e., removing information that has not been used for HR decisions, especially if it has been updated).
- Using the most valid procedures available, thereby minimizing erroneous acceptances and erroneous rejections.
- Treating applicants and employees with respect and consideration (i.e., by standardizing procedures for all candidates).

What can applicants do when confronted by a question they believe is irrelevant or an invasion of privacy? Some may choose not to respond. However, research indicates that employers tend to view such nonresponse as an attempt to conceal facts that would reflect poorly on an applicant. Hence applicants (especially those who have nothing to hide) are ill advised not to respond.[105] Clearly, it is the employer's responsibility to (1) know the kinds of questions that are being asked of candidates and (2) to review the appropriateness and job-relatedness of all such questions.

Whistle-Blowing

Just as a referee on a playing field can blow a whistle to stop action, former or current organization members can disclose illegal, immoral, or illegitimate practices under the control of their employers to persons or organizations that may be able to do something about them.[106] This practice is known as **whistle-blowing.** Research indicates that individuals can be conditioned to behave unethically (if they are rewarded for it), especially under increased competition,[107] but that the threat of punishment has a counterbalancing influence.[108] More important, when a formal or informal organizational policy that favors ethical behavior is present, ethical behavior tends to increase.[109]

IMPACT OF PROCEDURAL JUSTICE AND ETHICS ON PRODUCTIVITY, QUALITY OF WORK LIFE, AND THE BOTTOM LINE

As we have seen throughout this chapter, employees and former employees are very sensitive to the general issue of "justice on the job." On a broad range of issues, they expect to be treated justly, fairly, and with due process. Doing so certainly contributes to improved productivity and quality of work life, for grievances are both time consuming and costly. On the other hand, organizations that disregard employee rights can expect two things: (1) to be hit with lawsuits and (2) to find courts and juries to be sympathetic to tales of employer wrongdoing. Whistle-blower cases illustrate this trend clearly. As for employers contesting such suits, one corporate attorney noted: "Whistle-blower claims are the nastiest form of litigation we engage in. They take an incredible emotional toll on both employees and employers."[111] The monetary

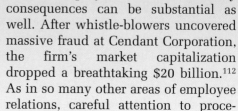

consequences can be substantial as well. After whistle-blowers uncovered massive fraud at Cendant Corporation, the firm's market capitalization dropped a breathtaking $20 billion.[112] As in so many other areas of employee relations, careful attention to procedural justice and ethical decision making yields direct as well as indirect benefits. The old adage "an ounce of prevention is worth a pound of cure" says it all.

Research with almost 8,600 employees of 22 federal agencies and departments revealed that those who had observed alleged wrongdoing were more likely to blow the whistle if they:

- Were employed by organizations perceived by others to be responsive to complaints.
- Held professional positions, had long service, and had positive reactions to their work.
- Had recently been recognized for good performance.
- Were male (although race was unrelated to whistle-blowing).
- Were members of large work groups.[110]

These findings are consistent with other research that has destroyed the myth that whistle-blowers are social misfits. Most of them are well-adjusted individuals who have strong personal values that they live by.[113]

Despite retaliation, financial loss, and high emotional and physical stress,[114] there are at least two reasons why more whistle-blowers are likely to come forward in the future. One, 40 states (and the federal government) now protect the jobs of workers who report wrongdoing by their companies.[115] Two, disclosure of fraud, waste, and abuse by federal contractors can lead to substantial financial gains by whistle-blowers. As a result of recent amendments to the federal False Claims Act of 1863, private citizens may sue a contractor for fraud on the government's behalf and share up to 30 percent of whatever financial recovery the government makes as a result of the charges. Such an incentive helped the government recover more than $1.2 billion from cheaters between 1987 and 1997. On the other hand, only about 11 percent of False Claims Act cases produce a recovery, and defending a claim, even if baseless, can cost $400,000.[116]

IMPLICATIONS FOR MANAGEMENT PRACTICE

Managers who fail to address employee concerns for ethics and procedural justice do so at their peril. Ethics programs are control systems whose objectives are to standardize employee behavior within the domains of ethics and legal compliance. Evidence now indicates that management, and especially top management, commitment to an ethics program affects both its scope and its control orientation. Programs of broad scope include multiple elements, dedicated staff, and extensive employee involvement. Control may be *compliance-oriented,* emphasizing adherence to rules, monitoring employee behavior, and disciplining misconduct, or it may be *values-oriented,* emphasizing commitment to shared values and encouraging ethical aspirations. Some programs strive for both internalization of values and compliance with rules, so that organizational values are not perceived as empty rhetoric.[119]

Remember that employees' perceptions influence their judgments about procedural justice. In fact, a recent **meta-analysis** (quantitative cumulation of research studies) of 183 studies of organizational justice confirmed the beneficial effects on employee attitudes and performance of procedural justice safeguards.[120] Provide explicit procedures for resolving conflicts, and make sure that all employees know how to use them. Treat all people with dignity and respect, and they will respond with high levels of performance and commitment.

Whistle-blowing is likely to be effective to the extent that (1) the whistle-blower is credible and relatively powerful, (2) he or she reports information that is clearly illegal and unambiguous, (3) the evidence is convincing, and (4) the organization itself encourages whistle-blowing and discourages retaliation against whistle-blowers. However, the more an organization depends on the wrongdoing (e.g., by covering up shoddy aircraft maintenance procedures), the less likely it is that internal whistle-blowing will be effective, and the more likely that external whistle-blowing will be effective.[117] If you have a tale to tell, here are some do's and don'ts[118]:

Do make sure your allegation is correct, keep careful records, research whether your state provides protection for whistle-blowers, and be realistic about your future.

Do talk to your family, and be prepared for a worst-case scenario.

Don't assume that a federal or state law will protect you as the "good guy." Legal protection for private-sector workers is often inadequate and varies from state to state.

Don't run to the media (check with an attorney first).

Don't expect a windfall if you're fired. Although some states allow punitive damages, you may be eligible only for back pay and reinstatement—in a place where you probably don't want to work anyway.

Conclusion

Ethical behavior is not governed by hard-and-fast rules. Rather, it adapts and changes in response to social norms. This is nowhere more obvious than in human resource management. What was considered ethical in the 1950s and 1960s (deep-probing selection interviews; management prescriptions of standards of dress, ideology, and lifestyle; refusal to let employees examine their own employment files) would be considered improper today. Indeed, as we have seen, growing concern for employee rights has placed organizational decision-making policies in the public domain. The beneficial effect of this, of course, is that it is sensitizing both employers and employees to new concerns.

To be sure, ethical choices are rarely easy. The challenge in managing human resources lies not in the mechanical application of moral prescriptions but rather in the process of creating and maintaining genuine relationships from which to address ethical dilemmas that cannot be covered by prescription.[121]

Human Resource Management in Action: Conclusion

ALTERNATIVE DISPUTE RESOLUTION: GOOD FOR THE COMPANY, GOOD FOR EMPLOYEES?

In a 2001 decision *(Circuit City Stores, Inc. v. Adams)*, the U.S. Supreme Court ruled that an employer can enforce a signed agreement that obligates an employee to take all employment-related disputes to arbitration rather than to court. While job applicants can be required to sign an agreement to arbitrate employment disputes as the exclusive remedy for claims against the company, current employees may require different treatment. The employer may encourage—but not require—current employees to sign such an agreement without some "additional consideration." Such consideration often takes the form of a one-time payment or bonus, or some form of time off. Now that there is no question about enforceability of such agreements, opponents might point to flaws in the procedural fairness of the process as a basis for a petition to a court to nullify an agreement.

This raises another issue, namely, what does a fair **alternative dispute resolution (ADR) program** look like? According to attorneys and HR professionals, a fair ADR program is neutral, is confidential, provides due process to the employee, and does not limit the remedies available to the employee. Moreover, it imposes fees (if any) that are no higher than what it would cost an employee to file a claim in court—generally about $100. In addition to these features, the Society for Human Resource Management suggests the following additional standards of fairness:

- Accessibility.
- Opportunity for a hearing before one or more neutral, impartial decision makers.
- Opportunity to participate in the selection of decision makers.
- Participation by the employee in assuming some portion of the costs of the dispute-resolution process.

Like other HR initiatives, ADR programs have both negative and positive features. On the one hand, ADR procedures may increase the number of employee claims, and unfavorable arbitration decisions are almost impossible to overturn. In addition, mandatory arbitration of employment disputes can keep employees who claim to be fired whistle-blowers from taking their claims to court.[122] On the other hand, employees can pursue the same claims in arbitration that they could in court, and claims can be resolved much more quickly. Arbitrators can award damages in the same fashion that a judge or jury can. On balance, therefore, programs that incorporate features designed to ensure procedural justice are good for both employers and employees. They will likely encourage both sides to make greater use of ADR in the future.

SUMMARY

The broad theme of this chapter is "justice on the job." This includes procedural justice, due process, and ethical decision making. Each of these processes should guide the formulation of policy in matters involving dispute resolution (e.g., through grievance procedures), arbitration, discipline, employment contracts, and termination for disciplinary or economic reasons. Indeed, such concerns for procedural justice and due process form the basis for many challenges to the employment-at-will doctrine.

Two of the most important employment issues of our time are employee privacy and ethical decision making. Three areas that involve employee privacy are receiving considerable emphasis: fair information practices in the Internet age, the assessment of job applicants and employees, and whistle-blowing. Although it is not possible to prescribe the content of ethical behavior in each of these areas, processes that incorporate procedural justice can lead to an acceptable (and temporary) consensus among interested parties regarding an ethical course of action.

DISCUSSION QUESTIONS

14–1. Discuss the similarities and differences in these concepts: procedural justice, workplace due process, and ethical decisions about behavior.

14–2. What advice would you give to an executive who is about to negotiate an employment contract?

14–3. Is it ethical to tape-record a conversation with your boss without his or her knowledge?

14–4. How can a firm avoid lawsuits for employment-at-will?

14–5. What are some guidelines to follow in determining a reasonable compromise between a company's need to run its business and employee rights to privacy?

KEY TERMS

alternative dispute resolution (ADR) programs

employee relations

justice

procedural justice

distributive justice

due process

ethical decisions about behavior

organizational citizenship behaviors

organizational support

employee voice

interactional justice

informational justice

just cause	retaliatory discharge
positive discipline	no-compete agreements
social learning theory	fiduciary duty of loyalty
progressive discipline	choice-of-law provision
red-hot stove rule	privacy
employment-at-will	ethical dilemma
public policy exception	whistle blowing
implied promises	meta-analysis

APPLYING YOUR KNOWLEDGE

Case 14–1   ***George Cotter Blows the Whistle***

Employees who find themselves in the dicey position of witnessing a breach of ethics, a crime, or a health or safety threat in the workplace need to proceed very cautiously. Protection for federal workers who expose fraud or wrongdoing is fairly broad, but this is not the case for many private-sector workers. A wrong step can leave an employee without a job and without legal recourse. Furthermore, it can ruin his or her reputation and make subsequent employment extremely difficult to obtain.

Take the case of George Cotter, an East Coast regional manager for Selton, a medium-size entertainment company. In 1995, Mr. Cotter noticed that something funny seemed to be going on at his company. Specifically, some higher-level executives were ordering big shipments of free compact disks (CDs) to recipients who were not, in fact, entitled to them. After doing some legwork to ensure that his suspicions were supported, Mr. Cotter took his findings to higher-level supervisors. In fact, he notified supervisors on three different occasions. His allegation was that the upper-level executives were receiving kickbacks for delivering free CDs to certain individuals. This was obviously costing Selton Company a large amount of money.

George Cotter expected to be thanked for his discovery. Instead, he got fired, supposedly for not adequately performing his job.

Six months later, Cotter filed a wrongful termination lawsuit with a superior court in his county. The preliminary ruling was in his favor, but Selton Company is presently in the process of appealing the case to the State Supreme Court.

Cotter is not as famous as Ernest Fitzgerald, the Air Force civil servant who identified billions of dollars in cost overruns at Lockheed in 1968, or as the Morton-Thiokol engineers who tried to stop the launch of the space shuttle *Challenger* because weather conditions were too cold. But Cotter is a classic whistle-blower. Unfortunately, Selton's response—firing him—also appears to be classic.

In theory, most managers agree that blowing the whistle is what they want employees to do. But in practice, many "ethical dissenters" can attest to the fact that they are treated like pariahs, if not fired outright, after fingering the wrongdoing in their organizations. The problem seems to be that laws protecting whistle-blowers are extremely spotty. Certain environmental laws and workplace safety regulations have whistle-blower provisions. But most states are loath to interfere with "at-will" employment contracts.

Questions

1. Under what circumstances are employees most likely to blow the whistle?
2. What steps should George Cotter have taken to help ensure that his whistle-blowing was received favorably by the organization and to help protect his job?

REFERENCES

1. Fossum, J. A. (1990). Employee and labor relations in an evolving environment. In J. A. Fossum (ed.), *Employee and labor relations.* Washington, DC: Bureau of National Affairs, pp. 4-1–4-22.

2. *Webster's new collegiate dictionary* (1976). Springfield, MA: Merriam-Webster, p. 628.

3. Barnard, C. I. (1938). *The functions of the executive.* Cambridge, MA: Harvard University Press.

4. Greenberg, J. (1987). Reactions to procedural injustice in payment distributions: Do the means justify the ends? *Journal of Applied Psychology, 72,* 55–61.

5. Colella, A. (2001). Coworker distributive fairness judgments of the workplace accommodation of employees with disabilities. *Academy of Management Review, 26,* 100–116.

6. Wesman, B. C., & Eischen, D. E. (1990). Due process. In J. A. Fossum (ed.), *Employee and labor relations.* Washington, DC: Bureau of National Affairs, pp. 4-82–4-133.

7. Cullen, J. B., Victor, B., & Stephens, C. (1989). An ethical weather report: Assessing the organization's ethical climate. *Organizational Dynamics, 18,* 50–62. See also Nielsen, R. P. (1989). Changing unethical organizational behavior. *Academy of Management Executive, 3*(2), 123–130.

8. Kanovsky, M. (2000). Understanding procedural justice and its impact on business organizations. *Journal of Management, 26,* 489–511.

9. Elovainio, M., Kivimaki, M., & Helkama, K. (2001). Organizational justice evaluations, job control, and occupational strain. *Journal of Applied Psychology, 86,* 418–424.

10. Colquitt, J. A., Conlon, D. E., Wesson, M. J., Porter, C. O. L. H., & Ng, K. Y. (2001). Justice at the millennium: A meta-analytic review of 25 years of organizational justice research. *Journal of Applied Psychology, 86,* 425–445.

11. Borman, W. C., & Motowidlo, S. J. (1993). Expanding the criterion domain to include elements of contextual performance. In N. Schmitt & W. C. Borman (eds.), *Personnel selection in organizations.* San Francisco: Jossey-Bass, pp. 71–98.

12. Moorman, R. H., Blakely, G. L., & Niehoff, B. P. (1998). Does perceived organizational support mediate the relationship between procedural justice and organizational citizenship behavior? *Academy of Management Journal, 41,* 351–357.

13. Naumann, S. B., & Bennett, N. (2000). A case for procedural justice climate: Development and test of a multilevel model. *Academy of Management Journal, 43,* 881–889.

14. Kanovsky, op. cit.

15. Colquitt, J. A. (2001). On the dimensionality of organizational justice: A construct validation of a measure. *Journal of Applied Psychology, 86,* 386–400.

16. Bies, R. J. (2001). Interactional (in)justice: The sacred and the profane. In J. Greenberg & R. Cropanzano (eds.), *Advances in organizational justice (pp. 89-118).* Lexington, MA: Lexington Press.

17. Masterson, S. S., Lewis, K., Goldman, B. M., & Taylor, M. S. (2000). Integrating justice and social exchange: The differing effects of fair procedures and treatment on work relationships. *Academy of Management Journal, 43,* 738–748.

18. Gopinath, C., & Becker, T. E. (2000). Communication, procedural justice, and employee attitudes: Relationships under conditions of divestiture. *Journal of Management, 26,* 63–83.

19. Mishra, A. K, & Spreitzer, G.M. (1998). Explaining how survivors respond to downsizing: The roles of trust, empowerment, justice, and work redesign. *Academy of Management Journal, 23,* 567–588. See also Brockner, J., & Wiesenfeld, B. M. (1996). An integrative framework for explaining reactions to decisions: Interactive effects of outcomes and procedures. *Psychological Bulletin, 120,* 189–208.

20. Sheppard, B. H., Lewicki, R. J., & Minton, J. W. (1992). *Organizational justice: The search for fairness in the workplace.* New York: Lexington.

21. Arnold, J. A., & O'Connor, K. M. (1999). Ombudspersons or peers? The effect of third-party expertise and recommendations on negotiation. *Journal of Applied Psychology, 84,* 776–785.

22. Sheppard et al., op. cit.

23. Ibid.

24. Tyler, T. R., & Bies, R. J. (1990). Beyond formal procedures: The interpersonal context of procedural justice. In J. S. Carroll (ed.), *Applied psychology and organizational settings.* Hillsdale, NJ: Erlbaum, pp. 77–98.

25. Sheppard et al., op. cit.

26. Cropanzano, R., Aguinis, H., Schminke, M., & Denham, D. L. (1999). Disputant reactions to managerial conflict resolution tactics: A comparison among Argentina, the Dominican Republic, Mexico, and the United States. *Group and Organization Management, 24,* 124–154. See also Konovsky, op. cit.

27. Giaccobe-Miller, J. K., Miller, D. J., & Victorov, V. (1998). A comparison of Russian and U.S. pay allocation decisions, distributive justice judgments, and productivity under different payment conditions. *Personnel Psychology, 51,* 137–163.

28. Kozan, M. K. (1997). Culture and conflict management: A theoretical framework. *The International Journal of Conflict Management, 8,* 338–360.

29. Konovsky, op. cit.

30. Ewing, J. B. (1989, Oct.23). Corporate due process lowers legal costs. *The Wall Street Journal,* p. A14.

31. Bencivenga, op. cit. See also Taking it to arbitration (1985, July 16). *The Wall Street Journal,* p. 1.

32. Drost, D. A., & O'Brien, F. P. (1983). Are there grievances against your non-union grievance procedure? *Personnel Administrator, 28*(1), 36–42.

33. Ibid.

34. Hendriks, E. S. (2000, June). Do more than open doors. *HRMagazine,* pp. 171–181.

35. Seeley, R. S. (1992, July). Corporate due process. *HRMagazine,* pp. 46–49.

36. Wesman & Eischen, op. cit.

37. Falcone, P. (1997, Feb.). Fundamentals of progressive discipline. *HRMagazine,* pp. 90–94. See also Belohlav, J. (1983). Realities of successful employee discipline. *Personnel Administrator, 28*(3) 74–77, 92.

38. Hymowitz, C. (1998, July 28). Managers struggle to find a way to let someone go. *The Wall Street Journal,* p. B1.

39. Rubis, L. (1999, Aug.). Disciplining employees made easy, or at least easier. *HR News,* p. 47.

40. Baum, L. (1986, June 16). Punishing workers with a day off. *BusinessWeek,* p. 80.

41. Fossum, J. A. (1999). *Labor relations: Development, structure, process* (7th ed.). Burr Ridge, IL: McGraw-Hill/Irwin. See also O'Reilly, C. A., III, & Weitz, B. A. (1980). Managing marginal employees: The use of warnings and dismissals. *Administrative Science Quarterly, 25,* 467–484.

42. Franke, R., & Karl, J. (1978). The Hawthorne experiments: First statistical interpretation. *American Sociological Review, 43,* 623–643. See also O'Reilly & Weitz, op. cit.

43. Bandura, A. (1986). Social foundations of thought and action: A social cognitive theory. Englewood Cliffs, NJ: Prentice-Hall.

44. Trevino, L. K. (1992). The social effects of punishments in organizations: A justice perspective. *Academy of Management Review, 17,* 647–676.

45. O'Reilly, C. A., III, & Puffer, S. M. (1989). The impact of rewards and punishments in a social context: A laboratory and field experiment. *Journal of Occupational Psychology, 62,* 41–53.

46. Rubis, op. cit.

47. Klaas, B. S., & Feldman, D. C. (1994). The impact of appeal system structure on disciplinary decisions. *Personnel Psychology, 47,* 91–108. See also Klaas, B. S., & Dell'omo, G. G. (1991). The determinants of disciplinary decisions: The case of employee drug use. *Personnel Psychology, 44,* 813–835.

48. Klaas, B. S., & Wheeler, H. N. (1990). Managerial decision making about employee discipline: A policy-capturing approach. *Personnel Psychology, 43,* 117–134.

49. Falcone, op. cit.

50. Israel, D. (1983). The Weingarten case sets precedent for co-employee representation. *Personnel Administrator, 28*(2), 23–26.

51. *NLRB v. Weingarten* (1975). 420 U.S. 251, 95 S. Ct. 959.

52. *Epilepsy Foundation of Northeast Ohio,* 331 NLRB 92, 164 LRRM 1233 (July 20, 2000). See also Roberts, V. (2001, Dec.) Court upholds extending *Weingarten* rights to nonunion workers. *HR News,* p. 13.

53. Weingarten rights include prior consultation (1992, Aug.). *Mountain States Employers Council Bulletin,* p. 4. See also Clark, M. M. (2002, Jan.). Nonunion employers face choices in investigating misconduct. *HR News,* p. 9.

54. Employee's "Weingarten" rights limited by NLRB (1993, Jan.). *Mountain States Employers Council Bulletin,* p. 4.

55. Israel, op. cit.

56. Siegel, M. (1998, Oct.26). Yes, they *can* fire you. *Fortune,* p. 301.

57. Lorber, L. Z., Kirk, J. R., Kirschner, K. H., & Handorf, C. R. (1984). *Fear of firing: A legal and personnel analysis of employment-at-will.* Alexandria, VA: American Society for Personnel Administration.

58. Geyelin, M. (1989, Sept. 7). Fired managers winning more lawsuits. *The Wall Street Journal,* p. B13.

59. Geyelin, M., & Moses, J. M. (1992, Apr. 7). Rulings on wrongful firing curb hiring. *The Wall Street Journal,* p. B1.

60. Stern, G. (1993, May 5). Companies discover that some firings backfire into costly defamation suits. *The Wall Street Journal,* pp. B1, B7.

61. Mitchell, B. (1999, Jan. 25). At-will employment isn't safe harbor for companies. *The Denver Post,* p. 5L. See also Spurgeon, H., & Howbert, P. A. (1985). *Ready, fire! (aim): A manager's primer in the law of terininations.* Colorado Springs, CO: Author.

62. Koys, D. J., Briggs, S., & Grenig, J. (1987). State court disparity on employment-at-will. *Personnel Psychology, 40,* 565–577.

63. Stern, op. cit. See also Geyelin, op. cit.

64. Siegel, op. cit.

65. Click, J. (1999, July). Handbook created contract employer can't unilaterally alter. *HR News,* p. 8. See also Heshizer, B. (1984). The implied contract exception to at-will employment. *Labor Law Journal, 35,* 131–141.

66. Bakaly, C. G., Jr., & Grossman, J. M. (1984, Aug.). How to avoid wrongful discharge suits. *Management Review,* pp. 41–46.

67. Siegel, op. cit.

68. Wermiel, S. (1988, June 7). Justices expand union workers' right to sue. *The Wall Street Journal,* p. 4.

69. Yoder, S. K., & Lambert, W. (1990, Dec.21). California rulings may limit worker suits. *The Wall Street Journal,* p. B6. See also Schlender, B. R. (1988, Dec. 30). California ruling curtails damages in dismissal suits. *The Wall Street Journal,* p. B1.

70. Geyelin, pp. cit.

71. Click, op. cit. See also Handbooks (1994, Jan.). *Mountain States Employers Council Bulletin,* p. 2. See also Fulmer, W. E., & Casey, A. W. (1990). Employment at will: Options for managers. *Academy of Management Executive, 4*(2), 102–107.

72. Lorber, L. Z. (1984). Basic advice on avoiding employment-at-will troubles. *Personnel Administrator, 29*(1), 59–62.

73. Falcone, op. cit. See also Engel, P. G. (1985, Mar. 18). Preserving the right to fire. *Industry Week,* pp. 39–40.

74. Obdyke, L. K. (1998, Spring). Written employment contracts—When? Why? How? *SHRM Legal Report,* pp. 5–8.

75. Baig, E. C. (1997, Mar. 17). Beware the ties that bind. *Fortune,* pp. 120, 121.

76. Personal affairs (1983, June 6). *Forbes,* pp. 174, 178.

77. Sandler, D. R. (1998, Winter). Noncompete agreements: Considering ties that bind. *SHRM Legal Report,* pp. 5–8.

78. Lancaster, H. (1998, Feb. 17). How to loosen the grip of a noncompete pact after your breakup. *The Wall Street Journal,* p. B1. See also Baig, op. cit. See also Wadman, M. K. (1992, June 26). More firms restrict departing workers. *The Wall Street Journal,* pp. B1, B3. See also You'll never eat lunch in this industry again (1991, Nov.11). *BusinessWeek,* p. 44.

79. Egler, T. D. (1996, May). A manager's guide to employment contracts. *HRMagazine,* pp. 28–33.

80. Stickney, J. (1984, Dec.) Settling the terms of employment. *MONEY,* pp. 127, 128, 132.

81. Geyelin, op. cit.

82. Nearly 2 million laid off in 2001. Retrieved from the World Wide Web at www.CBSMarketwatch.com on January 22, 2002.

83. Warner, M. (2001, Jan. 22). Pity the poor dot-commer (a little bit). *Fortune,* p. 40.

84. Bing, S. (1997, Feb. 3). Stepping up to the firing line. *Fortune,* pp. 51, 52. See also Sweet, D. H. (1989). *A manager's guide to conducting terminations.* Lexington, MA: Lexington Books.

85. Youngblood, D. (1987, June 22). Supervisors offered guidelines to "humane" firing. *Rocky Mountain News,* p. 62.

86. Coleman, F. T. (2001). *Ending the employment relationship without ending up in court.* Alexandria, VA: Society for Human Resource Management. See also Sweet, op. cit.

87. Youngblood, op. cit.

88. Sweet, op. cit., p. 56.

89. Folger, R., & Skarlicki, D. P. (1998). When tough times make tough bosses: Managerial distancing as a function of layoff blame. *Academy of Management Journal, 41,* 79–87.

90. Brockner, J., Grover, S., Reed, T. F., & Dewitt, R. L. (1992). Layoffs, job insecurity, and survivors' work effort: Evidence of an inverted-U relationship. *Academy of Management Journal, 35,* 413–425. See also Brockner, J. (1988). The effect of work layoffs on survivors: Research, theory, and practice. In B. M. Staw & L. L. Cummings (eds.), *Research in organizational behavior* (vol. 10). Greenwich, CT: JAI Press, pp. 213–255.

91. Sweet, D. H. (1989). Outplacement. In W. F. Cascio (ed.), *Human resource planning, employment, and placement.* Washington, DC: Bureau of National Affairs, pp. 2-236–2-261.

92. Piller, C. (1993, July). Privacy in peril. *Macworld,* pp. 124–130.

93. Privacy (1999, Apr. 5). *BusinessWeek,* pp. 84–90. See also Time to move on Internet privacy (2000, Feb 28). *BusinessWeek,* p. 174.

94. Peticolas, S., & Heslin, K. R. (1999, Winter). Electronic communications in the workplace: A new challenge in employment law. *SHRM Legal Report,* pp. 5–9. See also Behar, R. (1997, Feb. 3). Who's reading your e-mail? *Fortune,* pp. 57–70.

95. Brown, E. (1997, Feb. 3).The myth of e-mail privacy. *Fortune,* p. 66. See also Piller, C. (1993, July). Bosses with X-ray eyes. *Macworld,* pp. 118–123.

96. Armstrong, L. (2000, July 10). Someone to watch over you. *BusinessWeek,* pp. 189, 190.

97. Ibid.

98. Seglin, J. (2001, July 23). When an employee about to be axed asks for advice. . . . *Fortune,* p. 268.

99. Armstrong, op. cit. See also Workers, surf at your own risk (2000, June 12). *BusinessWeek,* pp. 105, 106. See also Wingfield, N. (1999, Dec. 2). More companies monitor employees' email. *The Wall Street Journal,* p. B6. See also When the devil is in the emails (2000, June 26) *BusinessWeek,* pp. 72, 74.

100. Dowd, A. R. (1997, Aug.). Protect your privacy. *MONEY,* pp. 104–114.

101. 2000 workplace privacy survey (2000). Alexandria, VA: Society for Human Resource Management and West Group. See also A model employment-privacy policy (1993, July). *Macworld,* p. 121.

102. Borrus, A. (2000, July 17). Web privacy: That's one small step. *BusinessWeek,* p. 50. See also When the devil is in the emails, op. cit. See also Cook, S. H. (1987). Privacy rights: Whose life is it anyway? *Personnel Administrator, 32*(4), 58–65.

103. London, M., & Bray, D. W. (1980). Ethical issues in testing and evaluation for personnel decisions. *American Psychologist, 35,* 890–901.

104. Mael, F. A., Connerley, M., & Morath, R. A. (1996). None of your business: Parameters of biodata invasiveness. *Personnel Psychology, 49,* 614–650

105. Stone, D. L., & Stone, E. F. (1987). Effects of missing application-blank information on personnel selection decisions: Do privacy protection strategies bias the outcome? *Journal of Applied Psychology, 72,* 452–456.

106. Miceli, M. P., & Near, J. P. (1992). *Blowing the whistle.* New York: Lexington.

107. Nielsen, op. cit.

108. Jansen, E., & Von Glinow, M. A. (1985). Ethical ambivalence and organizational reward systems. *Academy of Management Review, 10,* 815–822.

109. Hegarty, W. H., & Sims, H. P., Jr. (1979). Organizational philosophy, policies, and objectives related to unethical decision behavior: A laboratory experiment. *Journal of Applied Psychology, 64,* 331–338.

110. Miceli, M. P., & Near, J. P. (1988). Individual and situational correlates of whistle-blowing. *Personnel Psychology, 41,* 267–281.

111. Mathiason, M. cited in Jacobs, M. A. (1998, Aug. 6). Arbitration policies are muting whistle-blower claims. *The Wall Street Journal,* pp. B1, B4.

112. Nelson, B., & Lublin, J. S. (1999, Aug. 13). Buy the numbers? How whistle-blowers set off a fraud probe that crushed Cendant. *The Wall Street Journal,* pp. A1, A8.

113. Gomes, L. (1998, April 27). A whistle-blower finds jackpot at the end of his quest. *The Wall Street Journal,* pp. Bl, B6.

114. Maxey, D. (1997, May 22). No place to hide. *The Wall Street Journal,* pp. R22, R23. See also Greenwald, J. (1993, June 21). A matter of honor. *Time,* pp. 33, 34.

115. Near, J. P., & Miceli, M. P. (1995). Effective whistle-blowing. *Academy of Management Review, 20,* 679–708.

116. Whistle-blowers on trial (1997, Mar. 4). *BusinessWeek,* pp. 172, 174, 178.

117. Near & Miceli, 1995, op. cit.

118. Dunkin, A. (1991, June 3). Blowing the whistle without paying the piper. *BusinessWeek,* pp. 138, 139.

119. Weaver, G. R., Trevino, L. K., & Cochran, P. L. (1999). Corporate ethics programs as control systems: Influences of executive commitment and environmental factors. *Academy of Management Journal, 42,* 41–57.

120. Colquitt et al., op. cit.

121. Cascio, W. F. (1998). *Applied Psychology in Human Resource Management* (5th ed.) Upper Saddle River, NJ: Prentice-Hall.

122. Jacobs, op. cit.

SAFETY, HEALTH, AND INTERNATIONAL IMPLICATIONS

This capstone section deals with two broad themes: organizational support for employees and the international implications of human resource management activities. Chapter 15 examines key issues involved in employee safety and health, both mental and physical. Chapter 16 considers key issues in international human resource management. Given the rapid growth of multinational corporations, it is perhaps in this area more than any other that employees and their families need special social and financial support from their firms.

15 SAFETY, HEALTH, AND EMPLOYEE ASSISTANCE PROGRAMS

Questions This Chapter Will Help Managers Answer

1. What is the cost-benefit trade-off of adopting measures to enhance workplace safety and health?
2. Which approaches to job safety and health really work?
3. What should an informed, progressive AIDS policy look like?
4. What are some key issues to consider in establishing and monitoring an employee assistance program?
5. Does it make sound business sense to institute a worksite wellness program? If so, how should it be implemented and what should it include?

SUBSTANCE ABUSE ON THE JOB PRODUCES TOUGH POLICY CHOICES FOR MANAGERS*

Experts estimate that 5 to 10 percent of employees in any company have a substance abuse problem (alcohol or drugs) serious enough to merit treatment. The situation may be even worse. Thus, over a 2-year period, unbeknown to employees and job applicants, ChevronTexaco Corp. carried out anonymous drug testing. About 30 percent of all applicants and 20 percent of all employees tested positive for illegal drug use.

What is an appropriate policy for managers to adopt in these circumstances? Certainly cost pressures are forcing some employers to reexamine their drug and alcohol treatment programs. After noting that the cost of a 21-day detoxification program runs from $4000 to $14,000, one health care professional commented, "People want to fire other people because they consume a lot of health-care dollars. Those of us in the . . . field are feeling [pressure]. We were feeling it before Valdez, and we'll feel it after. In terms of cutting their costs, they go for the most visible, and clearly the most visible are chemically dependent people."

Another professional in the field says that more hard-line companies simply demote people who have been in treatment. "They won't have a written policy, but they'll guide that person into a position of no strategic importance. If asked, the companies won't acknowledge it. They don't want the bad publicity of being a mean guy."

Buoying these hard-liners are some very public drug- and alcohol-related accidents, of which the ExxonMobil Valdez oil spill is probably the best known. Subsequently, three Northwest Airlines pilots were convicted of operating a commercial airliner while intoxicated. What should firms do? While dismissal and demotion are two obvious policy choices, rehabilitation is a third.

Among companies that endorse rehabilitation, however, there is considerable debate about whether employees should be returned to their jobs if they are successfully rehabilitated. Standard industry practice is to return people to their jobs after treatment, but Exxon bucked the industry trend following the wreck of its oil tanker ExxonMobil Valdez (and the environmental disaster that followed). The ship's captain had previously been treated for alcoholism and returned to work. After the accident, a blood test revealed a high level of alcohol in his system. ExxonMobil therefore adopted the policy that, following treatment, known alcohol and drug abusers won't be allowed to return to so-called safety-sensitive jobs such as piloting a ship, flying a plane, or operating a refinery, although they will be given other jobs. ExxonMobil was hit with 107 discrimination lawsuits as a result of that policy.[1]

Those who favor returning people to work after rehabilitation argue that this practice is not only more humane but also more effective. Refusing to return people to work—even in safety-sensitive positions—would be "short-sighted. It will make sure that no one who's an alcoholic ever gets help," according to the

---

*Sources: J. Smoyer, A practical approach to the issues of drug and alcohol testing, Apr. 1999, *www.shrm.org*, retrieved Aug. 31, 2001; S. Overman, Splitting hairs, *HRMagazine,* Aug. 1999, pp. 42–48. SHRM comments on notice of proposed rulemaking on procedures for transportation workplace drug and alcohol testing programs, Apr. 7, 2000, *www.shrm.org*, retrieved Aug. 31, 2001; Firms debate hard line on alcoholics, *The Wall Street Journal,* Apr. 13, 1989, p. B1.

medical director of United Airlines (which regularly returns pilots to their jobs after treatment). "As ubiquitous a disease as alcoholism is, you have two choices: you either have practicing alcoholics in the cockpits, or you have recovering ones." Those who take a more hard-line attitude toward drug and alcohol abuse point out that many companies are thinking through their policies, wondering how much criticism from the community they can tolerate.

Challenges

1.   What are some arguments for and against each of these policies: dismissal, demotion, return to the same job following rehabilitation, return to a different job following rehabilitation?
2.   Should follow-up be required after rehabilitation? If so, how long should it last and what form should it take?

As the chapter-opening vignette shows, managers face tough policy issues in the area of workplace health and safety. As we shall see, a combination of external factors (e.g., the spiraling cost of health care) and internal factors (e.g., new technology) are making these issues impossible to ignore. This chapter begins by examining how social and legal policies on the federal and state levels have evolved on this issue, beginning with workers' compensation laws and culminating with the passage of the Occupational Safety and Health Act. The chapter then considers enforcement of the act, with special emphasis on the rights and obligations of management. It also examines prevailing approaches to job safety and health in other countries. Finally it considers the problems of AIDS and business, employee assistance programs, and corporate "wellness" programs. Underlying all these efforts is a conviction on the part of many firms that it is morally right to improve job safety and health—and that doing so will enhance the productivity and quality of work life of employees at all levels.

THE EXTENT AND COST OF SAFETY AND HEALTH PROBLEMS

Consider these startling facts about U.S. workplaces[2]:

■   About 16 workers die on the job each day[3]; this number has been declining over the past 7 years.
■   More than 5.7 million workers (roughly 6.3 of every 100) either get sick or are injured every year because of their jobs. Of these, 1.8 million workers have ergonomics-related injuries, such as repetitive-stress injuries (RSIs). RSIs are classified as illnesses because of their long-term nature.[4] More than 600,000 workers miss time at work each year because of them.[5]
■   Being hit by an object is the most common workplace injury, followed by sprains, strains, slips, and falls.[6] Falls account for 12 percent of fatal work injuries.
■   Low-back injuries account for one-fourth of all workers' compensation claims, and cost an average of $8,300, more than twice the average workplace claim.[7]
■   Thirty-five million workdays are lost per year.

The number of workdays lost balloons to 75 million workdays lost when permanently disabling injuries that occurred in prior years are included. The cost? A staggering $40 billion in lost wages, medical costs, insurance administration costs, and indirect costs. At the level of the individual firm, a DuPont safety engineer determined that a disabling injury costs an average of roughly $29,000 (in 2001 dollars). A company with 1,000 employees could expect to have 27 lost-workday injuries per year. With a 4.5 percent profit margin, the company would need almost $17.5 million of sales to offset that cost.[8] At Southern California Edison, over an 8-year period, the average cost of an injury (disabling or not) was almost $7,300 (in 2001 dollars). Of this cost 41.2 percent represented lost productivity; 30 percent medical; and 28.8 percent direct, nonmedical costs.[9]

Regardless of one's perspective, social or economic, these are disturbing figures. In response, public policy has focused on two types of actions: *monetary compensation* for job-related injuries and *preventive measures* to enhance job safety and health. State-run workers' compensation programs and the federal Occupational Safety and Health Administration (OSHA) are responsible for implementing public policy in these areas. Since we discussed workers' compensation in some detail in Chapter 12, we focus here only on current trends in that area. We will devote more effort to covering OSHA.

Workers' Compensation: Current Trends

Today, stress-related disability claims are the most rapidly growing form of occupational illness within the workers' compensation system.[10] Perceptions of exposure to health and safety risks increases stress, and such stress is related directly to health-care costs.[11] Workers' compensation has also been awarded for injuries that occur in connection with work that the employer authorizes to be performed at home.[12] In addition to *compensation* for work-related injuries, public policy also mandates a federally administered program of *prevention* of workplace health and safety hazards. This program is enabled by the Occupational Safety and Health Act of 1970.

THE OCCUPATIONAL SAFETY AND HEALTH ACT

Purpose and Coverage

The purpose of the act is an ambitious one: To prevent work-related injuries, illnesses, and deaths.[13] Its coverage is equally ambitious, for the law extends to any business (regardless of size) that *affects* interstate commerce. Since almost any business affects interstate commerce, about 6.9 million U.S. workplaces and 105 million workers are included.[14] Federal, state, and local government workers are excluded since the government cannot easily proceed against itself in the event of violations.

Administration

The 1970 act established three government agencies to administer and enforce the law:

- **The Occupational Safety and Health Administration** (OSHA) establishes and enforces the necessary safety and health standards. However, a 1998 law prohibits OSHA from evaluating compliance officers and their supervisors on the basis of enforcement activities, such as the number of citations issued or penalties assessed.[15] The emphasis is therefore more on prevention and cooperation rather than on confrontation.
- **The Occupational Safety and Health Review Commission** (a three-member board appointed by the president) rules on the appropriateness of OSHA's enforcement actions when they are contested by employers, employees, or unions.
- **The National Institute for Occupational Safety and Health** (NIOSH) conducts research on the causes and prevention of occupational injury and illness, recommends new standards (based on this research) to the secretary of labor, and develops educational programs.

Safety and Health Standards

Under the law, each employer has a "general duty" to provide a place of employment "free from recognized hazards." Employers also have the "special duty" to comply with all standards of safety and health established under the act.

OSHA has issued a large number of detailed standards covering numerous environmental hazards. These include power tools; machine guards; compressed gas; materials handling and storage; and toxic substances such as asbestos, cotton dust, silica, lead, and carbon monoxide.

As an example, consider OSHA's blood-borne pathogen standard, which was revised in 2001. Workers exposed to blood and bodily fluids (e. g., health care providers, first-aid providers) are covered by the rule, but it does not apply to workers who give first aid as "good Samaritans." It requires facilities to develop exposure-control plans, to implement engineering controls and worker training to reduce the incidence of needlesticks, to provide personal protective equipment and hepatitis B vaccinations, and to communicate hazards to workers.[16]

To date, NIOSH has identified more than 15,000 toxic substances based on its research, but the transition from research findings to workplace standards is often a long, contentious process. Currently, it takes 38 to 46 months to set a standard, although OSHA's proposed ergonomics standards are taking much longer.[17]

Record-Keeping Requirements

As of 2002, covered employers are required to complete three new forms. These are:

- Log of Work-Related Injuries and Illnesses (OSHA 300) (see Figure 15–1)
- Injury and Illness Reporting Form (OSHA 301), and
- Summary of Work-Related Injuries and Illnesses (OSHA 300A)

Employees are guaranteed access, on request, to Form 300 at their workplaces, and the records must be retained for 5 years following the calendar

Figure 15–1

OSHA Form 200, log and summary of occupational injuries and illnesses.

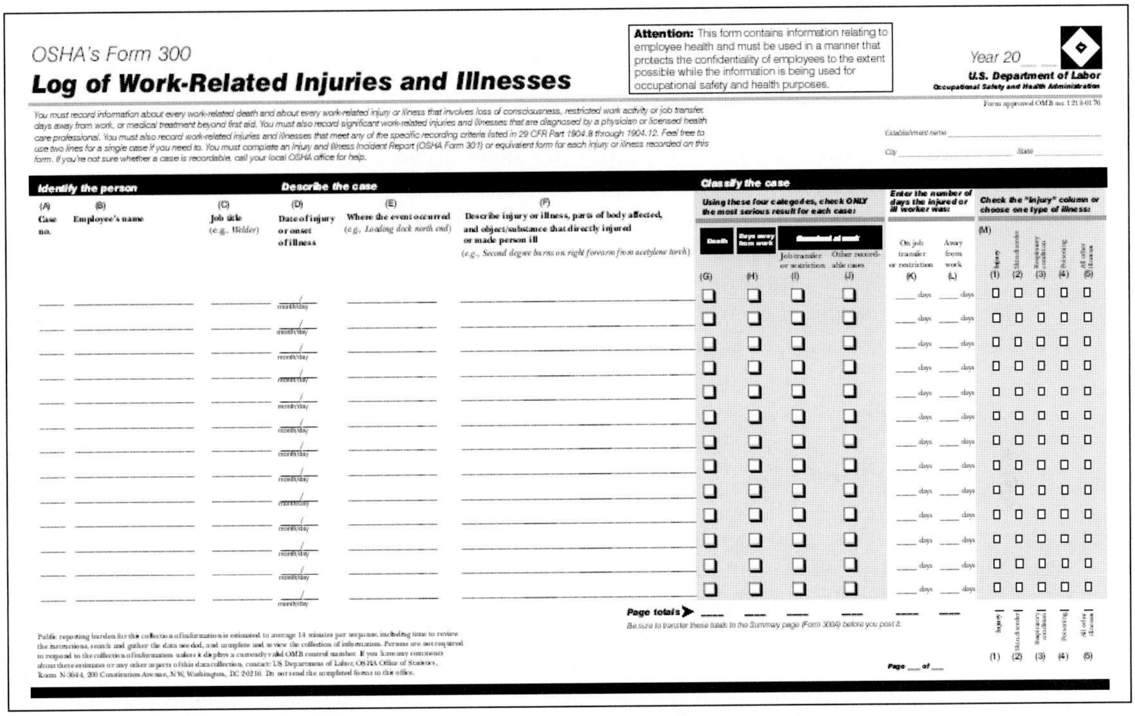

year they cover. The purpose of these reports is to identify where safety and health problems have been occurring (if at all). Such information helps call management's attention to the problems, as well as that of an OSHA inspector, should one visit the workplace. The annual summary must be sent to OSHA directly, to help the agency determine which workplaces should receive priority for inspection.

OSHA Enforcement

In administering the act, OSHA inspectors have the right to enter a workplace (but not the home office of a teleworking employee) and to conduct a compliance inspection.[18] However, in its *Marshall v. Barlow's, Inc.* decision, the Supreme Court ruled that employers could require a search warrant before allowing the inspector onto company premises.[19] In practice, only about 3 percent of employers go that far, perhaps because the resulting inspection is likely to be especially "close."[20] Employers are prohibited from discriminating against employees who file complaints, and an employee representative is entitled to accompany the OSHA representative during the inspection.

Since it is impossible for the 1,170 agency inspectors (most of whom are either safety engineers or industrial hygienists) to visit the nation's 6.9 million workplaces, a system of priorities has been established. OSHA assigns top priority to reports of imminent dangers—accidents about to happen. Second are fatalities or accidents serious enough to send three or more workers to the hospital. Third are employee complaints. Referrals from other government agencies are fourth, and special emphasis programs are fifth. These involve hazardous work such as trenching or equipment such as mechanical power presses.[21]

At the worksite, inspectors concentrate more on dangerous hazards than on technical infractions. For example, OSHA fined Samsung Guam, Inc. $8.3 million after a worker fell 50 feet to his death. The construction company had no railings or harness ropes, letting workers walk across steel beams with no protection.[22]

Considerable emphasis has been given to OSHA's role of *enforcement,* but not much to its role of *consultation.* Employers in every state who want help in recognizing and correcting safety and health hazards can get it from a free, on-site consultation service funded by OSHA. State governments or private-sector contractors provide this service using well-trained safety and/or health professionals (e. g., industrial hygienists). Primarily targeted for smaller businesses, this program is penaltyfree and completely separate from the OSHA inspection effort. An employer's only obligation is a commitment to correct serious job safety and health hazards.[23]

Penalties

Fines are mandatory where serious violations are found. For each **willful violation** (one in which an employer either knew that what was being done constituted a violation of federal regulations or was aware that a hazardous condition existed and made no reasonable effort to eliminate it), an employer can be assessed a civil penalty of up to $70,000. An employer who fails to correct a violation (within the allowed time limit) for which a citation has been issued can be fined up to $7,000 for each day the violation continues. Finally, a willful first violation involving the death of a worker can carry a criminal penalty as high as $70,000 and 6 months in prison. A second such conviction can mean up to $140,000 and a full year behind bars.[24]

Executives can also receive criminal penalties. Calling their conduct everything from assault and battery to reckless homicide, prosecutors in at least 14 states have sought hard time for employers who ignore warnings to improve safety on the job. They have jailed more than a dozen—handing one plant owner a sentence of nearly 20 years after 25 workers died in a fire at his food-processing plant. Investigators found that the high death count had been the result of illegally locked plant doors and the absence of a sprinkler system.[25]

Appeals

Employers can appeal citations, proposed penalties, and corrections they have been ordered to make through multiple levels of the agency, culminating with the Occupational Safety and Health Review Commission. The commission presumes the employer to be free of violations and puts the burden of proof on OSHA.[26] Further appeals can be pursued through the federal court system.

The Role of the States

Although OSHA is a federally run program, the act allows states to develop and administer their own programs if they are approved by the secretary of labor. There are many criteria for approval, but the most important is that the state program must be judged "at least as effective" as the federal program. Currently,

26 states have approved plans in operation. In 2000, for example, OSHA inspected 36,350 workplaces. The 26 states running their own OSHA programs conducted an additional 54,510 inspections.[27]

Workers' Rights to Health and Safety

Both unionized and nonunionized workers have walked off the job when subjected to unsafe working conditions.[28] In unionized firms, walkouts have occurred during the term of valid collective bargaining agreements that contained no-strike and grievance and/or arbitration clauses.[29] Are such walkouts legal? Yes, the Supreme Court has ruled, under certain circumstances[30]:

- Objective evidence must be presented to support the claim that abnormally dangerous working conditions exist.
- If such evidence is presented, a walkout is legal regardless of the existence of a no-strike or arbitration clause.
- It is an unfair labor practice for an employer to interfere with a walkout under such circumstances. This is true whether a firm is unionized or nonunionized.
- Expert testimony (e. g., by an industrial hygienist) is critically important in establishing the presence of abnormally dangerous working conditions.
- If a good-faith belief is not supported by objective evidence, employees who walk off the job are subject to disciplinary action.

OSHA's Impact

From its inception, OSHA has been both cussed and discussed, and its effectiveness in improving workplace safety and health has been questioned by the very firms it regulates. Employers complain of excessively detailed and costly regulations that, they believe, ignore workplace realities. Congress has cut its staff by one-fourth since 1980, and has underfunded it for years.[31] However, even critics acknowledge that the agency has made the workplace safer. Its cotton-dust standard has almost wiped out brown-lung disease among textile workers, and its excavation rules have helped reduce trench cave-ins by a third. On the other hand, OSHA has also been accused of overreaching, as when it issued proposed ergonomics standards that would be extremely costly to implement, or when it issued a letter applying its rules to home workplaces. Both of those actions were greeted with howls of protest, and both were withdrawn.[32] On the other hand, employers sometimes try to improve their competitiveness at the expense of safety. Here's an example.

PRODUCTIVITY VERSUS SAFETY IN A SMALL BUSINESS

COMPANY EXAMPLE

Preoccupied with staying in business, many small businesses skimp on safety information and worker training. That can be especially risky because such companies rely more heavily than do big companies on workers who are young or who speak little English. As an example, consider the case of Everardo Rangel-Jasso.

Mr. Rangel-Jasso was crushed to death at Denton Plastics, Inc., in Portland, Oregon. The 17-year-old was backing up a forklift, with a box high on its fork,

when he cut the rear wheels sharply and the vehicle tipped over. A posted sign, in English, warned forklift drivers to wear seat belts—but the Mexican youth didn't speak English. According to an OSHA investigator, a seat belt might have saved his life.

Employees told OSHA that Hispanic workers learned their jobs through "hand signals and body gestures." Mr. Rangel-Jasso hadn't received any forklift training; he lacked a driver's license and a juvenile's work permit. Federal and state officials levied more than $150,000 in fines against the company, and two senior managers faced criminal indictments. This is not an isolated incident. A computer analysis of 500,000 federal and state safety inspection records over a 4-year period showed that 4,337 workers died at inspected workplaces with fewer than 20 workers, but only 127 died at companies with more than 2,500 workers. According to an OSHA administrator: "[At many small businesses] it takes a serious accident or fatality for them to wake up."[33]

Management's willingness to correct hazards and to improve such vital environmental conditions as ventilation, noise levels, and machine safety is much greater now than it was before OSHA. Moreover, because of OSHA and the National Institute for Occupational Safety and Health, we now know far more about such dangerous substances as vinyl chloride, PCBs, asbestos, cotton dust, and a host of other carcinogens. As a result, management has taken at least the initial actions needed to protect workers from them.

Finally, any analysis of OSHA's impact must consider the fundamental issue of the *causes* of workplace accidents. OSHA standards govern potentially unsafe *work conditions* that employees may be exposed to. There are no standards that govern potentially unsafe *employee behaviors.* And while employers may be penalized for failure to comply with safety and health standards, employees are subject to no such threat. Research suggests that the enforcement of OSHA standards, directed as it is to environmental accidents and illnesses, can hope *at best* to affect 25 percent of on-the-job accidents.[34] The remaining 75 percent require *behavioral* rather than *technical* modifications.

ASSESSING THE COSTS AND BENEFITS OF OCCUPATIONAL SAFETY AND HEALTH PROGRAMS

Let's face it: accidents are expensive. Aside from workers' compensation *(direct)* costs, consider the **indirect costs of an accident:**

1. Cost of wages paid for time lost.
2. Cost of damage to material or equipment.
3. Cost of overtime work by others required by the accident.
4. Cost of wages paid to supervisors while their time is required for activities resulting from the accident.
5. Costs of decreased output of the injured worker after she or he returns to work.
6. Costs associated with the time it takes for a new worker to learn the job.
7. Uninsured medical costs borne by the company.

8. Cost of time spent by higher management and clerical workers to investigate or to process workers' compensation forms.

On the other hand, safety pays, as the following examples illustrate.

SAFETY PAYS AT DUPONT AND ALCOA   COMPANY EXAMPLE

At DuPont Corp., safety experts provide feedback while engineers observe workers and then redesign valves and install key locks to deter accident-causing behavior. When injuries do happen, the company reports them quickly to workers to provide a sense of immediacy, trying to show the behavior that caused the accident without naming the offender. It also fosters peer pressure to work safely by giving units common goals—this way, workers are working together instead of independently. DuPont offers carrots, too. Its directors regularly give safety awards, and workers win $15 to $20 prizes if their divisions are accident-free for 6 to 9 months. The company's incentive for doing this is not altogether altruistic—it estimates its annual cost savings to be $150 million.

At Aluminum Company of America, Inc. (Alcoa), which introduced a "brother's keeper" slogan in the workplace, all employees must submit safety improvement suggestions, and even the lowest-level workers can stop production lines if they suspect a safety problem. The company's chairman has made safety a top priority as well. Have these efforts paid off? Most assuredly. Alcoa improved its safety record by 25 percent in 3 years and estimates it saves $10,000 to $12,000 in workers' compensation for each accident avoided.[35]

Like many other problems of the marketplace, safety and health programs involve what economists call **externalities**—social costs of production that are not necessarily included on a firm's profit-and-loss statement. The employer does not suffer from the worker's injury or disease and therefore lacks the full incentive to reduce it. As long as the outlays required for preventive measures are less than the social costs of disability among workers, higher fatality rates, and the diversion of medical resources, the enforcement of safety and health standards is well worth it and society will benefit.[36]

ORGANIZATIONAL SAFETY AND HEALTH PROGRAMS

As noted earlier, accidents result from two broad causes: *unsafe work conditions* (physical and environmental) and *unsafe work behaviors.* Unsafe physical conditions include defective equipment, inadequate machine guards, and lack of protective equipment. Examples of unsafe environmental conditions are noise, radiation, dust, fumes, and stress. In one study of work injuries, 50 percent resulted from unsafe work conditions, 45 percent resulted from unsafe work behaviors, and 5 percent were of indeterminate origin.[37] However, accidents often result from an *interaction* of unsafe conditions and unsafe acts. Thus, if a particular operation forces a worker to lift a heavy part and twist around to set it on a

Figure 15–2

Causes of and re-
sponses to work-
place accidents.

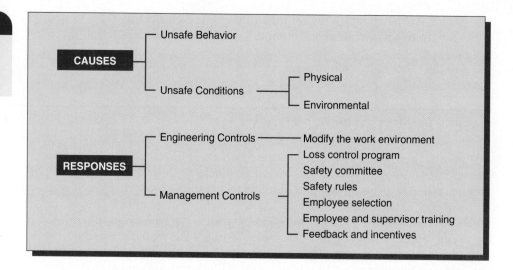

bench, the operation itself forces the worker to perform an unsafe act. Telling the worker not to lift and twist at the same time will not solve the problem. The *un-safe condition itself* must be corrected, either by redesigning the flow of material or by providing the worker with a mechanical device for lifting.

To eliminate, or at least reduce, the number and severity of workplace accidents, a combination of management and engineering controls is essential. These are shown in Figure 15–2. **Engineering controls** attempt to eliminate unsafe work conditions and to neutralize unsafe worker behaviors. They involve some modification of the work environment: for example, installing a metal cover over the blades of a lawn mower to make it almost impossible for a member of a grounds crew to catch his or her foot in the blades. **Management controls** attempt to increase safe behaviors. The following sections examine each of the elements shown in Figure 15–2.

Loss Control

Management's first duty is to formulate a safety policy. Its second duty is to implement and sustain this policy through a **loss-control program.** Such a program has four components: a safety budget, safety records, management's personal concern, and management's good example.[38]

To reduce the frequency of accidents, management must be willing to spend money and to budget for safety. As we have seen, accidents involve direct as well as indirect costs. Since the national average for indirect costs is 4 times higher than the average for direct costs, it is clear that money spent to improve safety is returned many times over through the control of accidents. Detailed analysis of accident reports, as well as management's personal concern (e.g., meeting with department heads over safety issues, on-site visits by top executives to discuss the need for safety, as practiced at Alcoa; and publication of the company's accident record), keeps employees aware constantly of the need for safety.

Study after study has shown the crucial role that management plays in effective safety programs.[39] Such concern is manifest in a number of ways: appointment of a high-level safety officer, rewards to supervisors on the basis of their subordinates' safety records, and comparison of safety results against preset objectives. Evidence indicates that employees who perceive their organizations as supporting safety initiatives and those that have high-quality relationships with their leaders are more likely to feel free to raise safety-related concerns. Such safety-related communication, in turn, is related to safety commitment, and, ultimately, to the frequency of accidents.[40]

Management's good example completes a loss-control program. If hard hats are required at a particular operation, then executives should wear hard hats even if they are in business suits. If employees see executives disregarding safety rules or treating hazardous situations lightly by not conforming with regulations, they will feel that they, too, have the right to violate the rules. In short, organizations show their concern for loss control by establishing a clear safety policy and by assuming the responsibility for its implementation.

The Role of the Safety Committee

Representation of employees, managers, and safety specialists on the safety committee can lead to a much higher commitment to safety than might otherwise be the case. Indeed, merely establishing the committee indicates management's concern. Beyond that, however, the committee has important work to do:

- Recommend (or critique) safety policies issued by top management.
- Develop in-house safety standards and ensure compliance with OSHA standards.
- Provide safety training for employees and supervisors.
- Conduct safety inspections.
- Continually promote the theme of job safety through the elimination of unsafe conditions and unsafe behaviors.

As an example of recommendations that such a committee might make, consider some possible policies to reduce the incidence of **repetitive-motion injuries** (more broadly, musculoskeletal disorders, or MSDs). Such injuries afflict not only meatpackers and pianists, but also telephone and computer operators and supermarket checkout clerks who repeatedly slide customers' purchases over price scanners.

BEST PRACTICES IN REDUCING REPETITIVE STRESS INJURIES   COMPANY EXAMPLE

Aetna Life & Casualty Co. installed ergonomically designed chairs with lower-back supports, adjustable seats, and armrests. Quest created "Worksmart," a one-on-one telephone operator–training program. Operators' work habits are videotaped and analyzed for work speed and posture. Exercises help stretch hands and wrists, and a metronome helps operators work at a smooth pace.[41] At 3M, when workers complained about discomfort on a packaging line, an ergonomics team analyzed the entire process. The workers were packing an epoxy product that included two different size pails, gloves, and a stir stick. The team's solution was to go to a separate sealed pouch, eliminating the need

for the pails and stir stick. Getting rid of the pails decreased the need for warehouse space, and cut costs because the plastic pouches were cheaper. It also decreased reaching motions by the workers, made the product easier for the customer to use, and saved $250,000 per year. These two approaches, modifying equipment and analyzing the way work is done, are the two most common preventive actions by employers. Best practices also include upper-management support, employee participation, an early reporting system, and proactive evaluation of hazards.[42]

Safety Rules

Safety rules are important refinements of the general safety policies issued by top management. To be effective, they should make clear the consequences of not following the rules, for example, progressive discipline. Evidence indicates, unfortunately, that in many cases the rules are not obeyed. Take protective equipment, for example.

OSHA standards require that employers *furnish* and employees *use* suitable protective equipment (e. g., hard hats, goggles, face shields, earplugs, respirators) where there is a "reasonable probability" that injuries can be prevented by such equipment. Companies often find that it is in their own best interests to do so as well. Thus a 5-year study of 36,000 Home Depot, Inc. employees found that back-support devices reduced low-back injuries by about a third. The study compared the incidence of such injuries before and after the company made corsets mandatory for all store employees.[43] As the following data show, however, "You can lead a horse to water, but you can't make it drink"[44]:

- Hard hats were worn by only 16 percent of workers who sustained head injuries, although 40 percent were required to wear them.
- Only 1 percent of workers suffering facial injuries were wearing facial protection.
- Only 23 percent of workers with foot injuries were wearing safety shoes or boots.
- Only 40 percent of workers with eye injuries were wearing protective equipment.

Perhaps the rules are not being obeyed because they are not being enforced; but it is also possible that they are not being obeyed because of flaws in employee selection practices, because of inadequate training, or because there is simply no incentive for doing so.

Employee Selection

To the extent that keen vision, dexterity, hearing, balance, and other physical or psychological characteristics make a critical difference between success and failure on a job, they should be used to screen applicants. However, there are two other factors that also relate strongly to accident rates among workers: *age* and *length of service*.[45] Regardless of length of service, the younger the employee, the higher the accident rate. In fact, accident rates are substantially higher during the first month of employment than in all subsequent time periods, regardless of age. When workers of the same age are studied, accident rates decrease as length of service increases. One large-scale study found that work-ers over age 55 are a third less likely than their younger colleagues to be injured at work seriously enough to lose work time.[46] This is true in industries as di-verse as mining, retail trade, transportation, public utilities, and services. The lesson for managers is clear: *New worker equals high risk!*

Training for Employees and Supervisors

Accidents often occur because workers lack one vital tool to protect them-selves: information. Consider the following data collected by the Bureau of Labor Statistics[47]:

- Nearly 1 out of every 5 workers injured while operating power saws re-ceived no safety training on the equipment.
- Of 724 workers hurt while using scaffolds, 27 percent had received no in-formation on safety requirements for installing the kind of scaffold on which they were injured.
- Of 554 workers hurt while servicing equipment, 61 percent were not told about lockout procedures that prevent the equipment from being turned on inadvertently while it is being serviced.

On the other hand, a study of work injuries among employed adolescents (ages 16–19) suggested that training by itself is not the answer either. Rather, employers need to pay more attention to the design of jobs, specifically, to re-duce employees' exposure to physical hazards, heavy workloads, and job bore-dom. Supervisors also need to learn about and look for signs of substance abuse on the job, for it relates strongly to the incidence of work injuries. Evidence in-dicates that these three factors, employee training, job design, and employer monitoring, can contribute to safer workplaces.[48] So also can "right-to-know" rules, which affect workers exposed to high levels of chemicals or other possi-ble causes of disease.

The notification rules come under OSHA's "hazard communication" stan-dard. The rules apply to about 575,000 hazardous chemicals and 320,000 man-ufacturing businesses and affect some 32 million workers.[49] They require every workplace in the United States to identify and list hazardous chemicals being used ("from bleach to bowl cleaner")[50] and to train employees in their use. Such "right-to-know" requirements have helped to avoid situations like the following.

RIGHT-TO-KNOW RULES IN THE CHEMICAL INDUSTRY   COMPANY EXAMPLE

Cathy Zimmerman, a 26-year-old lab technician at Hercules, Inc., in Wilming-ton, Delaware, was pouring chemicals last year when she noticed that the bot-tles were labeled "mutagen" and "teratogen." She went to her dictionary, which said that a mutagen can alter chromosomes and a teratogen can cause malfor-mations in fetuses. "I said, 'O, my God!'" she recalls. "When I saw that, I talked to my boss and told him I was scared. I didn't want to take a chance." Right-to-know rules had not yet taken effect.

Mrs. Zimmerman, who is expecting her first child, has since been trans-ferred to Hercules's flavoring division, where she works with less hazardous

materials. But she hopes that a new right-to-know training program required by OSHA will prevent such surprises in the future. "With right-to-know, we'd have gone over it first, before it came into the lab," she says. "We didn't have that before."

Some employees are alarmed to discover that they have been working with certain hazardous chemicals. Others are overwhelmed by the detailed labeling, which they say makes it even harder to distinguish really dangerous materials. Meanwhile some businesses claim that fearful workers are demanding unnecessary and costly changes. At the same time, however, OSHA defends the measure, arguing that heightened awareness, and even anxiety, will help reduce work-related accidents. As one spokesperson for OSHA commented, "I'd rather be anxious and alive than calm and dead."[51]

Lack of information and training is unfortunate, but a problem that is just as serious occurs when safety practices that are taught in training are not reinforced on the job. Regular feedback and incentives for compliance are essential.

Feedback and Incentives

Previous chapters have underscored the positive impact on the motivation of employees when they are given feedback and incentives to improve productivity. The same principles can also be used to improve safe behavior. Thus, in one study of a wholesale bakery that was experiencing a sharp increase in work accidents, researchers developed a detailed coding sheet for observing safe and unsafe behaviors. Observers then used the sheets to record systematically both safe and unsafe employee behaviors over a 25-week period before, during, and after a safety-training program. Slides were used to illustrate both safe and unsafe behaviors. Trainees were also shown data on the percentage of safe behaviors in their departments, and a goal of 90 percent safe behaviors was established. Following all this, the actual percentage of safe behaviors was posted in each department. Supervisors were trained to use positive reinforcement (praise) when they observed safe behaviors. In comparison to departments that received no training, workers in the trained departments averaged almost 24 percent more safe behaviors. Not only did employees react favorably to the program, but the company was able to maintain it. One year prior to the program, the number of lost-time injuries per million hours worked was 53.8. Even in highly hazardous industries, this figure rarely exceeds 35. One year after the program, it was less than 10.[52]

Newport News Shipbuilding and Dry Dock Co. cut its injury rate in half by using a similar behavioral approach to safety management. The company's bottom-up approach empowers employees to correct others' unsafe behavior and to take it upon themselves to fix unsafe things they observe.[53] The results of these studies suggest that training, goal setting, and feedback provide useful alternatives to disciplinary sanctions to encourage compliance with the rules. As one safety consultant noted: "It's better to recognize a guy for success than to beat him up for failure."[54]

As we have seen, in the United States there is considerable pressure to improve plant safety. The international application on the next page describes the situation in other countries.

For many office workers, video display terminals are essential tools.

HEALTH HAZARDS AT WORK

The Need for Safeguards

The National Institute of Occupational Safety and Health has identified more than 15,000 toxic substances, of which some 500 might require regulation as carcinogens (cancer-causing substances). The list of harmful chemical, physical, and biological hazards is a long one. It includes carbon monoxide, vinyl chloride, dusts, particulates, gases and vapors, radiation, excessive noise and vibration, and extreme temperatures. When present in high concentrations, these agents can lead to respiratory, kidney, liver, skin, neurological, and other disorders. Scary, isn't it?

There have been some well-publicized lawsuits against employers for causing occupational illnesses as a result of lack of proper safeguards or technical controls.[62] The U.S. Supreme Court has ruled that the states can prosecute company officials under criminal statutes for endangering the health of employees, even if such hazards are also regulated by OSHA.[63] Nevertheless, some of the criticism against employers is not fair. To prove negligence, it must be shown that management *knew* of the connection between exposure to the hazards and negative health consequences and that management *chose* to do nothing to reduce worker exposure. Yet few such connections were made until recent years. Even now, alternative explanations for the causes of disease or illness cannot be ruled out in many cases. Responsibility for regulation has been left to OSHA.

The primary emphasis to date has been on installing engineering controls that *prevent* exposure to harmful substances, for example, by installing improved ventilation systems.[64] Thus after OSHA established or toughened workplace exposure limits for 376 toxic chemicals, compliance cost employers $788 million a year. While this figure might sound steep, consider that an estimated $30 billion is spent annually just to treat preventable cancer. The benefits? According to OSHA, the new limits should save nearly 700 lives a year and reduce work-related illnesses, such as cancer, liver and kidney impairments, and respiratory and cardiovascular illnesses, by about 55,000 cases a year.[65] But is cost-benefit analysis appropriate when lives are literally at stake?

The Supreme Court recognized this problem in its 1981 "cotton dust" decision. It held that OSHA need not balance the costs of implementing standards

INTERNATIONAL APPLICATION
HEALTH AND SAFETY—THE RESPONSE BY GOVERNMENTS AND MULTINATIONAL FIRMS IN LESS DEVELOPED COUNTRIES

In 1984, 45 tons of lethal gas leaked from the Union Carbide (India) Ltd. pesticide plant in the central Indian city of Bhopal, killing more than 3,800 people and disabling more than 20,000 in history's worst industrial disaster. Subsequently, the Indian Supreme Court ordered Union Carbide to pay $470 million in damages to victims of the disaster (although dissatisfied survivors could still file claims in the United States as well)[55]; and an Indian judge ordered the seizure of all of Carbide's Indian assets as part of continuing criminal proceedings against the company.[56]

These events produced important consequences. U.S. multinational firms found out that liability for any Bhopal-like disaster could be decided in U.S. courts under the *Alien Torts Claims Act.* Such claims were still being litigated in 2000 in New York.[57] This, more than pressure from third-world governments, has forced companies to tighten safety procedures, upgrade plants, supervise maintenance more closely, and educate workers and communities in their far-flung empires.[58] In India, despite the outcry against Union Carbide, the country continues to welcome foreign investment and technology.

In Mexico, a gas explosion at Pemex, the state-owned oil monopoly, killed at least 500 people and wounded thousands of others at about the same time as the Bhopal disaster. One year later, little had been done to improve the conditions that caused the explosion. After years of neglect and rampant pollution at Pemex facilities, the government was loath to clamp down because that would focus attention on the main culprit: the Mexican government itself.[59]

Neither the Bhopal nor the Pemex incident had any noticeable effect on multinational investment in Mexico. In fact, all the developing countries in one survey seem to rely on the multinationals, rather than on draconian new regulations, to prevent a repeat of Bhopal.

This is true in South Korea, China, Taiwan, Egypt, and Thailand, for example. In Thailand, a fire at a toy factory killed more than 240 workers. There were no fire escapes, fire alarms, sprinkler systems, or other safety features. Experts say such negligence is common throughout the region, where labor unions are weak, there is lax enforcement of labor laws, and corruption is often endemic.[60] As these few examples make clear, in many of the less developed countries around the world, foreign investment is a political and economic issue, not a safety issue.

This may be changing, for the rapid globalization of business now links manufacturers, investors, and consumers everywhere. Increasingly consumers can see how their shirts and sneakers actually are made, peering into Indonesian factories and Honduran sweatshops. Under pressure from U.S. consumer and labor groups, firms such as Nike, Kmart, and Wal-Mart announced new codes for overseas contract labor. Thus after an audit by Ernst & Young, ordered by Nike, subcontractors now are keener about ensuring that workers wear protective gloves and masks and that fire extinguishers are properly maintained. Yet conditions remain tough. In Indonesia, military police regularly enter factories to keep workers under control. Overtime is mandatory, and workers complain that exhausted colleagues regularly faint from overwork. If consumers refuse to buy goods produced under sweatshop conditions, then economic pressure may force firms to become trendsetters as much in labor as they are in fashion.[61]

against the benefits expected. OSHA has to show only that it is *economically feasible* to implement the standards. The decision held that Congress had already decided the balance between costs and benefits in favor of the worker when it passed the law.[66] On one issue all parties agree: The nature of cancer itself makes it virtually impossible for workers to protect themselves from exposure to cancer-causing substances. In recent years, another killer has entered the workplace. While its origins lie outside the workplace, businesses cannot ignore either its costs or its consequences. That killer is AIDS.

AIDS and Business

Acquired immune deficiency syndrome (AIDS) is a medical time bomb. With 40,000 newly diagnosed cases per year in the United States and 850,000 people infected with the human immunodeficiency virus (HIV) that causes AIDS, employers are fast having to deal with increasing numbers of AIDS victims in the workplace. Unlike other life-threatening illnesses, such as Alzheimer's or heart disease, the vast majority of those dying from AIDS are of working age—between 25 and 44. It's a bottom-line business issue.[67] Consider these facts and prognoses about the disease:

- As of 2000, 33 million people worldwide were infected with HIV. Yet AIDS, a killer, can itself be killed through education and the adoption of safe behavior.[68]
- With no cure in sight for at least 20 years, the Health Insurance Association of America estimates that the AIDS medical bill may be as much as $11 billion a year. By 2000, the disease had already killed 21.8 million people world wide.[69]
- The cost of treating an AIDS patient from diagnosis to death is about $102,000. This figure will escalate over time as people with AIDS live longer—largely due to the development of better drugs to fight the disease and the growing availability of AIDS-related health care. While the death rate from HIV/AIDS has dropped by about half as a result of combination drug, or "cocktail" therapy, the average time period from infection with HIV to the development of AIDS is 8–11 years.[70] The cost of treating AIDS is higher than the average cost of treating leukemia, cancer of the digestive system, a heart attack, or paraplegia from an auto crash.
- The cumulative costs of long-term disability payments to people with AIDS are expected to exceed $2 billion.
- Direct costs to companies will escalate in three ways: through (1) increased medical premiums to cover their employees with AIDS, (2) increased medical premiums to cover AIDS victims without insurance, and (3) an increased Medicaid burden.
- Indirect costs will also affect the bottom line in at least three ways. One is through lost work time of AIDS patients. Since the Americans with Disabilities Act protects the jobs held by AIDS-affected persons (as well as job applicants who have the disease), others have to do their work while they are out, and the substitutes may be less productive. Two, productivity may suffer if coworkers refuse to work with an AIDS-infected employee. Three, recruitment costs will increase to the extent that AIDS-infected employees can no longer work, and to the extent that those employees (or

coworkers who quit rather than work with an AIDS-infected employee) must be replaced.

Progressive firms are taking action. Four years ago, for example, Volkswagen established an AIDS-care program in Brazil that installed condom machines in company bathrooms and provided HIV-positive workers with medical care. By 1999 the company found that hospitalizations were down 90 percent and HIV costs were down 40 percent.[71] Here's how Levi Strauss & Company is tackling the issue.

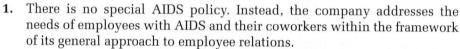

COMPANY EXAMPLE   ## LEVI STRAUSS & CO.'s AIDS-RELATED CORPORATE PHILOSOPHIES[72]

1. There is no special AIDS policy. Instead, the company addresses the needs of employees with AIDS and their coworkers within the framework of its general approach to employee relations.
2. There is no preemployment testing of any sort for AIDS, and there are no AIDS screening questions on employment applications.
3. Employees with AIDS are treated with compassion and understanding—as are employees with any other life-threatening disease.
4. Employees with AIDS can continue to work as long as they are medically cleared to do so; they are also eligible for work accommodation.
5. Employees are assured of confidentiality when seeking counseling or medical referral.
6. Company medical coverage, disability-leave policy, and life insurance do not distinguish between AIDS and any other life-threatening disease.
7. The company's medical plan supports home-health and hospice care for the terminally ill.
8. A case-management strategy is implemented whenever an employee becomes critically ill.
9. Managers are held accountable for creating a work environment that is supportive of an employee with AIDS.
10. The company has assumed responsibility for educating employees so that neither unwarranted fear nor prejudice affects the work environment of people with AIDS.
11. Individual, family, or group counseling is available to employees and their families through the company's employee assistance program or through outside agencies.
12. The EAP staff conducts department and management counseling sessions on request about issues such as how to handle rumors about AIDS, how to deal directly with people's feelings when a colleague becomes ill with AIDS, what colleagues can do to be helpful to a person with AIDS, and how to deal with grief associated with the death of a colleague.

How do these policies work in practice? According to CEO Robert Haas: "It's a kaleidoscope of combined efforts with literally thousands of people in Levi Strauss & Co. [worldwide] contributing to our broad commitment to employee education, to humane care, to outreach, and to our various publics; and that's a model for how we do business here. . . . it creates enormous commitment, better decisions, a lot of energy, and results that speak for themselves."[73]

EMPLOYEE ASSISTANCE PROGRAMS

Another (brighter) side of the employee health issue is reflected in **employee assistance programs** (EAPs). Such programs represent an expansion of traditional work in occupational alcoholism treatment programs. From a handful of programs begun in the 1940s (led by DuPont), today more than 80 percent of the largest companies in the United States, and many others in Canada, offer EAPs, as do about a third of all worksites with more than 50 employees.[74]

The very title "employee assistance program" signals a change both in application and in technique from the traditional occupational alcoholism treatment program. Modern EAPs extend professional counseling and medical services to all "troubled" employees. A **troubled employee** is an individual who is confronted by unresolved personal or work-related problems.[75] Such problems run the gamut from alcoholism, drug abuse, and high stress to marital, family, and financial problems. While some of these may originate "outside" the work context, they most certainly will have spillover effects to the work context.

Do Employee Assistance Programs Work?

A recent large-scale review of the cost-effectiveness of EAPs concluded: "There is no published evidence that EAPs are harmful to corporate economies or to individual employees. . . . All of the published studies indicate that EAPs are cost-effective."[76] By offering assistance to troubled employees, the companies promote positive employee-relations climates, contribute to their employees' well-being, and enhance their ability to function productively at work, at home, and in the community.[77]

From a business perspective, well-run programs seem to pay off handsomely. In well-run programs, management at various levels expresses support for the program, educates employees about the program and provides necessary training on its use, makes the program accessible to employees, and ensures that it operates in a confidential, credible, and neutral manner.[78] Here are two examples of well-run programs.

General Motors Corp., whose EAP counsels more than 6,500 employees with alcohol problems each year, reports a 65 to 75 percent success rate and estimates that it gains $3 for every $1 spent on care. In addition, blue-collar workers who resolve their alcohol and drug-abuse problems through an EAP file only half as many grievances as they did before treatment. The EAP at McDonnell Douglas (now part of Boeing) serves about 100,000 employees and 250,000 dependents. It estimates a 4:1 return on its investment. Workers treated for alcohol or drug dependency missed 44 percent fewer days of work after the EAP was set up, as compared to pre-EAP years. Turnover among these employees also dropped from 40 percent to 8 percent after the EAP had been in effect for four years.[79]

EAPs cost $20 to $30 per employee per year,[80] but, as we have seen, data on their effects are impressive. Nevertheless, it is important to be cautious. Often there is a "rush to evaluate" EAPs and other occupational programs. This can lead to premature claims of success or, equally likely, premature condemnation. *Beware of making strong statements about a program's impact at least until repeated evaluations have demonstrated the same findings for different groups of employees.*[81] It is also important to emphasize that findings do not generalize across studies unless the EAP is implemented in the same way. For example, in some companies counselors are available on site. In others, it is only possible to access an EAP counselor through a toll-free telephone number. Evidence indicates that when counselors are available on site, as opposed to being accessible through a toll-free number, the programs are more effective.[82]

How Employee Assistance Programs Work

There are five steps involved in starting an EAP[83]:

1. **Develop a written statement** of the objectives of the program, consistent with organizational policy. Confirm the company's desire to offer help to employees with behavioral or medical problems, and emphasize that such help will be offered on a personal and confidential basis.
2. **Teach managers, supervisors, and union representatives what to do**—and what not to do—when they confront the troubled employee and when they use the program to resolve job performance problems. Both the supervisor and the steward need to be trained to recognize that they are helping, not hurting, the employee by referring her or him to the EAP.
3. **Establish procedures for referral** of the troubled employee to an in-house or outside professional who can take the time to assess what is wrong and arrange for treatment.
4. **Establish a planned program of communications** to employees to announce (and periodically to remind them) that the service is available, that it is confidential, and that other employees are using it.
5. **Continually evaluate** the program in terms of its stated objectives.

More on the Role of the Supervisor

In the traditional alcoholism-treatment program, the supervisor had to look for symptoms of alcoholism and then diagnose the problem. Under an EAP, however, the supervisor is responsible only for identifying declining work performance. If normal corrective measures do not work, the supervisor confronts the employee with evidence of his or her poor performance and offers the EAP. Recognize, however, that classic warning signs, such as chronic tardiness and absenteeism, are not always evident at companies where some employees telecommute, or where workers may be geographically separated from their supervisors. Nevertheless, here are some recommendations on how to proceed.[84]

1. Once you suspect a problem, begin documenting instances in which job performance has fallen short. Absenteeism (leaving early, arriving late for work, taking more days off than allowed by policy), accidents, errors, a

slackened commitment to completing tasks, and a rise in conflicts with other employees (due to mood swings) may become evident.

2. Having assembled the facts, set up a meeting. Keep the discussion focused on performance, and don't try to make a diagnosis. Outline the employee's shortcomings, insist that improvement is necessary, and then say, "I need to bring you to the medical department, something isn't right here.... I'm taking you to the experts."

3. Often managers are scared of potential liability and scared to be wrong. They worry, "Can the person sue me?" As long as the discussion focuses on declining job performance, legal experts say that a defamation claim is highly unlikely. Besides, confrontation without focusing on job performance is usually ineffective.

This approach leaves the diagnosis and treatment recommendations to trained counselors. But you can increase the odds of success, according to the medical director of United Airlines, by "telling them that if performance doesn't improve they'll be disciplined."[85] As difficult as it is, such intervention often works.[86]

Now that we understand what EAPs are, their effects, and how they work, let us examine three of today's most pressing workplace problems. These are alcoholism, drug abuse, and violence.

Alcoholism

Management's concern over the issue is understandable, for alcohol misuse by employees is costly in terms of productivity, time lost from work, and treatment. How prevalent is alcoholism, and how costly is it? At the outset we should note that while many figures are bandied about, a critical review of the development and reporting of knowledge about employee alcoholism treatment programs has shown these estimates to be supported by limited empirical data.[87] Nevertheless, according to the National Council on Alcoholism and Drug Dependence[88]:

- About 16 percent of full-time employees have serious drinking problems. This percentage has remained constant for the past 15 years.
- Annual deaths due to alcohol number about 105,000.
- Of all hospitalized patients, about 25 percent have alcohol-related problems.
- Alcohol is involved in 47 percent of industrial accidents.
- Fully half of all auto fatalities involve alcohol.

The cost? A staggering $86 billion in costs due to lower productivity and treatment, premature death, and accidents, crime, and law enforcement.

Alcoholism affects employees at every level, but it is costliest at the top. Experts estimate that it afflicts at least 10 percent of senior executives. As an example, consider an executive who makes $100,000 per year, is unproductive, and files large health claims. That cost is certainly far higher than a $10,000 treatment program.[89]

A study done for McDonnell Douglas Corp. shows how expensive it is to ignore substance-abuse problems in the workplace. The company found that in the previous 5 years each worker with an alcohol (or drug) problem had been absent 113 more days than the average employee and had filed for $23,000 more in medical claims. Their dependents also filed some $37,000 more in claims than the average family. Intervention works, as long as it includes ongoing case management and post-treatment monitoring.[90] Recovered alcoholics frequently credit such programs with literally saving their lives. Companies win, too—by reclaiming employees whose gratitude and restored abilities can result in years of productive service.

Drug Abuse

Drug abuse is no less insidious. It cuts across all job levels and types of organizations and, together with employee alcohol abuse, costs U.S. businesses more than $120 billion in annual productivity losses.[91]

Evidence clearly shows that drug abuse affects on-the-job behaviors.[92] Here is a profile of the "typical" recreational drug user in today's workforce. He or she:

- Is late 3 times as often as fellow employees.
- Requests early dismissal or time off during work 2.2 times as often.
- Has 2.5 times as many absences of 8 days or more.
- Uses 3 times the normal level of sick benefits.
- Is 5 times as likely to file a workers' compensation claim.
- Is involved in accidents 3.6 times as often as other employees.
- Is one-third less productive than fellow workers.

A longitudinal study of 5,465 applicants for jobs with the U.S. Postal Service found that after an average of 1.3 years of employment, employees who had tested positive for illicit drugs (typically about 5 percent) had an absenteeism rate 59.3 percent higher than employees who had tested negative. Those who had tested positive also had a 47 percent higher rate of involuntary turnover than those who had tested negative. However, there was no relationship between drug test results and measures of injury and accident occurrence.[93] This may not be true in other occupations, however.

Said a construction union leader in California: "Sometimes 90 percent of the crew's been doing uppers. I just leave the jobs when the guys are dopers. Would you want to work on a four-story building knowing the guy with the blowtorch next to you is doing drugs?"[94]

Remember, the Americans with Disabilities Act protects rehabilitated alcohol and drug abusers from discrimination in employment. However, the ADA Technical Assistance Manual specifically states: "Employees who use drugs or alcohol may be required to meet the same standards of performance and conduct that are set for other employees."[95] As we have seen, rehabilitation under an EAP can be effective. From an employment perspective, however, the key issue is documented evidence of decreased job performance.

Violence at Work

What do Xerox, Fireman's Fund, and the U.S. Postal Service have in common? Histories of employees who died violently while at work. Nationally, an average of 20 workers are murdered and 18,000 workers are assaulted each week.[96]

It is important to emphasize, however, that a large majority of workplace homicides do *not* involve murderous assaults between coworkers in an organization. Rather they occur in connection with robberies and related crimes.[97] Those most at risk are taxi drivers, police officers, retail workers, people who work with money or valuables, and people who work alone or at night.

Violence disrupts productivity, causes untold damage to those exposed to the trauma, is related to workplace abuse of drugs or alcohol and absenteeism, and costs employers millions of dollars.[98] In a stressed-out, downsized business environment, people are searching for someone to blame for their problems. With the loss of a job or other event the employee perceives as unfair, the employer may become the focus of a disgruntled individual's fear and frustration. Under these circumstances, some form of **workplace aggression,** that is, efforts by individuals to harm others with whom they work, or have worked, or their organization itself, is likely.[99]

What can organizations do? Prehire drug testing, detailed questions about previous employment, and criminal-record checks can go a long way toward identifying violence-prone individuals.[100] Fair treatment (procedural justice) on the job, adequate compensation, a climate of honesty by leaders, communicating a policy about counterproductive behavior, consistently punishing unacceptable behavior, and taking steps to reduce job stress can reduce the likelihood of workplace violence and aggression.[101] In addition, both employees and supervisors should be alert to warning signs, such as[102]:

- **Verbal threats.** Take seriously remarks from an employee about what he or she may do. Experts say that individuals who make such statements usually have been mentally committed to the act for a long period of time. It may take very little provocation to trigger the violence.
- **Physical actions.** Employees who demonstrate "assaultive" physical actions at work are dangerous. The employer, working with experts trained to assess a possibly violent situation, needs to investigate and intervene. Failure to do so may be interpreted as permission to do further or more serious damage.
- **Behaviors.** Watch for changes such as irritability and a short temper. Is the employee showing a low tolerance to work stress or frustrations?[103]

Here are some additional preventive steps.[104]

- **Consult specialists**—professionals in the area of facility security, violence assessment, EAP counseling, community support services, and local law enforcement—to formulate a plan for identifying, defusing, and recovering from a violent event.
- **Create and communicate to all employees a written policy** that explains the organization's position on intimidating, threatening, or violent behavior and establishes a procedure for investigating any potentially violent talk or action.
- **Establish a crisis management team** with the authority to make decisions quickly. This group will evaluate problems, select intervention techniques, and coordinate follow-up activities, such as counseling for victims and dealing with the media.
- **Offer training and employee orientation.** Train supervisors and managers in how to recognize aggressive behavior, identify the warning signs of

violence, be effective communicators, and resolve conflict. (Untrained supervisors often escalate violent situations.) Orient all employees on facility-security procedures and on how to recognize and report threats of violence in the workplace.

- **Help employees adjust to change**—for example, in the event of a downsizing, a merger, or an acquisition give employees advance notice. Under the Worker Adjustment and Retraining Act (WARN) of 1988, covered employers are required to give 60 days' notice to employees affected by mass layoffs or plant closings. Keeping employees informed about impending changes and providing additional benefits, such as severance pay or EAP stress-management counseling, can help employees adjust to the change.

- **Be aware of potential risks and respond appropriately.** Remarks such as "I'll kill you" or "I'd like to put out a contract on him" should not be taken lightly. Experts say that in many cases an individual who becomes violent has given multiple clues of potentially violent behavior to a number of people within the organization. However, these warnings were overlooked or dismissed. Be proactive; don't assume the employee doesn't mean it, because when employees feel powerless there is a greater likelihood of violence. Report the incident to management for investigation.

CORPORATE HEALTH PROMOTION: THE CONCEPT OF "WELLNESS"

Consider these sobering facts:

- U.S. companies spend, on average, about 26 percent of their earnings (13. 6 percent of their payrolls) on health care costs.[106] Fully 70 percent of such costs are spent on preventable illnesses.[107]
- Fully 60 percent of U.S. adults are overweight. This costs companies an estimated $5.5 billion per year in lost productivity due to absenteeism and

---

IMPACT OF SAFETY, HEALTH, AND EAPs ON PRODUCTIVITY, QUALITY OF WORK LIFE, AND THE BOTTOM LINE

We know that the technology is available to make workplaces safe and healthy for the nation's men and women. We also know that legislation can never substitute for managerial commitment to safe, healthy workplaces based on demonstrated economic and social benefits. Consider just one example. Based on an analysis of 3,896 disability cases, Northwestern National Life Insurance Company calculated that the average cost of rehabilitating an employee disabled because of stress was $1,925 ($2,850 in 2001 dollars). If he or she is not rehabilitated, companies will need to hold in reserve an average of $73,270 ($108,450 in 2001 dollars) or more to cover disability payments for each employee disabled by job-related stress.[105] On balance, commitment to job safety, health, and EAPs is a win-win situation for employees and their companies. Productivity, QWL, and the bottom line all stand to gain.

weight-related chronic disease.[108] Common backaches alone account for about 25 percent of all workdays lost per year, for a total cost of $15 to $20 billion in lost productivity, disability payments, and lawsuits.[109] For employees who miss time due to back problems, the median time away from the job is 6–7 days.[110]

- Business spends some $700 million per year to replace the 200,000 employees aged 45–65 who are killed or disabled by heart disease.

Keep in mind that health plans do not promise good health. They simply pay for the cost of ill health and the associated rehabilitation. Because 8 of the 10 leading causes of death are largely preventable, however, managers are beginning to look to *disease prevention* as one way to reduce health-care spending. The old saying "An ounce of prevention is worth a pound of cure" is certainly true when one compares the costs of a workshop to help employees stop smoking with the price tag on an average coronary-bypass operation.[111]

Is it possible that health care costs can be tamed through on-the-job exercise programs and health-promotion efforts? Convinced that if people were healthier, they would be sick less often, two out of three U.S. businesses with more than 50 employees have some form of health-promotion program in place.[112] Do such programs work? In a moment we will consider that question, but first let's define our terms and look at the overall concept.

The process of corporate health promotion begins by promoting health awareness, that is, knowledge of the present and future consequences of behaviors and lifestyles and the risks they may present. The objective of **wellness programs** is not to eliminate symptoms and disease; it is to help employees build lifestyles that will enable them to achieve their full physical and mental potential. Wellness programs differ from EAPs in that wellness focuses on prevention, while EAPs focus on rehabilitation. **Health promotion** is a four-step process[113]:

1. Educating employees about health-risk factors—life habits or body characteristics that may increase the chances of developing a serious illness. For heart disease (the leading cause of death), some of these risk factors are high blood pressure, cigarette smoking, high cholesterol levels, diabetes, a sedentary lifestyle, and obesity. Some factors, such as smoking, physical inactivity, stress, and poor nutrition, are associated with many diseases.[114]
2. Identifying the health-risk factors that each employee faces.
3. Helping employees eliminate or reduce these risks through healthier lifestyles and habits.
4. Helping employees maintain their new, healthier lifestyles through self-monitoring and evaluation. The central theme of health promotion is "No one takes better care of you than you do."

To date, the most popular programs are smoking cessation, blood-pressure control, cholesterol reduction, weight control and fitness, and stress management. In well-designed programs, 40 to 50 percent of employees can be expected to participate.[115] However, it's the 15 to 20 percent of high-risk employees who account for up to 80 percent of all claims who are the most difficult to reach.[116] Here is why it is important to try.

Linking Unhealthy Lifestyles to Health Care Costs

A 4-year study of 15,000 Control Data employees showed dramatic relationships between employees' health habits and insurance claim costs. For example, people whose weekly exercise was equivalent to climbing fewer than five flights of stairs or walking less than half a mile spent 114 percent more on health claims than those who climbed at least 15 flights of stairs or walked 1.5 miles weekly. Health care costs for obese people were 11 percent higher than those for thin ones. Workers who routinely failed to use seat belts spent 54 percent more days in the hospital than those who usually buckled up. Finally, people who smoked an average of one or more packs of cigarettes a day had 118 percent higher medical expenses than nonsmokers.[117] This study was the first to tie health costs to workers' behavior. It was corroborated in another longitudinal study that appeared at about the same time.[118] Together, such results may form the basis for incentive programs to (1) improve workers' health habits and (2) reduce employees' contributions to health insurance costs or increase their benefits. Here's what two companies are doing.

COMPANY EXAMPLE

HOW JOHNSON & JOHNSON AND QUAKER OATS REACH "HIGH-RISK" EMPLOYEES

At J&J, employees get $500 discounts on their insurance premiums if they agree to have their blood pressure, cholesterol, and body fat checked and to fill out detailed health-risk questionnaires. Among the more than 150 questions are these: Do you drive within the speed limit? How often do you eat fried foods? Do you exercise regularly, and if not, why not?

Workers found to be at high risk for health problems receive letters urging them to join a diet and exercise program. Those who refuse lose the $500 discount. Before the discount was offered, only 40 percent of the company's 35,000 U.S. employees completed the health assessments. After offering the discount, more than 96 percent did.

Quaker Oats Co. gives employees up to $140 credit in the company's flexible-benefit program if they make a "healthy lifestyle pledge." The more promises they make, the more benefit credits they earn. Pledging to exercise aerobically three times a week is worth $20 in credit, as is a commitment to wear seat belts. Drinking in moderation and refraining from smoking are worth $50 each. The program runs on the honor system.[119]

Evaluation: Do Wellness Programs Work?

Few controlled studies exist,[120] and the movement's doctrines remind some medical doctors of earlier measures that also seemed as unassailable as apple pie—annual physicals, annual Pap smears, and mass health screening. Unfortunately, none of these provided the huge health benefits that seemed almost guaranteed.

Wellness programs are especially difficult to evaluate, for at least six reasons[121]:

1. Health-related costs that actually decrease are hard to identify.
2. Program sponsors use different methods to measure and report costs and benefits.
3. Program effects may vary depending on when they are measured (immediate versus lagged effects).
4. Program effects may vary, depending on how long they are measured.
5. Few studies use control groups.
6. Data on effectiveness are limited in the choice of variables, estimation of the economic value of indirect costs and benefits, estimation of the timing and duration of program effects, and estimation of the present value of future benefits.

At a general level, four key questions need to be answered:

1. Do health-promotion programs in fact eliminate or reduce health-risk factors?
2. Are these changes long-lasting?
3. If the changes are long-lasting, will illness and its subsequent costs be reduced?
4. Are the savings great enough to justify the expense?

Based on a number of independent studies, the answers to the first two questions appear to be yes—especially when programs incorporate systematic outreach and follow-up counseling.[122] For example, one longitudinal study measured the following health-risk factors: blood pressure, cholesterol levels, number of pounds over ideal mean weight, seat belt usage, salt intake, dietary fat intake, smoking, alcohol intake, exercise, and stress.

Although there was some variation in improvement in various categories and between age groups, there was nearly a 20 percent improvement in health-risk scores after 18 months, and the gains were sustained at 30 months. While the effect of age on the rate of change diminished over time, the effect of educational level did not. Those with more education had lower health-risk scores at the beginning of the study and also made the most improvement. In general, these results suggest that participation in an organized health-promotion program results in improved health.[123]

The answer to the third question also appears to be positive, based on an analysis of 200 corporate wellness programs. The best such programs cut medical claims by up to 20 percent. If such "demand reduction" could be extended to all Americans, according to the researchers, the nation could cut $180 billion from its health care bill.[125]

With respect to the fourth question, several studies have focused on *costs that would have been incurred if a wellness program had not been available.* This was the approach taken by the Adolph Coors Co. in evaluating its mammography-screening program for breast cancer. By calculating exactly how many examinations showed breast cancer in the early stages, Coors was able to calculate the costs avoided, assuming that without mammography the problem would have gone undetected and the cancer would have matured. Coors spent $232,500 to perform 2500 screenings and avoided $828,000 in health care costs. This yielded a net saving of $595,000, and a return on investment (ROI) of greater than 3.5 to 1.[126]

Ethical Dilemma
Should Employees Be Punished For Unhealthy Lifestyles?[124]

Johnson & Johnson Health Management, Inc., which sells wellness programs to companies, estimates that 15 to 25 percent of corporate health-care costs stem from employees' unhealthy lifestyle conditions. As a result, individuals may not be hired, might even be fired, and could wind up paying a monthly penalty based on their after-hours activities. Here are some examples:

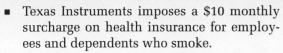

- Texas Instruments imposes a $10 monthly surcharge on health insurance for employees and dependents who smoke.
- Turner Broadcasting won't hire smokers.

- U-Haul International imposes a biweekly $5 charge for health insurance for employees who smoke or chew tobacco or whose weight exceeds guidelines.
  - Multi-Developers won't hire anyone who engages in what the company views as high-risk activities: skydiving, piloting a private aircraft, mountain climbing, or motorcycling.

Existing civil rights laws generally don't protect against **lifestyle discrimination** because smokers and skydivers aren't named as protected classes. Should employers be able to implement "lifestyle policies"?

The medical director at Eli Lilly & Co. estimated that an advanced case of breast cancer costs Lilly more than $100,000 a case in lost work time and medical costs. Mammography equipment costs about $80,000. While it might appear that a compelling case can be made for purchasing such equipment, experts estimate that a company needs to employ at least 1,000 to 2,000 women to justify starting such a program. For smaller companies that cannot afford to buy their own equipment, one option is to contract with mobile mammography-screening programs to bring vans to company premises once a year.[127] Here are some other company examples of cost-benefit analyses of worksite wellness programs:

- Travelers Insurance reported saving $7.8 million in benefit costs by using its "Taking Care" program for its 34,700 participating employees. Each dollar spent yielded a return of $3.40.[128]
- Pillsbury claims that every dollar spent on its "Be Your Best" wellness program produced $3.63 in health-related cost savings.[129]
- Quad/Graphics of Sussex, Wisconsin, offers its 8,700 workers a gym with martial arts instructors and personal trainers, cooking classes, weight and stress reduction, and health checks. According to an outside actuarial firm, health-care costs at Quad/Graphics are 18 percent below those of similar companies.[130]
- Small businesses too are saving money by claiming insurance discounts for group-life premiums if they offer some type of wellness program to their employees. Thus Babson Brothers, a dairy-farm equipment maker in Naperville, Illinois, saved $5000, or 5 percent, on its group-life premiums because it has a no-smoking policy and fitness programs.[131]
- A comprehensive review of three large-scale computer simulations of the effects of worksite wellness programs found that such programs may be cost

beneficial, that economic benefits primarily stem from increases in productivity and less so from decreases in health-care costs, and that program effects vary considerably both within organizations (from year to year) and also between organizations.[132]

Wellness Programs and the Americans with Disabilities Act (ADA)

Employers that *require* employees to submit to wellness initiatives, such as health-risk appraisals (questionnaires about one's health history and current lifestyle) and assessments (physical and biomedical tests that screen for specific health conditions), are violating the ADA. This is so because the act forbids employers from conducting mandatory medical exams once an employee is hired, unless the inquiry is "job-related and consistent with business necessity."

Employers also must be careful when tying financial incentives or disincentives (e. g., cash bonuses, lower health-insurance contributions) to test results. The employer can offer an incentive only upon verification that the employee went for the test. The incentive cannot be tied to the test results. Under the ADA, employers cannot discriminate in pay or benefits based on a legally protected disability. In addition, any test results from wellness screening must be kept confidential.

What types of wellness programs do not violate the ADA? Educational wellness programs that encourage people to sign up for tests and instruct them on how to improve their lifestyles.[133] By helping employees to take an interest in their future health, employers should ultimately be able to keep at least a loose lid on claims and major expenses.

SUBSTANCE ABUSE ON THE JOB PRODUCES TOUGH POLICY CHOICES FOR MANAGERS

Human Resource Management in Action: Conclusion

Given the amounts of time and money invested in employees, especially highly skilled knowledge workers, many firms try to rehabilitate those with substance abuse problems. But how do firms get "problem" employees into rehabilitation programs? The most popular approaches are self-referral and referral by family and friends. Among pilots who have gone through the airline industry's alcohol-rehabilitation program (which has been in effect since 1973) 85 percent were initially turned in by family, friends, or coworkers.

According to the Air Line Pilots Association, one of the hallmarks of the industry's program is a willingness of people to turn in an alcoholic pilot. That willingness, in turn, depends on knowing that the pilot can return to work. If people know that by turning in a pilot they will also be taking away his or her livelihood, they may not do it.

The key to returning to work, in the opinion of most professionals in the field of substance abuse, is follow-up, because substance abuse is a recurring disease. Prior to the Exxon Valdez accident, ExxonMobil really had no systematic policy on how to handle employees after treatment. The company depended solely on the judgments of local managers.

Under United's program, rehabilitated pilots are monitored for at least 2 years. During this time, the pilot is required to meet monthly with a committee

IMPLICATIONS FOR MANAGEMENT PRACTICE

In the coming years, we can expect to see three developments in occupational safety and health:

1. More widespread promotion of OSHA's consultative role, particularly as small businesses recognize that this is a no-cost, no-penalty option available to them.

2. Wider use of cost-benefit analysis by regulatory agencies; industry is demanding it, and Executive Order 12292 endorses it.

3. Broadening of the target group for EAPs and wellness programs to include dependents and retirees.

The high costs of disabling injuries and occupational diseases, together with these three trends, suggest that the commitment of resources to enhance job safety and health makes good business sense over and above concerns for corporate social responsibility.

---

comprising counselors and representatives of both union and management in a kind of group therapy session with other recovering pilots. They may also be required to undergo periodic surprise alcohol or drug tests. United has never had an alcohol-related accident.

Although experts don't always agree on how long follow-up should last, programs most commonly require 6 months of intensive contact, such as weekly meetings, and 1 year after that of monthly contact. Longer-term follow-up may last as long as 4 years.

SUMMARY

Public policy regarding occupational safety and health has focused on state-run workers' compensation programs for job-related injuries and federally mandated preventive measures to enhance job safety and health. OSHA enforces the provisions of the 1970 Occupational Safety and Health Act, under which employers have a "general duty" to provide a place of employment "free from recognized hazards." Employers also have the special duty to comply with all standards of safety and health established under the act. OSHA's effectiveness has been debated for more than a decade, but it is important to note that workplace accidents can result either from *unsafe work conditions* or from *unsafe work behaviors.* OSHA can affect only unsafe work conditions. There are no standards that govern potentially unsafe employee behaviors.

A major concern of employers today is with the possible health hazards associated with high technology, such as video display terminals and semiconductors, with diseases related to radiation or carcinogenic substances that may have long latency periods, and with AIDS.

In response, OSHA has established or toughened workplace exposure limits for many carcinogenic substances. Management's first duty in this area is to develop a safety and health policy. Management's second duty is to establish controls that include a loss-control program, a safety committee, safety rules, careful selection of employees, extensive training, and feedback and incentives for maintaining a safe work environment.

Employee assistance programs represent a brighter side of the health issue. Such programs offer assistance to all "troubled" employees. Under an EAP, supervisors need be concerned only with identifying declining work performance, not with involving themselves in employee problems. Treatment is left to professionals. Finally, health-promotion, or "wellness," programs differ from EAPs in that their primary focus is on prevention, not rehabilitation. Both EAPs and wellness programs hold considerable promise for improving productivity, quality of work life, and profits.

DISCUSSION QUESTIONS

15–1. Should OSHA's enforcement activities be expanded? Why or why not?

15–2. What advantages and disadvantages do you see with workers' compensation?

15–3. Discuss the relative effectiveness of engineering versus management controls to improve job safety and health.

15–4. If the benefits of EAPs cannot be demonstrated to exceed their costs, should EAPs be discontinued?

15–5. Should organizations be willing to invest more money in employee wellness? Why or why not?

KEY TERMS

willful violation

indirect costs of accidents

externalities

engineering controls

management controls

loss-control program

repetitive-motion injuries

employee assistance program

troubled employee

workplace aggression

wellness programs

health promotion

lifestyle discrimination

APPLYING YOUR KNOWLEDGE

Skyline Machine Shop

Case 15–1

Skyline Machine Shop is a medium-size firm located in San Jose, California. It employs almost 1,000 workers when business is good. Skyline specializes in doing precision machining on a subcontract basis for several large aerospace companies. Skilled machinists are always in short supply, and therefore command high salaries and generous benefit packages.

Recently, one of the plant foremen, Len Fulkner, paid a visit to Skyline's human resources manager, Jamie Trenton, to discuss an HR problem.

Fulkner: You know, Jamie, I've been around the barn a time or two. I've seen all kinds of people-type problems over the years. But I guess maybe I'm over the hill—53 is no spring chicken you know! The other day I ran into a situation like I've never seen before, and I need your help.

Trenton: What happened Len?

Fulkner: Well, last Thursday one of my best machinists, Harry Boecker, began acting really weird. He seemed in a daze, couldn't seem to concentrate on the part he was milling, and began dropping tools and engineering drawings all over. At first I thought he'd been drinking. But I smelled his breath and couldn't smell anything. When I asked him what was wrong, he mumbled something about "coke."

Trenton: What did you do?

Fulkner: I sent him home for the rest of the day. I didn't know what else to do, but I knew he was a danger to himself and others so I had to get him out of the plant. I hope I did the right thing. I'm really worried about the guy, Jamie. I'd hate to lose a good machinist like that, but I don't know the first thing about drugs or how to handle workers who have been taking them. Can you help me?

The next day, Jamie Trenton had a meeting scheduled with the president of Skyline. Jamie had been thinking for some time about recommending an employee assistance program to the president, and her conversation with Len Fulkner convinced her that now was the appropriate time. Quite a few other firms in the San Jose area had instituted EAPs—seemingly with some success. However, Jamie knew that Skyline's president was skeptical of "follow-the-leader" approaches to employee benefit packages.

Questions

1. Did Len Fulkner handle the situation with Harry Boecker correctly? Why or why not?
2. Prepare an outline for a cost-benefit analysis that Jamie Trenton could use in presenting her EAP proposal to Skyline's president. In particular, what categories of benefits might be quantifiable?
3. If Jamie's proposal is accepted, what key steps would you recommend to her in implementing a new EAP at Skyline Machine Shop?

REFERENCES

1. Seligman, D. (1996, Dec. 9). Keeping up. *Fortune*, p. 60.
2. *OSHA Facts. www.osha.gov/as/opa/oshafacts/html.* Retrieved Aug. 24, 2001.
3. *Census of Fatal Occupational Injuries Summary. www.bls.gov/news/release/cfoi. nr0.htm.* Retrieved Aug. 24, 2001.
4. Kuntz, P. (2000, Sept.18). What a pain: Proposed OSHA rules for workplace injuries make companies ache. *The Wall Street Journal*, pp. A1, A14.
5. OSHA ergonomics rules draw flak (2000, Nov. 14). *The Denver Post*, p. 3A.
6. Labor letter (1993, Sept. 14). *The Wall Street Journal*, p. A1.
7. Rundle, B. (1996, Oct. 9). Back corsets receive support in UCLA study. *The Wall Street Journal*, pp. B1, B2.
8. Labor letter (1987, Apr. 14). *The Wall Street Journal*, p. 1.
9. Dieterly, D. (1994). *Industrial injury cost analysis by occupation in an electric utility.* Occupational Research Division, Southern California Edison Co., Rosemont, CA.
10. Danna, K., & Griffin, R. W. (1999). Health and well-being in the workplace: A review and synthesis of the literature. *Journal of Management, 25,* 357–384.
11. Manning, M. R., Jackson, C. N., & Fusilier, M. R. (1996). Occupational stress, social support, and the costs of health care. *Academy of Management Journal, 39,*

738–750. See also McLain, D. L. (1995). Responses to health and safety risk in the work environment. *Academy of Management Journal, 38,* 1726–1743.

12. Click, J. (2000, May). Employer liable for slip and fall at home that caused quadriplegia. *HR News,* p. 6.

13. *OSHA: Frequently-Asked Questions. www.osa.gov/as/opa/osha-faq.html.* Retrieved Aug. 24, 2001.

14. OSHA Facts, op. cit.

15. OSH Act is changed to emphasize cooperation. (1998, Sept.). *HR News,* p. 14.

16. OSHA Facts, op. cit. See also New OSHA bloodborne pathogen standards (1992, Sept.). *Mountain States Employers Council Bulletin,* p. 4.

17. Kuntz, op. cit. See also Minehan, M. (2001, Jan.). OSHA ergonomics regs draw immediate fire. *HR News,* pp. 1, 3.

18. OSHA kept out of homes (2000, Feb.28). *The Denver Post,* p. 4A.

19. *Marshall v. Barlow's, Inc.* (1978). 1978 OSHD, Sn. 22,735. Chicago: Commerce Clearing House.

20. Etter, I. B. (1993, Sept.). You can't hide from an OSHA inspector. *Safety & Health,* p. 3.

21. OSHA: Frequently-Asked Questions, op. cit.

22. Work week (1995, Oct.31). *The Wall Street Journal,* p. A1.

23. OSHA: Frequently-Asked Questions, op. cit. See also U.S. Department of Labor, Occupational Safety and Health Admimstration (1996). *Consultation services for the employer.* Washington, DC: U.S. Government Printing Office.

24. OSHA: Frequently-Asked Questions, op. cit.

25. Davis, A. (1997, Feb.26). Treating on-the-job injuries as true crimes. *The Wall Street Journal,* pp. B1, B6. See also The price of neglect (1992, Sept. 28). *Time,* p. 24.

26. OSHA: Frequently-Asked Questions, op. cit. See also U.S. Department of Labor (1983, Mar.). *Program highlights: Job safety and health.* Washington, DC: U.S. Government Printing Office, Fact Sheet No. OSHA-83-01 (rev.).

27. OSHA: Frequently-Asked Questions, op. cit.

28. *NLRB V. Jasper Seating Co.* (1988). CA 7, 129 LRRM 2337. See also *Whirlpool Corporation v. Marshall* (1981, Feb. 26). *Daily Labor Report,* Washington, DC: Bureau of National Affairs, pp. D3–D10.

29. *Gateway Coal Co. v. United Mine Workers of America* (1974). 1974 OSHD, Sn. 17,085. Chicago: Commerce Clearing House.

30. Ledvinka, J., & Scarpello, V.G. (1991). *Federal regulation of personnel and human resource management* (2d ed.). Boston: PWS-Kent.

31. Bernstein, A. (1998, Feb.23). The workplace cops could use some backup. *BusinessWeek,* p. 42.

32. Kuntz, op. cit.

33. Marsh, B. (1994, Feb. 3). Workers at risk. *The Wall Street Journal,* pp. A1, A8.

34. Cook, W. N., & Gautschi, F. H. (1981). OSHA plant safety programs and injury reduction. *Industrial Relations, 20*(3), 245–257.

35. Champ, B. (1997). The safety culture revolution: Making it happen. *Canadian Chemical News, 49,* 12. See also Milbank, D. (1991, Mar. 29). Companies turn to peer pressure to cut injuries as psychologists join the battle. *The Wall Street Journal,* pp. B1, B3.

36. Ashford, N. A. (1976). *Crisis in the workplace: Occupational disease and injury.* Cambridge, MA: MIT Press. See also Burtt, E. J. (1979) *Labor in the American Economy.* New York: St. Martin's Press.

37. Follmann, J. F., Jr. (1978). *The economics of industrial health.* New York: AMACOM.

38. *Inside OSHA: The role of management in safety* (1975, Nov. 1). New York: Man and Manager, Inc.

39. Hofmann, D. A., & Morgeson, F. P. (1999). Safety-related behavior as a social exchange: The role of perceived organizational support and leader-member exchange. *Journal of Applied Psychology, 84,* 286–296. See also LaBar, G. (1997). OSHA has a

strategic plan. Do you? *Occupational Hazards, 59*, 10. See also Manuele, F. A. (1997). A causation model for hazardous incidents. *Occupational Hazards, 59*, 160–164.

40. Hofmann & Morgeson, op. cit. See also Hofmann, D. A., & Stetzer, A. (1998). The role of safety climate and communication in accident interpretation: Implications of learning from negative events. *Academy of Management Journal, 41*, 644–657.

41. Kuntz, op. cit. See also Repetitive stress: The pain has just begun (1992, July 13). *BusinessWeek*, pp. 142, 143. See also Crippled by computers (1992, Oct. 12). *Time*, pp. 70, 71.

42. Grossman, R. J. (2000, April). Make ergonomics go. *HRMagazine*, pp. 36–42. See also Repetitive motion complaints (1996, Aug. 15). *USA Today*, p. B1.

43. Rundle, op. cit.

44. U.S. Department of Labor, op. cit.

45. Liao, H., Arvey, R. D., & Butler, R. J. (2001). Correlates of work injury frequency and duration among firefighters. *Journal of Occupational Health Psychology, 6*(3), 229–242. See also Graham, S. (1996, Jan.). Debunk the myths about older workers. *Safety & Health*, pp. 38–41. See also Siskind, F. (1982). Another look at the link between work injuries and job experience. *Monthly Labor Review, 105*(2), 38–41. See also Root, N. (1981). Injuries at work are fewer among older employees. *Monthly Labor Review, 104*(3), 30–34.

46. Leary, W. E. (1982, Aug. 2). Management concern affects mine safety. *Denver Post*, p. 1C. See also Liao et al., op. cit.

47. U.S. Department of Labor, op. cit.

48. Frone, M. R. (1998). Predictors of work injuries among employed adolescents. *Journal of Applied Psychology, 83*, 565–576.

49. *Chemical hazard communication* (rev. ed.) (1988). OSHA No. 3084. Washington, DC: U.S. Department of Labor.

50. Jacobs, S. L. (1988, Nov. 22). Small business slowly wakes to OSHA hazard rule. *The Wall Street Journal*, p. B2.

51. Hays, L. (1986, July 8). New rules on workplace hazards prompt intensified on-the-job training programs. *The Wall Street Journal*, p. 31.

52. Komaki, J., Barwick, K. D., & Scott, L. R. (1978). A behavioral approach to occupational safety: Pinpointing and reinforcing safe performance in a food manufacturing plant. *Journal of Applied Psychology, 63*, 434–445.

53. Yandrick, R. M. (1996, Feb.). Behavioral safety helps shipbuilder cut accident rates. *HR News*, pp. 3, 11. See also Reber, R. A., & Wallin, J. A. (1984). The effects of training, goal setting, and knowledge of results on safe behavior: A component analysis. *Academy of Management Journal, 27*, 544–560.

54. Milbank, op. cit.

55. McMurray, S. (1991, Oct. 4). India's high court upholds settlement paid by Carbide in Bhopal gas leak. *The Wall Street Journal*, p. B3. See also Damages for a deadly cloud (1989, Feb. 27). *Time*, p. 53.

56. McMurray, S., & Harlan, C. (1992, May 1). Indian judge orders seizure of Carbide assets in country. *The Wall Street Journal*, p. B5.

57. One CEO's nightmare: Bhopal ghosts (still) haunt Union Carbide. (2000, Apr. 3). *Fortune*, pp. 44, 46.

58. Foreign firms feel the impact of Bhopal most (1985, Nov. 26). *The Wall Street Journal*, p. 24.

59. Ibid.

60. A crusader for industry's casualties (2000, Dec. 18). *BusinessWeek*, p. 188. See also Thailand fire shows region cuts corners on safety to boost profits (1993, May 13). *The Wall Street Journal*, p. A13.

61. Pangs of conscience: Sweatshops haunt U.S. consumers (1996, July 29). *BusinessWeek*, pp. 46–48.

62. *Illinois v. Chicago Magnet Wire Corp.* (1990, Oct. 24). 126 Ill. 2d 356, 534 N.E., 2d 962, 128 Ill.

63. Wermiel, S. (1989, Oct. 3). Justices let states prosecute executives for job hazards covered by U.S. law. *The Wall Street Journal,* p. A11.

64. Grossman, R. J. (2000, Oct.). Out with the bad air. *HRMagazine,* pp. 36–45.

65. Karr, A. R. (1989, Jan. 16). OSHA sets or toughens limits on 376 toxic chemicals in workplace. *The Wall Street Journal,* p. C16.

66. Stead, W. E., & Stead, J. G. (1983, Jan.). OSHA's cancer prevention policy: Where did it come from and where is it going? *Personnel Journal,* pp. 54–60.

67. Carrns, A. (2001, May 30). Blacks now account for half of all new HIV infections; homosexuality still taboo. *The Wall Street Journal,* pp. Bl, B4. See also Alliton, V. (1992, Feb.). Financial realities of AIDS in the workplace. *HRMagazine,* pp. 78–81.

68. Taking stock of the devastation (2000, July 17). *BusinessWeek,* pp. 84, 85.

69. Twenty years of AIDS in America (2001, May 30). *The Wall Street Journal,* p. B1.

70. Ibid.

71. Taking stock of the devastation, op. cit.

72. Levi Strauss & Co. in Tedlow, op. cit., p. 17.

73. Tedlow, R. S. (1993, June 18). *Levi Strauss & Co. and the AIDS crisis.* Harvard Business School, Case #9-391-198, p. 17.

74. Seppa, N. (1997, Mar.). EAPs offer quality care and cost-effectiveness. *APA Monitor,* pp. 32, 33. See also Is business bungling its battle with booze? (1991, Mar. 25). *BusinessWeek,* pp. 76–78.

75. Berg, N. R., & Moe, J. P. (1979). Assistance for troubled employees. In D. Yoder & H. G. Heneman, Jr. (eds.), *ASPA handbook of personnel and industrial relations.* Washington, DC: BNA, pp. 1.59–1.77.

76. Blum, T. C., & Roman, P. M. (1995). *Cost-effectiveness and preventive implications of employee assistance programs.* Washington, DC: U.S. Dept. of Health and Human Services.

77. Stone, D. L., & Kotch, D. A. (1989). Individuals' attitudes toward organizational drug testing policies and practices. *Journal of Applied Psychology, 74,* 518–521.

78. Milne, S. H., Blum, T. C., & Roman, P. M. (1994). Factors influencing employees' propensity to use an employee assistance program. *Personnel Psychology, 47,* 123–145.

79. Seppa, op. cit. See also Is business bungling its battle with booze? op. cit.

80. Seppa, op. cit.

81. Cascio, W. F. (2000). *Costing human resources: The financial impact of behavior in organizations* (4th ed.). Cincinnati, OH: South-Western. See also Foote, A., & Erfurt, J. (1981, Sept.–Oct.). Evaluating an employee assistance program. *EAP Digest,* pp. 14–25.

82. Collins, K. (2001, Apr.). HR must find new ways to battle substance abuse in the workplace. *HR News,* pp. 11, 16.

83. Ray, J. S. (1982). Having problems with worker performance? Try an EAP. *Administrative Management, 43*(5), 47–49.

84. How is drinking affecting the workplace? (1993, Aug.). *Mountain States Employers Council Bulletin,* p.5. See also How to confront—and help—an alcoholic employee (1991, Mar. 25). *BusinessWeek,* p. 78.

85. Ibid.

86. Pollock, E. J. (1996, Sept. 9). In leaner, meaner workplace, bosses get tough on addiction. *The Wall Street Journal,* pp. B1, B2.

87. Weiss, R. M. (1987). Writing under the influence: Science versus fiction in the analysis of corporate alcoholism programs. *Personnel Psychology, 40,* 341–356.

88. Collins, op. cit. See also Is business bungling its battle with booze? op. cit.

89. Pollock, op. cit.

90. Collins, op. cit.

91. Ibid. See also Farkas, G. M. (1989). The impact of federal rehabilitation laws on the expanding role of employee assistance programs in business and industry. *American Psychologist, 44,* 1482–1490.

92. Overman, S. (1999, Aug.). Splitting hairs. *HRMagazine,* pp. 42–48. See also Lehman, W. E. K., & Simpson, D. D. (1992). Employee substance abuse and on-the-job behaviors. *Journal of Applied Psychology, 77,* 309–321.

93. Drug tests keep paying off; but continued gains are tougher (1998, May 5). *The Wall Street Journal,* p. Al. See also Normand, J., Salyards, S. D., & Mahoney, J. J. (1990). An evaluation of pre-employment drug testing. *Journal of Applied Psychology, 75,* 629–639.

94. Taking drugs on the job (1983, Aug. 22). *Newsweek,* p. 55.

95. How is drinking affecting the workplace? op. cit.

96. OSHA issues guidelines on workplace violence (1996, Nov.–Dec.) *Mountain States Employers Council Bulletin,* p. 3.

97. Neuman, J. H., & Baron, R. A. (1998). Workplace violence and workplace aggression: Evidence concerning specific forms, potential causes, and preferred targets. *Journal of Management, 24,* 391–419.

98. After the shooting stops (2001, Mar. 12). *BusinessWeek,* pp. 98–100.

99. Neuman & Baron, op. cit. See also Adams, J. T. III (2001, Feb.). Workplace deaths decline, coworker homicides rise. *HRMagazine,* p. 12.

100. Fisher, A. (1997, May 26). Managing. *Fortune,* pp. 165, 166.

101. Neuman & Baron, op. cit.

102. Mountain States Employers Council and Nicoletti-Flater Associates (1997). *Violence goes to work: An employer's guide* (2d ed.). Denver: Mountain States Employers Council. See also Ferlise, W. G. (1995, Apr.). Violence in the workplace. *Personnel Testing Council of Metropolitan Washington Newsletter,* p. 9.

103. Kilborn, P. T. (1993, May 17). Inside post offices, the mail is only part of the pressure. *The New York Times,* pp. Al, A15.

104. Ferlise, op. cit. See also Violent employees. (1994, Feb.). *Mountain States Employers Council Bulletin,* p. 5.

105. Brody, J. E. (1991, July 10). As benefits and staff shrink, job stress grows. *The New York Times,* p. C11.

106. Lombino, P. (1992, Feb.). An ounce of prevention. *CFO,* pp. 15–22. See also Winslow, R. (1991, Jan. 29). Medical costs soar, defying firms' cures. *The Wall Street Journal,* p. B1.

107. Wellness plans cut U.S. firms' health cost (2000, June). *Manpower Argus,* no. 381, p. 8.

108. Pudgeball nation (2001, July 23). *BusinessWeek,* p. 16.

109. Rundle, op. cit. See also Hollenbeck, J. R., Ilgen, D. R., & Crampton, S. M. (1992). Lower back disability in occupational settings: A review of the literature from a human resource management view. *Personnel Psychology, 45,* 247–278.

110. Grossman, R. J. (2001, Aug.). Back with a vengeance. *HRMagazine,* pp. 36–46.

111. Lombino, op. cit.

112. Ibid.

113. Terborg, J. (1998). Health psychology in the United States: A critique and selected review. *Applied Psychology: an International Review, 47*(2), 199–217 See also Epstein, S.S. (1989). *A note on health promotion in the workplace.* Boston: Harvard Business School.

114. Stolberg, S. (1993, Nov. 10). Top underlying cause of death: Tobacco use. *The Denver Post,* p. 2A. See also Kahn, R. L., & Byosiere, P. (1992). Stress in organizations. In M.D. Dunnette & L. M. Hough (eds.), *Handbook of industrial and organizational psychology* (2d ed., vol. 3). Palo Alto, CA: Consulting Psychologists Press, pp. 571–650.

115. Mavis, B. E. (1992). Issues related to participation in worksite health promotion: A preliminary study. *American Journal of Health Promotion, 7*(1), 53–63. See also

Alexy, B. B. (1991). Factors associated with participation or nonparticipation in a workplace wellness center. *Research in Nursing and Health 14*(1), 33–39.

116. Lombino, op. cit.

117. Jose, W. S., Anderson, D. R., & Haight, S. A. (1987). The StayWell strategy for health care cost containment. In J. P. Opatz (ed.), *Health promotion evaluation: Measuring the organizational impact.* Stevens Point, WI: National Wellness Institute, pp. 15–34. See also Wellness plans cut U.S. firms' health cost, op. cit.

118. Parkes, K. R. (1987). Relative weight, smoking, and mental health as predictors of sickness and absence from work. *Journal of Applied Psychology, 72,* 275–286.

119. Jeffrey, N. A. (1996, June 21). "Wellness plans" try to target the not-so-well. *The Wall Street Journal,* pp. B1, B6.

120. Terborg, op. cit. See also Falkenberg, L. E. (1987). Employee fitness programs: Their impact on the employee and the organization. *Academy of Management Review, 12,* 511–522.

121. Cascio, op. cit.

122. Erfurt, J. C., Foote, A., & Heirich, M. A. (1992). The cost-effectiveness of worksite wellness programs for hypertension control, weight loss, smoking cessation, and exercise. *Personnel Psychology, 45,* 5–27. See also Viswesvaran, C., & Schmidt, F. L. (1992). A meta-analytic comparison of smoking cessation methods. *Journal of Applied Psychology, 77,* 554–561. See also Gebhardt, D. L., & Crump, C. E. (1990). Employee fitness and wellness programs in the workplace. *American Psychologist, 45,* 262–272.

123. Fries, J. F. (1992). Health risk changes with a low-cost individualized health promotion program: Effects at up to 30 months. *American Journal of Health Promotion, 6*(5), 367–380.

124. If you light up on Sunday, don't come in on Monday (1991, Aug. 26). *BusinessWeek,* pp. 68–72.

125. Fries, J. F., Koop, C. E., Beadle, C. E., Cooper, P. P., England, M. J., Greaves, R. F., Sokolov, J. J., & Wright, D. (1993). Reducing health care costs by reducing the need and demand for medical services. *New England Journal of Medicine, 329*(5), 321–325. See also Wellness plans cut U.S. firms' health cost, op. cit.

126. Johnson, S. (1988, June). Breast screening's bottom line—lives saved. *Administrative Radiology,* p. 4.

127. Petty, A. (1993, Sept. 17). More women get mammograms at work. *The Wall Street Journal,* pp. B1, B6.

128. Lombino, op. cit.

129. Rothman, H. (1992). Wellness works for small firms. *Nation's Business, 77*(12), 42–46.

130. Wellness plans cut U.S. firms' health cost, op. cit.

131. Wellness can mean a trim bottom line (1993, Aug. 16). *BusinessWeek,* p. 112.

132. Terborg, op. cit.

133. Matthes, K. (1992, Dec.). ADA checkup: Assess your wellness program. *HR Focus, 69*(12), p. 15.

16

INTERNATIONAL DIMENSIONS OF HUMAN RESOURCE MANAGEMENT

Questions This Chapter Will Help Managers Answer

1. What factors should I consider in "sizing up" managers, employees, and customers from a different culture?
2. What should be the components of expatriate recruitment, selection, orientation, and training strategies?
3. How should an expatriate compensation package be structured?
4. What kinds of career management issues should a manager consider before deciding to work for a foreign-owned firm in the United States?
5. What special issues deserve attention in the repatriation of overseas employees?

WHAT'S IT LIKE TO BE A GLOBAL MANAGER?*

My first day on the job is turning into a nightmare. I am about to meet with a promising young manager who has just botched a new assignment, and in just a few hours, I'm scheduled to make a strategy presentation to my new boss. But the phone won't stop ringing, and I'm being deluged with e-mail.

It's a good thing this isn't really happening. I'm at a makeshift office in suburban London taking part in a workplace-simulation exercise. It's just like the exercise hundreds of Motorola, Inc. executives around the world will go through in the coming months as part of a wide-ranging effort at the company to identify and evaluate tomorrow's top international managers.

Like many multinationals, Motorola is pressing to find talented leaders to run its increasingly complicated global business. As companies cross borders to make acquisitions and expand operations, the demand for employees with international management skills is growing exponentially. The consequences can be dire for firms that fail to build up a cadre of competent global managers. Poor decisions can lead to multi-billion-dollar flubs, as products flop and marketing campaigns go awry.

Motorola's Internet-based test, developed with Aon Consulting Worldwide, can be administered remotely any place in the world. As Aon executives explained to me how the simulation would work, I imagined myself enduring several hours of awkward play-acting. In practice, the experience is startlingly lifelike.

My role is Chris Jefferson, regional manager in the finance unit of a fictitious conglomerate, Globalcom. My laptop computer has been specially set up so that I can send and receive e-mail, look up information about my employer, and consult my calendar—where several meetings have already been scheduled. An Aon psychologist will play several roles, phoning me from an adjacent office and popping in at the end in the role of Jean Dubois, my boss.

As soon as I settle in to my windowless, brick-walled office, the telephone calls begin and unexpected visitors arrive. Urgent tasks come so fast and furiously that I quickly forget it is all a game. Several calls and e-mails concern a promising middle manager who has let several details of a critical new assignment fall through the cracks.

Another Aon psychologist is playing the role of the manager, and he enters my office for our meeting. I try teasing out of him information about what's going wrong. We talk for several minutes before a voice in the back of my brain reminds me that it's all only make-believe.

The meeting is over and I have less than 2 hours to get my presentation ready. I hurry to prepare, scouring my computer for information about Globalcom. I find things like market research, news reports, results of an employee survey and corporate press releases, but just like one of those bad dreams, I keep getting sidetracked by a steady stream of telephone calls. An irate customer rails shrilly at me about poor service and threatens to bolt to the competition. E-mails, some of them demanding immediate attention, keep popping up on my computer screen.

Source: Adapted from D. Woodruff, Distractions make global manager a difficult role, *The Wall Street Journal,* Nov. 21, 2000, pp. B1, B18. Reprinted by permission of *The Wall Street Journal,* © 2000 Dow Jones & Company, Inc. All rights reserved worldwide.

Challenges

1. Can you identify any differences between managing domestically versus internationally?
2. How accurate are such workplace simulations? In what form might results show up?
3. Do simulations like Motorola's "travel well"? That is, do you think they will work in different cultures?

Increasingly, the world is becoming a "global village" as multinational investment continues to grow. All the human resource (HR) management issues that have been discussed to this point are interrelated conceptually and operationally and are particularly relevant in the international context: HR planning, recruitment, selection, orientation, training and development, career management, compensation, and labor relations. In examining all these issues, as well as considering the special problems of repatriation (the process of reentering one's native culture after being absent from it), this chapter thus provides a capstone to the book.

THE GLOBAL CORPORATION: A FACT OF MODERN ORGANIZATIONAL LIFE

The demise of communism, the fall of trade barriers, and the rise of networked information have unleashed a revolution in business. Market capitalism guides every major country on earth. About $1.6 trillion of foreign exchange changes hands every day, goods and services flow across borders more freely than ever; and vast information networks instantly link nations, companies, and people. The result—21st-century capitalism.[1] To begin to appreciate the magnitude of this trend, consider a snapshot of the 2001 *Fortune* Global 500 (the largest 500 firms in the world). Their aggregate revenues were $14,065 billion, profits were $667 billion, their assets totaled $45,808 billion, and they employed more than 47.2 million of the world's people.[2]

Signs of Globalization

Globalization is the dominant driving force in the world economy, reshaping societies and politics as it changes lives. Moreover, an expanding high-tech, information-based economy increasingly defines globalization and shapes the business cycles within it. Much of the flow of capital, labor, services, and goods among Asia, America, and Europe are technology based. Without chips, screens, and software help from Asia, the U.S. economy would grind to a halt.[3] In this emerging economic order, foreign investment by the world's leading corporations is a fact of modern organizational life. Over 800 multinational companies have regional headquarters in Hong Kong alone![4] Today foreign investment is viewed not just as an opportunity for U.S. companies investing abroad but also as an opportunity for other countries to develop subsidiaries in the United States and elsewhere. Indeed, a global marketplace has been created by factors such as the following:

- Global telecommunications enhanced by fiber optics, satellites, and computer technology.[5]
- Giant multinational corporations such as Gillette, Unilever, and Nestlé, which have begun to lose their national identities as they integrate and coordinate product design, manufacturing, sales, and services on a worldwide basis.
- Growing free trade among nations (exemplified by the 1993 North American Free Trade Agreement among Mexico, the United States, and Canada).
- Financial markets' being open 24 hours a day around the world.
- From 1998 through the first quarter of 2001, foreign companies invested more than $600 billion in the United States, and U.S. multinationals invested similar amounts overseas.[6]
- Foreign control of about 6 percent of the U.S. workforce and 15 percent of manufacturing employees.[7]
- The emergence of global standards and regulations for trade, commerce, finance, products, and services.

The Backlash against Globalization

In no small part, the booming U.S. economy of recent years has been fueled by globalization. Open borders have allowed new ideas and technology to flow freely around the globe, accelerating productivity growth and allowing U.S. companies to be more competitive than they have been in decades. Yet there is a growing fear on the part of many people that globalization benefits big companies instead of average citizens—of America or any other country.[8] Five factors are driving this backlash[9]:

- **Insecurity.** As companies restructure and adapt to market forces, they are churning their workforces. Many operations are being sent overseas, as both blue- and white-collar workers watch their jobs migrate to India and Ireland.
- **Mistrust.** Big, multilateral institutions such as the International Monetary Fund (IMF), the World Bank, and the World Trade Organization (WTO) are losing their credibility. Their secret decisions, made behind closed doors, are not acceptable to citizens accustomed to transparent, democratic institutions.
- **Policy.** Long-held prescriptions for solving international financial crises are losing support. Bailing out private banks while depressing growth and forcing unemployment higher—a strategy the IMF initially pursued in response to the Asian financial crisis of 1997–1999—is no longer acceptable as the sole remedy to financial troubles overseas.
- **Priorities.** Whether business likes it or not, the environment and also labor standards overseas are genuine issues with growing support among high-tech workers, students, and the young in America. These are new issues on the global agenda and they won't go away.
- **Technophobia.** The battle against genetically modified food is just one indicator of the growing reaction against the dot.com world. In the United States, and especially in Europe, science and innovation are seen by many

as threats, not solutions. Preservation of traditional national values is most important.[10] Globalization is the enemy.

In the public eye, multinational corporations are synonymous with globalization. In all of their far-flung operations, therefore, they bear responsibility to be good corporate citizens, to preserve the environment, to uphold labor standards, to provide decent working conditions and competitive wages, to treat their employees fairly, and to contribute to the communities in which they operate. Some have done so admirably. Levi Strauss & Co. has ethical manufacturing standards for its overseas operations. Home Depot, Inc. has adopted an eco-friendly lumber supply program with the Rainforest Action Network. Starbucks is working with Conservation International to buy coffee from farmers preserving forests.[11] Actions like these make a strong case for continued globalization.

The fact is, thousands of firms have operations in many countries around the globe. Before proceeding further, let's define some terms that we will use throughout the chapter:

- A **global corporation** is one that has become an "insider" in any market or nation where it operates and is thus competitive with domestic firms operating in local markets.[12] Unlike domestic firms, however, the global corporation has a global strategic perspective and claims its legitimacy from its effective use of assets to serve its far-flung customers.
- An **expatriate,** or a *foreign-service employee,* is a generic term applied to anyone working outside her or his home country with a planned return to that or a third country.
- The **home country** is the expatriate's country of residence.
- The **host country** is the country in which the expatriate is working.
- A **third-country national** is an expatriate who has transferred to an additional country while working abroad. A German working for a U.S. firm in Spain is a third-country national.

Expatriates staff many, if not most, overseas operations of multinational firms, and the costs can be astronomical.

The Costs of Overseas Executives

One of the first lessons global corporations learn is that it is far cheaper to hire competent host-country nationals (if they are available) than to send their own executives overseas. Foreign-service employees typically cost 2 to 3 times the salary of a comparable domestic employee, and often many more times the salary of a local national employee in the assignment country (see Table 16-1).[13] Firms spend an average of $1 million per manager during a four-year assignment,[14] but companies send only about 15 percent of their overall managerial populations on overseas assignments.[15]

Consider these 2001 cost-of-living indexes for a three-person U.S. family at the $100,000 income level, where New York equals 100: Toronto, 51.3; Bombay, 55.5; Paris, 65.4; Mexico City, 77.6; Beijing, 84; London, 95.1; Singapore, 96.3; Moscow, 113.4; Tokyo, 138.8; and Seoul, 147.[16]

Table 16–1

TYPICAL U.S. EXPATRIATE COMPENSATION PACKAGE (ANNUAL EXPENSE): MARRIED WITH ONE CHILD

Category	U.S. compensation	Overseas compensation
Base salary	$85,000	$ 85,000
Overseas incentive		15%
Hardship		10%
Housing differential		35%
Furniture		12%
Utilities differential		20%
Car and driver		15%
Cost-of-living adjustment		40%
Club membership		2%
Education		12%
Total	$85,000	$221,850
U.S. Tax	24,000	24,000
Net annual compensation	$61,000	$197,850

Note: A complete expatriate package also includes the following: (1) annual transportation to the United States for home leave, (2) storage of U.S. household goods, (3) shipment of some goods to the foreign location, (4) U.S. auto disposal, (5) U.S. house management, (6) interim living expenses, (7) travel to new assignment and return, and (8) annual tax equalization.

The costs of doing business are often much higher overseas than in the United States. Consider office space as an example. In the United States, rent, taxes, and operating expenses per square foot average $42 in midtown Manhattan. By contrast, such costs (in U.S. dollars) average about $48 in Paris and Frankfurt, $84 in Tokyo, $80 in Moscow, $65 in Hong Kong, and $121 in London.[17] Of course, costs fluctuate with international exchange rates relative to the U.S. dollar. In view of these high costs, firms are working hard to reduce the failure rate in their expatriates—about 10 percent of expatriate assignments for companies based in North America and Europe, and about 15 percent for Asian firms.[18] For companies, the costs of mistaken expatriation include the costs of initial recruitment, relocation expenses, premium compensation, repatriation costs (i.e., costs associated with resettling the expatriate), replacement costs, and the tangible costs of poor job performance. When an overseas assignment does not work out, it still costs a company, on average, twice the employee's base salary. For employees, the costs are more personal: diminished self-esteem, impaired relationships, and interrupted careers.[19]

Although the costs of expatriates are considerable, there are also compensating benefits to multinational firms. In particular, overseas postings allow managers to develop international experience outside their home countries—the kind of experience needed to compete successfully in the global economy that we now live in.[20]

Nevertheless, it is senseless to send people abroad who do not know what they are doing overseas and cannot be effective in the foreign culture. As the manager of international HR at Hewlett-Packard remarked: "When you are sending someone abroad to work on an important agreement, it is terribly important that they have as much information as possible about how to do business in that country. The cost of training is inconsequential compared to the risk of sending inexperienced or untrained people."[21]

For all these reasons, companies need to consider the impact of culture on international HR management. But what is culture? **Culture** refers to characteristic ways of doing things and behaving that people in a given country or region have evolved over time. It helps people to make sense of their part of the world and provides them with an identity.

THE ROLE OF CULTURAL UNDERSTANDING IN INTERNATIONAL MANAGEMENT PRACTICE

Managers who have no appreciation for cultural differences have a **local perspective.** They believe in the inherent superiority of their own group and culture, and they tend to look down on those considered "foreign." Rather than accepting differences as legitimate, they view and measure alien cultures in terms of their own.

By contrast, managers with a **cosmopolitan perspective** are sensitive to cultural differences, respect the distinctive practices of others, and make allowances for such factors when communicating with representatives of different cultural groups. Recognizing that culture and behavior are relative, they are more tentative and less absolute in their interactions with others.[22]

Such cultural understanding can minimize "culture shock" and allow managers to be more effective with both employees and customers. The first step in this process is increasing one's general awareness of differences across cultures, for they deeply affect human resource management practices.

HUMAN RESOURCE MANAGEMENT PRACTICES AS A CULTURAL VARIABLE

Particularly when business does not go well, Americans returning from overseas assignments tend to blame the local people, calling them irresponsible, unmotivated, or downright dishonest. Such judgments are pointless, for many of the problems are a matter of fundamental cultural differences that profoundly affect how different people view the world and operate in business. This section presents a systematic framework, 10 broad classifications, that will help managers assess any culture and examine its people systematically. It does not consider every aspect of culture, and by no means is it the only way to analyze culture. Rather, it is a useful beginning for cultural understanding. The framework is composed of the following 10 factors[23]:

- Sense of self and space.
- Dress and appearance.
- Food and eating habits.

- Communication: verbal and nonverbal.
- Time and time sense.
- Relationships.
- Values and norms.
- Beliefs and attitudes.
- Work motivation and practices.
- Mental processes and learning.

Sense of Self and Space

Self-identity may be manifested by a humble bearing in some places, by macho behavior in others. Some countries (e.g., the United States) may promote independence and creativity, while others (e.g., Japan) emphasize group cooperation and conformity. Americans have a sense of space that requires more distance between people, while Latins and Vietnamese prefer to get much closer. Each culture has its own unique ways of doing things.

Dress and Appearance

Outer garments as well as body decorations have an effect on a person's appearance. Many cultures wear distinctive clothing—the Japanese kimono, the Indian turban, the Polynesian sarong, the "organization-man-or-woman" look of business, and uniforms that distinguish wearers from everybody else. Cosmetics are more popular and accepted in some cultures than in others, as is cologne or after-shave lotion for men.

Food and Eating Habits

The manner in which food is selected, prepared, presented, and eaten often differs by culture. Most major cities have restaurants that specialize in the distinctive cuisine of various cultures—everything from Afghan to Zambian. Utensils also differ, ranging from bare hands to chopsticks to full sets of cutlery. Knowledge of food and eating habits often provides insights into customs and culture.

Communication: Verbal and Nonverbal

The axiom "Words mean different things to different people" is especially true in cross-cultural communication. When an American says she is "tabling" a proposition, it is generally accepted that she means discussion of the proposition will be put off. In England, "tabling" means to discuss something now. Translations from one language to another can generate even more confusion as a result of differences in style and context. Coca-Cola found this out when it began marketing its soft-drink products in China.

The traditional Coca-Cola trademark took on an unintended translation when shopkeepers added their own calligraphy to the company name. "Coca-Cola," pronounced "ke kou ke la" in one Chinese dialect, translates as "bite the wax tadpole." Reshuffling the pronunciation to "ko kou ko le" roughly translates to "may the mouth rejoice."[24]

In many cultures, directness and openness are not appreciated. An open person may be seen as weak and untrustworthy, and directness can be interpreted as abrupt, hostile behavior. Providing specific details may be seen as insulting to one's intelligence. Insisting on a written contract may suggest that a person's word is not good.

Nonverbal cues may also mean different things. In the United States, one who does not look someone in the eye arouses suspicion and is called "shifty-eyed." In some other countries, however, looking someone in the eye is perceived as aggression. Just as communication skills are key ingredients for success in U.S. business, such skills are basic to success in international business. There is no compromise on this issue; ignorance of local customs and communications protocol is disrespectful.[25]

Time and Time Sense

To Americans, time is money. We live by schedules, deadlines, and agendas; we hate to be kept waiting, and we like to "get down to business" quickly. In many countries, however, people simply will not be rushed. They arrive late for appointments, and business is preceded by hours of social rapport. People in a rush are thought to be arrogant and untrustworthy.

In the United States, the most important issues are generally discussed first when making a business deal. In Ethiopia, however, the most important things are taken up last. While being late seems to be the norm for business meetings in Latin America, the reverse is true in Switzerland, Sweden, and Germany, where prompt efficiency is the watchword.[26] The lesson for Americans doing business overseas is clear: *Be flexible about time and realistic about what can be accomplished.* Adapt to the process of doing business in any particular country.

Relationships

Cultures designate human and organizational relationships by age, gender, status, and family relationships, as well as by wealth, power, and wisdom.[27] Relationships between and among people vary by category—in some cultures the elderly are honored; in others they are ignored. In some cultures women must wear veils and act deferentially; in others the female is considered equal, if not superior, to the male.

In some cultures (e.g., France, Japan, Korea, and to some extent the United States and Great Britain), *where* one went to school may affect one's status.[28] Often, lifelong relationships are established among individuals who attended the same school. In other cultures (e.g., Switzerland), one's rank in the military may affect one's job level and prospects for promotion. Finally, the issue of nepotism is viewed very differently in different parts of the world. While most U.S. firms frown upon the practice of hiring or contracting work directly with family members, in Latin America or Arab countries, it only makes sense to hire someone you can trust.[29]

Values and Norms

From its value system, a culture sets **norms of behavior,** or what some call "local customs." One such norm is that in Eastern countries businesspeople strive for successful business outcomes after personal relationships have been established, while Westerners develop social relationships after business interests have been addressed. International managers ignore such norms at their peril.[30] For example, consider the impact of values and norms on management styles and HR practices in the European Union.

HRM IN THE EUROPEAN UNION[31]

INTERNATIONAL
EXAMPLE

The EU comprises the following 15 countries: Austria, Belgium, Denmark, Finland, France, Germany, Ireland, Italy, Greece, Luxembourg, Netherlands, Portugal, Spain, Sweden, and the United Kingdom. Much has been written recently about the economic and political unification of Europe—the free movement of capital, goods, and people and the harmonization of European Union (EU) legislation. Does this mean that multinationals operating in Europe can deal with people in the various EU countries on a regional basis and in a universal manner? Is there such a thing as "European human resource management (Euro-HRM)"? A recent analysis of 12,965 articles published between 1975 and 1999 from 26 HR journals in the original nine languages of 10 EU countries indicates that the answer is no. So also do the results of in-depth interviews with 48 European HR experts (practitioners, consultants, and academics) in 14 different countries of the EU conducted on location in the original languages of the countries.

In spite of the economic, political, and social unification of Europe as a result of the EU, there is no harmonized manner in which HR services are delivered across or within the various European countries. Rather, Euro-HRM is a mosaic of practices that differ primarily on the basis of the size of the company, and the different national, cultural, legal, and geographic contexts. Outsiders should know eight key things about HRM in the EU countries:

1. Each country has a unique set of intricate laws that govern employment and labor relations.[32]
2. Each country has a unique culture that impacts management styles and the corporate cultures of companies.
3. Within some EU countries there are different subcultures that influence HRM.
4. The power of the labor unions is decreasing, but labor relations issues remain very important.
5. Each country has developed a set of institutions that reflects its traditions and influences the way HR is practiced.
6. Distinct underlying social models have an impact on the way HR is practiced in each country. For example, the Dutch social justice model emphasizes the widespread belief that the government should play an active, interventionist role to provide social justice in areas such as occupational health, safety, and terminations. In contrast, the Italian social model is a mixture of Christian and Marxist values. It emphasizes the individual's need for protection and solidarity, and is less meritocratic and competitive than Protestant cultures.
7. There are formal consultation processes in place that allow for greater involvement of employees and trade unions in the decision-making processes of companies.

8. Importing HR practices from abroad without attempting to localize them to the specific culture, laws, and languages of the country provides little chance of successful implementation.

Beliefs and Attitudes

To some degree, religion expresses the philosophy of a people about important facets in life. While Western culture is largely influenced by Judeo-Christian traditions and Middle Eastern culture by Islam, Oriental and Indian cultures are dominated by Buddhism, Confucianism, Taoism, and Hinduism. In cultures where a religious view of work still prevails, work is viewed as an act of service to God and people and is expressed in a moral commitment to the job or quality of effort.[33] In Japan, the cultural loyalty to family is transferred to the work organization. It is expressed in work-group participation, communication, and consensus.[34]

T. Fujisawa, cofounder of Honda Motor Co., once remarked: "Japanese and American management is 95 percent the same, and differs in all important respects." In other words, while organizations are becoming more similar in terms of structure and technology, people's behavior within those organizations continues to reveal culturally-based differences.[35]

Work Motivation and Practices

Knowledge of what motivates workers in a given culture, combined with (or based on) a knowledge of what they think matters in life, is critical to the success of the international manager. Europeans pay particular attention to power and status, which results in more formal management and operating styles in comparison to the informality found in the United States. In the United States individual initiative and achievement are rewarded, but in Japan managers are encouraged to seek consensus before acting, and employees work as teams. In one comparison of motivating factors for middle-aged Japanese and U.S. business managers, the Japanese showed more interest in advancement, money, and forward striving. Since these characteristics tend to be closely associated with success, it may be that achievement and advancement motivation are driving forces behind Japanese productivity, and that "team" action is only their method

Effective multinational managers are constantly open to new ideas, trying to learn from cultures other than their own.

of disciplining and rewarding it.[36] When a similar survey was conducted among German workers, 48 percent said higher income was the key motivating factor for them, followed by opportunities for promotion (25 percent) and more independence (25 percent).[37]

The determinants of work motivation may not be all that different in developing countries. In Zambia, for example, work motivation seems to be determined by six factors: the nature of the work itself, opportunities for growth and advancement, material and physical provisions (i.e., pay, benefits, job security, favorable physical work conditions), relations with others, fairness or unfairness in organizational practices, and personal problems. The effect of personal problems is totally negative. That is, *their presence impairs motivation, but their absence does not enhance it.*[38]

Mental Processes and Learning

Linguists, anthropologists, and other experts who have studied this issue have found vast differences in the ways people think and learn in different cultures. While some cultures favor abstract thinking and conceptualization, others prefer rote memory and learning. The Chinese, Japanese, and Korean written languages are based on ideograms, or "word pictures." On the other hand, English is based on precise expression using words. Western cultures stress linear thinking and logic, that is, A, then B, then C, then D. Among Arabic and Oriental cultures, however, nonlinear thinking prevails. This has direct implications for negotiation processes. That is, A may be followed by C; then back to B and on to D. Such an approach, in which issues are treated as independent and not linked by sequence, can be confusing and frustrating to Westerners because it does not appear "logical." What can we conclude from this? What seems to be universal is that each culture has a reasoning process, but each manifests the process in its own distinctive way.[39] Managers who do not understand or appreciate such differences may conclude (erroneously and to their detriment) that certain cultures are "inscrutable."

CULTURAL DIFFERENCES AMONG IBMers WORLDWIDE

COMPANY EXAMPLE

Geert Hofstede, a Dutch researcher, identified four dimensions of cultural variation in values among IBM employees in 60 countries.[40] He analyzed 116,000 questionnaires completed by respondents matched by occupation, gender, and age at different time periods. The four dimensions were power distance, uncertainty avoidance, individualism, and masculinity. Other researchers have generally confirmed these dimensions.[41]

Power distance refers to the extent that members of a culture accept inequality and whether they perceive much distance between those with power (e.g., top management) and those with little power (e.g., rank-and-file workers). Hofstede found the top power-distance countries to be the Philippines, Mexico, and Venezuela; the bottom ones were Austria, Israel, and Denmark.

Uncertainty avoidance is reflected in an emphasis on ritual behavior, rules, and stable employment. Countries that score high on this dimension tend to be more ideological and less pragmatic than those that score low. The countries

highest in uncertainty avoidance were Greece, Portugal, Belgium, and Japan; the lowest were Singapore, Denmark, Sweden, and Hong Kong. The United States is low on this dimension.

Individualism reflects the extent to which people emphasize personal or group goals. If they live in nuclear families that allow them to "do their own thing," individualism flourishes. However, if they live with extended families or tribes that control their behavior, collectivism—the essence of which is giving preference to in-group over individual goals—is more likely.[42] The most individualistic countries are the United States and the other English-speaking countries. The most collectivist countries are Venezuela, Colombia, and Pakistan.

Hofstede's fourth dimension, **masculinity,** is found in societies that differentiate very strongly by gender. Femininity is characteristic of cultures where sex-role distinctions are minimal. While the centrality of work in a person's life is greater in masculine cultures, feminine cultures emphasize quality of life and give more of their gross national product (GNP) to the third world. Hofstede found the most masculine cultures to be Japan, Austria, and Venezuela, while the most feminine were Sweden, Norway, and the Netherlands.

This work is valuable because it provides a set of benchmarks against which other studies can be organized conceptually. It also helps us to understand and place into perspective current theories of motivation, leadership, and organizational behavior.

Lessons Regarding Cross-Cultural Differences

There are three important lessons to be learned from this brief overview of cross-cultural differences:

1. **Do not export headquarters-country bias.** As we have seen, the HR management approach that works well in the headquarters country might be totally out of step in another country. Managers who bear responsibility for international operations need to understand the cultural differences inherent in the management systems of the countries in which their firms do business.
2. **Think in global terms**. We live in a world in which a worldwide allocation of physical and human resources is necessary for continued survival.
3. **Recognize that no country has all the answers.** Flexible work hours, quality circles, and various innovative approaches to productivity have arisen outside the United States. Effective multinational managers must not only think in global terms, but also be able to synthesize the best management approaches to deal with complex problems.

HUMAN RESOURCE MANAGEMENT ACTIVITIES OF GLOBAL CORPORATIONS

Before we consider recruitment, selection, training, and other international HR management issues, it is important that we address a fundamental question: is this subject worthy of study in its own right? The answer is yes, for two rea-

SHOULD YOU WORK FOR A FOREIGN-OWNED FIRM IN THE UNITED STATES?[43]

Increasing numbers of American managers are joining foreign-based companies that are doing business in the U.S. market. However, working for such a company can be difficult. Its offices typically are managed by expatriates, who are most comfortable with the culture, language, and customs of their mother country and are likely to import international management styles into the U.S. workplace. For their U.S. subordinates, that could mean fewer opportunities for advancement and a wide range of other cultural differences. Such problems arise frequently when a U.S. firm merges with or is acquired by a foreign one, such as Germany's Daimler and the American company, Chrysler. Executives from both companies seemed to understand that a successful merger would require the two companies to abandon their respective business cultures and to create a new and distinctive one. Yet from the beginning of the formal relationship, in late 1998, issues that should have been handled easily, like labor relations or differences in emission-control policies, got bogged down in turf battles. Instead of trying to blend the best of each company's culture, in the words of one senior executive, "It became a question of comparing the styles of the two and picking one." This had led to serious integration problems.

Does it help to know the language of the foreign firm? Yes, but even if people are linguistically capable, say experts, learning how to praise or criticize someone from a different culture is a difficult skill. Asking a Swiss or German boss for a performance appraisal would probably lead to a very specific answer, while a Japanese, Korean, or Chinese boss would tend to be more vague.

Depending on the corporate culture, the staffing of the U.S. office, and the nationality of the company, it is possible to work for a foreign firm and barely notice cultural differences. Such is the case at Ebel U.S.A. Inc., a U.S. sales agent of a Swiss watch company, or at the Los Angeles office of the National Bank of Canada. Other companies have become so international that they're essentially melting pots. Schlumberger, Ltd., for example, was founded by two French brothers, is incorporated in the Netherlands Antilles, has executive offices in New York and Paris, and does business in more than 100 countries. Says one manager: "When you join Schlumberger, you put your passport away."

Despite these difficulties, there will be healthy payoffs for those who can cross cultural boundaries. Many foreign-owned companies doing business in the United States offer competitive salaries and assignments abroad. In addition, working for a foreign company can promote empathy for other cultures and skill in working with people from around the world. Those are attractive characteristics in a global job market.

sons—scope and risk exposure.[44] In terms of *scope,* there are at least five important differences between domestic and international operations. International operations have:

1. More functions, such as taxation and coordination of dependents.
2. More heterogeneous functions, such as coordination of multiple-salary currencies.
3. More involvement in the employee's personal life, such as housing, health, education, and recreation.

4. Different approaches to management, since the population of expatriates and locals varies.
5. More complex external influences, such as from societies and governments.

Heightened *risk exposure* is a second distinguishing characteristic of international HR management.[45] A variety of legal issues confront companies in each country, and the human and financial consequences of a mistake in the international arena are much more severe. On top of that, terrorism is now an ever-present risk for executives overseas. The cost of a kidnapping may run $2 to $3 million, and it is estimated that there are 10,000–15,000 kidnappings a year worldwide.[46] As a result, companies often purchase kidnap-ransom/extortion insurance for their employees. The cost varies by country, and how much time employees spend there. For example, someone who does business in several Latin American countries 1 week a month might take out a $1 million policy for about $2,500. That can rise to as much as $100,000 for an executive who is in Colombia for a year. The policy covers the ransom and the cost of hiring a security firm to get you out.[47]

All this has had an important effect on how people are prepared for and moved to and from international assignment locations. In light of these considerations, it seems reasonable to ask, "Why do people accept overseas assignments?" Why *do* they go? As companies' global ambitions grow, fast-track executives at companies such as General Mills, Procter & Gamble, Gillette, General Electric, and ExxonMobil see foreign tours as necessary for career advancement.[48] Evidence indicates that U.S.-based multinationals actually do perform better when they have CEOs with international-assignment experience.[49]

Organizational Structure

Businesses tend to evolve from domestic (exporters) to international (manufacturing and some technology resources allocated outside the home country) to multinational (allocating resources among national or regional areas) to global (treating the entire world as one large company) organizations.[50] As an example of the latter, consider global powerhouse Asea Brown Boveri (ABB). It employs 210,000 people in 25 countries. It combines small-company entrepreneurialism with big-company economies of scale—a global paradox. ABB is at once international and local. It is a global federation of national companies employing and managed by their own nationals—all of whom are plugged into a global network.

Decentralization helps ABB avoid the "big-company syndrome." The company comprises 1,000 legal entities and 5,000 distinct profit centers and profit-and-loss balance sheets. With only five managers per profit center and three layers of management, ABB is very flat. The result? A small-company atmosphere in a big company. Within this framework, an elite cadre of 500 global managers assigns contracts, coordinates international purchasing, promotes standardization, and facilitates technology exchange throughout the corporation.[51]

Organizational structure directly affects all HR management functions from recruitment through retirement. Thus effective HR management does not exist in a vacuum but is integrated into the overall strategy of the organization. Indeed, from the perspective of strategic management, the fundamental problem is to keep the strategy, structure, and HR dimensions of the organization in direct alignment.[52]

Human Resource Planning

This issue is particularly critical for firms doing business overseas. They need to analyze both the local *and* the international external labor markets as well as their own internal labor markets in order to estimate the supply of people with the skills that will be required at some time in the future. Six other key issues in international HR planning are[53]:

1. Identifying top management potential early.[54]
2. Identifying critical success factors for future international managers.
3. Providing developmental opportunities.
4. Tracking and maintaining commitments to individuals in international career paths.
5. Tying strategic business planning to HR planning and vice versa.
6. Dealing with multiple business units while attempting to achieve globally and regionally focused (e.g., European, Asian) strategies.

In developed countries, national labor markets can usually supply the skilled technical and professional people needed. However, developing countries are characterized by severe shortages of qualified managers and skilled workers and by great surpluses of people with little or no skill, training, or education.[55] The bottom line for companies operating in developing countries is that they must be prepared to develop required skills among their own employees.

Recruitment

Broadly speaking, companies operating outside their home countries follow three basic models in the recruitment of executives: (1) They may select from the national group of the parent company only, (2) they may recruit only from within their own country and the country where the branch is located, or (3) they may adopt an international perspective and emphasize the unrestricted use of all nationalities.[56] Each of these strategies has both advantages and disadvantages.

Ethnocentrism: Home-Country Executives Only

A strategy of **ethnocentrism** may be appropriate during the early phases of international expansion, because firms at this stage are concerned with transplanting a part of the business that has worked in their home country. Hence, detailed knowledge of that part is crucial to success. On the other hand, a policy of ethnocentrism, of necessity, implies blocked promotional paths for local executives. If there are many subsidiaries, home-country nationals must recognize that their foreign service may not lead to faster career progress. Finally, there are cost disadvantages to ethnocentrism as well as increased tendencies to impose the management style of the parent company.[57]

Limiting Recruitment to Home- and Host-Country Nationals

This may result from acquisition of local companies. In Japan, for instance, where the labor market is tight, most people are reluctant to switch firms. Thus use of a local partner may be extremely important. Hiring nationals has other advantages as well. It eliminates language barriers, expensive training periods, and cross-cultural adjustment problems of managers and their families. It also allows firms to take advantage of (lower) local salary levels while still paying a premium to attract high-quality employees.

Yet these advantages are not without cost. Local managers may have difficulty bridging the gap between the subsidiary and the parent company, for the business experience to which they have been exposed may not have prepared them to work as part of a global enterprise.[58] Finally, consideration of only home- and host-country nationals may result in the exclusion of some very able executives.

Geocentrism: Seeking the Best Person for the Job Regardless of Nationality

At first glance it may appear that a strategy of **geocentrism** is optimal and most consistent with the underlying philosophy of a global corporation. Yet there are potential problems. Such a policy can be very expensive, it would take a long time to implement, and it requires a great deal of centralized control over managers and their career patterns. To implement such a policy effectively, companies must make it very clear that cross-national service is important and that it will be rewarded.

Colgate-Palmolive is an example of such a company. It has been operating internationally for more than 50 years, and its products (e.g., Colgate toothpaste, Ajax cleanser) are household names in more than 170 countries. Fully 60 percent of the company's expatriates are from countries other than the United States, and two of its last four CEOs weren't U.S. nationals. In addition, all the top executives speak at least two languages, and important meetings routinely take place all over the globe.[59] Let's now consider a very serious problem that confronts many executives offered overseas assignments.

PRACTICAL EXAMPLE   ## JOB AID FOR SPOUSES OF OVERSEAS EXECUTIVES

Today, families in which both parents are working have become the majority among married couples with children.[60] About 41 percent of employees transferred abroad have spouses who worked before relocating. At the same time, global companies are expanding into areas such as central and eastern Europe and the Middle East, where spouses of expatriates face particularly tough obstacles to finding jobs. Here is a scenario likely to become more and more common in the future. A company offers a promotion overseas to a promising executive. But the executive's spouse has a flourishing career in the United States. What should the company—and the couple—do?

Employers and employees are wrestling with this dilemma more often these days. As noted in Chapter 10, job aid for the so-called trailing spouse is already a popular benefit for domestic transfers. Now, 47 percent of employers are also providing informal or formal job help to the spouses of international transferees.[61]

HR officers may try to find a job for the spouse within the company, press a spouse's current employer for a foreign post, provide job leads through customers and suppliers, or plow through costly government red tape to get work permits. This kind of aid usually occurs in industries like banking, financial services, pharmaceuticals, and computers, all of which have significant numbers of high-level women executives. Other firms provide continuing education benefits that will finance either local or correspondence courses, or allowances for spouses to attend professional seminars and conferences so they can keep up with developments in their professions.

Despite company efforts, it is often very difficult to place spouses abroad. Where there are language barriers or barriers of labor laws, tradition, or underemployment, it can be almost impossible. Certain Middle Eastern nations frown on women working or even driving. In Switzerland and Kenya, expatriate spouses even need permission to work as volunteers.[62] Moreover, an international assignment can slow a spouse's professional progress and sometimes stir resentment. On the other hand, some spouses find their overseas experiences as personally and professionally rewarding as their spouses do. One American tax lawyer received permission to work in Brussels as an independent legal consultant. A German travel executive followed his wife to Britain and, 7 months later, landed a job organizing exhibitions between Britain and Germany. Not surprisingly, however, many experts believe that spousal income loss will be the single most important factor determining an executive's decision to accept or reject an overseas position.[63]

International Staffing

There are two important guidelines in this area: (1) do not assume that a job requires the same skills from one location to another, and (2) do not underestimate the effect of the local culture and physical environment on the candidate.[64] In many cultures, tribal and family norms take precedence over technical qualifications in hiring employees. African managers often hire relatives and members of their tribes.[65] Likewise, in India, Korea, and Latin America, family connections are frequently more important than technical expertise. For expatriates, technical competence and other factors, such as cross-cultural adaptability and flexibility, increase their chances of successful performance abroad.[66]

Selection criteria for international jobs cover five areas: *personality, skills, attitudes, motivation, and behavior.*[67] When success is defined in terms of completing the expatriate assignment, and also supervisory ratings of performance on the assignment, evidence indicates that three personality characteristics are related to ability to complete the assignment. These are **extroversion** and **agreeableness** (which facilitate interacting and making social alliances with host nationals and other expatriates), and **emotional stability. Conscientiousness** is a general work ethic that supervisors "see" in their subordinates, and this affects their performance ratings. Expatriate assignments require a great deal of persistence, thoroughness, and responsibility—all of which conscientious people possess and use.[68]

How common is such screening? While 50 percent of North American companies and 33 percent of European companies require psychological screening for both the employee and spouse or domestic partner, only 11 percent of Asian firms do.[69]

Highly developed technical skills, of course, are the basic rationale for selecting a person to work overseas. In some cases, unfortunately, technical skills are the *only* criterion for selection. This is a mistake, for technical competence per se has nothing to do with one's ability to adapt to a new environment, to deal effectively with foreign coworkers, or to perceive and if necessary, imitate, foreign behavioral norms.[70] In addition to technical skills, candidates should possess skills in communication (both home- and host-country languages, verbal, nonverbal, and written)[71]; interpersonal relations (in developing countries, native people will simply walk off the job rather than continue to work with disagreeable outsiders), and stress management (to overcome the inevitable "culture shock"—frustration, conflict, anxiety, and feelings of alienation—that accompanies overseas assignments).

Tolerant attitudes toward people who may differ significantly in race, creed, color, values, personal habits, and customs are essential for success in overseas work. People who look down smugly on other cultures as inferior to their own simply will not make it overseas.

High motivation has long been acknowledged as a key ingredient for success in missionary work. Who, for example, can forget the zeal of the Protestant missionaries in the book *Hawaii,* by James Michener, as they set out from their native New England? While motivation is often difficult to assess reliably, firms should at the very least try to eliminate from consideration those who are only looking to get out of their own country for a change of scenery.

The last criterion is behavior—especially concern for other members of a group, tolerance for ambiguity, displays of respect, and nonjudgmental behavior. These characteristics may be determined from tests or interviews. For example, the Foreign Assignment Selection Test (FAST) appraises candidates in terms of six critical criteria: cultural flexibility, willingness to communicate, ability to develop social relationships, perceptual abilities, conflict-resolution style, and leadership style. Research indicates that most of the FAST criteria are indeed related to expatriate adjustment at work and outside of work in a new cultural environment.[72]

COMPANY EXAMPLE   ## INTERVIEWING POTENTIAL EXPATRIATES AT AT&T

AT&T is a worldwide player, having experienced exponential growth in overseas markets. Here are some typical questions it uses to screen candidates for overseas transfers[73]:

- Would your spouse be interrupting a career to accompany you on an international assignment? If so, how do you think this will affect your spouse and your relationship with each other?
- Do you enjoy the challenge of making your own way in new situations?
- How able are you in initiating new social contacts?
- Can you imagine living without television?
- How important is it for you to spend significant amounts of time with people of your own ethnic, racial, religious, and national background?
- As you look at your personal history, can you isolate any episodes that indicate a real interest in learning about other peoples and cultures?

- Has it been your habit to vacation in foreign countries?
- Do you enjoy sampling foreign cuisines?
- What is your tolerance for waiting for repairs?

Applicability of U.S. Labor Laws to Multinational Employers. The Age Discrimination in Employment Act (as amended in 1984), Title VII (as amended by the Civil Rights Act of 1991), and the Americans with Disabilities Act apply to United States citizens employed abroad. They also apply to U.S. citizens of foreign corporations doing business in the United States, even if those corporations employ fewer than 20 workers in the United States. However, they do not apply to foreign employees of a U.S.-based multinational who are not U.S. citizens.[74]

A final issue involves government regulation of staffing activities in foreign countries. In several western European countries, for example, employment offices are operated by the government, and private agencies are not permitted. In Sweden, employer, union, peers, and subordinates all participate in the entire selection process for managers—from job analysis to the hiring or promotion decision.[75] Recognize also that the use of various selection practices, such as structured interviews, varies dramatically across countries.[76] These kinds of HR practices and regulations may require global corporations to modify their HR and industrial relations policies to operate successfully overseas.

Orientation

Orientation is particularly important in overseas assignments, both before departure and after arrival. Formalized orientation efforts—for example, elaborate multimedia presentations for the entire family, supplemented by presentations by representatives of the country and former expatriates who have since returned to the United States—are important. After all, approximately 80 percent of international assignees are accompanied by a spouse, children, or both.[77]

Some firms go further. Federal Express and Colgate-Palmolive, for example, actually send prospective expatriates and their families on familiarization trips to the foreign location in question. While there, they have to "live like the natives" do by taking public transportation, shopping in local stores, and visiting prospective schools and current expatriates.[78]

In fact, there may be three separate phases to orientation, all of which are designed to provide potential expatriates and their families with realistic assignment previews.[79] The first is called *initial orientation*, which may last as long as 2 full days. Key components are:

- **Cultural briefing.** Traditions, history, government, economy, living conditions, clothing and housing requirements, health requirements, and visa applications. (Drugs get a lot of coverage, both for adults and for teenagers—whether they use drugs or not. Special emphasis is given to the different drug laws in foreign countries. Alcohol use also gets special attention when candidates are going to Muslim countries, such as Saudi Arabia.)
- **Assignment briefing.** Length of assignment, vacations, salary and allowances, tax consequences, and repatriation policy.
- **Relocation requirements.** Shipping, packing, or storage; home sale or rental; and information about housing at the new location.

During this time, it is important that employees and their families understand that there is no penalty attached to changing their minds about accepting the proposed assignment. It is better to bail out early than reluctantly to accept an assignment that will be regretted later.

The second phase is *predeparture orientation,* which may last another 2 or 3 days. Its purpose is to make a more lasting impression on employees and their families and to remind them of material that may have been covered months earlier. Topics covered at this stage include:

- Introduction to the language.
- Further reinforcement of important values, especially open-mindedness.
- En route, emergency, and arrival information.

The final aspect of overseas orientation is *post-arrival orientation.* Upon arrival, employees and their families should be met by assigned company sponsors. This phase of orientation usually takes place on three levels, and a dedicated support staff may provide it. The purpose is to reduce the stress associated with clashing work and family demands.[80]

- **Orientation toward the environment.** Language, transportation, shopping, and other subjects that—depending on the country—may become understandable only through actual experience, such as dealing with local government officials.
- **Orientation toward the work unit and fellow employees.** Often a supervisor or a delegate from the work unit will introduce the new employee to his or her fellow workers, discuss expectations of the job, and share his or her own initial experiences as an expatriate. The ultimate objective, of course, is to relieve the feelings of strangeness or tension that the new expatriate feels.
- **Orientation to the actual job.** This may be an extended process that focuses on cultural differences in the way a job is done. Only when this process is complete can we begin to assess the accuracy and wisdom of the original selection decision.

Throughout the assignment, some companies arrange periodic company-sponsored social functions to provide opportunities for expatriates and their families to interact with host-country nationals. Doing so facilitates cross-cultural adjustment and overall satisfaction with the assignment.[81]

Cross-Cultural Training and Development

To survive, cope, and succeed, managers need training in three areas: the culture; the language; and practical, day-to-day matters.[83] Female expatriates (expected to account for 21 percent of expatriates by 2005) need training on the norms, values, and traditions that host nationals possess about women, and also on how to deal with challenging situations they may face as women.[84] Reviews of research on cross-cultural training found that it has a positive impact on an individual's development of skills, adjustment to the cross-cultural situation, and performance in such situations.[85] Evidence also indicates that training should take place prior to departure, and also after arrival in the new location.

INTERNATIONAL APPLICATION
How to Stay Safe Abroad[82]

Many parts of the world are dangerous, including many cities in the U.S. South and Central America are particular hot spots. In Colombia, kidnapping is almost a cottage industry. In China, extortion and other crimes are on the rise. In Paris, young hoodlums are boarding buses and holding up passengers and drivers. In Mexico, many cabs are driven by bandits who kidnap foreigners, force them to withdraw cash from an ATM, beat them, and dump them in remote locations. In Istanbul, bars catering to Westerners often present them with exorbitant bills, which they have no choice but to pay. According to experts in security, terrorism remains relatively rare, while crime is everywhere. Here are some tips to help keep you safe.

- Make photocopies of your passport, plane tickets, and other key documents. Leave copies at home with family or friends. Take nonstop flights whenever possible, and don't show hotel details on your luggage.
- Familiarize yourself with the current political and health situations in the areas you are visiting. Check out free State Department warnings on the Internet (*www.travel.state.gov/osac.html*), as well as Travel Health Online (*www.tripprep.com/index.html*).

- Divide your money in half and keep it in separate places, some in a wallet, some in a moneybelt or briefcase. Leave questionable reading material, expensive jewelry, and unneeded credit cards at home. Dress conservatively. Watch your drink being poured.
- In fundamentalist countries do not proselytize or wear religious symbols. Remember to smile, respect local customs, and mind your own business. Keep strong opinions to yourself.
- Don't use unmarked taxis. Be careful about getting into a cab with other passengers. This practice is a no-no in some countries (Russia), but quite common in others (Morocco).
- Ask for directions in a hotel, restaurant, or airport, rather than querying a stranger on the street. In some countries you may ask the police, but in Colombia, Cambodia, and Mexico it is not recommended.
- Know how to use local pay phones.
- Use the safe deposit box at your hotel. Upon leaving your room, hang a "Do not disturb" sign outside your door.
- Stay in touch with your office, but keep your itinerary confidential. Give your schedule only to relatives and coworkers with a need to know it.
- Above all, try not to look important or rich.

Formal mentoring for expatriates by host-country nationals also shows organizational support, and it can help to improve both language skills and the ability to interact effectively.[86]

In a 2001 Global Relocation Trends survey, 57 percent of multinationals reported that they provide cross-cultural preparation of at least one day's duration, and almost a third do so for the entire family. Fully 75 percent of expatriates (and in many cases their families as well) participated in the training.[87]

To a very great extent, expatriate failure rates can be attributed to the **culture shock** that usually occurs 4 to 6 months after arrival in the foreign country. The symptoms are not pleasant: homesickness, boredom, withdrawal, a need for excessive amounts of sleep, compulsive eating or drinking, irritability, exaggerated cleanliness, marital stress, family tension and conflict (involving children), hostility toward host-country nationals, loss of ability to work effectively, and physical ailments of a psychosomatic nature.[88]

To be sure, many of the common stresses of everyday living become amplified when a couple is living overseas with no support other than from a spouse. To deal with these potential problems, spouses are taught to recognize stress symptoms in each other, and they are counseled to be supportive. One exercise, for example, is for the couples periodically to list what they believe causes stress in their mates, what the other person does to relieve it, and what they themselves do to relieve it. Then they compare lists.[89] Some companies have taken a different tack to grooming global talent. Gillette, Inc., is a good example.

COMPANY EXAMPLE

GILLETTE'S INTERNATIONAL TRAINEE PROGRAM[90]

Gillette competes in three major consumer businesses: personal grooming products for men and women, stationery products, and small electrical appliances. Some of its brand names include Sensor and Mach3 (razors), Right Guard, Soft & Dri, Braun, Oral-B, Liquid Paper, Duracell Batteries, and Parker Pen. All these consumer-product businesses share common traits: They are No. 1 worldwide in their markets, profitable, fast-growing, and anchored by a strong technological base. Some 1.2 billion people around the world now use at least one Gillette product every day.[91]

Gillette's global deployment of people has created the need for individuals trained specifically to work in operations. The company's International Trainee Program is designed to do just that.

Gillette seeks top business graduates from prestigious universities internationally. In addition, trainees must be:

- Adaptable, having good social skills.
- Younger than 30 years old.
- Mobile and oriented toward an international career.
- Single.
- Fluent in English.
- Enthusiastic and aggressive.

Junior trainees typically work at the Gillette subsidiaries in their home countries for 6 months. After that, Gillette management may choose to transfer them to one of the firm's three international headquarters (Boston, London, or Singapore) for 18 months. Assignments usually depend on which world region their subsidiaries are part of. Current trainees come from Argentina, Brazil, China, Colombia, Egypt, Guatemala, India, Indonesia, Malaysia, Morocco, New Zealand, Pakistan, Peru, Poland, Russia, South Africa, Turkey, and Venezuela.

Upon completion of their terms, graduates return to their home countries to assume entry-level managerial positions. If they are successful, they move on to other assignments in other countries. Eventually, they end up back in their home countries as general managers or senior operating managers.

The intent of the program is not to fill short-term vacancies. Rather, the objective is to hire and develop people who want careers with global proportions. At the top ranks of the corporation, two of Gillette's four executive vice presidents, the traditional steppingstone to the top, are Europeans. In some countries, Gillette management rivals the U.N. for diversity. For example, a Frenchman heads its business in the former Soviet Union. His management team includes an Egyptian controller, and English sales director, and officers from Pakistan and Ireland. As this example shows, the global workforce is a reality now.

A key characteristic of successful global managers is adaptability. Empirical research has revealed eight different dimensions of adaptability: handling emergencies or crisis situations; handling work stress; solving problems creatively; dealing with uncertain and unpredictable work situations; learning work tasks, technologies, and procedures; demonstrating interpersonal adaptability; cultural adaptability; and physically oriented adaptability.[92] This implies that an effective way to train employees to adapt is to expose them to situations like they will encounter in their assignments that require adaptation. Such a strategy has two benefits: (1) it enhances transfer of training, and (2) it is consistent with the idea that adaptive performance is enhanced by gaining experience in similar situations.

Integration of Training and Business Strategy

Earlier, we noted that firms tend to evolve from domestic (exporters) to international (or multidomestic) to multinational to global. Not surprisingly, the stage of globalization of a firm influences both the type of training activities offered and their focus. In general, the more a firm moves away from the export stage of development, the more rigorous the training should be, including its breadth of content. At the multinational and global stages, managers need to be able to socialize host-country managers into the firm's corporate culture and other firm-specific practices. This added managerial responsibility intensifies the need for rigorous training.[93]

An example of such integration is Federal Express Corporation (FedEx). FedEx has integrated the latest information technology into its corporate strategy, the core of which is to use IT to help customers take advantage of international markets. In fact, FedEx sees itself more as an IT company than as a transporter of goods (2.8 million packages a day in 210 countries). Today more than two-thirds of FedEx customers handle orders and deliveries online. "We decided years ago," says chairman and CEO Frederick W. Smith, "that the most important element in this business is information technology, and we have geared everything to that philosophy—recruitment, training, and compensation. Fail-safe precision is the key to it all."[94]

International Compensation

Compensation policies can produce intense internal conflicts within a company at any stage of globalization. Indeed, few other areas in international HR management demand as much top-management attention as does compensation.

The principal problem is straightforward: *Salary levels for the same job differ among countries in which a global corporation operates.* Compounding this problem is the fact that fluctuating exchange rates require constant attention in order to maintain constant salary rates in U.S. dollars.

Ideally, an effective international compensation policy should meet the following objectives:

- Attract and retain employees who are qualified for overseas service.
- Facilitate transfers between foreign affiliates and between home-country and foreign locations.
- Establish and maintain a consistent relationship between the compensation of employees of all affiliates, both at home and abroad.
- Maintain compensation that is reasonable in relation to the practices of leading competitors.[95]

As firms expand into overseas markets, they are likely to create an international division that becomes the home of all employees involved with operations outside the headquarters country. Three types of expatriate compensation plans typically found during this stage of development are[96]:

- Localization.
- "Higher-of-home-or-host" compensation.
- Balance sheet.

Localization refers to the practice of paying expatriates on the same scale as local nationals in the country of assignment. It implies paying a Saudi a British salary and benefits in London, and an American an Argentine package in Buenos Aires. Salary and benefits may be supplemented with one-time or temporary transition payments.

Localization works well under certain conditions, for example when transferring an employee with very limited home-country experience, such as a recent college graduate, to a developed country. It also works well in the case of permanent, indefinite, or extremely long (e.g., 10-year) transfers to another country.

Higher-of-home-or-host compensation localizes expatriates in the host-country salary program, but establishes a compensation floor based on home-country compensation so that expatriates never receive less than they would be paid at home for a comparable position.

This approach frequently is used for transfers within regions—notably in Latin America and in the European Union—and for assignments of unlimited duration. It is less appropriate for an expatriate on a series of assignments of 2–3 years.

The **balance-sheet approach** is by far the most common method used by North American, European, and, increasingly, Japanese global organizations to compensate expatriates. Its primary objective is to ensure that expatriates neither gain nor lose financially compared with their home-country peers. If there is no financial advantage to being in one country instead of another, then this objective will be realized. It also facilitates mobility among the expatriate staff in the most cost-effective way possible.[97]

Nonmonetary differences in the attractiveness of individual assignments (if they are not already reflected in base pay) may be compensated with separate allowances (premiums) and incentives. For example, expatriates often receive "hardship" allowances if they are sent to culturally deprived locations, those with health or safety problems, or other unusual conditions.[98] Figure 16–1 illustrates this approach.

Figure 16–1

The balance-sheet approach to international compensation.
(*Source: Compensation basics for North American expatriates: Developing an effective program for employees working abroad.* American Compensation Association, Scottsdale, AZ, 1995, p. 8. Used with permission.)

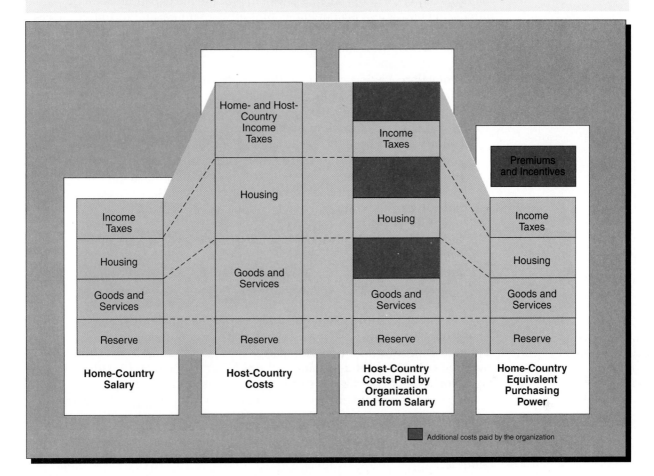

Note the labels at the bottom of each of the four columns of Figure 16–1. The first is "Home-Country Salary." Each of the four categories identified in this column is a "norm" that represents the typical proportion of income that someone at the stated income level and family size spends (e.g., a $75,000-a-year manager with a wife and two small children). Each category behaves differently as income increases and family size changes. In most countries, as income rises, income taxes and the reserve (net disposable income that can be saved, invested, or spent at home) increase at increasing rates, while housing and goods and services increase at decreasing rates.

"Host-Country Costs" (income taxes, housing, and goods and services) tend to be higher abroad than in most home countries, while the reserve remains the same. The column labeled "Host-Country Costs Paid by Organization and from Salary" demonstrates that if expatriates are responsible for the same level of expenditures abroad as at home and overall purchasing power is maintained, the employer becomes responsible for costs that exceed "normal" expatriate home-country costs. Thus if housing is more expensive abroad than at home, the employer is responsible for the remainder. These differentials are shown as gray blocks in the third column of Figure 16-1.

The column labeled "Home-Country Equivalent Purchasing Power" illustrates the objective of the balance sheet: to provide the expatriate with the same purchasing power as a peer at home, plus any premiums and incentives necessary to induce an employee to accept a particular foreign assignment.

Two philosophies characterize the balance-sheet approach:

1. **Protection.** Paying expatriates the supplements in home-country currency suggested by the gray blocks in third column of Figure 16–1.
2. **Equalization or "split pay."** In a process known as **equalization,** the employer pays the reserve in home-country currency after deducting home-country norms from the expatriate's salary for income taxes, housing, and goods and services. The company pays all income taxes through the expatriate, while making payments to the expatriate in local currency to provide housing and purchasing power for goods and services comparable to the purchasing power of a home-country peer.

The most important advantages of the balance-sheet approach are:

- It preserves the purchasing power of expatriates in a cost-effective manner.
- It facilitates mobility among expatriates.

This is not to imply that companies are not using alternative approaches. Small companies with very few expatriates, for example, may rely on *negotiation* of the overall compensation package on a case-by-case basis. Others use a **modified balance-sheet approach** that ties salary to a region (Asia-Pacific, Europe, North America) rather than to the home country.[99]

In an analysis of the international compensation package, two major components are: (1) benefits and (2) pay adjustments and incentives. Let's consider each of these.

Benefits

Benefits may vary drastically from one country to another. For example, in Mexico an **acquired rights law** requires that if a benefit, service, or bonus is paid 2 years in a row, it becomes an employee's right. Both India and Mexico mandate profit sharing—10 percent of pretax profits must be distributed to employees.[100] Most developed and emerging economies have some form of national health care supplied by employer- and employee-paid premiums. In Russia, benefits are a major strategic tool for employers, who offer scarce goods and services, medical care, improved housing, and access to quality products.[101] In Europe employees have various statutory rights that vary from country to country. These include pensions, sick pay, minimum wages, holiday pay, overtime pay, minimum work time, and dismissal procedures (including legally required severance benefits). In Japan, a supervisor whose weekly salary is modest (by U.S. standards) may also get benefits that include family income allowances (Toyota provides about $180 per month for the first dependent and about $50 per month for additional dependents), housing or housing loans, subsidized vacations, year-end bonuses that can equal 3 months' pay, and profit sharing.[102]

Global corporations commonly handle benefits coverages in terms of the **best-of-both-worlds benefits** model. Here is how it works. Wherever possible, the expatriate is given home-country benefits coverage, for example, with respect to pensions and medical coverage.[103] However, in areas such as disability insurance, where there may be no home-country plan, the employee may join the host-country plan.

Most U.S. multinationals also offer various types of premiums and incentives. Their purpose is to provide for the difference in living costs (that is, the costs of goods, services, and currency realignments) between the home country and the host country. Premiums may include any one or more of the following components:

- **Housing allowance.**
- **Education allowance.** Compensation for schools, uniforms, and other educational expenses that would not have been incurred had the expatriate remained in the United States.
- **Income tax equalization allowance.** (As described earlier.)
- **Hardship pay.** Usually a percentage of base pay provided as compensation for living in an area with climactic extremes, political instability, or poor living conditions.
- **Hazardous-duty pay.** Compensation for living in an area where physical danger is present, such as a war zone. Such a premium can be as high as 25 percent of base pay in some Middle Eastern and African countries.[104]
- **Home leave.** Commonly one trip per year for the entire family to the expatriate's home country. Hardship posts normally include more frequent travel for rest and relaxation.
- **School allowance.** As a rule, companies will pay for private schooling for the children of their expatriates.[105]

Finally, it is common practice for companies to pay for security guards in many overseas locations, such as in Middle Eastern countries, in the Philippines, and in Indonesia.

Pay Adjustments and Incentives

In the United States, adjustments in individual pay levels are based, to a great extent, on how well people do their jobs, as reflected in a performance appraisal. In most areas of the third world, however, objective measures for rating employee or managerial performance are uncommon. Social status is based on characteristics such as age, religion, ethnic origin, and social class. Pay differentials that do not reflect these characteristics will not motivate workers. For example, consider Japan. Although the situation is changing, especially among large companies, rewards are based less on the nature of the work performed or on individual competence than on seniority and personal characteristics such as age, education, or family background. A pay system based on individual job performance would not be acceptable since group performance is emphasized, and the effect of individual appraisal would be to divide the group.[106] Needless to say, exportation of U.S. performance appraisal practices to these kinds of cultures can have disastrous effects.

Despite such differences, research indicates that there are also important similarities in reward-allocation practices across cultures. The most universal

Table 16–2

SOME CHARACTERISTICS OF PERFORMANCE APPRAISAL SYSTEMS IN THE UNITED STATES, SAUDI ARABIA, AND KOREA

Issue	United States	Saudi Arabia	Korea
Objective	Administrative decisions, employee development	Placement	Develop relationship between supervisor and employee
Done by?	Supervisor	Manager several layers up who knows employee well	Mentor and supervisor
Authority of appraiser	Presumed in supervisor role	Reputation (prestige determined by nationality, age, sex, family, tribe, title, education)	Long tenure of supervisor with organization
Style	Supervisor takes the lead, with employee input	Authority of appraiser is important; never say "I don't know"	Supervisor takes the lead, with informal employee input
Frequency	Usually once/year	Once/year	Developmental appraisal once/month for 1st year; annually thereafter
Assumptions	Objective—appraiser is fair	Subjective appraisal more important than objective; connections are important	Subjective appraisal more important than objective; no formal criteria
Feedback	Criticisms are direct; may be in writing	Criticisms more subtle; not likely to be given in writing	Criticisms subtle and indirect; may be given verbally
Employee acknowledgement and possible rebuttal	Employee acknowledges receipt; may rebut in writing	Employee acknowledges receipt; may rebut verbally	Employee does not see or sign formal appraisal; would rarely rebut
How praised	Individually	Individually	Given to entire group
Motivators	Money, upward mobility, career development	Loyalty to supervisor	Money, promotion, loyalty to supervisor

Note: Characteristics of the Saudi Arabian approach to appraisal come from P. R. Harris & R. T. Moran, *Managing cultural differences* (3d ed.), Gulf Publishing, Houston, 1990.
Source: W. F. Cascio & E. Bailey, International HRM: The state of research and practice. In O. Shenkar (ed.), *Global perspectives of human resource management*, Prentice-Hall, Englewood Cliffs, NJ, 1995. p. 29.

of these seems to be the **equity norm,** according to which rewards are distributed to group members based on their contributions.[107] In general, the more expatriates perceive that the methods the parent organization uses to plan and implement decisions are fair (procedural justice), the better their adjustment and performance in overseas assignments.[108]

In implementing performance appraisal overseas, therefore, first determine the purpose of the appraisal. Second, whenever possible, set standards of performance against quantifiable assignments, tasks, or objectives. Third, allow more time to achieve results abroad than is customary in the domestic market. Fourth, keep the objectives flexible and responsive to potential market and environmental conditions. Table 16–2 illustrates characteristics of performance appraisal in a Western culture (the United States), a Middle Eastern culture (Saudi Arabia), and a Far Eastern culture (Korea). Perhaps the most important lesson of this table is that a foreign manager could be completely misled by assuming that the approach that "works" in his or her own culture will work elsewhere.[109]

More and more U.S. companies that are exploring strategic compensation approaches at home are beginning to adopt similar approaches for their senior executives worldwide. As an example, consider the balance-sheet approach to expatriate compensation. It is most appropriate to the business strategies of an organization that is in the export or international stage of globalization. However, as firms evolve from multinational to global, they want their expatriates to understand that the greatest organizational growth—and their fastest career development opportunities—are outside their home or base country. Hence a large part of the compensation of these individuals will be performance-based, and not a package of costly allowances and premiums that represent fixed costs.[110]

For these reasons, as the international operations of multinational firms evolve, they begin to introduce local and regional performance criteria into their pay plans, and they attempt to qualify the plans under local tax laws. Why do this? In order to create stronger linkages between executives' performance and long-term business goals and strategies; to extend equity ownership to key executives (through stock options); and, in many instances, to provide tax benefits.[111]

Ethical Dilemma:
Bribery to Win Business?

In the United States, the Foreign Corrupt Practices Act of 1977 (amended in 1988 to increase criminal fines for organizations and civil sanctions for individuals) prohibits payments by U.S. firms and their managers to win foreign business. It has cost them billions. In France and Germany, however, companies may offset payments to foreign officials against tax charges.[112] In Korea, bribes are a way of life. Former president Roh Tae Woo amassed a $650 million slush fund (prior to its exposure and ensuing scandal and reforms in 1995), and even mid-level bureaucrats who wield regulatory powers demand payments. How much? About 1.2 percent of annual sales for big companies, and about 0.8 percent for small- and medium-sized companies.[113] Is this ethical?

Korea (and Russia) wish to join the 29 member countries of the Organization for Economic Cooperation and Development (OECD), but they will have to change their ways to do so. In 1997, OECD member countries agreed to negotiate a binding international convention to criminalize the bribery of foreign public officials, "irrespective of the value or the outcome of the bribe, of perceptions of local custom, or of the tolerance of bribery by local authorities."[114]

Labor Relations in the International Arena

Labor relations structures, laws, and practices vary considerably among countries.[115] Unions may or may not exist. Management or government may dictate terms and conditions of employment. Labor agreements may or may not be contractual obligations. Management may conclude agreements with unions that have little or no membership in a plant or with nonunion groups that wield more bargaining power than the established unions do. Principles and issues that are relevant in one context may not be in others, for example, seniority in layoff decisions or even the concept of a layoff.[116]

In general, unions may constrain the choices of global companies in three ways: (1) by influencing wage levels to the extent that cost structures may become noncompetitive, (2) by limiting the ability of companies to vary employment levels at their own discretion, and (3) by hindering or preventing global integration of such companies (i.e., by forcing them to develop parallel operations in different countries).[117]

One of the most intriguing aspects of international labor relations is multinational collective bargaining. Unions have found global corporations particularly difficult to deal with in terms of union power and difficult to penetrate in terms of union representation.[118] Here are some of the special problems that global corporations present to unions:

1. While national unions tend to follow the development of national companies, union expansion typically cannot follow the expansion of a company across national boundaries, with the exception of Canada. Legal differences, feelings of nationalism, and differences in union structure and industrial relations practices are effective barriers to such expansion.

2. The nature of foreign investment by global corporations has changed. In the past, they tended to invest in foreign sources of raw materials. As a result, the number of processing and manufacturing jobs in the home country may actually have increased. However, in recent years there has been a shift toward the development of parallel, or nearly parallel, operations in other countries.[119] Foreign investment of this type threatens union members in the home country with loss of jobs or with a slower rate of job growth, especially if their wages are higher than those of workers in the host country. This threat is very real in Germany, for example, where labor costs are 25 percent higher than in the United States, and 33 percent higher than in Japan.[120]

3. When a global corporation has parallel operations in other locations, the firm's ability to switch production from one location shut down by a labor dispute to another location is increased. This, of course, assumes that the same union does not represent workers at each plant or that, if different unions are involved, they do not coordinate their efforts and strike at the same time. Another assumption is that the various plants are sufficiently parallel that their products are interchangeable.

One solution to the problems that global corporations pose for union members is multinational collective bargaining. For this to work, though, coordination of efforts and the cooperation of the unions are required. What is called for is an "international union" with the centralization of authority characteristic of

U.S. national unions. Yet two persistent problems stand in the way of such an international union movement[121]:

1. National and local labor leaders would have to be willing to relinquish their autonomy to an international level. This is a major stumbling block because the local union or enterprise union is essentially an autonomous organization.
2. Political and philosophical differences pose a further barrier to any international union movement. For example, a French labor leader committed to a communist form of economic organization is unlikely to yield authority willingly to an international union patterned after the United Auto Workers or any other union committed to the capitalist economic system. Conversely, the leaders of the United Auto Workers are unlikely to relinquish their autonomy to a communist international labor union.

Toward International Labor Standards

In view of the lack of success with multinational collective bargaining, unions have taken a different tack. Labor unions in the United States, for example, are attempting to influence the international labor practices of U.S.-based corporations, arguing that U. S.-based employees are unable to compete with overseas workers who are paid below-market wages and benefits. Toys 'R Us has been the target of several such campaigns over the past several years, including a "toycott" to force the retailer to stop selling goods allegedly manufactured with prison or child labor in China, and a union-led boycott to protest the company's refusal to allow unionization of its workers.[122] Self-policing by multinationals has not worked, but outside audits by independent bodies, such as the Worker Rights Consortium, have begun to lift the veil of secrecy that often shrouds factory work in less-developed countries.[123] While companies such as Reebok, Nike, Liz Claiborne, and Mattel have begun to enforce their codes of conduct that require contractors to fix harsh or abusive working conditions, experts estimate that 90 percent of western companies charged with such abuses have done nothing meaningful to address them.[124]

Four forces are driving the trend toward adoption of international labor standards: labor unions, pressure from social advocacy groups, resentment in some developing countries against multinationals, and U.S. and European proposals for linkages between trade policy and human rights. The international labor standards advocated by these groups include:

- Prohibitions on child labor.
- Prohibitions on forced labor.
- Prohibitions against discrimination.
- Protection for workers' health.
- Payment of adequate wages.
- Provision of safe working conditions.
- Freedom of association.

In addition, some developing countries are beginning to hold Western-based multinationals responsible for their foreign labor practices. Vietnam, for example, recently passed a law requiring that Vietnamese managers working for a foreign-owned company be paid at the same rate as any expatriate managers residing in Vietnam.[125] Managers with international responsibilities should therefore monitor developments closely and begin to consider an appropriate strategic response. Another strategic development is regional trading blocks, of which the North Atlantic Free Trade Agreement (NAFTA) is just one example.

The North American Free Trade Agreement

Economic competition in the 21st century consists not of scattered countries nibbling at one another, but of major regions operating as economic units on the global playing field.[126] Begun in 1994, NAFTA will eliminate trade barriers on goods and services within the United States, Canada, and Mexico over 15 years, and it creates a region of 370 million consumers with $6.5 trillion in output. It is North America's strategic response to the global economy.

How has it worked? U.S. imports from Mexico in 2000 amounted to less than 1.5 percent of U.S. gross domestic product. That implies that the direct effect on U.S. jobs—either negative or positive—has been relatively small. However, employment in the **maquiladora** border factories—which import auto parts and electronics, process them, and send them north again, all duty-free—has boomed. Since 1993, maquiladoras have created almost 800,000 jobs. Indeed, Mexican real manufacturing wages rose almost 6 percent in 2000, and the U.S. deficit with Mexico is only 10 percent of total trade with that country (exports plus imports). By contrast, the U.S. deficit with the European Community equals 14 percent of trade; with Japan, 38 percent; and with China, 72 percent.[127]

The relatively small direct impact of NAFTA actually conceals its pervasive, but subtle, indirect effects. For example, outsourcing of low-skill jobs to low-wage countries is an unstoppable trend. However, the NAFTA free-trade zone has given U.S. companies a way of taking advantage of cheap labor while still keeping close links to U.S. suppliers. Mexican assembly plants get 82 percent of their components from U.S. suppliers. By contrast, factories in Asia use far fewer U.S. parts. If General Motors relies on a plant in Matamoros, Mexico, to build wire harnesses for car audio systems, that's far better for the U.S. economy than if the carmaker buys its harnesses from, say, Taiwan. Says one economist, "Without NAFTA entire industries might be lost, rather than just labor-intensive portions."[128]

In Mexico, labor, management, and the government are working together toward a common goal: world-class levels of productivity. To illustrate this, consider the case of Volkswagen de México.

COMPANY EXAMPLE

DEALING WITH UNION DISSIDENTS AT VOLKSWAGEN DE MÉXICO

Conflict erupted when the government-controlled union at VW, based in Puebla, Mexico, agreed with management on a massive restructuring plan to raise productivity. VW management insisted the new agreement was vital for global competitiveness. This was hardly idle talk, since VW supplies the entire North American market from Puebla. Fearing layoffs, however, a group of dissidents opposed the plan. After weeks of a bitter strike, the government gave VW permission to rip up the union contract. The company promptly fired

14,000 workers and rehired all of them, minus some 300 dissidents, under a new contract. Within days, VW instituted a new HR management system; seniority as a basis for promotion is out, while training, and lots of it, is in. Workers are now promoted according to skills and performance.[129] The federal government has long had enormous control over unions in Mexico, a situation that reformers are trying to change.[130]

Today, the most favored union leaders in Mexico preach the gospel of productivity—and it's paying off. Already Nissan de Mèxico is exporting Sentras to Canada and light trucks back to Japan, while Ford's super-efficient Hermosillo plant builds Escorts and Tracers for U.S. consumption.[131]

Perhaps an unanticipated effect of NAFTA is that it has set the stage for unprecedented levels of cooperation among labor groups across national borders. U.S. unions are now using the treaty to help organize and support workers in Mexico. Why? Because if Mexican wages rise, so the thinking goes, companies won't be so apt to move their plants to Mexico. This is why workers at a Ford Plant in St. Paul, Minnesota sent money to workers at a Ford plant north of Mexico City, who were battling the company over layoffs and work rules.[132]

REPATRIATION

The problems of **repatriation,** for those who succeed abroad as well as for those who do not, have been well documented. All repatriates experience some degree of anxiety in three areas: personal finances, reacclimation to the U.S. lifestyle, and readjustment to the corporate structure.[133] They also worry about the future of their careers and the location of their U.S. assignments. Precisely the same issues have been found in studies of Japanese and Finnish expatriates.[134]

Financially, repatriates face the loss of the foreign-service premium and the effect of inflation on home purchases. Having become accustomed to foreign ways, upon reentry they often find home-country customs strange and, at the extreme, annoying. Such **reverse culture shock** may be more challenging than the culture shock experienced when going overseas![135] Finally, almost 4 out of every 5 returning American expatriates complain that their assignments upon return to the United States are mundane and lack status and authority in comparison to their overseas positions.[136] Possible solutions to these problems fall into three areas: planning, career management, and compensation.

Planning

The expatriation assignment and the repatriation move should be examined as parts of an integrated whole—not as unrelated events in an individual's career.[137] To do this, it is necessary to define a clear strategic purpose for the move. Prior to the assignment, therefore, the firm should define one or more of the three primary purposes for sending a particular expatriate abroad: executive development, coordination and control between headquarters and foreign operations, and transfer of information and technology.[138] Research shows that unless there is a planned purpose in repatriation, the investment of as much as $1 million to send an expatriate overseas is likely to be squandered completely.

Increasingly, multinational corporations are seeking to improve their HR planning and also to implement it on a worldwide basis. Careful inclusion of expatriation and repatriation moves in this planning will help reduce uncertainty and the fear that accompanies it.

Career Management

The attrition rate for repatriated workers is among the highest in corporate life, as high as 50 percent within 2 years.[139] Firms such as 3M, IBM, Ford, and Disney appoint a "career sponsor" (usually a group vice president or higher)[140] to look out for the expatriate's career interests while she or he is abroad and to keep the expatriate abreast of company developments. The development of global electronic-mail networks certainly has made that job faster and easier than it used to be. Sponsors also must be sensitive to the "job shock" the expatriate may suffer when she or he gets back and must be trained to counsel the returning employee (and her or his family as well) until resettlement is deemed complete.[141] To accelerate this process, some firms assemble a group of former expatriates to give advice and offer insights based on their own experiences.[142]

Compensation

The loss of a monthly premium to which the expatriate has been accustomed is a severe shock financially, whatever the rationale. To overcome this problem, some firms have replaced the monthly foreign-service premium with a one-time **mobility premium** (e.g., 3 months' pay) for each move—overseas, back home, or to another overseas assignment. A few firms also provide low-cost loans or other financial assistance so that expatriates can get back into their hometown housing markets at a level at least equivalent to what they left. Finally, there is a strong need for financial counseling for repatriates. Such counseling has the psychological advantage of demonstrating to repatriates that the company is willing to help with the financial problems that they may encounter in uprooting their families once again to bring them home.[143]

Human Resource Management in Action: Conclusion

WHAT'S IT LIKE TO BE A GLOBAL MANAGER?

Says Kelly Brookhouse, an industrial and organizational psychologist who directs Motorola's executive-development program, "We put people into a simulated environment and throw business challenges at them to see how they respond. We get a fairly comprehensive picture of people's leadership profile.

"It was hard. A lot harder than I had expected," says Mandy Chooi, a Beijing-based HR executive at Motorola who recently went through the exercise. "It's surprising how realistic and demanding it is."

Companies that use such assessments often see a quick payoff. French food group Danone SA reduced its failure rate among expatriate managers to 3 percent from about 35 percent in the 3 years since it started using such assessment programs.

Back in suburban London, I'm starting to sweat. Ms. Dubois is going to walk through the door in about 20 minutes, and I'm far from ready. There's a

IMPACT OF INTERNATIONAL HRM ON PRODUCTIVITY, QUALITY OF WORK LIFE, AND THE BOTTOM LINE

The ways in which a company operates overseas can have fundamental, long-term impacts on all three of these indicators. Recognize that poor conditions in an organization's international facilities can generate intense negative publicity, if discovered. In a recent poll, 51 percent of consumers surveyed said that a company's record on fairness and equality in hiring influences their buying choices. However, only 16 percent of company executives mentioned this record as a potential factor. Issues such as child and forced labor are particularly inflammatory to Western consumers.

Levi Strauss & Co. found a way to minimize the use of child labor in its international facilities without repudiating local custom. It pays would-be child laborers to go to school, and offers them a position in its factories once the children have reached the legal minimum age of 14. Using this strategy, the company is able to maintain commitment to its principles without alienating local families who often depend on their children's wages to survive.[144] The strategy also has the benefits of enhancing productivity, quality of work life, and profits.

IMPLICATIONS FOR MANAGEMENT PRACTICE

No one has discovered a single best way to manage. But before a company can build an effective management team, it must understand thoroughly its own culture, the other cultures in which it does business, and the challenges and rewards of blending the best of each.

In the immediate future, there will certainly be international opportunities for managers at all levels, particularly those with the technical skills needed by developing countries. In the longer run, global companies will have their own cadres of **globalites,** sophisticated international executives drawn from many countries, as firms like Gillette, Nestlé, and Sumitomo do now.[145] There is a bright future for managers with the cultural flexibility to be sensitive to the values and aspirations of foreign countries.

Finally, there is one thing of which we can be certain. Talent—social, managerial, and technical—is needed to make global business work. Competent HR management practices can find that talent, recruit it, select it, train and develop it, motivate it, reward it, and profit from it. This will be the greatest challenge of all in the years to come.

flip chart on an easel in the corner, but my handwriting is illegible. So I'm feverishly typing up a sheet of key points to hand her.

The phone rings. "Damn," I mutter. A persistent colleague wants me to send a team member to Holland for 3 months to help land a big new client. I put her off politely and promise to call back later. But I've lost precious time, and when Ms. Dubois strolls in, the presentation is still humming through the printer on my desk.

Sounds a lot like real life, doesn't it?

SUMMARY

Foreign investment by the world's leading corporations is a fact of modern organizational life. For executives transferred overseas, the opportunities are great, but the risks of failure are considerable. This is because there are fundamental cultural differences that affect how different people view the world and operate in business. The lesson for companies doing business overseas is clear: Guard against the exportation of home-country bias, think in global terms, and recognize that no country has all the answers.

Recruitment for overseas assignments is typically based on one of three basic models: (1) ethnocentrism, (2) limiting recruitment to home- and host-country nationals, or (3) geocentrism. Selection is based on five criteria: personality, skills, attitudes, motivation, and behavior. Orientation for expatriates and their families often takes place in three stages: initial, predeparture, and post-arrival. Cross-cultural training may incorporate a variety of methods and techniques, but to be most effective it should be integrated with the firm's long-range global strategy and business planning. International compensation presents special problems since salary levels differ among countries. To be competitive, firms normally follow local salary patterns in each country. Expatriates, however, receive various types of premiums (foreign service, tax equalization, cost of living) in addition to their base salaries—according to the balance-sheet approach. Benefits are handled in terms of the best-of-both-worlds model. An overseas assignment is not complete, however, until repatriation problems have been resolved. These fall into three areas: personal finances, reacclimation to the U.S. lifestyle, and readjustment to the corporate structure. Finally, since global companies operate across national boundaries while unions typically do not, the balance of power in the multinational arena clearly rests with management. To provide a more level playing field, unions are pushing hard for international labor standards.

DISCUSSION QUESTIONS

16–1. What advice would you give to a prospective expatriate regarding questions to ask before accepting the assignment?

16–2. Discuss the special problems that women face in overseas assignments.

16–3. How can the balance of power between management and labor be restored in international labor relations?

16–4. Describe the conditions necessary in order for a geocentric recruitment policy to work effectively.

16–5. Should foreign-language proficiency be required for executives assigned overseas? Why or why not?

KEY TERMS

global corporation	culture
expatriate	local perspective
home country	cosmopolitan perspective
host country	norms of behavior
third-country national	power distance

uncertainty avoidance
individualism
masculinity
ethnocentrism
geocentrism
extroversion
agreeableness
emotional stability
conscientiousness
culture shock
localization
balance-sheet approach

protection
equalization
modified balance-sheet approach
acquired rights law
best-of-both worlds benefits
equity norm
maquiladora
repatriation
reverse culture shock
mobility premium
globalites

APPLYING YOUR KNOWLEDGE

Expatriate Orientation Role Play   *Exercise 16–1*

American business is increasingly international in scope. Many problems can arise when Americans attempt to conduct business in foreign countries without an awareness of the local culture and customs. The obvious solution to these problems is education and training—in particular, a series of briefings (provided by the HR department) for expatriates before they are sent on overseas assignments.

The purpose of this exercise is to familiarize you with the culture and customs of one foreign country and with the process of developing and implementing a cultural briefing program for expatriates.

Procedure

Select a foreign country in which you have some interest. Then go to your college library and find several resources that discuss the customs and cultural dimensions of your chosen country that would be important for a businessperson to know.

On the basis of the information you have collected, develop a mock cultural briefing to be given to the rest of the class. Your cultural briefing should cover such topics as traditions, history, living conditions, clothing and housing requirements, health requirements, drug and alcohol laws, and political and economic climate.

Collect visual aids for your briefing. For instance, your library or a campus professor may have slides, videotapes, photos, or visual aids available through online services that you can borrow to give students a visual overview of the country you have chosen. A local travel agency may have some brochures that you could pass around as part of your presentation. Another possibility is to develop a brief role play which demonstrates a "rude" American insulting his or her host through ignorance of local customs. Such a demonstration can be built right into your overall cultural briefing.

Be creative! The main idea is to teach the other students in your class about the conduct of business in another country and the importance of a cultural briefing for expatriates before they leave the United States.

REFERENCES

1. Fox, J. (2001, July 23). First, baby it's cold outside. *Fortune,* pp. 30–33. See also Garten, J. (2001, May 14). What business should be telling the president. *Business-Week,* p. 34. See also 21st century capitalism: New rules for the global economy (1996, Jan. 14). *BusinessWeek,* Special Advertising Section. See also Thurow, L. (1992). *Head to head.* NY: Warner Books.
2. Fortune 2001 global 500 (2001, July 23). *Fortune,* pp. 143–152.
3. Globalization: Lessons learned (2000, Nov. 6). *BusinessWeek,* p. 228.
4. Kraar, L. (1997, May 26). The real threat to China's Hong Kong. *Fortune,* pp. 85–94.
5. White, J. B. (1998, May 7). Global mall: "There are no German or U.S. companies, only successful ones." *The Wall Street Journal,* pp. A1, A11.
6. The U.S. is awash in foreign money. That's a problem (2001, July 23). *Business-Week,* p. 40. See also Europe's cash is flooding into the U.S. (2000, Oct. 2). *Business-Week,* p. 144.
7. Pearlstein, S. (2001, Aug. 6). Foreign firms' layoffs hit home for U.S. workers. *The Washington Post,* pp. A1, A8.
8. Backlash: Behind the anxiety over globalization (2000, Apr. 24). *BusinessWeek,* pp. 38–44.
9. Time to regroup (2001, Aug. 6). *BusinessWeek,* pp. 26, 27. See also What's behind the global backlash (2000, Apr. 24). *BusinessWeek,* p. 202.
10. Schrage, M. (2000, Nov. 13). Nationality matters more than ever. That's no joke. *Fortune,* p. 462.
11. Confronting anti-globalism (2001, Aug. 6). *BusinessWeek,* p. 92.
12. Ohmae, K. (1990). *The borderless world.* New York: Harper Business.
13. Sheridan, W. R., & Hansen, P. T. (1996, Spring). Linking international business and expatriate compensation strategies. *ACA Journal,* pp. 66–79.
14. Bennett, R. (1999, Apr.). Selection criteria, procedures and success indicators for managers in international assignments. Society for Human Resource Management White Paper. Retrieved from the Web on Jan. 8, 2000. www.shrm.org.
15. Carpenter, M. A., Sanders, G., & Gregersen, H. B. (2001). Bundling human capital with organizational context: The impact of international assignment experience on multinational firm performance and CEO pay. *Academy of Management Journal, 44,* 493–511.
16. Where expats spend the most (2001, June 25). *BusinessWeek,* p. 30.
17. Office space at a royal price (1998, Nov. 9). *BusinessWeek,* p. 30.
18. Thompson, R. W. (1998, Mar.). Study refutes perception that expatriation often fails. *HR News,* p. 2.
19. Shaffer, M. A., & Harrison, D. A. (1998). Expatriates' psychological withdrawal from international assignments: Work, nonwork, and family influences. *Personnel Psychology, 51,* 87–118.
20. Bennett, op. cit. See also Mortensen, R. (1997, Nov.). Beyond the fence line. *HRMagazine,* pp. 100–109. See also McClenahen, J. S. (1997, Jan. 20). To go—or not to go? *Industry Week,* pp. 33, 36.
21. Copeland, L. (1984). Making costs count in international travel. *Personnel Administrator, 29*(7), 47.
22. Hesketh, B., & Bochner, S. (1994). Technological change in a multicultural context: Implications for training and career planning. In H. C. Triandis, M. D. Dunnette, & L. M. Hough (eds.), *Handbook of industrial and organizational psychology* (vol. 4). Palo Alto, CA: Consulting Psychologists Press, pp. 191–240.
23. Harris, P. R., & Moran, R. T. (1990). *Managing cultural differences* (3d ed.). Houston: Gulf Publishing.
24. Ricks, D. A. (1993). *Blunders in international business.* Oxford, England: Blackwell.

25. Catlin, L. B., & White, T. F. (2001). *International business: Cultural sourcebook and case studies* (2nd ed.). Cincinnati, OH: South-Western.

26. Lord, R. (1998). Succeed in business: Germany. Portland, OR: Graphic Arts Center Publishing. See also Axtell, R. E. (1996). *Do's and taboos around the world.* NY: John Wiley & Sons.

27. Harris & Moran, op. cit.

28. Dunn, C., Kim, J. H., Kim, Y. N., Koh, S. J., Mann, R., Matthews, W., & Suoo, M. (1997, May). Human resource management in South Korea. Working paper, Graduate School of Business, University of Colorado–Denver.

29. Copeland, op. cit.

30. Schweitzer, M. E., & Kerr, J. L. (2000). Bargaining under the influence: The role of alcohol in negotiations. *Academy of Management Executive, 14*(2), 47–57. See also Ralston, D. A., Gustafson, D. J., Elsass, P. M., Cheung, F., & Terpstra, R. H. (1992). Eastern values: A comparison of managers in the United States, Hong Kong, and the People's Republic of China. *Journal of Applied Psychology, 77,* 664–671.

31. Claus, L. (2001). *Euro-HRM.* Monterey, CA: Monterey Institute of International Studies.

32. For more on this see, for example, Baker & McKenzie. (2000, May). The global employer. *Global Labor, Employment, and Employee Benefits Bulletin, 5*(2), 1–43. Available at *www.bakernet.com.*

33. Ibrahim, Y. M. (1994, Feb. 3). Fundamentalists impose culture on Egypt. *The New York Times,* pp. A1, A10.

34. Harris & Moran, op. cit.

35. Adler, N. J., Doktor, R., & Redding, S. G. (1986). From the Atlantic to the Pacific century: Cross-cultural management reviewed. *Journal of Management, 12,* 295–318.

36. Howard, A., Shudo, K., & Umeshima, M. (1983). Motivation and values among Japanese and American managers. *Personnel Psychology, 36*(4), 883–898.

37. Employee motivation in Germany (1989, Mar.). *Manpower Argus,* no. 246, p. 6.

38. Machungwa, P. D., & Schmitt, N. (1983). Work motivation in a developing country. *Journal of Applied Psychology, 68*(1), 31–42.

39. Harris & Moran, op. cit.

40. Hofstede, G. (1991). *Cultures and organizations.* London: McGraw-Hill. See also Hofstede, G. (1980). *Culture's consequences.* Beverly Hills, CA: Sage.

41. Sondergaard, M. (1994). Research note: Hofstede's consequences: A study of reviews, citations, and replications. *Organization Studies, 15,* 447–456.

42. Triandis, H. C. (1998). Vertical and horizontal individualism and collectivism: Theory and research implications for international comparative management. In J. L. C. Cheng (ed.), *Advances in International Comparative Management, 12,* 7–35.

43. Lessons from a casualty of the culture wars (1999, Nov. 29). *BusinessWeek,* p. 198. See also Lancaster, H. (1996, June 4). How you can learn to feel at home in a foreign-based firm. *The Wall Street Journal,* p. B1. See also Lipin, S., & Deogun, N. (2000, Oct. 30). Big mergers of the '90s prove disappointing to shareholders. *The Wall Street Journal,* pp. C1, C21.

44. Dowling, P. (1999). Completing the puzzle: Issues in the development of the field of international human resource management. *Management International Review, 39,* 27–43. See also Schuler, R. S., Dowling, P. J., & De Cieri, H. (1993). An integrative framework of strategic international human resource management. *Journal of Management, 19*(2), 419–459.

45. Bussey, J. An evening at gunpoint in Mexico (1998, Feb. 26). *The Wall Street Journal,* pp. B1, B6. See also Pasquarelli, T. (1996, Oct.). Dealing with discomfort and danger. *HRMagazine,* pp. 104–110.

46. Taylor, S. (1999, Apr.). When workers travel abroad, caution is advisable. *HR News.* pp. 13, 15. See also Solomon, C. M. (1997, Jan.). Global business under siege. *Global Workforce,* pp. 18–23.

47. Taylor, op. cit. See also When peril lurks overseas (1997, June 16). *BusinessWeek,* pp. 150, 151.

48. The next CEO's key asset: A worn passport (1998, Jan. 19). *BusinessWeek,* pp. 76, 77. See also Lublin, J. S. (1996, Jan. 29). An overseas stint can be a ticket to the top. *The Wall Street Journal,* pp. B1, B5.

49. Carpenter et al., op cit.

50. Sheridan & Hansen, op. cit. See also Reynolds, C. (1995a). *Compensating globally-mobile employees.* Scottsdale, AZ: American Compensation Association. See also Briscoe, D. (1995). *International human resource management.* Englewood Cliffs, NJ: Prentice-Hall.

51. 21st century capitalism, op. cit.

52. Schuler, et al. op. cit. See also Bartlett, C. A. (1986). Building and managing the transnational: The new organizational challenge. In M. E. Porter (ed.), *Competition in global industries.* Boston: Harvard Business School Press, pp. 367–404.

53. Cascio, W. F. (1993). International human resource management issues for the 1990s. *Asia-Pacific Journal of Human Resource Management, 30*(4), 1–18. See also Dowling, P. J., Schuler, R. S., and Welch, D. E. (1999). *International dimensions of human resource management* (3d ed.). Belmont, CA: Wadsworth.

54. Spreitzer, G. M., McCall, M. W., Jr., & Mahoney, J. D. (1997). Early identification of international executive potential. *Journal of Applied Psychology, 82,* 6–29.

55. Marquardt, M. J., & Engel, D. W. (1993). *Global human resource development.* Englewood Cliffs, NJ: Prentice-Hall. See also Safavi, F. (1981). A model of management education in Africa. *Academy of Management Review,* 6(2), 319–331.

56. Dowling et al., op. cit. See also Briscoe, op. cit.

57. Reynolds (1995a), op. cit.

58. Solomon, C. M. (1994, Jan.). Staff selection impacts global success. *Personnel Journal,* pp. 88–101.

59. Ibid.

60. Lewin, T. (2000, Oct. 24). Working parents: Two-income families now the norm. *The Denver Post,* pp. 1A, 15A.

61. Lublin, J. S. (1992, Aug. 19). Spouses find themselves worlds apart as global commuter marriages increase. *The Wall Street Journal,* pp. B1, B4.

62. Rosen, B. (1995, June 19). Trailing spouses get the chance to re-create their careers abroad. *International Herald Tribune,* p. 9.

63. Ibid. See also Roberts, K., Kossek, E. E., & Ozeki, C. (1998). Managing the global workforce: Challenges and strategies. *Academy of Management Executive, 12*(4), 93–106.

64. Black, J. S., Gregersen, H. B., & Mendenhall, M. E. (1992). *Global assignments.* San Francisco: Jossey-Bass.

65. Marquardt & Engel, op. cit. See also Safavi, op. cit.

66. Jenkins, L. (1995, Summer). Overseas assignments: Sending the right people. *International HR Journal,* pp. 41–43.

67. Cascio, W. F. (1991, Sept.). International assessment and the globalization of business: Riddle or recipe for success? Keynote address prepared for the National Assessment Conference, Minneapolis, MN.

68. Caligiuri, P. M. (2000). The big five personality characteristics as predictors of expatriates' desire to terminate the assignment and supervisor-rated performance. *Personnel Psychology, 53,* 67–88.

69. Thompson, op. cit.

70. Mendenhall, M. E., & Oddou, G. (1995). The overseas assignment: A practical look. In M. E. Mendenhall & G. Oddou (eds.). *Readings and cases in international human resource management* (2d ed.), Cincinnati, OH: South-Western, pp. 206–216.

71. Ronen, S. (1989). Training the international assignee. In I. L. Goldstein (ed.), *Training and development in organizations.* San Francisco: Jossey-Bass, pp. 418–453.

72. Black, J. S. (1990). Personal dimensions and work-role transitions: A study of Japanese expatriate managers in America. *Management International Review, 30*(2), 119–134.

73. Fuchsberg, G. (1992, Jan. 9). As costs of overseas assignments climb, firms select expatriates more carefully. *The Wall Street Journal,* pp. B1, B5.

74. Carmell, W. A. (2001, May–June). *Application of U.S. antidiscrimination laws to multinational employers: Legal Report.* Alexandria, VA: Society for Human Resource Management.

75. Lévy-Leboyer, C. (1994). Selection and assessment in Europe. In H. C. Triandis, M. D. Dunnette, & L. M. Hough (eds.), *Handbook of industrial and organizational psychology* (vol. 4). Palo Alto, CA: Consulting Psychologists Press, pp. 173–190.

76. Ryan, A. M., McFarland, L., Baron, H., & Page, R. (1999). An international look at selection practices: Nation and culture as explanations for variability in practice. *Personnel Psychology, 52,* 359–391.

77. Shaffer, M. A., Harrison, D. A., Gilley, K. M., & Luk, D. M. (2001). Struggling for balance amid turbulence on international assignments: work-family conflict, support, and commitment. *Journal of Management, 27,* 99–121.

78. Pucik, V., & Saba, T. (1999). Selecting and developing the global versus the expatriate manager: A review of the state of the art. *Human Resource Planning,* 40–54. See also Odds and ends (1992, Nov. 11). *The Wall Street Journal,* p. B1.

79. Shaffer & Harrison, op. cit. See also Black, et al., op. cit. See also Solomon (1994), op. cit. See also Conway, M. A. (1984). Reducing expatriate failure rates. *Personnel Administrator, 29*(7), 31–38.

80. Shaffer et al., op. cit. See also Aryee, S., Fields, D., & Luk, V. (1999). A cross-cultural test of a model of the work-family interface. *Journal of Management, 25,* 491–511.

81. Shaffer, M. A., & Harrison, D. A. (2001). Forgotten partners of international assignments: Development and test of a model of spouse adjustment. *Journal of Applied Psychology, 86,* 238–254. See also Shaffer & Harrison (1998), op. cit.

82. Jossi, F. (2001, June). Buying protection from terrorism. *HRMagazine,* pp. 155–160. See also Bensimon, H. F. (1998, Aug.). Is it safe to work abroad? *Training & Development,* pp. 20–24. See also Bussey, op. cit. See also Taylor, op. cit. See also When peril lurks overseas, op. cit. See also Solomon (1997), op. cit.

83. Dowling et al., op. cit.

84. Caligiuri, P., & Cascio, W. F. (2000). Sending women on global assignments. *WorldatWork Journal, 9*(2), 34–40. See also Expatriate activity still expanding, but at a slower rate, survey shows (2001, Feb.) *HR News,* p. 10. See also Fisher, A. (1998, Sept. 28). Overseas, U.S. businesswomen may have the edge. *Fortune,* p. 304.

85. Harrison, J. K. (1992). Individual and combined effects of behavior modeling and the cultural assimilator in cross-cultural management training. *Journal of Applied Psychology, 77,* 952–962. See also Black, J. S., & Mendenhall, M. (1990). Crosscultural training effectiveness: A review and a theoretical framework for future research. *Academy of Management Review, 15,* 113–136.

86. Kraimer, M. L., Wayne, S. J., & Jaworski, R. A. (2001). Sources of support and expatriate performance: The mediating role of expatriate adjustment. *Personnel Psychology, 54,* 71–99.

87. Expatriate activity still expanding, op. cit.

88. Linowes, R. G. (1993). The Japanese manager's traumatic entry into the United States: Understanding the American-Japanese cultural divide. *Academy of Management Executive, 7*(4), 21–40. See also Black et al., op. cit.

89. Chronis, P. G. (1983, Feb. 6). They're learning how to live overseas . . . in Boulder. *Denver Post,* pp. 1C, 8C–9C.

90. Gillette's edge (1998, Jan. 19) *BusinessWeek,* pp. 70–77. See also Laabs, J. J. (1993, Aug.). How Gillette grooms local talent. *Personnel Journal,* pp. 65–76.

91. Gillette's edge, op. cit. See also Grant, L. (1996, Oct. 14). Gillette knows shaving—and how to turn out hot new products. *Fortune,* pp. 207–210.

92. Pulakos, E. D., Arad, S., Donovan, M. A., & Plamondon, K. E. (2000). Adaptability in the workplace: Development of a taxonomy of adaptive performance. *Journal of Applied Psychology, 85,* 612–624.

93. Black et al., op. cit.

94. Garten, J. E. (1998, Mar. 23). Why the global economy is here to stay. *Business-Week,* p. 21.

95. Sheridan & Hansen, op. cit.

96. Reynolds (1995a), op. cit.

97. Ibid.

98. Bensimon, op. cit.

99. Milkovich, G. T., & Newman, J. M. (2002). *Compensation* (7th ed.). Burr Ridge, IL: McGraw-Hill/Irwin.

100. Flynn, G. (1994, Aug.). HR in Mexico: what you should know. *Personnel Journal,* pp. 34–44.

101. Milkovich & Newman, op.cit.

102. Deloitte Touche Tohmatsu International (1997). *The hidden costs of employment: A comparative study of income tax and additional employment costs across Europe.* St. Albans, UK: Author. See also Milkovich & Newman, op. cit. See also Corporate benefits as a competitive tool in Japan (1990). *Japan Economic Institute Report.* Washington, D.C.: Japan Economic Institute.

103. Overman, S. (2000, Mar.). Check the vitality of health care abroad. *HRMagazine,* pp. 77–84.

104. U.S. Department of Labor (1996, July). *U.S. Department of State indexes of living costs abroad, quarters allowances, and hardship differentials.* Washington, DC: U.S. Government Printing Office.

105. Reynolds, C. (1995b). *Compensation basics for North American expatriates.* Scottsdale, AZ: American Compensation Association.

106. Sano, Y. (1993, Feb.). Changes and continued stability in Japanese HRM systems: Choice in the share economy. *International Journal of Human Resource Management,* pp. 11–27.

107. Kim, K. I., Park, H. J., & Suzuki, N. (1990). Reward allocations in the United States, Japan, and Korea: A comparison of individualistic and collectivistic cultures. *Academy of Management Journal, 33,* 188–198.

108. Garonzik, R., Brockner, J., & Siegel, P. A. (2000). Identifying international assignees at risk for premature departure: the interactive effect of outcome favorability and procedural fairness. *Journal of Applied Psychology, 85,* 13–20.

109. Cascio, W. F., & Bailey, E. (1995). International HRM: The state of research and practice. In O. Shenkar (ed.), *Global perspectives of human resource management.* Englewood Cliffs, NJ: Prentice-Hall, pp. 15–36.

110. Sheridan & Hansen, op. cit.

111. Ibid. See also Brooks, B. J. (1988). Long-term incentives: International executives need them too. *Personnel, 65*(8), 40–42.

112. Bray, N. (1997, May 27). OECD ministers agree to ban bribery as means for companies to win business. *The Wall Street Journal,* p. A2.

113. Glain, S. (1995, Nov. 21). South Koreans say bribes are part of life. *The Wall Street Journal,* p. A11. See also Running scared in Seoul: The scandal may signal the end of the corrupt old ways (1995, Nov. 27). *BusinessWeek,* pp. 58, 59.

114. Bray, op. cit.

115. Rothman, M., Briscoe, D., & Nacamulli, R. (eds.). (1993). *Industrial relations around the world.* Berlin: Walter de Gruyter.

116. Gatley, S. (1996). *Comparative management: A transcultural odyssey.* London: McGraw-Hill. See also Gaugler, E. (1988). HR management: An international comparison. *Personnel, 65*(8), 24–30.

117. Movassaghi, H. (1996). The workers of nations: Industrial Relations in a global economy. *Compensation & Benefits Management, 12*(2), 75–77. See also Dowling et al., op. cit.

118. Mills, D. Q. (1994). *Labor-management relations* (5th ed.). New York: McGraw-Hill. See also Levine, M. J. (1988). Labor movements and the multinational corporation: A future for collective bargaining? *Employee Relations Law Journal, 13*, 382–403.

119. Sera, K. (1992). Corporate globalization: A new trend. *Academy of Management Executive, 6*(1), 89–96.

120. Time to leave the cocoon? (1993, Oct. 18). *BusinessWeek,* pp. 46, 47.

121. Levine, op. cit.

122. International labor standards gain attention (1997, Mar.–Apr.). *Workplace Visions International,* pp. 3–6.

123. Lee, L., & Bernstein, A. (2000, June 12). Who says student protests don't matter? *BusinessWeek,* pp. 94, 96. See also A life of fines and beatings (2000, Oct. 2). *BusinessWeek,* pp. 122–128.

124. A world of sweatshops (2000, Aug. 28). *BusinessWeek,* pp. 84, 86.

125. International labor standards gain attention, op. cit.

126. Gomez, J. A. (1994, Dec. 10). Competition and collaboration in a new marketplace: Implications for U.S. and Canadian managers operating in Mexico. *Proceedings: Business practices under NAFTA: Developing common standards for global business.* Institute for International Business, University of Colorado–Denver, pp. 12–18. See also Davis, B. (1995, Oct. 26). Two years later, the promises used to sell NAFTA haven't come true, but its foes were wrong, too. *The Wall Street Journal,* p. A24. See also Bradley, B. (1993, Sept. 16). NAFTA opens more than a trade door. *The Wall Street Journal,* p. A14.

127. NAFTA's scorecard: So far, so good (2001, July 9). *BusinessWeek,* pp. 54, 56. See also

128. Ibid., p. 56.

129. The Mexican worker (1993, Apr. 19). *BusinessWeek,* pp. 84–92.

130. Now, Mexico's unions have a real chance at freedom (1998, Jan. 26). *BusinessWeek,* p. 46.

131. Border crossings (1993, Nov. 22). *BusinessWeek,* pp. 40–42.

132. Raised fists in the developing world (2000, Aug. 28). *BusinessWeek,* pp. 130–132.

133. Whitman, M. F. (1999, Mar.). Antecedents of repatriates' intent to leave the organization: Repatriation adjustment, job satisfaction, and organizational commitment. Executive summary of a dissertation. See also McClenahen, op. cit. See also Black, J. S., &, Gregersen, H. B. (1991). When Yankee comes home: Factors related to expatriate and spouse repatriation adjustment. *Journal of International Business Studies, 22*(4), 671–695.

134. Gregersen, H. B., & Black, J. S. (1996). Multiple commitments upon repatriation: The Japanese experience. *Journal of Management, 22,* 209–229. See also Black et al., op. cit.

135. Gregersen, H. B. (1992). Commitments to a parent company and a local work unit during repatriation. *Personnel Psychology, 45,* 29–54.

136. Dobrzynski, J. H. (1996, Aug. 18). The out-of-sight Americans: Executives pay later for their stints abroad. *International Herald Tribune,* pp. 1, 7.

137. Whitman, op. cit. See also Before saying yes to going abroad (1995, Dec. 4). *BusinessWeek,* pp. 130, 132.

138. Roberts et al., op. cit. See also Black et al., op. cit.

139. Whitman, op. cit. See also Work week (1997, Jan. 7). *The Wall Street Journal,* p. A1. See also Dobrzynski, op. cit.

140. Taking steps can cut risk of rocky return from overseas stint (1993, Aug. 25). *The Wall Street Journal,* p. B1.

141. Ibid. See also Bennett, R. (1993, Sept.–Oct.). Meeting the challenges of repatriation. *Journal of International Compensation & Benefits,* pp. 28–33.

142. Savich, R. S., & Rodgers, W. (1988). Assignment overseas: Easing the transition before and after. *Personnel, 65*(8), 44–48.
143. Thompson, op. cit. See also Work week, op. cit. See also Bennett, op. cit.
144. Strategy suggestions (1997, Mar.–Apr.). *Workplace Visions International,* p. 8.
145. Roberts et al., op. cit.

GLOSSARY

absenteeism Any failure of an employee to report for or to remain at work as scheduled, regardless of reason.

absolute rating systems Rating formats that evaluate each employee in terms of performance standards, without reference to other employees.

acceptability The extent to which a performance measure is deemed to be satisfactory or adequate by those who use it.

accepting diversity Learning to value and respect styles and ways of behaving that differ from one's own.

acquired rights law A Mexican labor law stipulating that if a benefit, service, or bonus is paid 2 years in a row, it becomes an employee's right.

action learning A process in which participants learn through experience and application.

action programs Programs, including the activities of recruitment, selection, performance appraisal, training, and transfer, that help organizations adapt to changes in their environments.

active listening Listening in which five things are done well: taking time to listen, communicating verbally and nonverbally, not interrupting or arguing, watching for verbal and nonverbal cues, and summarizing what was said and what was agreed to.

adjustment The managerial activities intended to maintain compliance with the organization's human resource policies and business strategies.

adverse impact discrimination Unintentional discrimination that occurs when identical standards or procedures unrelated to success on a job are applied to everyone, despite the fact that such standards or procedures lead to a substantial difference in employment outcomes for the members of a particular group.

affirmative action Action intended to overcome the effects of past or present discriminatory policies or practices, or other barriers to equal employment opportunity.

age grading Subconscious expectations about what people can and cannot do at particular times of their lives.

agency shop A union security provision stipulating that although employees need not join the union that

agency shop *(cont.)* represents them, in lieu of dues they must pay a service charge for representation.

agreeableness The degree to which an individual is cooperative, warm, and agreeable, versus cold, disagreeable, and antagonistic.

alternative dispute resolution (ADR) A formal, structured policy for dispute resolution that may involve third-party mediation and arbitration.

alternation ranking A ranking method in which a rater initially lists all employees on a sheet of paper, and then chooses the best employee, worst employee, second best, second worst, and so forth until all employees have been ranked.

annuity problem The situation that exists when past merit payments, incorporated into an employee's base pay, form an annuity (a sum of money received at regular intervals), allowing formerly productive employees to slack off for several years while still earning high pay.

antidiscrimination rule A principle that holds that employers can obtain tax advantages only for those benefits that do not discriminate in favor of highly compensated employees.

applicant group Individuals who are eligible for and interested in selection or promotion.

assessment center method A process that evaluates a candidate's potential for management on the basis of multiple assessment techniques, standardized methods of making inferences from such techniques, and pooled judgments from multiple assessors.

assessment phase of training The phase whose purpose is to define what the employee should learn in relation to desired job behaviors.

attitudes Internal states that focus on particular aspects of or objects in the environment.

authority For managers at all levels, the organizationally granted right to influence the actions and behavior of the workers they manage.

authorization cards Cards, signed by employees, which designate the union as the employee's exclusive representative in bargaining with management.

661

baby-boom generation   People born between 1946 and 1964, currently 55 percent of the workforce, who believe that the business of business includes leadership in redressing social inequities.

balance   In a pay system, the relative size of pay differentials among different segments of the workforce.

balance-sheet approach   A method of compensating expatriates in which the primary objective is to ensure that the expatriates neither gain nor lose financially compared with their home-country peers.

bargaining impasse   The situation that occurs when the parties involved in negotiations are unable to move further toward settlement.

bargaining unit   A group of employees eligible to vote in a representation election.

behavior costing   An approach to assessing human resource systems that focuses on dollar estimates of the behaviors of managers, measuring the economic consequences of managers' behaviors.

behavior modeling   Acting as a role model. The fundamental characteristic of modeling is that learning takes place by observation of the role model's behavior or by imagining his or her experience.

behaviorally anchored rating scales (BARSs)   Graphic rating scales that define the dimensions to be rated in behavioral terms and use critical incidents to describe various levels of performance.

behavior-oriented rating method   An appraisal method in which employee performance is rated either by comparing the performance of employees to that of other employees or by evaluating each employee in terms of performance standards without reference to others.

benchmark jobs   Jobs that are characterized by stable tasks and stable job specifications; also known as *key jobs.*

"best-of-both-worlds" benefits   In global corporations, an approach to benefits coverage stating that wherever possible, the expatriate is given home-country benefits coverage, but if there is no home-country plan in a certain benefit area, the employee may join the host-country plan.

blended life course   A lifestyle with balance in the ongoing mix of work, leisure, and education.

bona fide occupational qualifications (BFOQs)   Otherwise prohibited discriminatory factors that are exempted from coverage under Title VII of the Civil Rights Act of 1964 when they are considered reasonably necessary to the operation of a particular business or enterprise.

break-even value   The length of time an observed training effect would need to be maintained in order to recover the cost of the training program.

business game   A situational test in which candidates play themselves, not an assigned role, and are evaluated within a group.

cafeteria benefits   A package of benefits offered to workers; both "basic" and "optional" items are included, and each worker can pick and choose among the alternative options.

card check   A process in which a union secures authorization cards from more than 50 percent of employees, giving it the right to ask management directly for the right to exclusive representation.

career   A sequence of positions occupied by a person during the course of a lifetime; also known as one's *objective career.*

career paths   Logical and possible sequences of positions that could be held in an organization, based on an analysis of what people actually do in the organization.

career planning   A support mechanism to help employees plan out their long-term career goals.

career sponsor   An individual (usually a group vice president or higher) who is appointed to look out for an expatriate's career interests while she or he is abroad, to keep the expatriate abreast of company developments, and to counsel the expatriate when she or he returns home.

career success   The measure of career development and satisfaction over a period of time.

cascading process   Periodic review of work plans by both supervisors and subordinates in order to identify goals attained, problems encountered, and the need for training.

case law   The courts' interpretations of laws and determination of how those laws will be enforced, which serve as precedents to guide future legal decisions.

cash balance plan   A pension plan in which each employee receives steady annual credit toward an eventual pension, adding to his or her pension account "cash balance."

central tendency   In rating employees, a tendency to give employees an average rating on each criterion.

certiorari   Discretionary review by the Supreme Court when conflicting conclusions have been reached by lower courts or when a major question of constitutional interpretation is involved.

change facilitator   An individual who anticipates the need for change in strategy and prepares the organization for that change; a key role of a human resource professional.

checkoff   A union security provision under which an employee may request that union dues be deducted from her or his pay and be sent directly to the union.

circumstantial evidence   Statistical evidence used as a method of proving the intention to discriminate systematically against classes of individuals.

closed shop   A union security provision stipulating that an individual must join the union that

closed shop *(cont.)*
represents employees in order to be considered for employment.

collaborator An individual who works well both inside and outside an organization, and who shares information rather than promoting competition; a key role of a human resources professional.

collective bargaining unit The group of employees eligible to vote in a representation election.

collectivism The extent to which members of a culture give preference to an in-group over individual goals.

community of interest A defined unit that reflects the shared interests of the employees involved.

compensable factors Common job characteristics that an organization is willing to pay for, such as skill, effort, responsibility, and working conditions.

compensation The human resource management function that deals with every type of reward that individuals receive in return for performing organizational tasks.

compensatory damages In civil cases, damages that are awarded to reimburse a plaintiff for injuries or harm.

competency-based pay system A pay system under which workers are paid on the basis of the number of jobs they are capable of doing, that is, on the basis of their skills or their depth of knowledge.

competitive strategies The means that firms use to compete for business in the marketplace and to gain competitive advantage.

conciliation agreement An agreement reached between the Office of Federal Contract Compliance Programs and an employer to provide relief for the victims of unlawful discrimination.

concurrent engineering A design process that relies on teams of experts from design, manufacturing, and marketing working simultaneously on a project.

conscientiousness The degree to which an individual is hard-working, organized, dependable, and persevering versus lazy, disorganized, and unreliable.

consideration The aspect of leadership behavior that reflects management actions oriented toward developing mutual trust, respect for subordinates' ideas, and consideration of their feelings.

conspiracy doctrine A claim by employers that employees are conspiring against them in restraint of trade (for instance, that they are not working until their wages are raised).

contract compliance Adherence of contractors and subcontractors to equal employment opportunity, affirmative action, and other requirements of federal contract work.

contrast effects A tendency among interviewers to evaluate a current candidate's interview performance

contrast effects *(cont.)*
relative to the performances of immediately preceding candidates.

contrast error A rating error occurring when an appraiser compares several employees with one another rather than with an objective standard of performance.

contributory plans Group health care plans in which employees share in the cost of the premiums.

control group design A study design in which training is provided to one group but not to a second group that is similar to the trained group in terms of relevant characteristics.

cosmopolitan managers Managers who are sensitive to cultural differences, respect the distinctive practices of others, and make allowances for such factors when communicating with representatives of different cultural groups.

cosmopolitan perspective A perspective that comprises sensitivity to cultural differences, respect for distinctive practices of others, and making allowances for such factors in communicating with representatives of different cultural groups.

cost control The practice of keeping business costs at the lowest possible level in order for the business to be competitive.

cost shifting In health care, a situation in which one group of patients pays less than the true cost of their medical care.

cost-reduction strategy A competitive strategy with the primary objective of gaining competitive advantage by being the lowest-cost producer of goods or provider of services.

critical incidents In job analysis, vignettes consisting of brief actual reports that illustrate particularly effective or ineffective worker behaviors; a behavior-oriented rating method consisting of such anecdotal reports.

criteria The standards used to measure performance.

culture The characteristic customs, social patterns, beliefs, and values of people in a particular country or region, or in a particular racial or religious group.

culture shock The frustrations, conflict, anxiety, and feelings of alienation experienced by those who enter an unfamiliar culture.

debarment The act of barring a contractor or subcontractor from any government-contract work because of violations of equal employment opportunity and affirmative action requirements.

decertification Revocation of a union's status as the exclusive bargaining agent for the workers.

decision support system (DSS) An interactive computer program designed to provide relevant information and to answer what-if questions; may be used to enhance communication about and understanding of employee benefit programs.

defined-benefit plans Pension plans under which an employer promises to pay a retiree a stated pension, often expressed as a percentage of preretirement pay.

defined-contribution plan A type of pension plan that fixes a rate for employer contributions to a pension fund; future benefits depend on how fast the fund grows.

Delphi technique A structured approach for reaching a consensus judgment among experts, consisting of successive rounds in which experts independently generate information that is summarized by an intermediary and fed back to the experts for revision until there is a convergence of expert opinion.

demotions Downward internal moves in an organization that usually involve cuts in pay and reduced status, privileges, and opportunities.

dental HMOs Health maintenance plans for dental care that operate in the same way as medical HMOs.

desirable qualifications In job specifications, those qualities and skills that are advantageous but are not absolutely necessary for the performance of a particular job.

destructive criticism Criticism that is general in nature; that is frequently delivered in a biting, sarcastic tone; and that often attributes poor performance to internal causes.

development The managerial function of preserving and enhancing employees' competence in their jobs by improving their knowledge, skills, abilities, and other characteristics.

direct contracting In health care, a system in which doctors are free to charge, organize, and treat patients as they choose.

direct evidence An open expression of hatred, disrespect, or inequality, knowingly directed against members of a particular group, revealing pure bias.

direct measures Measures that deal with actual costs, such as accumulated direct costs of recruiting.

disability A physical or mental impairment that substantially limits one or more major life activities.

disability management A method of controlling disability-leave costs that emphasizes a partnership among physician, employee, manager, and human resources representative.

discrimination The giving of an unfair advantage (or disadvantage) to the members of a particular group in comparison with the members of other groups.

distributed practice Practice sessions with rest intervals between the sessions.

distributive bargaining In negotiations, the bargaining posture that assumes that the goals of the parties are irreconcilable; also known as *win-lose bargaining*.

distributive justice Justice that focuses on the fairness of the outcomes of decisions, for example, in the

distributive justice *(cont.)* alcation of bonuses or merit pay, or in making reasonable accommodations for employees with disabilities.

diversity-based recruitment with preferential hiring An organization's recruitment policy that systematically favors women and minorities in hiring and promotion decisions; also known as a *soft-quota system.*

doctrine of constructive receipt The principle that holds that an individual must pay taxes on benefits that have monetary value when the individual receives them.

downsizing The planned elimination of positions or jobs in an organization.

due process In legal proceedings, a judicial requirement that treatment of an individual may not be unfair, arbitrary, or unreasonable.

dynamic characteristics of jobs Characteristics of jobs that change over time, like those of public accountants or lifeguards.

economic strikes Actions by a union of withdrawing its labor in support of bargaining demands, including those for recognition or organization.

efficiency wage hypothesis The assumption that payment of wage premiums by employers to attract the best talent available will enhance productivity and thus offset any increase in labor costs.

employee assistance programs Programs that offer professional counseling, medical services, and rehabilitation opportunities to all troubled employees.

employee relations All the practices that implement the philosophy and policy of an organization with respect to employment.

employee stock ownership plans (ESOPs) Organizationwide incentive programs in which employees receive shares of company stock, thereby becoming owners or part owners of the company; shares are deposited into employees' accounts and dividends from the stock are added to the accounts.

employee voice A method of ensuring procedural justice within an organization by providing individuals and groups with an opportunity to be heard—a way to communicate their interests upward.

employment-at-will An employment situation in which an employee agrees to work for an employer but there is no specification of how long the parties expect the agreement to last.

engineering controls Modifications of the work environment that attempt to eliminate unsafe work conditions and neutralize unsafe worker behaviors.

enterprise unions Unions in which membership is limited to regular employees of a single company regardless of whether they are blue-collar or white-collar employees.

entrepreneurs Enterprising, decisive managers who can thrive in high-risk environments and can respond rapidly to changing conditions.

equal employment opportunity (EEO) Nondiscriminatory employment practices that ensure evaluation of candidates for jobs in terms of job-related criteria only, and fair and equal treatment of employees on the job.

equal employment opportunity (EEO) for women The raising of awareness of issues among both men and women so that women can be given a fair chance to think about their interests and potential, to investigate other possibilities, to make intelligent choices, and then to be considered for openings or promotions on an equal basis with men.

equalization An approach to international compensation in which an employer deducts home-country norms from the expatriate's salary for income taxes, housing, and goods and services, and then pays the balance, in home-country currency.

equity The fairness of a pay system, assessed in terms of the relative worth of jobs to the organization, competitive market rates outside the organization, and the pay received by others doing the same job.

equity norm A reward-allocation practice, common across cultures, in which rewards are distributed to group members on the basis of their contributions.

erroneous acceptance In the selection of personnel, the selection of someone who should have been rejected.

erroneous rejection In the selection of personnel, the rejection of someone who should have been accepted.

essential functions Job functions that require relatively more time and have serious consequences of error or nonperformance associated with them.

ethical decisions about behavior Decisions that concern one's conformity to moral standards or to the standards of conduct of a given profession or group; decisions that take into account not only one's own interests but also, equally, the interests of all others affected by the decisions.

ethical dilemmas Situations that have the potential to result in a breach of acceptable behavior.

ethnic Pertaining to groups of people classified according to common traits and customs.

ethnic minorities People classified according to common traits and customs.

ethnocentrism The view of an organization that the way things are done in the parent country is the best way, no matter where the business is conducted.

evaluation phase of training A twofold process that involves establishing indicators of success in training as well as on the job and determining exactly what job-related changes have occurred as a result of the training.

exclusive representation The concept that one and only one union, selected by majority vote, will exist in a given job territory, although multiple unions may represent different groups of employees who work for the same employer.

exempt employees Employees who are exempt from the overtime provisions of the Fair Labor Standards Act.

expatriate Anyone working outside her or his home country with a planned return to that or a third country; also known as a *foreign-service employee.*

experience-based interview An employment interview in which candidates are asked to provide detailed accounts of how they reacted in actual job-related situations.

expert system (ES) An interactive computer program that combines the knowledge of subject-matter experts and uses this information to recommend a solution for the user; may be used to enhance communication about and understanding of employee benefit programs.

external criteria Measures of behavior and results that indicate the impact of training on the job.

external equity "Fairness" in the wages paid by an organization, in terms of competitive market rates outside the organization.

externalities Social costs of production that are not necessarily included on a firm's profit-and-loss statement.

extraversion Gregariousness, assertiveness, and sociability in an individual, as opposed to reserved, timid, and quiet.

fact finding A dispute-resolution mechanism in which each party submits whatever information it believes is relevant to a resolution of the dispute, and a neutral fact finder then makes a study of the evidence and prepares a report on the facts.

fairness As it pertains to employee performance rewards, the employees' perceptions that rewards are given honestly and impartially, without favoritism or prejudice; an employee's perception depends on a comparison with the reward received and some comparison standard, such as rewards received by others, rewards received previously, or rewards promised by the organization.

family-friendly firms Organizations with policies, such as on-site child care and flexible work schedules, that take into account the families of employees.

featherbedding Requiring an employer in a labor-contract provision to pay for services that are not performed by hiring more employees than are needed or by limiting production.

feedback Evaluative or corrective information transmitted to employees about their attempts to improve their job performance.

femininity The extent to which members of a culture consider sex-role distinctions to be minimal and emphasize quality of life, as opposed to work, as the central value in a person's life.

fiduciaries Pension trustees.

fiduciary duty of loyalty An obligation by employees to maintain all trade secrets with which their employers have entrusted them; also provides a former employer with legal recourse if an executive joins a competitor and reveals trade secrets.

financial rewards The component of an organizational reward system that includes direct payments, such as salary, and indirect payments, such as employee benefits.

flexible benefits Benefits provided under a plan that allows employees to choose their benefits from among the alternatives offered by the organization.

flexible-spending accounts Accounts into which employees can deposit pretax dollars (up to a specified amount) to pay for additional benefits.

flextime A strategy that allows any employee the right, within certain limitations, to set his or her own workday hours.

forced distribution A rating method in which the overall distribution of ratings is forced into a normal, or bell-shaped, curve, under the assumption that a relatively small portion of employees is truly outstanding, a relatively small portion is unsatisfactory, and all other employees fall in between.

foreign-service employee Anyone working outside her or his home country with a planned return to that or a third country; also known as an *expatriate*.

formal recruitment sources External recruitment channels, including university relations, executive search firms, employment agencies, and recruitment advertising.

401(k) plan A defined-contribution pension plan in which an employee can deduct a certain amount of his or her income from taxes and place the money into a personal retirement account; if the employer adds matching funds, the combined sums grow tax-free until they are withdrawn, usually at retirement.

free-speech clause The right of management to express its opinion about unions or unionism to employees, provided that it does not threaten or promise favors to employees to obtain antiunion actions.

gain sharing An organizationwide incentive program in which employee cooperation leads to information sharing and employee involvement, which in turn lead to new behaviors that improve organizational productivity; the increase in productivity results in a financial bonus (based on the amount of increase), which is distributed monthly or quarterly.

gatekeeper A primary-care physician who monitors the medical history and care of each employee and his or her family.

Generation X People born between 1965 and 1977, who grew up in times of rapid change, both social and economic; also known as baby busters.

Generation Y People born between 1977 and 1997; includes offspring of baby boomers as well as an influx of immigrants through the 1990s. These people have grown up and are growing up with sophisticated technologies, having been exposed to them much earlier in life than members of Generation X.

generational diversity Important differences in values, aspirations, and beliefs that characterize the swing generation, the silent generation, the baby boomers, Generation X, and Generation Y.

geocentrism In the recruitment of executives for multinational companies, a strategy with an international perspective that emphasizes the unrestricted use of people of all nationalities.

glass ceiling The barrier faced by women in breaking through to senior management positions, so called because although women can see the top jobs, they cannot actually reach them.

global challenge Training needs stimulated by the expansion of many firms into global markets. Such needs involve the training of local nationals, as well as preparing employees from the home country to work in foreign markets.

global corporation A corporation that has become an "insider" in any market or nation where it operates and is thus competitive with domestic firms operating in local markets.

globalization The interdependence of business operations internationally; commerce without borders.

globalites Sophisticated international executives drawn from many countries.

goal theory The theory that an individual's conscious goals or intentions regulate her or his behavior.

goals and timetables Flexible objectives and schedules for hiring and promoting underrepresented group members to ensure compliance with equal opportunity employment and affirmative action requirements.

grandfather clause A plan that allows older workers to stay enrolled in the original pension plan if the organization decides to change plans.

grievance An alleged violation of the rights of workers on the job.

grievance arbitration The final stage of the grievance process, which consists of compulsory, binding arbitration; used as an alternative to a work stoppage and to ensure labor peace for the duration of a labor contract.

grievance procedures Procedures by which an employee can seek a formal, impartial review of a decision that affects him or her; a formal process to help the parties involved resolve a dispute.

group life insurance Life insurance benefits, usually yearly renewable term insurance, provided for all employees as part of a benefits package.

halo error A rating error occurring when an appraiser rates an employee high (or low) on *many aspects* of job performance because the appraiser believes the employee performs well (or poorly) on some *specific aspect.*

hard quotas In an organization's recruitment and selection process, a mandate to hire or promote specific numbers or proportions of women or minority-group members.

headhunter An executive recruiter.

health awareness Knowledge of the present and future consequences of behaviors and lifestyles and the risks they may present.

health maintenance organization (HMO) An organized system of health care, with the emphasis on preventive medicine, that assures the delivery of services to employees who enroll voluntarily under a prepayment plan, thereby committing themselves to using the services of only those doctors and hospitals that are members of the plan.

health promotion A corporation's promotion of health awareness through four steps: educating employees about health-risk factors; identifying health-risk factors faced by employees; helping employees eliminate these risks; and helping employees maintain the new, healthier lifestyle.

high-performance work practices Work practices that maximize the fit between the company's social system and technology.

high-performance work systems challenge Increasingly sophisticated technological systems that will impose training and retraining requirements on the existing workforce.

home country An expatriate's country of residence.

host country The country in which an expatriate is working.

hostile environment harassment Verbal or physical conduct that creates an intimidating, hostile, or offensive work environment or interferes with an employee's job performance.

"hot cargo" agreements Refusals by the management or union members of a company to handle another employer's products because of that employer's relationship with a particular union.

human resource accounting An approach to assessing human resource systems that considers only the

human resource accounting *(cont.)* investments made in managers and not the returns on those investments.

human resource forecasts The human resource planning activity that predicts future human resource requirements, including the number of workers needed, the number expected to be available, the skills mix required, and the internal versus external labor supply.

human resource information system The method used by an organization to collect, store, analyze, report, and evaluate information and data on people, jobs, and costs.

human resource management (HRM) system An overall approach to management, comprising staffing, retention, development, adjustment, and managing change.

human resource planning (HRP) An effort to anticipate future business and environmental demands on an organization, and to provide qualified people to fulfill that business and satisfy those demands; HRP includes talent inventories, human resource forecasts, action plans, and control and evaluation.

in-basket test A situational test in which an individual is presented with items that might appear in the in-basket of an administrative officer, is given appropriate background information, and is directed to deal with the material as though he or she were actually on the job.

in-house temporaries Temporary workers who work directly for the hiring organization, as opposed to those supplied from temporary agencies.

in-plant slowdowns The action of union workers of staying on the job instead of striking, but carrying out their tasks "by the book," showing no initiative and taking no shortcuts.

incentives One-time supplements, tied to levels of job performance, to the base pay of employees, including nonexempt and unionized employees.

income-maintenance laws Laws designed to provide employees and their families with income security in case of death, disability, unemployment, or retirement.

indirect costs of accidents Costs that cannot be avoided by a corporation when an employee has an accident, such as wages paid for time lost, cost of damage to material or equipment, and any other expense created in conjunction with the accident.

indirect labor Workers who provide essential services to line workers.

indirect measures Measures that do not deal directly with cost; expressed in terms of time, quantity, or quality.

individual analysis In the assessment of training needs, the level of analysis that determines how well

individual analysis *(cont.)* each employee is performing the tasks that make up his or her job.

individual equity Determination of whether or not each individual's pay is "fair" relative to that of other individuals doing the same or similar jobs.

individualism The extent to which members of a culture emphasize personal rather than group goals.

informal recruitment sources Recruitment sources such as walk-ins, write-ins, and employee referrals.

informational justice Justice expressed in terms of providing explanations or accounts for decisions made.

initial screening In the employee recruitment and selection process, a cursory selection of possible job candidates from a pool of qualified candidates.

initiating structure The aspect of leadership behavior that reflects the extent to which an individual defines and structures her or his role and those of her or his subordinates toward task accomplishment.

innovation strategy A competitive strategy with the primary objective of developing products or services that differ from those of competitors.

innovator An individual who creates new approaches to motivating and managing people rather than relying on past procedures; a key role of a human resource professional.

institutional memories Memories (primarily of workers with long service) of corporate traditions and of how and why things are done as they are in an organization.

integrative bargaining In negotiations, the bargaining posture that assumes that the goals of the parties are not mutually exclusive, that it is possible for both sides to achieve their objectives; also known as *win-win bargaining.*

integrity tests Overt (clear-purpose) tests that are designed to assess directly attitudes toward dishonest behaviors and personality-based (disguised-purpose) tests that aim to predict a broad range of counterproductive behaviors at work.

interactional justice The quality of interpersonal treatment that employees receive in their everyday work.

interest arbitration A dispute-resolution mechanism in which a neutral third party hears the positions of both parties and decides on binding settlement terms.

internal criteria Measures of reaction and learning that are concerned with outcomes of the training program per se.

internal equity Determination of whether or not pay rates are fair in terms of the relative worth of individual jobs to an organization.

international alliance A collaboration between two or more multinational companies that allows them jointly to pursue a common goal.

interpersonal challenge The need, as more firms move to employee involvement and teams in the workplace, for team members to learn behaviors such as asking for ideas, offering help without being asked, listening and feedback skills, and recognizing and considering the ideas of others.

interrater reliability An estimate of reliability obtained from independent ratings of the same sample of behavior by two different scorers.

inventories Standardized measures of behavior, such as interests, attitudes, and opinions, that do not have right and wrong answers.

job analysis The process of obtaining information about jobs, including the tasks to be done on the jobs as well as the personal characteristics necessary to do the tasks.

job description A written summary of task requirements for a particular job.

job evaluation Assessment of the relative worth of jobs to a firm.

job families Job classification systems that group jobs according to their similarities.

job posting The advertising of available jobs internally through the use of bulletin boards (electronic or hardcopy) or in lists available to all employees.

job satisfaction A pleasurable feeling that results from the perception that a job fulfills or allows for the fulfillment of its holder's important job values.

job sharing An approach that allows two employees to share the job responsibilities normally handled by only one employee, and to receive salary and benefits in proportion to their contribution.

job specification A written summary of worker requirements for a particular job.

just cause As it pertains to arbitration cases, the concept that requires an employer not only to produce persuasive evidence of an employee's liability or negligence, but also to provide the employee a fair hearing and to impose a penalty appropriate to the proven offense.

justice The maintenance or administration of what is just, especially by the impartial adjustment of conflicting claims or the assignment of merited rewards or punishments.

key jobs Jobs that are characterized by stable tasks and stable job specifications; also known as benchmark jobs.

knowledge capital The value of the knowledge possessed by people at all levels of an organization.

labor market A geographical area within which the forces of supply (people looking for work) interact with the forces of demand (employers looking for people) and thereby determine the price of labor.

leaderless group discussion (LGD)   A situational test in which a group of participants is given a job-related topic and is asked to carry on a discussion about it for a period of time, after which observers rate the performance of each participant.

leniency   The tendency to rate every employee high or excellent on all criteria.

liability without fault   The principle that forms the foundation for workers' compensation laws, under which benefits are provided not because of any liability or negligence on the part of the employer, but as a matter of social policy.

Likert method of summed ratings   A type of behavioral checklist with declarative sentences and weighted response categories; the rater checks the response category that he or she thinks best describes the employee and sums the weights of the responses that were checked for each item.

local perspective   A viewpoint that includes no appreciation for cultural differences.

localization   The practice of paying expatriates on the same scale as local nationals in the country of assignment.

lockout   The shutting down of plant operations by management when contract negotiations fail.

long-term disability (LTD) plans   Disability insurance plans that provide benefits when an employee is disabled for 6 months or longer, usually at no more than 60 percent of base pay.

loss-control program   A way to sustain a safety policy through four components: a safety budget, safety records, management's personal concern, and management's good example.

maintenance of membership   A union security provision stipulating that an employee must remain a member of the union once he or she joins.

managed care   A health care system in which a doctor's clearance for treatment is required for the employee before he or she enters the hospital.

managed health   Total health and productivity management in which patients are treated under the same health-care delivery system, regardless of whether they became ill or were injured at work or on their own time.

managed-disability programs   Disability insurance plans that focus on making sure that disabled employees receive the care and rehabilitation they need to help them return to work quickly.

management by objectives (MBO)   A philosophy of management with a results-oriented rating method that relies on goal-setting to establish objectives for the organization as a whole, for each department, for each manager, and for each employee, thus providing

management by objectives (MBO)   *(cont.)* a measure of each employee's contribution to the success of the organization.

management controls   Measures instituted by management in an attempt to increase safe worker behaviors.

managing change   The ongoing managerial process of enhancing the ability of an organization to anticipate and respond to developments in its external and internal environments, and to enable employees at all levels to cope with the changes.

managing diversity   Establishing a heterogeneous workforce (including white men) to perform to its potential in an equitable work environment where no member or group of members enjoys an advantage or suffers a disadvantage.

maquiladoras   Border factories that import auto parts and electronics, process them, and send them north again, all duty-free.

market-based pay system   A pay system that uses a direct market-pricing approach for all of a firm's jobs.

masculinity   The extent to which members of a culture differentiate very strongly by gender and the dominant cultural values are work-related.

massed practice   Practice sessions that are crowded together.

meaningfulness of material   Material that is rich in associations for the trainees and is therefore easily understood by them.

mediation   A process by which a neutral third party attempts to help the parties in a dispute reach a settlement of the issues that divide them.

mentor   One who acts or is selected to act as teacher, advisor, sponsor, and confidant for a new hire or a small group of new hires in order to share his or her knowledge about the dynamics of power and politics, facilitate socialization, and improve the newcomers' chances for survival and growth in the organization.

merged-gender mortality tables   Mortality tables that, rather than treating males and females separately, show the combined number of persons living, the combined number of persons dying, and the merged-gender mortality rate for each age.

merit guide charts   Charts that are used to determine the size of an employee's merit increase for a given level of performance; the intersection on the chart of the employee's performance level and his or her location in a pay grade identifies the percentage of pay increase.

merit pay systems   Pay systems, most commonly applied to exempt employees, under which employees receive permanent increases, tied to levels of job performance, in their base pay.

meta-analysis   A statistical cumulation of research results across studies.

mid-career plateauing Performance by mid-career workers at an acceptable but not outstanding level, coupled with little or no effort to improve performance.

mixed-motive case A discrimination case in which an employment decision was based on a combination of job-related as well as unlawful factors.

mobility premium A one-time payment to an expatriate for each move—overseas, back home, or to another overseas assignment.

modified balance sheet approach In terms of international compensation, linking salary to a region rather than to the home country.

modular corporation A new organizational form in which the basic idea is to focus on a few core competencies—those a company does best—and to outsource everything else to a network of suppliers.

mommy wars Personal conflicts experienced by women in the workforce, especially those in demanding executive positions, as they juggle work and family roles.

money-purchase plan A defined-contribution pension plan in which the employer contributes a set percentage of each vested employee's salary to his or her retirement account; annual investment earnings and losses are added to or subtracted from the account balance.

motion study A method of studying how a job is done.

needs assessment The process used to determine whether training is necessary.

negligent hiring The failure of an employer to check closely enough on a prospective employee, who then commits a crime in the course of performing his or her job duties.

neuroticism The degree to which an individual is insecure, anxious, depressed, and emotional, versus calm, self-confident, and cool.

no-compete agreements Clauses in a contract that bar an individual from working for a competitor for 6 months to 2 years if he or she is fired, if the job is eliminated, or if the individual leaves voluntarily.

noncontributory plan The employer pays the full cost of insurance premiums for employees.

nonfinancial rewards The component of an organizational reward system that includes everything in a work environment that enhances a worker's sense of self-respect and esteem by others, such as training opportunities, involvement in decision making, and recognition.

norms of behavior Local customs created from a culture's value system.

objective career A sequence of positions occupied by a person during the course of a lifetime; commonly referred to simply as one's *career*.

objective personality and interest inventories Inventories that provide a clear stimulus and a clear set of responses from which to choose.

obsolescence As it pertains to human resource management, the tendency for knowledge or skills to become out of date.

ombudspersons People designated to investigate claims of unfair treatment or to act as intermediaries between an employee and senior management and recommend possible courses of action to the parties.

O*Net (Occupational Information Network) A national occupational system that provides comprehensive descriptions of the attributes of workers and jobs.

open-door policies Organizational policies that allow employees to approach senior managers with problems that they may not be willing to take to their immediate supervisors.

openness to experience The degree to which an individual is creative, curious, and cultured, versus practical with narrow interests.

operational planning Short-to middle-range business planning that addresses issues associated with the growth of current or new operations, as well as with any specific problems that might disrupt the pace of planned growth; also known as *tactical planning*.

operations analysis In the assessment of training needs, the level of analysis that attempts to identify the content of training—what an employee must do in order to perform competently.

organization In business, a group of people who perform specialized tasks that are coordinated to enhance the value or utility of some good or service that is wanted by and provided to a set of customers or clients.

organization analysis In the assessment of training needs, the level of analysis that focuses on identifying where within the organization training is needed.

organization development Systematic, long-range programs of organizational improvement.

organizational citizenship behaviors Discretionary behaviors performed outside an employee's formal role, which help other employees perform their jobs or which show support for and conscientiousness toward an organization.

organizational commitment The degree to which an employee identifies with an organization and is willing to put forth effort on its behalf.

organizational culture The pattern of basic assumptions developed by an organization in learning to adapt to both its external and its internal environments.

organizational entry The process of becoming more involved in a particular organization.

organizational reward system A system for providing both financial and nonfinancial rewards; includes anything an employee values and desires that

organizational reward system   *(cont.)* an employer is able and willing to offer in exchange for employee contributions.

organizational support   The extent to which an organization values employees' general contributions and cares for their well being.

orientation   Familiarization with and adaptation to a situation or an environment.

outsourcing   Shifting work other than the organization's core competencies to a network of outside suppliers and contractors.

overlearning   Practicing far beyond the point where a task has been performed correctly only several times to the point that the task becomes "second nature."

paired comparisons   A behavior-oriented rating method in which an employee is compared to every other employee; the rater chooses the "better" of each pair and each employee's rank is determined by counting the number of times she or he was rated superior.

paradigm shift   In management philosophy, a dramatic change in the way of thinking about business problems and organizations.

parallel forms reliability estimate   The coefficient of correlation between two sets of scores obtained from two forms of the same test.

passive nondiscrimination   An organization's commitment to treat all races and both sexes equally in all decisions about hiring, promotion, and pay, but with no attempt to recruit actively among prospective minority applicants.

pattern bargaining   Negotiating the same contract provisions for several firms in the same industry, with the intent of making wages and benefits uniform industrywide.

Paul Principle   The phenomenon that over time, people become uneducated, and therefore incompetent, to perform at a level at which they once performed adequately.

pay compression   A narrowing of the ratios of pay between jobs or pay grades in a firm's pay structure.

peer nomination   A method of peer assessment that requires each group member to designate a certain number of group members as highest or lowest on a performance dimension.

peer ranking   A method of peer assessment that requires each group member to rank the performance of all other members from best to worst.

peer rating   A method of peer assessment that requires each group member to rate the performance of every other group member.

pension   A sum of money paid at regular intervals to an employee who has retired from a company and is eligible to receive such benefits.

performance appraisal   A review of the job-relevant strengths and weaknesses of an individual or a team in an organization.

performance definition   A way to ensure that individual employees or teams know what is expected of them, and that they stay focused on effective performance by paying attention to goals, measures, and assessment.

performance encouragement   Provision of a sufficient amount of rewards that employees really value, in a timely, fair manner.

performance facilitation   An approach to management to which roadblocks to successful performance of employees are eliminated, adequate resources to get a job done right and on time are provided, and careful attention is paid to the selection of employees.

performance management   A broad process that requires managers to define, facilitate, and encourage performance by providing timely feedback and constantly focusing everyone's attention on the ultimate objectives.

performance standards   Criteria that specify *how well,* not *how,* work is to be done, by defining levels of acceptable or unacceptable employee behavior.

placement   In the employee recruitment and selection process, the assignment of individuals to particular jobs.

plateaued workers   Employees who are at a standstill in their jobs, either organizationally, through a lack of available promotions, or personally, through lack of ability or desire.

point-of-service plans   Health-care plans that offer the choice of using the plan's network of doctors and hospitals (and paying no deductible and only small copayments for office visits) or seeing a physician outside the network (and paying 30 to 40 percent of the total cost); an in-network gatekeeper must approve all services.

portability   Tax-free transfer of vested benefits to another employer or to an individual retirement account if a vested employee changes jobs and if the present employer agrees.

positive discipline   An alternative discipline procedure that includes the following steps: an oral reminder; a written reminder; and a decision-making leave, which is the employee's last chance to reform.

power distance   The extent to which members of a culture accept the unequal distribution of power.

preferential shop   A union security provision stipulating that union members be given preference in hiring.

preferred-provider organization (PPO)   A health-care system, generally with no gatekeeper, in which medical care is provided by a specified group of physicians and hospitals; care from outside the network is available at additional cost to the individual employee.

premium-price options Stock options granted at a price higher than the market price.

pretest–post-test only design A study in which a control group is not used and the performance of the trained group is evaluated before and after the training program.

prima facie case A case in which a body of facts is presumed to be true until proved otherwise.

privacy The interest employees have in controlling the use that is made of their personal information and in being able to engage in behavior free from regulation or surveillance.

procedural justice Justice that focuses on the fairness of the procedures used to make decisions—the extent to which the decisions are consistent across persons and over time, free from bias, based on accurate information, correctable, and based on prevailing moral and ethical standards.

process In a process-based organization of work, a collection of activities cutting across organizational boundaries and traditional business functions that takes one or more kinds of input and creates an output that is of value to a customer.

productivity A measure of the output of goods and services relative to the input of labor, material, and equipment.

profit sharing An organizationwide incentive program in which employees receive a bonus that is normally based on some percentage of the company's profits beyond some minimum level.

progressive discipline A discipline procedure that proceeds from an oral warning to a written warning to a suspension to dismissal.

projective measures Measures that present an individual with ambiguous stimuli (primarily visual) and allow him or her to respond in an open-ended fashion.

promotions Upward internal moves in an organization that usually involve greater responsibility and authority along with increases in pay, benefits, and privileges.

psychological success The feeling of pride and personal accomplishment that comes from achieving one's most important goals in life.

public-policy exception An exception to employment at will; an employee may not be fired because he or she refuses to commit an illegal act, such as perjury or price fixing.

punitive damages In civil cases, damages that are awarded to punish a defendant or to deter a defendant's conduct.

pure diversity-based recruitment An organization's concerted effort to expand actively the pool of applicants so that no one is excluded because of past or

pure diversity-based recruitment *(cont.)* present discrimination; the decision to hire or to promote is based on the best-qualified individual regardless of race or sex.

Pygmalion effect The phenomenon of the self-fulfilling prophecy; with regard to training, the fact that the higher the expectations of the trainer, the better the performance of the trainees.

qualified individual with a disability An individual with a disability who is able to perform the essential functions of a job with or without accommodation.

qualified job applicants Applicants with disabilities who can perform the essential functions of a job with or without reasonable accommodation.

quality challenge Ongoing needs to meet the product and service needs of customers.

quality of work life (QWL) A set of objective organizational conditions and practices designed to foster quality relationships within the organization; employees' perceptions of the degree to which the organizational environment meets the full range of human needs.

quality-enhancement strategy A competitive strategy with the primary objective of enhancing product or service quality.

quid pro quo harassment Sexual harassment that is a condition of employment.

quotas Inflexible numbers or percentages of underrepresented group members that companies must hire or promote to comply with equal employment opportunity and affirmative action requirements.

race norming Within-group percentile scoring of employment-related tests.

realistic job preview (RJP) A recruiter's job overview that includes not only the positive aspects but also the unpleasant aspects of the job.

reasonable accommodations Adjustments in the work environment to allow for the special needs of individuals with disabilities.

recency error A rating error occurring when an appraiser assigns a rating on the basis of the employee's most recent performance rather than on long-term performance.

recruitment A market-exchange process in which employers attempt to differentiate their "products" (job opportunities) among "consumers" (job applicants) who vary in their levels of job-relevant knowledge, abilities, and skills.

recruitment pipeline The time frame from the receipt of a résumé to the time a new hire starts work.

red-hot-stove rule The theory that discipline should be immediate, consistent, and impersonal, and should include a warning.

redeployment   Transfer of an employee from one position or area to another—often resulting from a business slowdown or a reduced need for certain skills and usually coupled with training for the transition to new job skills and responsibilities.

reengineering   Review and redesign of work processes to make them more efficient and to improve the quality of the end product of service.

relative rating systems   Rating formats that compare the performance of an employee with that of other employees.

relevance   In an effective appraisal system, a requirement that there be clear links between the performance standards for a particular job and the organization's goals, and clear links between the critical job elements identified through a job analysis and the dimensions to be rated on an appraisal form.

relevant labor market   Determined by which jobs to survey and which markets are relevant for each job, considering geographical boundaries as well as product-market competitors.

reliability   The consistency or stability of a measurement procedure.

repatriation   The process of reentering one's native culture after being absent from it.

repetitive motion injuries   Injuries caused by performing the same task (or similar tasks) repeatedly, such as typing or using a computer mouse, for extended periods of time.

representation election   A secret-ballot election to determine whether a particular union will be certified as the exclusive bargaining representative of all the employees in the unit.

required qualifications   In job specifications, those qualities and skills that are absolutely necessary for the performance of a particular job.

restructuring   The process of changing a company by selling or buying plants or lines of business, or by laying off employees.

results-oriented systems   Rating formats that place primary emphasis on what an employee produces.

Resumix Human Skills Management System   An automated résumé-processing system that uses electronic technology to process résumés, input data into an applicant database, and provide online access to résumé and skills information on available job candidates.

retaliatory discharge   The situation that exists when an employee is terminated for what she or he considers unreasonable, outrageous reasons; in such cases, the employee may seek damages under an exception to the employment-at-will doctrine.

retention   Initiatives taken by management to keep employees from leaving, such as rewarding employees

retention   *(cont.)*
for performing their jobs effectively; ensuring harmonious working relations between employees and managers; and maintaining a safe, healthy work environment.

return on investment (ROI)   A measure comparing a training program's monetary benefits with its cost.

reverse culture shock   A condition experienced by an expatriate who has become accustomed to foreign ways and who, upon reentry, finds his or her home-country customs strange and even annoying.

reverse discrimination   Discrimination against whites (especially white males) and in favor of members of protected groups.

reverse mentoring   A mentoring program in which an older manager meets with a younger subordinate to learn about technologies such as the Internet and e-commerce.

right-to-work laws   Laws that prohibit compulsory union membership as a condition of continued employment.

secondary boycott   A boycott occurring when a union appeals to firms or other unions to stop doing business with an employer who sells or handles struck products.

selection ratio   The percentage of applicants hired, which is used in evaluating the usefulness of any predictor.

self-assessment   A process in which employees focus on their own career goals.

seniority   Privileged status attained by length of employment.

seniority system   An established business practice that allots to employees ever-improving employment rights and benefits as their relative lengths of pertinent employment increase.

sensitivity   The capability of a performance appraisal system to distinguish effective from ineffective performers.

"70 percent comfortable" rule   Saturn Corporation's guideline for reaching consensus among team members: each team member must feel at least 70 percent comfortable with any decision made by the team.

severity   The tendency to rate every employee low on the criteria being evaluated.

severance pay   Payments, usually based on length of service, organization level, and reason for termination, provided to employees whose employment is terminated.

sexual harassment   Unwelcome sexual advances, requests for sexual favors, and other verbal or physical conduct of a sexual nature when submission to or

sexual harassment *(cont.)*
rejection of this conduct explicitly or implicitly affects an individual's employment; unreasonably interferes with an individual's work performance; or creates an intimidating, hostile, or offensive work environment.

shrinkage Losses due to bookkeeping errors and employee, customer, and vendor theft.

silent generation People born between 1930 and 1945, who dedicated themselves to their employers, made sacrifices to get ahead, and currently hold most positions of power in the country.

simplified employee pension A defined-contribution pension plan under which a small-business employer can contribute a certain percentage or amount of an employee's salary tax-free to an individual retirement account; the employee is vested immediately for the amount paid into the account but cannot withdraw any funds before age 59½ without penalty.

situational interview An employment interview in which candidates are asked to describe how they think they would respond in certain job-related situations.

situational tests Standardized measures of behavior whose primary objective is to assess the ability to *do* rather than the ability to *know* through miniature replicas of actual job requirements; also known as *work-sample tests.*

skip-level policy An organizational policy that allows an employee with a problem to proceed directly to the next higher level of management above his or her supervisor.

social challenge In the context of training, it refers to the number of unskilled and undereducated youth who will be needed for entry-level jobs, and the need to train currently underutilized groups of racial and ethnic minorities, women, and older workers.

social learning theory The theory that individuals in groups learn appropriate behaviors and attitudes from one another.

socialization In the employee recruitment and selection process, the introduction of new employees to company policies, practices, and benefits through an orientation program; the mutual adaptation of the new employee and the new employer to one another.

soft-quota system An organizational recruitment policy that systematically favors women and minorities in hiring and promotion decisions; also known as *diversity-based recruitment with preferential hiring.*

spatial relations ability The ability to visualize the effects of manipulating or changing the position of objects.

speed strategy A competitive strategy with the primary goal of being the fastest innovator, producer,

speed strategy *(cont.)*
distributor, and responder to customer feedback; also known as a *time-based strategy.*

staffing The managerial activities of identifying work requirements within an organization; determining the numbers of people and the skills mix necessary to do the work; and recruiting, selecting, and promoting qualified candidates.

status In an organization, the value ascribed to an individual because of his or her position in the organization's hierarchy.

stock options The right (primarily of executives) to buy a company's stock sometime in the future at a fixed price, usually the price on the day the options are granted.

strategic human resource management (HRM) An approach to human resource management that has the goal of using people most wisely with respect to the strategic needs of the organization, ensuring that people from all levels of the organization are working to implement the strategy of the business effectively.

strategic job analyses Future-oriented analyses that identify skill and ability requirements for jobs that do not yet exist.

strategic partner An individual who works with managers to help them better understand the value of people and the consequences of ineffective or effective HRM; a key role of an HR professional.

strategic planning Long-range business planning that involves fundamental decisions about the very nature of the business, including defining the organization's philosophy; formulating statements of identity, purpose, and objectives; evaluating strengths, weaknesses, and competitive dynamics; determining organizational design; developing strategies; and devising programs.

subjective career A sense of where one is going in one's work life based on one's perceived talents and abilities, basic values, and career motives and needs.

succession plans Internal labor supply forecasts—consisting of setting a planning horizon, identifying replacement candidates for each key position, assessing current performance and readiness for promotion, identifying career development needs, and integrating the career goals of individuals with company goals—that are used to ensure the availability of competent executive talent.

swing generation Those people born between 1910 and 1929, who struggled through the Great Depression, fought in World War II, and rebuilt the American economy after that war.

sympathy strikes Refusals by employees of one bargaining unit to cross a picket line of a different bargaining unit.

system   A network of interrelated components.

systemic discrimination   Any business practice that results in the denial of equal employment opportunity.

systems approach   An approach to managing human resources that provides a conceptual framework for integrating the various components within the system and for linking the human resource management (HRM) system with larger organizational needs.

tactical planning   Short- to middle-range business planning that addresses issues associated with the growth of current or new operations, as well as with any specific problems that might disrupt the pace of planned growth; also known as *operational planning.*

talent inventory   The human resource planning activity that assesses current human resources skills, abilities, and potential, and analyzes how those resources are currently being used.

team   A group of individuals who are working together toward a common goal.

telecommuting   An approach, made possible by the use of personal computers, fax machines, and electronic mail, in which an employee works either full-time or part-time from his or her home.

test-retest reliability   An estimate of reliability obtained from two administrations of the same test at two different times.

tests   Standardized measures of behavior, such as math and vocabulary skills, that have right and wrong answers.

third-country national   An expatriate who has transferred to an additional country while working abroad.

"Three-C" logic   An approach to organizational design based on the strategies of command, control, and compartmentalization.

time study   A study conducted to determine how fast a job should be done.

time-based strategy   A competitive strategy with the primary goal of being the fastest innovator, producer, distributor, and responder to customer feedback; also known as a *speed strategy.*

total health and productivity management   A developing trend toward integrating disability coverage with workers' compensation and, eventually, with group health care; also known as *managed health.*

total quality management (TQM)   A management approach that emphasizes the continuous improvement of products and processes to ensure long-term customer satisfaction; TQM has a group problem-solving focus that encourages employee empowerment.

tournament model of upward mobility   A model of career success based on the assumption that an individual must have a challenging first job and receive

tournament model of upward mobility   *(cont.)* quick, early promotions in order to be successful in his or her career; so called because, as in a tournament, everyone has an equal chance in the early contests but the losers are not eligible for the later, major contests.

training   Planned programs designed to improve performance at the individual, group, and/or organizational levels.

training and development phase of training   The phase of training whose purpose is to design the environment in which to achieve the objectives defined in the assessment phase by choosing methods and techniques and by delivering them in a supportive environment based on sound principles of learning.

training outcomes   The effectiveness of a training program based on cognitive, skill-based, affective, and results outcomes.

training paradox   The seemingly contradictory fact that training employees to develop their skills and improve their performance increases their employability outside the company while simultaneously increasing their job security and desire to stay with their current employer.

transfer   The extent to which competencies learned in training can be applied on the job.

transfer of training   The use of knowledge, skills, and behaviors learned in training on the job.

troubled employee   An individual with unresolved personal or work-related problems.

trust gap   A frame of mind in which employees mistrust senior management's intentions, doubt its competence, and resent its self-congratulatory pay.

turnover   Any permanent departure of employees beyond organizational boundaries.

two-tier wage schemes   Wage practices that set lower starting pay and smaller increments in pay for new employees.

type A behavior pattern   A hard-driving, aggressive, competitive, impatient pattern of behavior.

unauthorized aliens   Foreign-born U.S. residents not legally authorized to work in the United States.

uncertainty avoidance   The extent to which members of a culture feel threatened by ambiguous situations and thus emphasize ritual behavior, rules, and stability.

uncontrollable costs   Costs that are beyond the control of an organization.

unequal treatment   Disparate treatment of employees based on an intention to discriminate.

unfair-labor-practice strikes   Strikes that are caused or prolonged by unfair labor practices of the employer.

union shop A union-security provision stipulating that, as a condition of continued employment, an individual must join the union that represents employees after a probationary period.

union-security clause In a contract, a clause designed to force all employees to join the union in order to remain working.

unprotected strikes Both lawful and unlawful work stoppages, such as sit-down strikes, slowdowns, and wildcat strikes, in which participants' jobs are not protected by law; thus the participants may be discharged by their employer.

utility analysis A method of converting measures of staffing or training outcomes into the metric of dollars.

validity Evidence regarding the appropriateness or meaningfulness of inferences about scores from a measurement procedure.

validity generalization The assumption that the results of a validity study conducted in one situation can be generalized to other similar situations.

variable-pay systems Pay programs that are linked to profit and productivity gains.

vesting Guarantee as a legal right with no contingencies, of an employee's retirement benefits after a certain length of employment.

virtual corporation A new organizational form in which teams of specialists come together to work on a project and then disband when the project is finished.

virtual organization An organizational form in which teams of specialists come together through technology to work on a project, and disband when the project is finished.

virtual workplace A new organizational form based on the idea of working anytime, anywhere—in real space or in cyberspace.

visioning Conceptualizing what should be happening in the future, and having the ability to excite and inspire others in making the vision a reality.

voice systems Organizational systems that provide individuals and groups with the capacity to be heard, with a way to communicate their interests upward.

weighted application blanks (WABs) Statistically significant relationships between responses to questions on application forms and later measures of job performance.

***Weingarten* rights** Rights defined by the Supreme Court in *NLRB v. J. Weingarten, Inc.,* stating that a union employee has the right to demand that a union representative be present at an investigatory interview that the employee reasonably believes may result in disciplinary action; *Weingarten* rights also extend to nonunion employees.

wellness programs Programs that focus on prevention to help employees build lifestyles that will enable them to achieve their full physical and mental potential.

whistle-blowing Disclosure by former or current organization members of illegal, immoral, or illegitimate practices under the control of their employers.

willful violations Violations of OSHA requirements in which an employer either knew that what was being done constituted a violation of federal regulations or was aware that a hazardous condition existed and made no reasonable effort to eliminate it.

win-lose bargaining In negotiations, the bargaining posture that assumes that the goals of the parties are irreconcilable; also known as *distributive bargaining.*

win-win bargaining In negotiations, the bargaining posture that assumes that the goals of the parties are not mutually exclusive, that it is possible for both sides to achieve their objectives; also known as *integrative bargaining.*

work-life program An employer-sponsored benefit or working condition that helps employees to balance work and nonwork demands.

"Work-Out" program General Electric's program to involve every employee in improving efficiency and to foster communication between lower-level employees and bosses.

work-sample tests Standardized measures of behavior whose primary objective is to assess the ability to do rather than the ability to *know* through miniature replicas of actual job requirements; also known as *situational tests.*

workers' compensation programs Programs that provide payments to workers who are injured on the job, or who contract a work-related illness.

workforce planning Identification of the numbers of employees and the skills needed to perform available jobs, based on an understanding of available competencies and changes in jobs required by corporate goals.

workforce utilization A means of identifying whether the composition of the workforce—measured by race and sex—employed in a particular job category in a particular firm represents the composition of the entire labor market available to perform that job.

workload standards Standards that provide relatively objective definitions of jobs, give employees targets to shoot for, and make it easier for supervisors to assign work equitably.

yearly renewable term insurance Group life insurance in which each employee is insured one year at a time.

CREDITS

PHOTO CREDITS

NAME INDEX

679

SUBJECT INDEX